WARRING FOR AMERICA

View of the Capitol of the United States after the Conflagration in 1814.

WARRING FOR AMERICA

Cultural Contests in the Era of 1812

Edited by NICOLE EUSTACE
and FREDRIKA J. TEUTE

Published by the
OMOHUNDRO INSTITUTE OF
EARLY AMERICAN HISTORY AND CULTURE,
Williamsburg, Virginia,
and the
UNIVERSITY OF NORTH CAROLINA PRESS,
Chapel Hill

The Omohundro Institute of
Early American History and Culture
is sponsored by the College of William and Mary.
On November 15, 1996, the Institute
adopted the present name in honor of a bequest
from Malvern H. Omohundro, Jr.

© 2017 The University of North Carolina Press
All rights reserved

Portions of the essay by Dawn Peterson, "Domestic Fronts in the
Ear of 1812: Slavery, Expansion, and Familial Struggles for Sovereignty
in the Early-Nineteenth-Century Choctaw South," were first published in
Dawn Peterson, *Indians in the Family: Adoption and the Politics of Antebellum
Expansion* (Cambridge, Mass., 2017), 81–106. Copyright © 2017 by
the President and Fellows of Harvard College.

Library of Congress Cataloging-in-Publication Data
Names: Eustace, Nicole, editor. | Teute, Fredrika J., editor.
Title: Warring for America : cultural contests in the era of 1812 /
edited by Nicole Eustace and Fredrika J. Teute.
Description: Williamsburg, Virginia : Omohundro Institute of Early American
History and Culture ; Chapel Hill : University of North Carolina Press, [2017] |
Includes bibliographical references and index.
Identifiers: LCCN 2017008687 | ISBN 9781469631516 (cloth : alk. paper) |
ISBN 9781469688411 (pbk. : alk. paper) | ISBN 9781469631769 (ebook) |
ISBN 9798890853776 (pdf)
Subjects: LCSH: United States—History—War of 1812—Social aspects. |
National characteristics, American—History—19th century.
Classification: LCC E354 .W394 2017 | DDC 973.5/2—dc23
LC record available at https://lccn.loc.gov/2017008687

COVER AND FRONTISPIECE
"View of the Capitol of the United States, after the Conflagration, in 1814."
Frontispiece in Jesse Torrey, *A Portraiture of Domestic Slavery, in the United
States* ... (Philadelphia, 1817). Courtesy, Special Collections Research Center,
Swem Library, College of William and Mary

PREFACE

When the British marched into Washington, D.C., on August 24, 1814, and torched the city, reducing the Capitol and other federal buildings to rubble, they struck not just a physical but also a symbolic blow to the center of the new nation. The invasion revived fears about the danger of internal insurrection by blacks, the dissolution of the Union, and, if it survived, the abandonment of Washington as its capital. These anxieties, brought to the fore by wartime, had deeper roots in the upheavals of the Revolution, which had let loose competing claims on America but left them unreconciled. The War of 1812 for many inhabitants only magnified the issues at stake in the country; it did not resolve them.

Rather than focusing on the war itself, then, this volume offers a wider lens on the decades before and after 1812 to bring into view a range of clashing objectives that made the early Republic such an unsettled and unsettling period. The essays grew out of the 2011 conference "Warring for America, 1803–1818," held in the James Madison Memorial Building of the Library of Congress. The idea for this conference originated with a question posed by Mendy C. Gladden, former associate editor of publications at the Institute: Why is there not more published about the period around the War of 1812? A working group of Nicole Eustace, Robert G. Parkinson, Mendy, and myself formulated the intellectual rationale for the conference; after Mendy's departure, the remaining three of us implemented the proposal and constituted the program committee. The proceedings of the conference appear at the back of the volume in gratitude to all the participants. In their presentations and comments, they fulfilled the intent of the conference call to explore the conflicting visions of liberty, territorial reach, cultural affiliation, and power structures in the early national period. The productive discussions during the meeting were the first step toward conceptualizing a publication.

Given the centrality of the Federal City to the events of the era, Washington was the obvious place to convene the meeting. But this was not such a simple thing to effect. A number of people and institutions were instrumental in making it possible, and we acknowledge our gratitude to their contributions.

Ronald Hoffman, then director of the Omohundro Institute, convener of conferences nonpareil, put a great deal of effort into bringing together a group of sponsors and locating a venue. Carolyn T. Brown, director of the Office of Scholarly Programs and of the John W. Kluge Center, Library of Congress, responded positively to his call and provided the space. Her assistants Joanne Kitching and Alicia Robinson facilitated the process. Daniel E. Rose, special events coordinator at the Library of Congress, managed the requirements for permitting a two-day meeting within the building.

To put on a conference takes money and people. Ron backed the project from the first planning meeting. Nicole Eustace approached the chair of her history department at New York University, Lauren Benton, who responded with matching funds. And Roy Ritchie, then W. M. Keck Foundation Director of Research at the Huntington Library, joined the financial collaboration in underwriting "Warring for America." Kim Foley, Sally Mason, Meg Musselwhite, and Beverly Smith of the Omohundro Institute coordinated the interlocking parts of the conference—paper proposals, meeting arrangements, brochure, and registration. The monetary support from the three institutions and the professional input of staff were essential to the conference's success and to the volume resulting from it.

Shaping conference papers into a publishable collection of essays requires scholarly commitment from editors and authors alike. Niki took the lead and pushed the work forward. Her mark is on every page of the volume. Two outside readers, Michael Meranze and Andrew Cayton, gave insightful critiques and offered constructive observations on the themes and organization of the whole. The contributors responded to the editorial input with thoughtful revisions. Associate Editor Nadine Zimmerli exercised a firm grip on the materials of fifteen different contributors and set them in train for the publication process. Managing Editor Virginia Montijo Chew wielded her deft expertise in copyediting the essays and melding them into a whole. Senior Project Editor M. Kathryn Burdette assisted her in some of the copyediting, and Institute editorial apprentices Anna Roberts, Nicole Penn, Kasey Sease, Katherine Cartwright, and Brandon Munda checked the sources in each of the pieces. Paul W. Mapp, interim editor of books, took over the desk in time to ease the book's way to the University of North Carolina Press. Volumes of essays always involve extensive collaboration; *Warring for America* is the outcome of the many individuals who contributed to its creation.

> Fredrika J. Teute
> *Editor of Publications, Emerita*
> *Omohundro Institute of Early American History and Culture*

CONTENTS

Preface	v
List of Illustrations	ix
Introduction *Nicole Eustace*	1

PART I. SLAVERY, NATION, AND THE ONGOING REVOLUTION

Minstrelization and Nationhood: "Backside Albany," Backlash, and the Wartime Origins of Blackface Minstrelsy *David Waldstreicher*	29
Meditating on Slavery in the Age of Revolution: Barbary Captivities and the Whitening of American Democracy *Carroll Smith-Rosenberg*	56
"Murder, Robbery, Rape, Adultery, and Incest": Martha Meredith Read's *Margaretta* and the Function of Federalist Fiction *Duncan Faherty*	95
Conceptual Traffic: The Atlantic Slave Trade and the War of 1812 *Christen Mucher*	127
The Radicalism of the First Seminole War and Its Consequences *Nathaniel Millett*	164

PART II. REPRESENTING THE REPUBLIC

For the Love of Glory: Napoleonic Imperatives in the Early American Republic *Matthew Rainbow Hale*	205
Military Service and Racial Subjectivity in the War Narratives of James Roberts and Isaac Hubbell *James M. Greene*	250

Naval Biography, the War of 1812, and the
    Contestation of American National Identity
    Tim Lanzendörfer — 278

The Self-Abstracting Letters of War:
    Madison, Henry, and the Executive Author
    Eric Wertheimer — 313

"Can You Be Surprised at My Discouragement?" Global Emulation
    and the Logic of Colonization at the New York African Free School
    Anna Mae Duane — 331

PART III. EXPANSION AND THE INTIMACY OF BORDERS

Widening the Scope on the Indians' Old Northwest
    Jonathan Todd Hancock — 359

Domestic Fronts in the Era of 1812:
    Slavery, Expansion, and Familial Struggles for Sovereignty
    in the Early-Nineteenth-Century Choctaw South
    Dawn Peterson — 386

"Borders Thick and Foggy": Mobility, Community, and
    Nation in a Northern Indigenous Region
    Karen L. Marrero — 419

"Hindoo Marriage" and National Sovereignty in the
    Early-Nineteenth-Century United States
    Brian Connolly — 445

Conference Program — 479

List of Contributors — 481

Index — 485

ILLUSTRATIONS

The Battle of Plattsburg 30
Backside Albany 35
Backside Albany; and Jack of Guinea 36
Andrew Jackson Allen 51
Champlain, Plattsburgh[, New Orleans]; Honor to the Bra[ve];
Splendid Battles! 53
Rembrandt Peale, *William Henry Harrison* 217
Gilbert Stuart, *Major-General Henry Dearborn* 218
James Akin, "Dress, the Most Distinguishing Mark of
a Military Genius" 220
"Don't Give Up the Ship" Banner 224
John Wesley Jarvis, *Oliver Hazard Perry* 225
Benjamin West, *The Death of General Wolfe* 226
John Trumbull, *George Washington before the Battle of Trenton* 228
Antoine Jean Gros, *General Napoleon Bonaparte
at the Bridge of Arcole, November 17, 1796* 229
John Wesley Jarvis, *Andrew Jackson* 242
John Wesley Jarvis, *General Andrew Jackson* 243
Jean François de la Vallée, *Andrew Jackson* 244
Charles Willson Peale, *Andrew Jackson* 245
Anna Claypoole Peale, *Andrew Jackson* 246
William Rush, *General Andrew Jackson* 247
John Vanderlyn, *Andrew Jackson* 248
Oliver Hazard Perry 302
Columbia Seizing the Trident of Neptune 309
James Trenchard, *Temple of Liberty* 318

INTRODUCTION

Nicole Eustace

When Noah Webster presented the first-ever American-authored dictionary of the English language to the reading public in 1806, thirty years had passed since America had declared independence from Great Britain. In those three decades, the nation had undergone a revolution, two national constitutions, and innumerable state and local ones. It had engaged in protracted debates about the nature of authority, the location of territorial borders, the form of economy, and the definition of citizenry. At the moment that Webster published, the legal trade in Atlantic slavery was about to end though the domestic trade thrived as never before; the British had largely vacated western forts but continued to threaten the nation from the fringes and from the sea; the Louisiana Purchase had just doubled the nation's territory only to redouble the intensity of its conflicts with Native Americans; and New Jersey was about to become the last state to revoke women's suffrage even as citizenship requirements for white men had been relaxed. Meanwhile, Haiti was on the rise, Napoleon was on the march, American sailors faced Barbary pirates, and revolutionary movements were sweeping through Spanish America. In another half-dozen years, in 1812, the nation would make its first-ever formal declaration of war. In this time of change and challenge, Webster offered the nation the weapon of words.[1]

Webster explained his decision to publish a dictionary, despite the existence of well-regarded British-authored ones, by asserting: "In every country where the English language is used, improvements will continually demand the use of new terms.... A new system of civil polity in the western world, originates new ideas." He insisted that, with the innovation in political structures, the United States required a vocabulary of its own distinct from Britain's.[2]

Civic changes required cultural shifts. Webster handed out words as tools, not as pummels for beating the nation into prescribed and pre-existing

---

1. Noah Webster, *A Compendious Dictionary of the English Language* ... (New Haven, Conn., 1806).
2. Webster, "Preface," ibid., xxii.

forms, but as shears with which to cut novel patterns of thought, new modes of social, political, and economic life. As he further explained, "From the changes in civil policy, manners, arts of life and other circumstances attending the settlement of English colonies in America ... with numerous variations arising from difference of climate, plants, animals, arts, manufactures, [and] manners ... a distinct dialect of the language will be gradually formed." For, although Webster anticipated that a single "distinct dialect" would emerge to distinguish the United States from Britain while binding Americans to one another, he acknowledged in the same breath that "numerous variations" existed in the "arts, manufactures, [and] manners" of the new nation. This still undefined country offered open terrain for warring visions of inclusion and exclusion.[3]

The history of the early Republic is one of struggle to define the physical and cultural parameters of the nation. In the years when the manifold tensions endemic to the new nation were intensified by the imminence of war, Americans of all kinds—from presidents to pupils in the African Free School, from hack magazine writers to Choctaw mothers—fought for country on the battleground of belonging. The dangers of wartime emergency amplified calls for national unity. Yet, one of the signal features of the 1812 era was that, even as it intensified interest in the American democratic project, it did not produce any clear consensus on the ideal contours of the country. Rather, the Americans portrayed in these essays wrestled over how to shape material circumstances and social relations in accordance with often divergent values and customs.

The notion that national culture functions as a medium for the cultivation of common purpose and unified identity has a long history. The Revolu-

---

3. Ibid., xxii. Webster has more often been portrayed as a Federalist politico intent on improving American attitudes and consolidating American character by recording American language. Without challenging this view of Webster's politics or aims, well documented in Jill Lepore, *A Is for American: Letters and Other Characters in the Newly United States* (New York, 2002), esp. 21, this essay adds a counterweight by foregrounding Webster's own assertions that language is not a force amenable to simple political containment or to social control. The classic statement on Webster as Federalist manipulator is Richard M. Rollins, "Words as Social Control: Noah Webster and the Creation of the *American Dictionary*," *American Quarterly*, XXVIII (1976), 415–430. An update appears in Tim Cassedy, "'A Dictionary Which We Do Not Want': Defining America against Noah Webster, 1783–1810," *William and Mary Quarterly*, 3d Ser., LXXI (2014), 229–254.

tionary leader Gouverneur Morris summed up American aspirations on this point in a letter to John Jay in 1784: "National spirit is the natural result of national existence ... the present generation ... will ... give place to a race of Americans." When Joyce Appleby affirmed his comments by adding her own assessment that "Morris's 'race of Americans' disclosed the creative potential that had long been coiled like a spring within Britain's North American colonies," she did no more than reprise the conventional wisdom of two centuries. After years of Revolutionary ferment, the period on which Appleby focused, 1790 to 1830, has long been regarded as a time of relative calm and consensus, one in which Americans' creativity and spirit allowed them to emerge as a well-defined and distinctive people, indeed as a "race" apart.[4]

The problem with such consensus views of American identity is that they fly in the face of an equally long and distinguished tradition of noticing the fractures and fissures that split American society from the outset. To Webster's apt enumeration of American "variations," we could add any number of other divisions: of race, class, and gender, of region, religion, and affiliation. A country of scrabblers, strivers, settlers, raiders, runaways, and border crossers became ever more intently engaged in the contest to define the image of a nation that seemed to be always receding, mirage-like, before them. As Appleby has also noted, foreign observers of the United States remarked from the start on this national deficit. She quotes the French traveler La Rochefoucauld, who concluded in 1799 that America is "a country in flux," seemingly in perpetuity: "That which is true today as regards its population, its establishments, its prices, its commerce will not be true six months from now." Such comments cast in high relief the absence of any clear consensus holding Americans together.[5]

Americans of all stripes disagreed on who and what constituted the United States. Multiple points of division within the country, not simply the continuing external influence of Great Britain, created the crucial pivots on which the 1812 era turned. Many articulations of national character in the first decades of the nineteenth century came out of contests over choices, opportunities, and self-definition among different segments of the domestic

---

4. Gouverneur Morris to John Jay, Jan. 10, 1784, in Henry P. Johnston, ed., *The Correspondence and Public Papers of John Jay* ..., III (New York, 1891), 104-105, cited in Joyce Appleby, *Inheriting the Revolution: The First Generation of Americans* (Cambridge, 2000), 3.

5. La Rochefoucauld-Liancourt, *Voyages dans les États-Unis d'Amérique, fait en 1795, 1796 et 1797* (Paris, [1799]), I, xi, cited in Appleby, *Inheriting the Revolution*, 6.

population. Noah Webster perceived that, in a nation only recently formed and still unsettled in its political, social, and economic structures, culture would prove to be an effective instrument through which varied people and groups would seek to implement competing national visions.[6]

Still, a legacy of underlying Anglocentrism runs through early Republic historiography from the nineteenth century to the present, framing the emergence of the United States by its independence from Great Britain rather than by power struggles among its own disparate peoples and territories. From the nineteenth-century historian Henry Adams to current scholars of the early Republic like Gordon S. Wood, a long train of historical interpreters have cast the War of 1812 as America's second war of independence. In 1891, Adams declared: "Until 1815 nothing in the future of the American Union was regarded as settled.... In 1815 for the first time Americans ceased to doubt the path they were to follow. Not only was the unity of their nation established, but its probable divergence from older societies was also well defined." Similarly, in 2009, Wood stated that, "in the end many Americans came to believe that they had to fight another war with Great Britain in order to reaffirm their national independence and establish their elusive identity." Wood is far less concerned with addressing American internal divisions than with highlighting the potential of political nationalism to offset the lingering impact of Great Britain on the identity of the new United States.[7]

---

6. Alan Taylor has emphasized Britain's role in inhibiting the United States from forming a coherent identity in this period, given that both "the republic and the empire competed for the allegiance of the peoples of North America" in the era of 1812. Taking this insight into consideration, this volume pivots to exploring other aspects of North American divisions in this period, the internal ones created by many competing and contesting groups. As Taylor himself notes, "We underestimate the fluid uncertainty of the postrevolutionary generation, when the new republic was so precarious and so embattled." See Taylor, *The Civil War of 1812: American Citizens, British Subjects, Irish Rebels, and Indian Allies* (New York, 2010), 8.

7. Henry Adams, *History of the United States of America during the Second Administration of James Madison*, III (1891; New York, 1921), 219–220 (this book constitutes volume IX of the full series, also published in 1921); Gordon S. Wood, *Empire of Liberty: A History of the Early Republic, 1789–1815* (New York, 2009), 40, 42. In fact, the idea that the United States shed its cultural dependence on Great Britain even after 1812 has been considered with skepticism. On the United States as a postcolonial nation, see Leonard Tennenhouse, *The Importance of Feeling English: American Literature and the British Diaspora, 1750–1850* (Princeton, N.J., 2007); Elisa Tamarkin, *Anglophilia: Def-*

For Wood, politics is the sole arena of national definition, and war the primary means of national enunciation. The twofold problem with such an argument lies in the primacy it grants Britain in the negative definition of the United States and in the centrality it credits to politics as the site of such negotiations. Whereas Webster saw the need for a new common culture to meld the disparate parts, Adams and Wood understood the unifying medium to be high politics. Adams regarded politics as the only real field of national conflict; victory there meant everything else could be regarded as close enough to "settled." Adams affirmed that, "as far as politics supplied a test ... the American, in his political character, was a new variety of man." Wood claims that "what held ... diverse and ultimately incompatible sectional and social elements together was a comprehensive and common ideology ... Republican ideology." To this day, the propensity to cast the terms of American identity in relation to European social forms shifts focus away from the more trenchant domestic divisions among Euro-Americans, the alienation of African Americans, and the resistance of Native Americans in the early national period. But in the days of the early Republic not everyone thought that politics alone sufficed to define the nation.[8]

Unlike historians from Adams to Wood, Webster understood that national formation began and ended with broader negotiations over social habits and communal values. At the time of the War of 1812, Webster, like many Americans, particularly Federalists, regarded that confrontation as a fabricated and unnecessary distraction from polarizing debates and entrenched differences within the United States. Regardless, scholars like Wood have preferred the emphasis of Adams to that of Webster.

True enough, American history cannot be understood without due attention to politics; there can be no disputing Webster's claim that the emergence of the United States inaugurated a "new system of civil polity in the western world." The creation of the globe's first constitutional democracy was heralded. Yet, high politics alone could not define the new nation, its character, or its essence. The story of enfranchised white men, a small minority of the population, cannot serve as the summation of the history of

---

erence, Devotion, and Antebellum America (Chicago, 2008); Sam W. Haynes, *Unfinished Revolution: The Early American Republic in a British World* (Charlottesville, Va., 2010); and Kariann Akemi Yokota, *Unbecoming British: How Revolutionary America Became a Postcolonial Nation* (Oxford, 2011).

8. Wood, *Empire of Liberty*, 172; Adams, *History of the United States*, III, 221.

the entire nation. If the creation of the United States augured the rise of republicanism, it also contributed to codifying the structures of patriarchy, slavery, imperialism, and capitalism. The critical contests that emerged out of these concomitant developments arose from the divergent experiences of the vast majority of Americans. The political sphere was not coterminous with American identity, nor was it capable alone of creating a culture of consensus. Rather, the current volume argues for the importance of understanding diverse people's lived lives as a ground of conflict.[9]

Summing up his view of the nation's situation in the wake of the War of 1812, Henry Adams contended that, by 1815, "American character was formed, if not fixed." Rather than concede that there was anything like a fully formed "character" for America in 1815, this book stresses the second half of the formulation Adams offered. Precisely because American character was not firmly fixed, the "America" of these essays emerges less as a simple ideal worth fighting for than as a complex of ideas worth fighting over.[10]

If some practitioners of high political history have proven reluctant to concede culture's significance, social historians have sometimes appeared all too persuaded of the insidious power of this historical approach. James Cook warns: "Culturalism has been accused of many crimes. It threatens to 'obliterate the social.' It 'displace[s] our gaze from the poor and powerless.' ... Sometimes it even shares a 'secret affinity with an emergent logic of capitalist development.'" Yet, social and cultural history emerged in tandem, not in opposition.[11]

The eminent founding social historian E. P. Thompson declared that cultural history and material history belonged together. In Thompson's view,

---

9. Gordon S. Wood, "History in Context: The American Vision of Bernard Bailyn," *Weekly Standard*, Feb. 23, 2015, http://www.weeklystandard.com/history-in-context/article/850083. On the world-historical significance of the founding political philosophy of the United States, see David Armitage, *The Declaration of Independence: A Global History* (Cambridge, Mass., 2007).

10. Adams, *History of the United States of America*, III, 345.

11. James W. Cook, "The Kids Are All Right: On the Turning of Cultural History," *American Historical Review*, CXVII (2012), 763. A useful retrospective on twentieth-century American cultural studies can be found in David W. Noble, *Death of a Nation: American Culture and the End of Exceptionalism* (Minneapolis, Minn., 2002). See also Michael Holzman, "The Ideological Origins of American Studies at Yale," *American Studies*, XL, no. 2 (Summer 1999), 71–99.

"Any evaluation of the quality of life must entail an assessment of the total life-experience, the manifold satisfactions or deprivations, cultural as well as material, of the people concerned." In fact, culture was a key component in shaping the American political economy from the earliest days of the nation.[12]

In the spirit of Webster himself, consider the working definition of the term "culture" in the early Republic. In his 1806 dictionary entry, Webster provides important clues to both the explanatory allurements long promised by the concept of culture and the intellectual objections it sometimes provokes. On page 74 of the now smudged and faded pages of the first edition of his book, Webster defined "Culture, *n.*" as "the act of cultivation," while "Cultivate, *v.t.*," meant "to till, manure, improve, refine." English-speakers in the early United States regarded agriculture as the basis of all culture, an attitude that encapsulated in a single term a political ideology that equated settled farming with advanced civilization, land use with the conversion of native property rights to Euro-American title, and elevation of personal taste with advancement of the nation. To ground the investigation of culture on such an eighteenth-century Enlightenment platform would necessarily limit the scope of cultural history, but concepts of culture are no more fixed than the range of early American subjects' experiences.[13] Although the current definition of "culture" still retains the meanings "cultivation, tillage" as well as "enlightenment and excellence of taste," it also contains additional connotations: "The customary beliefs, social forms, and material traits ... shared by people in a place or time." Over the course of more than two hundred years, Americans have come to a deliberate recognition that the social is embedded in the cultural. As Gabrielle M. Spiegel has argued, cultural history has always maintained "a belief in the objective reality of the social world, and thus might more profitably have been labeled sociocultural history." For Noah Webster as well, given his ideas on the "arts of life," arts and

---

12. E. P. Thompson, *The Making of the English Working Class* (London, 1963), 444. In a 2013 essay in *Labor*, Lara Kriegel argues for the need to "reignite cultural history" fifty years after E. P. Thompson, crediting him with being "ahead of his time in seeking to understand the relationships among the material, cultural, and affective contours of class." Nonetheless, she "remind[s] us of the importance of keeping both material practice and social location in play" as we return to the critical analysis of culture. See Kriegel, "How It Feels to Be Fifty: E. P. Thompson and Cultural History, Past, Present, and Future," *Labor*, X, no. 3 (Fall 2013), 31–34 (quotations on 34).

13. Webster, *A Compendious Dictionary*, 74. For a recap of "settler political theory" in early America, see Craig Yirush, *Settlers, Liberty, and Empire: The Roots of Early American Political Theory, 1675-1775* (New York, 2011), esp. 264–270.

manufactures, manners and ideas—that is to say material and sociocultural forces in history—were intimately intertwined.[14]

Indeed, early American historians have linked the realization and rationalization of material aims through cultural means. Elite white men across the periods of the Revolution and the early Republic manifested their disproportionate material advantages by deploying culture extensively—in the form of social norms and cultural conventions—in efforts to distinguish themselves from their subordinates. Conversely, when members of the lower orders developed countercultures, they called into question the authenticity of elite claims to mastery. Early American studies has attempted to define and describe a range of historical identities while also paying tribute to acts of cultural contestation. Whether scanning the popular crowds at political parades or listening in on the political exchanges occurring in ladies' parlors, historians have found rich lodes of evidence for writing narratives of resilience in the records of culture.[15] The danger has been the sacrifice of the hard analysis of political economy for soft-focus celebrations of self-expression. The challenge, of course, has been to balance focus on the symbolic forms of resistance and agency with attention to the emergence of systemic inequalities in early America.[16]

---

14. Merriam-Webster, Online ed., s.v., "culture," accessed June 16, 2014, http://www.merriam-webster.com/dictionary/culture; Thompson, *Making of the English Working Class*, 444; Gabrielle M. Spiegel, "Comment on *A Crooked Line*," *American Historical Review*, CXIII (2008), 406–416 (quotation on 409); Michael Meranze, *Laboratories of Virtue: Punishment, Revolution, and Authority in Philadelphia, 1760–1835* (Chapel Hill, N.C., 1996), 35, 146.

15. A short list includes: Elliott J. Gorn, "'Gouge and Bite, Pull Hair and Scratch'": The Social Significance of Fighting in the Southern Backcountry," *American Historical Review*, XC (1985), 18–43; David Waldstreicher, *In the Midst of Perpetual Fetes: The Making of American Nationalism, 1776–1820* (Chapel Hill, N.C., 1997); Waldstreicher, "Reading the Runaways: Self-Fashioning, Print Culture, and Confidence in Slavery in the Eighteenth-Century Mid-Atlantic," *WMQ*, 3d Ser., LVI (1999), 243–272; Simon P. Newman, *Parades and the Politics of the Street: Festive Culture in the Early American Republic* (Philadelphia, 1997); Susan Branson, *These Fiery Frenchified Dames: Women and Political Culture in Early National Philadelphia* (Philadelphia, 2001); Catherine Allgor, *Parlor Politics: In Which the Ladies of Washington Help Build a City and a Government* (Charlottesville, Va., 2000); Rosemarie Zagarri, *Revolutionary Backlash: Women and Politics in the Early American Republic* (Philadelphia, 2007); Kate Haulman, *The Politics of Fashion in Eighteenth-Century America* (Chapel Hill, N.C., 2011).

16. Seth Rockman, *Scraping By: Wage Labor, Slavery, and Survival in Early Baltimore* (Baltimore, 2009), 11.

As Jean-Christophe Agnew describes this scholarly reassessment in a 2006 article, even a practitioner as prominent as James Scott (author of *Domination and the Arts of Resistance*) "would readily admit that his analysis of domination ... privileged 'the issues of dignity and autonomy' over 'material exploitation.'" The clear concern is that historians who focus on culture put symbol over substance—to the detriment of efforts to discern the structural inequalities of early America. Yet we now realize that enslaved people's insubordinate culture had clear material correlates, from the existence of underground slave market exchanges to the maintenance of geographic mobility. Ultimately, enslaved people used the "hidden transcripts" documented by James Scott as a deep cultural reservoir from which to draw on during the long struggle to reshape their material circumstances. This, of course, is no more than what E. P. Thompson long ago led us to expect.[17]

Keeping in mind Thompson's endeavor to understand the relationships among the material, cultural, and affective aspects of class, historians have at hand in culture not only a useful analytic lens but also the very instrument used by many of their subjects. For, as Michael Meranze has argued, the realm of culture is not a "discrete sphere" in which "meaning or value" is preserved in pristine form, "effectively separated ... from systems of governance, power, and constraint." In early America, "one fundamental form of politics was the explosive interface between the effort to exercise culture over others and those others' efforts to exercise culture over themselves." It is just this kind of combat over the terms of authority and authorization that the authors of the essays in *Warring for America* address.[18]

That early American cultural contests occurred in the midst of many overlapping armed conflicts—from real and imagined slave insurrections, to widespread U.S.-Indian military confrontations, to a formally declared war

---

17. Jean-Christophe Agnew, "Capitalism, Culture, and Catastrophe: Lawrence Levine and the Opening of Cultural History," *Journal of American History*, XCIII (2006), 772–791, esp. 783; James C. Scott, *Domination and the Arts of Resistance: Hidden Transcripts* (New Haven, Conn., 1990). For two prominent examples of more recent approaches to slave resilience, see Stephanie M. H. Camp, *Closer to Freedom: Enslaved Women and Everyday Resistance in the Plantation South* (Chapel Hill, N.C., 2004); and Anthony E. Kaye, *Joining Places: Slave Neighborhoods in the Old South* (Chapel Hill, N.C., 2007).

18. Michael Meranze, "Culture and Governance: Reflections on the Cultural History of Eighteenth-Century British America," *WMQ*, 3d Ser., LXV (2008), 713–744 (quotations on 714, 716, 743).

with Britain—only heightened the stakes of struggle. Moreover, although property-holding white men enjoyed a nearly unassailable advantage in any dispute occurring on economic or political terrain, the cultural field opened a degree of opportunity for all. Americans of many kinds engaged in fractious negotiations over lines of power and authority during the war era, underscoring both the limits of national sovereignty and the extent of new democratic possibilities in the early Republic.[19]

To fight for one's country meant many things. At the literal level, it meant taking up arms on behalf of the new United States. But a fight for America was also always a fight over America, over the right to the land, no matter whether the combatants were poor white soldiers hoping to win family farms or members of Indian nations campaigning to preserve their sovereignty. More broadly, in a country whose territorial borders and civic boundaries remained nebulous, to fight for country could also refer aptly enough to the struggles of the disenfranchised and dispossessed to claim national belonging—or independent sovereignty—for themselves. Ultimately, these many forms of combat amounted to a contest to define what "America" itself could mean.

From its inception, cultural rivalries defined the United States as much as military competition. Throughout the eighteenth and early nineteenth century, the British and their American successors sought to justify territorial and economic goals on moral grounds. Each relied in turn on invocations of liberty, rights, and civility as defining values that both motivated and legitimated acts of aggression and dispossession, from seizures of Indian land to claims on enslaved people's lives. At the moment of Anglo-American rupture marked by the Revolution, each side accused the other of betraying the true principles of liberty.[20]

American Revolutionaries had initially positioned themselves as the true sons and sole heirs of English liberty. The independence movement's alliance with the French empire, however, undercut centuries of rivalry that had cast French papists as the ultimate enemies of freedom. In place of popular

---

19. More than two decades ago, Edward W. Said challenged scholars to recognize that "culture can even be a battleground on which causes expose themselves to the light of day and contend with one another." See Said, *Culture and Imperialism* (New York, 1993), xiii.

20. See Matthew Mason, "The Battle of the Slaveholding Liberators: Great Britain, the United States, and Slavery in the Early Nineteenth Century," *WMQ*, 3d Ser., LIX (2002), 665–696. See also Mason, *Slavery and Politics in the Early American Republic* (Chapel Hill, N.C., 2006); and Christopher Leslie Brown, *Moral Capital: Foundations of British Abolitionism* (Chapel Hill, N.C., 2006).

rights vested in English common law, Revolutionaries championed instead a new Franco-American emphasis on natural rights. Yet the events of the late eighteenth century, which saw not only a revolution in the name of liberty in France but also, by 1804, the establishment of the hemisphere's first free black republic in Haiti, proved deeply disturbing to the fragile new American status quo.[21]

Far from settling the dust, the years after independence brought new storms of internal debate as intense as the external ones. In the decades after the Revolution, Euro-Americans split on whether, as many Federalists believed, the mission of the new nation was simply to preserve the commitment to Protestantism and refine the traditions of English common law endangered in Britain or whether its purpose was instead, as Republicans soon came to insist, to promote the rise of natural rights and encourage maximal freedom of circulation in all realms of life, from the economic and political to the social and cultural. Meanwhile, leading men's reliance on the ideal of liberty, however defined, served only to highlight the anomalous position of the majority of the population of former royal subjects—Indians, free and enslaved Africans, white men without property, and women of every rank—who were not privileged to be reborn as American citizens.

Among the noncitizen majority of American inhabitants, goals and strategies varied widely, from designs for full inclusion in the nation to efforts at asserting autonomy. Native Americans converted to Christianity or revitalized their own traditions of spirituality, signed over lands to the new United States or entered into new indigenous alliances and imperial configurations. African Americans variously escaped to maroon communities, advocated new schemes of colonization, rebelled against slaveholders, or staked citizenship claims through national service. Women elaborated new forms of family ties, from marriage to motherhood, the proxy for exercising authority on the national stage, while patriarchy faced mounting challenges as the model for governance. Against these competing claims, the "nation" itself could seem to be an empty signifier, dependent on the various actors' efforts to imbue it with meaning for their lives or to reject its legitimacy altogether. The 1812 era exposed these countervailing tensions but did little to resolve

21. On anti-papist and anti-French rhetoric from the colonial period through Jacksonian America, see Rachel Hope Cleves, *The Reign of Terror in America: Visions of Violence from Anti-Jacobinism to Antislavery* (New York, 2009); Owen Stanwood, *The Empire Reformed: English America in the Age of the Glorious Revolution* (Philadelphia, 2011); and Robert Englebert and Guillaume Teasdale, eds., *French and Indians in the Heart of North America, 1630–1815* (East Lansing, Mich., 2013).

them. The war for America played out in a wider Atlantic and transcontinental context that predated, postdated, and exceeded the confines of the War of 1812 itself.²²

By connecting these many metaphorical senses of "warring for America," contributions in this volume broaden the compass of issues in contention. The collection as a whole can be understood as addressing pressures on the malleable boundaries, subjective and geopolitical, of the nation. Debates over participation, dissent, and status take place in a rich array of sites—printed page, high seas, battlefields, borderlands, portraits, schools, family. The essays are organized into three parts to highlight themes that, although they run throughout the volume, especially resonate among the essays in each group and emphasize a particular set of problems bedeviling the early Republic. The unfinished business of the Revolution haunts the entire period, from the 1790s to the 1830s. The first part revolves around race and slavery in relation to membership in the new nation. Matters of inclusion and exclusion, precipitated by the War of Independence, became doubly charged leading up to the War of 1812. This second revolution waged over American self-mastery reinforced, rather than resolved, internal divisions over the rightful legatees of the Republic. The focus of the second part is on American elites, who, deprived of colonial and imperial props to their authority, had to establish their hegemony anew. They endeavored to corner the market on virtue even as they sought to aggregate material gains exclusively to themselves. The third part engages questions of sovereignty, both of literal self-determination and of national political control, which plagued individuals, families, communities, and state entities. Noncitizens employed varied strategies to carve a place for themselves on the continent, sometimes within the rubric of the United States and at other times beyond. Americans of every description struggled with problems of national definition because the nation itself was being built on shifting sands.

As the essays in Part 1, "Slavery, Nation, and the Ongoing Revolution," suggest, the decades of Revolutionary tumult witnessed the amplification of contending stakeholders' claims of their right to belong. The expansion of print provided a crucial arena in which varied Americans could sketch competing national visions. Even as white males felt the pressure from the

---

22. Many of these themes are introduced in Nicole Eustace, *1812: War and the Passions of Patriotism* (Philadelphia, 2012).

upheavals spreading across the Atlantic to delineate their privileged status in the political community, African Americans were developing a small but vibrant counterpublic that challenged the normative assertions of many whites about national membership. The Constitution was barely implemented when its delimitations of scope came under challenge. Black combatants countered their reduction to three-fifths of a person with their actions and words in the War of 1812. Though the gateways to print were far narrower for blacks than for whites, free African Americans used what openings they found to pry wide debates about the nature and limits of American liberty.[23]

Free blacks' assertions of their continued presence formed a crucial counter to every attempt to force them into civic invisibility. In his essay, "Minstrelization and Nationhood: 'Backside Albany,' Backlash, and the Wartime Origins of Blackface Minstrelsy," David Waldstreicher invites us to consider the unexpected implications of the fact that the first appearance of "blackface" minstrel shows took place in the context of the War of 1812. The black population of the United States was never more dangerous to underestimate than in the midst of a wartime emergency that made every body matter. Waldstreicher explores the challenge that the figure of the black sailor posed to efforts to ignore African American contributors to the early United States. Whites in blackface might have intended nothing but dismissive mockery of blacks' claims to national belonging, yet Waldstreicher argues that such performances inevitably registered African Americans' participation in nation making. Authorized only as a figure of fun, the black sailor nonetheless subverted the exclusionary assumptions of white audiences.

In this age of revolutions, many leading men claimed commitment to universal natural rights even as they simultaneously worked to establish a political economy of privilege. The racial exclusion of blacks, the territorial dispossession of Indians, the restriction of the franchise to the propertied, and the marginalization of women under the legal cover of patriarchy consigned the majority to live their lives in "zones of exception." Those formally recognized as full citizens who celebrated life in a land of liberty secured their claims through intertwined processes of political omission and material appropriation—even as they invoked arguments of nature and culture to assert that the disenfranchised and dispossessed owed their anomalous

---

23. See Joanna Brooks, "The Early American Public Sphere and the Emergence of a Black Print Counterpublic," *WMQ*, 3d Ser., LXII (2005), 67–92.

position in the Republic to their innate lack of the qualifying characteristics of rights-bearing subjects. Still, the rhetorical work required for sustaining such casuistry created innumerable cultural vulnerabilities for the property-possessing, liberty-endowed citizenry. Those who founded their own putatively universal freedoms on the denial of freedom to others were ultimately subject to persistent public and private challenges.[24]

If democratic self-rule entailed the right to define citizenship in the nation—and to restrict the rights to vote and hold office to men of property—then what was to be done in situations where this right of the people conflicted with the equally basic inalienable rights of the excluded? This is just the question posed by Carroll Smith-Rosenberg in her essay, "Meditating on Slavery in the Age of Revolution: Barbary Captives and the Whitening of American Democracy." The many countervailing pressures of the early American Republic threatened to create a sort of civic paralysis. If U.S. citizens thought they could solve this dilemma by associating whiteness with freedom, the revolutionary forces of black republicanism in Haiti coupled with the enslavement of white Americans in Barbary unbalanced this easy equation. As a direct result, Smith-Rosenberg finds American popular prints in the early Republic awash in panicked tales of white slaves and black revolutionaries, twin literary strains with genesis in the same political dilemma. In effect, the representations of white Barbary captives turned their slavery into badges of citizenship, denying the equivalency of the black experience of enslavement and reinforcing the equation of whiteness with belonging.

Not only blacks but also Federalist Party members and sympathizers paid a political price for demurring from the emerging post-Revolutionary settlement. Opposed to the War of 1812 and the ensconcement of the new Democratic Party on the twin pillars of plantation slavery and expansive white male entitlement, Federalists found their power in the national government severely diminished in the era of 1812. Yet, again, countervailing possibilities for asserting cultural hegemony complicate the picture of complete Federalist eclipse.

For Federalist politicians fading from national power, literary authorship

---

24. On the concept of "zones of exception," see Lisa Lowe, *The Intimacies of Four Continents* (Durham, N.C., 2015), 16. Robert G. Parkinson has written extensively on the role of racial exclusion in the Revolutionary formation of the American nation. See Parkinson, *The Common Cause: Creating Race and Nation in the American Revolution* (Chapel Hill, N.C., 2016).

became a last resort for reclaiming an effective measure of public influence and authority. Duncan Faherty's essay, "'Murder, Robbery, Rape, Adultery, and Incest': Martha Meredith Read's *Margaretta* and the Function of Federalist Fiction," presents *Margaretta* as an example of Federalist writers in the period of Republican ascendancy exerting renewed national influence in spite of their formal political decline. Federalists opposed to every element of Republican Francophilia—from French physiocrats' denunciations of the sort of trade protections preferred by Federalist merchants to French revolutionaries' embrace of radical democratization—mounted symbolic displays of the dangers of American "Jacobinism."[25]

The plot of *Margaretta* offered the perfect vehicle for inserting Federalist concerns into public debates; the novel portrayed a heroine threatened by the mercenary ambitions of an adoptive father who sought to marry her off to the highest bidder, a man who epitomized the selfish ambition and acquisitive nature that characterized America's emerging democratic order. Estranged from her erstwhile father, Margaretta fled, first to Saint Domingue and then to England, only to find the one a seat of violent radicalism and the other a land of aristocratic exploitation. For Margaretta, only a return to the United States to live in a well-ordered Federalist household after many harrowing journeys in the Caribbean and the Atlantic could resolve the tensions between freely mobile individuals and traditional communal obligations. In explicating the Federalist message of *Margaretta*, Faherty opens to view the fissures within the dominant culture over the allocation of power.[26]

Of course, for some whites, the very existence of a commitment to liberty

---

25. Work such as this amplifies the findings on Federalist uses of culture as a form of political influence presented by scholars such as Albrecht Koschnik, *"Let a Common Interest Bind Us Together": Associations, Partisanship, and Culture in Philadelphia, 1775–1840* (Charlottesville, Va., 2007) and Cleves, *Reign of Terror*. On the direct influence of French physiocrats on the nationally dominant Republican Party, see Eustace, *1812*. On early American political economy more broadly, see Steven Watts, *The Republic Reborn: War and the Making of Liberal America, 1790–1820* (Baltimore, 1989); John L. Brooke, *Columbia Rising: Civil Life on the Upper Hudson from the Revolution to the Age of Jackson* (Chapel Hill, N.C., 2010), esp. chaps. 8 and 9.

26. Catherine O'Donnell Kaplan also presents culture as a realm beyond politics in which men might nevertheless enjoy public influence, a prospect of special appeal to out-of-power Federalists in the early Republic but also useful to leading men generally. See Kaplan, *Men of Letters in the Early Republic: Cultivating Forms of Citizenship* (Chapel Hill, N.C., 2008).

provided ideological cover for the economic recommitment to slavery. Christen Mucher suggests that merchant sailors in the 1812 era might have used the U.S. government's tacit approval of their evasions of British naval blockades—officially circumvented in the name of free trade—to find a means for extending the era of Atlantic slavery even after the British-mandated end of the trade. In "Conceptual Traffic: The Atlantic Slave Trade and the War of 1812," Mucher contends convincingly that we should regard the War of 1812 era as the beginning of the clandestine period of the Atlantic slave trade. Mucher charts the existence of a thriving trade in contraband between France and the United States even at the height of military blockades and posits that this illicit inventory likely included slaves. Despite the formal legal end to the trade in 1808, a vital black market in enslaved blacks persisted on the Atlantic. She urges us to see that the very language of "free trade and sailors rights," which on the surface consisted of claims about freedom of movement and the importance of consent, cloaked a dispute about vested economic interests.

Although some Americans, in the pursuit of self-interest, circumvented the one clause in the Constitution that, however indirectly, recognized the Atlantic slave trade as a wrong to be eliminated, principles of universal rights did afford opportunities for the dispossessed to stand their ground. Indeed, the very warriors fighting military battles used the moral capital of liberty as a weapon. As Nathaniel Millett describes in a biographical sketch with geopolitical implications, when Britons fought Americans for the mantle of freedom they could do so on the strength of an abolitionist ideology honed in revolutionary Saint Domingue. In "The Radicalism of the First Seminole War and Its Consequences," Millett presents the story of a Royal Marine named Edward Nicolls who arrived in Florida fresh from fighting alongside revolutionaries in Haiti, providing a living link between rebelling former slaves in the Caribbean and those in mainland Florida. Nicolls consciously positioned himself as an opposition leader fighting against the related American projects of engrossing Indian territory in the Southeast and enslaving the African Americans needed to work these new lands. Leading a combined force of formerly enslaved blacks, Red Sticks, and Seminoles against the United States, he brought the ideals of the freedom struggle from Haiti to the eager hands of rebels in America. Combatants in the Seminole War were more than ready to meet U.S. claims to champion liberty with an overt rejection of the U.S. commitment to slavery and colonial expansion. These warriors struggled, not for freedom within, but rather for freedom from the United States. In effect, they were attempting to redraw the zones defining American exception.[27]

Part 2, "Representing the Republic," addresses the cultural imperatives involved in shaping the contours of republican culture and in establishing the criteria for status claims. Without the benefit of inherited justifications for their supremacy, American elites embraced republican liberty and virtue to burnish their ambitions with an ideological glow of legitimacy. But, as they projected ideals of the republican subject that mirrored themselves, the image splintered. In trying to model the exemplary citizen while at the same time appropriating authority and material assets, white males introduced new instabilities in the equation between equality and democracy. People on all sides could access the principles of universal rights to assert their own version of moral worth.

Yet black and white soldiers, even when they offered comparable service, gained vastly different returns on their national investments. Whereas black soldiers found racial attitudes often overwhelmed the value of armed efforts, white military men could compound the interest earned on their military service by adding a veneer of honor to their right to rule. In his essay, "For the Love of Glory: Napoleonic Imperatives in the Early American Republic," Matthew Rainbow Hale describes the importance of Napoleonic ideas of glory in the culture and politics of the nineteenth-century United States. The shift from the self-sacrificing virtue once proclaimed by many leaders in the Revolutionary era to officers' ambitious pursuit of glory embodied in the cult of Napoleon brought an intensified militaristic element to American culture. Nothing better defined an exclusively white and masculine brand of virtue and merit than military valor exerted on behalf of the national effort to extend into new territories. Self-aggrandizement worked hand in hand with geopolitical expansion. If one current reaching United States waters came from the Caribbean freedom movements that inspired fighters like the Seminoles, the reactionary Napoleonic imperative to preserve racial privilege at all costs proved to be a riptide with a wide Atlantic reach.

James M. Greene offers us a meditation on the outcomes experienced by black soldiers who took up arms for the United States. In "Military Service and Racial Subjectivity in the War Narratives of James Roberts and Isaac Hubbell," Greene compares two memoirs of the War of 1812 written

---

27. Christopher Leslie Brown has been influential in demonstrating the usefulness of "moral capital" as a historical concept. See Brown, *Moral Capital*.

on the eve of the Civil War, one voiced by an apologist for slavery and the other by a free black man, in order to reveal the methods by which white men of "merit" claimed exemption from the requirements of republican self-sacrifice. He reminds us that, for blacks, service as an avenue to citizenship was a path strewn with perils. So often, the dispossessed paid with their very lives in the effort to counteract civic death. Greene emphasizes that black servicemen more often won only continued subjugation. In a nation built in no small part on measuring marks of merit, whiteness itself became an important form of cultural capital. The correlation between property in whiteness and property in land—between the racial and the material—deepened significantly as each was expanded for Euro-Americans through the 1812 era and beyond.[28]

Continuing the theme of biography and autobiography, this time by scrutinizing the form, rather than simply analyzing the contents, Tim Lanzendörfer offers a close examination of biographical writing about naval officers in "Naval Biography, the War of 1812, and the Contestation of American National Identity." Lanzendörfer dissects wartime writers' attempts to portray naval officers as "eidolons," heroes who embodied the nation, in order to infuse the empty idea of the American nation with patriotic meaning. Yet, even within this very narrowly defined literary form, Lanzendörfer documents multiple conflicting strategies for defining American identity, from claims of lineal kinship to Britain to strict denials of such ties. In the incoherence of even such a tightly scripted form of nationalist cultural production, Lanzendörfer finds further evidence of the fractured nature of the early Republic.

The contradictions permeating claims to belong in the nation arose out of the related difficulty of fixing the true source of national authority. Precisely because the nation was not yet bound by any agreed-upon definition, even acknowledged leaders struggled to assert their place. Eric Wertheimer dissects a very specific yet highly illuminating instance of this problem in his essay, "The Self-Abstracting Letters of War: Madison, Henry, and the Executive Author," in which he plays with the connections between political authority and literary authorship. Werthheimer begins by noting that James Madison, principal author of the American Constitution, was also

---

28. For a discussion of how state recognition of black citizenship often arrived only in time for the punishment of black men designated as criminal offenders—and on the implications for all of having free black citizenship forever linked to "culpable personhood"—see Jeannine Marie DeLombard, *In the Shadow of the Gallows: Race, Crime, and American Civic Identity* (Philadelphia, 2012).

the author of the nation's first declared war. Paradoxically, in authoring the Constitution, Madison had removed declarations of war from executive purview to the legislative realm, in effect deauthorizing his future self. Madison the president thus made an uneasy heir to Madison the architect of the Constitution.

Madison's political problem required a cultural remedy. Using the newspaper publicity surrounding a purported espionage scandal, he experimented with manipulating public opinion. In so doing, he found a new source of leverage, one stemming from the people. In this telling, regular people, including even those without the vote, gained new influence as public commentators. Yet, crucially, Wertheimer argues that ordinary individuals could exert only diluted influence as members of collectives. By contrast, a leading man like Madison, with disproportionate access to the press and to the bully pulpit, could play a decisive role in molding public opinion in his own right. Madison thus gained new power even as he appeared to abstract himself from authority.

However much the idea of popular sovereignty—which accounted for Madison's diminution of executive power in favor of legislative power—affirmed the participation of white Americans in the polity, for free black Americans national membership brought few tangible privileges. Anna Mae Duane's essay, "'Can You Be Surprised at My Discouragement?' Global Emulation and the Logic of Colonization at the New York African Free School," reminds us of the extent to which whites by the 1820s were willing to go in imagining a nation without blacks and the lengths to which free blacks had to go to overturn such ideas. The white board members who directed the African Free School also numbered among the most prominent proponents of the African Colonization Society, whose goals were to remove all free blacks from the United States to some new colony. The school's directors intended the circulation of knowledge begun at the school as the precursor for the circulation of black bodies. The imagined outcome of their efforts was not socioeconomic mobility so much as literal physical mobility, the removal of educated blacks to their own fledgling nation.

Duane's work revives the laments of James Fields, the 1819 valedictorian of the African Free School, who used his valedictory speech to publicize his concern that he would never be accepted into full citizenship. His speech boldly exposed the limited impact of even the most impressive black achievements in the context of whites' unremitting economic exploitation. The problem stemmed directly from the goals of colonizationists like Matthew Carey, who claimed that "no merit, no services, no talents can ever elevate them [freed blacks] to a level with the whites" and that as a result free African Americans should agree to migrate beyond the nation. James Fields defied the removal project of the colonizationists. As important, he decried black economic exclusion from the nation on the basis of culturally mediated ideas about merit that not even demonstrated academic excellence could combat. American blacks rejected whites' attempts to resolve the paradox of slavery within freedom — and to tighten the links between blackness and bondage — by ejecting them from the nation.[29]

The essays in Part 3, "Expansion and the Intimacy of Borders," look at the blurred boundaries of territories and of disparate societies existing on the edges of the United States. Like free blacks, America's first inhabitants also refused to accede to the early Republic's ideological projections onto them. Native Americans employed varied strategies in efforts to counter the hegemonic encroachments of the United States on their lives and lands. Throughout the many confrontations of the 1812 era, Indian groups from the Creeks in the South to the Potowatomis in the old Northwest took divergent approaches to the common goal of preserving their own domains while resisting that of the United States. In his essay, "Widening the Scope on the Indians' Old Northwest," Jonathan Todd Hancock dismantles the scholarly binary of accommodationist versus nativist Indians to reveal that Indians drew on their own cultural systems to make continuing strategic adjustments to one another and to the United States. Comparing Indians' reactions across the middle of the country to a series of earthquakes that convulsed the continent, Hancock analyzes an array of Indian responses that both reflected Indians' rich and vibrant philosophical repertoires and anticipated the diverse tactics they would bring to struggles for sovereignty.

Tribal quests for sovereignty were paralleled by the efforts of individual Indians to assert autonomy in sometimes highly counterintuitive fashion. In "Domestic Fronts in the Era of 1812: Slavery, Expansion, and Familial Struggles for Sovereignty in the Early-Nineteenth-Century Choctaw South," Dawn Peterson untangles the simultaneously interlocking and countervailing family formations of U.S. whites and Choctaw Indians. Peterson recounts the stories of Molly McDonald, a Choctaw mother, and Silas Dinsmoor, the

---

29. M[atthew] Carey, *Reflections on the Causes That Led to the Formation of the Colonization Society: With a View of Its Probable Results* ... (Philadelphia, 1832), 16. Such research adds to the portrait of the intersections of cultural racism and institutionalized forms of unequal social and labor relations offered in Joanne Pope Melish, *Disowning Slavery: Gradual Emancipation and "Race" in New England, 1780–1860* (Ithaca, N.Y., 1998).

Indian agent whom she willingly allowed to adopt her son James. Dinsmoor viewed the agreement as the ultimate demonstration of his paternalistic power. Yet this Choctaw woman's apparent acceptance of a white man's authority was in actuality a bid to incorporate him in a kinship network of her own design—and to use that family constellation to her own material advantage. By forging this relationship with Dinsmoor, McDonald gained the leverage she needed to preserve her landholdings when many Choctaws were losing theirs. In a nation where power relied so heavily on dominant authority structures, Peterson's essay demonstrates the impact that divergent family strategies could have on economic and political struggles. Subordinated people could and did appropriate prevailing social systems and expectations to their own economic purposes.

If the bounds of authority were challenging to maintain, they were equally difficult to ascertain. When Peterson writes of the "Choctaw South" (a placename probably never used on any historical map, yet no less accurate for that), she reminds us that the very geography of American sovereignty remained fluid and uncertain in this era. Karen L. Marrero's essay, "'Borders Thick and Foggy': Mobility, Community, and Nation in a Northern Indigenous Region," captures the pervasive unease among diverse peoples from the United States to Canada about porous national parameters. Studying the edge-land region of the Great Lakes between Canada and the United States, and tracking the paths of the U.S. migrants, Potawatomis, and indigenized French who traversed that ground through the 1830s, Marrero argues that Indians' adherence to the standard of birthright tribal membership ensured that for them not even profound displacement could impose total cultural dislocation. In fact, the Potowatomis would continue to maintain, even in the midst of mass migrations, that blood ties, language, and culture were the keys to identity irrespective of geography. Their nationality was something they carried with them in their bodies no matter where they might be forced to migrate, a crucial reminder of the material body's role in transmitting culture.

White Americans wished to rely on boundary staking to further the task of nation making. They designed their exacting (if ever-expanding) geopolitical maps in deliberate contrast to the Indian view of nations as floating and flexible nets of affiliation. And yet, like so many other supposedly signal traits of the United States, the borders of national authority were far less well defined than nationalists tried to assert. From white women like Duncan Faherty's Margaretta, who crossed over U.S. borders in defiance of the limits of patriarchy, to black men, whether sailors, soldiers, or students, who refused to be fenced out of the nation, many Americans did not respect or recognize the lines leading men tried to draw. In fact, in the final essay by Brian Connolly, the outlines of America remained nebulous precisely because there never was any fully formed and authentically autonomous nation around which a bold line could have been drawn.

Connolly starts by describing a legal conundrum vexing the new nation: gaining international recognition of American sovereignty—a key requirement for finalizing and institutionalizing the new nation's independence and financial solvency—required limiting that sovereignty in instances where U.S. law conflicted with the laws of other nations. The new nation could not hope to gain legitimacy on the international stage unless it in turn recognized the reach of international law. In his essay, "'Hindoo Marriage' and National Sovereignty in the Early-Nineteenth-Century United States," he shows that international variations in marriage law became an especially dramatic instance of this dilemma. Dissecting popular discussions of "Hindoo marriage," featured widely in national newspapers and magazines throughout the first decades of the nineteenth century, Connolly reveals that, regardless of their legal validity, only certain kinds of marriages merited recognition. Even if the U.S. government could not legally invalidate foreign marriages that contradicted American statutes, popular American attitudes could fatally undermine their acceptance. Here, again, we can appreciate that hegemonic values could trump the exigencies of national public policy.

White Christian patriarchy runs like an invisible thread through many of these essays and the historical events they consider. Articles on "Hindoo marriage" invited American women to regard their own unions as free contracts, in contrast to the coerced sales of virgins supposedly conducted by "Hindoos." Time after time in this period, whether in the case of the heroine Margaretta, who fled a false father across the oceans but then came home to a true husband, or in the case of Molly McDonald, who co-opted the patriarchal expectations of a white patron to further female property rights, the terms of women's political and economic exclusion were tested, if not overturned, in the midst of struggles over the reach of white male dominance.

For the people in these essays, America was a country that they did not just fight for in the War of 1812; it was a place they fought over from the post-Revolutionary decades through the 1820s and 1830s. The very definition of the nation was a crucial battleground. During this era, the territory of the United States doubled, incorporating alien populations of French and Spanish along with Africans who had lived under these rival colonial regimes as well as new native groups on the land. A United States that could not identify its borders, much less defend them, became an arena for continuing campaigns over who belonged and who could be excluded. In a nation that yet possessed little in the way of formal infrastructure, it took considerable cultural work to alternately reinforce or creatively reshape a political and economic system subject to continual jolts. That most of the constituent populations did not count as American citizens underscored the inadequacy of a narrow definition of the nation. As the work of military war and cultural contest began to converge in the early Republic, the equation grew ever tighter between literal and symbolic forms of power and property. Still, shoring up national sovereignty often required drawing on contributions from the very people and groups officially excluded from the polity.

For Noah Webster, as for the scholars contributing to this volume, the very point of documenting cultural shifts was to mark the progress of social and political change. As he explained in 1806: "English, like every living language, is in a state of progression, as rapid now as at any former period.... It is fruitless to attempt to fix that which is in its nature, changeable, and to fix which beyond the power of alteration, would be the greatest evil that could happen to a living language." Webster believed that languages "progressed" in tandem with "improvements" in society. Without adopting his obvious belief in American exceptionalism outright, we can take seriously his contention that culture holds a crucial key to understanding the mechanisms of the early Republic.[30]

Webster took to print not only to describe differences in American and British vocabulary but also, and as importantly, to articulate an American philosophy of culture markedly at variance with British ones. He set his work against that of Samuel Johnson, claiming that Johnson had foolishly "flattered himself that he might fix the language and put a stop to alterations." Webster chortled, "How short [s]ighted was that learned man!" Whereas Johnson sought to retard what he regarded as the decline of English, Webster positively celebrated the shifting uses of language along with the transformations in the "civil polity" enabled by cultural alterations.[31]

---

30. Webster, "Preface," in *A Compendious Dictionary*, xxii.
31. Ibid.

Despite their oppositional positions on the desirability of cultural change, both the British Johnson and the American Webster recognized fundamental connections between language and society or, as we might put it, between culture and political economy. Advocating that the English language should be crystalized at the height of "perfection," Johnson claimed, "Tongues, like governments, have a natural tendency to degeneration; we have long preserved our constitution, let us make some struggles for our language." Webster gleefully skewered this view. Of certain British usages beloved by Johnson, he exclaimed, "Most of the language ... of the old feudal and hierarchical establishments of England, will become utterly extinct in this country—much of it already forms a part of the neglected rubbish of antiquity." If Americans in the early Republic maintained only the most fractured vision of democracy, they had nevertheless embarked on a novel course in world history. Though they were as often at odds with one another as with their erstwhile British adversaries, the people "warring for America" in the era of 1812 understood that they were engaged in a crucial contest over the definition and direction of the new.[32]

The signal image of *Warring for America* is the frontispiece from Jesse Torrey's antislavery tract, *A Portraiture of Domestic Slavery, in the United States*, published in 1817. The caption reads: "View of the Capitol of the United States, after the Conflagration, in 1814." Rubble from the Capitol lies in the foreground, foreboding clouds hanging overhead. A white gentleman gestures toward the building's ruins, as if giving an admonitory lecture, while looking back over his shoulder to a coffle of enslaved black people, adults and children, their wrists chained. One of them seems to be giving attention to the lecture, while others gaze past the scene to a sight beyond the frame, perhaps even seeking eye contact with us, the viewers. They are all being herded by a staff-wielding slave driver toward a covered wagon, itself a potential reminder of the nation's insistent westward expansion onto Native lands. The image evinces the terrible destruction at the center of the Republic caused by the War of 1812 and links it to a far more enduring struggle over the terms on which that Republic is based. Hovering above the clouds in a spot of sunlight are two allegorical figures. Columbia, seated with a pole bearing a liberty cap, points toward a young maiden of the Republic,

---

32. Samuel Johnson, *A Dictionary of the English Language ...*, 2 vols. (London, 1755), [last page of unnumbered preface], 36; Webster, "Preface," in *A Compendious Dictionary*, xxii. On the long shadow of monarchy in American life, see Paul Downes, *Democracy, Revolution, and Monarchism in Early American Literature* (Cambridge, 2002).

whose hand is lifted toward heaven. These female cultural symbols direct their gaze at the viewers, enjoining all to raise their sights to the inclusive cause of freedom. That Torrey himself was animated by both his condemnation of slave trafficking and his commitment to the political economy of property rights—including property in people—in the United States adds shaded meaning to the tableau. The scene vivifies the deeply ambivalent attitudes of many Americans in this uncertain era, aware of the fault lines beneath the foundation of the society they were struggling—in concert and in conflict—to build from the ground.[33]

33. Jesse Torrey, *A Portraiture of Domestic Slavery, in the United States: With Reflections on the Practicability of Restoring the Moral Rights of the Slave, without Impairing the Legal Privileges of the Possessor; and a Project of a Colonial Asylum for Free Persons of Colour: Including Memoirs of Facts on the Interior Traffic in Slaves, and on Kidnapping; Illustrated with Engravings* (Philadelphia, 1817). For more on the sharp limits of Torrey's antislavery politics, see Eustace, *1812*, esp. chapter 5.

PART I

SLAVERY, NATION, AND THE ONGOING REVOLUTION

MINSTRELIZATION AND NATIONHOOD
"BACKSIDE ALBANY," BACKLASH, AND THE WARTIME ORIGINS OF BLACKFACE MINSTRELSY

David Waldstreicher

The first blackface minstrel song debuted as a stage piece, "sung in the Character of a Black Sailor," as the Boston broadside version put it, at the Green Street Theatre in Albany, New York, a few weeks after the American victory in the Battle of Plattsburgh, in a play about that campaign. Later titled for its provocative first line, "Backside Albany" was not only "one of the most popular songs written and sung during the war," according to the mid-nineteenth-century chronicler Benson J. Lossing, it was also "the most popular song in the United States during the winter of 1814–15" (see Figure 1). The lyrics appeared in at least fifteen songsters before 1830 and remained a favorite during the subsequent elaboration of blackface minstrelsy into what we now remember as "the minstrel show." During an 1834 interview with U.S. Army commanding general Alexander Macomb, hero of the Battle of Plattsburgh, a journalist tried hard to concentrate but found himself "thinking all the while of"

> BACKside Albany stan' Lake Champlain
> One little pond, half full a' water.

The writer could be sure that his readers would get the joke because the song that referred to Macomb four times had proven at least as memorable as the general. Even two generations later, a local historian of Westport, New York, could barely contain her disgust at the memory that "no social occasion was complete without it for many years."[1]

The author would like to thank Corey Capers, Nicole Eustace, Sarah Gronningsater, Michael Meranze, Heather S. Nathans, Jason Shaffer, Fredrika Teute, Eran Zelnik, and members of the CUNY Early American Republic Seminar for helpful readings.

1. "Congressional Sketches," *Saratoga Sentinel* (Saratoga Springs, N.Y.), Jan. 7, 1834, [2]; *The Battle of Plattsburg — Tune, ... Banks of the Dee; together with the Siege of Plattsburg, Sung in the Character of a Black Sailor ...* ([Boston], [1814?]) (all lyrics to this song cited in the text are from this edition); "[By Request] Siege of Plattsburg," *Republican*

THE BATTLE OF PLATTSBURG. Tune,...Banks of the DEE.
Together with the Siege of Plattsburg, sung in the Character of a Black Sailor.—Tune.—"Boyn-Water."

TWAS autumn, around me the leaves were descending,
And lonely the wood-pecker peck'd on the tree :
Whilst thousands their freedom & rights were defending,
The din of their arms sounded dismal to me,
For Sandy, my love, was engag'd in the action,
His death would have ended my life in distraction ;
Without him I valued this world not a fraction,
As lonely I stray'd on the Banks of Champlain.
  Then turning to list to the cannons' loud thunder,
My elbow I lean'd on a rock near the shore :
The sound nearly parted my heart strings asunder,
I thought I should see my dear shepherd no more,
But soon an express all my sorrows suspended,
My thanks, to the Father of Mercies, ascended ;
My shepherd was safe and my country defended,
By freedom's brave sons, on the banks of Champlain.
Wip'd from my eyes the big tears that had start d,
And hastened to parents the news for to bear
Who sad for the loss of relations departed,
And wept at the tidings that bani-hed all care,
The cannon ceas'd roaring, the drums still were beating,
The foes of our country, for the North were retreating.
The neighboring damsels each other were greeting,
With songs of delight, on the Banks of Champlain.
  They sung of the heroes whose valor had made us,
Sole nation on earth, independent and free ;
And so we'll remain, with kind Heaven to aid us,
In spite of invaders, by land or by sea:
New York, the Green Mountain, M'Comb, & M'Donnough
The Farmer, the soldier, the sailor, and Gunner ;
All parties united had plighted their honor,
To conquer or die, on the Banks of Champlain.
Our squadron triumphant, our army victorious,
With laurels unfaded, our spartans' return'd ;
My eyes never dwelt on a scene half so glorious,
My heart with such raptures, before never burn'd,
For Sandy my darling, that moment appearing,
His presence to ev'ry countenance cheering,
Was render'd to me more than doubly endearing,
By the feats he'd perform'd, on the Banks of Champlain.
  But should smiling peace, with her blessings & treasures,
Soon visit the plains of Columbia again,
What pen can describe the enrapturing pleasures,
Which I shall experience, through life, with my swain,
For now no wild savage will come to alarm us,
No worse British foe, send their millions to harm us ;
But nature and art will continue to charm us,
While so happy we'll live, on the Banks of Champlain.

BACK side Albany stan' Lake Champlain,
  One little pond, half full a' water,
Plat-te-bug dare too, close pon de main,
  Town small, he grow bigger do hereafter.
    On Lake Champlain
    Uncle Sam set he boat,
  And Massa M'Donough he sail 'em,
    While Gen'ral M'Comb
    Make Plat-te-bug he home,
Wid de army, who courage nebber fail 'em.

On 'lebenth day of Sep tem-ber,
  In eighteen hund'red an fourteen,
Gubbener Probose, an he British soger,
Come to Plat-te-bug a tea party courtin ;
  An he boat come too
  Arter uncle Sam boat;
Massa Donough do look sharp out de winder,
  Den Gen'ral Mc Comb.
  (Ah ! he always at home.)
Catch fire too, jis like a tinder.

Bang ! bang ! bang !! den de cannons gin
  t' roar.
In Plat-te bug an all 'b ut dat quarter ;
Gubbener Probose try he hand 'pon de shore,
While he boat take he luck 'pon de water,
  But Massa M'Donough
  Knock he boat in he head,
Break he heart broke he shin, 'teve he caf-
  fin in,
  An General Mc Comb,
  Start ole Probose home,
Tot me soul den, I mus die a laffin.

Probose scare so, he lef all behine,
Powder, ball, cannon, tea-pot an kittle,
Some say he catch a cole., trouble in he mine,
Cause he eat so much raw an cole vittle.
  Uncle Sam berry sorry,
  To be sure, for he pain ;
Wish he nuss heself up well an hearty,
For Gen'ral Mc'Comb, an Massa 'Donough
  home,
When he notion for a nudder tea party.

Printed by Nathaniel Coverly, Jun.

Figure 1. *The Battle of Plattsburg—Tune,... Banks of the Dee; together with the Siege of Plattsburg, Sung in the Character of a Black Sailor* ... ([Boston], [1814?]). Courtesy, Boston Public Library

Not so differently, during the late twentieth century "Backside Albany" became alternately a joke and an embarrassment to the sophisticated scholars who stressed the ambivalence and multivocality of blackface minstrelsy in its formative years. The song elicited such scholarly schadenfreude because, although it initiated the rapid expansion of a distinct genre or repertoire with racial denigration as its core (or, more importantly, at its performative surface), the tune hardly appears to be about race or black people at all. For what it is about, indisputably, is the War of 1812: the seemingly whitest war in American history. Even for those who insist that 1830s–1850s minstrelsy was usually also about class, about gender, about manifest destiny, and about the politics of slavery, this focus on the war is just too much— or rather too little?—to square with either the newer sense of the genre's multiple meanings or with its lasting, if not original, sin of racism. It has been easier to banish a song written, performed, and possibly printed in 1814 to "after the War of 1812": a postwar period quickly turned "antebellum" and imagined to have little to do with the War of 1812. As a result, a question that might seem obvious has remained unasked: Why was the first popular blackface song—the first tune sung in black dialect in blackface about specifically American characters and events, then reproduced in print, then later remembered as the first of its kind—about a northern front victory in 1814?[2]

Farmer (Bridgeport, Conn.), July 5, 1815, [4]; "Siege of Plattsburgh," *The Aeolian Harp; or, Songster's Cabinet* ..., 2 vols. (New York, 1817), II, 51–52; "The Seige of Plattsburgh," *The Columbian Songster* ... (Pittsburgh, Pa., 1818), 40–41; "Independence," *New-York American*, July 4, 1823; *Hornet and Peacock, and Battle of Plat-te-bug* (Boston, [1829]); Benson J. Lossing, *The Pictorial Field-Book of the War of 1812* ... (New York, 1896), 876– 877 n. 3; John R[andolph] Spears, *The History of Our Navy from Its Origin to the Present Day* (New York, 1897), III, 184; Ken Emerson, *Doo-dah! Stephen Foster and the Rise of American Popular Culture* (New York, 1997), 71; William J. Mahar, "'Backside Albany' and Early Blackface Minstrelsy: A Contextual Study of America's First Blackface Song," *American Music*, VI (1988), 2; Vera Brodsky Lawrence, "Micah Hawkins, the Pied Piper of Catherine Slip," *New-York Historical Society Quarterly*, LXII (1978), 151; S. Foster Damon, "The Negro in Early American Songsters," *Papers of the Bibliographical Society of America*, XXVIII (1934), 143–144, 155–162; Caroline Halstead Royce, *Bessboro: A History of Westport, Essex Co., N.Y.* ([Westport, N.Y.], 1902), 278.

2. Dale Cockrell, *Demons of Disorder: Early Blackface Minstrels and Their World* (Cambridge, 1997); Michael Rogin, *Blackface, White Noise: Jewish Immigrants in the Hollywood Melting Pot* (Berkeley, Calif., 1996), 27; Eric Lott, *Love and Theft: Blackface Minstrelsy and the American Working Class* (New York, 1993), 44; Robert C. Toll, *Blacking Up: The Minstrel Show in Nineteenth-Century America* (New York, 1974), 3, 26. De-

Perhaps the question ought to be why we find this so surprising. Minstrelsy emerged from a musical theater culture that expanded in reach and significance because of its successes in representing war and performing national identities.³ In subsequent blackface minstrelsy, the War of 1812 remained a touchstone, as it did in so many other arenas of U.S. popular and political culture during the 1820s and beyond. T. D. Rice's genre-solidifying "Original Jim Crow" (1832) referred in its third through fifth verses (of ninety-eight) to the Battle of New Orleans, reinforcing a sense of the war as a significant, recognized moment not just of American pride but also of African American boldness and distinctiveness. That Tuckahoe's Jim Crow, beginning his prodigious riverine wanderings, promises to "cotch de Uncle Sam" to "de place / Where dey kill'd Packenham" and further boasts that New Orleans made him "feel so full of fight" that he "hit a man" so hard it

---

spite his important 1988 article on "Backside Albany," William J. Mahar focused on the 1840s and beyond in his *Behind the Burnt Cork Mask: Early Blackface Minstrelsy and Antebellum American Popular Culture* (Urbana, Ill., 1999).

As Robert Christgau observes, even "postmodern minstrelsy studies" obsess over, when they do not fall for, the origin myth of Jim Crow as black stablehand observed by Thomas D. Rice in 1830—a story that obviates the need to consider an earlier period. See Christgau "In Search of Jim Crow: Why Postmodern Minstrelsy Studies Matter," in JT Leroy, ed., *DaCapo Best Music Writing 2005* (New York, 2005), 17-40. For exceptions that reach back instead to urban interracialism at Catherine Slip, New York City, circa 1820, where Micah Hawkins's grocery was located, see W. T. Lhamon, Jr., *Raising Cain: Blackface Performance from Jim Crow to Hip Hop* (Cambridge, Mass., 1998), 7-8; and Peter G. Buckley, "'The Place to Make an Artist Work': Micah Hawkins and William Sidney Mount in New York City," in *Catching the Tune: Music and William Sidney Mount* (Stony Brook, N.Y., 1984), 26-28. Lhamon, in particular, while putting forward Catherine Slip as an alternative primal scene, leaves open the likelihood that these dynamics of "Atlantic popular culture" go back further and has declined to posit a move from early Republic simplicity to industrial-era complexity: "Postmodernism has nothing on popular culture from the early Republic." See Lhamon, "Core Is Less," *Reviews in American History*, XXVII (1999), 567-568. For transatlantic approaches that also stress earlier examples of blackface performance, see Jenna M. Gibbs, *Performing the Temple of Liberty: Slavery, Theater, and Popular Culture in London and Philadelphia, 1760-1850* (Baltimore, 2014), esp. 6, 14, 116-117, 177-179, 198-199; and Elizabeth Maddock Dillon, *New World Drama: The Performative Commons in the Atlantic World, 1649-1849* (Durham, N.C., 2014).

3. For theater and war in contemporary British context, see Gillian Russell, *The Theatres of War: Performance, Politics, and Society, 1793-1815* (Oxford, 1995). For the Revolutionary War context in England, see Daniel O'Quinn, *Staging Governance: Theatrical Imperialism in London, 1770-1800* (Baltimore, 2005); and O'Quinn, *Entertaining Crisis in the Atlantic Imperium, 1770-1790* (Baltimore, 2011).

left nothing of him "'Sept a little grease spot" suggests more racial politics in the war, and more war in the racial politics, than either the scholarship on 1812 or on minstrelsy allows.[4]

Both the underrating of the War of 1812 as the moment of minstrelsy's emergence and the neglect of minstrelsy's wartime origins derives from a larger difficulty in placing the making of race and the making of nationalism in relation to one another, as each were invented and redeveloped during the post-Revolutionary decades. Considered in a context of black sailors and emerging black political and literary culture in the North and of identity confusion during the war fought over possession of borderlands and over the bodies of English-speaking sailors, the Battle of Plattsburgh's "Backside Albany" can be seen as much a part of the War of 1812's reinvention of American nationhood—and shaped as much by that conflict's multifront particularities—as the war's better-known musical syntheses, New Orleans's "Hunters of Kentucky" and Baltimore's "Star-Spangled Banner." Indeed, the story of "Backside Albany" helps us understand the African American referents in these other battle-inspired anthems of 1815, and thus their larger contexts as well.

We might then be in a position to comprehend how "Backside Albany" served as the pivot that allowed minstrelsy to begin to do its political and cultural work, how it became the specifically originating instance of a larger process Eric Lott has called *minstrelization*. In minstrelization, performers of minstrelizing forms, live and in print, simultaneously racialized African Americans and, by ventriloquizing them, nationalized themselves as Americans.[5] The racializing aspects appear to have depended upon the national-

---

4. "The Original Jim Crow" (New York, 1832), in W. T. Lhamon, Jr., ed., *Jump Jim Crow: Lost Plays, Lyrics, and Street Prose of the First Atlantic Popular Culture* (Cambridge, Mass., 2003), 96; Jon W. Finson, *The Voices That Are Gone: Themes in Nineteenth-Century American Popular Song* (New York, 1994), 164-165, 170. Paul Gilje observes that, despite the profusion of work on race and slavery in U.S. history and culture, "there has been little done to place the War of 1812 in this larger narrative." "Instead we have little snippets of stories about black activity during the war.... Most of the standard histories of race and slavery seem to jump over the war as if nothing important happened." See Gilje, "Interchange: The War of 1812," *Journal of American History*, LXXXIX (2012), 544-545. This gap, of course, reflected the scholarship on the war itself, at least until the appearance, the year following Gilje's published remarks, of Alan Taylor, *The Internal Enemy: Slavery and War in Virginia, 1772-1832* (New York, 2013); and Gene Allen Smith, *The Slaves' Gamble: Choosing Sides in the War of 1812* (New York, 2013).

5. Lott, *Love and Theft*, 40-41; Rogin, *Blackface, White Noise*, 49-52. Both Rogin and Lott emphasized the striking presence of non-U.S.-born performers in the genre.

izing framework. What scholars usually mean by blackface minstrelsy—and (with some contemporaries) locate as a distinctly American form of popular culture—was a nationalist variation in a transatlantic tradition of blackface performances that already had both antislavery and proslavery variants. Minstrelsy might have fermented in particular urban borders in the North and South—New York, Louisville, Kentucky—but it improved upon a particular nationalist idiom and arrived to do the work of nationhood.[6]

"Backside Albany" had a generating force, and it did ultimately fit neatly into the developing minstrelsy playlist, as the ragtag image that appeared with the sheet music in 1837 suggests most immediately (see Figures 2 and 3). Yet the seeming problem of the song being about the war (and thus, thanks to our whitened memory of the war, not about black people) has ob-

---

I have earlier analyzed ventriloquism in the literary blackface of the "Bobalition broadsides" in *In the Midst of Perpetual Fetes: The Making of American Nationalism, 1776-1820* (Chapel Hill, N.C., 1997), 336-342. For other, compatible anaylses, see especially, Shane White, "'It Was a Proud Day': African Americans, Festivals, and Parades in the North, 1741-1834," *Journal of American History*, LXXXI (1994), 35-38; Shane White and Graham White, *Stylin': African American Expressive Culture from Its Beginnings to the Zoot Suit* (Ithaca, N.Y., 1998), 108-114; Joanne Pope Melish, *Disowning Slavery: Gradual Emancipation and "Race" in New England, 1780-1860* (Ithaca, N.Y., 1998), 166-183; John Wood Sweet, *Bodies Politic: Negotiating Race in the American North, 1730-1830* (Baltimore, 2003), 378-392; Corey Capers, "Black Voices, White Print: Racial Practice, Print Publicity, and Order in the Early American Republic," in Lara Langer Cohen and Jordan Alexander Stein, eds., *Early African American Print Culture* (Philadelphia, 2012), 107-126; Gibbs, *Performing the Temple of Liberty*, 43-50; Douglas A. Jones, Jr., *The Captive Stage: Performance and the Proslavery Imagination of the Antebellum North* (Ann Arbor, Mich., 2014), 40-49.

6. For a transatlantic emphasis, see Gibbs, *Performing the Temple of Liberty*. Dillon argues specifically that Jim Crow "assists in defining U.S. nationalism by erasure of a prior, Atlantic history" (*New World Drama*, 218). Following Mahar, "'Backside Albany' and Early Blackface Minstrelsy," Robert Nowatzki has argued that "Backside Albany" demonstrates how "nationalism trumps racism" at minstrelsy's origins, a useful corrective that nevertheless posits a false dichotomy. See Nowatzki, *Representing African Americans in Transatlantic Abolitionism and Blackface Minstrelsy* (Baton Rouge, La., 2010), 107. Compare Hans Nathan, *Dan Emmett and the Rise of Early Negro Minstrelsy* (Norman, Okla., 1962), 34-35, who depicted the song as the refreshing emergence of a real black American voice on the stage, in contrast to earlier and later stereotypes. Reflecting on the presence and erasure of Crispus Attucks, another black sailor, Tavia Nyong'o observes a "simultaneity of inclusion and exclusion" and proceeds to note that minstrelsy would evoke both scorn and a sense of possibility from blacks because it did not completely erase blacks from the national-popular. See Nyong'o, *The Amalgamation Waltz: Race, Performance, and the Ruses of Memory* (Minneapolis, Minn., 2009), 47, 132.

Figure 2. *Backside Albany* ... (New York, 1837). Courtesy, the Lester S. Levy Collection of Sheet Music, Sheridan Libraries, Johns Hopkins University

BACK SIDE ALBANY.

And he boat come too arter Uncle Sam boat.

AND JACK OF GUINEA.

Battle of Plat-te-bug.

Back side Albany stan' Lake Champlain,
One little pond, half full a' water;
Plat-te-bug dare too, close pon de main—
Town small—he grow biger do herearter.
On Lake Champlain Uncle Sam set he boat,
And Massa M'Donnough he sail 'em,
While Gen'ral M'Comb make Plat-te-bug he home,
Wid de army, who courage nebber fail 'em.

On lebenth day of Sep-pe-tem-ber,
In eighteen hundred an fourteen,
Gubbenur Probose, an he British soger,
Come to Plat-te-bug a tea party courtin;
An he boat come too arter Uncle Sam boat,
Massa 'Donnough do look sharp out de winder,
Den General M'Comb (ah! he always a home,)
Catch fire too, jiss like tinder.

Bang—Bang—Bang den de cannons 'gin t' roar
In Plat-te-bug, an all about dat quarter;
Gubbenur Probose try he hand 'pon de shore,
While he boat he take he luck 'pon de water;
But Massa M'Donnough knock he boat in he head,
Broke he hart, broke he shin, 'tove in he caffin,
An General M'Comb start ole Probose home,
Tot me soul den I muss die a laffin.

Ole Probose scare so, he lef all behine,
Powder, ball, cannon, tea-pot an kittle—
Some say he cotch a cole, trouble in he mine,
'Cause he eat so much raw an cole vittle.
Uncle Sam berry sorry to be sure, for he pain;
Wish he nuss himself up well and hearty—
And have Gen. M'Comb an Massa Donnough home
When he notion for nudder tea party.

Jack of Guinea.

Great way off at sea, when at home I've been ee,
Buckra man fetch me from the coast of Guinea;
Christian massa pray, he call'd me heathen doggy,
Den I run away for very much he floggy.
Ri tol lol, &c.

White man bring me here, and good christian make me,
Lady fair, O dear! for a footman take me,
Stand behind her chair she faro play for guinea;
Always she play fair, yet she always winnee.
Ri tol lol, &c.

Lady run away, lawyer man now take me,
Latin word he say, and great rogue he make me;
Poor man dare I saw go to law so funny,
He get all the law, but massa all the money.
Ri tol lol, &c.

Actor man so gay for a sarvy hire me,
Tragedy he play—play-house never tire me;
Massa often die, den good wine he quaffee,
All the people cry, I and massa laugh ee.
Ri tol lol, &c.

After dat I go with a doctor liv'ee,
Hold him hand out so, den de fee dey givee,
Dey he fool enough, massa make great fussee,
He give de patient stuff, it make the poor man worse.
Ri tol lol, &c.

Negro girl I see, love her sweet as honey,
Soon she marry me, she and I get money,
Happy on we go, she be so bewitching,
While I jump Jim Crow, she can "Clar de kitchen."
Ri tol lol, &c.

Sold wholesale and retail by Hunts & Shaw, No. 2 Mercantile wharf, and head of City wharf, North Side.

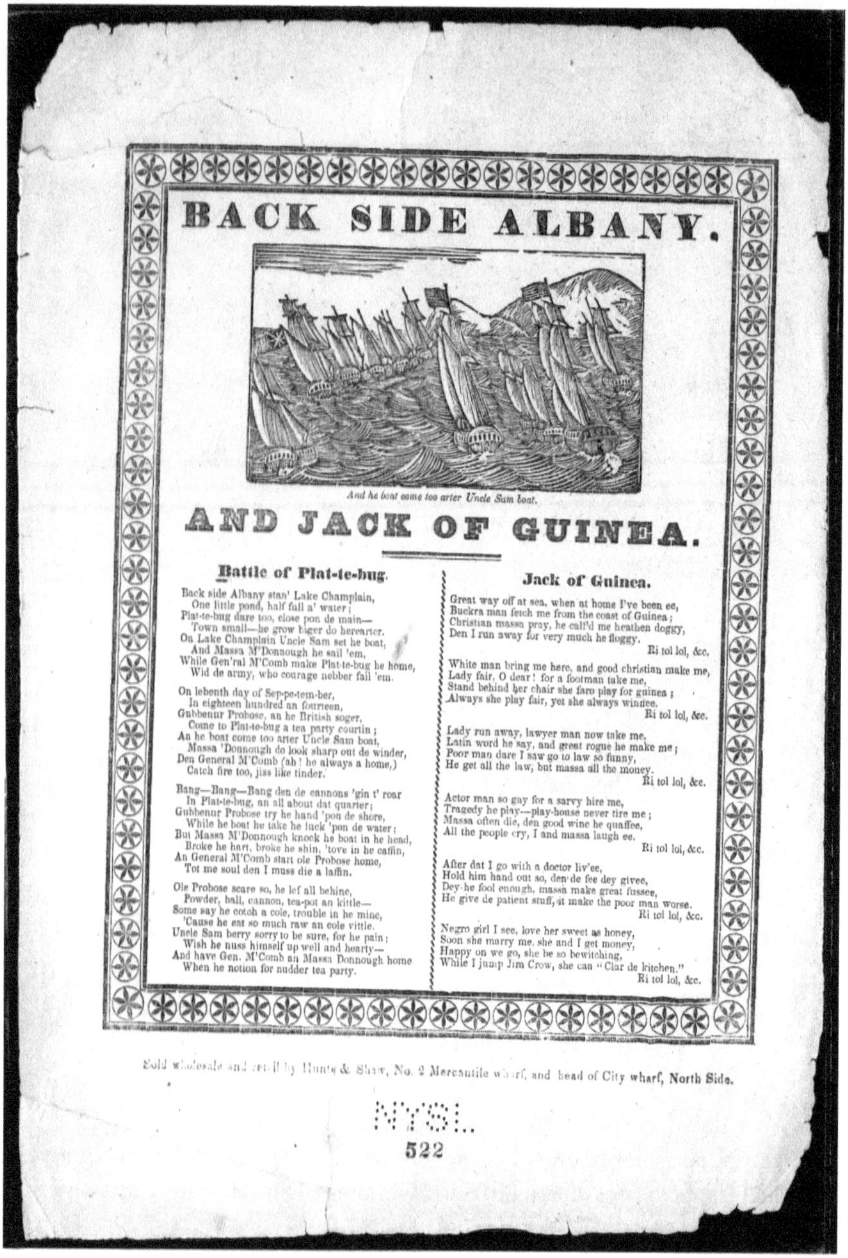

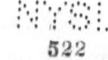

Figure 3. *Backside Albany; and Jack of Guinea* (Boston, 1837–1841?). Courtesy, Manuscripts and Special Collections, New York State Library

scured the evidence the song provides of whites dealing, strenuously, with the meaning of black participation in the war. Minstrelization could not perform its nationalizing and racializing cultural work without suggesting and to some extent working through how Africans and their descendants had moved to the center stage in the United States, both through their own actions and as a result of the nation's nascent integration as a polity and an economy. The meaning of minstrelsy, even at this early stage, lay in its simultaneous recognition and displacement of black centrality, in the desire of whites to perform their way out of the seizure of public, political significance by African Americans, slave and free, whose actions not only haunted but also informed nation making and remaking. The War of 1812 continued a post-Revolutionary process in which blacks and sailors alike reinvented themselves and experienced forced migrations, along the way causing international and interregional incidents. If "managing ethnic divisions was the essence of empire" circa 1812, emergent minstrelsy in 1814 began to do the hard work of making the undeniable fact of blacks on ships—and in full voice—safe for a revised, and revived, nationalism.[7]

From the first performance, the audience always knew the singer was supposed to be black *and* a sailor. This understanding was reinforced by the black and maritime dialect fully detectable as early as the song's third line, "Plat-te-bug dare too, close pon de main." The song's first phrase, "BACK-side Albany stan' Lake Champlain," has to be considered as a crucial introduction to its considerable pleasures: a double entendre, geographic and urban (buildings have back sides, but do towns? Perhaps so, if they are on a

---

7. Alan Taylor, *The Civil War of 1812: American Citizens, British Subjects, Irish Rebels, and Indian Allies* (New York, 2010), 91; Denver Brunsman, "Subjects vs. Citizens: Impressment and Identity in the Anglo-American Atlantic," *Journal of the Early Republic*, XXX (2010), 570, 585. The most probing account of whites managing diversity and inventing race in the early Republic is Carroll Smith-Rosenberg, *This Violent Empire: The Birth of an American National Identity* (Chapel Hill, N.C., 2010); but see also David Kazanjian, *The Colonizing Trick: National Culture and Imperial Citizenship in Early America* (Minneapolis, Minn., 2003); Andy Doolen, *Fugitive Empire: Locating Early American Imperialism* (Minneapolis, Minn., 2005); Kariann Akemi Yokota, *Unbecoming British: How Revolutionary America Became a Postcolonial Nation* (New York, 2011), 213–225; Lawrence J. Friedman's neglected *Inventors of the Promised Land* (New York, 1975); and Ronald T. Takaki's classic *Iron Cages: Race and Culture in Nineteenth-Century America* (New York, 1979).

river like Albany) and embodied, even profane (backside as posterior). Composer Micah Hawkins, a decidedly New York City figure—grocer and coach maker and bartender as well as musician and later playwright—seems to be depicting the black sailor as an urban as well as a marine Yankee, the type for whom upstate New York, and even the state capital of Albany, remains, two centuries later, in the sticks. Such folk do not know and do not want to know that Lake Champlain is nowhere near any side of Albany. Much as in Saul Steinberg's *View of the World from Ninth Avenue* (1976), the famous *New Yorker* cover in which Gotham dwarfs the mere continents beyond, the point is that, from a Manhattan perspective, it simply does not matter. The sense of urbane yet provincial geographical ignorance is only reinforced by the reference to the 435-square-mile Lake Champlain as "One little pond, half full a' water."[8]

Is the black sailor ignorant, or is he an urban dandy in the know? Is the great occasion of celebrating the American victory—as a victory seen then, if not always since, as strategically important—also to be an opportunity for mocking black pretensions to geopolitical knowledge? Absolutely, yes, and no, or not only that. The very next line places the singer as a booster of the nation's expansive prospects: "Town small ... he grow bigger de herearter." This is just the first of the celebratory distinctions the black sailor makes for the audience in a joking yet confiding and concise manner, confirming the sense of victory over the British. The singer invokes a series of markers of national-popular identification that appear here even earlier than we might expect, chronologically speaking: "Uncle Sam" setting his boat, for example, and "Gubbener Probose" (Sir George Prevost, 1st Baronet, commander of the British forces in Canada during the war) "a tea party courtin" when the very term "tea party" had been banished from polite, printed discourse because it reminded contemporaries of *the people's* raucous, rowdy, and perhaps socially transformative revolution.[9]

---

8. One historian of minstrelsy detects a shift toward American rather than West Indian Black English with "Backside Albany." See Joseph Boskin, *Sambo: The Rise and Demise of an American Jester* (New York, 1986), 72. For Lake Champlain's dimensions, see David Curtis Skaggs, *Thomas Macdonough: Master of Command in the Early U.S. Navy* (Annapolis, Md., 2003), 59. For black urban sophistication in early national New York, see especially, Shane White, *Stories of Freedom in Black New York* (Cambridge, Mass., 2002); White, "The Death of James Johnson," *American Quarterly*, LI (1999), 753–795; White, "Freedom's First Con: African Americans and Changing Notes in Antebellum New York City," *Journal of the Early Republic*, XXXIV (2014), 385–409.

9. Alfred F. Young, *The Shoemaker and the Tea Party: Memory and the American*

As the tea party reference suggests, the language of "Backside Albany" is allusive and metaphorical throughout, what sympathetic contemporaries would expect of a cannily observant African American character or of a sailor, with their equally distinctive lingo. He is also on top of the details: the precise date of the battle, its origins in a British advance, its simultaneous engagement of army and naval forces. It is not a precise reckoning, but it is hardly less so than other contemporary victory songs, which stressed when they could the world-turned-upside-down aspects of American victories over British forces and the humor in these reversals. If the black sailor is laughing at the British in a distinctly black fashion ("Tot me soul den, I mus die a laffin"), he is in the act of laughing in the same position as the audience for the equally popular "Noble Lads of Canada," a mocking portrait of invaders who get "burgoyned" and transformed from brave marchers to terrified stay-at-homes.[10]

For the humblest of American tars to ridicule the British may be all the more effective. The last verse of "Backside Albany" domesticates and shames General Prevost, who "scare so, he lef all behine, / Powder, ball, cannon, tea-

---

Revolution (Boston, 1999), 162. For arguments that the Lake Champlain and Plattsburgh engagements changed British strategic options and proved decisive in bringing them to the table only to be deemphasized in the wake of Baltimore and the Battle of New Orleans, see Henry Adams, *History of the United States of America during the Administrations of James Madison* (New York, 1986), 982–988; Harry L. Coles, *The War of 1812* (Chicago, 1965), 171; Skaggs, *Macdonough*, 135; David G. Fitz-Enz, *The Final Invasion: Plattsburgh, the War of 1812's Most Decisive Battle* (New York, 2001); Daniel Walker Howe, *What Hath God Wrought: The Transformation of America, 1815–1848* (New York, 2007), 69; Troy Bickham, *The Weight of Vengeance: The United States, the British Empire, and the War of 1812* (New York, 2012), 169–170. For more skeptical views of Plattsburgh, see Donald R. Hickey, *Don't Give Up the Ship! Myths of the War of 1812* (Urbana, Ill., 2006), 75–77; Jon Latimer, *1812: War with America* (Cambridge, Mass., 2007), 402.

10. "The Victories at Plattsburg," *American Historical Record*, III, no. 26 (February 1874), 67–69; "Noble Lads of Canada," lyrics from Stan Ransom's CD, *The Battle of Plattsburgh: Music from the War of 1812* (Cadyville, N.Y., 2001), which also includes "Siege of Plattsburgh." For seminal discussions of nineteenth-century African Americans' ability to say (or sing) one thing and mean another, or to signify differently to different audiences, and for whites' responses, see Gilbert Osofsky, "Introduction: Puttin' on Ole Massa: The Significance of Slave Narratives," in Osofsky, ed., *Puttin on Ole Massa* (New York, 1969), 9–44; Lawrence W. Levine, *Black Culture and Black Consciousness: Afro-American Folk Thought from Slavery to Freedom* (New York, 1977); Roger D. Abrahams, *Singing the Master: The Emergence of African American Culture in the Plantation South* (New York, 1992); Shane White and Graham White, *The Sounds of Slavery: Discovering African American History through Songs, Sermons, and Speech* (Boston, 2005), 72–96.

pot an kittle," no small thing amid the logistical challenges of the frontier and border war. Whereas patriot forces had been limited by the lack of supplies in this campaign, that condition, both epidemiological and psychological, comes in the end to characterize the British high command, as the sailor spreads the word: "Some say he catch a cole, trouble in he mine, / Cause he eat so much raw an cole vittle." Starving, disoriented officers: who better to tell the story of complete role reversal than the humblest of the victors? The sailor claims the final joke as his own while taking on the identity of Uncle Sam:

> Uncle Sam berry sorry,
> *To* be sure, for he pain;
> Wish he nuss heseff up well an hearty,
> For Gen'ral Mc'Comb, an Massa 'Donough-
> home,
> When he notion for a nudder tea party.

The trope of the tea party appears in precisely the way that ordinary Bostonians had originally invoked it: as an inversion of the genteel ritual of taking tea into a deliberately celebratory event—the people and their will on top. The black sailor-narrator of "Backside Albany" is racialized, is mocked, at the outset and perhaps implicitly throughout, even if the black dialect is relatively accurate in terms of contemporary black English. Yet he ends as the knowing spokesperson of the national-popular will.[11]

Why this ambivalence, which seems to advance an argument for black citizenship even as it emphasizes racial difference? The key to understanding the distancing embrace of a black speaker is his identity as a black sailor. It is impossible to imagine why this earlier original Jim Crow would be a sailor without knowing what contemporaries knew about maritime life and the attendant political controversies: people of African descent were dispro-

---

11. Mahar, "'Backside Albany' and Early Blackface Minstrelsy," *American Music*, VI (1988), 5–6, 13, stresses the accuracy of the battle account and of the Black English. See also Buckley, "'The Place to Make an Artist Work,'" in *Catching the Tune*, 28; Louis S. Gerteis, "Blackface Minstrelsy and the Construction of Race in Nineteenth-Century America," in David W. Blight and Brooks D. Simpson, eds., *Union and Emancipation: Essays on Politics and Race in the Civil War Era* (Kent, Ohio, 1997), 86. The penultimate line may suggest that the black sailor remains unfree in fact or in mind because he refers to his superior as "Massa Donough." But this may not be as much of a choice as it might seem, as Thomas Macdonough's rank at the time was master commandant.

portionately represented on the crews of both British and American ships. They partook of the ability of English speakers to switch loyalties when it suited them—or when it suited British press gangs and their officers. Two of the four men seized in the *Chesapeake* affair of 1807 were of African descent. The U.S. Congress officially authorized the enlistment of free blacks in the navy on March 8, 1813; they served as approximately 10 to 20 percent of the sailors thereafter. Blacks participated in well-publicized volunteer efforts to build fortifications at Baltimore, New York, and Philadelphia: one wartime song, "Patriotic Diggers," described "Men of every age, color, rank, profession, / Ardently engaged, labor in succession."[12]

Contemporaries also knew that things could, and did, sometimes go the other way, that people of African descent were also a potentially decisive fifth column in the War of 1812. In the Southeast, fugitive slaves played a key role in the Red Stick War in Florida and at the Negro Fort subsequently. According to some estimates, at least two thousand and as many as thirty-four hundred Chesapeake slaves fled to freedom as a result of the British invasion: "Black initiative transformed the British conduct of the war," argues Alan Taylor. Six hundred black mariners were recruited by the British and participated at the Battle of Bladensburg and the burning of Washington, D.C., a fact that Francis Scott Key worked into one of the forgotten verses of "The Defence of Fort McHenry" (later "The Star-Spangled Banner"), which associates the failed invaders with "the hireling and the slave." Shortly after the Battle of Plattsburgh, the New York legislature, still under threat of invasion, authorized the enlistment of two thousand blacks, including slaves, promising pay for the masters and freedom for the bondmen.[13]

12. Paul A. Gilje, *Liberty on the Waterfront: American Maritime Culture in the Age of Revolution* (Philadelphia, 2004), 166; Taylor, *The Internal Enemy*, 3, 359, 441-442; Smith, *The Slaves' Gamble*; "Patriotic Diggers," in liner notes to *War of 1812: Sung by Wallace House with Lute,* Folkways Records, FP 5002, Smithsonian Center for Folklife and Heritage, 2004 Smithsonian Folkways Recordings / 1954 Folkways Records, http://media.smithsonianfolkways.org/liner_notes/folkways/FW05002.pdf. W. Jeffrey Bolster goes so far as to place black sailors "at the center of the War of 1812"; see Bolster, *Black Jacks: African American Seamen in the Age of Sail* (Cambridge, Mass., 1998), 20, 103. A more restrained Donald R. Hickey grants them "a significant role on both sides"; see Hickey, *Don't Give Up the Ship!* 185, 189.

13. Nicole Eustace, *1812: War and the Passions of Patriotism* (Philadelphia, 2012), 182; Gerald Horne, *Negro Comrades of the Crown: African Americans and the British Empire Fight the U.S. before Emancipation* (New York, 2012), 35, 39-40, 45-65; Claudio Saunt, *A New Order of Things: Property, Power, and the Transformation of the Creek Indians, 1733-1816* (New York, 1999), 236-288; Christopher T. George, "Mirage of Free-

Black patriotism and black rebellion, in other words, were not so much identity choices or, in retrospect, equally justifiable fights for black freedom; they also existed in an inseparable, mutually reinforcing relationship. That Governor Daniel Tompkins and other state officials were later said to have been present at the first Albany performance of "Backside Albany" suggests the proximity of events, policy, and representations of blacks-in-arms in 1814. The more patriotic the black performance, in arms or on stage, the more it suggested the possibility of something else: the fifth column that slavery and discrimination had made just as likely. Whether as internal enemy or as potential hero, the black sailor at war could not be taken for granted in 1814.

In this context, the strolling of the blackfaced Jack Tar onto the stage in Albany (and, soon after, New York), just weeks after the event he sings about (which was just a few weeks after Bladensburg and the invasion of Washington, D.C.), to sing a song that satirized the British and the black sailors themselves suggests a multitude of wartime anxieties relieved by a victory. The strategic importance, ambiguous loyalties, and sheer theatricality of all the Jack Tars, white and black, English and American, were certainly in play. To be a sailor had always been to project a distinctly visible and audible identity in speech, clothing, and bodily movement, but this had become even more true and more consequential for the sailors and for the polity when the precise (or imprecise) national identities of sailors came to be considered a national security matter and even a reason to fight. The course of the impressment controversy, reaching a height during these years, can be seen as a crisis caused in part by sailors' acting skills and their refusal to abide by—or their desperate need to improvise upon—juridical *and* vernacular distinctions of race and nation. Sailor talk, in other words, had come to be considered both dubious and important precisely because it could be so cre-

---

dom: African Americans in the War of 1812," *Maryland Historical Magazine*, XCI (1996), 427–450; Peter J. Kastor, *The Nation's Crucible: The Louisiana Purchase and the Creation of America* (New Haven, Conn., 2004), 171–173; Adam Rothman, *Slave Country: American Expansion and the Origins of the Deep South* (Cambridge, Mass., 2005), 122–124, 139–162; Leslie M. Harris, *In the Shadow of Slavery: African Americans in New York City, 1626–1863* (Chicago, 2003), 72–73, 93–94; David R. Roediger, *The Wages of Whiteness: Race and the Making of the American Working Class* (London, 1991), 44; Stephen Budiansky, *Perilous Fight: America's Intrepid War with Britain on the High Seas, 1812–1815* (New York, 2010), 330–332, 364; Jack D. Foner, *Blacks and the Military in American History: A New Perspective* (New York, 1974), 22–23; Taylor, *Civil War of 1812*, 332–333; Smith, *The Slaves' Gamble*, 131; Taylor, *The Internal Enemy*, 213; "The Victories at Plattsburg," *American Historical Record*, III, no. 26 (February 1874), 69.

atively and expertly performed by those boastful humble men, whom everyone would be hearing, if not singing, about soon.

British and American soldiers and sailors indexed the essentially theatrical aspects of military and naval service by displaying their own enthusiasm for dramatic performances both in camp and when on leave. Theaters responded by regularly producing spectacles about battles and also producing the eighteenth century's most popular songs of empire, like "Heart of Oak" (1760) and "Rule, Britannia" (1740). Although the text of *The Battle of Lake Champlain*, the production in which "Backside Albany" first appeared, does not survive, there is a reference to the play having included actual ships on water reenacting the naval battle. Audiences apparently delighted in both the outrageousness and the verisimilitude of war's representation on stage, recognizing in either case an engagement with, and a sometimes parody of, war's theatrical dimensions.[14]

Gillian Russell depicts the two faces of the image of soldiers and sailors in contemporary British theater: they were heroes and the scum of the earth. In the United States, sailors might have become symbols of national identity during a war about free trade and sailors rights, but not in any simple or complete way—not during a war opposed by some people in the very seaports sailors knew best, and not during an era when sailors exemplified both the extraordinary freedoms of leaving home (or running away) and the extraordinary unfreedoms enforced by press gangs and the lash. Not coincidentally, the theaters themselves became "places of self-definition, especially for the sailor" ashore—the very locus of the "Jolly Jack Tar" stereotype. In New York, sailors were sometimes invited to formal dinners in celebration of naval victories, and certain plays were performed specifically in honor of sailors after celebrations. Paul Gilje has emphasized the ability of Jack Tars simultaneously to use and mock the rhetoric of free trade and sailors' rights, a tendency that could have only heightened the sense of anxiety, and curiosity, about where the ever-mobile sailor stood and what he meant for the nationalities he so often fudged to preserve a measure of freedom—or to save his skin from floggings.[15]

---

14. W[illiam] Davenport Adams, ed., *A Dictionary of the Drama: A Guide to the Plays, Playwrights* ..., I (Philadelphia, 1904), 124.

15. Russell, *Theatres of War*, 64–65, 98–99 (quotation on 98), 101, 105–106, 182; Bolster, *Black Jacks*, 120–122; Gilje, *Liberty on the Waterfront*, xiii; Isaac Land, *War, Nationalism, and the British Sailor, 1750-1850* (New York, 2009), 9; Dan Hicks, "Broadsides on Land and Sea: A Cultural Reading of the Naval Engagements in the War of 1812," in Paul A. Gilje and William Pencak, eds., *Pirates, Jack Tar, and Memory: New Directions*

Were black Jack Tars especially theatrical, as suggested by their leading role in putting on plays in Dartmoor Prison? Did they exemplify, and even push further, the synergies of theater and war, of players and sailors so familiar by 1814? If the sailor had to sing the victory for it to be complete in this war, is it significant that the "black sailor" in *The Battle of Lake Champlain* vocalized that "character" in a particularly black way? The performance seems a kind of compromise of black aspirations and white control. The singer gets to tell the story of the movement of generals rather than being subject to forced movement himself. This is the black man as free man, not slave—claiming citizenship, the escape from impressment, and the ability to narrate the national story—even while honoring General Macomb and Master Commandant Macdonough and racializing himself by calling Macdonough "Massa." What is being theatricalized here is the essential Jack Tar dilemma—Who is he? Can he be a source of national identity? Can he, will he, affirm the embrace?—as the dilemma of the African in the new nation that was part slave and part free. That black sailors had in fact literally embodied the nation in the *Chesapeake* affair, and held U.S. protection papers that did not discriminate on the basis of race, made the black sailor at once a test of whether either blacks or sailors could be the American citizens they claimed to be. On the other hand, in "Backside Albany" the potentially equalizing similarity of blacks and whites playing sailor and playing American is minstrelized, which is to say racialized, and thus contained.[16]

As Robert P. Forbes has argued, during the 1810s the possibility of African American citizenship, or the question of African American nationality—as black or as American—held the greatest promise, or threat, for blacks and whites alike. Federalist cries of "slave representation" reached new heights in 1812. The number of free African Americans in New York rose by almost 150 percent between 1800 and 1810, from 10,417 to 25,333; as a result, "the black electorate expanded dramatically," and by 1808 "Federalist-leaning black men were beginning to organize themselves publically and formally in advance of elections." Voters encountered challenges at the polls. Free black votes determined the outcome of the New York state election in 1813,

---

in *American Maritime History* (Mystic, Conn., 2007), 141, 158; Gilje, "'Free Trade and Sailors' Rights': The Rhetoric of the War of 1812," *Journal of the Early Republic*, XXX (2010), 17.

16. For protection papers, sailors' experiences of impressment, and the politics of impressment more generally, see Joshua J. Wolf, "'The Misfortune to Get Pressed': The Impressment of American Seamen and the Ramifications on the United States, 1793–1812" (Ph.D. diss., Temple University, 2015).

spurring formal moves to disfranchise them. This would have been reason enough for New Yorkers such as Micah Hawkins to wonder what blacks-in-arms might mean for the postwar scene.[17]

Just whose party was "a nudder tea party"? The period 1810–1816 saw a rash of domestic slave revolts and rumors of revolt. It was also a particularly fertile period in northern black self-representation. Celebrations of the end of the slave trade in Boston, New York, and Philadelphia criticized the continuance of slavery in the nation and told a public story of an injured African nation-within-a-nation that still insisted, vigorously, on its American belonging. Dickson D. Bruce, Jr., has pointed to this era as the emergence of "an alternative discursive community taking a critical perspective on emerging forms of white American nationalism," evident in a sudden profusion of printed pamphlets. Around 1815, more whites began to respond by harassing black celebrants on some occasions and by patronizing the new genre of Bobalition broadsides, which employed black dialect to ridicule the slave trade abolition fetes and other black public expressions. After 1816, the colonization movement formed another attempt to deal with antislavery and black assertions of citizenship. The critical free black response included assertions of patriotic service in the War of 1812 as well as in the Revolution—and critiques of white hypocrisy in forgetting both.[18]

Persistent national myths notwithstanding, to suggest that whites were unaffected by northern as well as southern black assertiveness in the early Republic is, in light of contemporary scholarship, no longer credible, no matter what realm of society, politics, or culture one chooses to examine.

17. Robert Pierce Forbes, "'The Cause of This Blackness': The Early American Republic and the Construction of Race," *American Nineteenth Century History*, XIII (2012), 84–85; Matthew Mason, *Slavery and Politics in the Early American Republic* (Chapel Hill, N.C., 2006), 42–74, 107–111; Rachel Hope Cleves, *The Reign of Terror in America: Visions of Violence from Anti-Jacobinism to Antislavery* (New York, 2009), 172–179; Dixon Ryan Fox, "The Negro Vote in Old New York," *Political Science Quarterly*, XXXII (1917), 257; Sarah Levine-Gronningsater, "Delivering Freedom: Gradual Emancipation, Black Legal Culture, and the Origins of Sectional Crisis in New York, 1759–1870" (Ph.D. diss., University of Chicago, 2014), 237–257, quotations on 238, 243; Paul J. Polgar, "'Whenever They Judge It Expedient': The Politics of Partisanship and Free Black Voting Rights in Early National New York," *American Nineteenth Century History*, XII (2011), 1–23.

18. Herbert Aptheker, *American Negro Slave Revolts* (New York, 1943), 244–261; White and White, *Stylin'*, 108–114; Waldstreicher, *In the Midst of Perpetual Fetes*, chap. 6; Dickson D. Bruce, Jr., *The Origins of African American Literature, 1680–1865* (Charlottesville, Va., 2001), 95; Doolen, *Fugitive Empire*, 174–175.

Mechal Sobel's study of dream narratives in early American culture suggests the psychological dimension of these challenges for the white audiences to whom "Backside Albany" appealed. During the post-Revolutionary period, until about 1820, a cohort of men "partially realized that they were dependent on blacks for crucial aspects of their selves but were determined to restrengthen hierarchies and 'keep blacks in their place.'" This tendency overlapped with the emergence, after 1810, of dream accounts that display "conflicted self-fashioning in which whites were more actively demeaning blacks to achieve a sense of unity and superiority and were not overtly conscious of the fact that they were dependent on them for crucial emotions and values." Black advances, in other words, did not lead only, or even primarily, to antislavery and antiracism. They also inspired ambivalence and a renewal of racism: a backlash, indeed, more modern than it might at first seem.[19]

The first minstrel song seems to partake of both of these kinds of white self-fashioning—perhaps playing a role in the movement toward more active, and ultimately less self-conscious, demeaning of blacks by both stressing racial difference and using it to distract from black contributions to national as well as individual self-fashioning. "Backside Albany" explicitly, theatrically acknowledges the black other by having a white American not only dress the black part but also voice quintessential American sentiments: celebrating victory over England. The black sailor is thus acknowledged as American while contained as a racialized subject. Yet, in light of what would happen with minstrelsy, we must also see the emerging potential that minstrelization had for "actively demeaning blacks" in particular new ways that more effectively responded to black self-assertion and, in doing so, crafted a more secure white identity. Sobel's description of a psychological transition to a more active form of demeaning, and a seeming regression to less self-consciousness about depending on blacks for making white selves, articulates not only *how* but also *why* American blackface developed new forms— Bobalition and minstrelsy—at this particular time to enact such impulses. So strange and yet so familiar to us, so disturbing as to upend our sense of (northern) progress away from slavery, it can best be explained as a response to the selves and the collectivities that blacks themselves were making as well as the difference that the war made in that process. Such a focus on the fuller range of what blacks were doing besides singing and dancing and even signifying, which had to be represented if it was to be repressed somehow,

---

19. Mechal Sobel, *Teach Me Dreams: The Search for Self in the Revolutionary Era* (Princeton, N.J., 2000), 61–62.

helps account for the timing as well as the manner of blackface minstrelsy's rapid spread in its increasingly nationalist idioms.²⁰

For historians of the War of 1812, the payoff for white Americans of a minstrelized national identity should be more obvious, in terms of who won that conflict and what, indeed, was won. After all, it has long been known that westerners engaged in a similar quest for respectability and incorporation, and they found postwar easterners playing an anthem for them, too, in "The Hunters of Kentucky" (1815?), a paean to the Battle of New Orleans and General Andrew Jackson. The black sailor of "Backside Albany," like Jim Crow of 1832, has more than a little in common with the hunters of Kentucky, including taking the stage to epitomize the importance of ordinary fighters as arbiters of the war's meaning. Like Kentucky's backwoods marksmen, the bold and boastful black sailors of 1814 are simultaneously embraced and kept at a distance in urban popular culture's remix of wartime conflicts.²¹

20. Ibid., 84. Joseph Roach writes of a related process of "surrogation" in *Cities of the Dead: Circum-Atlantic Performance* (New York, 1996); see also Smith-Rosenberg, *This Violent Empire*.

21. John William Ward, *Andrew Jackson: Symbol for an Age* (New York, 1955), 13–29; Finson, *The Voices That Are Gone*, 165–167. The dating of "Hunters of Kentucky" remains uncertain, with some archives dating broadside versions to 1815, while other scholars, including Ward, date it to sometime between 1818 and 1824. Eran Zelnik has identified a dialect song published in eight newspapers in April and May 1815 that highlights at the end of its third stanza the self-description of backwoods American fighters as "one half horse, Half an alligator!"—thus appearing to be a direct inspiration for "Hunters of Kentucky." It is also likely a direct adaptation of "Backside Albany" to Bladensburg and the Battle of New Orleans, for it is sung in the voice of an African-born Virginia fugitive slave liberated in the Chesapeake campaign who joins the "Admiral" to fight at New Orleans. See Zelnik, "The Comical Style in America: Humor, Settler Colonialism, and the Making of a White Man's Democracy, 1790–1840" (Ph.D. diss., University of California, Davis, 2016), 241–242.

The notion of the simultaneous, related emergence of minstrelsy and the comic backwoodsman extends as far back as Constance Rourke, *American Humor: A Study of the National Character* (1931; rpt. Tallahassee, Fla., [1986]), 98–104. See also Michael Rogin, "The Two Declarations of American Independence," *Representations*, LV (1996), 16–17; Lara Langer Cohen, *The Fabrication of American Literature: Fraudulence and Antebellum Print Culture* (Philadelphia, 2012), 86–87. Matthew Rebhorn, who highlights T. D. Rice's first performance of Jim Crow in *The Kentucky Rifle*, sees 1830s minstrelsy as a "(re)presentation of the frontier," but his argument, too, presumes minstrelsy's emer-

But, seen in relation to one another, the shadows of rising antiblack racism and proslavery politics loom over the Kentucky hunter, as it does over an emerging "Jacksonianism" too often divorced from the southwesterner Jackson's own wartime rise. Jackson's victory and emergence as a national figure depended on blacks-in-arms—the slaves who built fortifications and the free black militia he recruited into his army at New Orleans (despite the official refusals of the Madison administration to accept black soldiers) but who subsequently did not get fully incorporated into the body politic in Louisiana. In "Hunters of Kentucky," the brave riflemen prevent Edward Pakenham, commander of British forces in North America, from gaining access to New Orleans's "cotton bags" and "girls of every hue it seems, / from snowy white to sooty," allowing westerners and urban easterners alike to imagine and enjoy their national repossession of both the "beauty" and the "booty." A deeper and more accurate depiction of the Jacksonian alliance would be hard to come by.[22]

In such a light, it is interesting that "Backside Albany" came first and that, although it is the most northern of the war's three national anthems in origin, the black sailor in the play *The Siege of Plattsburg* was originally named "Gumbo," suggesting his role as a stand-in not only for the black sailors of the ports but also for a larger, diverse community of African Americans, and perhaps especially those of New Orleans. By contrast, in the aforementioned forgotten verse of "The Star-Spangled Banner," the "slave" is present but depersonalized, identified with the British and their "hireling" and all too

---

gence in 1830, after Edwin Forrest's redface *Metamora*, without noting that Forrest was also doing blackface during the 1820s. In arguing for the frontier's surrogation of black voices as a response to events of 1812–1815, I do not mean to preclude other ways of understanding the relation of "frontier" performance and blackface during the 1830s and beyond. See Rebhorn, *Pioneer Performances: Staging the Frontier* (Oxford, 2011), 73.

22. *Hunters of Kentucky* (Providence, R.I., 1815); William W. Freehling, "Andrew Jackson, Great President?" in Paul Finkelman and Donald R. Kennon, eds., *Congress and the Emergence of Sectionalism: From the Missouri Compromise to the Age of Jackson* (Columbus, Ohio, 2008), 132–151; Smith, *The Slaves' Gamble*, 165. The War of 1812 "made the rapid expansion of slavery not only possible but also blameless," observes Jason M. Opal in "Interchange: The War of 1812," *Journal of American History*, XCIX (2012), 527. See also Robin Blackburn, *The Overthrow of Colonial Slavery, 1776–1848* (London, 1988), 289; Rothman, *Slave Country*; Taylor, *The Internal Enemy*, 10, 345. The phrase "beauty and booty" had been widely but falsely reported as the British password on the eve of the Battle of New Orleans. See Eustace, *1812*, 212–218, 233–234. The earlier April 1815 blackface antecedent of "Hunters of Kentucky" (see Note 21, above) also invoked "booty." See Zelnik, "Comical Style in America," 241, 248.

wishfully consigned, in the next line, to "the terror of flight, or the gloom of the grave." And in "The Hunters of Kentucky," the African American male as soldier or sailor is somehow rendered completely absent in New Orleans — precisely where, by any measure of military importance, he should be most present. An American memory of the War of 1812 that went down more easily with slaveholders took the foreground when the free colored militia was rendered invisible and African American women were rhymed into spoils of war ("sooty"/"booty"). This is particularly true insofar as the particular theme of "The Hunters of Kentucky" is the identification of the ordinary militia man, in victory, with the great general.[23]

Andrew Allen, the man who first performed "Backside Albany" in blackface as the character named "Gumbo," personally furthered this shift from recognizing and minstrelizing the black sailor to lionizing and electing the white frontiersman. After his minstrelizing innovation in Albany, in 1815 Allen created a play based on the Battle of New Orleans, impersonating Andrew Jackson on stage — and on horseback — in Pensacola, Florida. Back in Albany in 1816, he opened a "New-Orleans Hotel" across the street from the theater. He returned to Pensacola in 1818, during the First Seminole War, and General Jackson apparently took an interest. According to a friend of Allen, the publicity-savvy general sent him a note pledging "lasting friendship" — which for Jackson would have entailed patronage as well as affection. Allen later bragged that he had been "friend and adviser of General Jackson, at Pensacola, during the Creek campaign." The general also showed up at a benefit performance for Allen in Philadelphia in 1820. Allen returned the favor by making a pilgrimage to the Hermitage in Nashville the next year. Well before Jackson became president in 1828, the actor later known

---

23. For the singer of "Backside Albany" in *The Battle of Lake Champlain* as "Gumbo," see "Questions and Answers," *New York Sun*, Sept. 12, 1909, [3]; H. R., "First Negro Song Sung on the American Stage," *Philadelphia Inquirer*, Nov. 28, 1922. I have not located any earlier reference to the name of this character or others in the play. On the slave in the forgotten verse of "The Star-Spangled Banner," see *Defence of Fort M'Henry* (1814), in Vera Brodsky Lawrence, *Music for Patriots, Politicians, and Presidents: Harmonies and Discords of the First Hundred Years* (New York, 1975), 205. Francis Scott Key was a colonizationist, slaveholder, and, later, an ardent anti-abolitionist. See John Picker, "Two National Anthems," in Greil Marcus and Werner Sollors, eds., *A New Literary History of America* (Cambridge, Mass., 2009), 87–88; Seth Rockman, *Scraping By: Wage Labor, Slavery, and Survival in Early Baltimore* (Baltimore, 2009), 262; Jefferson Morley, *Snow-Storm in August: Washington City, Francis Scott Key, and the Forgotten Race Riot of 1835* (New York, 2012), 40–42, 56.

as the "father of the American stage" had renamed himself Andrew Jackson Allen—with the general's permission, he insisted. He wore his hair like Jackson and dressed in a blue coat with brass buttons, standard Jackson attire from his military years (see Figure 4). Allen continued to do his Jackson-face regularly in *Old Hickory; or, A Day at New Orleans* and, after 1829, in Richard Penn Smith's *Eighth of January*, a piece often staged on the anniversary of the Battle of New Orleans. He became an active Jackson partisan offstage as well, and even claimed to have given the first public toast to Jackson as a presidential candidate at a public dinner in Alabama.[24]

Moreover, there is a direct link between Allen's postwar performances and blackface's breakout hit, T. D. Rice's "Jim Crow," which, as we have seen, explicitly references the Battle of New Orleans. During the mid-1820s, Allen began to travel as the costumer for Edwin Forrest, who performed slave

24. Sol Smith, "The Father Of The American Stage," *Spirit of the Times: A Chronicle of the Turf, Agriculture, Field Sports, Literature and the Stage*, Nov. 1, 1845, 420; Smith, *Theatrical Management in the West and South for Thirty Years* (New York, 1868), 138–139; "Andrew Jackson Allen," *Spirit of the Times*, Nov. 12, 1853, 463; "American Poets—No. III. By M.C. and J.M. Fields," ibid., July 6, 1844, 218; Laurence Hutton, "The Negro on the Stage," *Harper's New Monthly Magazine*, LXXIX (June 1889), 134–135; T. Allston Brown, *A History of the New York Stage from the First Performance in 1732 to 1901* (New York, 1903), I, 105; Henry Dickinson Stone, *Personal Recollections of the Drama ...* (Albany, N.Y., 1873), 177–180; Mark R. Cheatham, *Andrew Jackson, Southerner* (Baton Rouge, La., 2013), 77, 80–81; Winona L. Fletcher, "Andrew Jackson Allen, 'Internal and External Costumer' to the Early Nineteenth Century American Theatre" (Ph.D. diss., Indiana University, 1968), 12, 23, 45, 51–52, 64, 216–218; H[enry] P[itt] Phelps, *Players of a Century: A Record of the Albany Stage* (Albany, N.Y., 1880), 145–146; Walter J. Meserve, *An Emerging Entertainment: The Drama of the American People to 1828* (Bloomington, Ind., 1977), 252; Doutor Judd, "Dummy Allen: The Eccentric Old-Time Actor," *Billboard*, Oct. 14, 1905, 31. For Allen as an active Jacksonian party man, see "Democratic Jackson Festival," *Philadelphia Inquirer*, July 11, 1831; *Age* (Augusta, Maine), Dec. 9, 1842; A. J. Allen, "In Honor of Andrew Jackson," *Albany Argus*, Dec. 28, 1843.

Vera Lawrence casts doubt on Allen's performance of "Backside Albany" in Albany in "Micah Hawkins," *New-York Historical Society Quarterly*, LXII (1978), 150–154, and suggested instead Hopkins Robinson, who clearly sang the song in New York in June 1815, but she seems to have been unaware of Fletcher's work. Douglas S. Harvey also places Allen at the Green Street Theatre in Albany regularly after 1811. See Harvey, *The Theatre of Empire: Frontier Performances in America, 1750–1860* (London 2010), 197 n. 21; Buckley, "'The Place to Make an Artist Work,'" in *Catching the Tune*, 27. Bert Williams, who was in a position to hear all the lore around minstrelsy, knew of Allen as the author of the entire play about Plattsburgh and as connected to early blackface; see Williams, "The Negro on the Stage," *New York Age*, Nov. 24, 1910.

Figure 4. *Andrew Jackson Allen.*
Courtesy, University Library, University of Illinois at Urbana-Champaign

parts, blacked up, as early as 1820. A few years later, Allen returned for some time to the Tivoli Theatre in Pensacola. Rice is listed as performing "comic songs" there and in nearby Mobile, Alabama, in 1829, the year before his famous debut of "Jim Crow" in Louisville during a performance of a play called *The Kentucky Rifle*.[25]

These appear to be the peregrinations that allowed blackface minstrelsy to wheel about and turn about and embody the Jacksonian ascendancy, just so. The process appears to be confirmed in an 1826 Cincinnati broadside that sandwiches "Backside Albany" between "The Hunters of Kentucky" and a new riff on both, "CUFFEE's Poetical Review of Champlain, Plattsburgh and Orleans VICTORIES!" (see Figure 5). The Plattsburgh campaign had merely to be repackaged with, or as, New Orleans, a telling reminder of how the seemingly exceptional Southwest came to play the tunes to which even the northern frontier would dance. The dissolution of the black sailor's war into that of the southwestern frontiersman and the hero of New Orleans was itself a central part of the alchemy that turned the war, and the slavery crisis of 1819–1821, into the opportunity to recreate a renewed, and more explicitly white, version of American political identity. We can call this the minstrelization of American politics as well as culture, for there remains much wisdom in Alexander Saxton's argument that minstrelsy and Jacksonian democracy were two sides (cultural and political) of the same coin of the realm.[26]

But African Americans did not forget the liberating ambitions, the wartime ferment, or the backlash that minstrelized American nationalism. William Alexander Brown and James Hewlett, the impresario and the great actor of the African Theatre in New York City during the early 1820s, had both been ship's stewards. Brown first imagined his theater as a pleasure garden for black stewards segregated from other establishments. They put

---

25. Dian Lee Shelley, "Tivoli Theatre of Pensacola," *Florida Historical Quarterly*, L (1972), 347, 350–351; W. T. Lhamon, Jr., "Introduction: An Extravagant and Wheeling Stranger," in Lhamon, ed., *Jump Jim Crow*, 33–34; Lhamon, "Turning around Jim Crow," in Stephen Johnson, ed., *Burnt Cork: Traditions of Blackface Minstrelsy* (Amherst, Mass., 2012), 20.

26. *Champlain, Plattsburgh[, New Orleans]; Honor to the Bra[ve]; Splendid Battles!* (Cincinnati, 1826); Alexander Saxton, *The Rise and Fall of the White Republic: Class Politics and Mass Culture in Nineteenth-Century America* (New York, 1990), 95–182. Elizabeth Dillon argues that the very conception of minstrelsy as an indigenous performance genre, by the same performers who like Forrest were playing Indian, effaces the colonizing process. See Dillon, *New World Drama*, 215–261.

Figure 5. *Champlain, Plattsburgh[, New Orleans]; Honor to the Bra[ve]; Splendid Battles!* (Cincinnati, 1826). Courtesy, American Antiquarian Society

on plays with Atlantic, maritime themes and developed "a preexistent tradition of whiteface minstrelsy" in explicitly riffing on both English actors' performances of Shakespeare and on the plays of the New York newspaper editor, sometime diplomat, and soon-to-be Jacksonian partisan Mordecai M. Noah.[27]

Noah was a worthy target. In Noah's war play *She Would Be a Soldier* (1819), which featured Edwin Forrest as an Indian in redface, all the virtuous Anglo- and Euro-American characters are ethnically marked—but there are no African Americans, despite their increasing prominence elsewhere on the stage in the early Republic. For Noah, the Missouri crisis proved the necessity of turning against antislavery and free black suffrage. As a journalist, he became the scourge of New York's African Americans and a begrudging critic of the African Theatre that performed some of his own plays.[28]

Scholars of the African Theatre depict the minstrelizing moves of New Yorkers like Noah as responses to the brilliant challenge posed by the black thespians, themselves former sailors. In this spirit, the story can be pushed a couple of steps, or perhaps we should say stages, back to the war and the black sailors themselves. Who we put at the center of the story and where we begin and end it makes all the difference in how we construe the meaning of a war and its culture—and, no less importantly, the relationship of war to culture. In the case of the War of 1812, the real war was not even remotely as white as a minstrelized nation remembered. Much like the Revolutionary War, the War of 1812 advanced powerfully liberating and reactionary trends:

---

27. George A. Thompson, Jr., *A Documentary History of the African Theatre* (Evanston, Ill., 1998), 9, 42; Marvin McAllister, *White People Do Not Know How to Behave at Entertainments Designed for Ladies and Gentlemen of Colour: William Brown's African and American Theater* (Chapel Hill, N.C., 2003), 2, 5–7.

28. Rebhorn, *Pioneer Performances*, 43; Jonathan D. Sarna, *Jacksonian Jew: The Two Worlds of Mordecai Noah* (New York, 1980), 110–111, 167; White, *Stories of Freedom in Black New York*, 74–75, 84–86, 127–184, 203–210; Levine-Gronningsater, "Delivering Freedom," 262–263, 268; Michael Warner et al., "A Soliloquy 'Lately Spoken at the African Theatre': Race and the Public Sphere in New York City, 1821," in Warner, *Publics and Counterpublics* (New York, 2002), 225–268; Dillon, *New World Drama*, 224–245. For the strikingly ambivalent presence of African Americans in early Republic theater, see Jeffrey H. Richards, *Drama, Theatre, and Identity in the American New Republic* (New York, 2005); Heather S. Nathans, *Slavery and Sentiment on the American Stage, 1787–1861: Lifting the Veil of Black* (Cambridge, 2009); Peter P. Reed, *Rogue Performances: Staging the Underclasses in Early American Theatre Culture* (New York, 2009); Gibbs, *Performing the Temple of Liberty*. I owe the characterization of Noah's plays to Heather Nathans, personal communication.

blacks' specific actions both advanced antislavery and, in response, provided whites a reason to re-create the color line.[29]

We should not be so surprised, therefore, that "Backside Albany" itself remained popular until the 1850s, when the fugitive slave controversy provided so much new material for remixing black agency and whites' ambivalence about it. We should not—we cannot—underestimate the damage that blackface minstrelsy did. There are nevertheless costs to our understanding of national history in construing racism and its cultural forms as overwhelming constants or unmitigated tidal waves, much less as subject only to a gradual decline or much later civil rights revolutions. To do so misses why, as well as when, minstrelsy began to become what it became. Blacks were pushing back at the nation's origins, politically and theatrically. For this reason, by 1814 popular culture was already a political force field and a racial minefield. Blackface minstrelsy emerged in a backlash, in whites dealing with blacks center stage. Indeed, the Jim Crowing of the multifront, multiracial war may be another way in which the War of 1812 reenacted the American Revolution: from one vantage point reprising its notable successes, from another turning its tragedy into farce.[30]

---

29. Robert G. Parkinson, "'Manifest Signs of Passion': The First Federal Congress, Antislavery, and Legacies of the Revolutionary War," in John Craig Hammond and Matthew Mason, eds., *Contesting Slavery: The Politics of Bondage and Freedom in the New American Nation* (Charlottesville, Va., 2011), 49–68. Alan Taylor has noted the manner in which the war "generated a brand of racialized nationalism"; see Taylor, *The Internal Enemy*, 10.

30. Lawrence, "Micah Hawkins," *New-York Historical Society Quarterly*, LXII (1978), 151. The classic delineation of the War of 1812 as a farce, against which serious historians of the conflict still strain, is Adams, *History of the United States*. The classic depiction of history happening "the first time as tragedy, the second as farce" is Karl Marx, *The Eighteenth Brumaire of Louis Bonaparte* (1852) (New York, 1963), 15. For the American Revolution as disturbingly shaped by its construction of black enemies (and by its actual black enemies), see Robert G. Parkinson, *The Common Cause: Creating Race and Nation in the American Revolution* (Chapel Hill, N.C., 2016); Gerald Horne, *The Counter-Revolution of 1776: Slave Resistance and the Origins of the United States of America* (New York, 2014).

MEDITATING ON SLAVERY IN THE AGE OF REVOLUTION
BARBARY CAPTIVITIES AND THE WHITENING OF AMERICAN DEMOCRACY

Carroll Smith-Rosenberg

American democracy rests on the solid base of racial exclusion. For nearly a century and a half, it coexisted, first with chattel slavery and then with the peonage of millions of African Americans whose legal subjecthood it denied, whose political rights it refused, and whom it systematically subjected to physical and psychological violence.[1] From the nation's founding, inclusion in and exclusion from the body politic has been racialized. Citizenship and whiteness have been defined in opposition to slavery and blackness, the free white man celebrated as the prototype of the liberty-loving American citizen.[2] Systems of racialized and gendered exclusion, initially written into the Constitution, have been repeatedly reenacted in court decisions, federal and state legislation, the policing of populations, popular culture, and, above all, in white America's national sense of self. "The very structure of American citizenship is white," political scientist Joel Olson argues, its exclusionary nature the result of "a successful political struggle in which certain persons won the right to proclaim themselves white and therefore citizens ... largely by distinguishing themselves from slaves and free Black persons." Political philosopher Judith N. Shklar concurs. "From the first," she points out, "the most radical claims for freedom and political equality were played out in counterpoint to chattel slavery.... Black chattel slavery stood at the opposite social pole from full citizenship and so defined it." David Waldstreicher, Pa-

---

1. This is not to deny that some white Americans criticized slavery as inhuman and tyrannical. Certainly, by the mid-nineteenth century, slavery had become a burning political issue for some Americans. Still until the Civil Rights movement, most white Americans lived comfortably with the worst forms of racist violence and segregation. To this day, the Supreme Court attempts to conceptualize Affirmative Action with race obliterated as an issue.

2. We can see this in the United States' very first naturalization act (1790), which excluded all of African descent from naturalization processes.

draig Riley, Seth Cotlar, and Andrew Shankman provide historical contexts: Waldstreicher points to the way "We the People" wrote the defense of slavery into the Federal Constitution, whereas Riley, Cotlar, and Shankman trace how the Jeffersonian coalition of northern political and economic radicals and southern planters established unalienable natural rights as the white man's exclusive property, the United States as a white man's republic.[3]

Yet American democracy took form during one of the most radical periods in human history: the Age of Revolution, that moment of chaos and transformation when the political world appeared remade and the promise of freedom, unlimited. Between the 1770s and the 1820s, increasingly radical political uprisings crisscrossed the Atlantic from Philadelphia to Paris, Dublin, and beyond, then back across the Atlantic to Saint Domingue and Gran Colombia. Tumbling one after another in intense interaction, these revolutions proclaimed all men free, equal, and endowed with unalienable rights; challenged the concept of absolute monarchies and the empires they spawned; gave birth to postcolonial republics throughout the Americas; questioned the legitimacy of human slavery for the first time in history—and, bringing all these revolutionary challenges together, spearheaded the torturous processes by which democratic citizenship took form.

For a few magical moments in the mid- and late 1790s, Enlightenment liberalism's universal promises seemed within grasp. Western Pennsylvania farmers, muskets primed, rose up against elite Federalist rule. Women invaded Jacobin meetings and led the sansculottes through Paris streets. Most dramatically, slaves on the rich Caribbean island of Saint Domingue linked the rights of man to the right to violent revolution. Going far beyond participants in either the United States or the French Revolution, Haitian revolutionaries imagined a world built upon the freedom and political sovereignty

---

3. Joel Olson, *The Abolition of White Democracy* (Minneapolis, 2004), xv, 32; Judith N. Shklar, *American Citizenship: The Quest for Inclusion* (Cambridge, Mass., 1991), 1, 16; David Waldstreicher, *Slavery's Constitution: From Revolution to Ratification* (New York, 2009); Padraig Riley, *Slavery and the Democratic Conscience: Political Life in Jeffersonian America* (Philadelphia, 2016); Andrew Shankman, *Crucible of American Democracy: The Struggle to Fuse Egalitarianism and Capitalism in Jeffersonian Pennsylvania* (Lawrence, Kans., 2004); Seth Cotlar, *Tom Paine's America: The Rise and Fall of Transatlantic Radicalism in the Early Republic* (Charlottesville, Va., 2011). See, as well, Douglas Bradburn, *The Citizenship Revolution: Politics and the Creation of the American Union, 1774–1804* (Charlottesville, Va., 2009). I have adopted the concept of whiteness as property from Cheryl I. Harris, "Whiteness as Property," *Harvard Law Review*, CVI (1993), 1707–1745.

of all men, regardless of race and place of birth—a vision the French Republic momentarily embraced when, in 1794, it abolished slavery throughout its empire and welcomed former slaves as delegates to its National Assembly. The Haitian Revolution, Laurent Dubois tells us, "generated what we view today as the true thinking of the Enlightenment—a concrete and radical universalism that overthrew profit for principle and defended human rights against the weapons of empire and the arguments of racial hierarchy." Born of such momentous times, how were American citizenship and American democracy constituted as powerful instruments of racial exclusion?[4]

A time of decisive transformations, the Age of Revolution was, as well, a time of uncertainty, confusion, and fear. The very revolution that, Dubois tells us, signaled the high point of Enlightenment universalism sent shockwaves across the revolutionary Atlantic. Was the white Atlantic ready to celebrate the equality of *all* men—indeed, of all *women?* As critically, of what did the rights of man consist? Like the new republics they legitimated, the new rights were philosophical abstractions, detached from history, from established institutions. Could the new republican citizen be certain what his natural rights actually comprised, who could claim them, or how they could be implemented? Uncertainties and paradoxes multiplied. What if the rights claimed by one group conflicted with those of other groups—the human rights of slaves, for example, with the property rights of slaveowners? Indeed, how did the new republicans reconcile their egalitarian principles with the centuries-old practice of chattel slavery? Even more pressing, how did the new citizens use slavery to articulate their understanding of liberty and of citizenship?[5]

---

4. Laurent Dubois, "An Enslaved Enlightenment: Rethinking the Intellectual History of the French Atlantic," *Social History,* XXXI (2006), 1–14, esp. 12–14.

5. This article seeks to engage with current European discussions of liberalism and democracy—particularly with both Chantal Mouffe's *Democratic Paradox* (London, 2005) and Étienne Balibar's *Equaliberty: Political Essays,* trans. James Ingram (Durham, N.C., 2014). Both explore the contradictions and paradoxes they see destabilizing liberal and democratic political thought. Although I differ from Mouffe and Balibar in critical ways, we are all investigating contradictions critical to liberal political thought, especially the tensions between liberalism's universalism and fear of difference.

Robert Bernasconi and Anika Maaza Mann trace the conundrum of conflicting rights back to the Glorious Revolution and Locke's *Two Treatises of Government,* stressing the tensions between Locke's condemnation of slavery in his *First Treatise* and his authorship of the *Fundamental Constitutions of Carolina,* in which he affirms the slaveowner's absolute control over his slaves. See their essay "The Contradictions of Racism: Locke,

Equal rights were not the Age of Revolution's only radical innovation. The birth of postcolonial republics was another, equally electrifying and challenging. How were republican *citizens,* long used to identifying as *subjects* of Europe's great empires, to constitute new national identities grounded, not on ancient cultural memories and historical practices, but on the abstract theories of universal Natural Rights? Reconstructing their sense of self and their right to political agency was a monumental task, but only one of the challenges facing the new citizens. The new republics linked their universally proclaimed liberal rights to national citizenship, but nations are, by nature, exclusionary instruments. They need to demarcate themselves from other nations, their citizens from other peoples whom they brand as different and at times as dangerous and threatening. Yet Enlightenment liberalism insisted on the universality of liberal rights and the sameness, the equality of all men. How could the new republicans negotiate their national need for constituting Others with their commitment to the sameness, the equality of all men—and their romantic vision of revolutionary cosmopolitanism? Enigmas and paradoxes destabilized Enlightenment political thought and practice in ways that proved particularly vexing to the new U.S. Republic, its national identity so fresh, so fragile.[6]

Slavery, and the *Two Treatises,*" in Andrew Valls, ed., *Race and Racism in Modern Philosophy* (Ithaca, N.Y., 2005), 89–107.

6. "Identity's constitution," Ernesto Laclau reminds us, "is always based on *excluding* something and establishing a violent hierarchy between the two resultant poles." Stuart Hall elaborates, "Identities can function as points of identification and attachment only because of their capacity to exclude, to leave out, to render 'outside,' abjected." See Hall, "Introduction: Who Needs 'Identity'?" in Hall and Paul Du Gay, eds., *Questions of Cultural Identity* (London, 1996), 1–17, esp. 5, quoting Ernesto Laclau, *New Reflections on the Revolution of Our Time* (London, 1990), 32. For a detailed historical discussion of the nation-state and citizenship as exclusionary instruments, see Engin F. Isin, *Being Political: Genealogies of Citizenship* (Minneapolis, Minn., 2002). For a discussion of the role exclusion played in the processes by which an American national identity took form, see Carroll Smith-Rosenberg, *This Violent Empire: The Birth of an American National Identity* (Chapel Hill, N.C., 2010), esp. x–xi.

I initially came to the problem of liberalism's exclusionary practices from a feminist perspective. For decades, feminist critical legal scholars and cultural critics have examined the ways liberal political theory and legal systems have systematically treated women as different, and therefore outside the normal protections male rights conferred. See, for example, the work of Drucilla Cornell, Kimberlé Crenshaw, Angela Harris, Carol Pateman, Joan Scott, and Nancy Stepan, to mention only a few: Drucilla Cornell, *The Imaginary Domain: Abortion, Pornography, and Sexual Harassment* (New York, 1995);

This essay examines American republican citizens' struggle with those paradoxes by engaging in a close reading of one of America's newest literary genres: Barbary captivity narratives, popular depictions of the enslavement of American sailors by Barbary "pirates." Focusing on the 1790s, the epic moment when the revolution in Saint Domingue made the contradictory interplay of Atlantic slavery and universal rights impossible to ignore, this essay explores the role popular representations of slavery played in the construction of a new American national identity—explores and contextualizes. The Barbary captivity narratives must be read against the twinned backdrop of the French and Haitian Revolutions, which radically expanded the rights of all men at the same time that they revealed the violence and chaos revolutions bring forth. Exaltation and fear warred in American breasts as America's new republicans found themselves adrift in a sea of uncertainty, caught between revolutionary exuberance and fear of disorder, between the rights of man and the rights of property.

Building a New Nation

The Barbary narratives were a by-product of the United States' post-Revolutionary commercial expansion as merchants, barred from traditional trade routes within the British Empire, sought new commercial partners in the Caribbean and southern Europe. The costs of this expansion, as experienced by captains and crew, were heavy as American ships and crews, no longer under British imperial protections, were seized by predatory North African corsairs. Images of white American men—and some women—enslaved far from home, subject to the absolute will of tawny strangers, excited horror and patriotic zeal among the new Republic's reading public. A cadre of ambitious printers played upon those feelings. In the process, they initiated a new literary genre. But they simultaneously helped to consolidate and strengthen the new national government at a time when it lacked a strong western army, a navy, and a diplomatic corps. Representations of the capture and ruthless treatment of hundreds of American citizens by Barbary "pirates" dramatized the Republic's national weakness, leading many to stress the urgency of expanding the federal government and designing

---

Adrien Katherine Wing, ed., *Critical Race Feminism: A Reader*, 2d ed. (New York, 2003); Carole Pateman, *The Sexual Contract* (Stanford, Calif., 1988); Joan Wallach Scott, *Only Paradoxes to Offer: French Feminists and the Rights of Man* (Cambridge, Mass., 1996); Nancy Leys Stepan, "Race, Gender, Science, and Citizenship," *Gender and History*, X (1998), 26–52.

a tax structure that would replenish the national treasury, strengthen the western army, develop a diplomatic corps, build a navy—and establish the United States' diplomatic and military independence among the nations of the world.[7]

Although depicting Americans' weakness and victimization, the widely popular captivity narratives contributed to still another critical aspect of nation building. They buttressed American's growing sense of national identity and legitimacy by fabricating a system of binary oppositions between the new, white American citizen and his dangerous, racialized Others: barbaric infidels of North Africa, debased and enslaved sub-Saharan Africans, and—hovering always at the narratives' margins—white America's original defining Other, the savage Native American.[8]

At the same time, the captivity narratives permitted authors and readers to explore the nature of republican citizenship, especially who could claim full and active citizenship and what claims those citizens could make upon their new government. Questions concerning divisions within the nascent Republic spilled forth. Did captivity trump class distinctions, entitling all Americans to the sympathy and support of their fellow citizens, or did the captivity narratives reveal that deeply embedded class and regional divisions destabilized the Republic? As race and class were never far from the surface in these narratives, neither were gender and sexuality. And, like race, both gender and sexuality, apparently stabilizing factors in the construction of

---

7. For general historical analyses of the Barbary Wars and captivity narratives, see Frank Lambert, *The Barbary Wars: American Independence in the Atlantic World* (New York, 2005); Paul Baepler, ed., *White Slaves, African Masters: An Anthology of American Barbary Captivity Narratives* (Chicago, 1999); Lawrence A. Peskin, *Captives and Countrymen: Barbary Slavery and the American Public, 1785–1816* (Baltimore, 2009); James R. Lewis, "Savages of the Seas: Barbary Captivity Tales and Images of Muslims in the Early Republic," *Journal of American Culture*, XIII (1990), 75–84. That the Barbary pirates' exploits bared the new Republic's deficiencies is an argument both Baepler (*White Slaves*, 1–2) and Lambert (*Barbary Wars*, 3–13) make.

8. We cannot forget that the Barbary captivity narratives mimicked and played upon a far older and even more popular early American captivity narrative: the so-called Indian captivity narrative. We must see the Barbary narratives as constituting a complex triangle of Othering as critical to the formation of a U.S. national identity—the savage North African doubling the savage Native American, both as Constitutive Others for the pure, liberty-loving, white U.S. republican. See Paul Baepler's analysis of the Barbary captivity narratives in relation to the Indian captivity narratives in his *White Slaves, African Masters*. See, as well, Smith-Rosenberg, *This Violent Empire*, 207–249.

the new national identity, actually destabilized it in significant ways. As a result, a genre designed to strengthen white Americans' sense of themselves as freedom-loving, virtuous citizens revealed the fragility of that identity.

White Slaves

Between 1784 and the early 1800s, nearly 500 American sailors were seized by North African corsairs and sold in Algerian, Tunisian, and Tripolitan slave markets. The seizures came in waves. In the mid-1780s, when independence deprived the new United States of British naval protection, 2 U.S. merchant ships, 20 crew members, and 2 captains were seized by Algerian xebecs. In the mid-1790s, when the end of a ten-year truce between Portugal and Algiers again freed Algerian corsairs to cruise the Mediterranean and the Atlantic (Americans saw Britain's fine imperial hand in the truce's termination), 140 crew members and their captains were captured. In 1803, the capture of the navy warship *Philadelphia*, pursuing a Tripolitan cruiser during the U.S. blockade of Tripoli, led to the seizure of a U.S. warship and the enslavement of its 305 crew members and officers.[9]

Like the ship's seizures, the captivity narratives also came in waves. News of the first two captures in 1784 reached America's reading public slowly, primarily in the form of letters from merchants in Europe writing to their American correspondents and later in letters from the captives themselves, especially from their two captains, Richard O'Brien of Philadelphia and Isaac Stephens of Salem. Most of these letters were then published in both British and U.S. newspapers. (British merchants and newspapers thus played a critical role in the dissemination of these early descriptions.) Following the second and third waves of seizures, book-length captivity narratives began to appear, along with histories of North Africa, plays, poems, and novels focusing on the North Africans' enslavement of U.S. citizens.[10]

All the narratives stressed what one captive called "the Horrors of Slavery," graphically depicting the enslavement of "true-born" American citizens—heirs of Bunker Hill and Yorktown—by tawny-skinned Muslims. Deploy-

---

9. Lambert, *The Barbary Wars*.

10. Peskin's *Captives and Countrymen*, 22, presents a detailed analysis of these letters, the amount of time they took to reach American correspondents, and the ways they circulated from northern to southern newspapers. Reporting on his sample of four U.S. newspapers between 1785 and 1797, he found at least 285 items relating to the Algerian crisis. Surprisingly, he found little copying from one newspaper to another, indicating, he felt, that there were numerous letters for local newspapers to choose from, and they were not reduced to copying from one another.

ing deception and stealth, the Barbary "pirates" preyed on innocent, neutral ships found far from the protection of their native shores. Most of the American ships attacked were unarmed brigs or brigantines, their crews ranging from 8 to 15 men. The Barbary corsairs, in contrast, were heavily armed frigates, xebecs, and caravels. Their crews numbered between 300 and 450 men, the majority heavily armed and battle-hardened marines. Flying a false flag, the corsairs would approach the American ship. When close enough to fire, they attacked, easily overwhelming the Americans.[11]

John Foss, a youthful crew member aboard the *Polly* in 1793, painted such a scene in a narrative that sought to arouse his readers' sense of outrage. It all started, Foss explained, when they spotted a distant ship fast approaching the *Polly*.

> We supposed her to be an English Privateer.... She hailed us in English. ... The man who hailed us, was dressed in the Christian habit.... [But] by this time the Brig was under our stern, we then saw ... by their dress, and their long beard, that they were Moors.... Our feelings at this unwelcome sight, are more easily imagined than described.... We heard a most terrible shouting.... And saw a great number of men rise up ... drest in the Turkish habit.... about one hundred of the Pirates, jumped on board, all armed; some, with Scimitres and Pistols, others with pikes, spears lances, knives, etc.

Those who resisted were "lashed like ... dog[s] ... spurned and spit at by all the piratical crew." "Bemoaning our hapless fate," they trembled at the thought of what awaited them.[12]

---

11. Lambert, *Barbary Wars*, 39.
12. John Foss, *A Journal, of the Captivity and Sufferings of John Foss: Several Years a Prisoner in Algiers; together with Some Account of the Treatment of Christian Slaves When Sick: —and Observations on the Manners and Customs of the Algerines* (Newburyport, Mass., [1798]), 5–6, 9. For another description of the first moments of capture, see *Original Account of the Desperate Engagement and Capture of the General Washington, Alexander Boyle, Commander, Which Was Attacked by Two Barbary Corsairs, up the Mediterranean...* (London, [1804]), 9–10. No author is attributed on the title page, and it does not seem to have been Commander Boyle. The authenticity of this narrative is therefore suspect. See, as well, James Wilson Stevens, *An Historical and Geographical Account of Algiers: Comprehending a Novel and Interesting Detail of Events relative to the American Captives* (Philadelphia, 1797), 70–71; *An Affecting Narrative of the Captivity and Sufferings of Thomas Nicholson ...* (Boston, [1815]), 5. William Penrose, captain of the *President*, captured by an Algerian corsair November 4, 1793, complained that the

But it was not until they arrived in Algiers that Americans' misery truly began. Thomas Nicholson, a young man captured on his first Atlantic voyage, described his treatment on reaching the city in a narrative published in 1815: "We were taken charge of by the Dey's troops, who confined us in a stinking and dismal apartment of the castle." The following day, their rags were removed and they were washed and dressed in Turkish garments. They were then "blindfolded and followed by an immense rabble, who were permitted to pelt us with clubs and stones until we came to the palace of the Dey." And it was here that they came face to face with their abject position. "The Dey," Nicholson continued,

> was seated upon a low stage covered with rich carpeting ... and on each side about 1000 of his fort guards [or so the number of his troops appeared to the terrified eyes of captured Americans] were drawn up in the form of a half moon.... We were directed by turns to approach the foot of the eminence; when within a few paces, we were made to throw ourselves upon the earth and creep towards the Dey licking the dust as a token of reverence and submission.

The following day, those captives not chosen for castle service (the dey had a predilection for boys and young men, one narrator reported, undoubtedly adding to his readers' revulsion) were again stripped naked. "A narrow piece of cloth was wrapped around our loins.... We were then exposed to public sale in the market place," a large space where creatures of all sorts were offered for sale "whether for appetite or use." Camels, mules, asses, goats, hares, dromedaries, women and men jostled for space and attention. And here, the Americans found, humiliation piled upon humiliation. "The barbarians," Nicholson explained, "were very critical in their examination of our limbs to see if they were free from any defect; they made us walk, turn, lie down and lift large stones of 70 pounds weight. I was purchased by a young man ... who compelled me to lie down in the street and take his foot and placed it upon my neck as a token of submission and obedience to him."

Americans were given "a few old rags that would scarcely cover our nakedness ... I was forced to lay on the poop, and the wind being at E.N.E. it almost perished me" ("Letter from William Penrose, Captain of the Ship President, to His Owners, Dated Algiers, November 4, 1793," in [Mathew Carey], *A Short Account of Algiers, and of Its Several Wars* ... [Philadelphia, 1794], 37). Stevens had been a crew member on a captured U.S. ship but chose to structure his narrative as a history of North Africa.

How low could an American citizen sink? Nicholson seemed to be asking his white American readers. Nor could parallels to slave sales in the United States have escaped American readers.[13]

Ironically, stories designed to incite nationalism and patriotic zeal represented the new American citizens in the language of pathos and victimization. Heart-wrenching appeals to readers' sympathies followed hard upon appalling depictions of capture and enslavement. Drawing upon the discourses of romanticism and the sympathies, the narrators called on readers to shed tears for fellow Americans doomed to slavery, starvation, and hard labor. Thus John Foss began his narrative predicting that "tears of sympathy will flow from the humane and feeling, at the tale of the hardships and sufferings of their unfortunate fellow countrymen, who had the misfortune to fall into the hands of the Algerines—whose tenderest mercies towards Christian captives, are the most extreme cruelties." "Teach me to feel another's woe," Salem minister Isaac Story cried as he called on his congregation to imagine themselves enslaved, "and subjected to all the hardships and distresses of that situation ... denied the humble boon of rest, the lot of all the brutal herd."[14]

Drawing a clear line between her imagined white American readers and the "savage barbarians" who helped forge the readers' new national identity, Mary Velnet, one of the few women to write a captivity narrative, added, in a similar vein: "To witness the distress, and to hear the dispairing groans of these miserable people, could not fail to draw a tear from the eye of any one but a savage barbarian!" Describing the first scene that greeted her eyes on arriving on the Barbary coast, she continued,

---

13. Nicholson, *Affecting Narrative*, 6-8; Stevens, *Historical and Geographical Account*, 72. For discussions of the abolition movement in the late-eighteenth-century Atlantic, see, among others, Christopher Leslie Brown, *Moral Capital: Foundations of British Abolitionism* (Chapel Hill, N.C., 2006); Thomas P. Slaughter, *The Beautiful Soul of John Woolman, Apostle of Abolition* (New York, 2008); Brycchan Carey, *From Peace to Freedom: Quaker Rhetoric and the Birth of American Antislavery, 1657-1761* (New Haven, Conn., 2012); Robin Blackburn, *The American Crucible: Slavery, Emancipation, and Human Rights* (London, 2011); Seymour Drescher, *Abolition: A History of Slavery and Anti-Slavery* (New York, 2009); Sue Peabody, *"There Are No Slaves in France": The Political Culture of Race and Slavery in the Ancien Régime* (New York, 1996).

14. Isaac Story, *A Discourse, Delivered February 15, 1795, at the Request of the Proprietors' Committee; as Preparatory to the Collection, on the National Thanksgiving, the Thursday Following, for the Benefit of Our American Brethren in Captivity at Algiers* (Salem, Mass., 1795,) title page, 13; Foss, *Journal*, [1].

> Here for the first time, I had a melancholly prospect of my unhappy fellow slaves, whose countenances as they stole a pitying glance toward me, bespoke more than the tongue could express! ... those employed to load the waggons, had large collars about their necks, *made much after the form of those worn by the West-India negroes.* ... Under the heavy weight of the lash, they were compelled to perform tasks which we should judge impossible for human nature to support; naked, and apparently half starved, their scorched and lacerated bodies afforded a frightful proof of the brutality exercised toward them by their unprincipled masters.

Velnet's casual reference to "West-India negroes" leads us to wonder: Was the most unsettling aspect of Barbary slavery the harsh treatment American citizens suffered or the collapse of racial distinctions, as Americans were treated in Africa as enslaved Africans were treated in America?[15]

Echoing abolitionists' descriptions of the harsh treatment of African enslavement (consciously or unconsciously), the Barbary narratives detailed the taxing nature of slave labor, which, they insisted, tested human endurance. Most captured Americans were forced to labor on Algerian and Tunisian waterfront defenses, hauling boulders of twenty tons or more, heaving them through the water, placing them in the forts' breakwaters. Most of the slaves assigned to this work were shackled with heavy chains to prevent their escape. Captured in the seizure of the *Philadelphia* in 1803, William Ray presented the most detailed description of a marine slave's sufferings. "It was now the coldest season of the year," Ray wrote.

> We were almost naked, and were driven into the water up to our arm-pits. We had to shovel the sand from the bottom of the water, and carry it in baskets to the banks.—The chilling waves almost congealed our blood.... We were kept in the water from sunrise until about two o'clock, before we had a mouthful to eat.... We were driven again into the water, and kept there until sunset. Having no clothes to change, we were obliged to sleep on the ground in our wet ones; which gave many of us severe colds, and caused one man to lose the use of his limbs for upwards of a year afterwards.

15. *An Affecting History of the Captivity and Sufferings of Mrs. Mary Velnet, an Italian Lady, Who Was Seven Years a Slave in Tripoli; Three of Which She Was Confined in a Dungeon, Loaded with Irons, and Four Times Put to the Most Cruel Tortures Even Invented by Man: Written by Herself* (Boston, [1800?]), 9–11, 14–15 (emphasis added).

He ended his description on a note of despair. "With such usage life became insupportable, and every night when I laid my head on the earth to sleep, I most sincerely prayed that I might never experience the horrors of another morning."[16]

Narrative after narrative depicted the captives' dire living conditions: vermin-infected dungeons, earthen or rocky floors with only one blanket or rotten tree branches to sleep upon, food that was scanty, often moldy. William Penrose reported that Americans long enslaved frequently died of starvation. Certainly, fear of starvation was a constant theme. When William Ray received a loaf of white bread as an unexpected present from a captured but better-treated American navy officer, he found only poetry adequate to express his joy—as well as his ongoing sense of shame and despair. "To life-wasting hunger, to heart-piercing cold," he wrote his benefactor, "To scourges of tyrants a prey; / Midst demons of slavery too fierce be told ... / From you the first crust of regard I receiv'd— / From you the first crumb of esteem."[17]

No captivity narrative was complete without dismaying descriptions of brutal punishments. Floggings of a hundred lashes or more were commonplace for slaves who failed to meet their work quotas. For those accused of minor rule infractions, bastinadoing was the rule. Mathew Carey, in his *Short Account of Algiers, and of Its Several Wars* (which he hastily published in 1794, just as news of the second wave of Barbary captures reached America),

---

16. William Ray, *Horrors of Slavery; or, The American Tars in Tripoli ... Written during Upwards of Nineteen Months' Imprisonment and Vassalage among the Turks* (Troy, N.Y., 1808), 104. The captain of the *Minerva* complained that he and his men were kept "at hard labor from day light till dark, with an iron chain which reaches from our legs to our hips; about 50-lb. weight, and treated with great severity by our masters." He then added, "The wheel-barrow men in your city [Philadelphia] lived a genteel life to what we do." (One wonders: Was this last a reference to Philadelphia's practice of having prisoners work with wheelbarrows around the city, to African American day- or enslaved laborers, or to Philadelphia's newly arrived Irish immigrants? In all events, wheelbarrows in the city signaled loss of the status of free men.) The captain's report was reprinted in Carey, *Short Account*, 39. James Wilson Stevens described a similar chain gang being propelled through the streets of Algiers. These unfortunate men were "attended by a crew of savage drivers, who goaded them forward whenever they halted or happened to falter under the pressure of their burdens. The extremity of their sufferings in this laborious employment is better conceived than expressed" (Stevens, *An Historical and Geographical Account of Algiers*, 76; Foss, *Journal*, 18–19, 28).

17. Nicholson, *Affecting Narrative*, 8; Penrose, "Letter," in Carey, *Short Account*, 39; Ray, *Horrors of Slavery*, 100.

reported that "Christian slaves are ... sometimes burned, or rather roasted alive." Slaves charged with killing a Muslim, Foss noted, were thrown off the city walls onto iron hooks. Here, "they hang in this manner in the most exquisite agonies for several days before they expire." Even more ghastly scenes awaited those who had attempted to escape. As Thomas Nicholson reported,

> To detail minutely the horrid proceedings of these merciless barbarians, would too much wound the sensibility of my humane readers; suffice it to say, that after they had striped the sufferer naked, they inserted the iron pointed stake into the lower termination of the vertebrae, and thence forced it up near his backbone, until it appeared between his shoulders avoiding the vital parts. The stake was then raised in the air, and the poor sufferer exposed to the view of the other slaves, writhing in all the contortions of insupportable agony. In this shocking situation he remained about half an hour when he was taken down and beheaded.

Others were crucified, "nailed to the gallows, by one hand and the opposite foot, and in this manner they expire, in the most undescribable torture." All were forced to witness these executions.[18]

Women slaves also experienced cruel and inhuman punishments. Mary Velnet claimed that those compelled to work in the kitchens preparing food for their fellow slaves were frequently forced to stand on hot coals for punishment, or stripped of their clothing, held close to a roaring fire "until our bodies were nearly covered with blisters!" One woman died when her overseer, having stripped her naked, covered her body in burning rice. "But we were slaves, and to a barbarous and unprincipled nation!" Velnet lamented. "Deprived of our liberties, we were compelled like beasts of burden to toil under the heavy yoke of bondage!"[19]

Death through boiling rice was the least of the afflictions Velnet's narrative presented. As the centerpiece of her narrative, Velnet described an

---

18. Carey, *Short Account*, 15; Nicholson, *Affecting Narrative*, 9–10; Foss, *Journal*, 24–25. Ray presents his readers with a detailed description of bastinadoing: "A man sits on his [the slave's] back, and two more with each a bamboo, as large as a walking-staff, and about three feet long, hard and heavy, apply it to the soles of the feet with all their might and vengeance. In this manner, they punished several of our men for various offences.... The men thus flogged were put in heavy irons for two or three days" (William Ray, *Poems, on Various Subjects, Religious, Moral, Sentimental, and Humorous* ... [Auburn, N.Y., 1821], 232–233).

19. Velnet, *An Affecting History*, 35–36.

unusual torture machine that she claimed had been "made in imitation of a Genoese Shaving Mill, and when set in motion was so calculated as to cut the unhappy person into as small pieces as one's little finger." Slaves caught trying to escape were pushed into this machine—as other slaves were forced to watch the execution, until "there appeared nothing of him but a mass of goared flesh, cut into a thousand pieces."[20]

Through the darkness and horror of African enslavement, however, one bright vision shone forth—that of the American Republic as a beacon of freedom around the globe. Far removed "from the clanking of the tyrant's chain ... remote from the view of slavery's pallid visage, or the sound of her grief-extorted groans," the America the narratives held up to their readers was an "unrivalled region of liberty and independence," home to valiant republicans who valued their freedom and rights above life itself. Referencing America's Revolutionary patriots, John Foss closed the narrative of his captivity with David Humphreys's poetic celebration of Americans as "Men of firm nerves who spurn at fear and sloth, / Men of high courage like their sires of old." "Arise and spread thy virgin charms abroad," Humphrey/Foss called out to Columbia; "Ope[n] new prospects for th' enr..ptur'd eye / See a new aera on this globe begun." A proud, powerful, and liberty-loving Republic, America must strike out against slavery, inhumanity, and piracy— and must rescue her enslaved sons. Similarly calling upon American patriotism, William Ray cried out to his fellow Americans for rescue: "VOTARIES of freedom arm! / ... / Vet'rans of seventy-six, / Awake the slumb'ring sword!"[21]

In sharp contrast to the image of America as the home of the free and the brave, the narratives presented North Africa as "a region of horror," a land

20. Ibid., 44, 46; see also 84–87.

21. Ray, *Horrors of Slavery*, 18–19; Foss, *Journal*, 77–78. In poem after poem, Ray heaped accolades on American military heroes who had helped free Barbary captives, praising "EATON, *unexampled* brave / Who fought to rescue, and who bled to save / *Three hundred captive souls* from chains and death"; Preble, who, "to free the captive, ... wing'd his aid, / And more firm valor never was display'd"; and most of all Decatur, "Bold shall he chase yon demons of the wave, / For all who know him,—know him to be brave." Ray's celebration of Eton and Decatur points to the resentment at least some of the captives felt toward the slowness of their rescue. At times despairing of ever being released, some pointedly asked why the United States government did not simply invade the Barbary states. Complaints of being abandoned and forgotten by friends and country dotted these narratives. In this way, the narratives addressed the responsibility the new Republic must assume to protect its citizens from abuse (Ray, *Poems*, 77–79, 81, 83–86). At the same time, we must note Foss's unconscious irony of addressing the new, virile American nation as "she," a gender shift that the name "Columbia" necessitated.

of "hellish tortures and punishments," "its very atmosphere seems fraught with the most detestable depravity." A land of political tyranny and abject slaves, it could lay no claim to progress and prosperity. Thus James Stevens predicted in his history of North Africa, "The spirit of discovery will ever be retarded [here].... Since the destruction of Carthage, civilization seems not an attribute of the kingdom of Algiers, or of any of the states of Barbary." Slavery and "ferocious" savagery born of "the virulence of Mahometan antipathy to every thing that bears the name of Christian," he concluded, characterized the area. Even the mild-toned Reverend Story called Algiers "the City of bondage and death,... that cruel and barbarous city."[22]

In a more pragmatic, though equally disdainful, tone, Mathew Carey's *Short Account of Algiers* similarly stressed North Africa's economic backwardness. "Such is the gross ignorance of the natives in whatever concerns domestic improvement," he wrote, "that there is not a single bridge over any of these rivers.... ferry boats are unknown." Of course, William Ray's depiction of North Africa's backwardness and savagery was the most dramatic. "Ye lurid domes!" he expostulated in "Description of Tripoli" (written in 1803, while he was still imprisoned there), "whose tott'ring columns stand, / Marks of the despot's desolating hand: / Whose weed-grown roofs and mould'ring arches show / The curse of tyranny, a nation's woe; / In ev'ry ruin—ev'ry pile I find / A warning lesson to a thoughtful mind."[23]

What a series of powerful binaries the captivity tales strove to constitute for readers struggling to understand what it meant to be citizens in a republic barely ten years old. Narrative after narrative contrasted American liberty to North African slavery; American civilization to North African barbarism; Christianity to Islam; citizenship to lawless tyranny; free and productive trade to piracy; progress to declension; light to darkness; America to Africa. An idealized vision of America emerged, a critical component of the national identity American republicans were fashioning.

But, on closer reading, these narratives reveal that America's burgeoning national identity was riven with multiple contradictions, denials, and ellipses. America's identity, along with understandings of the meaning of liberty, rights, and citizenship, was, at best, explorative, experimental. On the narratives' pages, the binary oppositions so critical to the new Republic's self-presentation repeatedly collapsed. Color, religion, and gender are

---

22. Stevens, *Historical and Geographical Account*, v; Foss, *Journal*, [2]–4; Story, *Discourse*, 13.

23. Carey, *Short Account*, 3; Ray, *Poems*, 79–81, esp. 79.

revealed as uncertain markers of difference; the enslaved, as enslavers. Indeed the very structures of the narratives themselves inscribed uncertainty. Far from being simple depictions of the captives' genuine experiences, the narratives reveal themselves to be pastiches of borrowed descriptions and purported events lifted from one another's tales and from readily available ethnographic descriptions of North Africa. What had the captive truly experienced and seen? Who had written them, and for what purpose?[24]

No narrative exemplifies this counterfeit nature more powerfully than Mary Velnet's *Affecting History of the Captivity and Sufferings of Mrs. Mary Velnet, the Italian Lady, Who Was Seven Years a Slave in Tripoli*, published in 1800. Despite the title page's reassurance that the narrative was "Written by Herself," it reads far more like a sensationalist gothic romance designed to make its mark in late-eighteenth-century Britain's pornographic market. The book's most striking feature is its frontispiece, which depicts a barebreasted Velnet covered in chains, the graphic embodiment of her lengthy subtitle: "An Italian Lady, Who Was . . . Confined in a Dungeon, Loaded with Irons, and Four Times Put to the Most Cruel Tortures Ever Invented by Man." Tellingly, Velnet's narrative differs sharply both from those of the sailors, which stress brutal punishments but make no reference to sexual oppression, and from that of another female-authored narrative, *An Authentic Narrative of the Shipwreck and Sufferings of Mrs. Eliza Bradley, Wife of Capt. James Bradley*, which features neither potentates nor torture but tells only of poor, struggling nomads and the lack of material comforts.[25]

Other discrepancies render the text's authenticity suspect. Is it likely that in 1800 Velnet would have represented herself as an "Italian" rather than as a "Neopolitan," a "Roman," or a "Venetian"? And would she have dotted her

---

24. Two examples underscore these confusions. Borrowing from British ethnographic descriptions of the Barbary states, both Thomas Nicholson and John Foss end their narratives of brutal and inhuman slavery with descriptions of a cultured North Africa, its cities filled with public baths, coffeehouses, and bustling piazzas where "the inhabitants delight to loll, to drink sherbet, [and] sip coffee." Nicholson reports that Algiers boasts of "twenty thousand houses, one hundred and sixty thousand believers, twenty-five thousand Jews, and six thousand Christian slaves." Readers are left to wonder where the Reverend Story's "City of bondage and death" or William Ray's "lurid domes" and "weed-growing roofs" had disappeared to, or Mathew Carey's region without bridges or ferries. See Nicholson, *Affecting Narrative*, 15–16; Foss, *Journal*, 51–58.

25. Velnet, *An Affecting History*, frontispiece, 6–10; *An Authentic Narrative of the Shipwreck and Sufferings of Mrs. Eliza Bradley, Wife of Capt. James Bradley, of Liverpool, Commander of the Ship Sally, Which Was Wrecked on the Coast of Barbary, in June 1818: Written by Herself* (Boston, 1821).

texts with references to "political liberties" lost rather than threats to her religious faith, as Mrs. Bradley did? As an "Italian" woman in the 1790s, what "political liberties" had Velnet been deprived of? Whether or not Velnet "herself" wrote the narrative, it seems likely that she—or the actual author—adopted sections of existing U.S. or British male narratives about lost liberties and then enriched these plagiarisms with salacious engravings and sadistic tidbits.[26]

But far more serious contradictions and inconsistencies destabilized the narratives' representations of America as the home of freedom, modernity, and rights and of Africa as its multiply defining Other. William Ray's depiction of his enslavement as one of the crew on the U.S. warship *Philadelphia* abounds with such disruptions, especially his insistence that growing class divisions within the new Republic undercut its reputed commitment to the equality and rights of all men. Ray's narrative begins with a description of the economic adversities that led him to join the U.S. Navy. A child of the Revolution, Ray claimed to have read widely in Enlightenment political texts, most specifically those of Voltaire and Thomas Paine. He was thus one of many educated young men struggling to find a foothold in America's rapidly modernizing economy. His troubles began when his country store went bankrupt in 1802 as a result of the Jeffersonian embargo. Rather than turning Ray into a resentful Federalist critic of Jefferson, however, his economic misfortunes appear to have deepened his radical political perspective.

---

26. We should note that just about every stereotypic captivity scene possible takes place on the opening pages of Velnet's narrative, which was apparently first published in the United States in 1800, in keeping with its gothic character. Unlike those of Ray, Foss, or Nicholson, Velnet's narrative revolves around dark dungeons, "infernal place[s]" dramatically lit by oil lamps suspended from iron hooks, machines of torture, whips, chains, a circle of six "wretches" who administer the tortures—and, finally, deus ex machina, as she suddenly learns that the Italian government has paid her ransom and an Italian ship is waiting in the harbor to bear her home to her husband and daughter (Velnet, *An Affecting History*, 79). That the tale was then repeatedly reissued with a different woman's name on the title page—Mrs. Maria Martin—ruins the suspension of disbelief. This is especially so when one compares Velnet's narrative to that of Mrs. Eliza Bradley, the wife of "Capt. James Bradley, of Liverpool, Commander of the Ship Sally, Which Was Wrecked on the Coast of Barbary, in June 1818." In sharp contrast to Velnet's sadomasochistic frontispiece, Bradley's presents her fully dressed and carrying a Bible—which, Bradley tells us, was her constant companion and comfort during the year she spent separated from her husband, anxiously awaiting ransom (Bradley, *An Authentic Narrative*). Nevertheless, Paul Baepler informs us, the Velnet / Martin narrative was one of the most popular Barbary narratives, reprinted from 1807 until 1818 (Baepler, *White Slaves*, 11–12).

As Ray explained his situation, saddled by debts, set upon "by a ruthless hord of exorbitant, vindictive, and insatiable creditors," he fled home and family, moving to Philadelphia in search of a position in the city's growing printing industry. But no sooner had Ray arrived in Philadelphia than he fell "dangerously ill," lost the printing position he had been promised, was robbed by his callous landlord and hounded by Pennsylvania creditors. "The surly, unsociable, churlish, and suspicious curmudgeons of the interior of Pennsylvania," Ray thundered, "shun an itinerant stranger in distress, as they would a rattle-snake or a viper." In an amazing disruption of the self-Other binary that lies at the heart of the Barbary narratives, Ray continues: "You might with more hopes of success, expect friendship or relief from the Esquimaux of America, or the wandering Arabs of Asia, than from the *black-Dutch Pennsylvanians;* especially, if you add ... the appearance of poverty." Only equally impoverished Irish immigrants offered him aid, helping him in spite of their own indigence. Significantly, immigration had divided Pennsylvanians throughout the 1790s, with conservative Federalists seeking to bar most immigrants and Jeffersonian Republicans embracing them. Ray positioned himself within the radical Jeffersonian Republican camp at the same time as he challenged the idyllic Jeffersonian vision of the United States as an egalitarian yeoman republic.[27]

Despairing of finding employment on land, Ray enlisted in the navy. Here, his situation went from bad to worse. Ray embarked upon the ill-fated *Philadelphia* only to discover that no rations had been sent aboard to sustain the common sailors. The inherent inequality between Ray's situation and that of wealthy civilians on shore was not lost on him. "Our enterprising tars" were left to subsist on river water and whatever food they could scavenge, "while the high-fed, rich and slothful epicureans of our sea-ports

---

27. Ray, *Horrors of Slavery*, 23, 29 (emphasis added). We must bear in mind that Ray wrote in the shadow of the turbulent 1790s, when Jeffersonian Republicans battled Federalists and the Whiskey and Fries's Rebellions laid bare the economic and political conflicts at the heart of the Republic. Indeed, in so many ways, Ray's narrative tells the story of those conflicts. For explorations of political and economic conflicts in the young Republic with a special focus on the rise of the Jeffersonian Republican coalition, see Riley, *Slavery and the Democratic Conscience;* Andrew Shankman, "Malcontents and Tertium Quids: The Battle to Define Democracy in Jeffersonian Philadelphia," *Journal of the Early American Republic*, XIX (1999), 43–72; Terry Bouton, *Taming Democracy: "The People," the Founders, and the Troubled Ending of the American Revolution* (New York, 2007). For a discussion of growing class disparities among post-Revolutionary white Americans, see Shankman, *Crucible of American Democracy*.

were gorging the dainty luxuries of various climes, and different oceans." Far worse was the treatment those "tars" received from navy officers, more often than not "cruel, vain, and magisterial coxcomb[s] ... [who] display[ed] ... [their] diabolical disposition[s], by punishing men for frivolous faults or errors, with the austerity of *a West-Indian slave-driver, and inhumanity of a Tripolitan or Algerine.*" Ray pointed to the severe beating one sailor received for holding an opinion different from an officer's and then calling that officer "no gentleman." "You thought!" the outraged officer responded, "You have no right to think, damn your blood; you tell an officer he is no gentleman—I'll cut you into ounce pieces"—reminding one of Mary Velnet's Genoese Shaving Mill. "He was then," Ray continued, "flogged without feeling or mercy." Ray, a true disciple of Tom Paine, then provides us with a crash course in eighteenth-century epithets:

> That a man had no right to *think*, was a theorem I had never heard of before, not even under the most arbitrary governments.... It was worse ... than the Bastile of France. Votaries of Justice! What do you think of a smockfaced, pickshank, fopdoodle of an officer, sporting with the feelings, the liberty, and the very life and health of one of our gallant tars ... an effeminate, pragmatical, fopling of an officer?[28]

Ray assures us this was no isolated incident. On another occasion, Ray watched as a boatswain, just released from slavery in Tripoli, was given twenty-four lashes despite his weakened state. His crime: his bare feet (impoverished, he had no shoes) had soiled the gangplank. "That a man, but just escaped from the sanguinary clutches of Tripolitan barbarians," Ray fumed,

> weak, palid, and broken with toils, chains, and hunger, should so soon be *treated worse than by those savages*—beaten, among his own countrymen, for not performing impossibilities, was enough to awaken the spirit of indignation in the bosom of a fainted anchorite. Shades of departed heroes! who fought, bled and died in the sacred cause of liberty, how are your blessed [names] insulted.[29]

As U.S. Navy officers were revealed as more inhumane than "a West-Indian slave-driver ... a Tripolitan or Algerine" and the *"black-Dutch Penn-*

---

28. Ray, *Horrors of Slavery*, 20, 51, 55 (emphasis added).
29. Ibid., 62–63 (emphasis added).

sylvanians" as "more void of humanity than Turkish barbarians," the distinctions between freedom-loving Americans and Barbary slave drivers in Ray's and other narratives eroded. The earlier image of America as "the consecrated of liberty" committed to "equality and inalienable right[s]" for "all men" fractured. The new Republic was revealed as deeply divided socially, economically, and ideologically—at best, a republic in the process of becoming. But what kind of a republic would it be? Whose rights, what rights would be protected? In 1803, as Ray wrote and Haiti emerged as an independent, sovereign nation, these issues remained hotly contested and unresolved.[30]

Nothing, however, disrupted the Barbary narratives' elaborate system of Othering as much as the strong parallels the narratives revealed between the injustice of Barbary slavery and the injustice of slavery in the United States, between the intolerable sufferings European Americans experienced as slaves in North Africa and the sufferings of enslaved Africans in the United States. That these parallels went largely unacknowledged, perhaps even unobserved, by their authors makes the ironic comparison all the more pointed. As European American captives detailed their experiences— of being stripped naked, examined, and purchased in Algiers' slave market, of their professed masters' "inhumane" arrogance, of being driven by the lash and mercilessly flogged—how could their readers not draw parallels to descriptions of Atlantic slavery found in the works of Anthony Benezet, Abbé Raynal, or Granville Sharp? Even the descriptions of slaves' being crucified or speared on hooks and hanging until they died were familiar to readers of John Stedman's widely published *Narrative, of a Five Years' Expedition, against the Revolted Negroes of Surinam*, those images made particularly powerful by William Blake's engravings.[31]

---

30. Ibid., 23.

31. The second half of the eighteenth century and the opening years of the nineteenth saw a plethora of antislavery publications. See, for example: Ant[hony] Benezet, *A Caution to Great Britain and Her Colonies, in a Short Representation of the Calamitous State of the Enslaved Negroes in the British Dominions* (Philadelphia, 1767); Benezet, *The Case of Our Fellow-Creatures, the Oppressed Africans, Respectfully Recommended to the Serious Consideration of the Legislature of Great-Britain, by the People Called Quakers* (London, 1784); Granville Sharp, *An Appendix to the Representation; (Printed in the Year 1769,) of the Injustice and Dangerous Tendency of Tolerating Slavery, or of Admitting the Least Claim of Private Property in the Persons of Men in England* (London, 1772); *Letter from Granville Sharp, Esq. of London, to the Maryland Society for Promoting the Abolition of Slavery, and the Relief of Free Negroes and Others, Unlawfully Held in Bond-*

Yet none of the narrators who reported their experiences of enslavement in North Africa drew the connection between their experiences and those of Africans enslaved in the United States and the Caribbean. Rather, the narrators frequently displayed a tone bordering on disdain when referring to enslaved Africans. As already noted, Mary Velnet's narrative expressed outrage that she and other Barbary captives were treated in ways similar to West Indian slaves. John Foss was deeply offended when he discovered that one of the pirates who enslaved him was a black African. As we have seen, even William Ray wrote with disdain of being "manacled, stripped, castigated, flayed, and mangled worse than *the vilest Virginian slave.*"[32]

How can we understand the narrators' silence on issues that so roiled the revolutionary Atlantic? One explanation might lie in the unsettled nature of their identities as both Americans and republican citizens. At a time when so much was new and tentative, did racial difference offer white Americans an unqualified sense of self and social order? Since John Locke had published his *First Treatise of Government,* freedom and unalienable rights had been seen as the white man's property. Proclaiming oneself no different than a black slave presumed a sameness, an exchangeability between white and black that might threaten the Americans' claims to the privileges of whiteness. It was one thing for a white man secure in his freedom and inalienable rights to sympathize with an enslaved Other, but for the white slave to em-

---

age: *Published by Order of the Society* (Baltimore, 1793); Abbé Raynal, *A Philosophical and Political History of the Settlements and Trade of the Europeans in the East and West Indies* ... (London, 1788); Olaudah Equiano, *"The Interesting Narrative" and Other Writings,* ed. Vincent Carretta (New York, 1995); John Stedman, *Expedition to Surinam: Being the Narrative of a Five Years Expedition against the Revolted Negroes of Surinam in Guiana ... from the Year 1772 to 1777* ... (London, 1963). Stedman's *Narrative* was translated and published in six European countries in addition to its British publication. It is interesting, however, that it was not printed in the United States. Of course, its British publication made it available to U.S. audiences; nevertheless, the failure of U.S. publishers to exploit a volume European publishers found profitable is significant and may indicate the difficulty U.S. readers had with Stedman's romantic depiction (and open defense) of miscegenation.

32. Foss, *Journal,* 7; Ray, *Horrors of Slavery,* 18–19 (emphasis added). Ray's poem, written twenty years after his own enslavement but included in a reissue of his captivity narrative, may be the sole exception. Embracing enslaved African Americans as "a kindred race," he criticized the proposed Missouri Compromise and the contradictions of slavery: "Land of *freedom*—land of *slaves!* / State of *patriots*—state of *knaves,*" Ray intoned, "Sticklers for that traffic base, / Which degrades the human soul— / Which enchains a kindred race, / Till their tears in blood-drops roll" (Ray, *Poems,* 163–169).

pathize with a black slave seemed difficult for even the most radical of the Barbary narrators. On a more global scale, if race proved an unstable social marker, where, in an Atlantic world torn by revolution, could the new republicans find stability?

It was not, however, the parallels between the experiences of white and black slaves that most threatened the narratives' system of binary oppositions; it was the parallels between the behavior of North African and North American slaveowners. The 1790s and early 1800s saw the proliferation of British, American, and French antislavery tracts that depicted the Atlantic slave trade as barbaric and the treatment of slaves arrived in the Americas as sadistic. Once those comparisons were drawn, barbarism ceased to be a marker of difference between America and Africa. The distinction between the white American subject and his African Other, the distinction upon which the coherence of America's national identity depended, blurred.[33]

Although Americans who had actually suffered Barbary enslavement failed to acknowledge similarities between North African and American slaveholders, other Americans did. Not surprisingly, African Americans were particularly astute at connecting the dots. Discussing his hopes for alleviating the condition of African Americans enslaved in the United States, Prince Hall, a leading spokesman for the free blacks of Boston, rather pointedly praised God for the speed with which Congress had delivered European Americans enslaved in North Africa: "How sudden were they delivered by the sympathising members of the Congress of the United States, who now enjoy the free air of peace and liberty, to their great joy and surprize, to them and their friends." Hall then demanded, "Where is the man that has the least spark of humanity, that will not rejoice with them?" The contrast to the centuries-long enslavement of Africans in America hovered over his text.[34]

White abolitionists also began to draw the connection between Barbary

---

33. See note 13 for references to the early abolitionist movement in the United States and Great Britain.

34. Prince Hall, "A Charge" (1797), rpt. in Richard Newman, Patrick Rael, and Philip Lapsansky, eds., *Pamphlets of Protest: An Anthology of Early African-American Protest Literature, 1790–1860* (New York, 2001), 45–50, esp. 49. See, as well, Richard S. Newman, *Freedom's Prophet: Bishop Richard Allen, the AME Church, and the Black Founding Fathers* (New York, 2008); Joanne Pope Melish, *Disowning Slavery: Gradual Emancipation and "Race" in New England, 1780–1860* (Ithaca, N.Y., 1998). For a discussion of the role black women played in the antislavery movement, see Catherine Adams and Elizabeth H. Pleck, *Love of Freedom: Black Women in Colonial and Revolutionary New England* (New York, 2010), esp. 165–184.

and Atlantic slavery. As early as 1788, shortly after the first wave of Algerian enslavements, the Pennsylvania Society for Promoting the Abolition of Slavery voted to include the enslavement of Americans in the Barbary states among its causes, suggesting an equivalency between the enslavement of white Americans and Africans. Even more telling was a satirical article the society's president, Benjamin Franklin, published pointing to the hypocrisy of white American criticism of North African slavery. In a Franklinesque fusion of sarcasm and moral outrage, he placed the proslavery arguments of Georgia representative James Jackson in the mouth of Sidi Mehemet Ibrahim, "a member of the Divan of Algiers." Eloquently defending Algerian enslavement of white Americans, Ibrahim / Franklin mimicked U.S. slaveholders' defense of the peculiar institution. "If we cease our cruises against the christians, how shall we be furnished with the commodities their countries produce, and which are so necessary for us? If we forbear to make slaves of their people, who, in this hot climate, are to cultivate our lands?" Furthermore, did not the "Alcoran" prescribe slavery, as it urged, *"Masters treat your slaves with kindness: Slaves serve your masters with cheerfulness and fidelity"?*[35]

Fellow Philadelphian Mathew Carey, another sharp critic of slavery, was more direct, though far less humorous, in his insistence that American slaveholders were at least as barbaric as North African slaveholders. In his 1794 *Short Account of Algiers,* Carey insisted: "For this practice of buying and selling slaves, we are not entitled to charge the Algerines with any exclusive degree of barbarity. The Christians of Europe and America carry on this commerce an hundred times more extensively than the Algerines." Having established parallels between Algerian and American slaveholders, Carey directed his admonitions to the situation in Philadelphia. Writing in the aftermath of the burning of Le Cap and the flight of large numbers of Saint Domingue slaveholders (with their slaves) to Philadelphia, Carey denounced the "diabolical ... advertisements" for runaway slaves that began appearing with ever-greater frequency in Philadelphia newspapers. "The French fugitives from the West-Indies," Carey continued,

> have brought with them a croud *[sic]* of slaves. *These most injured people* sometimes run off, and their master advertises a reward for apprehending

---

35. Benjamin Franklin [Historicus], "To the Editor of the Federal Gazette," *Federal Gazette and Philadelphia Evening Post,* Mar. 25, 1790, [3].

them. At the same time, we are commonly informed, that his [the master's] sacred name is marked in capitals, on their breasts; or in plainer terms, it is stamped on that part of the body with a red hot iron. Before therefore we reprobate the ferocity of the Algerines, we should enquire whether it is not possible to find, in some other regions of the globe, a systematic brutality still more disgraceful?

Philadelphia newspapers provided Carey with ample evidence. A year before Carey wrote, *Dunlap's American Daily Advertiser*, edited by Franklin's grandson, Benjamin Franklin Bache, carried the following ad:

EIGHT DOLLARS REWARD.
RAN AWAY last evening, from the Citizen LaSalle, living near the Hospital, TWO NEGROES; one about eighteen years of age, five feet none inches high, smooth faced, with a small beard; he is stamped [branded] upon the right side of his breast; speaks bad French. The other is about fourteen years of age. Whoever takes up said Negroes, shall receive the above Reward, by applying to the printer.

Of course, Carey neatly displaced U.S. responsibility for barbarous slavery onto Saint Domingue planters, but a crucial connection had been made.[36]

None drew a closer connection between American and North African slavery than Royall Tyler in his 1797 work *The Algerine Captive*, an early American novel posing as a captivity narrative. Tyler's book predates actual American captivity narratives, often by five to ten years. Yet it presages the captives' descriptions of their experiences almost exactly. Like captivity narratives, *The Algerine Captive* is a rough stitching together of diverse discourses and genres. Indeed, it might well be described as three loosely connected books, all of which problematize the United States' self-image as a virtuous republic. The first book (or section) consists of light, satirical commentary on rural America, north and south, as it lampoons pompous clergymen and college professors, quack doctors, illiterate old maids hungry for

---

36. Carey, *Short Account*, 16, emphasis added; *Dunlap's American Daily Advertiser*, Aug. 4, 1793. Peskin presents an interesting analysis of Carey's *Account*, pointing out that large sections of it were hardly original but rather interwove ethnographic and historical accounts of North Africa (largely taken from British sources) with material drawn from early captivity accounts (often in the form of letters to Carey), finally adding Carey's own attack on U.S. slavery (Peskin, *Captives and Countrymen*, 165–168).

young husbands, and southern preachers far more interested in flogging their slaves and racing their horses than in God or theology.[37]

In the second section, Tyler's narrator, Updike Underhill, in order to escape imprisonment for his mounting debts, signs up as a ship's doctor. (Here, especially, we should note the similarities between Tyler's fictional Underhill and William Ray, in flight from his accumulated debts. Both works represented young men struggling to gain a foothold in an emerging capitalist economy, as, indeed, Tyler was himself.) Underhill unwittingly signs on to a slave ship, ironically named *Sympathy*, headed for Goree Island on the coast. Once the *Sympathy* reaches Africa, the tone of the novel changes dramatically. Underhill's first response on discovering he has embarked on a slave ship is alarm—and then a concerted effort to distance himself from any responsibility for what he sees happening. Commenting on conversations he hears among the ship's captain and officers, he confesses, "To hear these men converse upon the purchase of human beings, with the same indifference, and nearly in the same language, as if they were contracting for so many head of cattle or swine, shocked me exceedingly." When Underhill, as one of the ship's officers, is offered the opportunity to take a share in the cargo, "I rejected my privilege with horror, and declared I would sooner suffer servitude than purchase a slave." His remonstrance is met "with repeated bursts of laughter"—and, on a more serious level, with

---

37. Tyler, *Algerine Captive*. It almost seems as if history were enacting fiction rather than the reverse. One could, of course, hypothesize that both Tyler's novel and later American captivity narratives mimicked earlier British narratives of empire and enslavement on the Barbary Coast—except for their celebration of American love of liberty and frequent attacks on British tyranny. In the young Republic, patriotic ideology molded both fiction and autobiographical writing. For British captivity narratives, see Linda Colley, *Captives: The Story of Britain's Pursuit of Empire and How Its Soldiers and Civilians Were Held Captive by the Dream of Global Supremacy, 1600–1850* (New York, 2002). For another study of early British captivity narratives, see Daniel J. Vitkus, ed., *Piracy, Slavery, and Redemption: Barbary Captivity Narratives from Early Modern England* (New York, 2001). For literary historical studies of *The Algerine Captive*, see, among others: Cathy N. Davidson, "Reading *The Algerine Captive*," in Davidson, *Revolution and the Word: The Rise of the Novel in America* (New York, 1986), 192–211; Cathy N. Davidson and Arnold E. Davidson, "Royall Tyler's *The Algerine Captive*: A Study in Contrasts," *Ariel*, VII (1976), 56–67; Larry R. Dennis, "Legitimizing the American Novel: Royall Tyler's *The Algerine Captive*," *Early American Literature*, IX (1974), 71–80; Sarah Ford, "Liberty Contained: Sarah Pogson's 'The Young Carolinians; or, Americans in Algiers,'" *EAL*, XLI (2006), 109–128.

his crewmates' growing suspicion of him. From this point on, Underhill becomes an outsider.[38]

But he is one deeply immersed in the proceedings and practices of Atlantic slavery. Willful ignorance, even disdain, *The Algerine Captive* tells us, does not offer a moral reprieve. Anyone slavery touches at whatever remove bears responsibility. At first, Underhill refuses to accept this obligation. As he watches a train of 150 men, women, and children marched into the slave dungeons on Goree Island, chained in pairs, iron collars around their necks, an iron rod connecting the pairs in a long line of shuffling figures (very much like the scene of white slaves Mary Velnet described some ten years later), he flees to the ship to avoid further contact. Only then does he discover that one of his principal tasks as ship's doctor is to examine each of the captives to ascertain whether, as the captain explains, "our owners were not shammed off with unsound flesh." Having become a suspect figure, Underhill is forced to carry on his examinations under the watchful eye of the ship's clerk, who sees that it is "transacted with all that unfeeling insolence which wanton barbarity can inflict upon defenceless wretchedness ... equally insulting to humanity and common decency." Close parallels connect Tyler's description with that Thomas Nicholson published more than twenty years later—again, with fiction foretelling actual events.[39]

Forced to participate in the African slave trade, Underhill becomes a moral witness. His goal: awakening Americans to what was done in their name and subject to their republican governance. Watching those captives deemed a "sound" purchase loaded onto the ship, chained, manacled, guarded by crew members armed with cutlasses and cat-o'-nine-tails, Underhill tells his readers, a "more affecting group of misery was never seen." Long before the slave ship is ready to leave Africa, more than two-thirds of the slaves are seriously ill. Certainly, Underhill does little to spare his readers' feelings, detailing the filth that results from cramming so many bodies into such small spaces—"the stagnant confined air ... the stench of the faeces ... putrid diseases." Again and again deploying the language of the sympathies, Underhill forces his readers to confront the slaves as human beings, little different from themselves. Not simply dirty, sweating, dying bodies were chained down in the hold but husbands and wives, loving fathers and mothers, weeping children, terrified young girls used "to gratify the brutal lust of the

---

38. Tyler, *Algerine Captive*, 96, 98, 99.
39. Ibid., 100.

sailors"—all with feelings little different from those of European Americans. The text's deployment of sameness continues as Tyler repeatedly deploys the very language Revolutionary Americans used to describe American victims of British impressments.[40]

Tyler's invocation of sameness and the consequent disruption of racialized categories of difference only intensifies as Tyler suddenly and unexpectedly positions Underhill as the Atlantic slave trade positioned Africans. As the ship waits for still more slaves to be loaded aboard, Underhill persuades the captain to permit him to take the sickest slaves ashore, hopefully to recover away from the ship's fetid air. It is at this point that a sharp reversal of conditions occurs. While Underhill and his convalescing slaves are still on shore, an Algerian corsair approaches. The slave ship's captain, to save his cargo, flees, abandoning Underhill to capture and enslavement. Suddenly, white privilege becomes white vulnerability, captor becomes captive. The transformation happens so quickly, in the space of a few short pages, that readers cannot fail to see the parallels between American and Barbary slavery, slaves and slaveholders. The horrors that so sickened Underhill when he viewed the enslavement of black men and women are now his to experience. Like them, he is stripped naked, tossed into the black hold of the ship, denied adequate food and water, pressed down by fear and despair. Once ashore, he is taken to the public slave market, where his naked body is carefully examined and evaluated—as he examined and evaluated black bodies on Goree Island—to determine whether he is of unsound flesh, to paraphrase the slaver's captain. He is then condemned to hard labor, whipped, starved, brought nigh to death. In the midst of all these sufferings, one of the Africans he had befriended on the slave ship slips him food and water, sufficient to keep him alive (just as Underhill had worked to keep the black slave alive when their situations were reversed). When Underhill realizes who has been succoring him, he is "oppressed with gratitude. Is this, exclaimed I, one of those men whom we are taught to vilify as beneath the human species, who brings me sustenance, perhaps at the risk of his life, who shares his morsel with one of those barbarous men who had recently torn him from all he held dear, and whose base companions are now transporting his darling son to a grievous slavery?" This act of empathy and kindness transforms Tyler's vision of human brotherhood, his nation, and his political vision. "Grant me," he cries out,

40. Ibid., 101–105. It scarcely needs to be pointed out that Tyler borrowed extensively from abolitionist literature to paint this abject picture.

once more to taste the freedom of my native country, and every moment of my life shall be dedicated to preaching against this detestable commerce. I will fly to our fellow citizens in the southern states; I will on my knees conjure them, in the name of humanity, to abolish a traffic which caused it to bleed in every pore. If they are deaf to the pleadings of nature, I will conjure them for the sake of consistency to cease to deprive their fellow creatures of freedom, which their writers, their orators, representatives, senators, and even their constitutions of government, have declared to be the unalienable birth-right of man.

Seeing black and white enslavement cheek by jowl has led Underhill to embrace human connectedness. He has become a spokesman for Enlightenment liberalism's celebration of the sameness of all men and the universality of rights.[41]

However, this black slave is not the only one to befriend and aid Underhill. Perhaps the most admirable character Tyler presents in his lengthy bildungsroman is the "Mollah," or Muslim "priest," who visits Underhill when harsh treatment has rendered Underhill close to death. The Mollah helps Underhill recover his health and then invites him to visit his college, there to learn more about Islam and, possibly, to consider conversion. While persisting in his Christian faith, Underhill goes and discovers the Mollah to be a pious man with a high sense of personal moral responsibility. Gentle and cosmopolitan, the Mollah respects other races and religions and sympathizes with all who suffer. No contrast could be sharper than that between the Mollah and the cruel and avaricious captain and crew members of the slave ship, the French and Portuguese slave traders of Goree Island—or, indeed, the Christian ministers Underhill/Tyler spent much of the early part of his narrative lampooning. The Mollah, far more than any of Tyler's Christian characters, espouses the Enlightenment's celebration of reason, science, and human brotherhood. Out of charity, the Mollah convinces Underhill's cruel owner to sell him to an Algerian hospital, where Underhill both introduces western medical practices and grows familiar with North African drugs and medicine, enriching his western training (another example of

---

41. Tyler, *Algerine Captive*, 107, 108–111, 126–128. In another example of captivity narratives' imitating fiction, Tyler describes a scene that parallels one Nicholson would describe later—of being forced by his new owner to "lie in the street and take the foot of my new master, and place it upon my neck—making to him what the lawyers call atonement" (118–119).

an Enlightenment embrace of cultural diversity and social usefulness, made possible through the Mollah's efforts and foresight).[42]

Nor is the Mollah the only courteous and helpful Algerian to guide Underhill on his road to greater understanding. A wealthy, educated Jewish merchant also befriends Underhill, advising him how to accumulate money from his medical services so that he will be able to ransom himself. Encouraged by the Mollah and the Jew, Underhill gains permission to travel throughout North Africa, from Algiers to Medina, the birthplace of the Prophet (sections of the book are clearly copied from ethnographies of North Africa). Underhill is fascinated and charmed by much of what he sees. The result is an image of the Barbary states that differs radically from the one of savagery and declension featured in actual captivity narratives. Instructed by the Mollah, Underhill is now able to appreciate difference without placing it in a hierarchical system of superior / inferior.[43]

Of course, at some point, the *Algerine Captive* has to reverse fields and reaffirm the hierarchical binary that privileges freedom-loving America and denigrates savage North Africa. Not surprisingly, the figure that restores difference to its identity-confirming role is that archfiend of the Christian imaginaire, the duplicitous, avaricious Jew. The kind Jew who advised Underhill has a conniving son, who steals Underhill's carefully hoarded savings and sells him back into slavery. Only the deus ex machina of a storm at sea and the providential rescue by a Portuguese frigate restore Underhill to freedom, the United States, and his loving parents. *The Algerine Captive* closes with white Christian patriarchal order restored. But it is a far wiser Underhill who returns, alive to the faults of his countrymen and sensitive to the virtues of Others—possessed of a cosmopolitan, universalist vision the novel's contrived ending cannot efface. Yet the abruptness of the closure, its numerous loose ends, and its ambivalence leave us wondering how Royall Tyler would answer our two fundamental questions: At the height of the Age of Revolution, what rights could republican citizens claim? Who could claim to be a man, a citizen?[44]

The *Algerine Captive* was not the only fictional account to link slavery in North Africa and the United States. In 1801, seven years after *The Algerine Captive* first appeared, *Humanity in Algiers; or, The Story of Azem: By an American, Late a Slave in Algiers* was published in Troy, New York.

---

42. Ibid., 131–142, 150–159.
43. Ibid., 211–216, 219–232.
44. Ibid., 234–240.

Financed largely by subscriptions from farming families in Vermont and northern New York State, *Humanity in Algiers* echoed Tyler's critique of Atlantic slavery and his universalist vision of freedom and human brotherhood. (We should remember that Vermont's Revolutionary constitution was the first state constitution to abolish slavery.) Like Tyler, as well, the anonymous author refused the captivity narratives' dualistic vision of the United States as the unquestioned home of liberty and of the Barbary states as the realm of declension and despotism. Echoing Mathew Carey, the author insisted that, though loath to admit it, white Americans were far more guilty of the sins of slavery than Algerians. "Unconscious of our own crimes, or unwilling the world should know them," *Humanity in Algiers* commenced, "we frequently condemn in others the very practices we applaud in ourselves; and, wishing to pass for patterns of uprightness, or blinded by interest, pass sentence upon the conduct of others less culpable than ourselves."

> "A vile, piratical set of unprincipled robbers," is the softest name we can give them; forgetful of our former depredations on the coasts of Africa, and the cruel manner in which we at present treat the offspring of those whom we brought from thence. When the Algerines yoke our citizens to the plough, or compel them to labour at the oar, they only retaliate on us for similar barbarities.[45]

Humanity in Algiers presents three distinct tales of enslavement: that of an American captured on the high seas by an Algerian corsair and sold into slavery in Algiers; that of a Senegalese captured in war; and that of an innocent African farming family by "barbaric" slave hunters, an example only too familiar to readers of eighteenth-century antislavery tracts. Not only did the novel unequivocally condemn each form of slavery; it repeatedly drew parallels between slavery in Africa and the United States. Its message: slavery was cruel and unjust wherever it existed. It insisted, as well, on the barbaric nature of all slaveowners no matter where they lived or what color their skin.[46]

Even for Vermont readers, however, such radicalism had its limits. Despite Vermont's history of militantly defending its own independence

---

45. *Humanity in Algiers; or, The Story of Azem: By an American, Late a Slave in Algiers* (Troy, N.Y., 1801), 3–4. Concerning its publication history, at the conclusion of the novel, the publisher lists the towns in Vermont and New York State from which subscriptions were raised. For a secondary analysis of *Humanity in Algiers*, see Baepler, *White Slaves, African Masters*, 46.

46. *Humanity in Algiers*, esp. 8, 10–43, 60–70.

from both Britain and New York State, *Humanity in Algiers* does not condone slaves' violent resistance. Rather, all the enslaved characters, despite their keen sense of the injustice of their enslavement, rely on God and the humanity of others, not their own actions, for their emancipation. Time and again, the novel insists, the slave must not fight for his own liberation but wait upon God's mercy. In the very years when rampaging slaves in Saint Domingue battled aggressively to gain their freedom and establish a self-governing black state, this was a truly conservative message—one that posed no threat to the continuation of slavery in the United States.

In contrast to the didactic tone adopted by both *The Algerine Captive* and *Humanity in Algiers*, Susanna Rowson's *Slaves in Algiers; or, A Struggle for Freedom* takes the form of a rollicking comedy. *A Play, Interspersed with Songs*, it was first performed in Philadelphia on June 30, 1794—at the height of the slave rebellion in Saint Domingue, the same year that the French National Assembly abolished slavery and in the immediate aftermath of the yellow fever epidemic many felt fleeing Saint Domingue planters had brought with them. Popular at the time and much studied since, Rowson's comic opera plays with—and thoroughly disrupts—the captivity narratives' hierarchicalized vision of difference. In a light, comedic form, it enacts the most transgressive challenge imaginable to hierarchical systems of difference in late-eighteenth-century America: it plays with miscegenation, then goes on to fuse miscegenation with a radical inversion of gendered roles. Rowson thus challenges two of the fundamental axes upon which Atlantic societies rested—race and gender distinctions—all in the name of meditating on the incompatibility of Americans' love of liberty and acceptance of slavery.[47]

In the opening scenes of *Slaves in Algiers*, two of its female protagonists—one, a Jew raised as a Muslim, the other, a Muslim princess—appropriate the classic republican rhetoric that galvanized European Americans to challenge British imperialism and proclaim their own freedom and independence. Fearlessly, these two women defy patriarchal power, personified by a licentious dey, putting their desire for liberty above love of family or country.

47. Susanna Haswell Rowson, *Slaves in Algiers; or, A Struggle for Freedom*, ed. Jennifer Margulis and Karen M. Poremski (Acton, Mass., 2000). For analyses of this play, see, among others, Marion Rust, *Prodigal Daughters: Susanna Rowson's Early American Women* (Chapel Hill, N.C., 2008); Benilde Montgomery, "White Captives, African Slaves: A Drama of Abolition," *Eighteenth-Century Studies*, XXVII (1996), 615–630; Elizabeth Maddock Dillon, "Slaves in Algiers: Race, Republican Genealogies, and the Global Stage," *American Literary History*, XVI (2004), 407–436.

Assuming the role of virile republican heroes, they devise a plot to rescue enslaved American sailors and carry them off to freedom.[48]

Not only does Rowson's comic opera present foreign women as classic republican heroes; it gives its boldest, most freedom-affirming speeches to the plaything of the Orientalist imaginaire, the harem slave Fetnah—in this case, doubly Othered as a Jewish Moor born in England, the ultimate figure of (con)fused identities. In the play's opening lines, Fetnah (having just been sold to the dey by her father, Ben Hassan, a greedy Jew turned Muslim) declares that, despite the luxuries that now surround her, she would relinquish all to regain her liberty. "It's all vastly pretty, the gardens, the house and these fine clothes," she tells an astonished fellow slave, "but I don't like to be confined.... I wish for liberty." Seeking to convince her amazed fellow harem slave, she continues: "Is the poor bird that is confined in a cage ... consoled for the loss of freedom. No! tho' its prison is of golden wire ... its little heart still pants for liberty ... nor once regrets the splendid house of bondage." Fetnah thus challenges the misogynous assumptions that women happily trade independence for luxuries and that harem slaves luxuriate in licentiousness. Referring significantly to her British birth, like a true citizen of a revolutionary world, Fetnah insists, "I feel that I was born free, and while I have life, I will struggle to remain so."[49]

Fetnah is as good as her word. At one point, using wit and inventiveness, she saves the life of a Christian slave (Frederic) found in the dey's harem garden (the most dangerous place for a white Christian man to be found), and when she has to leave him alone with the dey she worries. Without her quick wit to protect him, "what will become of him?" Later, stealing clothes from the dey's son so she can dress as a boy, she seeks out a desperate group of enslaved Christian men hiding in a cave by the coast. When the men offer

48. Rowson, *Slaves*, ed. Margulis and Poremski, esp. acts 1, 3.

49. Rowson, *Slaves*, ed. Margulis and Poremski, act 1, scene 1 (13, 17). We should note that Muslim women are the absent presence in captivity narratives. The male captives wonder about them but never see them. Here, Rowson places two Muslim women on the public stage, front and center, as the play's most powerful actors. Women's frivolous and foolish nature was a hotly debated issue in late-eighteenth-century women's texts, as not only Rowson's but Wollstonecraft's and other texts demonstrate. See Mary Wollstonecraft, *A Vindication of the Rights of Woman; with Strictures on Moral and Political Subjects* (Philadelphia, 1792). Interestingly, Mathew Carey published a slightly later edition and was the publisher of Rowson's *Slaves*. For more on Wollstonecraft's complex political position on feminism and gender, see Barbara Taylor, *Mary Wollstonecraft and the Feminist Imagination* (Cambridge, 2003).

to lead her to a place of safety, she replies with scorn: "Do you take me for a coward? ... A woman can face danger with as much spirit, and as little fear, as the bravest man amongst you." She then adds authoritatively, "Do you lead the way; I'll follow to the end." The men, awed, respond, "She's a devil of a spirit. — It's a fine thing to meet with a woman that has a little fire in her composition."[50]

In a paired scene, Zoriana, the dey's daughter (a figure purportedly modeled on Voltaire's *Zaire*), brings the authority of class privilege to her role as republican hero. Ziriana devises a daring plot to rescue the Christian slaves when she discovers that Olivia, an enslaved American woman, has the keys to the dey's palace but has never thought to use them to secure an escape. Amazed at Olivia's passivity, in another telling inversion of European American self-presentations, Zoriana seizes the keys, declaring, "To-morrow night shall set us all at liberty." Zoriana has already been helping Henry, another enslaved American, supplying him with money and jewels to buy his own freedom and those of his companions. She now summons Henry (the play's central American protagonist) to the dey's garden, explains her rescue plans, and orders him and his men to assemble the next night, break open the dey's prison doors, and rescue Olivia's father, another captive. When Olivia hesitates to join the conspiracy because she fears that they will all be captured, Zoriana coolly proclaims, "These are groundless fears."[51]

Rebecca is the play's remaining woman protagonist. She is usually presented as the most outspoken exemplar of Americans' love of freedom. Indeed, Fetnah attributes her own newfound passion for liberty to Rebecca's influence. "It was she, who nourished in my mind the love of liberty, and taught me, woman was never formed to be the abject slave of man. Nature made us equal with them, and gave us the power to make ourselves superior."

---

50. Rowson, *Slaves*, ed. Margulis and Poremski, act 1, scene 2 (38–43, 47, 49–52, esp. 43).

51. Rowson, *Slaves*, ed. Margulis and Poremski, act 1, scene 3 (26–28), act 2, scene 1 (35–36). Literary critics, Marion Rust in particular, argue that the character Zoraida from Cervantes's *Don Quijote* provided the model for Rowson's *Slaves* and especially the character Zoriana (Rust, *Prodigal Daughters*, 228). However, Mozart's comedia del arte masterpiece, *The Abduction in the Seraglio*, has at least as good a claim. The basic plotline is much the same: British lovers are enslaved in North Africa, along with their lower-class servants. Ferocious Moorish soldiers and lyrical harem girls parade around the stage. An escape is foiled until the Dey relents and releases the two couples. A joyous finale completes the opera. Fears of fierce Turks, who, in reality, had long threatened Vienna, are rendered a humorous and delightful digression.

But it is actually Fetnah, not Rebecca, who speaks these lines. Although, in the end, Rebecca uses her wealth to free the central Christian protagonists, she makes no proud declarations of liberty until the play's final scene. It is only then that she finally speaks, admonishing Christians planning to enslave Muslims they had captured during their escape. In a pointed rebuke of American slaveholders, she declares: "By the Christian law, no man should be a slave." Paraphrasing Locke's opening words in the *First Treatise of Government*, Rebecca continues: "It [slave] is a word so abject, that, but to speak it dyes the cheek with crimson. Let us assert our own prerogative, to be free ourselves, but let us not throw on another's neck, the chains we scorn to wear."[52]

Through much of the play, however, Rebecca embodies the good Republican Mother, as described by Linda K. Kerber. We first meet Rebecca as she worries about the fate of her young son, Augustus, who has been auctioned off as a slave by Fetnah's father. "Must a boy born in Columbia, claiming liberty as his birth-right, pass all his days in slavery?" she laments. "Oh! my adored boy! must I no more behold his eyes beaming with youthful ardor, when I have told him, how his brave countrymen purchased their freedom with their blood." (But pause a moment to consider the irony of naming an emblem of U.S. republican ardor after the Roman emperor who oversaw the demise of the Roman Republic. Was Rowson, a former British loyalist, questioning the longevity of the U.S. Republic or its claims to civic virtue?) Later, Rebecca tells Augustus directly: "Can I be happy while you are a slave? My own bondage is nothing." She thus gives voice to the mediated sense of freedom appropriate to the Republican Mother, who was designed to experience her sense of citizenship and freedom vicariously through her sons and husband, never through independent political actions of her own. Noticeably, though mourning for her captive son, Rebecca takes no part in the slave rebellion. In the end, it is her son who rushes into the dey's palace to rescue his mother. Olivia, similarly, as the virtuous republican daughter, places her father's and her fiancé's liberty above her own. "Oh! heavens," Olivia cries out to Zoriana, "could I but see him [her father or her fiancé; the reference is ambiguous] once more at liberty, how gladly would I sacrifice my own life."[53]

---

52. Rowson, *Slaves*, ed. Margulis and Poremski, act 1, scene 1 (16–17) act 3, scene 7 (67, 73). Significantly, it is at this point that Fetnah attributes her love of liberty not only to Rebecca's American influence but to her own birth in Britain. For examples of Rebecca as the champion of American freedoms, see Rust, *Prodigal Daughters*, 216, 218, 223.

53. Linda K. Kerber, *Women of the Republic: Intellect and Ideology in Revolutionary*

Two enslaved American men grace the stage in *Slaves in Algiers*. However, their claims to heroic republican virtue are somewhat suspect, since they spend most of the play's opening scenes longing for the embraces of beautiful Muslim women. Henry, the leading male, not only is romantically involved with Zoriana but, exploiting her sexual interest in him, has procured her assistance (that is, her money) to gain his ransom, scarcely the behavior we would expect from a virtuous republican. Not only does it render a young man dependent on a wealthy woman, but we soon discover that Henry is, in fact, engaged to Olivia, Zoriana's dearest friend. Frederic, Henry's boon companion, is infatuated with Fetnah and as dependent on her as Henry is on Zoriana. As we have seen, it was Fetnah's swift wit and self-possession that saved Frederic from the dey's vengeance.[54]

As already suggested, however, these gender inversions were not Rowson's most transgressive move. (After all, bluestocking women from London to Paris to Philadelphia had been challenging traditional gender roles and the restraints of coverture for nearly half a century.) It is when Rowson suggests the possibility of miscegenation, of racial "amalgamation," that ultimate fusion of difference, that she comes close to crossing the pale. The first hint we have of such a possibility occurs when Zoriana confesses to Olivia that she "love[s] a Christian slave, to whom I have conveyed money and jewels sufficient to ransom himself and several others." Then, in the very next scene, Frederic tells Henry of his dependence on and desire to rescue "the fair Zoriana," and Frederic responds with envy. Oh, that he could find a beautiful, Moorish woman who would love him and whom he could love. Zoriana's and Henry's affair ends abruptly when Henry discovers that Olivia lives and is in the dey's palace. But the possibility lingers. When Olivia chooses not to leave with the escaping Henry, Frederic, and Zoriana, she insists that should she, Olivia, not be able to follow them, Zoriana must "be a daughter to my poor father ... let him not feel the loss of his Olivia." She then adds, "Be to my Henry ... a friend, to soothe him in his deep affliction; pour consolation on his wounded mind, and love him ... as I have done." Having established the Christian American's / Moorish princess's interchangeability and thus their exchangeability as daughter / lover / wife, Olivia then "Exits" the scene.[55]

America (Chapel Hill, N.C., 1980); Rowson, *Slaves*, ed. Margulis and Poremski, act 1, scene 1 (16–17), act 3, scene 2 (54).

54. Rowson, *Slaves*, ed. Margulis and Poremski, act 1, scene 4 (29–31), act 2, scene 1 (32–37).

55. Ibid., act 2, scene 1 (36–37).

Slaves in Algiers's very next scene repeats the possibility of miscegenation, as Fetnah and Frederic meet in early dawn in the dey's garden and fall in love. Calling Fetnah "my charmer," "beautiful creature," "sweet," and "bewitching," Frederic asks, "Do you indeed love me?" Fetnah instantly responds, "Yes, I do, better than any body I ever saw in my life." Frederic then asks the follow-up question: "You will go away with me?" and Fetnah answers: "To be sure, I will, that's the very thing I wish." Later, in the cave, she reiterates her pledge. "I came with a full intention to go with you, if you will take me, the whole world over." Of course, the play suggests that Fetnah is more interested in freedom and travel than in the bald Frederic. Nevertheless, she is quite willing to go with him "the whole world over," and their words indicate that physical attraction as well as pragmatism is at work. On first seeing Frederic, Fetnah sighs in a stage whisper: "Oh dear! what a charming man. I do wish he would run away with me."[56]

The play balances these provocative couplings with two condemned from their inception: the dey's melodramatic passion for Olivia and its comic reprise, Ben Hassan's for Rebecca. Both American women make it clear that, in Rebecca's words, "a daughter of Columbia, and a Christian, [would never] tarnish her name by apostasy, or live the slave of a despotic tyrant." We should note, as well, that the misogynous couplings the play explores involve racialized women and American men, whereas the suggestion of an American woman marrying a racialized man would be condemned as un-American—and un-Christian.[57]

Of course, the word "play" is key. From the opening prologue, everything turns topsy-turvy as a Federalist woman author publicly proclaims "the Rights of Man." *Slaves in Algiers* is a farce, complete with comedic figures: the bearded and mustached Mustapha, the even more ludicrous and ultimately cross-dressing Ben Hassan, and a sexually inept and unattractive dey. (We should remember the depiction of the Algerian dey as unusually fond of attractive slave boys.) Certainly, he wins neither Fetnah's heart nor her respect: "He is old and ugly," she informs us, "and when he makes love, he looks so grave and stately, that I declare, if it was not for fear of his huge seymetar [scimitar], I shou'd burst out alaughing in his face." Even Fetnah and Frederic are comedic characters. Indeed, it is Fetnah's double entendres and her obvious phallic references that mark *Slaves in Algiers* as a comedy. A com-

---

56. Ibid., act 2, scene 3 (37–40), act 3, scene 1 (49–51).
57. Ibid., , act 1, scene 2 (20–22), scene 3 (26), act 3, scene 3 (57–58), scenes 6 and 7 (64–66).

edy is not serious; the function of humor is to challenge, but not overthrow, order. Humor is possible only because author and audience are secure in the knowledge that the social order is not endangered. As Mary Douglas points out: "The joke merely affords opportunity for realising that an accepted pattern has no necessity. Its excitement lies in the suggestion that any particular ordering of experience may be arbitrary and subjective. It is frivolous in that it produces *no real alternative*, only an exhilarating sense of freedom from form in general."[58]

In 1795, William Cobbett, in his bitter condemnation of *Slaves in Algiers*, predicted that the play would inspire American women to organize politically, replace men in Congress, even disrupt Congressional debates by giving birth on the floor of Congress—making a mockery of republican self-governance. As with most of Cobbett's Hobbesian predictions, that never happened. Despite the efforts of certain elite women to assert their political voice in post-Revolutionary Philadelphia and revolutionary Paris, patriarchal power was not at risk. Women's demands faded in the face of the effective political backlash against women that, Rosemarie Zagarri argues, characterized the late eighteenth and early nineteenth centuries. It is true, there were moments in the revolutionary Atlantic world when it did appear that the world might turn upside down—as already noted, 1794 was undoubtedly one such moment, with slavery abolished throughout the French Empire, Pennsylvania farmers rising in arms against the U.S. government, and the United Irishmen readying for pitched battle against the British. But, by the decade's end, white patriarchal order had been restored across much of the Atlantic. *Slaves in Algiers* appears to have been little more than an entertaining fantasy built with the smoke and mirrors of impossible desires. It provided "an exhilarating sense of freedom from form in general," but it "produce[d] *no real alternative*."[59]

---

58. Ibid., prologue (9), act 1, scene 1 (14); Mary Douglas, "The Social Control of Cognition: Some Factors in Joke Perception," *Man*, III (1968), 361–376, esp. 364, 368–369.

59. Peter Porcupine [William Cobbett], *A Kick for a Bite; or, Review upon Review; with a Critical Essay on the Works of Mrs. S. Rowson; in a Letter to the Editor, or Editors, of the American Monthly Review* ... (Philadelphia, 1795), rpt. in David A. Wilson, ed., *Peter Porcupine in America: Pamphlets on Republicanism and Revolution* (Ithaca, N.Y., 1994); Rosemarie Zagarri, *Revolutionary Backlash: Women and Politics in the Early American Republic* (Philadelphia, 2007). For the long-term effects of this misogynous backlash, see Linda K. Kerber, *No Constitutional Right to Be Ladies: Women and the Obligations of Citizenship* (New York, 1998). Although there are moments when *Slaves in Algiers*, playing with miscegenation, appears far more radical than either the actual

It did, however, permit Rowson, the daughter of a British army officer and a loyal British subject until her return to America in 1793, to tweak white American claims to a superior love of liberty and of man's unalienable rights. From the Stamp Act crisis through the Revolution and far into the nineteenth century, white Americans depicted their revolution as a battle between American republicanism and British tyranny, enslavement, and corruption—depictions the British deeply resented, as Samuel Johnson's quip, "We hear the loudest *yelps* for liberty among the drivers of negroes," demonstrates. A loyalist throughout the war and for the decade following, Rowson would have been very familiar with such critiques. One wonders whether continued British resentment might have informed Rowson's presentation of her American captives as less devoted to freedom than the brave Muslim women who rescued them, especially since one of those women (Fetnah) announces that she was born in England. Did Rowson, like Tyler, refuse the racialization of difference, deliberately satirizing the images of a barbaric Africa and a freedom-loving America? She certainly suggests that racial "amalgamation," rather than being a dirty little plantation secret, could be both romantic—and ennobling. Nor can we forget that Rowson chose to write a comic opera, rife with satire and double entendres. As the opera ends with all the characters heralding the new U.S. Republic as a bastion of liberty in a tyrannical world, we must ask: Did she intend that, too, as a joke—upon her patriotic American audiences?[60]

Conclusion

The Age of Revolution was a time of tumult and transformation, of unprecedented political creativity and utopian dreaming. It was also a time of fear, a moment when radical universalism came face-to-face with slavery's centrality to American politics, economic well-being, and the emerging national identity. It was a time when white Americans, northerners and southerners, rich and poor, eastern elites and laborers, sturdy western farmers and frontier squatters, bitterly debated what rights republican citizens could claim and, even more fundamentally, who among the United States' diverse

---

captivity narratives or Tyler's *Algerine Captive*, Elizabeth Maddock Dillon is right: binary oppositions hold. But the whiff of subversive desires lingers as the curtain descends. See Dillon, "Slaves in Algiers," *American Literary History*, XVI (2004), esp. 428–429.

60. Samuel Johnson, *Taxation No Tyranny: An Answer to the Resolutions and Address of the American Congress, 1775*, in *The Works of Samuel Johnson* (Troy, N.Y., 1903), XIV, 93–144.

population could claim them. It was during these momentous years that slavery emerged as a critical political issue as white and black Americans, both northern and southern, argued over the pros and cons of slavery, emancipation, and colonization; read U.S. and British abolitionist tracts; parsed Equiano's *Narrative;* watched anxiously as slaves rose up in Saint Domingue and slave revolts ignited around the Caribbean, Central America, and, indeed, as far north as Virginia; and observed the French Republic abolish slavery and admit African-born former slaves as members of its National Assembly.

The popular press's representation of white Americans' enslavement by Barbary rulers opens a small window onto these discussions. It helps us locate the ellipses, the moments of racial blindness, when the fears and needs of white men blinkered them to the ideological contradictions embedded in their deep-seated commitments to liberal universalism. It permits us to map the gradual process by which the United States emerged as a white man's republic, unalienable rights as the exclusive property of white men. But it also helps us see that citizenship and rights are changing concepts that emerge out of virulent, ongoing political struggle. Our experience of being an American, a citizen, a rights-bearing political agent is endlessly, relentlessly contradictory, contested, always in process.

"MURDER, ROBBERY, RAPE, ADULTERY, AND INCEST"
MARTHA MEREDITH READ'S *MARGARETTA* AND THE FUNCTION OF FEDERALIST FICTION

Duncan Faherty

In a series of columns originally published in the *Connecticut Courant* throughout the early fall of 1800, the staunchly Federalist "Burleigh" warned against the dangers of electing Thomas Jefferson as president. Historians have long cited Burleigh's electric prose as representative of the contentious rhetoric surrounding the revolution of 1800. They have done so with good cause, as Burleigh vividly indexed the partisanship of the era. If the Federalists lost power, Burleigh proclaimed, "murder, robbery, rape, adultery, and incest, will be openly taught and practised, the air will be rent with the cries of distress, the soil soaked with blood, and the nation black with crimes." Burleigh represented a potential Jeffersonian victory as an abandonment of the Republic's foundational principles. A public toleration of incest, rape, and adultery would shatter normative familial bonds; similarly, if homicide and theft were unpunished, several of the primary guarantees of the Constitution—concerning life, liberty, and property—would be rendered meaningless. The consequences of such a present would sabotage cultural cohesion for generations, condemning the Republic's future citizens to a recursive struggle to secure cardinal freedoms they already possessed.[1]

I would like to thank Elizabeth Maddock Dillon and Catherine O'Donnell for their comments on the earliest version of this essay, which was presented at the "Warring for America, 1803–1818" conference organized by the Omohundro Institute of Early American History and Culture. Many thanks as well to Fredrika Teute and Nicole Eustace for their generative editorial labors with this piece and this volume. Double thanks to Christopher Eng, Andy Doolen, and Ed White for their readings and comments about this piece along the way.

1. There were at least thirteen columns published under the pseudonym "Burleigh" that originally appeared in the *Connecticut Courant* (Hartford) in the late summer and early fall of 1800. The tenor of these articles is demagogic Federalism, as Burleigh seems

Barely submerged within Burleigh's fears resided the terror that Washington would become both a pre- and a post-Revolutionary Cape François (present-day Cap Haitien), a space where, many white Americans believed, degenerate cultural mores had licensed unbridled revolution. Federalists had long employed literary conventions to address foreign traumas, especially through their use of gothic tropes to rail against the violent energies of Jacobism. Burleigh seized upon this long-standing tradition—and domesticated it—by inferring that a vote for Jefferson essentially endorsed an importation of the corruptions of Caribbean plantation culture. Burleigh's jeremiad conflated sexual behaviors and cultural stability, and he plotted his fears along a Caribbean axis in order to depict Jeffersonian ideals as alien to a Federalist landscape. The horrors of Saint Domingue haunted, and deeply inflected, Burleigh's notion of a national future "black with crimes" by his implicit references to the kinds of depravity long configured as synonymous with the island. By echoing commonplace tropes about Saint Domingue, Burleigh discursively deployed patterns deeply familiar to his audience and frequently associated with a Jeffersonian francophilia. His rhetoric, in other words, invoked fears about racial revolution by conflating the acts of vio-

---

intent on terrifying voters into supporting his party's cause. The columns were widely reprinted in Federalist newspapers across the country and were likewise consistently cited by Democratic-Republican papers as prime examples of the partisanship of their opposition. Burleigh's weekly screeds, for example, were reprinted by Federalist venues across September and October 1800—in such papers as the *South-Carolina State Gazette, and Timothy's Daily Advertiser* (Charleston), the *Massachusetts Mercury* (Boston), the *Pennsylvania Gazette* (Philadelphia), the *New-York Gazette and General Advertiser*, the *Washington Federalist* (Georgetown, D.C.), and *Jenk's Portland Gazette* (Maine). Democratic-Republican newspapers openly rebutted Burleigh's accusations before the printer's ink was barely dry. The *Impartial Observer* (Providence, R.I.) decried him as "a hot-headed, violent, and strenuous party-man" intent on slander and malice (Sept. 1, 1800, [1]). This piece, signed by the "Friends to Truth," is but one instance of these direct replies to Burleigh, and, indeed, a majority of the issues of the *Impartial Observer* contain a response to Burleigh in September and October 1800. For examples of historians who have cited Burleigh, see Michael A. Bellesiles, "'The Soil Will Be Soaked with Blood,': Taking the Revolution of 1800 Seriously," in James Horn, Jan Ellen Lewis, and Peter S. Onuf, eds., *The Revolution of 1800: Democracy, Race, and the New Republic* (Charlottesville, Va., 2002), 59–86; John Ferling, *Adams vs. Jefferson: The Tumultuous Election of 1800* (New York, 2004); and David Hackett Fischer, *The Revolution of American Conservatism: The Federalist Party in the Era of Jeffersonian Democracy* (New York, 1965). Burleigh's predications about murder and incest can be found in "No. XII. To the People of the United States," *Connecticut Courant*, Sept. 20, 1800, [1].

lence that had destroyed planter culture on the island with the predictable outcomes of a Jeffersonian victory.[2]

The future of the United States would be dislodged, Burleigh declared, if the nascent Republic abandoned the stabilizing influence of properly structured kinship networks in favor of these illicit foreign practices. In this imagined future, there would no longer be any consequences for an unbounded sense of liberty, and the contractual relationships embodied within such configurations as father and child, husband and wife, personal and public, and free citizen and enslaved person would no longer have traction. The battery of ruptures in the social compact (often taking the form of sexual aberrations) that Burleigh cataloged exhibited a pattern operant in the first decade of the nineteenth century; indeed, such representations functioned as key metaphors for expressing the crisis of cultural authority that circulated around the revolution of 1800. Figurations of non-normative (or unacknowledgeable) social reproduction, in short, served as a discursive trope by which early-nineteenth-century writers debated the terms of individual and collective rights.

Inflamed passions surrounding the revolution of 1800 were far from limited to the Federalist cause, as leaders of both parties checked the stocks of local armories, plotted counterinsurgencies, and cast weary eyes across the circum-Atlantic world for evidence of foreign infiltration and clandestine support. Given the zealous saber rattling, describing the period as the "era of ungood feelings" might best encapsulate the heightened tension surrounding the election of 1800 and its aftermath. When Jefferson was finally, after thirty-six Congressional ballots, peaceably elected, his marginal victory did little to foreclose simmering tensions. Alternative outcomes had been entirely possible—even momentarily probable—across the contentious campaign, leaving the nation with a host of unanswered, and far-reaching, questions. These uncertainties helped structure an already prevalent urgency about the imbrication of the post-1800 nation in a world of empires, increasing global economic integration, racialized violence, and seemingly endless revolutions. From continuing paranoia sparked by the Haitian Revolution, or the Burr Conspiracy, or the Louisiana Purchase, or abiding conflicts with Native Americans, or Gabriel's Rebellion, or the economic ramifications of

2. See Rachel Hope Cleves, "On Writing the History of Violence," *Journal of the Early Republic*, XXIV (2004), 641–665. For more information on the manifold connotations of the Haitian Revolution, see Laurent Dubois, *Avengers of the New World: The Story of the Haitian Revolution* (Cambridge, Mass., 2004).

the Embargo and Non-Intercourse Acts, the first decade of the nineteenth century was marked by widespread anxieties about the Republic's future.

The affective register that Burleigh reproduced and fueled did not vanish during the inauguration in March 1801, and, by focusing on the absence of a physical aftershock, scholars have routinely neglected the reverberations encoded in textual figurations of cultural life in the wake of 1800. Although these rippling tensions eventually attenuated, their force early in the century demonstrates an almost commonplace recognition of the tenuous state of social cohesion in the emerging Republic. The idea that the dyspeptic election had subverted national stability hastened apprehensions about whether Jefferson's victory was just a foreshock of change or the epicenter of a cataclysmic breach. Was the election a harbinger of future ruptures, or was it a ravaging singularity from which recovery might still be imaginable? In a variety of discursive mediums, Federalists explored the notion that a corrupted present might divorce the Republic from its past praxis and undermine reasoned national expansion. Burleigh's columns project such a disjointed future: one bereft of the anchor of a stable family because of an epidemic of overly permissive sexual practices and an utter devaluation of property rights. Imperiled households, rent by misaligned desires, served as a locus for such figurations because they grounded the contrasting spatial dimensions quartered within the word *domestic*. Yet, much more than this, the distorted kinship that Burleigh feared would undermine the Republic was a hallmark of colonial plantocracies; as such, his paranoid figurations simultaneously reflect prevalent apprehensions about the creolization of the United States.

If Saint Domingue had long been understood as a slumbering volcano, Burleigh conjured a relocation of that potential for devastation to domestic shores. By prognosticating that the twin specters of planter depravity and racialized violence might triumph in the United States, Burleigh displayed how such a transplantation would infest the emerging Republic. The imputation that Jefferson would foster illicit behaviors allowed Burleigh to connect Democratic-Republican rule to the erosion of U.S. civil society. Burleigh's rhetoric fixed Jefferson as emblematic of a planter class whose actions had already proven disastrous in the Caribbean. The violence of the Haitian Revolution demonstrated the results of unmediated personal liberty as defined by the wayward ethos of an extreme French radicalism, and Burleigh's language equated that apocalyptic present with a future "black with crimes." In essence, Burleigh gothically crumpled time so that the future of the United States perilously mirrored the corrupt past of colonial Cape François and the frenzied furnace of its revolutionary present.[3]

Burleigh's essays cataloged a Federalist fantasy writ large, one that circulated far and wide in the months before and after the conclusion of the revolution of 1800. Forced from the center of political power, Federalists were compelled to locate a new means of animating the development of U.S. sociality beyond simply representing it as imperiled. Grappling with their overt loss of authority was but the first step; the more daunting task facing Federalists remained reassembling their positions as actors within the new unfolding social network. This counterassemblage, more often than not, sought to reconstitute national character by depicting the benefits emanating from properly constituted households. The reordering of genealogies—the return to a whitewashed linear form of development—would prevent a devolution into the more multivalent kinship networks (acknowledged or not) embodied in plantation economies. These nascent counterassemblages, in essence, associated citizenship and stability with northern Federalism, while simultaneously figuring southern U.S. Democratic-Republicans as directly linked to unstable creolized social structures.[4]

An unorganized Federalist intelligentsia continued to deploy this dystopian rhetoric in newspaper articles, political speeches, sermons, essays, and

---

3. From as early as 1789, when the Comte de Mirabeau noted that the planter class was living as if they slept "at the foot of Vesuvius" ([Jean]-P[hilippe] Garran[-Coulon], *Rapport sur les troubles de Saint-Domingue* ... [Paris, 1789–1799], IV, 18), through the middle of the nineteenth century, when Herman Melville compared the *San Dominick* to "a slumbering volcano" in *Benito Cereno* (1855) (see *The Piazza Tales* [New York, 1856], 163), writers have seized on the image of Haiti as a barely dormant powder keg ready to erupt. See C. L. R. James, *The Black Jacobins: Toussaint Louverture and the San Domingo Revolution* (New York, 1938); Alfred N. Hunt, *Haiti's Influence on Antebellum America: Slumbering Volcano in the Caribbean* (Baton Rouge, La., 1988); and Gordon S. Brown, *Toussaint's Clause: The Founding Fathers and the Haitian Revolution* (Jackson, Miss., 2005).

4. This potential loss of authority was especially true of Federalist women because, as Rosemarie Zagarri has argued, "the triumph of Republicanism meant that women were excluded from politics primarily, and not incidentally, because of their sex." Zagarri's sense of that exclusion matches up with the tendency to imagine the period as dominated by a cult of Republican Motherhood, a catchall phrase quite literally antithetical to Federalist ambitions for moral suasion. See Zagarri, "Gender and the First Party System," in Doron Ben-Atar and Barbara B. Oberg, eds., *Federalists Reconsidered* (Charlottesville, Va., 1998), 134.

private correspondence in the aftermath of Jefferson's ascendency. Yet perhaps the best record of its complex gesticulations resides in the oft-neglected literary culture of the period. After the revolution of 1800, an emergent Federalist literary movement sought to overwrite the conditions of its displacement by dramatizing the traumas of national declension. Since predictions like Burleigh's failed to become realities after the election, dispossessed Federalist writers needed access to a new generic form to continue their critiques. Fiction fulfilled these needs, allowing the exploration of the ramifications of sexual disorder, as a coded embodiment of political disarray, to seamlessly transition into a new medium. The novel, in particular, accommodated a prolonged juxtaposition of properly ordered domestic relationships—socially anchoring marriages and parental relationships—and their dangerous counterparts. These Federalist writers sought to coercively fashion new models of subjectivity aimed at reforming public behavior because they had lost their ability to legislate public interactions. As these writers staged the potential victims of misrule and sexual misconduct, they used traumatic disarray as a pedagogic exercise. In so doing, they turned to the themes of adultery, robbery, incest, and rape as tropes capable of charting how improper domestic relationships weakened social, cultural, and political order.

By interrogating the threats to cultural stability as domestic dramas, these writers routinely considered the relationship between protean households and mismanaged desires. Fiction allowed Federalists to sound out the contours of individual liberty and to stress ordered sexual relationships (as microcosms of political ones) as foundational aspects of social unity. Moreover, the form of the novel allowed them to explore the class dimensions of sexual relationships as well as model appropriate patterns of behavior. This often unrecognized agenda percolated in a range of literary texts published in the first decade of the nineteenth century—novels like Charles Brockden Brown's *Jane Talbot* (1801), the pseudonymously published *Moreland Vale; or, The Fair Fugitive* (1801), and Tabitha Tenney's *Female Quixotism* (1801). These novels explore the effects of radical social philosophies and consider the stabilizing potential of clearly defined social hierarchies. By forging questions about desire and identification to consider the alterations in political power, these novels personified the fears that Burleigh had so ominously sketched; Federalist writers renovated the tenets of the sentimental and seduction novel and fictionalized the Federalist loss of authority. The import of these texts was not in their literal capacity to effect change but in their prevalent sense of urgency about shifts in the sociopolitical character of the United States.

Representing the dangers of democracy via the language of seduction was, of course, a commonplace, and John Adams's plaintive quip, "Democracy is Lovelace, and the people are Clarissa.... The artful villain will pursue the innocent lovely girl to her ruin and her death," merely stands as the most famous instance of a popular metaphorical connection. Adams's reference to Samuel Richardson's paradigmatic seduction novel, *Clarissa; or, The History of a Young Lady* (1747–1748), moves to prophesy the inevitable corruption of the Republic at the hands of a smooth-talking seducer. Yet, for all the homage afforded this metaphor, relatively little attention has been paid to the complexities of the social conservatism embedded in this sentiment. Indeed, scholars have become accustomed to reading U.S. novels of the 1790s as radical interrogations of cultural formation, favoring readings of texts that frame the early U.S. novel as a veritable catalog of the Revolutionary struggle to fashion a national identity. This legacy functions as a kind of critical *doxa* so pervasive that scholars have embraced a long-standing myth that the 1790s was the zenith of literary production in the early Republic and that the questions of the 1790s stand as the central concerns of the early U.S. novel. Such pervasive logic has manufactured a warped portrait of the early U.S. novel as radical and liberal in aims.[5]

---

5. John Adams to William Cunningham, Mar. 15, 1804, *Correspondence between the Hon. John Adams, Late President of the United States, and the Late W. Cunningham, Esq., Beginning in 1803, and Ending in 1812* (Boston, 1823), 19. The tendency to imagine early U.S. fiction as framed around the Revolutionary struggle to form a nation largely stems from the foundational work of Cathy N. Davidson in articulating the field of early U.S. literary studies. Davidson's temporal range in *Revolution and the Word: The Rise of the Novel in America* (New York, 2004) spans three decades, but her focus on the "coemergence of the new U.S. nation and the new literary genre of the novel" has unintentionally canonized texts overtly concerned with nation formation (vii). All too often literary historiography misrepresents the period between 1800 and 1820 as one of declension, describing it as marked by a plummet both in the numbers of novels published and the number of initiate authors. The root of this generalization can be traced back to Lillie Deming Loshe's important bibliographic work, *The Early American Novel* (New York, 1907). Yet, in fact, just as many if not more domestically authored novels were published between 1800 and 1810 than during the previous decade. That Loshe's incomplete statistics have long held sway underscores the potency of the desire to read the early U.S. novel as principally and inherently about nation formation. Moreover, during the first decade of the nineteenth century, the majority of published novels appeared anonymously and

Continuing to assume that on or about 1800 novel production in the United States waned for two decades only to be resuscitated by the emergence of the historical novel will only maintain the faulty master narratives already circulating concerning U.S. literary development. To modify this incomplete portrait, we need to acknowledge that our collective disregard of the first decade of the nineteenth century springs from our misapprehension of the political and aesthetic work undertaken by these neglected texts. Many of these post-1800 writers understood fiction as a generic ground on which to battle for continued cultural influence, and they seized upon the literary conventions of seduction, sentimentality, and the gothic to represent the upheaval of a Democratic-Republican ascendancy. The rhetorical distinctions between Burleigh's paranoid tone and more traditionally configured literary forms like the novel are not as stark as one might suspect, and we would find a more accurate accounting of the communities of discourse in the early Republic if we examined these voices in concert. If democracy (as Adams prognosticated) was Lovelace and the people Clarissa, Federalist fictions of the early nineteenth century sought to tabulate the violations enacted on the seduced and abandoned social order. Like the end turn of Richardson's novel, the protagonists of these Federalist fictions produced a corrective after their violation in an attempt to "undo" the damage rendered by misplaced trust and false associations. The primacy of the imperiled subject—in need of suitably secure contractual protections—furnished Federalist writers with a site of potential instruction.[6]

By delimiting historical flashpoints as the spark for literary interpretation, early Americanists have relied on historians to define their objects of study. Yet, just as literary critics have oversimplified the tenor of this period's textual production, so, too, have historians reduced the operant sense of Federalism into redacted notions of elite social hierarchy or a pragmatic sense of institutionalism (as well as their routine insistence that partisan tensions faded after Jefferson's ascension). Deploying a counterfactual narrative strategy allowed these Federalist writers to privilege properly configured domestic relationships, to unfold a qualified but sympathetic attachment

---

pseudonymously, and, although linking texts without authors to prevailing conversations about national identity is complex, the obvious lack of biographical inroads at least partially explains the neglect of this period.

6. The connection between these two seemingly discrete discourse communities is even more apparent if we begin to account for the importance of serialized publication for fiction and political polemics alike. For more on the importance of serialization, see Jared Gardner, *The Rise and Fall of Early American Magazine Culture* (Chicago, 2012).

to England, and to underscore the dangers of even a passing connection to Francophone influence. Seizing upon a set of readily available rhetorical tropes, these texts transmogrify the seduction and gothic genres into a sustained campaign to restore a semblance of Federalist authority. The vexed and bitter partisan rhetoric of the era troubles attempts to read these texts as informing master narratives about progressive development. Indeed, many of these texts invest more in the closing off of possibilities as a means of regaining cultural control by quarantining undesirable social elements. This analysis does not imply that these novels were not inherently complex, that their political messages were not fraught and tangled, for indeed they were, but no more so than any other outlet of political thinking during the period.[7]

Many of these writers, in the struggle to find a narrative strategy that could accurately reflect their nostalgia for a residual order, their concerns about the wayward course of present authority, and their deep-seated anxieties about national development, blurred the boundaries between past, present, and future in such a way as to represent them as indistinguishable. In short, many of these neglected texts deployed a conflated narrative temporality that portrayed the U.S. Revolution as unfolding within a contiguous ambit of the French and Haitian Revolutions. They represent time as a process of accumulation, and their attempts to map futurity are deeply linked to the incorporation and resuscitation of past compounded histories. This multidimensional landscape, or, more accurately, this chronoscape, afforded early-nineteenth-century novelists a means of exploring the potentiality of revolutionary aggregation. This essay explores an emblematic instance of these attempts to re-imagine a Federalist Republic, allowing us to move beyond our habitual abridgement of this era's complexity. The literary public sphere is thus a space in which to restructure the feelings of the nation, to avert the presumptive permissiveness of Jeffersonism, and to heal the breach opened up by the revolution of 1800.[8]

---

7. The fear of a French influence was always racially coded in the United States in the early nineteenth century, in large part because Haiti stood as a dramatic reminder of what an attraction to French revolutionary logic entailed.

8. In *Specters of the Atlantic,* Ian Baucom challenges our normative figuration of the past as a temporal modality distinct from the "time of the now." Following Walter Benjamin's articulation of the past and the present as complicated constellations, Baucom provocatively argues that "time does not pass . . . it accumulates." See Ian Baucom, *Specters of the Atlantic: Finance Capital, Slavery, and the Philosophy of History* (Durham, N.C., 2005), 34 (quotation). As Michel Serres has suggestively argued, "Time does not always flow according to a line" but rather "according to an extraordinary com-

Burleigh's polemics against Jefferson, his fears that "murder, robbery, rape, adultery, and incest, will be openly taught and practised," are thus more than just hyperbolic political objections; he endeavored to use the generic tropes to fashion a compelling, albeit alarmist, argument. Murder, robbery, rape, adultery, and incest served as central tenets of the early-nineteenth-century U.S. novel, and perhaps no more so than in Martha Meredith Read's *Margaretta; or, The Intricacies of the Heart* (1807), a Federalist imaginary similar to that recorded by Burleigh's invectives. Crafted amid the aftershocks of the revolution of 1800, Read's novel promoted a counterrevolution to the loss of power suffered by the Federalist cause. Read subjected her eponymous heroine to almost all of the trials that Burleigh warned against in order to sound out the consequences of such unrest on social development. The novel archives the dangers of murder, robbery, rape, adultery, and incest as alien crimes, allowing Read to delineate between foreign and domestic behaviors. In so doing, she asserts the role of moral suasion in nourishing a counterreformation for remaking a culture that is adrift. Read resettles planter degeneracy outside the United States so that she can imagine a northern mid-Atlantic region free from chattel slavery and its attendant depravities. Margaretta's trials are not enacted to reductively underscore what a Jeffersonian ascendency had wrought, but rather to insure a new stable social order despite that shift in political culture.[9]

Laura Doyle provocatively describes the seduction of Charlotte Temple as occurring "within an Atlantic ring of forces." Her topography graphs how Susanna Rowson weaves a triangle of desire using the pivots of England, France, and North America. The trilateral angles of Rowson's most famous novel chart the orbit of a long-standing sense of the transatlantic world. Yet, as the work of Sean Goudie, Stephen Shapiro, and Chris Iannini (among others) has demonstrated, this mapping precariously plots the geography of late-eighteenth-century literary production since it fails to consider the expansive Euro–North American interest in the Caribbean. Indeed, as

---

plex mixture, as though it reflected stopping points, ruptures, deep wells, chimneys of thunderous acceleration,... all sown at random, at least in a visible disorder." See Serres with Bruno Latour, *Conversations on Science, Culture, and Time*, trans. Roxanne Lapidus (Ann Arbor, Mich., 1995), 57.

9. [Martha Meredith Read], *Margaretta; or, The Intricacies of the Heart* (Charleston, S.C., 1807). All references to the novel are to this edition and will be cited parenthetically within the essay.

Stephen Shapiro succinctly argues, "No aspect of the early American Republic has gone so under recognized as the importance of Haitian trade to the United States," and as such we need a fuller accounting of the early U.S. novel's reflection of this often-unacknowledged orientation. This influence on early-nineteenth-century cultural production intensifies, as Marlene L. Daut, Michael Drexler, Elizabeth Maddock Dillon, and Ashli White have argued, as the Republic attempted to reconcile what ruptures in that trade network meant for the United States.[10]

Early-nineteenth-century U.S. fiction curates an apparent obsession with the impact of the Haitian Revolution—sometimes encoded in passing allusions to the events themselves, or in muted discussions of a fractured market economy, or referenced by the promotion of domestic production (of locally harvested maple sugar, for example) or a turn toward East Indies trade routes. In effect, these references became a hub for probing the "legitimation crisis" so poignantly central to Federalist discursive practices in the first decade of the nineteenth century. Just as Burleigh implied a connection between a disintegration in social cohesion and the moral laxity of planter decadence, these post-1800 novels similarly gestured toward Haiti and its potential to unsettle the Republic. Economic and political concerns become embedded within constellations of domestic relationships, as many of these novels framed questions around the possibilities and limitations of interpersonal exchanges (marriage and paternal duty) to foster cultural stability. Figuring companionate marriage as the lynchpin of social cohesion, these texts decried the permissiveness of contingent associations by presenting them as detrimental to identity formation. Often unacknowledged in these figurations is their racial and class coding, as marriage is inevitably under-

---

10. Laura Doyle, *Freedom's Empire: Race and the Rise of the Novel in Atlantic Modernity, 1640–1940* (Durham, N.C., 2008), 160; Sean X. Goudie, *Creole America: The West Indies and the Formation of Literature and Culture in the New Republic* (Philadelphia, 2006); Stephen Shapiro, *The Culture and Commerce of the Early American Novel: Reading the Atlantic World-System* (University Park, Pa., 2008), esp. 105; and Christopher P. Iannini, *Fatal Revolutions: Natural History, West Indian Slavery, and the Routes of American Literature* (Chapel Hill, N.C., 2012). See also Marlene L. Daut, *Tropics of Haiti: Race and the Literary History of the Haitian Revolution in the Atlantic World, 1789–1865* (Liverpool, U.K., 2015); Michael Drexler, "The Displacement of the American Novel: Imagining Aaron Burr and Haiti in Leonora Sansay's *Secret History*," *Common-Place*, IX, no. 3 (April 2009), http://www.common-place-archives.org/vol-09/no-03/drexler/; Elizabeth Maddock Dillon, *New World Drama: The Performative Commons in the Atlantic World, 1649–1849* (Durham, N.C., 2014); and Ashli White, *Encountering Revolution: Haiti and the Making of the Early Republic* (Baltimore, 2010).

stood as concretizing elite whiteness, and conditional relationships are often ghosted by the specters of interracial or interclass connections. Although, as Andrew Cayton has argued, early-nineteenth-century fiction "nurtured a fluid community of people" across the Atlantic basin to imagine their commonalities, it did so in large part by fashioning a stable sense of a color line and by asserting the necessity of maintaining that boundary as firm. The familiar geography of the early American canon often ignores, or fails to plot, the perils felt by that fluid community from the dangerous possibilities of creolization, and, as such, obscures the more sprawling territorial concerns of early-nineteenth-century novels.[11]

Martha Meredith Read's *Margaretta* (and the attempted seductions of its titular character) unfolds within a more fluctuating circum-Atlantic ring of forces, a multinodal geography that recognizes the interconnectedness of the United States and the Caribbean. The trajectory of Read's novel begins in a small North American village, ventures to a pre-revolutionary Cape François, and then moves to metropolitan England. In each of these spaces the characters are haunted by planter decadence, an ominous weight they can escape only when they finally return to a reconfigured and decidedly Federalist United States. Although the outset of the novel nominally graphs geographical referents, it also implies that it is possible for isolated locations to remain disconnected from larger political and social dimensions. By the end of the novel, such a naive faith in geographic isolation is replaced by a more-nuanced sense of mobility and interconnection. Indeed, as the action of the novel crosses international boundaries, these markers become more vivid and pronounced until finally the only seemingly local North American scene coalesces as part of the larger configuration of "the United States."[12]

---

11. Andrew Cayton, "The Authority of the Imagination in an Age of Wonder," *Journal of the Early Republic*, XXXIII (2013), 10. Forced from the center of political power, Federalists were, as Joseph Fichtelberg argues, compelled to "reexamine the social order they had formerly defended, and to explain its loss of coherence." The daunting task at hand was nothing less than addressing "a legitimation crisis," as Federalists had to not only make sense of the loss of overt authority but also to secure some kind of stable position moving forward. See Fichtelberg, "Friendless in Philadelphia: The Feminist Critique of Martha Meredith Read," *Early American Literature*, XXXII (1997), 207.

12. The phrase "United States" appears in the novel seven times, with its first appearance occurring about midway through the novel on page 195. In this first instance, the phrase is uttered during a conversation by two Creole women in Cape François who mock Margaretta in part via this geopolitical marker. The phrase appears twice in the exchange

The transformation in territorial designation springs from the juxtapositions produced by Margaretta's movement, as if the characters can discover the meaning of a national identity only after they have passed through divergent forms of political and social organization. Within the novel, Read allegorizes these various structuring forms as different regions replete with myriad social codes. Margaretta's dispossession culminates in her reintegration into a Federalist household, which not only ends her vagrant wanderings but also by extension anchors a wider social landscape. Read replaces the typical seduction narrative's claustrophobic exploration of domestic interiority with an expansive geographical inquiry into the complexities of social reproduction in the circum-Atlantic world. While Margaretta and her eventual husband, the reformed rake William De Burling, do find projected happiness (in a union defined by mutual affection and painstakingly acquired respect), they do so only after Margaretta resists a virtual battery of seduction attempts. Indeed, almost every character in the novel, ranging from a Philadelphia society lady to a lecherous superannuated West Indian plantation owner to her own aristocratic uncle, petitions Margaretta in sexually charged ways. Love (early-nineteenth-century) American style—*Margaretta* assures us—is never an easily obtained thing.

Read's novel traffics settings almost as rapidly as it exchanges would-be seducers, and this expansive cartographic imagination allows her to catalog how U.S. history and sociality stem from participation in a fluid circum-Atlantic world. This transnational interest drives Read to place roughly one-third of the novel in the three most important nodes of connection in the long eighteenth century: the United States, Saint Domingue, and England. Deploying a contrapuntal spatiality enables Read to map the formation of an American identity by plotting its associations with extranational spaces and institutions. Margaretta's serial resettlement in a variety of subordinate positions—from quasi ward to imperiled captive to imagined courtesan—enables Read to plot the social geography of the circum-Atlantic basin by virtue of an imperiled white subjectivity. The contours of this mapping orient her readers to an upper-class perspective eventually embodied by the heroine through her rediscovered class status. The rapid increase in threats to Margaretta mirrors her assumption of a self-assertive agency, as the multi-

---

about economic orders between Vernon and the Creole planter, and then it appears four times in the last twenty pages of the book when it has been recast as the privileged site to which all the generative characters in the text seek to return.

plicity of correspondents of the first portion of the novel disappear and are replaced by Margaretta's own letters, which dominate the final two-thirds of the book. Alongside this shift in voice, from multiple perspectives to Margaretta's textual centrality, emerges Read's interest in Margaretta as symbolic of the United States. As Margaretta surfaces as the only commentator on her story of near ruin and recovery, she projects her history as a record of future possibilities. This evolution in Margaretta's self-fashioning models a way for isolated citizens to enter into properly constructed networks of association and for elite versions of those networks to regulate those around (and beneath) them in sustaining ways.[13]

The plot's movement across these divergent spaces is complicated by the way the novel staggers back and forth across a transtemporal chronoscape, as the distinct regional settings occur within inconsistent historical moments. Even as the headings of the novel's epistles depict the events as unfolding over the course of several months, constructing an accurate chronology for the novel remains impossible. Although the conclusion of the novel occurs around the turn to the nineteenth century in the United States, hinted at by an allusion to the watershed election of 1800, Margaretta's time in Cape François is spent in a locale totally undisturbed by the Haitian Revolution. Such a disjointed chronology cannot be explained by a linear conception of history, nor does Read take any pains to craft a logical explanation. Like Burleigh before her, Read essentially renders the nonsynchronous as simultaneous in order to think about how both a pre- and post-revolutionary Cape François combine to shape cultural development in the United States. In effect, Read deploys a fluid sense of historical accumulation to reveal the contingencies of the past within the present, even if they are not overtly accounted for. The legacies of contentious histories, recognized as hallmarks of particular kinds of economic orders, do not vanish with shifts in political agency; rather, they remain compounded within the contemporary moment. Read's complex admixture of colonial past and republican present and federalist future refigures cultural legacies in order to sketch a potentially new social landscape. The erasure of racialized revolution in favor of cultural placidity (if the novel's temporal continuity followed historical realities) is a case of staggering misdirection and begs an examination of Read's interest

---

13. To borrow a term Anna Brickhouse deploys to describe the "blindness" and narrowness of a "nationalist narrative of US literary history," Read's novel has a circum-Atlantic, not a "binocular," imagination. See, Brickhouse, *Transamerican Literary Relations and the Nineteenth-Century Public Sphere* (Cambridge, 2004), 22.

in a pre-revolutionary Saint Domingue as a foil for her vision of the development of the United States.[14]

The ambiguous temporality of the novel mirrors the discontinuity of Margaretta's own fractured geographical connections; by marrying these issues, Read considers national formation not simply by focusing on an individual's origins but also on the processes by which cultural legacies are mobilized to establish group identities. Read's use of novelistic weeks to obscure decades of change is not the result of bad craft; instead, her later narrative attempts to present history as multilayered and accumulative rather than causal and linear. Indeed, her other extant novel *Monima* (1801) explicitly traces a sequential link between the tyranny of the French Revolution and the struggle for self-emancipation in the Caribbean. This earlier novel traces the flight of the Fontanbleu family from the Reign of Terror to the imagined safety of Saint Domingue; but, of course, shortly after their arrival in Cape François the chaos of another revolution drives them to Philadelphia. The bankrupt family drifts along all the revolutionary currents of the late-eighteenth-century Atlantic basin, as Read surveys a conservative reaction to the diasporic movement of families dispossessed by circum-Atlantic instabilities. *Monima*'s accurate representation of historical contexts exhibits Read's fears about revolutionary contagions and her capacities to mold them into a temporally coherent narrative form; her intricate interweaving of historical episodes in *Margaretta* intentionally plots a different course.

If a reader grants *Margaretta* its historical anachronisms (or the ways in which it aligns nonsimultaneous events simultaneously), Read's intent in the novel crystalizes around her desire to think about foreign violence alongside the election of 1800. Margaretta's captivity narrative, the attempt to imprison her on a sugar plantation in Saint Domingue, stands in for any sustained consideration of race, as if to highlight that colonial planter degeneracy underwrites such extreme licentiousness and clouds racial as well as social distinctions. Indeed, the novel goes so far as to define the brutalities of slavery and its horrific agricultural practices as Caribbean—and not northern U.S.—problems. In a sustained conversation between two plant-

---

14. At the novel's conclusion, the ill-educated farmer who raised Margaretta (her presumptive father for most of the text) returns from casting his vote "elated with a hope that the republican ticket would carry" (414). By having a bad patriarch (a man more invested in selling off his daughter than in allowing her to find happiness) be a visible supporter of the Democratic-Republican cause, Read again highlights how domestic surety is undercut by unqualified and unfeeling heads of houses (or states).

ers, one West Indian and one an American who ventured to Cape François to secure his fortune, Read contrasts what she sketches as two different culture-defining agricultural practices. Disgusted by the brutal assault on an aged enslaved laborer who dared to address an overseer without first deferentially uncovering his head, Vernon (the American planter) declares, "I shall sell off my property, and move to the northern part of the country of the United States, there, each man who owns a spot of ground, works it himself, and when his daily labour is done, he can retire and enjoy the fruits of his industry with a peaceful conscience" (235). Vernon argues that northern U.S. "gentlemen" have no need for enslaved laborers, as they use their wealth to "hire ... at just and equitable wages" workers to till their land (235).

In contradistinction to chattel slavery, Read edenically populates the northern portion of the United States with noble yeoman farmers. As Vernon unfolds his plans to divest from a slave economy and purchase a mid-Atlantic estate, he characterizes the cultural orders of the two regions as outgrowths of their economic systems. The complete absence of any reference to a southern U.S. plantation economy effectively subsumes that region in an extended circum-Caribbean sphere of influence, as if to surreptitiously align the geographical stronghold of the Democratic-Republicans with the cultural practices of sybaritic French planters. Vernon's vision also removes the enslaved population from the northern United States, imagining this reconfigured region as wholly disconnected from the horrors of the peculiar institution. The possibilities for social reproduction appear intimately defined by regional economic systems, so the misalignments of planter society stand as totalizing. In the world of this novel, Vernon breaks his connection to a plantation economy that will erupt (as it had already historically) into revolution in order to suggest the ways in which a timely shift in economic connections could shield one from the dangers of racial violence.

The debate about regional economic systems echoes the differences in the threats posed to Margaretta depending on her geographical location. In North America, the seduction attempts she braves are largely rhetorical and fleeting, but as she ventures elsewhere they become increasingly physical. In Cape François, she suffers sustained physical imprisonment and isolation (from other whites), a period of quasi captivity that culminates in one of the most brutally vivid depictions of sexualized violence in an early U.S. text. In England, she is mistaken as a courtesan by an elderly aristocrat who brazenly propositions her. By manufacturing such a stark division between economic practices and aligning them with the issue of Margaretta's safety, Read affirms her protagonist's function for her readers. In rewriting patterns of mobility and settlement, Read recalibrates the impact that regional and economic affiliations had on social formation across the Atlantic basin. The threats endured in colonial and aristocratic spaces are not possible within her frame of the United States, even as the safety of a refigured national family prohibits lingering connections to foreign spaces. Transforming Margaretta's endangered virtue into a palimpsest of settlement patterns allows Read to demonstrate that the fabrication of a generative social order first requires a realignment of embedded influences.

Read began serially publishing pieces of "Margaretta; or, The Village Maid," in the *Ladies' Monitor* in the fall of 1801. The narrative originally appeared alongside several installments of *Monima* and Read's reworking of Mary Wollstonecraft in "A Second Vindication." As Joseph Fichtelberg has argued, this period was a time of intense productivity for Read (from what we have been able to identify of her written work). No extant evidence remains to indicate why the publication of "Margaretta" broke off (although the magazine did undergo a change in ownership and editorial control), and it would be another six years before a reconfigured *Margaretta; or, The Intricacies of the Heart* (1807) would be published in book form in both Philadelphia and Charleston. Whatever the cause for the break, the seeds of the text that would become the expanded novel were initially planted during the first months of Jefferson's presidency, which makes Read's reference to that event at the novel's conclusion an interesting repository of her potential intent. Little biographical information about Read remains, as is the case with many early American women writers, but she was the daughter of Samuel Meredith, niece of Lambert Cadwalader, wife of John Read, and daughter-in-law of George Read. The proximate connections between Read and supplanted Federalist power offers a window into the intricate plot of *Margaretta*, a means of decoding how the novel translates the complexities of circum-Atlantic settlement histories and addresses the vexing questions posed by the Federalist displacement. Like many of her male relatives across the first decade of the nineteenth century, Read's titular protagonist did not simply faint in the face of dissolution; she struggled to discover a new stabilized and generative social position.[15]

15. Read's "A Second Vindication of the Rights of Women," which was published under the pen name "An American Lady," appeared in the August 22 and September 5, 1801, issues of the *Ladies' Monitor* (New York). The September 12, 1801, issue of the magazine announced that "a new Novel, entitled, 'Margaretta; or The Village Maid,' will shortly be handed for publication," further adding that "it is written by the authoress of the Second Vindication of the Rights of Women, Beggar Girl. etc. etc." From September

The early life of Margaretta Wilmot, who was raised in the semi-isolated town of Elkton, Maryland, by impoverished farmers she assumes to be her biological parents, was largely uneventful. This situation rapidly changes as the novel opens, and her recent experiences (the weeks constituting the novel's opening third) are an unparalleled series of disruptions and oscillations. Margaretta's troubles begin when a stagecoach en route from Baltimore to Philadelphia breaks down in the rural way station of Elkton. The three main passengers, Miranda Stewart (an unmarried thirty-three-year-old Philadelphia society lady), William De Burling (the son of a wealthy planter with ties to both Philadelphia and Saint Domingue), and Captain Waller (an elderly sea merchant with a bit of a salty past), each instantaneously falls in love with Margaretta, establishing a narrative pattern wherein Margaretta continually becomes an object of unmitigated desire. Indeed, almost every figure in the novel—man, woman, aristocrat, subsistence farmer, widower, betrothed, stranger, relative, single, young, or superannuated—at some point manifests an errant devotion toward her. The sheer number of presumptive lovers and seducers has no corollary in either the early U.S. or the eighteenth-century British novel: the sheer number of dangerous liaisons would make Clarissa or Charlotte Temple swoon beyond recovery. Although the trials forced upon Margaretta's heart borrow from

---

12 to October 3, 1801, portions of "Margaretta; or, The Village Maid" serially appeared in the magazine, although they are substantively different from the final form they would take in Read's novel. For more information on Read's scant biography, the publication history of *Margaretta*, and about the dates of her composition, see Fichtelberg, "Friendless," *EAL*, XXXII (1997), 207; and Joseph Fichtelberg, "Heart-felt Verities: The Feminism of Martha Meredith Read," *Legacy*, XV (1998), 125–138. Aside from Fichtelberg, the only critic to offer an extended examination of *Margaretta* is Richard Pressman, in "*Margaretta* as Federalist Fantasy," *Literature in the Early American Republic*, IV (2012), 11–40. Read's father, Samuel Meredith (1741–1817), was a decorated officer during the Revolutionary War, a member of the Pennsylvania Assembly, and the first secretary of the Treasury in the United States, a cabinet position he held from 1789 until 1801, when (after Jefferson's election) he resigned for health reasons. Read's uncle, Lambert Cadwalader (1743–1823), was also a decorated Revolutionary War veteran and a two-term Federalist congressman from Pennsylvania (1789–1791 and 1793–1795). Read's father-in-law, George Read (1733–1798), was a signer of the Declaration of Independence and a close ally of Alexander Hamilton; he served two terms in the Senate before becoming the chief justice of the Supreme Court of Delaware in 1793. Read's husband, John Read (1769–1854), was a confidant of John Adams, who appointed him the agent general of the United States for the Jay Treaty (a position he occupied until 1809). John Read was among those Federalists who remained in an important federal position after Jefferson's election.

a host of preceding narratives, Read multiplies the themes of these earlier productions to an extreme. Unlike a range of earlier models of female virtue, Margaretta struggles not simply to resist one aggressive suitor but to stay chaste despite unending pursuits from every element of the social spectrum.

The novel opens with a broken stagecoach—a trope that literally signals a rupture in circuits of mobility—as a means of broadcasting Read's interest in fluidity, communication, and socioeconomic exchange. Stranded in Elkton, these passengers lament the village's isolation, despite its location on a principal commercial artery almost exactly midway between Philadelphia and Baltimore; it is also, as the northeasternmost harbor of the Chesapeake Bay estuary, a peripheral port of some note. Yet the stalled passengers taxonomize Elkton as a sleepy hamlet sprung out of a bucolic imaginary. Even as they lament delayed business dealings and their imagined dislocation, these accidental tourists all discover a new fetish object—Margaretta—that quells their disquietude. Shunting aside their external responsibilities, each of these delayed travelers rapidly estimates Margaretta's value as a potential commodity. Presented as naturally patrician, she appears as both the paragon of unspoiled rustic virtue and differentiated from all the other "cottagers" by her noteworthy rarity (2). By the novel's conclusion, Read safely accredits Margaretta's innate nobility to her biological parentage (both her mother and father turn out to be English aristocrats, not the subsistence farmers who raise her). Margaretta's secret history evinces that the rustic paradise of Elkton is not as isolated as some characters had naively imagined, since her genealogy proves long-standing global connections between this imagined fringe and the larger world. Indeed, the overall effect of deflating this fantasy of a backcountry disconnected from global networks—of information, of bodies, of goods—proves to readers and characters alike that surface realities often mask deeper associations. Moreover, the text highlights the potency of these submerged histories to resurface and to impinge upon cultural formation. Read's unpacking of the intricacies of Margaretta's history allows for a reframing of these legacies to contain their excesses. In order to prove this point, Read dislocates Margaretta and depicts her as a circum-Atlantic castaway adrift on uncertain social currents.

Margaretta's speculative resettlement in Saint Domingue materializes as the first mappable instantiation of Read's interest in demonstrating the fluidity of circum-Atlantic social development. Margaretta is conned by De Burling's fiancée, Arabella Roulant, into venturing to Cape François under the pretense that it will be a haven of security. She makes this tragic blunder—a misstep that places Margaretta at the mercy of Roulant's nefarious father, an opulent Creole planter—only after the man she has assumed to be her father awkwardly peddles her off to a variety of ill-fitting suitors as a means of repairing his insolvency. Exiled from her birthplace by her adoptive father for refusing his mercenary dictates, Margaretta succumbs to thinking of Cape François as a "place of refuge" (155). On the verge of her first circum-Atlantic crossing, Margaretta takes stock of her miserable situation and asks: "But who are my friends? And where is my home?" (154). Read examines these questions across the rest of the novel, and they signal the movement of the text from a farcical explosion of the conventions of the sentimental narrative into a more pointed critique of the dangers of foreign spaces. Saint Domingue's anarchical permissiveness of noncontractual social relations subverts the cultural power of properly ordered domestic connections. Such a potential fermentation of discord jeopardizes a Federalist vision predicated on legible social connections as a superstructure for cultural cohesion. Margaretta's geographical movements diagram the interconnectedness of the post-revolutionary nation-state within networks of circum-Atlantic exchange. This narrative strategy allows Read to render a variety of historical and economic forces as foreign while still noting how they inflect the development of the Republic. By entering into the inverted (and temporally displaced) world of Cape François, Margaretta severs her generative relationships to inhabit a public sphere devoid of any viable moral or juridical legitimation.

While early-nineteenth-century American novels reference (albeit often in muted ways) the immersion of the United States in circum-Atlantic economies, Read moves beyond passing remarks about West Indian or East Indian speculations to highlight the actual movement of characters across global networks. Such a focus allows for a detailed consideration of the ebb and flow of human traffic and its impact on the concretizing of a particular definition of citizenship. As Margaretta becomes a nomadic figure, a subject wandering without a fixed home, she quickly enters into a situation of near enslavement (or a kind of white slavery) on the outskirts of Cape François. This section of the novel positions Margaretta as a vehicle for exploring the precarious ramifications of having no legitimate social connections. Removed by the elder Roulant to an isolated plantation, the Almond Bowery, Margaretta finds herself at his mercy and surrounded by enslaved women with whom she cannot communicate (since she cannot speak French). A break from causal history occurs when Margaretta moves into the licentiousness of the Almond Bowery and thus retreats into a pre–Haitian revolutionary landscape. Here Roulant attempts to seduce Margaretta, and when rebuffed he threatens her with rape and murder; only the fortuitous arrival of another presumptive guardian narrowly disrupts the final execution of Roulant's violent crimes.

Margaretta's movement through the horrors of the prerevolutionary past of Cape François allows Read to measure the U.S. futurity against the legacies that these foreign contagions signify. At Cape François, young women procure concubines for their fathers, figure their relationships to their fiancés and husbands as adversarial, embrace sexual promiscuity, and endlessly slander one another to manipulate public perception—all set against the backdrop of a slave society. The disassembling households of Cape François shelter degenerate actors and practices, and Read rejects this model of traumatic social formation to posit a different set of possibilities for U.S. stability. She spurns the murder, robbery, rape, adultery, and incest born from a cultural order black with crimes in favor of rescuing a superseded future past. The displaced future that Read tries to recapture was ostensibly interrupted by the ascension of Jeffersonian authority, which bore with it the horrors of both colonial decadence and the violence of struggles for self-emancipation. Read's juxtaposition of these two spaces also marks a distinction between nation and colony, as the United States begins to be framed as an independent (politically, socially, and economically) state, whereas Saint Domingue remains a colonial imaginary, a creolized space whose dependence, exploitation, and desire render it subservient and fractured. The present state of Cape François as a site of subaltern struggle was routinely imagined as intimately intertwined with its violent past, a fact that would not have been lost on Read's audience as they encountered her renditions of the misaligned social practices of the island.

After Mr. Montanan interrupts Roulant's attempted rape, he persuades Margaretta to accompany him to England since Cape François remains so dangerous. Like every other figure in the novel, Montanan soon becomes utterly devoted to Margaretta, and he proposes to her (although they both possess some inner reluctance to move beyond a platonic connection). The wider public suspects the engagement to be a sham connection intended to disguise Margaretta's position as Montanan's mistress. Despite Margaretta's continual innocence, the English relentlessly slander her. Indeed, the English social sphere she inhabits entirely revolves around gossip, sexual intrigue, and petty vindictiveness. As a result of the public perception of her as a concubine, the profligate Sir Henry Barton feels emboldened to menacingly proposition her. This repeated threat of sexual violence serves as Read's way of equating the aristocratic drawing rooms of England with the decadent plantations of Cape François, as she charts the corruption of social mores in each space via a depiction of aggressive men who lustfully prey on isolated women. The absence of a visible juridical or political order in either location suggests that nothing exists to secure individual rights; instead, those rights can be guaranteed only by the surety of one's economic position. These safeguards born from capital accumulation are precisely the kinds of connections that Margaretta does not possess. When she imagines herself as abject, Margaretta simultaneously confesses the absence of any generative links to surrounding economic networks beyond utter dependency. Her struggle to regain her independence succeeds because she has the capacity, unlike those actually abject, to attain a stable position in larger legitimate networks of association.

A series of convoluted plot twists reveal that Montanan is Margaretta's biological father and that his long-feared-dead wife (and Margaretta's mother and Barton's sister) has been in England under another name. Barton refuses to believe this new information, and his ardent desire for Margaretta overwhelms his ability to comprehend either her innocence or their biological relationship. When Margaretta understands that Barton remains undaunted by the revelation of her history, she argues that "there is a law for women, which will, independent of her voice, plead for me" (365). Sir Barton very tellingly replies, "Young lady, you will remember you are not in America," as if to emphasize that her voluntary removal from the United States vacated any protections she might have against his aristocratic status (365). This second near rape, just as narrowly averted as Roulant's attack at the Almond Bowery, crystalizes the connections between Cape François and England. Neither cultural system recognizes Margaretta's rights to self-determination; neither understands her as a subject with access to legal or social protections. Just as Margaretta found no generative haven in the illusory shelter of Cape François, England provides her no sustained protection from slander or attack.

At the crucial turning point when Margaretta decides to leave the United States for the *safety* of Cape François, she suggests that, for individuals without a national home, "each place is alike interesting or indifferent," and she concludes by noting that such a subject "is a citizen of the world" (154–155). Comparing herself to a virtual early-nineteenth-century catalog of subaltern people, Margaretta likens herself to "the African, the Indian, the Hottentot," as an individual displaced from her native space and left to be "moulded by the hand of heaven" (155). She surrenders herself to the consignment of divine protection and imagines that "providence" will "provide me a home"

(155). Such a disavowal of national citizenship echoes the most radical sentiments expressed by Thomas Paine in the *Rights of Man* (1791–1792). Declaring that "my country is the world," Paine argued, "I view things as they are, without regard to place or person." Paine's axiomatic depiction of universal citizenship, of the most radical version of republicanism, stands antithetical to a Federalist vision for collectivity. In having the most naive figure in her novel echo Paine's sentiments, Read effectively deflates the delusory promises of extreme versions of Liberté, Égalité, Fraternité. In so doing, she accentuates how such radical definitions of citizenship particularly alienate women, as Margaretta's renunciations subject her to serious physical and gendered dangers that coterminously subvert larger patterns of cultural cohesion.[16]

After Margaretta effectively vacates her citizenship, she figuratively crosses the never stable but ever present color line; indeed, her universal citizenship locates her in the same abject position as enslaved and colonized peoples from around the globe. In her unmoored position, Margaretta embodies, not a state of clarity, but one of disjointed discontinuity. Adopting Paine's radical sentiments about universal citizenship means she sacrifices any concrete relationship to the past, present, or future. In this positon, all three temporal zones blur into a confused haze where meaning and orientation are always fractured. She emerges out of this disaggregated temporality only by disavowing ungenerative colonial and revolutionary legacies. Perhaps, more importantly, she learns to recognize the difference between citizenship and subjecthood. At the moment of her greatest self-deception, Margaretta dreams of the possibility of being a citizen of the world, but the cost of such an ungrounded position manifests as soon as she sails out of Philadelphia. The novel presents citizenship as a subjectivity available only in the United States; outside its borders the world is populated by exploitative aristocrats and planters on the one hand, and subjects, captives, near victims, and the enslaved on the other. Those, for Read, are the alternate legacies of monarchism and revolutionary radicalism, and they spur the very traumas that Margaretta has to overcome in order to find shelter in the United States.

Unlike the handful of familiarly canonized early U.S. seduction narratives,

---

16. Thomas Paine, *Rights of Man*, in Mark Philip, ed., *Rights of Man, Common Sense, and Other Political Writings* (New York, 1998), 281. I am thankful to one of the anonymous reviewers of this essay for pointing out the similarities between Read's language and that of Paine.

such as William Hill Brown's *Power of Sympathy* (1789), Susanna Rowson's *Charlotte Temple* (1794), and Hannah Webster Foster's *The Coquette* (1797), *Margaretta* does not feature geographical stasis, social claustrophobia, or gendered passivity. More interested in the "intricacies of the heart" than in passing postmortem judgment, *Margaretta* nevertheless embodies a counterstrand of early U.S. sentimental narratives, one that our received critical narratives (largely limited to a 1790s canon) cannot adequately accommodate. Instead, the novel might best be described as concerned with what Elizabeth Maddock Dillon has suggestively termed "creole social reproduction." While the question of social reproduction obviously concerns the more familiarly canonical seduction narratives, Dillon's injunction of the qualifier "creole" moves us beyond reading these novels as attempts to invent a new U.S identity within the closed system of an isolationist imaginary (or even simply within a residually configured Atlantic ring of forces).[17]

Unlike the geographical scope of, for instance, *The Coquette,* which figures New Haven as a familiar world away from Hartford, *Margaretta* roams across the circum-Atlantic basin. Margaretta's final letter—postmarked in London, containing details about her time in Saint Domingue and addressed to a recipient in rural Maryland—exemplifies the broad terrain of the novel; indeed, one might say, readers inhabit a different universe from the one in which Lucy Freeman writes to Eliza Wharton from opposite ends of the *cosmopolitan* state of Connecticut. Read's concerns are not about the intricacies of local scandals; rather, they address the flux of global networks and the havoc such circulations carry in their wake. To think of it another way, Read's novel, unlike more familiar seduction narratives, does not focus on a crisis about internal guidance; instead, it probes the threats to the privileges of "whiteness" (embodied in a stable elite family) within the fluctuations of global economic circulation. Following the displacement of Federalists from authority, Read seems intent on demonstrating that an overwrought passivity could not persevere against the more visceral challenges of the early-nineteenth-century circum-Atlantic world. Margaretta's

17. Elizabeth Maddock Dillon, "The Secret History of the Early American Novel: Leonora Sansay and Revolution in Saint Domingue," *Novel,* XL (2006–2007), 99. For an example of this tendency to cast the genre as routinely populated by "the same array of cruel libertines, foolish coquettes, heartbroken parents, ruined women, stillborn babies, and destinies misshapen by desire," and as regurgitating the same "oft-repeated story with only minor variations," see Leonard Tennenhouse, *The Importance of Feeling English: American Literature and the British Diaspora, 1750–1850* (Princeton, N.J., 2007), 45.

survival, in other words, can only be guaranteed after the transformation of the larger social nexus, as her staid interiority will eventually fail to buffer her against a ceaseless onslaught of disruptions.

After being supplanted by the Democratic-Republicans, Federalists admittedly no longer possessed the authority to regulate transit across circum-Atlantic networks. Forced from the political sphere, many early-nineteenth-century U.S. conservatives sought, as William C. Dowling has argued, "sanctuary" in "a specific realm of literary or aesthetic values." From this new vantage point, these dispossessed figures addressed the crisis of authority that the revolution of 1800 enacted. Read's *Margaretta* advances Dowling's account of Federalist cultural production insofar as it crafts a sanctuary out of a careful deployment of aesthetic values. Instead of succumbing to seduction and ruin, Margaretta resists it in every conceivable form and emerges as a wellspring of a wider nexus of security. Margaretta's narrative functions, not to reproduce one more cautionary tale, but to provide a positive model for resistance. In effect, Read positions Margaretta as an exemplar of domestic (in both senses of that word) virtue to provide readers with easily emulated signposts for fashioning a new social order.[18]

Drifting away from Elkton severs Margaretta from any familial connections and subjects her to the pull of contending tides of possession and consumption. As the plot unfolds, she casts her lot (sometimes willingly, sometimes not) with a number of assumptive protective figures who contrive to manipulate her. Margaretta's transformation from potential victim into self-sufficient citizen concludes only after she unravels the mystery of her real ancestry, as if by virtue of inheriting a proper familial lineage she can be liberated from delusory ones. Until this disclosure, the novel presents an Atlantic world system wherein anonymity and mobility have attenuated social cohesiveness. The unpacking of Margaretta's secret history inaugurates a reverse migration in the text, suggesting that her encounters with cacophonous social orders and nonbiological connections can be harmonized only by the reestablishment of contractual relations. The plot importantly does not end with this Anglophilic restoration but rather deploys this discovery to underwrite a foundational household in North America (one that divests from the illusory foundations of aristocratic privilege).

Read clarifies this shift away from titled prerogative by attaching it to her most overt endorsement of Federalism. "My [biological] father," Margaretta

---

18. William C. Dowling, *Literary Federalism in the Age of Jefferson: Joseph Dennie and "The Port Folio," 1801–1812* (Columbia, S.C., 1999), ix.

writes, "is a true republican, though placed in a barony, the name of which he will not assume," and, as such, his "political principles are founded upon a system of united federalism" (398). Possessed with an innate sense of "equal rights and equal liberties between man and man" (398), Margaretta's biological father fervently longs to become a U.S. citizen, a desire that allows Read to locate Federalism as the defining essence of a real republican. The reunited family, natural Federalists all, sell off their holdings in England and momentarily pause in Cape François to sever their economic connections to the colony. With both the trauma of past and present Cape François and the rigid titled hierarchy of past and present England safely closed off, Margaretta and her family look for a new future in the United States. Read's narrative then constructs a post-1800 Federalist vision of a reconstituted household, one that rejects the instabilities of the plantation economy, aristocratic privilege, and the commodification of women (which, among other things, delimits their political agency) more generally.

Read's novel performs an act of historical interpolation, one aimed at altering the reader's perceptions of the past. In so doing, *Margaretta* breaks from a notion of causal history to speculate about the impact of multiple pasts alongside one another. Margaretta's dispossession is not theological; rather, Read imagines history and temporality in such a way as to figure multiple spaces and moments as intertwined. Depicting a world wherein both her titular character and the national landscape withstand crises of authority, Read's novel contributes to the efforts of a dispersed Federalist intelligentsia to curtail the loss of coherence engendered by their own displacement. The novel's movement toward permanent transplanting coincides with the emergence in the text of a more specific rendering of geography, as Read's cartographic lexicon solidifies and more forcefully orients characters and readers alike in relation to other places and populations. Throughout the course of the novel, Margaretta ranges farther and farther from home, while simultaneously winnowing down a definition of what she has left behind. Read solves the displacement crisis by rewriting the historical legacies that brought it into being, offering a counterfactual version of history to construct a more usable present upon which to erect a foundational Federalist fantasy.

By foreclosing the possibilities of illegitimacy, sexual or social, in favor of contractual and regularized domestic relationships, Read returns Margaretta to the United States so that her newfound validity can anchor a larger regional community. Read breaks away from the epistolary form to construct this final vision of domestic stability and thus deploys a narrative authority absent from the fractured communication networks that have constituted the bulk of the novel. The emergence of this omniscient narrative voice solves the problems of temporality and geography, of one-sided conversations and confused interchanges that have plagued characters up to this juncture. Margaretta's restoration to the United States also realigns political and economic boundaries as her newly constituted family casts off its connections to England and Saint Domingue. By undertaking these various tacks, Margaretta resumes—and more fervently clings to—her vacated citizenship. Forsaking these disruptive foreign entanglements, her family rechristens themselves—despite their own varying national and economic affiliations—jubilantly federated citizens of the Republic. Indeed, the novel concludes with Margaretta settling with her extended family "upon a charming spot, on the banks of the beautiful Susquehannah," with their hearts now "warmed with a noble enthusiasm for the rights and liberties of the citizens of Columbia" (417).

The discovery of these New World rights, and the newfound understanding of the limits and the possibilities of these liberties, flows out of Margaretta's experiences in foreign spaces. In essence, Read constructs a series of misadventures in improper social arenas to assert a newly articulated American national identity—one necessarily inflected by Margaretta's participation in the fluctuations (economic, social, temporal, and cultural) of the early-nineteenth-century circum-Atlantic world. "Laying their title on the altar of liberty, as a sacrifice to equality, peace and independence," Margaretta's parents become the paradigmatic naturally noble elite American family (417). The end of Read's novel prefigures the intent of James Fenimore Cooper's more famous *The Pioneers; or, The Sources of the Susquehanna* (1823), which also concludes with the establishment of an estate that radiates charitable guidance to those around it. Margaretta's reconstituted household underwrites a faith in the domestic sphere to function as stabilizing bedrock, a material and symbolic shelter for cultural development even in a climate defined by a retrograde political system. Preceding Cooper's similarly conservative turn by sixteen years, Read's long-neglected novel moved to solve central facets of the displacement crisis by underscoring that a Federalist vision of wealthy yeoman farmers—willfully divorced from degenerative webs of economic and cultural association—could provide a rootedness that the political sphere no longer offered. By ending unnecessary transnational mobility, the structures of feeling dislodged by the crisis in authority are imaginatively replotted in Margaretta's remodeled domestic landscape. Within *Margaretta,* Read argues that the Republic needs to divest itself from the horrors of Democratic-Republican plantocracy and circum-Atlantic slavery, to eschew commercialism and foreign trade in order to posit the stabilizing potential of a renovated Federalism grounded in republican principles. Self-preservation, on both the scale of the individual and the scale of the nation, could emerge only when the instabilities of the past were fully accounted for and safely reordered by active disassociation. Margaretta's independence, her immunity from past and present discords, allows Read to envision a secure future for the Republic regardless of whatever political authority holds sway.

Early Americanists have migrated away from mining the exceptionalist roots of domestic cultural production to a more geographically expansive survey of the multidimensional routes of bodies, information, and texts. This circum-Atlantic turn manifests the ways in which early U.S. novels do not, as traditionally upheld, constitute a sense of national identity through an isolationist imaginary. Much is to be (and has already been) gained, for example, from thinking about the neglected circum-Atlantic concerns of such familiar texts as Thomas Jefferson's *Notes on the State of Virginia* (1785) or Charles Brockden Brown's *Arthur Mervyn* (1799). Still, even as these critical developments would seemingly endorse the necessity of expanding our archival practices to craft a more saturated portrait of early U.S. cultural development, they have only slightly altered our received scholarly canon. Indeed, that these emergent critical movements have not significantly altered our received scholarly canon underscores how much more work remains to be done.[19]

The primary aberration to this canonical stasis remains Leonora Sansay's *Secret History; or, The Horrors of St. Domingo* (1808), which has garnered a wealth of critical attention because it vibrantly indexes U.S. anxieties about the Haitian Revolution and circum-Atlantic networks of association. The rapid canonization of *Secret History* affirms that its rediscovery has reshaped our understanding of the field. Without question, Sansay's novel grants scholars direct access to subjects and subjectivities sorely marginal-

---

19. For an example of the kinds of expansive geographies contained within the early U.S. novel, see Nancy Armstrong and Leonard Tennenhouse, "The Problem of Population and the Form of the American Novel," *American Literary History*, XX (2008), 667–685.

ized by intranationalist figurations of U.S. literary history. It is a remarkable text, but its critical popularity, arguably, stems from refracting it as another version of a radical interrogation of social formation; or, again, the critical questions that often frame our sense of the novels of the 1790s have been transplanted to convey the significance of Sansay's text. In part, this can be measured by the frequency with which the *Secret History* is positioned against texts from the 1790s, and, moreover, by critics' interpretations of the novel as emphasizing the possibilities of resistance to a patriarchal hegemony.[20]

Although such readings of Sansay fruitfully decode her complex considerations of the Caribbean, all too often scholars have abstracted from this solitary text a paradigmatic endorsement of a positivist spin on cosmopolitan circulation. Such a sweeping classification negates the alterity of more conservative texts: novels, like *Margaretta*, that highlight the flow of goods, bodies, and information to explore ways of halting such orbits of transit. Read's concluding turn establishes the United States as a site-specific nation; it accomplishes this redrawing by first roaming outside presumptive boundaries to sever the potentialities of dangerous foreign connections. When they return to the United States, Margaretta and her expanded social circle stand inoculated against unsettlement because they have divested from improper systems of accumulation. Projecting their future course, they radiate security by charitably attending to those around them. In contrast, *Secret History* declares no such sense of restoration. Sansay's text concludes with a slippery investment (undercut by the novel's dedication to Aaron Burr) in the idea that more mobility and a return to misaligned social connections will somehow undo the oscillating state of sociality that the novel charts. For the protagonists of Sansay's novel, this hope is, at best, oblique. Exhibiting a different strand of the secret history of the early U.S. novel, Read promotes fixed legible social connections as a countermeasure to the murky and tenuous ones that had compelled Margaretta to relinquish her citizenship. Although both novels feature heroines who eventually migrate

20. Given the ways in which Sansay's text accentuates a focus on people forced to the margins, it is no surprise that Armstrong and Tennenhouse turn to the *Secret History* as their primary example (Armstrong and Tennenhouse, "The Problem of Population," *American Literary History*, XX [2008], 667–685). Globalization is not an inherently new development but one that we have muted by the ways in which scholars have interacted with our archives. This practice has for too long distorted our perception of the cultural production of the early Republic.

back to the United States, the social landscape that they sketch could not be more dissimilar.[21]

The circum-Atlantic turn prompts a chance to rethink the spatial and temporal dynamics of the early Republic and to move beyond only recovering textual objects that reflect our inherited sense of canon formation. In a nuanced critique of the cosmopolitan turn in literary studies, Bruce Burgett cautions scholars to attend very specifically not only to moments of transit but also to consider the import of the pronounced restrictions on mobility (of bodies and of goods) that these texts also record. In essence, Burgett warns against replacing a domestically imagined community with a thinly examined cosmopolitan one and enjoins a deeper examination of the "specific historical conditions" influencing "the production and circulation" of texts to interpret the arguments they might contain about "the inevitably racialized and racializing contours of 'peoples' and 'populations.'"[22]

Margaretta achieves an increasing awareness of her own identity as an American by virtue of her movement away from its specific conditions, and as such she progressively represents the idea of a national subject. The conclusion of the novel imagines the formation of an ordering household that structures the surrounding landscape. A carefully articulated discourse of national fraternity tempers the elite nature of this household, but it simultaneously constructs, as Ed White observes about Benjamin Franklin's famous Junto, a kind of "network of subordinate units that do not realize they are subordinate"—in other words, the invention of a federated system of social collectivism. Following this logic, Read's postulation that properly remodeled households (disassociated from ungenerative practices and racializing contours) could ballast a range of subordinate family units signals the migration of Federalist logic to the semiprivate sphere. Instead of looking to politicians or the state to radiate cohesion, federated family units can fill the power vacuum created by the revolution of 1800.[23]

At the end of the novel, Read positions Margaretta as a dispenser of

---

21. For more information on the complexities of early-nineteenth-century cultural referents to Aaron Burr, see Michael J. Drexler and Ed White, *The Traumatic Colonel: The Founding Fathers, Slavery, and the Phantasmatic Aaron Burr* (New York, 2014).

22. Bruce Burgett, "Every Document of Civilization Is a Document of Barbary? Nationalism, Cosmopolitanism, and Spaces between: A Response to Nancy Armstrong and Leonard Tennenhouse," *American Literary History*, XX (2008), 686–694 (quotations on 694).

23. Ed White, *The Backcountry and the City: Colonization and Conflict in Early America* (Minneapolis, Minn., 2005), 193.

community-sustaining benevolence, transforming her into the very figure that could have prevented her own turbulent emigration. Securely housed along the Susquehanna, Margaretta labors to prevent future citizens from becoming vagrants indifferent to their own geographical positions. Read promotes the value of citizenship by positioning it against the tainted positions of English subjects and Haitian captives. She liberally frames her novel around the concerns of captivity and mobility, not to embrace or endorse the radical political ramifications of such fluctuation, but to reject them. The final section of the novel demonstrates that a national unity can counter such flux and replace it with a carefully camouflaged unfolding of federated collectivity—one predicated on a middle-class white subjectivity.

The purple prose of the novel's dedication, which lauds the ladies of the Female Association of Philadelphia, for the Relief of Women and Children, in Reduced Circumstances for their charitable works, lays the cornerstone for this vision of sociality. It does so by praising networks of like-minded individuals locally mobilizing to shepherd needy flocks. These ladies, Read maintains, "well know how to appreciate virtue for virtue's sake" (iii). Their selfless acts extend their influence over the "helpless," the infirm, and the "indigent" alike, knowing full well that they will only be repaid by "a consciousness of having discharged the claims of humanity" (iii). The dedication concludes by proclaiming that the "example" of this "institution" is "worthy [of] the emulation of every virtuous mind" (iv). The altruistic ladies of the Female Association of Philadelphia serve as a post-Revolutionary Junto capable of authoring and emanating social cohesion; simultaneously, they also provide an easily reproducible model for other interested parties to emulate. Read hopes her novel will function similarly, by exemplifying how a federated unit can—acting for the good of humanity—stabilize cultural order by a pronounced dedication to virtuous benevolence. Initially victimized by her lack of access to such benefits, Margaretta becomes reintegrated into society through her newly inclusive connections. Those bodies that cannot foster such legibility remain excised from the imagined nation at the conclusion of the novel.

Read sutures the ruptures enacted by the revolution of 1800 through a replotting of the tenets of seduction and captivity narratives. In so doing, she formulates a new Federalist proposition. Read's version of Federalism accentuates an appreciation for the rights and liberties of U.S. citizenship, not predicated on political authority, but rather emerging from a properly ordered home, one capable of rooting more than just a single family into a reconceived social landscape devoid of the uncertainties attached to the

Democratic-Republican ascendancy. Although Margaretta does not venture precisely into the world of "murder, robbery, rape, adultery, and incest" that Burleigh predicted, her experiences inscribe a near match: she is nearly murdered; she is kidnapped several times; she barely escapes a brutal rape; and she unknowingly almost enters into an incestuous marriage. Within the social ambit of Read's novel at least, Burleigh's factious rhetoric lives on, as if the futurity he projected had indeed—just a calendar year later in terms of Read's first work on the novel—become a present the United States occupied. Emblematic of early-nineteenth-century Federalist fictions that were engaged in warring to reconstitute their lost authority, Read's novel represents a neglected strand of U.S. literary production that sought to circumnavigate a loss of agency by counterfactually authoring social cohesion in the wake of dissolution.

CONCEPTUAL TRAFFIC
THE ATLANTIC SLAVE TRADE
AND THE WAR OF 1812

Christen Mucher

> Take the American slave-trade, which we are told by the papers, is especially prosperous just now.... In several states this trade is a chief source of wealth. It is called (in contradistinction to the foreign slave-trade) *"the internal slave-trade."* It is, probably, called so, too, in order to divert from it the horror with which the foreign slave-trade is contemplated. That trade has long since been denounced by this government as piracy. It has been denounced with burning words from the high places of the nation as an execrable traffic. To arrest it, to put an end to it, this nation keeps a squadron, at immense cost, on the coast of Africa. Everywhere, in this country, it is safe to speak of this foreign slave-trade as a most inhuman traffic, opposed alike to the laws of God and of man. The duty to extirpate and destroy it, is admitted even by our doctors of divinity. In order to put an end to it, some of these last have consented that their colored brethren (nominally free) should leave this country, and establish themselves on the western coast of Africa! It is, however, a notable fact that, while so much execration is poured out by Americans upon all those engaged in the foreign slave-trade, the men engaged in the slave-trade between the states pass without condemnation, and their business is deemed honorable.
>
> FREDERICK DOUGLASS,
> "The Meaning of July Fourth for the Negro," 1852

When Frederick Douglass was invited to deliver a Fourth of July oration to the Rochester Ladies' Anti-Slavery Sewing Society in 1852, he famously spoke about the shame, rather than the glory, of the national anniversary. Although his speech was supposed to celebrate the day marking the "politi-

---

Many thanks to Bruno Gravellier at the United States Consulate for Aquitaine, Poitou-Charentes, and Limousin, France; the Archives départementales de la Gironde; the Jeanette Campbell Chetwood Trust; Françoise Aphesbero; and Fredrika Teute.

cal freedom" of the American people, Douglass took the opportunity to highlight the hypocrisy of jubilee in a country that still practiced slavery and the trade in human beings. "What, to the American slave, is your 4th of July?" he asked, and then answered: "a day that reveals to him, more than all other days in the year, the gross injustice and cruelty to which he is the constant victim." At that very moment, Douglass exclaimed, the United States was "guilty of practices more shocking and bloody" than any nation, leading to great "national inconsistences" in America's understanding of freedom. The first hypocritical practice was the continued existence of slavery, the "great sin and shame of America," under the Republic. The second was that the United States maintained, "at immense cost," a naval unit dedicated to suppressing the "foreign slave-trade," while it allowed the "internal slave-trade" to flourish. On that day in Rochester, Douglass exhorted his listeners to abolish the "execrable traffic" of all slave markets, to challenge the recent Fugitive Slave Act (1850), and to extinguish any remaining tolerance for slavery in a land that—especially on Independence Day—prided itself on principles of "justice, liberty, and humanity." Seemingly contrasting the deauthorized, accursed practice of foreign slave trading with the so-called honorable internal trade in enslaved people, Douglass in fact implied that the activities were one and the same; the latter had merely been renamed and reconceptualized to "divert it from the horror" of the former.[1]

When Douglass spoke to the Rochester abolitionists in 1852, both the foreign and domestic trade in enslaved persons persisted in the United States: enslaved foreign laborers filtered through the nation's southern and western borders, and domestic ones were sent from the upper South to the markets in Louisiana, Mississippi, and Alabama. In his speech, Douglass noted that

1. Frederick Douglass, "The Meaning of July Fourth for the Negro," in Philip S. Foner, ed., *Frederick Douglass: Selected Speeches and Writings* (Chicago, 1999), 189, 192, 195, 196, 197, 203. Arguments about the decreasing financial returns of the Atlantic slave trade in the late eighteenth and early nineteenth century begin at least as early as Eric Williams's *Capitalism and Slavery* (Chapel Hill, N.C., 1944) but were rethought by Seymour Drescher in *Econocide: British Slavery in the Era of Abolition* (Pittsburgh, 1977) and a subsequent generation of scholars (see *Econocide*, 2d ed. [Chapel Hill, N.C., 2010]). See also Steven Deyle, "An 'Abominable' New Trade: The Closing of the African Slave Trade and the Changing Patterns of U.S. Political Power, 1808–60," *William and Mary Quarterly*, 3d Ser., LXIV (1999), 833–850. New understandings of the South Atlantic and Indian Ocean trade have been crucial to this revaluation; see, for example, Jane Hooper and David Eltis, "The Indian Ocean in Transatlantic Slavery," *Slavery and Abolition*, XXXIV (2013), 353–375; and Patrick Harries, "Negotiating Abolition: Cape Town and the Trans-Atlantic Slave Trade," ibid., 579–597.

the federal legislation of March 2, 1807, which had outlawed the importation of enslaved Africans after January 1, 1808, effectively split the concept of the "slave-trade" into two different spheres: the "foreign" and the "internal" or "American slave-trade." The 1807 law did not ban the traffic of slavery outright—the legislation signed by Thomas Jefferson made it unlawful to "import or bring into the United States or the territories thereof from any foreign kingdom, place, or country, any negro, mulatto, or person of colour, with intent to hold, sell, or dispose of such ... as a slave"—but instead banned the introduction of a specific class of persons ("any negro, mulatto, or person of colour") for a specific purpose ("with intent to hold, sell, or dispose of such ... as a slave") from a specific place ("any foreign kingdom, place, or country") to the United States. In 1808, therefore, the previously undifferentiated concept of "slave trade" became subject to the scrutiny of who, how, and where. The result was a de facto legalization of all trade that did not qualify under the foreign ban. To Douglass's point, this conceptual redefinition enabled the condoning of one kind of trade because of the condemnation of the other, and he highlighted this consequence by echoing the language used by abolitionists since the first decades of the nineteenth century. For, although the text of the 1807 Act to Prohibit the Importation of Slaves referred to the importation and sale of enslaved Africans as "trade or business," abolitionists in the United States and Britain referred to their sale, not as trade, but as traffic: "nefarious traffic," "inhuman traffic," and "horrid traffic."[2]

Douglass's words amplified his message that the United States' criminalization of the slave trade changed the ways in which the trade was conceptualized—how it was commonly understood by promoters and opponents alike—rather than how it was practiced. For example, when the U.S. Congress adjusted the 1807 Act in 1819 and 1820, it declared that any citizen caught participating in the trade "shall be adjudged to be a pirate"; pirates, after all, were merely those who traded without authorization rather than those who committed criminal acts per se. Furthermore, piracy explicitly pertained to the activities of robbery and kidnapping on the "high seas," not

---

2. Douglass, "July Fourth," in Foner, ed., *Frederick Douglass*, 197; An Act to Prohibit the Importation of Slaves ..., Mar. 2, 1807, c. 22, 2 Stat., sec. 1, 2, in *The Statutes at Large of the United States of America* ..., ed. Richard Peters et al., 18 vols. (Boston, 1845–1878), II, 426; *Sixth Report of the Directors of the African Institution* ... (London, 1812), 8, 67, 161. It is referred to as "illegal speculation" and "illicit practices" in the African Institution's *Fourth Report of the Directors of the African Institution* ... (London, 1810), 4, 5. According to the *Oxford English Dictionary*, online ed., "traffic" often carries improper or sinister implications.

on the turnpikes of Virginia or waterways of the Mississippi. For Douglass, the difference was more conceptual than material, a rhetorical sleight of hand that turned some traders into traffickers while leaving others as honorable businessmen. Douglass's words from July 1852 indict not only the hypocrisies of 1776, 1807, and 1850 but also the systems of thinking that assigned horror and outrage to the foreign trade in enslaved Africans—which had long since been reconfigured as a military, rather than moral, concern—while looking upon the business of the "American slave-trade" as a source of national pride and prosperity. The same actions, in Douglass's opinion, were called "trade" on the one hand and "traffic" on the other.[3]

"Trade"—the processes of exchanging people as goods—has been an important, even dominating, analytic in the histories of Atlantic slavery and its abolition. It has also been one of the main themes for histories of the War of 1812, so often framed as a transatlantic disagreement over sovereignty summarized by the slogan "free ships make free goods." Although understandings of these two signal events in the early-nineteenth-century Anglo-American world focus on trade, they are rarely considered in relation to each other. Indeed, one scholar has written that the "slave trade was an additional, albeit minor, issue" in the War of 1812, and another explained that slavery "faded from America's political consciousness" between 1808 and 1819 (although the rapid expansion of the domestic slave trade and the persistence of a clandestine international trade indicate that it did not fade from the country's economic consciousness). Furthermore, the reported re-

---

3. An Act to Continue in Force "An Act to Protect the Commerce of the United States, and Punish the Crime of Piracy," and Also to Make Further Provisions for Punishing the Crime of Piracy, May 15, 1820, c. 113, 1 Stat., sec. 3, in *Statutes at Large*, ed. Peters et al., III, 600. The earlier Act in Addition to the Acts Prohibiting the Slave Trade, Mar. 3, 1819, c. 101, 2 Stat., sec. 1 (III, 532–533) had given the president the power to authorize the seizure of any ship or vessel "made to carry on the slave trade by citizens or residents of the United States." The 1820 Act was passed to address some of the initial failings of 1807, which had allowed for the assessment of up to twenty thousand dollars in fines to shipowners suspected of fitting out their vessels for contraband trade; by 1820, those shipowners no longer faced fees if suspected of preparing for the slave trade, but rather—along with any crew or company—execution as a pirate. The 1820 Act was most concerned with defining piracy and piratical acts; only sections 4 and 5 were devoted to the slave trade itself. The Mar. 31, 1824, Act for the More Effectual Suppression of the African Slave Trade (5 Geo. 4, c. 17 [Eng.]), likewise defined slave trading as piracy. For the legal space of the "high seas," see Lauren Benton, "Legal Spaces of Empire: Piracy and the Origins of Ocean Regionalism," *Comparative Studies in Society and History*, XLVII (2005), 700–724.

duction in transatlantic trade (usually taken as a consequence of the Napoleonic Wars and the War of 1812) as well as a decrease in the total number of enslaved Africans imported to the Americas after 1807 (presumably owing only to abolition in the United Kingdom and the United States) are not often believed to share influences or consequences, nor are they seen as components of the wider geopolitical and economic currents of the early nineteenth century. Shifts in the representation and conceptualization of trade during the period have long caused these two histories, unnecessarily, to stand apart from each other.[4]

Rhetorical and material gaps have thus limited scholars' ability to see the connections between Atlantic slavery and the War of 1812. Building on David Eltis's call to locate abolition within the "fundamental restructuring

4. Reginald Horsman, *The Causes of the War of 1812* (Philadelphia, 1962), 20; Donald R. Hickey, *The War of 1812: A Forgotten Conflict* (Urbana, Ill., 1989), 12; Jeremy Black, *The War of 1812 in the Age of Napoleon* (Norman, Okla., 2009), 27; Matthew Mason, "'Nothing Is Better Calculated to Excite Divisions': Federalist Agitation against Slave Representation during the War of 1812," *New England Quarterly*, LXXV (2002), 531. The themes of illegal search, seizure, and trade restriction remain important touchstones in later works, including Alan Taylor, *The Civil War of 1812: American Citizens, British Subjects, Irish Rebels, and Indian Allies* (New York, 2010); Troy Bickham, *The Weight of Vengeance: The United States, the British Empire, and the War of 1812* (New York, 2012); Nicole Eustace, *1812: War and the Passions of Patriotism* (Philadelphia, 2012); and Gene Allen Smith, *The Slaves' Gamble: Choosing Sides in the War of 1812* (New York, 2013). Matthew Mason has noted that, in the historiography, abolition and trade are "seemingly unrelated geopolitical issues"; see Mason, "The Battle of the Slaveholding Liberators: Great Britain, the United States, and Slavery in the Early Nineteenth Century," *WMQ*, 3d Ser., LIX (2002), 667. David Brion Davis argued that a consequence of the Napoleonic Wars was "the fatal weakening of slaveholding regimes in most parts of the New World" but did not specifically discuss the consequences of the War of 1812 (or the Napoleonic Wars) on the trade in enslaved Africans (Davis, *Inhuman Bondage: The Rise and Fall of Slavery in the New World* [New York, 2006], 270). There are two notable exceptions in the historiography: Roger Anstey concentrated on the connection of abolition to neutrality disputes through the figure of James Stephen in *The Atlantic Slave Trade and British Abolition, 1760–1810* (Atlantic Highlands, N.J., 1975), 350–357; and Ann M. Burton, in "British Evangelicals, Economic Warfare, and the Abolition of the Atlantic Slave Trade, 1794–1810," *Anglican and Episcopal History*, LXV (1996), 197–225, wrote that the "close connection" between abolition and the Anglo-American conflict had not yet been made (209). For links between U.S. economic growth, expansion, and the post-1808 slave trade, see David Eltis, *Economic Growth and the Ending of the Transatlantic Slave Trade* (New York, 1987), 249; and Ernest Obadele-Starks, *Freebooters and Smugglers: the Foreign Slave Trade in the United States after 1808* (Fayetteville, Ark., 2007).

of Atlantic slave systems that occurred in the last century of their existence," a better understanding of wartime trade agreements and the related issues of neutrality and contraband as well as more careful attention to the conceptual disaggregation of the foreign trade from the internal "slave-trade between the states" are necessary to challenge and amend the heretofore isolated narratives of trade and war in early U.S. history. To be clear, this is a suggestive rather than a conclusive argument, and there is much work—theoretical and empirical—left to be done. Nonetheless, contemporary ideologies of "free trade" and a patriotism underscored by Revolutionary nostalgia have obscured the significance of the slave trade to the War of 1812, and, in the twentieth and twenty-first centuries, nation-centered histories have imposed limits that conceal transnational commercial networks.[5]

French shipping records can help illuminate the impact of Atlantic trade on U.S. history during this time by providing indications of what U.S. records and histories have been missing. Documenting contraband and illicit activities—what Lawrence A. Peskin calls the "problem of secrecy"—in the surviving archive is difficult, however, especially when coupled with the changing representations of "trade" at the time. But connections, hitherto unseen, between neutrality disagreements, slavery, early-nineteenth-century U.S.-French commerce, and the history of the War of 1812 demonstrate that one kind of trade was not hived off from the other. For, if we continue to think of early-nineteenth-century transatlantic commerce as structured by who, how, and where—one as business and the other as piracy—we will continue to miss the histories hidden by, in Douglass's words, "a system begun in avarice, supported in pride, and perpetuated in cruelty."[6]

---

5. David Eltis, "Was Abolition of the U.S. and British Slave Trade Significant in the Broader Atlantic Context?" *WMQ*, 3d Ser., LXVI (2009), 723. Peter Andreas asserted that the tension between the United States and the United Kingdom over trade on the "high seas" was owing to U.S. Anglophobia; see Andreas, *Smuggler Nation: How Illicit Trade Made America* (New York, 2013), 133. This essay takes as its starting point work claiming that histories of slavery and the Atlantic slave trade operate under the legacies of colonialism, racism, and the challenge of what Michel-Rolph Trouillot termed (adapting Pierre Bourdieu) the "unthinkable." See Trouillot, *Silencing the Past: Power and the Production of History* (Boston, 1995). See also Ian Baucom, *Specters of the Atlantic: Finance Capital, Slavery, and the Philosophy of History* (Durham, N.C., 2005); and Sibylle Fischer, *Modernity Disavowed: Haiti and the Cultures of Slavery in the Age of Revolution* (Durham, N.C., 2004).

6. Archives départementales de la Gironde, Bordeaux, France (hereafter cited as AD33), 8M185; Lawrence A. Peskin, "Conspiratorial Anglophobia and the War of 1812,"

Free Trade

Contemporaries tended to understand the War of 1812 through the restriction of transatlantic trade; indeed, in 1807 there were two twinned attempts to restrict transatlantic trade: on the one hand, the British Orders in Council (January 7 and November 11) and the U.S. Embargo Act (December 22); on the other, the British Act for the Abolition of the Slave Trade (March 25) and the U.S. Act to Prohibit the Importation of Slaves (March 2). The Orders in Council and Embargo Act are understood to apply directly to the conditions of restricted transatlantic trade resulting from the Napoleonic Wars, whereas the abolition acts resulted, at least in part, from a surging Anglo-American antislavery movement. Although all these measures are fundamentally trade restrictions, rarely are they considered as such.[7] The Orders in Council and Embargo Act are usually seen in the light of deteriorating U.S.-U.K. diplomatic and economic relations in the lead-up to the War of 1812, whereas the slave trade laws are often interpreted—and celebrated—as transatlantic benevolence unconnected to increasingly restrictive politi-

---

Journal of American History, XCVIII (2011), 660; Douglass, "July Fourth," in Foner, ed., *Frederick Douglass*, 202. On the meaning of "free trade" during the war, see Paul A. Gilje, "'Free Trade and Sailors' Rights': The Rhetoric of the War of 1812," *Journal of the Early Republic*, XXX (2010), 1–23. All translations from French are my own.

7. In the United States, the 1807 Act to Prohibit the Importation of Slaves, which did not take effect until January 1, 1808, was the culmination of more than a decade of federal legislation limiting U.S. participation in the Atlantic slave trade. From 1774 to 1783, and again between 1787 and 1800, the United States was closed to the international slave trade: during the War of Independence, cutting economic ties with Britain meant refusing to dock slave ships at American ports. See David Brion Davis, *The Problem of Slavery in the Age of Revolution, 1770–1823* (Ithaca, N.Y., 1974), 65. In 1794, Congress passed a law prohibiting U.S. citizens from fitting out ships for the trade, or selling slaves in foreign ports, which was amended in 1800 and 1803; by then, Georgia and South Carolina had already reopened their ports. Owing to article I, section 9, of the Constitution, Congress could not end (but could regulate) the trade until January 1, 1808. Unlike the British law, the U.S. act did not outlaw the trade of slaves across the Atlantic, their importation into territories contiguous to the United States, or slave trading within the United States. In Britain, an 1805 Order in Council banning the slave trade to Guiana was expanded in 1806 to prohibit all trade to foreign or British territories, which ironically led many British merchants to invest in American slaving trips in 1806–1807 (Burton, "British Evangelicals," *Anglican and Episcopal History*, LXV [1996], 214–215). The British Act for the Abolition of the Slave Trade (47 Geo. 2 c.36 [Eng.]) came into effect on May 1, 1807, and abolished the trade of enslaved Africans within the British Empire (although slavery itself remained in effect until 1834).

cal and economic policies. Because of their commonality, both the concepts "trade" and "restriction" are profitable sites for investigating links between the War of 1812 and Atlantic slavery.⁸

To understand the meaning of "trade" in the period, it is important to analyze the familiar nationalist claim to neutrality—that "free ships make free goods"—as well as to examine the ways in which ships and goods exceeded national networks during the early nineteenth century. In order to negotiate the terms of Atlantic trade, in 1794 the United States and Great Britain signed the Treaty of Amity, Commerce, and Navigation—or Jay Treaty—which established the practice of "neutrality" between the two countries. It stated that, as long as a country was not the enemy or aiding the enemy, its commerce would be unaffected by declarations of war (specifically that of 1793 between Great Britain and France). Furthermore, the treaty outlined

---

8. The belief that Britain was impinging on American rights to trade neutrality, along with the sensitive issue of impressment, are keys to the ways in which the War of 1812 was understood at the time, as encapsulated by the slogan "Free Trade and Sailors' Rights" (Gilje, "'Free Trade,'" *JER*, XXX [2010], 1–23). William St Clair writes that the British navy purchased large numbers of enslaved Africans to serve as sailors, spending about one million pounds on 13,400 men for the West India regiment between 1795 and 1808; see St Clair, *The Door of No Return: The History of Cape Coast Castle and the Atlantic Slave Trade* (New York, 2006), 239. See also Kevin McCranie, "The Recruitment of Seamen for the British Navy, 1793–1815: 'Why Don't You Raise More Men?'" in Donald Stoker, Frederick C. Schneid, and Harold D. Blanton, eds., *Conscription in the Napoleonic Era: A Revolution in Military Affairs?* (New York, 2009), 84–101. Often, U.S. newspaper accounts cast impressment as retribution for U.S. commercial success and attempts by Britain to secure the gains of neutrality for themselves; see, for example, "Debates on the Bill concerning Commercial Intercourse with Great Britain and France and for Other Purposes," *National Intelligencer & Washington Advertiser*, Feb. 14, 1810, [2]. Hawkish rhetoricians often likened the British seizures to the transatlantic slave trade, as in "British Impressments," *Democratic Press* (Philadelphia), May 3, 1810, [2]. Yet, despite the ready connections made across impressment, commerce, and slavery, there has seldom been any association made between neutral trading and slave trading. Although Mason details the usefulness of slavery as a rhetorical tactic in terms of domestic factionalism, the slave trade and slavery cannot be disentangled from the way the war itself is understood (Mason, "Battle of the Slave-holding Liberators," *WMQ*, 3d Ser., LIX [2002], 696). Mason's own rhetorical slippage—from slave trade to slavery—is indicative of the systemic problem Douglass tried to describe in 1852 (678). On slavery as a metaphor during the late eighteenth century, see Peter A. Dorsey, "To 'Corroborate Our Own Claims': Public Positioning and the Slavery Metaphor in Revolutionary America," *American Quarterly*, LV (2003), 353–386; and Edward Cahill, *Liberty of the Imagination: Aesthetic Theory, Literary Form, and Politics in the Early United States* (Philadelphia, 2012).

exactly which items constituted "just objects of Confiscation," including gunpowder, saltpeter, and "Timber for Ship Building." Yet, although U.S. neutrality remained in effect at the turn to the nineteenth century, British ships nonetheless routinely boarded and seized U.S. vessels that crossed the Atlantic, whether or not they were carrying contraband items. Into the century's first decade, effects of the war between France and Britain rippled across the Atlantic as both European powers extended their trade restrictions to American ships, although the United States was still technically a neutral party. When Britain effectively established a blockade of Napoleonic Europe with its Orders in Council of January and November 1807—disrupting U.S. trade as well—Jefferson responded in December with the U.S. Embargo Act, prohibiting all U.S. ships from departing for foreign ports and intensifying the transatlantic restrictions. The British Orders in Council of 1809, as well as the U.S. Non-Intercourse Act of 1809 (prohibiting U.S. shipping to British and French ports), continued the restrictive trend.[9]

As a result, the period 1783-1815 was characterized by the development of networks for the neutral "carrying trade" as well as for contraband and privateering. The carrying trade had originally developed as a way for neutral U.S. merchants to exploit France's inability to truck with its Caribbean colonies during the late eighteenth century; eventually it fostered other commercial networks designed to outwit embargos, blockades, and bans. The interests

9. "The Jay Treaty," in Hunter Miller, ed. *Treaties and Other International Acts of the United States of America*, II, *Documents 1-40: 1776-1818* (Washington, D.C., 1931), 245-274 (quotations on 259). Even after the French decrees of Berlin and Milan of Nov. 21, 1806, and Dec. 17, 1807—which forbade French ships from trading with Great Britain or carrying British goods—the United States was still technically a neutral party. Hickey reasons that Britain increased its enforcement of the Rule of 1756, the neutrality protocol established during the Seven Years' War, in the lead-up to 1812 because "British officials, [were] jealous of American commercial success and suspecting frauds in the neutral trade" (Hickey, *The War of 1912*, 9). Though Britain did increase its enforcement of the 1756 law, attributing it to jealousy demonstrates the nationalism-inflected interpretation typical of the historiography of this period. The U.S. Non-Intercourse Act of March 1809 was answered by the British Order in Council of April 26, 1809, and the French Rambouillet Decree of May 20, 1810, which operated under the assumption that American boats were British boats in disguise. See Silvia Marzagalli, "Guerre et création d'un réseau commercial entre Bordeaux et les États-Unis, 1776-1815: L'Impossible économie du politique," in Marzagalli and Bruno Marnot, eds., *Guerre et économie dans l'espace atlantique du XVIe au XXe siècle* (Bordeaux, 2006), 385; Kevin H. O'Rourke, "War and Welfare, Britain, France, and the United States, 1807-14," *Oxford Economic Papers*, LIX (2007), 19-111.

were not strictly of one nation or another but were often spread across the Atlantic in transnational webs of family and extended relations. Furthermore, inconsistent definitions of citizenship often made it difficult to pinpoint a person's nationality. The intricacies of these transatlantic networks created opportunities for trade even when technically there were none.[10]

In 1805, British abolitionist and jurist James Stephen, who would later frame the 1807 Orders in Council as well as William Wilberforce's Abolition of the Slave Trade Act, wrote about the dangers of the neutral carrying trade. In the pamphlet he published anonymously, *War in Disguise; or, The Frauds of the Neutral Flags* (1805), Stephen called for the abolition of the neutral carrying trade, which he claimed was strengthening Britain's enemies in the fight against Napoleon. The United States had been benefiting from its neutrality, at Britain's expense, ever since the signing of the Jay Treaty, when

> the ports of the French islands were speedily crowded with their vessels.
> Of course, the cargoes they received there, as well as those they delivered, were all declared by their papers to be neutral property; but when instead of rum and molasses, the ordinary and ample exchange in the West India markets for the provisions and lumber of America, the neutral ship owners pretended to have acquired, in barter for those cheap and bulky commodities, full cargoes of sugar and coffee; ... It was evident, that the flag of the United States was, for the most part, used to protect the property of the French planter, not of the American merchant.

In stating that the U.S. flag protected French rather than American property, Stephen implied that the neutral trade not only served French instead of U.S. interests but also supported the motor of transatlantic slavery: the plantation economy. In exchange for nothing more than "cheap and bulky commodities," U.S. merchants acquired the valuable "West India" products of sugar and coffee. Whereas American foodstuffs and lumber were usually exchanged for ordinary goods like molasses—which the U.S. market preferred—allegedly neutral traders were suddenly keen to trade for luxury

---

10. Gene A. Smith, "U.S. Navy Gunboats and the Slave Trade in Louisiana Waters, 1808–1811," *Military History of the West*, XXIII (1993), 135–147; Silvia Marzagalli, *"Les boulevards de la fraude": Le négoce maritime et le Blocus continental, 1806–1813: Bordeaux, Hambourg, Livourne* (Paris, 1999); Faye Kert, "Cruising in Colonial Waters: The Organization of North American Privateering in the War of 1812," in David J. Starkey, E. S. van Eyck van Heslinga, and J. A. de Moor, eds., *Pirates and Privateers: New Perspectives on the War on Trade in the Eighteenth and Nineteenth Centuries* (Exeter, U.K., 1997).

goods. Instead of reaching buyers in the United States, Stephen implied, these items were being ferried across the Atlantic on U.S. ships. The supposedly restricted trade was in fact continuing as usual. Stephen noted the same situation after the renewal of suspended British-French hostilities in 1803, with the start of the Napoleonic Wars. By 1805, he explained,

> The commercial, and colonial interests of our enemies, are now ruined in appearance only, not in reality. They seem to have retreated from the ocean, and to have abandoned the ports of their colonies, but it is a mere *ruse de guerre*—They have, in effect, for the most part, only changed their flags, chartered many vessels really neutral, and altered a little the former routes of their trade. Their transmarine sources of revenue, have not been for a moment destroyed by our hostilities, and at present are scarcely impaired.

That U.S. ships were willfully trying to deceive the British authorities, according to Stephen, justified Britain's application of its wartime rights: it was Britain's patriotic duty to end the neutral carrying trade, and it would do so by stopping U.S. ships.[11]

Stephen exposed that transatlantic embargoes and blockades disrupted trade along national lines, but, in many instances, transatlantic restrictions also sent trade underground, or "in disguise," and encouraged the kinds of transnational alliances that made national legislation less effective. Furthermore, the "fraud of the flags"—specifically French ships disguised as U.S. ships—was not limited to vessels filled with Caribbean sugar and coffee.

Even though neutrality applied to the United States in terms of the Napo-

---

11. [James Stephen], *War in Disguise; or, The Frauds of the Neutral Flags* (London, 1805), 9, 20, 37. The popularity of Stephen's text (two editions were published in London and one in New York) caused many historians to claim that his arguments provided the basis for the 1807 Orders in Council. Stephen had gained his legal expertise practicing law in Saint Kitts from 1783 to 1794, where he represented American shipowners in the Admiralty court. See James Stephen, *The Memoirs of James Stephen: Written by Himself for the Use of His Children*, ed. Merle M. Bevington (London, 1954), 5, 18. He became an avowed abolitionist in the Caribbean and upon his return to Britain struck up a friendship with William Wilberforce and eventually became a member of the "Clapham Sect" of Wilberforce, Granville Sharp, and other evangelical abolitionists in London (14). Burton claims that it was Stephen's political maneuvering that led to the passing of the abolition acts and that *War in Disguise* was his "strategy for victory over both the slave trade and Bonaparte"; see Burton, "British Evangelicals," *Anglican and Episcopal History*, LXV (1996), 198, 204.

leonic Wars, importing enslaved Africans into the United States after 1808 violated U.S. law against the external slave trade. Thanks to the 1810 *Amedie* decision made by the British courts, neutrality was thus a moot point and opened suspected U.S. ships to seizure. The Charleston-registered *Amedie*—which had been seized on its way from Bonny, in West Africa, to Matanzas, Cuba, with African captives—was ultimately condemned on grounds that the voyage contravened U.S. law. This decision, on illegality rather than neutrality, set the precedent for subsequent British condemnations of allegedly neutral slave ships seized after 1807. To avoid the U.S. and U.K. restrictions, therefore, American slavers would often employ the tricks of the neutral carrying trade and sail under the colors of a country that had not yet outlawed the transatlantic trade—in 1809, for example, the flags of choice were those of Spain, Portugal, and Sweden—in order to continue the trade in enslaved Africans.[12]

The African Institution, a London-based charity that focused on abolition and the maintenance of the Sierra Leone colony, claimed in its *Fourth Report of the Directors* (1810) that the persons "who are by far the most deeply engaged in this nefarious traffic [of the slave trade], appear to be citizens of the United States of America." While flying foreign colors, U.S. ships "have carried on their slave-trading speculations, during the last year, to an enormous extent." During October 1809, the report noted, "the coast [of Africa] was crowded with vessels, known to be American, trading for slaves under Spanish and Swedish flags." Despite the abolition legislation, the report found, U.S. "ships are now the great carriers of slaves."[13]

In *The Suppression of the African Slave Trade* (1896), W. E. B. Du Bois cited the African Institution's 1819 *Report*, which explained the shift from the U.S. to the Spanish flag after the *Amedie* decision:

---

12. Christopher Lloyd, in *The Navy and the Slave Trade: The Suppression of the African Slave Trade in the Nineteenth Century* (London, 1968), erroneously claims that slave trading under American colors stopped entirely after *Amedie* (62). In 1810, the High Court heard four other cases of U.S. slave ships—including the *Nancy* and the *Tartar*, seized in 1807 and 1808, respectively—which also lost their appeals (Burton, "British Evangelicals," *Anglican and Episcopal History*, LXV [1996], 223–224). Matthew Mason has called this intrigue the "delicate dance of smuggling" in "Keeping Up Appearances: The International Politics of Slave Trade Abolition in the Nineteenth-Century Atlantic World," *WMQ*, 3d Ser., LXVI (2009), 809–832.

13. *Fourth Report of the African Institution*, 2–3. In the *Sixth Report of the African Institution*, the directors accused both American and British ships of disguising themselves as those from Spain and Portugal (7, 8).

Ships bearing the American flag continued to trade for slaves until 1809, when, in consequence of a decision in the English prize appeal courts, which rendered American slave ships liable to capture and condemnation, that flag suddenly disappeared from the coast. Its place was almost instantaneously supplied by the Spanish flag, which, with one or two exceptions, was now seen for the first time on the African coast, engaged in covering the slave trade. This sudden substitution of the Spanish for the American flag seemed to confirm what was established in a variety of instances by more direct testimony, that the slave trade, which now, for the first time, assumed a Spanish dress, was in reality only the trade of other nations in disguise.

Although the report claimed that U.S. traffic was being carried out by Spanish proxies, Du Bois also made clear that ships flying American flags—such as the *Paz, Rosa, Rebecca, Dorset,* and *Saucy Jack*—were trading along "the slave coast" as well. Indeed, "So notorious" had the participation of Americans in the clandestine traffic become that President James Madison addressed Congress on the issue in 1810 and again in 1816. As corroborated by new demographic estimates, importation of African captives—whether conducted "in disguise" or otherwise—continued even after the U.S. and British abolition acts went into effect in 1807 and 1808. David Eltis estimates that three million Africans were transported across the Atlantic after 1807.[14]

14. W. E. Burghardt Du Bois, *The Suppression of the African Slave Trade to the United States of America, 1638-1870* (1896) (Baton Rouge, La., 1969), 110, 112–113, 290. Obadele-Starks has estimated the number of enslaved Africans imported into the United States from 1808 to 1863 to be more than 750,000 (Obadele-Starks, *Freebooters and Smugglers*, 10, 11). James A. McMillin has shown that many extrapolations based on earlier estimates made by Philip D. Curtin (in turn based on census data collected by H. C. Carey in the 1850s) are flawed. This data shows a significant decline in late-eighteenth-century imports as compared to colonial-era numbers. Employing the "slave-carrying capacity method" of estimation, by which the cargo capacity for known slave trading vessels is substituted for more concrete records, McMillin has reestimated the volume of foreign importation, especially between the years 1783 and 1810, at just more than 170,000, a figure much higher than the original 70,000 estimation (McMillin, *The Final Victims: Foreign Slave Trade to North America, 1783–1810* [Columbia, S.C., 2004], 13–17, 23, 29–30, 39–40, 48, "Appendix B: North American Foreign Slave Arrivals, Slave Voyages, and Foreign Slave Sales, 1783-1810" [CD-ROM database]; Curtin, *The Atlantic Slave Trade: A Census* [Madison, Wis., 1969]). In 1813, for example, the African Institution had underestimated that 15,000 people were taken from Africa from 1796 to 1810 (McMillan, *Final Victims,* 44). Using various revised methods as well as new ma-

Lawful Prize

Before abolition, the foreign slave trade was at its height in the United States from 1803 to 1808. From January 1, 1804, to December 31, 1807, the period in which South Carolina re-legalized the foreign slave trade, more than seventy-five thousand captives were imported into the state. After 1805, shipments of enslaved Africans to Louisiana were legally required to pass through Charleston, accounting for some of these numbers, but, nonetheless, Charleston merchants alone sponsored more than sixty voyages to Africa during that time. In 1806 and 1807, Charleston was responsible for more slaving voyages than all other Atlantic ports except Liverpool.[15]

An example of Charleston's prominence in the pre-abolition nineteenth-century trade—and how much is still unknown about the post-abolition period—can be traced by following the sloop *Fox*, which on April 19, 1805, left Sierra Leone, captained by Vincent, for Charleston with forty-eight enslaved Africans on board. By the end of September, Captain Vincent sailed the *Fox* into Charleston harbor and disembarked forty captives. The "cargo"

---

terial gleaned mostly from newspapers, McMillin estimates that 109,200 Africans were imported to North America (including only North Carolina, South Carolina, Georgia, Florida, Mississippi, and Louisiana) from 1800 to 1810; while there are supposedly 497 documented voyages from Africa to North America from 1801 to 1810, records have not yet been found for all of them (45, 48). For McMillin's discussion of method, see 39–46. David Eltis and David Richardson have noted problems with McMillin's method in "A New Assessment of the Transatlantic Slave Trade," in Eltis and Richardson, eds., *Extending the Frontiers: Essays on the New Transatlantic Slave Trade Database* (New Haven, Conn., 2008), 55 n. 17. Eltis suggests that this 3 million figure may amount to only one-quarter of the total number of Africans forcibly displaced by the transatlantic slave trade between 1500 and 1867 (Eltis, "Was Abolition of the U.S. and British Slave Trade Significant?" *WMQ*, 3d Ser., LXVI [2009], 722).

15. "Frederick and Franz Diederichs and Co.," *City-Gazette and Daily Advertiser* (Charleston, S.C.), Nov. 2, 1808, 3 (the same advertisement was repeated until Feb. 17, 1809); McMillin, *Final Victims*, 86, 129. McMillin estimates that 8,795 captives entered South Carolina in 1805, 14,306 in 1806, 21,683 in 1807, and 887 in 1808 (32). In Louisiana, however, he estimates the 1809 and 1810 numbers at 3,460 and 1,488, respectively (32). Jed Handelsman Shugerman reveals that Charleston merchants profited from the reopened trade as middlemen: of the 202 ships from South Carolina during the period, 91 of the consignees were British, 10 French, 88 were from Rhode Island, but only 13 were from South Carolina. See Shugerman, "The Louisiana Purchase and South Carolina's Reopening of the Slave Trade in 1803," *JER*, XXII (2002), 263–290. See also Margaret Kinard Latimer, "South Carolina—A Protagonist of the War of 1812," *American Historical Review*, LXI (1956), 914–929; McMillin, *Final Victims*, 88; Obadele-Starks, *Freebooters and Smugglers*, 20.

of "Prime Windward Coast Slaves" was listed for sale in the *Charleston Courier*. In November, the *Fox* cleared Charleston for Africa again, arriving at the Rio Pongo in April 1806 and returning to Charleston that July. Apparently, there was a change at the helm: although Vincent is recorded as the captain in April, Edward Smith returned with sixty-seven captives in July. By August 15, 1806, the *Fox* had been cleared to leave Charleston for Africa once more, still captained by Smith. No record indicates where the *Fox* headed after it landed on the West African coast (or if it landed there at all). The incomplete state of Charleston's archives may be a reason for this omission: only one (relatively) complete set of duties and customs records exists for the period, and it derives from an 1820 government report on slave vessels arriving in Charleston from 1804 to 1807. In this report, the *Fox* is only listed for 1806, omitting the 1805 record altogether. Although Captain Smith might well have returned to the city's wharves after clearing Charleston in August 1806, without additional information it looks as though the *Fox* just stopped trading in 1806. Indeed, most estimates based on Charleston's partial archives imply that the slave trade significantly decreased in 1808 and by 1809 had dropped to zero. Yet advertisements in the port's *City Gazette* continued to list "Stocks and Bitts, Sad Irons" and "Swords for the African trade" at least until February 1809.[16]

16. David Eltis et al. *Voyages: The Trans-Atlantic Slave Trade Database* (2008), http://www.slavevoyages.org (hereafter cited as *Voyages*), voyage identification number (VID) 25437, 25461, 37130; "For Sale The Cargo of the sloop Fox, Captain Vincent,—consisting of—Prime Windward Coast Slaves" (Sept. 27, 1805), *Charleston Courier*, Oct. 2, 1805, [3]; Elizabeth Donnan, ed., *Documents Illustrative of the History of the Slave Trade to America*, IV, *The Border Colonies and the Southern Colonies* (Washington, D.C., 1935), 508, 512, 515, 516 (unlike *Voyages* and McMillin, Donnan records the arrival of the *Fox* in Charleston from Rio Pongo as July 24, 1806). *Voyages* reports no further record of this brig after it left Charleston in August, yet it also states that 69 captives were disembarked; this is confusing because the online record cites McMillin's database, but McMillin himself does not supply any disembarkation figures (McMillin, *Final Victims*, 32, 33). The 1820 government report was prepared for William Smith, the U.S. senator from South Carolina, who referenced the material during his December 1820 address regarding admission of Missouri into the Union ("Recapitulation of the African Trade ... from January 1, 1804, to December 31, 1807," and "Admission of Missouri," Dec. 8, 1820, in *The Debates and Proceedings in the Congress of the United States ..., Annals of Congress*, 16th Congress, Session 2 [Washington, D.C., 1855], 76–77, 51–76). Smith's report included a Charleston-registered *Fox* from 1806 and listed the proprietor as "J[ohn] S. Adams, R.I." (ibid., 74). Although McMillin derives some of his information from Smith's report, he mainly relies on articles from the *Charleston Courier* and *City Gazette* (McMillin, *Final Victims*, 33, 162 n. 39). References to the sloop *Fox* in McMillan's database can be found

Scholars have noted significant gaps in the records of slave trading ventures after 1808, despite evident traces of the post-1808 trade. Existing figures can be misleading: it may be that the numbers are greater before 1808 because trading truly stopped after that, or because the records of continued trade become harder to discern after abolition. Only after South Carolina lifted its ban in 1804, for example, did American slavers finally begin to report harassment by French and British privateers, but the *Amedie* case put a stop to any continued reporting. As before, smuggling occurred at great rates in places like Providence and Newport, Rhode Island, after 1808. Foreign slave trading was still active in New Orleans and surrounding areas in Louisiana, especially in Barataria Bay, which provided havens for piracy in the early nineteenth century as well. It is possible that smuggling was even more widespread.[17]

As early as 1969, Philip Curtin recognized the difficulty and controversy in producing estimates of the slave trade. For one, as abolition measures strengthened, information began to disappear. Traffickers seldom reported the seizure of slaving ships because U.S. trade to foreign ports was illegal, and they simply absorbed the losses as part of the risky, yet lucrative, business. For example, renowned smuggler Jean Laffite did not appeal the judgment against his sloop *Porpoise* on November 13, 1811, at the vice-admiralty court in Tortola. Charleston merchant Samuel Groves only appealed the decision in the case of the *Amedie* because the voyage was made before the 1808 ban went into effect. In 1810, Sir William Scott (later, Lord Stowell), the judge of the High Court of the Admiralty who tried the *Amedie* case, wrote: "It appears to me, that hardly any thing will put a stop to this abominable traffic. The profits are so extremely high, that if they save one cargo out of

---

on 1111, 1206, 1230, 1298, 1372, 1389. Adams was consignee on at least thirteen other ships that disembarked at Charleston a total of more than 2,000 enslaved Africans from 1804 to 1807 (McMillan, *Final Victims*, "Appendix B," 1042, 1117, 1266, 1288, 1289, 1328, 1487, 1514, 1636, 1731, 1735, 1736, 2237).

17. Obadele-Starks, *Freebooters and Smugglers*, 9, 11–12; McMillin, *Final Victims*, 102. For piracy and the Battle of New Orleans, see Robert C. Vogel, "Jean Laffite, the Baratarians, and the Battle of New Orleans: A Reappraisal," *Louisiana History*, XLI (2000), 261–276; and Obadele-Starks, *Freebooters and Smugglers*, 36–40. After the war, President James Madison granted the inhabitants of New Orleans and Barataria "a free and full pardon" for activities regarding trade and navigation ("By the President of the United States of America: A Proclamation," Feb. 6, 1815, in James D. Richardson, ed., *A Compilation of the Messages and Papers of the Presidents . . .*, I, *1789–1817* [Washington, D.C., 1896], 543–545).

three, they will still make money." Documentation is often missing because traders did not retain records of their illegal ventures and because much of the slave trading and smuggling went undetected or underdetected by official forces. Despite a calendar of fines for those who broke the 1807 law, enforcement in the United States was practically nonexistent during abolition's first decade. In the appendix to *The Suppression of the African Slave Trade*, Du Bois provides a list of the "Typical Cases of Vessels Engaged in the American Slave-Trade" but skips from the *Sally*, which landed a cargo of fifty slaves in Louisiana in 1804, to the *Saucy Jack*, which was apprehended in 1814 by British forces off the coast of West Africa. Judging from Du Bois's records, no slaving voyages were run by U.S. citizens, or supported by U.S. interests, between 1804 and 1814; however, Du Bois himself did not believe this was the case. He suggests the war as a possible explanation for lax enforcement. "Perhaps from 1808 to 1814, in the midst of agitation and war, there was some excuse for carelessness," he writes, implying that trade continued even if officials were too preoccupied to take note.[18]

A similar situation exists with regard to the French records. Although France abolished slavery in 1794, both slavery and the Atlantic slave trade were reintroduced by Napoleon in 1802; from 1802 to 1818, France saw its greatest numbers in "la traite négrière." Between February 1802 and January 1804 alone, Bordeaux sent at least fifteen ships to Africa, overtaking Nantes as the most important slave trading port in France. Yet sources on the history of the French slave trade imply that it halted from the end of the eighteenth century until 1815, making the search for information about the period 1800–1815 extremely difficult. As a consequence, a strictly material absence appears instead as a lack of activity.[19]

---

18. In *Atlantic Slave Trade*, Curtin proclaimed that the "dimensions of the nineteenth-century slave trade have always been a matter of controversy" and that abolition "mark[ed] the end of regular and official shipping data from the slave-trading nations" (231, 233). For a discussion of the debates around Curtin's work, see chapter 2 of Michael A. Gomez, *Exchanging Our Country Marks: The Transformation of African Identities in the Colonial and Antebellum South* (Chapel Hill, N.C., 1998). Although there were nine captives aboard the *Porpoise*, there is no record of this sloop in *Voyages*. See Great Britain, House of Commons, "Papers Relating to Slave Ships and Condemned," *Miscellaneous Accounts and Papers, Session 4 Nov 1813–30 July 1814*, XII (London, 1814), 325; *Fifth Report of the Directors of the African Institution* ... (London, 1811), 10–11; Du Bois, *Suppression*, 109, 290.

19. Hugh Thomas, *The Slave Trade: The Story of the Atlantic Slave Trade, 1400–1870* (New York, 1997), 547; Eric Saugera, *Bordeaux, port négrier: Chronologie, économie,*

Nonetheless, records remaining for the French trading port of Bordeaux in the key decade after Napoleon reopened the French slave trade hint at the possibility of continued U.S. participation even after 1808. Documents provide clear instances of ship manifests with gap-filled itineraries and cargos of slave-produced commodities that suggest, at the least, that many ships continued to sail the Atlantic slave trading circuits and, at most, that some of these ships might well have engaged in slave trading itself. This evidence, although not conclusive, offers one way to connect early-nineteenth-century disputes over the Atlantic trade—in goods and people—to the outbreak of war in 1812.

---

idéologie, XVIIe–XIXe siècles, new ed. (Paris, 2002), 7. The implication that slave trading diminished from 1800 to 1815 specifically owes to national periodization: that is, French scholarship usually places the beginning of the nineteenth century at 1815 but ends the eighteenth century with Napoleon Bonaparte's coup in 1799. The interstitial "Epoch of Napoleon," also known as the Consulate and First Empire (1799–1815), is often considered on its own. Thus, with the notable exception of Serge Daget's work, most of the French studies implicitly define the slave trade as a problem that existed before, not after, 1800. Even Daget's groundbreaking *Répetoire des expéditions négrières françaises à la traite illégale (1814–1850)* (Nantes, 1988) is interested chiefly in the "illegal trade," focusing on voyages after 1814. See Perry Viles, "The Slaving Interest in the Atlantic Ports, 1763–1792," *French Historical Studies*, VII (1972), 529–543; Jean Mettas, *Répertoire des expéditions négrières françaises au XVIIIe siècle*, ed. Serge Daget, 2 vols. (Paris, 1978–1984); Pierre Dardel, *Navires et marchandises dans les ports de Rouen et du Havre au XVIIIe siècle* (Paris, 1963); Gaston-Martin, *Nantes au XVIIIe siècle: L'ère des Négriers (1714–1774), d'après des documents inédits* (Paris, 1931). All define the slave trade, at least historiographically, as a problem of the eighteenth century. To give two examples: both Jean-Michel Deveau's *La France au Temps des Négriers* (Paris, 1994), 318–319, and Paul Butel's *Histoire des Antilles françaises: XVIIe–XXe siècle* (Paris, 2007), 274–275, skip directly from discussions of the French and Haitian Revolutions to 1815.

As in the United States, these gaps are also owing to material absences. In Bordeaux, most of the port and municipal (but not departmental or national) records were lost to fire in the mid-nineteenth and early twentieth century (Saugera, *Bordeaux, port négrier*, 19). Saugera's *Bordeaux, port négrier* thus fails to identify any voyages between the *Gustave* in 1804 and the 1815 *Belle*, which was ultimately captured by the British navy off the coast of Guadeloupe (Thomas, *Slave Trade*, 587–588). Opening the parameters of *Voyages* to include other French ports only adds the ninety-nine-ton brig the *Sénégalaise*, which left Nantes for Bonny on Dec. 3, 1814, and ultimately disembarked 279 of 339 captives in Martinique (*Voyages*, VID 34005). The U.S. consulate in Bordeaux lost its records during World War II.

The Fraud of Neutral Flags

Most studies of this period assume that transatlantic trade dwindled and then ceased, owing to the French, British, and U.S. trade restrictions. They often ignore the networks developed for contraband trading outlined by James Stephen. Furthermore, U.S. ships could obtain special licenses and papers to trade between the United States and France after the embargo of 1807, although these mechanisms, too, have not been sufficiently explored. Such was the case with the U.S. brig *Fox*, whose history is directly connected with issues of neutral trading and the War of 1812.

In February 1811, the *Fox* was granted a special imperial license to transport fine French goods from Bordeaux to a port in the United States. On March 7, 1811, Bordeaux local Jean Bosquet related the following to the prefect of the Gironde:

> I was informed that my agent at Bayonne was not at all able to benefit from the favor accorded me by His Excellency the Minister of the Interior authorizing me to apply my American permit ... to the brig *Fox*, in order to sail it from Bayonne to a port in the United States. The particular circumstances in which this ship is found have obligated me to relinquish the advantages gained by these arrangements.

Despite possessing a special export license granted in February, the *Fox* was held at Bayonne, a port city not far from the Spanish border, because of unspecified "particular circumstances." Bosquet requested permission to use the special export license for import instead; the prefect granted the request the following day. Nonetheless, under the direction of Captain Thomas Cullen, the *Fox* left Bayonne for Philadelphia on March 13, 1811, loaded with a cargo of one-third silk stuffs, one-third wine and brandies, and another third in "authorized objects."[20]

That April, the *Fox* returned to Philadelphia after an absence of almost two years. In October 1809, Captain Cullen had sailed the *Fox* from Philadelphia to San Sebastián, Spain, freighted with coffee and "white Havana

---

20. "Licences et permis de navigation 1809–1814, Ministre de l'Intérieur," AD33 8M185; "Authorized objects" refers to items not on the lists of restricted goods. The only vessels permitted to leave France during the spring of 1811 were those that had applied for a special imperial license, which required all bearers to export at least a third of their cargo in French silks. Because of the high demand for French goods in the French colonies, and because of the shortage created by the British blockade, it is possible that these items were destined for the French Caribbean rather than the United States.

sugar." When the brig landed in Spain, it was placed under commercial quarantine by Napoleon's forces for allegedly violating the imperial decrees of Berlin and Milan. Along with the *Eagle, Hawk, Andrew* (all from Philadelphia) and other U.S. vessels, the *Fox* was taken to Bayonne, where it was auctioned, along with its cargo, in late 1809. Presumably, this was how Bosquet's "agent in Bayonne" came to have dealings with the American brig. Thus, the "particular circumstances" to which Bosquet alluded in 1811 were those of the *Fox*'s condemnation as a prize of war, even though the United States was neutral under the terms of Napoleon's decrees. Although the *Fox* safely returned to Philadelphia eighteen months after it had departed, some of the other American vessels purchased as prizes in Bayonne and dispatched to the United States were then seized by the British Royal Navy while re-crossing the Atlantic. These ships were taken to Plymouth, England, and tried at the High Court of the Admiralty for violating the embargo and blockades between France, Great Britain, and the United States.[21]

While French forces were condemning the *Fox* in Bayonne, another *Fox*—also a U.S. brig—was captured sailing from Boston to Cherbourg in 1810. This *Fox* was held at Plymouth, also for sailing in contravention of the French decrees of Berlin and Milan (like the Philadelphia *Fox*), even though the captain believed the decrees to have been repealed. As a potential prize of war, the brig and its cargo of "Colonial produce, etc." were condemned, evaluated for sale, and held at Plymouth with other U.S. ships, some of which had been captured after their previous release from France. The incident became a flashpoint in the lead-up to the 1812 war. The Boston *Fox* became "a

---

21. Lestapies v. Ingraham, in Robert M. Barr, *Pennsylvania State Reports, Containing Cases Adjudged in the Supreme Court during Part of December Term 1846, March Term, and Part of June Term, 1847, and Some Previous Cases*, V (Philadelphia, 1869), 71–82; "Latest from France," *Balance, & State Journal* (Albany, N.Y.), Apr. 23, 1811, 135; "Foreign Intelligence," *Northern Centinel* (Burlington, Vt.), Feb. 28, 1811, [2]; Greg H. Williams, *The French Assault on American Shipping, 1793–1813: A History and Comprehensive Record of Merchant Marine Losses* (Jefferson, N.C., 2009), 149. "Extract of a Letter from an American Gentleman at Bayonne, Aug. 1, 1810," *American and Commercial Daily Advertiser* (Baltimore), Sept. 24, 1810, [2], lists some of the *Fox*'s cargo for sale ("Beans, 6 barrels") in August 1810. See the list of vessels condemned in "Extract: —Mr. J. S. Smith to the Secretary of State [July 20, 1811]," in Walter Lowrie and Matthew St. Clair, eds., *American State Papers: Documents, Legislative and Executive, of the Congress of the United States ...*, III (Washington, D.C., 1832), 422. The *Rose-in-Bloom* and the *Andrew* were two such vessels released from Bayonne only to be captured in 1810. They were condemned by the High Court of the Admiralty on June 21, 1811, and were valued at $12,000 each with a cargo of "Brandy, wine and silks" worth $25,000.

fresh instance" of what the Hudson, New York, newspaper the *Bee* termed "British rapacity and plunder."²²

In May 1811, Sir William Scott rendered judgment in the case of "The Fox and Others." Although the *Fox*'s captain had mistaken the validity of the French decrees—Napoleon's minister of foreign affairs, the duke of Cadore, had offered to revoke them only when Great Britain canceled its blockade—Scott did not see his gesture as sincere proof of the decree's repeal. Accordingly, he found the *Fox* and its twenty-seven associates in breach of the blockade established under the British Order in Council of April 26, 1809, making the vessels and their cargo "lawful prize." Most of the "Others" were condemned by early June 1811, and the funds resulting from their sales were forfeited to the crown and the capturing cruisers. American partisans were enraged. "A state of war can scarcely be more ruinous to our commerce, and it will put it in our power to punish and capture in turn," railed the Hudson *Bee*. The Richmond, Virginia, *Enquirer* cast the *Fox*'s significance in even more aggressive terms: "If the Fox, etc. be condemned, the dogs of rapine will be let loose, and the British may sail with a *broom* at their mast head to sweep our ships from their destination.... If such be her course the question between us and Great Britain—will be reduced to a nutshell—*We resist or strike our colors!!*"²³

In addition to determining whether vessels and cargo captured during wartime were indeed lawful prizes, the vice-admiralty courts in Britain's colonial territories—located in places such as Barbados, Tortola, Halifax, and Sierra Leone—also heard prize cases that involved allegations of slave trading after 1807. Since Britain and the United States had both outlawed the foreign slave trade by then, British ships assumed the authority to stop vessels suspected of violating the prohibition; these cases were then tried in

---

22. "Extract of a letter from Mr. J. S. Smith ...," *Savannah Republican*, Dec. 3, 1811, [2]; "British 'Protection,'" *Bee* (Hudson, N.Y.), Sept. 13, 1811, 2. The Boston brig was reported as valued alternately at $12,000 and $10,000, with its cargo listed at $29,500. See "Smith to the Secretary of State," in Lowrie and St. Clair, eds., *American State Papers*, III, 422; *State Papers and Publick Documents of the United States ...*, VII, *1809–11* (Boston, 1815), 479.

23. "Fox and Others," in Thomas Edwards, *Reports of Cases Argued and Determined in the High Court of Admiralty, Commencing with the Judgments of the Right Hon. Sir William Scott, Easter Term 1808* (London 1812), 311–326; "British 'Protection,'" *Bee*, Sept. 13, 1811, [2]; the Richmond, Virginia, *Enquirer*, quoted in *Alexandria Daily Gazette, Commerical and Political* (Va.), July 27, 1811, [3]. The same article was printed in the *Boston Gazette*, Aug. 1, 1811, [2], and the *Carolina Gazette* (Charleston, S.C.), Aug. 24, 1811, [3].

British courts. If the ships were not registered as British or were not under British direction, the captain, crew, and owners had to prove that slave trading was legal under the laws of their own nation. The *Amedie* was one such case.[24]

On December 22, 1807, a British cruiser stopped the U.S. ship *Amedie*, which had a cargo of 105 enslaved Africans—mostly children—on its way from Bonny, on the West Coast of Africa, to Matanzas, Cuba. The *Amedie* was owned by Charleston merchant Samuel Groves—who also owned the ship *Semiramis*, which sailed with the *Amedie* and successfully disembarked 201 captives in Cuba before being seized by a French privateer in early 1808— and had initially declared its intention to land the captives in Charleston. When the *Amedie* was seized, the captain explained that he had decided to land at Matanzas because he feared that he would not make it to Charleston before the January 1, 1808, abolition deadline. The vice-admiralty court in Tortola, where the case was referred in 1808, and then the Tribunal of the Privy Council in 1810, however, suspected the *Amedie* had always intended to go to Cuba. The captain had waited until September to depart from the African coast, despite clearance papers dated for June. Furthermore, the *Semiramis* was also headed from Bonny to Cuba. James Stephen argued against the *Amedie* for the crown on the grounds that slave trading was "inhuman traffic" and illegal according to the law of nations.[25]

---

24. "Amedie, Johnson, master," in Thomas Harman Acton, *Reports of Cases Argued and Determined Before the Most Noble and Right Honorable the Lords Commissioners of Appeals in Prize Causes ...*, I (London, 1811), 240–251. On vice-admiralty courts, see Eugene Kontorovich, "The Constitutionality of International Courts: The Forgotten Precedent of Slave-Trade Tribunals," *University of Pennsylvania Law Review*, CLVIII (2009), 39–115; Jenny S. Martinez, "Antislavery Courts and the Dawn of International Human Rights Law," *Yale Law Journal*, CXVII (2008), 550–641; Tara Helfman, "The Court of Vice Admiralty at Sierra Leone and the Abolition of the West African Slave Trade," ibid., CXV (2006), 1122–1156. Helfman maintains that the Sierra Leone vice-admiralty court was "the third pillar supporting the suppression of the slave trade" (1125). From 1807 to 1811, the Court freed 1991 slaves, although some were subsequently recaptured (1143).

25. "Amedie," in Acton, *Reports of Cases*, I, 240–249; "Fortuna," in John Dodson, *Reports of Cases Argued and Determined in the High Court of Admiralty; Commencing with the Judgments of the Right Hon. Sir William Scott, Trinity Term 1811* (London, 1815), 81–91. One sailor testified that not all of the cargo belonged to Groves, and he had overheard Robins speaking of a "Mr. de Poe," and, although this could not be confirmed, it nonetheless raised the court's suspicions: "When a witness is found stating, as from very competent authority, that the property is not such as the claimant's witnesses describe,

Ultimately, the *Amedie* was condemned because the voyage contravened U.S. law, even though the U.S. ban was not yet technically in effect when the ship was stopped off the coast of Cuba in December 1807. In his appeal, Groves's counsel explained that he

> had been long engaged in this species of traffic.... Mr. Groves, therefore, had a right not only to continue his trade, but to expect that the most liberal allowances would be made in his favor by his own government, should any unfavorable occurrence take place. He had a right to expect that upright intention [to follow the new law] would constitute, under such circumstances, a just claim to favor and indulgence.

Not only did Groves consider trading identical to any other "species of traffic," his counsel's use of the phrase "species of traffic" as a euphemism for the slave trade was similar to terms such as "African trade," "Guinea Trade," or "blackbirding." Groves's defense exposed that he believed the 1807 law would not be enforced immediately; instead, he expected to be allowed to withdraw his "capital at leisure from this traffic, a provision perfectly consistent with sound policy and common justice." When Scott referred in his opinion to Groves's complaints "of the injury and interruption he has sustained in carrying on his usual and lawful trade, that of importing slaves for

---

and the vessel is afterward found deviating to an enemy's colony; in such a case as this ... contrary to the conviction of the *American* Government of the disgraceful nature of this trade, and after it had even come to a resolution to abolish it altogether, it is but the exercise of a laudable caution on the part of the Court to look upon the whole train of evidence with a scrupulous exactness and suspicion" ("Amedie," in Acton, *Reports of Cases*, I, 240, 241). The *Amedie*'s outward voyage was captained by Martin Robin; after his death on the return voyage, it was captained by James Johnson, which caused a problem for the case because there was no way to cross-examine the captain on his original instructions. See *Voyages*, VID 7661, 25520; Burton, "British Evangelicals," *Anglican and Episcopal History*, LXV (1996), 222. The *Semiramis* was captained by Charles Collins, a slave trader and the former Bristol, Rhode Island, customs collector (McMillin, *Final Victims*, 44). For more on the significance of the *Amedie* case, see "Notes: American Slavery and the Conflict of Laws," *Columbia Law Review*, LXXI (1971), 74–99; David R. Murray, *Odious Commerce: Britain, Spain, and the Abolition of the Cuban Slave Trade* (New York, 1980), 40–41; Patricia M. Muhammad, "The Trans-Atlantic Slave Trade: A Forgotten Crime against Humanity as Defined by International Law," *American University International Law Review*, XIX (2004), 883–947; Martinez, "Antislavery Courts," *Yale Law Journal*, CXVII (2008), 565–566; and Jenny S. Martinez, *The Slave Trade and the Origins of International Human Rights Law* (New York, 2012), 25–26.

the purpose of sale," he demonstrated how easily "slave" was dropped from "slave trade" and how the focus, as Groves's counsel had hoped, was mainly on the rights of merchant neutrality. Two years later, Scott upheld the Tortola prize court's decision on appeal, deciding that it was a case of illegality, not neutrality.[26]

Sir William Scott's May 1810 decision in the *Amedie* case—rendered one year before "The Fox and Others"—ultimately depended on the understanding that humans could not be defined as property and that technically slaves were not covered under the prize court. He wrote: "A claimant can have no right upon principles of universal law, to claim the restitution in a Prize Court of human beings carried as his slaves.... In this case, the laws of the claimant's country allow of no right of property such as he claims. There can therefore be no right to restitution." As the *Amedie* case demonstrates, the de facto legal status of trade and what was being traded centered on the items—that is, the persons—restricted by the 1807 legislation. Because the United States had already outlawed the foreign slave trade, the court found Groves guilty of breaking U.S. law rather than the law of nations. But, even in cases such as this, enslaved captives were not always disaggregated from other goods of sale. Although the British law no longer saw the right to property in persons, incendiary U.S. rhetoric about seized property did not always recognize that difference. Nor did prize courts, newspaper reports, or political pamphlets always delineate between one kind of cargo and another. Furthermore, there remained the difficulty of drawing a line between the trade that was linked to slavery—but that was not explicitly trade in slaves (say, the trade in cotton, sugar, or arms)—and that which was not.[27]

26. "Amedie," in Acton, *Reports*, 247, 249. *Voyages* puts the date the ship departed as Aug. 1, 1807, the date it landed in Bonny as Sept. 12, 1807, and the date it left as Nov. 1, 1807. See Curtin, *Atlantic Slave Trade*, 250–251, for a discussion of the ways in which slavery was carried out in other names and guises.

27. "Privy Council Appeals," *Norfolk Gazette and Publick Ledger*, Oct. 10, 1810, [4] (as reprinted from the *Courier* [London], Aug. 4, 1810). As Lloyd pointed out in what is still the authoritative monograph on the subject, "slave trading and piracy were indistinguishable both in practice and in the eyes of the law ... the suppression of the former may be equally regarded as part of the task of policing the seas" (Lloyd, *The Navy and the Slave Trade*, xi). Unfortunately, Lloyd's study focuses on 1810 forward. Charles R. Foy cited the 1782 condemnation and sale of the African men Obadiah Gale and Edward Carter, who were considered, "along with lumber and tar found on the *Nancy*, to be cargo that could be sold as prize goods," in "Eighteenth Century 'Prize Negroes': From Britain to America," *Slavery and Abolition*, XXXI (2010), 379. For a South African perspective, see Anna Maria Rugarli, "Eyes on the Prize: The Story of the Prize Slave Present," *Quar-*

The *Amedie* case persisted in the U.S. press because it was an illustration of British authority established at the expense of U.S. citizens' property rights—one of the key complaints leading up to the war. It gained further attention because the enslaved Africans had been resold in the Caribbean once the *Amedie* was seized. Although the crown had sequestered only the ship and had freed the captives, they were later recaptured and sold; as a result, some in the United States assumed that Britain was gaining monetarily from the search-and-seizure actions. The fear that Britain was profiting from condemned goods—although the goods themselves were undefined—increased tensions over trade between the two nations.[28]

The Trade of Other Nations in Disguise

One difficulty of focusing on trade in this era is the usual assertion that there was almost no trading—slave trading or otherwise—out of U.S. or French ports from 1807 to 1812. Scholars have indeed documented significant trade disruptions and diminutions during the 1807–1814 period. Nonetheless, the system of "war in disguise," as Stephen described it in 1805, did not halt with the Orders in Council. Examples from the Departmental Archives of Gironde in Bordeaux demonstrate that, in fact, trade proceeded between the United States and France even during the years of the most severe restriction, 1810 and 1811. The following instances demonstrate the ways in which the trade between France and the United States has been underestimated for the period. The first involves the evaluations of import and export cargo in customs records from Bordeaux, and the second clarifies more fully the concept of trade "in disguise."[29]

---

terly *Bulletin of the National Library of South Africa*, LXII, no. 4 (October–December 2008), 161–172.

28. The 1807 Act did nothing to regulate the sale of confiscated captives (that is, free men of color), who were sold in the United States as "Prize Negroes"; the proceeds were often shared with the U.S. government (Rugarli, "Eyes on the Prize," *Quarterly Bulletin of the NLSA*, LXII, no. 4 [October–December 2008], 161). Even in 1815, a writer for the *Rhode-Island Republican* was still impassioned by the issue: "It is PROVED slaves captured from us during the war on the high seas (or rather on neutral territory) have been condemned and *sold in the West-Indies*." See "Captured Slaves," *Rhode-Island Republican* (Newport), Aug. 2, 1815, [3].

29. "Bureau de commerce—Relevé général de tableau partiel fourni par le directeur des douanes—par sorti et entrée de cour des navires par l'étranger ou des continues françaises," [April 1810–1811], AD33 8M183: "Il paraitrait que M. le d[ire]cteur de Douanes n'a commencé à fournir ces tableaux que depuis le mois d'avril 1810—jusqu'à ce jour—parmi de quel il y en beaucoup de *négatifs* et quelques un où des Bâtiments faut dé-

TABLE 1. *Imports and Exports at the Port of Bordeaux, 1810 and 1811*

Year	Exports (francs)	Imports (francs)
1810	443,316	3,664,345
1811	2,025,487.39	—

Note: For 1811 imports, the value is not indicated in the inventory.
Source: "Bureau de commerce—Relevé général de tableau partiel fourni par le directeur des douanes—par sorti et entrée de cour des navires par l'étranger ou des continues françaises," [April 1810–1811], AD33 8M183.

The French customs records give values for imports and exports in 1810 and 1811, and at face value these numbers seem to provide a clear picture of how much was going out and coming into the port of Bordeaux during the years of greatest U.S.-French trade restrictions (Table 1).

In 1811, it appears as though there were no imports at all, which would corroborate claims that little trade occurred that year. However, there are two pieces of evidence to bear in mind: the first is a note that headed the figures, seemingly written by a civil servant upon transcribing the records of the customs director; the second is a sample of the included inventories. "It seems that the Director of Customs," begins the note, "only kept his records from the month of April 1810 to the current moment, among which there are many missing entries and some which signify that the ships had to note 'ballast' for their cargoes." This note implies an undervaluation of the 1810–1811 cargoes, then, because many ships were excluded from the

---

signer au lest pour le chargement. Voici les résultats récapitulatifs par exportations et importation, des années 1810 et 1811." An examination of U.S. newspapers reveals continued exchange between France and the United States during the disputed period. For example, the *Balance, & New-York State Journal*, Aug. 14, 1810, [3], reports: "The ship George Dyer, Collard, from Bordeaux, is in the Bay. She sailed from Bordeaux 8th June. Capt. Jacobs, of this port, passenger on board, came up in a pilot boat this morning; he reports that there was no change in the relations between that country and this." In the same paper on Aug. 6, 1811, 254: "The schooner Maria of and from New-York arrived with a cargo at Lateste, she has a French license. The schooner Matchless is bound from this port for New-York, and I am told has a French license." The *Observer* (New York), Jan. 27, 1811, 64, reported that "the schr. Maria-Louisa, capt. Skiddy, arrived here this morning from Bordeaux, in 26 days: sailed thence on the first of January. Accounts respecting our commerce with the French are rather favourable." A good overview of the impact of the embargoes and blockades of this period is Kevin H. O'Rourke, "War and Welfare: Britain, France, and the United States, 1807–14," *Oxford Economic Papers*, LIX (2007), 18–130. O'Rourke uses the price of goods traded rather than quantity of trade for his analysis.

total, and some cargoes were marked as worth nothing. An import inventory from February 10, 1811, for a ship flying U.S. colors—along with that of two other ships arriving the same day—records the following cargo contents were all assigned "0 value": "129 bales of cotton, 2000 hides, 14 tons Campeche wood, 10 blocks of mahogany, 4 bales of serpentine." One from May 11, 1811, for a ship with "American permit #13/6" lists: "208 cases of sugar, 79 bales of cotton, 40 cakes of indigo, 200 hides, 7 tons Campeche wood. 0 value." Another, from July 20, 1811, notes that the ship did not have an American permit but nonetheless brought in: "2050 hundredweight fresh codfish, 70 hundredweight dried codfish, 17 cases dried codfish, 61 barrels codfish tongues, 7.5 sester fish oil. Value not indicated." The contents of these three inventories undercut claims that there were no U.S. imports to France during 1810–1811. Similarly, examining what exactly was being traded on these ships—whether the *Fox*'s sugar and coffee, the chief products of enslaved labor, or the Caribbean-sourced mahogany, indigo, and Campeche wood listed here—turns the attention from arguments about violated neutrality agreements and toward the significance of the trade items themselves and the ways in which they were traded.[30]

As Stephen described, it was common practice in the beginning of the nineteenth century for ships to operate with flags, crew, and goods from various nations. Evading trade restrictions by registering ships under the colors of a neutral country was termed, in the case of U.S.-French trade, "neutralization." In Bordeaux, ships were most easily neutralized by foreign nationals or immigrant merchants who lived in the city. In late 1809, for example, John Archer Morton—who was originally from Baltimore but had moved to Bordeaux and founded the firm J. A. Morton (later Morton and Russell) there—requested and was granted a license from the French minister of the interior to sail the *Virginia*, then in Bordeaux, under American colors. There were many Americans in Bordeaux at the time (in 1807, Bordeaux merchant Honorat Lainé announced that "Americans were arriving in droves"), and they maintained quite a few merchant houses, some of

30. See "10 fev. 1811 importation," "11 Mai 1811 import," "20 juillet 1811 import," AD33 8M183. Serpentine powder is used for gunpowder. It is possible that this entry notes "serpentaire" (snakeroot, *Ageratina altissima*, a poisonous herb) instead. The case against the Spanish *Severn* in 1811 appeared, at first, ill-founded because the cargo seemed to be legitimate (Obadele-Starks, *Freebooters and Smugglers*, 23). Looking into newspapers advertising the ship's cargo as an "outfit for the slave trade" provided the court evidence of the *Severn*'s trafficking plans. There is no record for the *Severn* in *Voyages*.

which dated to the eighteenth century. Thus, even during the restrictive first decade of the nineteenth century, the U.S. presence in Bordeaux remained strong.[31]

The neutralizing merchant did not have to be American, however; merchants who had family or other business ties with a foreign agent could also apply to neutralize their vessels under the flags of other countries. In 1809, Bordeaux merchant Jean Ducornau applied for official licenses for two ships, one under the Prussian flag *(Le Courrier d'Elbing)* and the other under the American flag *(James Madison)*. Even French ships without any direct American connections were regularly neutralized under American colors. Indeed, for a time the American Consulate in Bordeaux handled requests for American papers directly, skirting the French bureaucracy altogether. In 1805, the U.S. consul in Bordeaux, William Lee, admitted that forty-two of the fifty-one ships sailing under American colors from Bordeaux since 1803 appeared to be French-owned.[32]

---

31. License No. 213, granted Dec. 26, 1809, AD33 8M185. This license was for the importation of 274,490 kilos of flour on Jan. 15, 1809, from the *Virginia* as requested by Morton in Ducornau's name (AD33 8M183). Morton also received a license to send the *Dispatch* from Philadelphia to Bordeaux (AD33 8M185). In November 1812, the *Powhatan*, which was owned by Morton and Russell, managed to bring goods worth 119,748 francs from Bordeaux to New York without the permission of the French authorities (Marzagalli, *"Les boulevards de la fraude,"* 286). Similarly, a ship owned by Justin Foussat of Philadelphia, *Le Petit Ray*, headed for his hometown in March 1813 laden with a cargo worth 239,923 francs, including wine, brandy, corks, antimony, verdigris, and—most intriguingly, and certainly in contravention of neutrality agreements—"trade rifles" (AD33 8M183, quoted in Marzagalli, *"Les boulevards de la fraude,"* 149). The largest merchant houses were: Skinner, Fenwick, and Brown; Jonathan Jones; Peters, Strobel, and Martini Company; Gray and Hoskins; and Morton and Russell (Silvia Marzagalli, *Bordeaux et les Etats-Unis, 1776–1815: Politique et stratégies négociantes dans la genèse d'un réseau commercial* [Geneva, 2015], 383–384). In 1803, Lainé recommended Bousquet's firm "Bousquet and Anthoine," which traded in Philadelphia and New York, for its "solvency and good judgment," as well as Jones, Foussat, John Gernon, and Hourquebie Brothers (quoted in Marzagalli, *Bordeaux et les Etats-Unis*, 253). For U.S.-France trade during the Napoleonic Wars, see François Crouzet, "Itinéraires atlantiques d'un capitaine marchand américain pendant les guerres 'napoléoniennes,'" in Marzagalli and Marnot, eds., *Guerre et économie dans l'espace atlantique*, 27–41; and Silvia Marzagalli, "The Failure of a Transatlantic Alliance? Franco-American Trade, 1783–1815," *History of European Ideas*, XXXIV (2008), 456–464.

32. "Licences et permis de navigation 1809–1814, Ministre de l'Intérieur," AD33 8M185; Marzagalli, *"Les boulevards de la fraude,"* 96. Marzagalli has compiled lists of French ships that were "neutralisé" with American names and papers from 1795 to 1805,

In addition, French vessels often docked at neutral ports and changed paperwork (called a "double" or "broken" voyage): that is, earlier records of the cargo's provenance and the ship's course were replaced by new records acquired at a neutral port, such as Charleston, South Carolina. Furthermore, itineraries were often kept deliberately loose or "open" to allow for stopovers in the United States (where French goods were presumably exchanged for capital) before attaining the declared destination. The following letter from January 1811 refers to the "open itinerary" for *La Mélanie*, which was financed by the Bordeaux merchants François Coudère, Schwartz, and Ferrière:

[We have just] come from Mauritius to Bordeaux with the attached leave granted by the Captain General of Mauritius and the cargo has been accepted without reservation.... we intend to leave for Mauritius or Batavia in the said ship, which will be loaded with 15 tons of wine and other supplies for use in the colonies; during the outward voyage, the ship is expected to stop in the United States of America to drop off the part of its cargo that consists of cloth from Paris and Lyon ... of 140,000 f. The return cargo will be entirely charged in Mauritius or Batavia and the ship will sail directly from there to a port in France.

Open itineraries such as the one planned for *La Mélanie* left plenty of room and time for unrecorded exchanges. Sometimes approximate or altogether false destinations would appear on the manifest in order to aid in later claims to trading rights under the rules of neutrality.[33]

---

along with the names of their "real owners," as well as U.S. ships that left Bordeaux from 1795 to 1807 claiming false destinations (Marzagalli, *Bordeaux et les Etats-Unis*, 495–496, 517–524). There are no records before 1795 or after the second part of 1805, and quite a few of the later entries are marked as "suspicious." Marzagalli's list of U.S. ships captured by British forces leaving from or going to Bordeaux from 1793 to 1812 includes fifty-three from 1803 to 1812, but there are none listed between Dec. 23, 1807, and Nov. 2, 1810 (ibid., 472–475). A comparison of these details with the archives of the British Admiralty may reveal more information about exactly what each of these ships was transporting across the Atlantic. For Franco-American politics under the Consulate from the point of view of the U.S. consuls in France, see Jolynda Brock Chenicek, "Dereliction of Diplomacy: The American Consulates in Paris and Bordeaux during the Napoleonic Era, 1804–1815" (Ph.D. diss., Florida State University, 2008).

33. "Licences et permis de navigation 1809-1814, Ministre de l'Interieur," AD33 8M185; Burton, "British Evangelicals," *Anglican and Episcopal History*, LXV (1996), 208. During this time, ships would often carry two copies of their papers, one for insur-

In addition, cargo was often shipped to intermediate locations until it could be reexported. When the vessel *Patty*, registered in New York, was captured on its way to Guadeloupe in 1805, for example, officials found merchandise aboard that had been imported into New York from France on six different ships. Despite what the manifests and customs records recorded, the nature of the merchandise reveals that the sugar plantations of the French colonies, not the United States, had always been the planned destination of the French goods. Thus, the prevalence of "colonial goods"—such as sugar, coffee, cotton, and indigo—exported from U.S. ports but really coming from the Caribbean attests to the ways in which merchants manipulated the usual circuits of trade. When Stephen feigned surprise at the exchange of lumber and food for sugar and coffee, he was remarking that the American tastes, more accustomed to molasses than sugar, were telling a truth that the ships' manifests did not.[34]

Partial evidence presents a particular problem in the age of quantitative humanities research. Information provided by *Voyages: The Trans-Atlantic Slave Trade Database*, a collaborative, international undertaking led by David Eltis and David Richardson, provides one example. This impressive open-source database, which consists of both published and unpublished data sets covering American, British, Dutch, French, Spanish, Brazilian, Cuban, and Portuguese sources, is robust, easy to use, and makes analyzing

---

ance and another in case of seizure. Some papers would be swapped out again during the course of the journey. In *War in Disguise*, Stephen writes that the double voyage "is now the only mode, of American neutralization in the colonial trade" (40, 42). For an example of a "double voyage" or "broken journey," see Marzagalli's account of the *Deucalion/Orion* in *Bordeaux et les Etats-Unis*, 328–329. A few records are available in *Voyages* from different sources: VID 14124, *Ducalion* (a[lias]) *Deucalion* (1803), and VID 33600, *Deucalion* (1803). Although the final negotiations of the Congress of Vienna in 1815 bound the French—along with Britain, Austria, Russia, and Prussia—to abolish the transatlantic slave trade, ships with French flags continued to depart for Africa. After the formal abolition of the French trade in 1818, it was the rhetoric rather than the traffic that changed, with captains stating that they were headed to the Pacific or Indian Oceans or that they were trading in Africa legitimately when they were not (Thomas, *Slave Trade*, 626). This practice of vague or misleading record keeping was usual beforehand as well, as the example of *La Mélanie* demonstrates. Coudère is occasionally "Couderc"; see Marzagalli, *"Les boulevards de la fraude,"* 292; *Almanach du commerce de Paris: des départements de l'Empire français et des principales villes du monde* (Paris, 1811), 632.

34. Marzagalli, *Bordeaux et les Etats-Unis*, 193, 219. Marzagalli estimates that, from 1800 to 1810, a quarter of the ships that arrived in Bordeaux with "colonial goods" or "American products" came from New York (ibid., 213).

the aggregated data of ship crossings and slave trading relatively effortless. A sample search in *Voyages* reveals that, between 1800 and 1815, 20 separate voyages were made by vessels sailing U.S. colors that were stopped by British cruisers under the suspicion of slave trading (by contrast, 513 U.S.-flagged ships were not captured during the same period, although only 20 of these sailed between 1808 and 1812). Ten of the seized voyages occurred between 1808 and 1812, of which 6 left from Charleston and 1 each left from Havana, New York, Bristol, R.I., and an undocumented U.S. port. Most were condemned by British vice-admiralty courts, either in the Bahamas, Antigua, or Sierra Leone. From the query's results, it seems that relatively few slaving voyages occurred during 1808–1812 (and about a third of these were foiled), implying overall that little slave trading occurred during this period. Such detailed results belie incomplete data sets, causing it to seem as though a record for every slave trading voyage exists and is accessible online. Yet even a tool as powerful as *Voyages* is limited by its sources: there is no record in the database for the *Saucy Jack*, for example, the "notorious little schooner" from Charleston that was boarded by a British vessel under suspicion of slaving in 1814, as noted in Du Bois's 1896 study. Nor do *Voyages*'s results account for the oversampling of ships that were caught versus ones that were not: that is, like the *Saucy Jack*, ships that traded illicitly but went undetected usually do not show up in the database. As a result, the limits posed by *Voyages*'s sources tend to distort the historical account.[35]

35. George Coggeshall, *History of the American Privateers, and Letters-of-Marque: During Our War with England in the Years 1812, '13, and '14 ...* (New York, 1856), 6–7; Du Bois, *Suppression*, 112, 290. Little was recorded about the *Saucy Jack*'s illicit activities, which perhaps accounts for its absence from the database. For an overview of the history of *Voyages*, see Per O. Hernaes, *Slaves, Danes, and the African Coast Society: The Danish Slave Trade from West Africa and Afro-Danish Relations on the Eighteenth-Century Gold Coast* (Trondheim, 1995), 129–171; and David Eltis and David Richardson, ed., *Extending the Frontiers: Essays on the New Transatlantic Slave Trade Database* (New Haven, Conn., 2008). By year, the ten records produced by *Voyages* for 1808–1812 are: 1808: *Washington*, Grant (VID 25517), *Africa*, Connelly (7632), *Baltimore*, Slocum (36927), *Tartar*, Taylor (7501); 1810: *Fortuna* (alias *William and Mary*), Trenholm and Verissimo (7683), *Lucia* (alias *Albert*), Wing (7585); 1811: *Atrevido* (alias *Carolina*), Leon (7686), *Hawke*, Taylor (7580), *Amelia* (alias *Agent*), Campbell (7659); 1812: *Hope*, Milbury (7667). In fact, all but the *Washington* and *Baltimore* were tried at the vice-admiralty court, although the *Africa* (1808) was only condemned on appeal. Despite meeting the criteria, the *Two Cousins* (1809) (VID 7542) is consistently omitted. The query is available at: http://www.slavevoyages.org/voyages/eU1sR3xK. Referring to British records such as those from the African Institution reveals at least three missing cases of condemned U.S. ships carry-

Newspaper archives as well as unexplored commercial and insurance records help supplement an aggregating tool such as *Voyages* and can help continue stories that had seemed concluded, such as that of the Charleston *Fox*. In late April 1807, *American, and Commercial Daily Advertiser* recorded that a brig *Fox* sailing from Kingston, Jamaica, to Philadelphia was captured by the British privateer *Driver* and taken to the vice-admiralty court in Halifax, Nova Scotia, for violating the Orders in Council. Although it is likely that this is the same brig and that it had possibly been returning to Charleston on a broken voyage, there is nothing in the record to hint that the *Fox* had previously been a slaving ship. The *United States' Gazette* merely notes that the "Fox was originally a merchantman, owned by a citizen of the United States." The brig was condemned in Halifax, but, when it came to Philadelphia on an impressment mission that July, it was retaken by Americans. These newspaper sources are not enough, however, to complete the record.[36]

Fox and Others

French records reveal that, in 1804 and 1805, a *Fox* captained by Drummond left Bordeaux. In 1805 and 1806, Captain Vincent sailed a *Fox* between Charleston and West Africa. In 1806, Captain Smith took the *Fox* back to Africa. In 1807, a *Fox* was seized near Charleston on its way from Jamaica and condemned at the British court in Halifax. It then sailed to Philadelphia where it was recaptured by Americans. In 1809, Captain Cullen tried to sail a *Fox* from Philadelphia to Bordeaux, but it was impounded by French authorities in Spain and held at Bayonne, where it was purchased by an agent working for Jean Bosquet of Bordeaux. At the same time, a *Fox* was captured by British privateers off the coast of France, which was condemned, sold, and sailed to New York in 1811. That year, Cullen returned

---

ing African captives: the *Esperanza* (1809), Porpoise (1811), and *Rambler* (1813) (*Sixth Report of the African Institution*, 43–46 *[Esperanza]*; *Eighth Report of the Directors of the African Institution* ... [London, 1814], 15, 68 *[Porpoise, Rambler]*). See also "Appendix 13: "A Return of All Ships or Vessels, Brought into Any Port in the Colonies of Great Britain, and Condemned Therein, under Any of the Acts for the Abolition of the Slave Trade" (July 25, 1814), *Journals of the House of Commons*, LXIX (1813–1814), 849–856; High Court of Admiralty: Prize Court: Papers, HCA 32, The National Archives, Kew, U.K.

36. "Marine Intelligence, New York, May 12," *American, and Commercial Daily Advertiser* (Baltimore), May 15, 1807, [3]; American Citizen, "The British Armed Brig Fox," *United States' Gazette* (Philadelphia), July 22, 1807, [3].

the *Fox* to Philadelphia from Bayonne. Another *Fox*, captained by Gooday and held at Plymouth, was sold in 1812 to a merchant with U.S. or French ties. A *Fox* left New York for Philadelphia on February 2, 1812; in late July a Captain Negus sailed another *Fox* from Philadelphia for Swedish Saint Bartholomew; and, in early September 1812, a *Fox* arrived in Baltimore from Charleston. By November 1812, a Philadelphia-registered *Fox* left New York for France, loaded with cotton, potash, and furs worth $14,000. It arrived, captained by Singleton, in Bordeaux in February 1813. On April 13, 1813, *le Fox*, financed by the Bordeaux firm Beizat and Jean and sailed by Captain Singleton, was granted an export permit to sail to Philadelphia with a charge of wine, brandy, "divers objects," steel, and prunes, worth a total of F 82,501. A note in its French record states that this brig had arrived with a "certificate of origin" denoting it as a truly—rather than just technically—American vessel. In 1820, records for a *Fox* connected to Bordeaux surfaced again: this time the brig was sponsored by Bordeaux merchant Ferrand and undertook a voyage from Le Havre to Bonny to Guadeloupe. There were 294 captive Africans aboard. Most likely, this *Fox* sailed between the United States and France multiple times before navigating to Bonny and Guadeloupe. Although there is no decisive paper trail, the proliferating records of *Foxes* plowing the Atlantic—some carrying enslaved captives, some carrying "colonial goods," some seized according to violations of neutrality and inflaming patriotic passions—establish that brigs, ships, and sloops traveled between the United States and France between 1806 and 1820, during the time of supposed nonactivity. The locations touched by the *Foxes*—Bristol, New York, Baltimore, Philadelphia, Charleston, San Sebastián, Bayonne, Bordeaux, Le Havre, Plymouth, Havana, Point-au-Pitre, and Bonny—illustrate the networks of locations and people involved with the ongoing slave trade.[37]

37. Marzagalli, *Bordeaux et les Etats-Unis*, 495, 509; *Voyages*, VID 25437, 25461, 34165; "Marine Intelligence," *American, and Commercial Daily Advertiser*, May 15, 1807, [3]; "Licences et permis de navigation 1809–1814, Ministre de l'Intérieur," AD33 8M185; "Smith to the Secretary of State," in Lowrie and St. Clair, eds., *American State Papers*, III, 422; "Federal Gazette Marine List," *Federal Gazette* (Baltimore), Feb. 8, 1812, [3]; "Fresh Rice," ibid., Sept. 8, 1812, [1]; "From Our Correspondent, Philadelphia, Feb. 27," reprinted in *City Gazette* (Charleston), Mar. 10, 1813, [3]; "Licences exportateurs fév. 1812–fév. 1814," AD33 8M183; Williams, *French Assault*, 149. Although Drummond's *Fox* had been captured in 1806, in 1808 the *Alexandria Daily Advertiser* advertised goods available from "the brig Fox, capt. DRUMMOND, from Liverpool" ("Salt Afloat," Apr. 14, 1808, [1]). There are High Court of Admiralty Prize Court records for the ships *Fox* cap-

But, to return to the first *Fox*, the one condemned by Napoleon's order in 1809, the one whose history has belonged until now to the war of 1812 alone: that *Fox*'s original owner, Abraham Piesch of Philadelphia, was a "prominent shipping merchant," active in the "carrying trade" during the end of the eighteenth and beginning of the nineteenth century. In a tone characteristic of nineteenth-century profiles of patriot-capitalists, the *History of Philadelphia, 1609–1884* (1884) describes Piesch as a man who "braved the savage blacks of San Domingo in 1792–93, and in the midst of insurrection and civil war reaped the reward of his pluck and courage in a profit on coffee purchased at five cents per pound.... during the war of 1812–15 he had twelve schooners engaged in running the blockade." Piesch and another Philadelphia investor, John Du Barry, had been awarded damages for their confiscated ship and goods in the 1820s; but it was not until 1846 that the last indemnity claims for the 1809 seizure of the *Fox* and its cargo were finally settled in the Supreme Court of Pennsylvania. The evidence for the case revealed that articles aboard the *Fox*, which had sailed from Philadelphia for San Sebastián under Captain Thomas Cullen with John Ribaut as supercargo, were originally owned by a French-born Philadelphian, Adrian Lestapies, possibly of the Bordeaux firm Lestapies and Cie. An invoice signed by Anthony Laussat on October 10, 1809, indicated that the cargo included 130 bags of coffee (property of Lestapies and destined for Bordeaux merchant Justin W. Foussat) and 100 boxes of "white Havana sugar." Ultimately, the case hinged on the issues of Andrian Lestapies's identity and nationality. When questioned whether Lestapies was the same as one "J.G. Villanueva," a Peter Bosquet of Philadelphia testified in the affirmative. Eventually, the

---

tained by Drummond (1806), Goodday (1811), and Singleton (1813) as well another from 1809 and two from 1810 at the National Archives, Kew: see HCA 32/1434/1929 (Drummond), HCA 32/1742/285 (Goodday), HCA 32/1299/1429 (Singleton), HCA 32/1835, part 2, HCA 32/1456/2302 (Hamilton), HCA 32/1456/2303 (Porter). Most, although not all, of these ships were brigs. There is also a record of Negus's brig *Fox* planning to leave Philadelphia for Batavia on Sept. 23, 1812, and it is quite possible that the same *Fox* left Saint Bartholomew, proceeded to Philadelphia, and continued to a port in Africa instead of (or in addition to) going to Batavia, returning to France for naturalization on the way back to the American market ("Federal Gazette Marine List," *Federal Gazette*, July 31, 1812 [3]). The *Fox*'s papers, which stated that it was registered in Philadelphia and granted leave to sail to France in November 1812, were signed by James Madison and James Monroe; these papers were put up for auction in 2006; see "25036: Madison and Monroe Signed 1812 Ship's Papers," Nov. 20, 1812, *Heritage American Grand Format Auction Catalogue #629* (Dallas, Tex., 2006), 19.

court found that Lestapies had no grounds for the suit, because he was a French rather than a U.S. citizen, and therefore had no right to trade as a neutral in 1809.[38]

Thanks to the 1811 letter from Bosquet as well as the court and insurance records, it is finally possible to trace a connection between one set of the American and French *Fox* vessels. The 1811 letter supplies the missing context—the "particular circumstances"—for how the U.S. *Fox* came into French hands, and the court and insurance records fill in the gaps about what was being traded and by whom; understanding the networks of "neutralization" and the "trade in disguise" shows the way it all worked. At the very least, this *Fox* is a record of the vast political and commercial conflicts of the era; at most, it holds the connection between neutral trading and slave trading and brings together the histories of the War of 1812 and the Atlantic slave trade.

Conclusion

The rights of neutrality and search and seizure remained important issues throughout the first half of the nineteenth century; indeed, the United States did not sign a treaty guaranteeing the right of "mutual search" with the United Kingdom until 1862. An article in the *New York Times* for that year notes that, owing to the new treaty, the Atlantic slave trade had been dealt a "severe blow":

> Previous to the present Administration, that [U.S.] flag was the chosen shelter and shield of all slavers, because we would permit no searches under it. Year after year we exhibited to Christendom the amusing inconsistency of maintaining what we called the inviolability of our flag against interference by our national co-equals, and yet, by this very act, occasioning it to be violated, every day of the year, by men whom our own laws declared pirates—disallowing, as an insult and an injury, a foreign naval officer to step under it on an errand of humanity, and yet inviting the thousand-fold greater insult and injury of a foreign Slave-trader systematically driving under it the most inhuman of all earthly work.

The example of the French and U.S. *Foxes*, crisscrossing the oceans during a period of heightened neutrality disputes, shows just how connected the

---

38. J. Thomas Scharf and Thompson Westcott, *History of Philadelphia, 1609-1884*, 3 vols. (Philadelphia, 1884), III, 2212; Williams, *French Assault*, 149; Lestapies v. Ingraham, in Barr, *Pennsylvania State Reports*, V, 71-82.

issues of the War of 1812 were to those of the Atlantic slave trade and its eventual abolition. Nonetheless, conventional accounts of the lead-up to the war as well as discussions of the war itself have tended to miss or misunderstand this connection. Indeed, one of the gaps in historical thinking about the War of 1812 occurs in the connection of the period's oft-mentioned commerce in the "West India trade" or "African trade" with the trade in people. Much of these misunderstandings are owing to the limitations of the archive, for, similar to the way in which records of U.S. slave trading interests from 1794 to 1803 and after 1808 are nonexistent, inaccessible, or at least inscrutable, the systems of U.S.-French cooperation—so important to evading enemy ships and fooling naval authorities—also effectively limited the kinds of historical evidence that can be accumulated from the period. Moreover, certain conceptual changes, such as the transition from "merchant" to "pirate," hide a longer history of trade than is usually noted and expose arguments about the "inviolability of our flag" and "free ships make free goods" as mainly serving to protect the interests of a transnational network of traders after 1807 no matter what—or whom—they were trading. Like Douglass's speech, the evidence presented here exposes the falsehood that slave trading was ever truly conceived as "piracy," and it questions casting the issue of the "inviolability of our flag" as one of patriotism, thereby obfuscating the human costs.[39]

The incomplete empirical data provided here, showing the ways in which Atlantic trade continued during the first years of the nineteenth century despite wartime restrictions, traces only the outline of other data sets that could appear but do not: documentation of U.S.-sponsored slaving voyages carried out under the U.S. and French flags during 1804–1815; records of discontent in business communities owing to British seizures and condemnations of supposed slaving ventures; cases in which people were adjudicated as goods in the prize courts. Records such as these have not yet come to light and, if they ever existed, may still never do so. But the data from Bordeaux reveal the need to reexamine the patriotic corsair-chasing and blockade-running naval lore that has preoccupied the traditional studies of the War of 1812 and highlight the limitations of a historiography that relies too heavily on the material evidence that has survived. Consistently, slavery and the slave trade, as well as the capital gained from the chattel slavery system, the commercial networks supported by it, and the diplomatic relations

---

39. "Sentence of Another Slave-Trader," *New-York Times*, Nov. 17, 1862, [4]. The Lyons-Seward Treaty was concluded on Apr. 7, 1862, and proclaimed June 7, 1862.

that it influenced, have been omitted from analyses of the era. Historians must examine why questions of race and representation are seldom asked in the military and diplomatic histories of 1812 and consider the ways in which material evidence—or its lack—may collude with narratives of patriotism, trade, and "freedom of the seas."

THE RADICALISM OF THE FIRST
SEMINOLE WAR AND ITS CONSEQUENCES

Nathaniel Millett

Most historians of the First Seminole War recognize that the conflict was racialized in that it pitted the United States' armed forces against blacks and Indians, was connected to American territorial expansion, and was—to varying degrees—related to the Patriot War, Creek War, and War of 1812 in the Southeast. The Spanish Empire's inability to control the Floridas, filibusters, or meddling by the British also appear in many discussions of the conflict. Likewise, most treatments of the 1821 acquisition of Florida by the United States stress land greed, the early stirrings of Manifest Destiny, and a strong southern lobby as decisive factors in the American acquisition of the beleaguered Spanish colonies. In such studies, the First Seminole War is considered one of many influences in the transfer of the Floridas, but not a pivotal one.[1]

There are elements of truth in each of these interpretations; however, the

---

1. For the sake of clarification, I will refer to the conflict as the "First Seminole War," even though it would not have been known as such until the Second Seminole War (1835-1842). For the First Seminole War, see William S. Belko, ed., *America's Hundred Years' War: U.S. Expansion to the Gulf Coast and the Fate of the Seminole, 1763-1858* (Gainesville, Fla., 2011); James W. Covington, *The Seminoles of Florida* (Gainesville, Fla., 1993); David S. Hiedler and Jeanne T. Hiedler, *Old Hickory's War: Andrew Jackson and the Quest for Empire* (Mechanicsburg, Pa., 1996); Frank Lawrence Owsley, Jr., and Gene A. Smith, *Filibusters and Expansionists: Jeffersonian Manifest Destiny, 1800-1821* (Tuscaloosa, Ala., 1997); Robert V. Remini, *Andrew Jackson and His Indian Wars* (New York, 2002); J. Leitch Wright, Jr., *Creeks and Seminoles: The Destruction and Regeneration of the Muscogulge People* (Lincoln, Nebr., 1986). On American territorial expansion, see Philip Coolidge Brooks, *Diplomacy and the Borderlands: The Adams-Onis Treaty of 1819* (Berkeley, Calif., 1939); Hubert Bruce Fuller, *The Purchase of Florida: Its History and Diplomacy* (Gainesville, Fla., 1964); Paul E. Hoffman, *Florida's Frontiers* (Bloomington, Ind., 2002); Robert V. Remini, *Andrew Jackson and the Course of American Empire, 1767-1821* (New York, 1977); J. C. A. Stagg, *Borderlines in Borderlands: James Madison and the Spanish-American Frontier, 1776-1821* (New Haven, Conn., 2009); David J. Weber, *The Spanish Frontier in North America* (New Haven, Conn., 1992); William Earl Weeks, *John Quincy Adams and American Global Empire* (Lexington, Ky., 1992).

real story of the First Seminole War's origins, course, and impact lies in two intertwined strands. First, the conflict was shaped greatly by the actions of a handful of individuals; the most visible of these was Edward Nicolls, a Royal Marine who was a radical antislavery advocate. Nicolls arrived in Florida as a veteran of the revolutionary struggles in Santo Domingo and provided many blacks and Indians in the Southeast with a living link to the tactics and perspectives of contemporary black revolutionaries in the Caribbean. Second, hundreds of slaves and thousands of Seminoles and Red Sticks took advantage of Nicolls's intellectual, political, and material offerings to further their individual and group agendas of freedom and the protection of territorial and cultural sovereignty.

These two strands became interwoven during the War of 1812, when Nicolls led a British expedition to the Southeast to raise and train an army of American slaves as well as Red Sticks and Seminoles. First from Pensacola and then from Prospect Bluff (on the banks of the Apalachicola River, approximately thirty miles from the Gulf of Mexico), Nicolls recruited and trained hundreds of former slaves from across the Southeast and thousands of Red Sticks and Seminoles between August 1814 and May 1815. Contrary to his orders, and much to the consternation of his superiors, Nicolls came to conceptualize his mission to the Southeast as both an antislavery experiment and an opportunity to defend the rights of the Red Sticks and Seminoles. His black and Indian allies' embrace of this message, combined with both groups' ideas about freedom, sovereignty, inclusion, and geopolitics, presented a formidable challenge to the expanding American plantation complex in the Southeast. As a result, the participants in Nicolls's antislavery machinations and his Indian allies were key to the outbreak and course of the First Seminole War, both as trained, armed, and radicalized combatants and as the primary target of the American and Creek war effort. To many white and Indian observers, the actions of Nicolls and his allies represented the culmination of more than a century of racialized, cross-border tensions that had become too great of a threat to be tolerated anymore. In a word, these actions were the final event that convinced most white southerners the Floridas must be annexed as a matter of national security.[2]

A reexamination of the First Seminole War must begin with a close analysis of Nicolls's antislavery beliefs. His unusual convictions (that blacks were

---

2. None of these assertions are designed to undermine the agency of the black and Indian participants in the conflict. Nor, as this essay explores, is such an analysis of the First Seminole War overly linear or simplistic.

fully human and capable of equality with whites, and slavery was an evil institution that could legitimately be destroyed through violence) explain his actions during the War of 1812 and were central in shaping the thoughts and identity of his black recruits well into the nineteenth century. In turn, this antislavery radicalism greatly affected the nature and outcome of the First Seminole War.

The roots of Nicolls's principles lay in his upbringing and ethnic identity as an Ulster Protestant during the Age of Revolution. The eldest of six sons (the rest of whom died serving in the British military), he was born in Coleraine, in the north of Ireland, in 1779. During the late eighteenth century, Ireland was marked by deep-seated sectarian tensions as well as concerns that arose from oppressive British rule. Even successful Ulster Protestants, who enjoyed the benefits of Great Britain's immense international success, realized that they were peripheral figures in an empire that was English at its core.[3]

Nicolls's family was of the middling rank (his father was the surveyor of excise in Coleraine), with extensive ties to the British military. In a world where religious practices carried tremendous weight, young Edward received an intense religious upbringing. His mother, whose father was the rector of Coleraine, converted from Presbyterianism to Methodism before Edward's birth. After leaving home, Nicolls returned to Presbyterianism and remained devout throughout his life. Regardless of these shifts, he spent his life as a staunch Ulster Protestant, a religious outlook that informed the unbending morality that he brought to every facet of his existence. This personal standard was framed in absolute terms, and Nicolls attached himself to causes with both passion and violence.[4]

At the age of eleven, Nicolls enlisted in the Royal Navy, and in 1795, at the age of sixteen, he was commissioned as a second lieutenant in the Royal Marines. The 1790s were a turbulent time for a young man from the north of Ireland to begin his long military career. The Age of Revolution was enter-

---

3. See Jonathan Bardon, *A History of Ulster* (Belfast, 2005); Michael Hechter, *Internal Colonialism: The Celtic Fringe in British National Development, 1536–1966* (Berkeley, Calif., 1975); Kevin Kenny, ed., *Ireland and the British Empire* (Oxford, 2004).

4. E. B. Laird, "All I Know of My Mother's Forbears," July 11, 1906, MS, Arch 11/13/132, 20, Royal Marine Museum, Portsmouth, U.K. See David Hempton and Myrtle Hill, *Evangelical Protestantism in Ulster Society, 1740–1890* (London, 1992), for the religious context. Andrew R. Holmes, *The Shaping of Ulster Presbyterian Belief and Practice, 1770–1840* (Oxford, 2006), is a good overview of Ulster Presbyterianism and its effects on the society and culture of Northern Ireland.

ing its most intense stage, with Britain and France locked in an international war on which the survival of both nations appeared to rest and the Haitian Revolution sending shockwaves across the globe.[5]

This era of substantial intellectual, political, and social change forced many people to reconsider ideas about political power, inclusion, race, the state, economics, and social justice. Out of this climate emerged a series of organized movements to abolish the slave trade and, in some cases, slavery itself. Nicolls, with his unyielding morality, was quickly drawn to the idea of racial egalitarianism and the belief that slavery needed to be destroyed by any means.[6] Nicolls's outlook was further shaped by the fact that the British Empire was rapidly and self-consciously altering many of its ideological foundations as it was forced to reconfigure itself after American independence and in relation to the threat of the French Revolution. Britons were coming to see themselves as inhabiting an empire of liberty and liberalism that defended the rights of the citizens of the world against French

---

5. See Richard Brooks, *The Royal Marines: A History* (Annapolis, Md., 2002), for an introduction to the history of the Royal Marines. Nicolls's formal education was scanty and consisted of two years of schooling in Greenwich. The age of Nicolls's enlistment was unremarkable, but it is important to consider the brutality of the world he entered into as a mere boy. Corporal punishment, self-sacrifice, and rigid discipline under extreme conditions defined his military life. For good treatments of the Age of Revolution, see David Armitage and Sanjay Subrahmanyam, eds., *The Age of Revolution in Global Context, c. 1760–1840* (Basingstoke, U.K., 2010); E. J. Hobsbawm, *The Age of Revolution, 1789–1848* (Cleveland, 1962); Wim Klooster, *Revolutions in the Atlantic World: A Comparative History* (New York, 2009); Lester D. Langley, *The Americas in the Age of Revolution, 1750–1850* (New Haven, Conn., 1996); R. R. Palmer, *The Age of the Democratic Revolution: A Political History of Europe and America, 1760–1800*, 2 vols. (Princeton, N.J., 1959–1964); Simon Schama, *Citizens: A Chronicle of the French Revolution* (New York, 1989). In 1795, as young Nicolls began his career, the British Caribbean was burning in a series of racialized rebellions while thousands of British soldiers were bogged down in the horrors of the Haitian Revolution.

6. See Robin Blackburn, *The Overthrow of Colonial Slavery, 1776–1848* (London, 1988); Christopher Leslie Brown, *Moral Capital: Foundations of British Abolitionism* (Chapel Hill, N.C., 2006); David Brion Davis, *The Problem of Slavery in Western Culture* (Ithaca, N.Y., 1967); Davis, *The Problem of Slavery in the Age of Revolution, 1770–1823* (Ithaca, N.Y., 1975); Seymour Drescher, *Capitalism and Antislavery: British Mobilization in Comparative Perspective* (New York, 1987); Drescher, *Econocide: British Slavery in the Era of Abolition* (Pittsburgh, 1977); David Eltis, *Economic Growth and the Ending of the Transatlantic Slave Trade* (Oxford, 1987); Adam Hochschild, *Bury the Chains: Prophets and Rebels in the Fight to Free an Empire's Slaves* (Boston, 2005); Suzanne Miers, *Britain and the Ending of the Slave Trade* (New York, 1975).

aggression. Ultimately, Nicolls embraced an extreme version of empire and antislavery that diverged from more mainstream tendencies by combining activism and violent action.[7]

The seeds of Nicolls's antislavery thought began to blossom when he first directly encountered Africans and slavery in the midst of one of the most dramatic epochs in western history. This occurred when the Ulsterman gained much of his earliest combat experience in the revolutionary Caribbean. In 1803, he distinguished himself at Santo Domingo, and, in 1804, he led a successful siege of Curaçao. Nicolls intimately witnessed the collapse of slavery in Hispaniola and the reverberations across the region that were marked by chaos, black armies, and the general sense that order had broken down under racial and imperial pressures. For a moralistic twenty-four-year-old imperial outsider from Coleraine, this was an extraordinary firsthand introduction to slavery and antislavery (importantly, in the form of violent black liberation). His own background, when combined with such experiences and the broader intellectual and political climate of the day, led Nicolls to reflect on questions of race, political inclusion, military service, religion, and empire.[8]

Few people would have had a more profound or emotional understanding of what the British Empire represented, ideologically and practically, than Edward Nicolls at the end of the Napoleonic Wars. After his service in the Caribbean, Nicolls continued to distinguish himself, this time in the Middle East and Europe. By 1814, Nicolls had devoted nearly twenty years—or what amounted to *all* of his adult life—to fighting in extreme conditions on three

---

7. Brown, *Moral Capital.*

8. Nicolls's obituary contains lengthy accounts of every engagement he was involved in, including his service in the Caribbean (*Gentleman's Magazine and Historical Review,* n.s., XLIII [1865], 644–646). The best overviews of the British military's experience in the Caribbean during this period are Roger Norman Buckley, *The British Army in the West Indies: Society and the Military in the Revolutionary Age* (Gainesville, Fla., 1998); Michael Duffy, *Soldiers, Sugar, and Seapower: The British Expeditions to the West Indies and the War against Revolutionary France* (Oxford, 1987). The thoughts and actions of Nicolls and his black allies is reminiscent of discussions and debates about "Black Jacobins" and the Haitian Revolution. See C. L. R. James, *The Black Jacobins: Toussaint Louverture and the San Domingo Revolution* (London, 1938); Laurent Dubois, *Avengers of the New World: The Story of the Haitian Revolution* (Cambridge, Mass., 2004); David Patrick Geggus, "The Haitian Revolution," in Geggus, ed., *Haitian Revolutionary Studies* (Bloomington, Ind., 2002), 1–29; John K. Thornton, "'I Am the Subject of the King of Congo': African Ideology and the Haitian Revolution," *Journal of World History,* IV (1993), 181–214.

different continents in defense of the British Empire. By this point, Nicolls had become a member of the Philanthropic Society, where he would have discussed such topics while becoming increasingly involved with the antislavery movement.[9]

To numerous white onlookers, many of Nicolls's actions across his long career appeared to be the work of a reckless fanatic. It is safe to say that Nicolls was a radical opponent of slavery whose efforts to ideologically, intellectually, and physically destroy the institution across the Atlantic world had few equals. This antislavery ideology is succinctly captured in an 1841 letter to the editor of the *Times* that Nicolls wrote after the rebellion of the slaves aboard the *Creole*. Importantly, Nicolls began the letter by noting that he had developed these ideas by the time of his mission to the Southeast. Nicolls then recounted an incident at Fernando Pó when hundreds of Portuguese slaves, including a number belonging to the Portuguese governor's wife, escaped to British protection from nearby Prince's Island. When the governor asked for the slaves to be returned, Nicolls responded, "I knew of no such disgrace as that of having a slave under the British flag, that all persons in [Fernando Pó] were free, and must be so whilst they obeyed the law." When pressed more aggressively for the return of the slaves, Nicolls answered in kind: "It was more than my commission was worth, as a British officer, or my character as a magistrate, or a friend of Africa, to be guilty of so infamous an act as that of depriving a fellow-creature of his liberty." In the midst of this standoff, much to Nicolls's delight, word spread among the slaves on Prince's Island and Saint Thomas that freedom could be found with the British on Fernando Pó. Hundreds of slaves fled, which ignited an already combustible situation. The furious Portuguese governor accused Nicolls of encouraging slaves to flee and harboring "murderers and ... stolen goods," and he vowed to report Nicolls to the British government in what threatened to be a serious diplomatic incident. Far from deterred, Nicolls boasted, "It would be contrary to British law to give up a slave under any circumstances, particularly such as that of killing any one during a scuffle to

---

9. Vicente Sebastián Pintado to José de Soto, Apr. 29, 1815, Vicente Sebastián Pintado Papers, box 3, folder 1, Library of Congress, Washington, D.C. From 1829 to 1834, Nicolls served as the governor of Fernando Pó, which placed him in charge of British efforts to eradicate the lingering Atlantic slave trade and to resettle the trade's victims in Sierra Leone. Upon retirement from the Royal Marines in 1835, Nicolls became a full-time antislavery advocate who was a prominent and active member of the most important antislavery societies of the day. This included being a founding member of the hugely influential British and Foreign Anti-Slavery Society.

obtain his liberty, which the law of God and England justified, and nobly acknowledged to be the right of all mankind; that such killing was no murder." The governor's shock deepened when Nicolls claimed that "it was my duty as a Christian man and a governor to discourage crime of every description ... [but it was] a gross and unmerited insult, by even supposing or hinting that a British officer could possibly descend to become a slave-driver to a slave-dealer." The governor never pursued the matter with either the British or Portuguese governments.[10]

The second half of the letter elaborated on these ideas in relation to the *Creole*. Nicolls conveyed his hatred of slavery as an affront to his Christian faith, his conviction that slavery could not be reconciled with his understanding of the British Empire and the modern world, his belief that Africans were fully human, and his acceptance of violence as an entirely appropriate means with which to combat the institution. In other words, this letter captured Nicolls's radicalism.

Beginning with Nicolls's arrival in West Florida in August 1814, his antislavery stance affected the Southeast in a process that would last for years. Upon Nicolls's arrival, he and a detachment of Royal Marines entered Pensacola with permission from the Spanish governor before taking control of the city. From Pensacola, the British were successful in raising and training an army of hundreds of former slaves (many of whom were from the city and happily left their masters) and Indians. The very public situation created tremendous anxiety across the Southeast, as it challenged racial order throughout the region. As a result, in early November, Andrew Jackson led a large white and Creek assault on Pensacola that forced the British to flee to Prospect Bluff. Here, the British built a large and imposing fort above the Apalachicola River while continuing to recruit and train former slaves and Indians. This force launched a series of distracting raids across the Deep South in support of the larger British assault on New Orleans.[11]

The formal end of the War of 1812 in February 1815 did little to stem the activity of Nicolls and his black and Indian allies. During the winter and spring, Nicolls and George Woodbine (Nicolls's second-in-command, who energetically participated in this radical antislavery experiment) continued in what they perceived as their mission as hundreds of blacks and Indians

---

10. Edward Nicolls, "The Creole: To the Editor of the Times," *Times*, Feb. 16, 1842, [7].

11. For the British occupation of Pensacola, see Nathaniel Millett, "Britain's 1814 Occupation of Pensacola and America's Response: An Episode of the War of 1812 in the Southeastern Borderlands," *Florida Historical Quarterly*, LXXXIV (2005), 229–255.

joined them at Prospect Bluff. During this period, British officials in North America encouraged the Red Sticks to endorse the Treaty of Ghent, which formally concluded the War of 1812. The officials took this approach because of the inclusion of Article IX, which called for the restoration of Indian lands to their 1811 boundaries. (The Creek War of 1813–1814, concluded by the Treaty of Fort Jackson, had forced both the Creeks and Red Sticks to cede twenty million acres of land to the United States.) Accordingly, Alexander Cochrane, the commander of the North American Station, instructed Nicolls to "tell our Indian Allies that they have been included [in the treaty] and that they are placed as to territory as they were in 1811 if the peace shall not be ratified, you will have a large reinforcement sent to you at Apalachicola." The British saw the continued presence of Nicolls and his army in the Floridas as an important bargaining chip as well as a powerful contingency plan should the treaty negotiations fail.[12]

In early March, when it had become clear that the Treaty of Ghent would soon be ratified, Nicolls received a series of clearly worded orders concerning his pending evacuation from the Southeast to the British West Indies. The British valued their commitments to their Native American allies as much as they feared an American-controlled Florida; however, when American officials and citizens ignored Article IX and failed to return the Indians' land to them, the British were not prepared to risk more bloodshed and decided to arm heavily and supply their Native and black allies in the hope that they could, at least, fend off the encroachments of the United States and keep the Floridas in Spanish hands. The British also made it clear that they

---

12. Alexander Cochrane to Edward Nicolls, Feb. 18, 1815, *Tonnant* off Mobile Bay, Cochrane Papers, MS 2348, reel 5, 277, P. K. Yonge Library of Florida History (hereafter cited as PKY). In 1813, a civil war began within the Creek Nation in the Deep South. At the heart of the civil war were growing economic, cultural, political, ethnic/racial, and power issues as well as the pan-Indian prophetic movement of Tecumseh that tore at Creek society. The conflict pitted the dissident Red Stick faction, who had taken up Tecumseh's call, against the more wealthy and accommodationist leadership of the Creeks, who were allied with the United States in an effort to protect their interests. The Creeks were unwavering in their hostility to the British and their black and Indian allies through the conclusion of the First Seminole War. See Joel W. Martin, *Sacred Revolt: The Muskogees' Struggle for a New World* (Boston, 1991); Gregory Evans Dowd, *A Spirited Resistance: The North American Indian Struggle for Unity, 1745–1815* (Baltimore, 1992); Claudio Saunt, *A New Order of Things: Property, Power, and the Transformation of the Creek Indians, 1733–1816* (Cambridge, 1999); Kathryn E. Holland Braund, *Deerskins and Duffels: The Creek Indian Trade with Anglo-America, 1685–1815* (Lincoln, Nebr., 1993).

intended to continue their formal economic alliances with the Indians from the Caribbean, combined with a subtler and less official political alliance.[13]

The Seminoles and Red Sticks were far from content with these decisions. Nicolls shared the Indians' frustration. In a choice that was to have long-lasting repercussions, Nicolls took it upon himself to see the Seminoles and Red Sticks righted. The Indians embraced Nicolls's help because they understood acutely that a continued alliance with the British offered distinct, if not essential, material, military, and political advantages in their struggle against the United States and the Creeks. Since his arrival in North America, Nicolls "disgusted all the army as well as the navy" with his willingness to ignore orders and make bold decisions in the field that circumvented the chain of command. By the winter and spring of 1815, however, it had become clear that Nicolls was now waging an unsanctioned war alongside the Red Sticks and Seminoles against the United States that the British foreign secretary, Lord Bathurst, was "altogether unacquainted" with. The most pressing issue was that Nicolls, long after British officials had conceded the point to the Americans, aggressively defended the Red Stick position that the Treaty of Fort Jackson was null and void because it predated the Treaty of Ghent, and only a handful of Creek leaders allied to the United States had signed it. According to Nicolls, the Creeks lacked any authority to sign a treaty on behalf of the Red Sticks, who were their mortal enemies. To the ire of the United States and their Creek allies, Nicolls recognized the militant Red Sticks Hepoeth Micco, Cappachimico, and Hopoy Micco (whom he collectively referred to as the "Chiefs of the Muscogee nation") as the supreme leaders of the Creeks. U.S. leaders insisted that none of the three chiefs Nicolls recognized "has ever attended the national councils of the Creeks, or is in any way a part of their Executive Government," and that one was a Seminole.[14]

Soon, Nicolls and his Indian allies took an even more drastic step that provoked anger on both sides of the Atlantic. On behalf of Great Britain, Ni-

---

13. Pulteney Malcolm to Nicolls, Mar. 5, 1815, *Royal Oak* off Mobile Bay, MAL/106, 169, Pulteney Malcolm Papers, National Maritime Museum, Greenwich, U.K. (hereafter cited as NMM).

14. Edward Codrington's diary, Jan. 13, 1815, Headquarters near New Orleans, Codrington Papers, Cod/7/13, NMM; Henry Bunbury to John Barrow, Sept. 7, 1815, Downing Street, FO 5/140, National Archives, Kew, U.K. (hereafter cited as NA); Benjamin Hawkins to Nicolls, May 24, 1815, Creek Agency, Papers of Panton, Leslie, and Company, Dec. 17, 1814, through Oct. 30, 1816, microfilm, reel 20, University of West Florida, Pensacola.

colls signed an "offensive and defensive ... [treaty of] alliance ... as well as one of commerce and navigation" with the Red Sticks and Seminoles. Even though official British policy was merely to encourage an economic alliance with the Red Sticks and Seminoles, and Nicolls had no authority to create such a treaty on behalf of his government, he believed that it would be ratified. The United States strenuously objected to this and accused Nicolls of negotiating a farcical treaty with the "Creek nation ... [based solely on] the authority created by yourself for the purpose, [which] must be a novelty."[15]

The Red Sticks and Seminoles, meanwhile, celebrated Nicolls's message and believed that they had gained the long-term allegiance of the world's foremost military power. This perception factored significantly into the Indians' political and military calculations in coming years. The Indians felt "assured ... that, according to the treaty of Ghent, all the lands ceded by the Creeks, in treaty with General Jackson, were to be restored; otherwise, the Indians must fight for those lands, and that the British would in a short time assist them." The Red Sticks and Seminoles believed so thoroughly in the treaty of Ghent and Nicolls's other promises that, years later, they petitioned British officials in the Bahamas for aid against the United States because "we consider ourselves allies of Great Britain entitled to the full benefit of that ... when the British evacuated the Floridas ... we were *expressly informed so* by ... Nicolls." The Indians were equally convinced that Nicolls would return to Florida to make sure that they were treated fairly. Edmund Gaines believed, "So industriously have these impressions been circulated by the British and Spanish agents among the Indians, that, so far as I can learn, not only the chiefs, but the common warriors, are in the habit of saying that the British treaty with the Americans gives the Indians their lands taken by the treaty with General Jackson." If this failed, "a war must ensue; and ... their friends, the British, will re-establish them in the possession of these lands." The Indians' faith in Nicolls's promises and their conviction in the illegality of the Treaty of Fort Jackson shaped their decision to enter into the First Seminole War and strongly influenced their choices during the conflict.[16]

15. Nicolls to Hawkins, May 12, 1815, FO 5/107, NA. A copy of the treaty does not exist, nor did Nicolls list the signatories. It is highly likely that the signatories included the "Chiefs of the Muscogee nation." See Hawkins to Nicolls, May 28, 1815, Creek Agency, in C. L. Grant, ed., *Letters, Journals, and Writings of Benjamin Hawkins*, II, *1802–1816* (Savannah, Ga., 1980), 732–734.

16. Deposition of Samuel Jervais, May 9, 1815, Mobile, Papers of Panton, Leslie, and Company, reel 20; Petition of Cappachimico, McQueen, Emathlela Hadjo, Taitachy, Holochapco, Bowlick, and Micocpah, Nov. 8, 1816, in Alexander Arbuthnot to Charles

The coordinated actions between Nicolls and his black allies during these months—even bolder and more far-reaching than those undertaken with his Indian allies—are best regarded as part of an elaborate antislavery plan that resulted in one of the most remarkable maroon communities in Atlantic history: the so-called Negro Fort. The net result was hundreds of radicalized former slaves who regarded themselves as British subjects and were, beyond any other factor, the primary cause of the First Seminole War. The first step in the antislavery plan centered on ensuring that the black recruits were not returned to their masters. This was easy when the former slaves fled from the United States or its allies, since Nicolls's orders were to recruit exactly such people. In other cases, Nicolls lied about the origins of his recruits. Most often, he pretended he had been tricked into believing that many of the Spanish slaves were from the United States. When not outright lying, Nicolls could be highly technical in defending the origins of his recruits. In October 1814, when Governor Mateo González Manrique accused Nicolls of recruiting two slaves belonging to a Spanish subject, Nicolls maintained "that they were ... Property of an American Magistrate taken out of the Territory of the U.S., and *that my orders being to take all such men into our service, they must remain so.*" Nicolls justified his recruitment of Creek slaves by arguing that they were allies of the United States.[17]

Bagot, Jan. 8, 1817, Nassau, CO 23/66, NA (emphasis added); Hawkins to Alexander J. Dallas, July 14, 1815, Creek Agency, in Grant, ed., *Letters, Journals, and Writings of Benjamin Hawkins*, 740. To underscore his commitment to his Indian allies, Nicolls took an envoy of four chiefs with him to London in the fall of 1815. British officials were furious at Nicolls, and the prince regent refused to meet with the chiefs before ordering Nicolls to return the men to North America. This did not deter the Indians' commitment to Nicolls's message or their belief in the power of the treaty that they had entered into with him. See "Substance of Correspondence Relating to Indian Chiefs," Sept. 25, 1818, Colonial Department, FO 5/140, NA; Nicolls to Earl Bathurst, Aug. 24, 1815, Durham Lodge near Eltham, U.K., and Nicolls to J. P. Morier, Sept. 25, 1815, Durham Lodge, both in Joseph Byrne Lockey Documents Related to the History of Florida, PKY; General Gaines to Dallas, acting secretary at war, May 22, 1815, Headquarters at Fort Stoddart, Mississippi Territory, in Papers of Panton, Leslie, and Company, reel 20.

17. I have chosen not to refer to the maroon community as the "Negro Fort," since this label would have had no meaning to the community's inhabitants. For the maroon community at Prospect Bluff, see James W. Covington, "The Negro Fort," *Gulf Coast Historical Review*, V (1990), 78–91; Nathaniel Millett, "Defining Freedom in the Atlantic-Borderlands of the Revolutionary Southeast," *Early American Studies*, V (2007), 367–394; Owsley and Smith, *Filibusters and Expansionists*, chap. 6; Saunt, *New Order of Things*, chap. 12. Nicolls argued that many of the slaves from Pensacola "report themselves as having come from the united states, all speaking good English—it was a long

Two separate Spanish expeditions to retrieve slaves from Prospect Bluff during the winter and spring illuminate the extent of coordination between the Royal Marine and the former slaves. The first expedition was led by Lieutenant José Urcullo of Pensacola and arrived at Prospect Bluff on December 27. Urcullo learned that Nicolls was away and that Captain Robert Henry was temporarily in charge of the British forces there. Unbeknown to Urcullo, Henry was an active participant in Nicolls's antislavery plan. With the cooperation of the former slaves, Henry frustrated the Spanish official's efforts through elaborate subterfuge. First, Henry told the Spaniard that, without Nicolls present, he was unable to identify any slaves from Pensacola. Henry then argued that "it would be dangerous and imprudent to force these People into a Vessel without a strong Guard, as the moment that Lieut Urcullo's mission became public they expressed their sentiments of disapprobation in strong terms, such as to convince me of the danger which might attend those who would attempt to take them in a vessel unarmed." Urcullo concurred with Henry on this count and agreed to wait for Nicolls's return.[18]

---

time before [I] knew of their having come from Pensacola." And yet, in the same letter, he admitted that "he Enlisted or rather protected the Black Men who fled from Pensacola" with the provision that they not be fully enlisted until they returned to Prospect Bluff. In other words, Nicolls knew full well the origins of all of his black recruits. See British rebuttal, point 19, in John Forbes to Viscount Robert Stewart Castlereagh, May 20, 1815, Pensacola, enclosed in John Croker to William Hamilton, Apr. 7, 1818, FO 72/219, NA; Nicolls to Governor Mateo González Manrique, Oct. 22, 1814, Pensacola, Forbes-Innerarity Papers, microfilm, reel 2, PKY. Hawkins, the American agent to the Indians of the Southeast, found Nicolls's argument with regard to the Creek slaves to be "an erroneous one, as there is not one Creek who has negroes so situated" (Hawkins to Nicolls, May 24, 1815, Creek Agency, in Grant, ed., *Letters, Journals, and Writings of Benjamin Hawkins*, 728).

18. Henry to Nicolls, Sept. 20, 1814, Pensacola, FO 72/219, NA; Henry to Manrique, Jan. 12, 1815, Cruzat Papers, PKY; Report of Urcullo to Manrique, Jan. 23, 1815, Pensacola, Forbes-Innerarity Papers, reel 2. This force, when combined with the Fifth West India Regiment and the *pardo* and *moreno* soldiers, comprised one of the largest black military units in the Western Hemisphere. At the moment, the force was flaunting its strength in the faces of the British and Spanish officers. See Jane Landers, "Transforming Bondsmen into Vassals: Arming Slaves in Colonial Spanish America," 120–145, Hendrik Kraay, "Arming Slaves in Brazil from the Seventeenth Century to the Nineteenth Century," 146–179, Laurent Dubois, "Citizen Soldiers: Emancipation and Military Service in the Revolutionary French Caribbean," 233–254, and Peter Blanchard, "The Slave Soldiers of Spanish South America: From Independence to Abolition," 255–273, all in Christopher Leslie Brown and Philip D. Morgan, eds., *Arming of Slaves: From Classical*

Days turned to weeks, with no sign of Nicolls, leading Urcullo to lose all patience and demand permission from the British to leave on January 12, 1815. While preparing to depart, Urcullo received a shock when—out of the blue and after weeks of contrary actions and denials—Henry ordered the "slaves of Pensacola to be formed in line ... [where he informed them] that such as chose to voluntarily return to their masters might be shipped [with Urcullo]." What followed was a performance coordinated between Henry and the former Pensacola slaves, of which 133 of various ages, ethnicities, and both sexes lined up for the Spanish officer. Yet, the next morning, Urcullo was bitterly disappointed when, "at the time ... [for] them to go on board the greater part told me that ... they were free" and refused to return with him. The former Pensacola slaves participated in the exercise with a wink and nod because they knew that the Spanish were powerless to return them by force and that the British were committed to helping them maintain their freedom. Urcullo concluded that the former slaves stayed at Prospect Bluff because they "have been seduced by the English ... and carried to the river Appalachicola in the promises of having their liberty granted them—of this I have not any doubt the negroes themselves having [been] informed."[19]

The second Spanish mission was led by Vicente Pintado, the surveyor general of West Florida. Unfortunately for Pintado, his orders contained a fatal caveat that doomed the mission to failure: neither the Spanish nor the British could use force to compel the former slaves to return; both had to rely solely on persuasion. After a lengthy and difficult voyage, Pintado, Dr. Eugenio Sierra, and William McPherson arrived at Prospect Bluff on April 7. They presented themselves to Captain Robert Spencer, who had arrived before the Spaniards with orders to help recover Spanish slaves that volunteered to return. Spencer was sincerely trying to do his job and did not

---

Times to the Modern Age (New Haven, Conn., 2006); see also Peter M. Voelz, *Slave and Soldier: The Military Impact of Blacks in the Colonial Americas* (New York, 1993), 120–121, 139, 149, 270; Roger Norman Buckley, *Slaves in Red Coats: The British West India Regiments, 1795–1815* (New Haven, Conn., 1979), chap. 7.

19. Report of Urcullo to Manrique, Jan. 23, 1815, Pensacola, in Forbes-Innerarity Papers, reel 2. The aggrieved slaveowner (Edmund Doyle) further captured the frustration of events at Prospect Bluff when he lamented, "We all Know, by common report, and every Negroe I saw says they were seduced from their Masters," yet it would be so difficult to prove that the only possible way to retrieve a former slave would be "by the Black people who voluntarily return." See Doyle to unknown recipient, 1817, Marie Taylor Greenslade Papers, 3, PKY.

share Nicolls's antislavery beliefs. But Nicolls was also there to meet Pintado and temporarily feigned that "there was no opposition on his part." Spencer took each alleged former Pensacola slave aside and "expostulated with, encouraged, threatened, advised and did every thing short of what ought to have been done, as a dernier resort,—the application of force." Furthermore, he sought to "mak[e] them see the horrible and miserable state which they would be in after the evacuation of the place by the English troops ... and explaining to them the danger in which they were in of being caught by the Indians and delivered to their masters in hope of receiving a reward from them." On the surface, at least, Nicolls assisted Spencer by reiterating the captain's message to each former slave. Despite this message and the apparent cooperation of Nicolls, Pintado succeeded in convincing only 28 out of 128 former slaves to return, and 16 "disappear[ed]" before the Spanish left. According to the testimony of a number of former slave eyewitnesses, when offered a choice between "remain[ing] with the Indians as freemen, or to return to their masters ... few had agreed to return."[20]

Once again, Nicolls and his former slave recruits were playing a carefully orchestrated game with the Spanish that demonstrated extensive cooperation. Contrary to his message in front of Pintado, Nicolls took "infinite pains ... to persuade them, that having enlisted into the British Service the British

20. Pintado to Soto, Apr. 29, 1815, Pintado Papers, box 3, folder 1, LOC; John Innerarity to Forbes, May 22, 1815, Pensacola, Papers of Panton, Leslie, and Company, reel 20. Sierra was one of Pensacola's most important residents and an employee of the town's hospital; he would stand face-to-face with a number of his former slaves who would refuse to return to Pensacola with him. See Juan Ruiz de Apodaca to West Florida commander, Nov. 27, 1815, PC, legajo 158A, doc. 356, frame 654, PKY; Malcom to Manrique, Mar. 15, 1815, *Royal Oak* off Mobile Bay, Pulteney Malcolm Papers, MAL/106, 178, NMM. The former slaves allegedly from Pensacola were sent to nearby Saint Vincent Island so they would not be influenced by other blacks or the British while being interrogated by Spencer and Pintado. (Pintado to Soto, Apr. 29, 1815, Pintado Papers, box 3, folder 1, LOC; John Innerarity to Forbes, May 22, 1815). The names of the former slave eyewitnesses were not recorded. It was noted, however, that the witnesses consisted of "some negro men" who belonged to "Don McGill, of Mobile." See Gaines to Dallas, acting secretary of war, May 22, 1815, Headquarters, Fort Stoddert, Mississippi Territory, *American State Papers*, book 1, *Foreign Relations*, IV, 552, American Memory, LOC, http://memory.loc.gov/ammem/amlaw/lwsp.html. When the former slaves received the impression that Pintado and Spencer might attempt to return them to their masters by force, they simply vanished into the forest or threatened violence. See Pintado to Soto, Apr. 29, 1815, Pintado Papers, box 3, folder 1, LOC; "Memorandum (English)," May 21, 1815, St. George, Bermuda, in Papers of Panton, Leslie, and Company, reel 20.

Government would set them free ... [and] made use of all the influence that he had acquired over them to persuade them not to return." Pintado, Sierra, and McPherson all witnessed Nicolls promising the former slaves "perpetual freedom; lands in Canada or Trinadad [sic]; the assurance that the British Gov. would pay their masters for their value; his return, abundance of provisions to support them and a well constructed fort to defend them in the interim." He even insisted that, if the British government refused to reimburse their masters, "he was sure the Philanthropic Society of which he had the honor of being a member would."[21]

This performance by Nicolls and his black allies during Pintado's visit to Prospect Bluff vividly captured the intellectual and, ultimately, ideological struggle they were waging against the system of slavery. Integral in this struggle was the fact that, for the better part of a year, Nicolls had gone to great lengths to instill an antislavery mindset within the former slaves, which had, to a substantial degree, been honed in the revolutionary Caribbean. In a sneering reference to this process, an aggrieved slaveowner claimed that the former slaves "had all preciously received their lessons.... By his audaciousness, hypocrisy, address and all his battery of imposing arts, wiles and intrigues he even blinded Spencer.... this apostle of liberty and worthy member of the philanthropic Society held them spell bound." Although this language was highly loaded, such descriptions attest to the fact that the former slaves at Prospect Bluff had listened to Nicolls's antislavery "lessons" of "liberty" and tales of the "philanthropic Society." Listening was easy: Nicolls flaunted his antislavery credentials and rhetoric so publicly and made it so clear that he and his black allies were working together to further these interests that one of the slaveowners went so far as to lament to another who sought the return of his slavers from Prospect Bluff, "I fear that the far famed ... humanity of the African Association, Abolition Society and others of a like stamp will prove an inseparable bar to your Success [in recovering runaway slaves] — In the eyes of these Right Reverend, Right Honorable, Right Worshipful and Right Honest Gentry, Negro stealing is no crime, but rather the chief of virtues — of course they will protect their slaves." Also, as mentioned above, the former slaves at Prospect Bluff found Nicolls's antislavery message and the promise of freedom and land within the British Empire to be in line with their own ideas and aims. Nicolls's rhetoric did,

21. Forbes to Castlereagh, May 20, 1815, Pensacola, enclosed in Croker to Hamilton, Apr. 7, 1818, FO 72/219, NA; John Innerarity to Forbes, May 22, 1815, Pensacola, Papers of Panton, Leslie, and Company, reel 20.

however, add specific details to the former slaves' conceptualization of their freedom and status, while British material and military support placed the blacks in a position to acquire and then protect their freedom. As a result, they were something very rare: maroons who had a deep knowledge of a particular strand of antislavery thought. Like the Seminoles and Red Sticks, the former slaves also understood that a continued relationship with the British offered distinct material and military advantages that might prove to be invaluable in the future. This knowledge, alliance, and material support were central in the maroons' identity and sense of community, all of which influenced black resistance during the First Seminole War.[22]

Pintado's disappointment turned to astonishment when he inspected one of the former slaves' license of decommission, or discharge papers. The license contained "no mention of their color or state of slavery ... that each one of the licenses was a letter of freedom for only free men were admitted to the armed service and that they would pass as such in whatever place that they presented themselves with this document." Perhaps no single comment captures the essence of Nicolls's plan better than Pintado's observation. Ni-

---

22. As early as August, Nicolls, having just arrived in Pensacola, publicly issued a proclamation that unveiled his ideology and his beliefs that the natives of the Southeast had been systematically mistreated by citizens of the United States. The proclamation was a successful recruiting tool that also spread fear across the Southeast as word of its radical content passed rapidly among the region's inhabitants. See Millett, "Britain's 1814 Occupation of Pensacola," *Florida Historical Quarterly*, LXXXIV (2005), 237–243; John Innerarity to Forbes, May 22, 1815, Pensacola, Papers of Panton, Leslie, and Company, reel 20; Innerarity to Forbes, Aug. 12, 1815, Mobile, Elizabeth Howard West Collection, PKY. Many of these communities entered into treaties or other formal alliances with colonial governments and protected their freedom by minimizing contact with outsiders and frequently returned fugitives, owned slaves, and even fought in defense of colonial regimes. When, as was the case with many slaves across the hemisphere, maroons encountered antislavery ideas, it was usually through rumor or word of mouth and so understood in fairly general terms. At the same time, maroons exerted a tremendous impact on antislavery thought and actions across the globe. Their existence and struggles became a favorite topic of antislavery advocates who used maroon communities to highlight black desire for freedom and the cruelty of slavery. Likewise, maroons served as a powerful affront to slavery that threatened the stability of the plantation complex. More profoundly, they reminded the enslaved of their condition and fueled their desire for freedom. Again, maroons exerted this influence while usually lacking extensive knowledge of formal antislavery ideas. At Prospect Bluff, however, a maroon community enjoyed a close relationship with a radical antislavery advocate and had detailed knowledge of antislavery thought.

colls conceptualized his army as one of equals because his antislavery beliefs hinged on the limitless potential for black equality within the framework of the British Empire. Accordingly, Nicolls constructed an army of free soldiers in which their race or former status meant nothing. While Pintado tried to comprehend the full implications of this, Nicolls stunned the Spanish officer once more when he promised that the slaveowners would be reimbursed by the British government, "or lacking that, the philanthropic society, would satisfy the worthy masters for the price of the slaves who did not wish to return to the service of their masters, so that afterwards they might be considered *entirely free.*"[23]

In the end, the most insurmountable stumbling block in recovering the former slaves was revealed by Nicolls's sincere boast at a trial in England after the war that "neither myself nor the Government of that day ever gave, or thought of giving, up a slave." Nicolls went on to testify that "it may be natural for a Slave owner to think that a British Officer ought to persuade a man who had born arms under the British colors to return to Slavery: ... [I] would consider that British officer as infamous who did so." The audacious actions of Nicolls and his black recruits made their intentions clear. He freed, radicalized, armed, and trained hundreds of former slaves, and—try as he might to justify and rationalize, at least superficially, not returning them to their masters—they remained at Prospect Bluff as part of a coordinated antislavery plan in which they demonstrated their clear commitment to protecting their freedom in the face of repeated efforts to reenslave them.[24]

During Pintado's stay, the British garrison began its official evacuation from Prospect Bluff. Cochrane ordered that Nicolls's black recruits were to be either returned to their masters, enlisted in one of the West India Regiments, or settled in Trinidad. Spencer was to lead a flotilla of seven ships to evacuate "as many of the Black Corps as they can *conveniently* stowe." Yet, in reality, only a handful of the former slaves were ever evacuated from Pros-

23. Papeles de Cuba, legajo, 147 B, reel 483, 960, PKY; Pintado to Soto, Apr. 29, 1815, Pintado Papers, box 3, folder 1, LOC. It was even speculated that, with these papers, they could "pass for free throughout the United States, or wherever they went" (John Innerarity to Forbes, May 22, 1815, Pensacola, Papers of Panton, Leslie, and Company, reel 20). Not that any of the former slaves would have dared to test this theory, but this was an overstatement designed to make a point about the extent of official freedom promised in the license of decommission. See Pintado to Soto, Apr. 29, 1815; Nicolls, "Creole," *Times,* Feb. 16, 1842, [7].

24. British rebuttal point no. 24, in Forbes to Castlereagh, May 20, 1815, enclosed in Croker to Hamilton, Apr. 7, 1818, FO 72/219.

pect Bluff by British forces. As Nicolls eventually admitted, "On my leaving the post at the Bluff, in June 1815, I had not transports sufficient to take away 350 men, women, and children ... but they agreed to keep together, under protection of Indian Chiefs, until we had an opportunity of sending for them." Nicolls indeed lacked sufficient space to evacuate hundreds of former slaves, but he clearly intended to transport them elsewhere in the British Empire to begin their lives as free soldiers or farmers and keep his promise. According to a "good Indian authority," Nicolls vowed "to return in six months" to recover the former slaves.[25]

Before departing, Nicolls's plan reached its final stage, as he and his black allies took yet another bold step to insure that the former slaves were "entirely free." This step, which reverberated throughout the Southeast and circum-Caribbean for decades, occurred when Nicolls "left with each soldier or head of family a written discharge from the service, and a certificate that the bearer and family were, by virtue of the Commander-in-Chief's Proclamation, and their acknowledged faithful services to Great Britain, entitled to all the rights and privileges of true British subjects ... [with] a perfect right to their liberty." These documents were the single most important weapon in the intellectual battle that Nicolls and the former slaves were waging. Up to this point, physical freedom, military service, and Nicolls's antislavery message had left the former slaves with a strong sense of their newly achieved and multidimensional status. These documents, however, which they doubtless interpreted through Nicolls's radical lens, made the *"British Blacks"* full

---

25. Cochrane to Malcolm, Feb. 17, 1815, *Tonnant* off Mobile Bay, ADM 1/508, NA (emphasis added); Malcolm to Robert Spencer, Mar. 29, 1815, *Royal Oak* off Mobile Bay, Pulteney Malcolm Papers, MAL 106, 196–197, NMM. Nicolls's superiors had every intention of honoring the promises to the former slaves and aimed to organize them as units of the West Indian Regiments defending Britain's Caribbean colonies or to establish them as free landowners in Trinidad. All of the former slaves that were evacuated had originated in Bon Secours, and when asked in Bermuda "whether they were willing to return to their previous owners ... unanimously declared that they would not return but by force." See Forbes to Castlereagh, May 20, 1815, enclosed in Croker to Hamilton, Apr. 7, 1818, FO 72/219; Admiral Smith to Croker, Aug. 24, 1816, Halifax, ADM 1/510, NA; Nicolls to Barrow, Sept. 11, 1843, Shooter's Hill, London, Class B: *Correspondence on the Slave Trade with Foreign Powers ...* (London, 1844), 13; Hawkins to Gaines, June 14, 1815, Fort Hawkins, in Grant, ed., *Letters, Journals, and Writings of Benjamin Hawkins*, 735–736. Regardless of his sincere intentions, the Royal Navy would never be sent to retrieve the former slaves. Not for a second did the British government entertain the idea of sending a mission to recover hundreds of former slaves from North America after peace had been negotiated with the United States.

British subjects and served as the cornerstone of their freedom and identity until the last of them died nearly fifty years later.[26]

Evidence abounds from across the Atlantic world of the long-term impact that these documents, with all that they embodied, had on Nicolls's black recruits. Mary Ashley and her husband, who had served as one of Nicolls's soldiers, understood the documents as simply and powerfully being "free papers" that entitled them to all of the rights and privileges of British subjecthood. Nearly thirty years later, Ashley illustrated the extent to which she believed that their "free papers" entitled her and her children to the rights of British subjects after they had been illegally reenslaved in Cuba. She petitioned the British Embassy on the island, demanding that the diplomatic officials take immediate action to correct this injustice and secure their freedom. The British consul general in Cuba took her claims, as well as his government's obligation to them, so seriously that he immediately ordered a major international investigation to make sure that "their freedom and restoration may be demanded and secured." Even clearer examples of the documents' legal and symbolic power came from the Bahamas. In 1828, when refugees from Prospect Bluff were first detected on Andros Island, they presented the British with "their discharges from His Majesty's service" as proof of their status as British subjects. The officials were instantly convinced "that these negroes are as much under the protection of the British Government as any other free person ... [no] doubt can be supposed to exist either in the minds of the negroes themselves or ... any ... planter ... as to these people being considered as Free British Subject[s]." Twelve years later, during a hotly contested election, the *Nassau Guardian* reported that about a dozen of one of the candidate's supporters were "Americans" or their children who "had served as soldiers in the British Army, under Edward Nicolls in Florida. ... these persons possessing the other requisite qualifications were considered [to be] British subjects."[27]

---

26. Nicolls to Barrow, Sept. 11, 1843, *Correspondences with Foreign Powers on Slave Trade*, 13; James Innerarity to John Innerarity, Nov. 25, 1815, Mobile, Elizabeth Howard West Collection.

27. Joseph Crawford to earl of Aberdeen, June 12, 1843, Havana, *Correspondence on the Slave Trade with Foreign Powers*, 42–43. That Ashley's claim for freedom came nearly two decades after her time at Prospect Bluff does not undermine the usefulness of this incident as historical evidence. In fact, the evidence is particularly strong, given Ashley's attachment to her British status and her ability to describe the documents and Nicolls's promises so vividly that she convinced British officials of the justice of her claim after twenty years. See Crawford to Aberdeen, June 12, 1843; James Carmichael Smith to

Just before departing, Nicolls issued orders to his black allies. They were now free British subjects. They should remain armed, trained, and organized. They should become independent farmers at Prospect Bluff in case his return was delayed or thwarted. They should avoid contact with whites. All told, the former slaves were, for the moment, to receive all that had been promised to them—not in Trinidad or Nova Scotia, but far from the British Empire. This meant that the minds of these Afro-Britons were located squarely within the British Empire while their community was physically located in a contested Atlantic borderland on the edge of the rapidly developing American plantation complex.[28]

This volatile situation became even more so when, upon the British departure in May, Nicolls backed up his word by leaving the Indians and blacks in charge of the fort at Prospect Bluff. The Indians soon returned to their villages, as did William Hambly, an employee of Forbes and Company who had been instructed to oversee the community, meaning that the "post at Apalachicola [and all of its resources] is now under command of negros." To bolster this claim to the fort, Nicolls left his allies an immense amount of military hardware and tools, along with items vital to daily life, such as pots, pans, utensils, and storage vessels. A British deserter testified that the fort was armed with "Canon[s], 4 12 pounders, one howitzer and two cohorns, about 3,000 stand of small arms, and near 3,000 of powder." When the fort was destroyed in July 1816, American estimates of the "property taken and destroyed could not have amounted to less than two hundred thousand dollars ... [including] about three thousand stand of arms, from five to six hundred barrels of powder, and a great quantity of fixed ammunition, shot, shells, etc." All of this meant that, from a practical perspective, without Nicolls's material support, the scale of black and Indian resistance during the First Seminole War would not have been possible.[29]

Bathurst, Aug. 10, 1831, Government House, Bahamas, CO 23/78, NA. The former slaves were so quickly recognized to be full British subjects that a number of them drew up and signed a petition against the removal of Governor James Carmichael Smith in 1832. See Petition in Support of Sir James Carmichael Smith, May 7, 1832, CO 23/86, NA; *Nassau Guardian*, Nov. 23, 1844.

28. Nicolls to Barrow, Sept. 11, 1843, *Correspondences with Foreign Powers on Slave Trade*, 13.

29. Hawkins to John Sevier and William Barnett, Aug. 19, 1815, Fort Hawkins, in Grant, ed., *Letters, Journals, and Writings of Benjamin Hawkins*, 748; Gaines to Secretary of War, Dallas, May 22, 1815, Fort Stoddart, FO 5/107, NA; Duncan Clinch to Col. Robert Butler, Camp Crawford, Aug. 2, 1816, List of Vessels of the U.S. Navy, 1797–1816,

What emerged at Prospect Bluff after the departure of the British was extraordinary. The Prospect Bluff community was larger (it averaged approximately four hundred inhabitants), better supplied, healthier, and more diverse (its inhabitants were Anglo, French, and Spanish Creoles, Africans, maroons, and former Indian slaves—all of whom considered themselves British subjects) than most other maroon communities in the Western Hemisphere. Like other maroon communities, the Prospect Bluff settlement operated in a multiracial and multiethnic world, so the variety of relations that it enjoyed with outsiders was largely typical, with the notable exception of its relationship with the British.[30]

The maroons' intertwined understanding of radical antislavery thought and their faith in their British status was, however, truly unique. No other maroon community was so insistent that it represented a sovereign enclave of (British) subjects who enjoyed particular rights and inhabited a distinct space. Nor did other maroon communities believe that they had achieved complete equality with white full subjects or citizens of given empires or nation-states. Perhaps the closest contemporary parallel can be found in

---

RG 45, box 181, National Archives and Records Administration, Washington, D.C. (hereafter cited as NARA). This was a staggering amount of military hardware. The Americans found 48 shovels, 26 spades, 55 pickaxes, 2 hoes, 1 tin scale, 10 saws, 2 corn mills, various belts and shoes, and a myriad of smaller items. See Henry Williams to James Madison, July 28, 1816, Prospect Bluff, *James Madison Papers*, reel 16, LOC, http://lcweb2.loc.gov/ammem/collections/madison_papers/mjmabout2.html.

30. The literature on maroon communities in the Western Hemisphere is voluminous. Some of the best works include E. Kofi Agorsah, ed., *Maroon Heritage: Archaeological, Ethnographic, and Historical Perspectives* (Kingston, Jamaica, 1994); Kenneth M. Bilby, *True-Born Maroons* (Gainesville, Fla., 2005); Mavis C. Campbell, *The Maroons of Jamaica, 1655-1796: A History of Resistance, Collaboration, and Betrayal* (Granby, Mass., 1988); Michael Craton, *Testing the Chains: Resistance to Slavery in the British West Indies* (Ithaca, N.Y., 1982); Eugene D. Genovese, *From Rebellion to Revolution: Afro-American Slave Revolts in the Making of the Modern World* (Baton Rouge, La., 1979); Gad Heuman, ed., *Out of the House of Bondage: Runaways, Resistance, and Marronage in Africa and the New World* (London, 1982); Wim Hoogbergen, *The Boni Maroon Wars in Suriname* (New York, 1990); Barbara Kamon Kopytoff, "The Early Political Development of Jamaican Maroon Societies," *William and Mary Quarterly*, 3d Ser., XXXV (1978), 287–307; Gabino La Rosa Corzo, *Runaway Slave Settlements in Cuba: Resistance and Repression*, trans. Mary Todd (Chapel Hill, N.C., 2003); Stuart B. Schwartz, *Slaves, Peasants, and Rebels: Reconsidering Brazilian Slavery* (Urbana, Ill., 1992). The best places to start are Alvin O. Thompson, *Flight to Freedom: African Runaways and Maroons in the Americas* (Kingston, Jamaica, 2006); and Richard Price, ed., *Maroon Societies: Rebel Slave Communities in the Americas* (Baltimore, 1996).

Article XLIV of the 1816 Haitian Constitution. This guaranteed both freedom and full citizenship to all people of color, black or Indian, after one year of residency in Haiti. Article XLIV would have made sense to the maroons at Prospect Bluff as they sought to claim the political, legal, military, economic, and personal rights of British subjects. This claim, which combined Nicolls's message with the former slaves' knowledge and wants, represented the surest route to the fullest version of freedom available to the former slaves. In turn, this attachment to British status created a strong sense of community and identity that would eventually guide the black combatants through the First Seminole War.[31]

In July 1816, a large detachment of American soldiers and sailors and Creek warriors destroyed the British-built fort at Prospect Bluff. This was a blow to black and Indian resistance in the Southeast and a tremendous victory for Anglo-America's long-term effort to end the threat of racial disorder originating in Spanish Florida. The victory, however, was not nearly as total as many had imagined. Americans and their allies were soon to be dismayed to learn that, as one of the survivors from Prospect Bluff would relay to Nicolls with only a small degree of overstatement, "all of those who had been in the British service" had left Prospect Bluff before the explosion and had joined Seminole, Red Stick, or maroon villages. They also remained committed to protecting their freedom and to their belief that they were British subjects. Further alarming the Americans, "It was discovered that a hostile disposition was still entertained by the Seminole tribe ... aided by fugitive negroes, and instigated by foreign incendiaries." This assessment confirmed the *Army and Navy Chronicle*'s assertion that the destruction of the fort at Prospect Bluff was the "first and perhaps one of the most hazardous expeditions of the Seminole war."[32]

Those who escaped Prospect Bluff before the July explosion did so in more than one direction. One stream of refugees escaped to a maroon settlement known as Angola, which was located in southwestern Florida. The largest number of refugees from Prospect Bluff fled to a cluster of black and Seminole villages on the Suwannee River under the jurisdiction of the Seminole chief Bowlegs. In the past, Bowlegs had worried about the negative atten-

---

31. Ada Ferrer, "Haiti, Free Soil, and Antislavery in the Revolutionary Atlantic," *American Historical Review*, CXVII (2012), 40–66.

32. Nicolls to Barrow, Sept. 11, 1843; Committee on Military Affairs to Congress, Jan. 12, 1818, rpt. in *Niles' Weekly Register*, Jan. 16, 1819; *Army and Navy Chronicle* (Washington, D.C.), Feb. 25, 1836.

tion that the Prospect Bluff settlement was directing to the Floridas. After submitting to a great deal of external pressure from American, Spanish, and Creek officials, Bowlegs even instructed his warriors to capture members of the community and return them to their masters. However, as the Seminoles observed American forces encroaching more aggressively, remembered Nicolls's promises, and absorbed many Red Sticks, they were becoming increasingly radicalized and hostile toward the United States and the Spanish, "whom they now considered as American partizans to the last." In the fall of 1816, when a Spanish official pleaded with Bowlegs to help the Spanish recover former slaves that had joined his community, the chief's cold response was, "You think hard of your black people but I did not fetch them here they came here by persuasion of the British so if you can make good with the English you are welcome to them." Bowlegs was rebuffing the Spanish while recognizing that the majority of the blacks who had joined his community were refugees from Prospect Bluff, who had a special relationship with the British. Bowlegs told the governor of East Florida, "We cannot submit to their [American] shackles, and will rather die in defence of our country." His words and actions brought Nicolls's promise of freedom, along with his commitment to violence and military service, to fruition. With the destruction of the fort, each of these groups was keenly aware that they had to make common cause to have any chance of resisting the growing tide of American expansion. Their shared history, and the fact that both groups believed that they had a special relationship with the British, made the alliance that much stronger.[33]

The refugees from Prospect Bluff made it clear they were unshaken in

33. Canter Brown, Jr., "Tales of Angola: Free Blacks, Red Stick Creeks, and International Intrigue in Spanish Southwest Florida, 1812–1821," in Brown and David H. Jackson, Jr., eds., *Go Sound the Trumpet! Selections in Florida's African American History* (Tampa, Fla., 2005), 9. Angola was a maroon community that had much in common with the one at Prospect Bluff; see Kenneth Wiggins Porter, *The Negro on the American Frontier* (London, 1971), 221. In 1813, Bowlegs and his people were driven to Suwannee by an American assault on the Alachua savanna. See Francisco Caso y Luengo to Jackson, May 14, 1818, Pensacola, rpt. in *National Register* (Washington, D.C.), Mar. 13, 1819, 166; General Bowleg[s] to governor of Florida, Sept. 10, 1816, Suwanee, East Florida Papers, sect. 29, reel 43, PKY, quoted in *The Trials of A. Arbuthnot and R. C. Ambrister, Charged with Exciting the Seminole Indians to War against the United States of America* ... (London, 1819), 42. Nicolls attempted to instill his antislavery beliefs in both the Red Sticks and Seminoles with a degree of success. Likewise, Nicolls's actions disturbed slaveowning Creeks, who went to great lengths to silence him. In both cases, it appears that Nicolls's actions with blacks brought the Indians' evolving racial consciousness to the fore.

their belief that they were full British subjects and that they were going to continue, at all costs, to defend their freedom. Driven by this identity and goal, the refugees, while recognizing that they were living in Bowlegs's territory, sought to replicate the society that they had created at Prospect Bluff. The first step was setting up loosely associated villages that extended far along the river and maintained ties with Angola. Within these villages, men, women, and children soon rebuilt a similar economy to the one that had served them so well before. Living in large and well-built cabins surrounded by wooden fences, the inhabitants tended gardens of peas, beans, corn, and rice. Despite the devastating blow of the fort's destruction, families, friends, neighbors, and associates quickly rebuilt their lives and their British community.[34]

The maroons were equally quick to re-create the political system and military structure of Prospect Bluff at Suwannee. They chose Nero, Bowlegs's chief black advisor, as their leader. Nero was a refugee from Prospect Bluff who had spent his early life on an East Florida plantation before joining the Seminoles in 1812. He shared some of his power with "Negro Chiefs," many of whom must have been refugees from Prospect Bluff. Together, these men "sat in counsel" with the Seminoles in a process that demonstrated the nature of the union between the Indians and the blacks as well as the contours of their political system.[35]

The refugees remained committed to military participation as both a means to emphasize their British status and a way to defend themselves against the ever-present menace of American and Creek aggression. This commitment was both central to the maroons' identity and made their military a substantial threat to American and Creek interests. After they had chosen Nero as their leader, a Seminole reported that the refugees were "on parade ... about six hundred that bore arms. They have chosen officers of every description, and endeavor to keep up a regular discipline, and are very

---

34. Kenneth W. Porter, *The Black Seminoles: History of a Freedom-Seeking People* (Gainesville, Fla., 1996), 18; Kevin Mulroy, *Freedom on the Border: The Seminole Maroons in Florida, the Indian Territory, Coahuila, and Texas* (Lubbock, Tex., 1993), 15; Covington, *Seminoles of Florida*, 45.

35. Jane G. Landers, *Atlantic Creoles in the Age of Revolutions* (Cambridge, Mass., 2010), 183–185. Nero was a highly privileged local black and a skilled warrior. This meant that he could be relied on for quality military and political leadership. It also meant that he understood the region's geopolitics. These were the same qualities that had led to the rise of Garçon, Cyrus, and Prince, the leaders of the maroon community at Prospect Bluff. See *Trials of Arbuthnot and Ambrister*, 49.

strict in punishing violators of their military rules." This was a re-creation of Prospect Bluff's military system, which had been defined by regular drilling and a clear chain of command. Word quickly spread to the United States that the "Indians and negroes were collecting in companies." From an American perspective, more troubling news came in March 1817, when the Creek captain Barnard reported, "There are four hundred [blacks at Suwannee] fit to bear arms exclusive of the women and children and that they are well furnished with arms and ammunition." The report continued "that those blacks have a red pole set up in their town and are dancing the red stick dance." This growing black and Indian force was publicly "speak[ing] in the most contemptuous manner of the Americans, and threaten[ing] to have satisfaction for what has been done—meaning the destruction of the Negro Fort." The refugees "say they are in complete fix for fighting, and wish an engagement with the Americans, or McIntosh's troops [these were Creeks]; they would let them know they had something more to do than they had at Apalachicola." Those "who were saved from the Negro Fort ... would revenge themselves for the loss of their friends at that place." This was not the language of a ragtag assortment of bitter or desperate rebels who were on the run. These were the proclamations of people who felt that their homes, property, and community had been unfairly attacked by the Americans and Creeks and that many of their fellow subjects had been murdered during this illegal invasion. This was the language of war between two legitimate powers: the survivors from Prospect Bluff (who regarded themselves as Britons) and the United States and its Creek allies.[36]

Unsurprisingly, when one considers the preceding half-dozen years of mounting tension and strong emotions in play, war soon enveloped the Southeast yet again. Beginning in the spring of 1817, the Seminoles and their black allies began to launch destructive raids against American fron-

---

36. Extract of a Letter from George Perryman to Lieutenant Sands, Feb. 24, 1817, *American State Papers*, book 2, *Indian Affairs*, II, 155, American Memory, LOC, http://memory.loc.gov/ammem/amlaw/lwsp.html. Six hundred was clearly an overstatement. Rather, it is probable that between two and three hundred refugees from Prospect Bluff were at Suwannee, many of whom were armed and training. See Committee on Military Affairs to Congress, Jan. 12, 1818, rpt. in *Niles' Weekly Register*, Jan. 16, 1819; "Abstract of Report of Captain Barnard of the 25th March," contained in Clinch to Secretary of War, July 17, 1816, Camp Crawford, "Letters, Secretary of War," [microcopy 221], roll 69, NARA; Perryman to Sands, Feb. 24, 1817; Testimony of William Hambly, *Trials of Arbuthnot and Ambrister*, 48.

tier settlers. The Indians and blacks were trying to stem the tide of American expansion, demonstrate their continued anger over the Treaty of Fort Jackson, and avenge the loss of the fort at Prospect Bluff. The regional tension that arose from these actions was both intensified and complicated when it became clear that Nicolls had not forgotten his black and Indian allies and soon reestablished contact with them through a series of proxies. The first of these was Woodbine, who had joined Gregor MacGregor's filibustering army commissioned by the Venezuelan revolutionaries and was busy recruiting troops in the Caribbean for a mission to the Floridas. The majority of these recruits were West India Regiment veterans of Nicolls's expedition to the Southeast. Woodbine had already been to West Florida in late 1816, where he met with the blacks and Indians at Suwannee and informed them that "Colonel Nicols would be out here in three months." Next Woodbine traveled to Angola and then on to New Providence via Havana. To the refugees from Prospect Bluff, Woodbine served as a reminder of their relationship to Great Britain and the experiment that had begun under Nicolls. To his Indian allies, Woodbine's appearance was definitive proof that they might yet hope for British help in resisting the Americans and the boundaries of the Treaty of Fort Jackson. To whites and Creeks, Woodbine had ominously shown up to carry on Nicolls's radical antislavery plan with the "remnant of the slaves who escaped from the negro fort."[37]

Two other white Britons soon appeared in West Florida, each reemphasizing the maroons' and Indians' relationship with Great Britain. The first was Robert Ambrister. During the War of 1812, Ambrister, a young Bahamian, had served under Nicolls and become radicalized. After being decommissioned from the Royal Marines, Ambrister returned to the Bahamas, where Woodbine recruited him to join his revolutionary army. As his first mission, Ambrister went to Florida to establish a base and to begin train-

---

37. Charles Cameron to Bathurst, Nov. 12, 1817, Nassau, CO 23/65, NA. For MacGregor, see David Sinclair, *The Land That Never Was: Sir Gregor MacGregor and the Most Audacious Fraud in History* (Cambridge, Mass., 2003); Matthew Brown, "Gregor MacGregor: Clansman, Conquistador, and Coloniser on the Fringes of the British Empire," in David Lambert and Alan Lester, eds., *Colonial Lives across the British Empire: Imperial Careering in the Long Nineteenth Century* (Cambridge, 2006); Doyle to John Innerarity, Jan. 28, 1817, Prospect Bluff, Greenslade Papers. The Spanish first became aware of Woodbine's return to West Florida in early December 1816. See Commander Masot to C. G. Cienfuegos, Dec. 19, 1816, Pensacola, PC, legajo 1873, reel 129, 706, PKY; *New-York Daily Advertiser*, Mar. 23, 1818.

ing the refugees from Prospect Bluff, who were at Suwannee, with the goal to "see the Negroes righted." Ambrister, under the direction of Woodbine, energetically continued the project begun at Prospect Bluff by Nicolls, with whom he regularly corresponded. Because of this relationship, it was reported that Ambrister "had complete command of the Negroes who considered him as their captain," whereas, at Ambrister's trial months later, after he had been captured by Jackson, a witness testified that he was "a person vested with authority among the Negro leaders, and gave orders for their preparation for war ... and that the leaders came to him for orders." Nothing more clearly illustrates that Ambrister was acting as Nicolls's surrogate than a letter he had written to Nicolls while at Suwannee, stating that the refugees from Prospect Bluff "depend on your promises, and expect you are on the way out. They have stuck to the *cause*, and will always believe in the faith of you." The Americans saw the *"cause"* as the "savage, servile, exterminating war against the United States." In reality, however, the cause was the community, freedom, and British status that had been created by the maroons at Prospect Bluff. Ambrister's discussion of the cause captured the extent to which the maroons' identity and sense of mission had not changed—only their location had.[38]

In the fall of 1817, Alexander Arbuthnot, an aging Scottish merchant who had extensive experience trading with the Natives of the Floridas from a base in the Bahamas, was the third British subject to become conspicuously involved with blacks and Indians in the region. Arbuthnot can be described as a "humanitarian" who had a sincere respect and concern for the Red Sticks and Seminoles as well as a businessman who hoped to establish a lucrative trade with the Indians. In a fateful decision, Arbuthnot, who agreed with Nicolls's grievances concerning the Indians, became tribal advocate for the Seminoles and Red Sticks. He petitioned the Americans, Spanish, and British on behalf of the Natives. To the Americans, Arbuthnot appeared to be yet another dangerous British interloper in the Floridas who had suspicious designs with blacks and Indians and who was the "real successor of Nicolls in the work of stirring up mischief along their borders—It may also be added and of Woodbine too." To the Indians, he was another reminder of

---

38. Owsley and Smith, *Filibusters*, 147; Testimony of John Lewis Phenix, Testimony of Jacob Harrison, both in *Trials of Arbuthnot and Ambrister*, 63, 75; Robert Ambrister to Nicolls, Suwannee near Apalachicola, 1818, *American State Papers*, book 1, *Foreign Relations*, IV, 594, LOC; Adams to the Minister Plenipotentiary, Nov. 28, 1818, Washington, D.C. rpt. in *Philadelphia Register, and National Recorder*, Jan. 30, 1819.

their relationship with Great Britain that inspired hope Nicolls was soon to reappear and make good on his word.[39]

In the minds of whites and Creeks, heavily armed and radicalized maroons, meddling Britons, and hostile Seminoles and Red Sticks posed a grave danger to national and tribal security that threatened to embroil the plantation complex in racialized violence. This threat seemed particularly acute in light of the last six years of history and the increasingly tenuous Spanish grasp on the Floridas. Accordingly, the United States soon put in motion plans to end permanently the threat of ongoing black and Indian resistance and British meddling in the Floridas. Gaines had been instructed by his superiors to increase the American military presence along the Escambia River gradually and to rebuild Fort Scott, located on the Flint River just above the Florida border. During 1817, Gaines exchanged a number of testy letters with Bowlegs and the anti-American Seminole chief Kinache, demanding that the Seminoles cease their hostilities against the United States and return fugitive slaves, including the refugees from Prospect Bluff. The Seminoles responded that they had suffered violent American encroachments, that they harbored no blacks, and that, if American armed forces attempted to dislodge them, they would respond with force.[40]

Closer to Fort Scott, in what was American territory—according to the Treaty of Fort Jackson—stood a large Red Stick and black village known as Fowltown. Many of the refugees from Prospect Bluff had migrated there. At the same time that Gaines was exchanging letters with Bowlegs and Kinache, Major David Twiggs, the commander of Fort Scott, received a letter from Neamathla, the leader of Fowltown. The letter warned Twiggs "not to cross nor cut a stick of wood in the east side of the Flint. That land is mine. I am directed by the power above and power below to protect and defend it. I shall do so." At virtually the same time, Gaines received intelligence from the "friendly Indians" that the "hostile party [of Indians] and Blacks have been promised a British force to assist them, from New Providence. This promise, though made by Nichols and Woodbine, is nevertheless relied on by these deluded wretches, who, I have no doubt, will sue for peace, as they find their hopes of British aid to be without foundation." The news hastened the coming of war because it made the Americans nervous at the possibility

---

39. Owsley and Smith, *Filibusters*, 145; Richard Rush to Castlereagh, Jan. 12, 1819, FO 5/146, NA.

40. Owsley and Smith, *Filibusters*, 149; Covington, *Seminoles of Florida*, 41.

that it was true and, at the same time, strengthened the resolve of the Seminoles, Red Sticks, and blacks.[41]

Gaines wasted little time in ordering Mathew Arbuckle and a large American force to proceed to the village and arrest Neamathla, since Fowltown was located in American territory. The First Seminole War officially began on the morning of November 21, 1817, when Arbuckle's force was fired upon by Fowltown's defenders. The Americans returned fire, causing the inhabitants of Fowltown to disperse. Before torching the village, the Americans made a discovery that confirmed their suspicion that the Indians and blacks were working closely with Nicolls and his proxies. The Americans found "in the house of the Chief ... a British uniform coat (scarlet), with a pair of gold epaulets, and a certificate, signed by a British Captain of Marines, 'Robert White, in the absence of Colonel Nichols,' stating, that the Chief had always been a true and faithful friend to the British."[42]

From the Floridas, the Native and black response was swift and brutal. Days later, an American naval vessel commanded by Lieutenant Robert Scott was ambushed by Indians and blacks on the Apalachicola River, near the ruins of the fort at Prospect Bluff. Most of the soldiers on board were killed in the attack, but a number of women and children were taken prisoner before being tortured and killed. In December, as the conflict began to escalate, Fowltown warriors captured William Doyle and Edmund Hambly. The refugees from Prospect Bluff blamed both men for the fort's destruction because of the intelligence that they had given to the Americans. Doyle and Hambly were transported to the black towns on the Suwannee, where the two men stood trial. It was remarkable that, deep in the wilderness of the Floridas, in the midst of a war, the refugees did not revert to frontier justice to avenge their incredible loss. Rather, they conducted a formal trial, which reveals that the maroon community had developed a coherent political and legal system and that its members continued to adhere to its principles. In the end, Nero, himself a refugee from Prospect Bluff, intervened and turned the men over to the Spanish garrison at St. Marks.[43]

41. "The Humble Representation of the Chiefs of the Creek Nation, to His Excellency Governor Cameron," n.d., *Narrative of a Voyage to the Spanish Main in the Ship "Two Friends"* ... (London, 1819), 219, cited in Covington, *Seminoles of Florida*, 41; "American Intelligence: Engagement with the Indians," rpt. in *Times*, Jan. 15, 1818.

42. "American Intelligence," Nov. 21, 1817, rpt. in *Times*, Jan. 15, 1818.

43. Owsley and Smith, *Filibusters*, 151. One white American woman, a Mrs. Stewart, was spared and held as a prisoner by the blacks and Indians until April 1818, when American troops rescued her in an ordeal that was reminiscent of the most dramatic

The ambush on Scott and his detachment had further enlivened American opinion. Consequently, in the winter of 1818, Secretary of War John C. Calhoun ordered Andrew Jackson to raise as many troops as he deemed necessary to bring peace to the Southeast. Jackson proceeded to Fort Scott, where he arrived in March. Soon Jackson's combined Indian and American force numbered more than thirty-five hundred men. Jackson's goals for his 1818 invasion of the Floridas were the same as they had been in 1814 when he invaded Pensacola and in 1816 when he ordered the destruction of the maroon community at Prospect Bluff: to end the threat of British-instigated Indian and black racialized violence that threatened the security of America's expanding slave frontier. This time, however, Jackson was in an even stronger position than before. He was a national celebrity because of his role in the Battle of New Orleans; America was not engaged in a war with Great Britain; Spain had virtually lost control of the Floridas; and the call from the American lobby for the annexation of the Floridas was almost deafening.[44]

At the end of March 1818, Jackson's large force began its descent on the Florida peninsula. Led by Nicolls's old ally Kinache, their first target was the Lake Miccosukee village. After a brief skirmish, the vast majority of Seminoles, Red Sticks, and blacks were able to flee. While searching the abandoned village, the Americans made a shocking discovery. They found fifty fresh scalps that they believed had come from the raid on Scott's party and more than three hundred older scalps. The Americans then burned the village. In the following week, Jackson seized the Spanish garrison at St. Mark's with the justification that the fort was so weakly held, it might fall into the hands of the Indians and blacks. While at St. Marks, Jackson captured the hapless Arbuthnot as well as the Red Stick chief Hillis Hadjo.[45]

The British maroons were the primary anti-American combatants in the First Seminole War, and their destruction was the main goal of the American and Creek war effort. Accordingly, American forces soon turned their attention to Bowlegs Town and the associated black villages under Nero, where the largest number of the refugees from Prospect Bluff had settled. They were joined by the black and Indian evacuees from Miccosukee, many of

---

captivity narrative. See Edward Brett Randolph diary, Apr. 12, 1818, Southern Historical Collection, University of North Carolina, Chapel Hill; Porter, *Black Seminoles*, 20.

44. Covington, *Seminoles of Florida*, 43. Many of these men, both white and Indian, were hardened veterans of Jackson's years of wars against the Indians and blacks of the Southeast, including the destruction of the fort at Prospect Bluff.

45. Owsley and Smith, *Filibusters*, 154.

whom had originated at Prospect Bluff. This was now the epicenter of black and Indian activity in the region, where for months Ambrister had been helping train Nero's black army. Before his capture, Arbuthnot had sent a letter to Ambrister that warned the blacks and Indians along the Suwannee River: "The main drift of the Americans is to destroy the black population of Swany. Tell my friend, Boleck [Bowlegs], that it is throwing away his people to attempt to resist such a powerful force." Arbuthnot was addressing a fundamental truth about this assault in particular and the First Seminole War in general: the Americans were taking care of unfinished business, but their greatest concern was over black resistance and, more specifically, the refugees from Prospect Bluff. Even more pointedly, at Arbuthnot's trial, he recalled bluntly telling the Indians "that it was the Negroes, and not the Indians, the Americans were principally moving against." A black resident of Suwannee who was an eyewitness corroborated Arbuthnot's belief when he later testified, "The Indians have always said that they should not have been attacked at the Suwanee, if they had not had these negroes among them; that the hope of getting possession of them (the negroes) invited the attack and proved the destruction of the town." Gaines made this clear when he told the Seminoles: "You harbor a great many of my black people among you, at Sahwahnee. If you give me leave to go by you against them, I shall not hurt anything belonging to you." In Secretary of State John Quincy Adams's careful and telling opinion, this was a "Negro-Indian war" and not the other way around. An American soldier's diary echoed this from the field when he described being involved in the planning of an "attack on the negro and bowlegs town." The soldier's choice of word order made it clear that the primary aim of the assault was the black villages. The Seminoles and Red Sticks were dangerous and deeply resentful foes of the United States, but most observers were aware that Indians were a diminishing threat to American interests east of the Mississippi River. Yet, with the expansion of slavery, slave resistance had become the gravest internal danger facing the Deep South. During the First Seminole War, Jackson was doggedly pursuing the refugees of one of North America's most conspicuous acts of slave resistance.[46]

46. Porter, *Black Seminoles*, 21, 22; testimony of Arbuthnot, *Trials of Arbuthnot and Ambrister*, 58; "Testimony of John Prince, a Colored Man, Territory of Florida," Saint Augustine, Jan. 10, 1828, House Reports, No. 723, 27th Cong., 2d sess., III, May 20, 1842, 5–6; Gaines to the Seminole Chief, *Narrative of a Voyage to the Spanish Main*, 221–222, quoted in Jane Landers, *Black Society in Spanish Florida* (Urbana, Ill., 1999), 235; John Quincy Adams to the American minister in Madrid, Washington, D.C., Nov. 28, 1818, rpt.

Contrary to advice from Arbuthnot and desperate advice from the recently arrived Miccosukee refugees, the inhabitants of Suwannee decided to make a stand against the Americans. The defense would have to be mounted without Ambrister, who had fled before the American assault. Undeterred, Nero's army established its position on the western bank of the river after evacuating the women and children. For many of these people, this was the second time in two years that they had braced themselves for a large American and Creek assault. On April 16, the American attack on the black settlements began. The Battle of Suwannee proved to be the decisive engagement of the First Seminole War. More than three hundred black soldiers fought skillfully and with bravery that reflected their British training and commitment, but they quickly realized the hopelessness of their cause and executed a well-planned escape. The destruction of the towns along the Suwannee River was a major military setback for the blacks and Indians. This was compounded by Jackson's capture of Ambrister only days later, when the British agent, unaware that the Americans had captured the Suwannee towns, walked right into American hands. Before the end of April, Jackson had tried and executed Ambrister and Arbuthnot for continuing Nicolls's mission, in a decision that greatly angered both the American and British governments.[47]

Jackson's grip on the Floridas began to tighten during the coming months. In May, Jackson once again occupied Pensacola because he felt that Indian and black hostility from the Floridas would never cease until the United States acquired the territories. The governor of West Florida, Don José Mazot, sent Jackson a letter insisting that he had violated Spanish sovereignty by occupying Pensacola and that he must withdraw his forces immediately. In response, Jackson penned a vitriolic letter to the Spanish governor that succinctly captured his rationale for invading the Spanish province and engaging in the First Seminole War more generally. Drawing a direct line connecting the events of the War of 1812 with the First Seminole War, Jackson argued that, for years, he had been fighting a race war that was the result of Spanish weakness and British (in the form of Nicolls and his

---

in *Albion* (New York), Jan. 20, 1838; Edward Brett Randolph diary, Apr. 16, 1818, Southern Historical Collection.

47. Covington, *Seminoles of Florida*, 46; Edward Brett Randolph diary, Apr. 18, 1818, Southern Historical Collection; and see Deborah Rosen, "Wartime Prisoners and the Rule of Law: Andrew Jackson's Military Tribunals during the First Seminole War," *Journal of the Early Republic*, XXVIII (2008), 559–595.

proxies) intrigues with the blacks and Indians of the Southeast. He felt that the United States was legally, morally, and ethically justified in invading the Floridas for what, he asserted, would be the last time. Fewer than two weeks later, President Monroe delivered a speech to Congress in which he agreed with Jackson's argument that Spanish weakness and American self-defense had more than justified the invasion.[48]

With the Battle of Suwannee, the First Seminole War was essentially over. The United States and Spain had begun negotiations over the transfer of the Floridas. Yet hundreds of blacks remained unconquered, the vast majority of whom had continued their exodus farther south and had joined Angola. Now populated by its initial inhabitants as well as refugees from Prospect Bluff that had arrived in both 1816 and 1818, Angola was, for the moment, the last bastion of meaningful black resistance in the Floridas. Jackson, in his eagerness to finish the job that he had begun in 1813, quickly sent Lieutenant James Gadsden of the U.S. Engineer Corps to investigate Angola and its surrounding settlements. Gadsden reported that Angola was, indeed, the last bastion of black and Native resistance in the Floridas and that it was growing as a result of American success in the First Seminole War. He also reported that the settlement maintained ties with Nicolls. Jackson promptly asked Secretary of War Calhoun for permission to attack the community but was denied, in light of the international complications that his recent actions had caused with both the Spanish and the British. For the time being, the residents of Angola were free to rebuild their lives while requesting aid from the British and Spanish.[49]

At the conclusion of the First Seminole War, various American officials and citizens made it clear that they considered the maroons from Prospect Bluff, their Indian allies, and the specter of British meddling to be the cause of the conflict. Before the war had even concluded, John Quincy Adams, fearing that the latest American invasion of Spanish territory might result in a war with Spain or, more realistically, derail efforts to acquire the Floridas, was charged by the government with providing an official explanation of the conflict. Over the next year, as Adams collected all of the intelligence relating

48. Owsley and Smith, *Filibusters*, 161; Don José Mazot to Andrew Jackson, May 23, 1818, Pensacola, Jackson to Mazot, May 23, 1818, Headquarters, Division of the South, both in *National Register*, Mar. 13, 1819; James Monroe, "Independence of the Spanish Provinces: Communicated to the House of Representatives," Mar. 25, 1818, *American State Papers*, book 1, *Foreign Relations*, IV, 173–174, American Memory, LOC, http://memory.loc.gov/ammem/amlaw/lwsp.html.

49. Brown, "Tales of Angola," in Brown and Jackson, eds., *Go Sound the Trumpet!* 10.

to the First Seminole War, he came firmly to believe that Jackson—for whom he had no love lost—had been justified in invading the Floridas as an effort to end a British-instigated race war led by the refugees from the Prospect Bluff maroon community. Adams's explanation, which began in August 1814 with the arrival of Nicolls in West Florida, centered almost exclusively, and in great detail, on the role of Nicolls and the British in inducing the blacks and Indians to war against the United States. In Adams's estimation, the primary causes of the war were Nicolls's insistence that the Treaty of Fort Jackson was null, his arming of the maroons at Prospect Bluff, and the recent work of his proxies to continue hostilities. Adams believed that the core combatants were blacks and Indians that Nicolls had trained and recruited while in the Floridas. In uncharacteristically colorful language, Adams described recent events as being part of a "creeping and insidious war, both against Spain and the United States; this mockery of patriotism; these political philters to fugitive slaves and Indian outlaws ... all in the name of South American liberty, of the rights of runaway Negroes, and the wrongs of savage murderers ... [a] war, left us by Nicholls, as his legacy, reinstigated by Woodbine, Arbuthnot and Ambrister."[50]

Many white Americans shared Adams's opinion. At a trial concerning the execution of Arbuthnot and Ambrister, David Mitchell, the American agent to the Creek Indians, argued that the root cause of the First Seminole War was "the fugitives from the Creek war, and those under the influence of Nichols." In justifying Jackson's recent invasion of Florida, John Overton confidently argued, "From the year 1814 down to the termination of the Seminole war, this motley crew of black and red combatants had been uniformly instigated by British incendiaries, Spanish cupidity, and their own ferocity, to carry on a war of depredation and massacre upon the peaceful citizens of our frontier." In early 1819, a Congressional committee noted its disapproval of Jackson's handling of the executions of Arbuthnot and Ambrister but chose not to censure the general. The committee agreed that Jackson was forced to invade Spanish Florida to protect American citizens from British-instigated hostilities by blacks and Indians and that, by permitting these conditions to exist in its territory, the Spanish had forfeited Florida's neutral status.[51]

50. Adams to the Minister Plenipotentiary, Nov. 28, 1818, Washington, D.C., rpt. in *Philadelphia Register and National Recorder*, Jan. 30, 1819.
51. Mitchell Testimony, Nov. 17, 1818, *American State Papers*, book 5, *Military Affairs*, I, 748, LOC, American Memory, http://memory.loc.gov/ammem/amlaw/lwsp.html;

Jackson's invasion of the Floridas aided the transfer of the colonies to the United States by vividly illustrating to the Spanish the impossibility of maintaining any meaningful control over the territories' internal and external affairs. Spain's empire in the Western Hemisphere was crumbling, and its fortunes in Europe were equally dire. Expending manpower and resources to hold on to the Floridas seemed pointless, especially in the face of nearly constant American aggression. Antagonizing the Anglo plantation society to the north was no longer a viable defensive strategy but rather a dangerous provocation of an awakening regional power. To this end, the Adams-Onís Treaty was signed on February 22, 1819, and took effect two years later.

The single most important factor in the American decision to acquire the Spanish colonies was a burning desire to end, finally, the threat that conditions in the Floridas posed to racial order in the United States and the expanding plantation complex. The insatiable desire for land, the initial stages of Manifest Destiny, and a robust southern lobby were certainly important elements driving America to acquire the colonies; however, recent events, beginning with the Patriot War and ending with the First Seminole War, had brought American anxieties about racial order to a head. At the same time, nothing had factored more prominently in the creation of these conditions than the actions of Nicolls, his proxies, their Seminole and Red Stick allies, and the refugees from the Prospect Bluff maroon community. To white Americans, the exploits of the maroons, Britons, and Indians drove home the unique national security threat posed by Spain's continued control of the Floridas. The *Daily National Intelligencer* echoed this argument in a widely reprinted editorial that the paper ran during the First Seminole War, calling for the American acquisition of the Floridas. The author contended that the majority of the provinces' population would prefer annexation and that excellent timber and agricultural land was to be found across the Floridas. Tellingly, the majority of the piece was devoted to the argument that the actions of Nicolls, Woodbine, and the refugees from Prospect Bluff made it imperative that the United States acquire the Floridas. Territorial Florida's first newspaper, the *Floridian,* ran a four-part, pro-Jackson series titled "The Next President" among its initial printings. For four months, the young newspaper passionately described the role of race, with overwhelming atten-

---

John Overton, *A Vindication of the Measures of the President and His Commanding Generals, in the Commencement and Termination of the Seminole War, by a Citizen of the State of Tennessee* (Washington, D.C., 1819), 20; Committee on Military Affairs to Congress, Jan. 12, 1818, rpt. in *Niles' Weekly Register,* Jan. 16, 1819.

tion paid to Nicolls and the refugees from Prospect Bluff, and Andrew Jackson in the American acquisition of Florida. The paper only mentioned other "positive advantages" in passing at the end of the series. Lewis Edwards, like many white southerners, was happy to hear "the news of the cession of the Floridas ... [because it will] have the effect of disarming the Seminole Indians of their hostility, restoring the fugitive blacks, and giving entire security to the frontier." Jackson concurred with all of these arguments while watching Congress debate the "Florida question," noting that he hoped "that body will take measures to secure our southern frontier from ... [from] a renewal of all the horrid scenes of massacre ... that existed before the campaign." Jackson had already been assured by Secretary of War Calhoun that he and the entire administration "concur in the view which you have taken in relation to the importance of Florida to the effectual peace and security of our Southern frontier."[52]

The 1821 transfer of the Floridas to the United States was yet another blow to the blacks and Indians of the region as the advantageous conditions created by Spanish rule became a memory. Then Andrew Jackson was appointed as Florida's territorial governor. Acting in direct defiance of Secretary of War Calhoun, Jackson's first order of business was to send his Creek allies on a search-and-destroy mission against Angola, where the majority of the refugees from Prospect Bluff now lived, as firm as ever in their belief that they were British subjects. An eyewitness described the raid as having been orchestrated by "some men of influence and fortune residing some where in the western country, [who] thought of making a speculation in order to obtain Slaves for a trifle." According to the witness, approximately 200 Coweta

52. *Daily National Intelligencer,* Nov. 11, 1817; *Floridian,* May 24, July 19, Aug. 2, 1823; L[ewis] Edwards to Calhoun, Charleston, S.C., Apr. 3, 1819, in W. Edwin Hemphill, ed., *The Papers of John C. Calhoun,* IV, *1819-1820* (Columbia, S.C., 1969), 8; Jackson to James Monroe, Dec. 7, 1818, Hermitage, in Hemphill, ed., *The Papers of John C. Calhoun,* III, *1818-1819* (Columbia, S.C., 1967), 360, Calhoun to Jackson, Nashville, Department of War, Sept. 8, 1818, 110. The first installment outlined British activities during the War of 1812 with special attention to the community at Prospect Bluff and praised Jackson for his "unparalleled boldness and energy with which ... the Negro Fort was demolished ... [and] he subdued the Seminoles and Red Sticks." The second installment lauded Jackson for directing the First Seminole War and defeating "these individuals [that] were the hearts blood of a savage war." The final piece in the series boldly proclaimed: "We are now free from apprehension for the lives of our border settlers. Florida is no longer an asylum for our runaway negroes, and refugees from justice.... [these] evils are remedied by this accession to our territory, besides securing many positive advantages ... [for] the people of the United States" (*Floridian,* May 24, July 12, 19, Aug. 2, 1823).

Creek Indians proceeded down the west coast of Florida "in the name of the United States" to capture as many blacks as possible and to bring them to a "secret" location. When they arrived at Angola, the Indians "surprised and captured about 300 of them, plundered their plantations, set on fire all their houses, and then proceeding Southerly captured several others." For the residents of Angola, as refugees from Prospect Bluff via Miccosukee, this was the third time they had seen their community destroyed by the United States and its Indian allies. As was illustrated by Mary Ashley's relentless pursuit of her rights and freedom thirty years later in Cuba, even those people unfortunate enough to be reenslaved never gave up in their belief that they were British subjects by virtue of what had happened at Prospect Bluff.[53]

Not all of the maroons were captured or killed in the Indian raid. Most important, one stream of refugees from Angola escaped to Andros Island in the Bahamas. Here, they were able to continue what they had begun at Prospect Bluff and fully realize what Nicolls had promised them. After their detection by British officials in 1828, the former slaves were immediately recognized as full British subjects who were allowed to participate in the island's government. As had been the case at Prospect Bluff, the former slaves owned property and became successful farmers and businessmen who formed an important part of Andros Island's economy. Furthermore, they had fulfilling spiritual and cultural lives, and their children were educated at a local, state-run school. All of these actions were so seamless because the refugees did not need an education in their rights as British subjects; they were merely continuing what they had begun under Nicolls's tutelage. Of unmistakable symbolism, the refugees lived in a village they had named "Nicholls Town," where their descendants still live today.[54]

Nicolls's decision to liberate, radicalize, arm, and then grant British subjecthood to hundreds of former slaves both incited and shaped the First Seminole War. The former slaves' embrace of the message Nicolls brought

---

53. Brown, "Tales of Angola," in Brown and Jackson, eds., *Go Sound the Trumpet!* 11; An Eye Witness, "Advice to the Southern Planters," *City Gazette and Commercial Daily Advertiser* (Charleston, S.C.), Nov. 24, 1821, [2].

54. One small group of refugees from Angola fled the raid and merged with a number of Red Sticks. Together they formed a community called "Minatti" at the Peace River headwaters (Brown, "Tales of Angola," in Brown and Jackson, eds., *Go Sound the Trumpet!* 12). Other refugees managed to escape and join scattered bands of their Seminole and Red Stick allies. In twenty years, many of these blacks and Indians, along with their children, would fight the United States armed forces once again in the Second Seminole War.

to North America via the revolutionary Caribbean, along with material and technical support and their own ideals, made the maroons formidable adversaries to American and Creek interests. These convergent factors meant that the black combatants in the First Seminole War were driven by a strong sense of community, identity, and mission that fueled their resistance to the United States. The relationship between Nicolls and the Seminoles and Red Sticks equally strengthened and shaped the Indians' resolve in resisting the United States during the conflict. After more than a century of Anglo anxiety over, and efforts to end, the threat to racial order posed by Spanish Florida, the Prospect Bluff maroon community—its radicalized black inhabitants who thought of themselves as British subjects, their Indian allies, and both groups' role in the First Seminole War—were the decisive factors in the American acquisition of the Floridas.

PART II

REPRESENTING THE REPUBLIC

FOR THE LOVE OF GLORY
NAPOLEONIC IMPERATIVES IN THE EARLY AMERICAN REPUBLIC

Matthew Rainbow Hale

In the War of 1812's aftermath, Americans were awash in glory, or so said that conflict's enthusiasts. "The brilliant events by sea and land, and the glorious termination of the late contest, has placed our country on exalted ground," ninety-two New York state legislators proclaimed, while the Lexington, Kentucky, *Western Monitor* reprinted a New Hampshire *Portsmouth Oracle* piece hailing the "blaze of glory, which has surrounded our gallant navy." In a widely reprinted speech lauding Andrew Jackson and his soldiers for their Battle of New Orleans victory, Georgia senator George Troup employed either the word "glory" or "glorious" four times in the span of three sentences.[1] Speaker of the House Henry Clay, meanwhile, used the 1816 debate on a direct tax bill to deliver a defiant discourse on American glory in particular and the concept of glory in general. "The glory acquired by our gallant tars—by our Jacksons and our Browns on the land,—is that nothing?" he asked in a speech excerpted in American rhetoric textbooks from the 1830s to the 1920s.

For constructive criticism, suggestions, and inspiration, the author thanks Nicole Eustace, Fredrika Teute, Peter Onuf, Goucher College History faculty, the two anonymous readers, the audience members at the 2011 "Warring for America, 1803–1818" conference—especially Jane Kamensky, Toby Ditz, and Rob Parkinson—students in my 2010 "Revisiting the War of 1812" seminar, and Bradley Hale. Kis Robertson Hale and Kelly Crawford created the elegant Graphs 1A and 1B. A 2009 Society for Historians of the Early American Republic Fellowship and a 2009 Goucher College Faculty Affairs Grant enabled me to conduct research for this essay. Finally, the earliest iteration of this essay took the form of a 2007 lecture for the Maryland Chapter of the Jane Austen Society, and I thank Goucher librarian Nancy Magnuson for arranging the invitation to speak.

1. New York legislators, in the *Enquirer* (Richmond), Apr. 26, 1815, [2]; *Western Monitor* (Lexington, Ky.), Apr. 21, 1815, [2]; *Daily National Intelligencer* (Washington, D.C.), Feb. 17, 1815, [3]; *Enquirer*, Feb. 25, 1815, [1]; *City Gazette and Commercial Daily Advertiser* (Charleston, S.C.), Feb. 25, 1815, [2]; *Rutland Vermont Herald*, Mar. 1, 1815, [3]; *New-Hampshire Gazette* (Portsmouth), Mar. 11, 1815, [1].

Is there a man who could not desire a participation in the national glory acquired by the war?—Yes, national glory, which however the expression may be condemned by some, must be cherished by every genuine patriot. What do I mean by national glory? Glory such as Hull of the Constitution, Jackson, Lawrence, Perry, have acquired.... I love true glory.... It is this sentiment which ought to be cherished; and in spite of cavils and sneers and attempts to put it down, it will finally conduct this nation to that height to which God and nature have destined it.[2]

The popular affinity for glory in the War of 1812 era is hard to swallow. It is shameless and self-serving. It is explicitly bombastic and implicitly ethnocentric. And it is blind to the rather poor performance of the United States military throughout the War of 1812.

Yet the rhetoric remains, and scholars miss an opportunity to understand important themes in the early Republic if they dismiss in toto paeans to glory.[3] New scholarship on Napoleonic Europe, moreover, invites historians

---

2. Henry Clay, "Speech on the Direct Tax and Public Affairs," Jan. 29, 1816, in Clay, *Papers*, ed. James F. Hopkins and Mary W. M. Hargreaves et al., II (Lexington, Ky., 1961), 148–149; John J. Harrod, *The Academical Reader* (Baltimore 1830), 193–194; John Frost, *The American Speaker* ... (Philadelphia, 1845), 116–118; Worthy Putnam, *The Science and Art of Elocution and Oratory* ... (New York, 1858), 79–81; John D. Philbrick, *The American Union Speaker* ... (Boston, 1870), 178–179; M. W. Hazen, *Hazen's Fifth Reader* (Philadelphia, 1896), 517–518; D. Barton Ross, *A Southern Speaker* ... (New York, 1901), 232–233; Henry Gaines Hawn, *Hawn Course in Public Speaking, for Self-Instruction* (New York, 1921), 158–159. According to Paxton Hibben, Henry Ward Beecher practiced Clay's speech "over and over again"; see Hibben, *Henry Ward Beecher: An American Portrait* (1927; rpt. New York, 1942), 35.

3. David Curtis Skaggs, in *Oliver Hazard Perry: Honor, Courage, and Patriotism in the Early U.S. Navy* (Annapolis, Md., 2006), 19, notes the importance of "glory" but does not elaborate. Christopher McKee has a section on ambition in his naval officer corps history, but the focus is on institutional promotion rather than the political-cultural meaning of glory; see McKee, *A Gentlemanly and Honorable Profession: The Creation of the U.S. Naval Officer Corps, 1794–1815* (Annapolis, Md., 1991), 269–325. Ricardo A. Herrera has a chapter titled "Questing for Personal Distinction: Glory, Honor, and Fame" in *For Liberty and the Republic: The American Citizen as Soldier, 1775–1861* (New York, 2015), but he conceives of glory narrowly—as a premodern reliance on God's favor—and spends only four pages on the topic. Moreover, his emphasis on self-regulating republicanism leads him to overlook Napoleonic self-aggrandizement. My essay builds upon Douglass Adair, "Fame and the Founding Fathers," in Trevor Colbourn, ed., *Fame and the Founding Fathers: Essays by Douglass Adair* (Indianapolis, Ind., 1974), 3–26.

of the early United States to take seriously the concept of glory.[4] Undoubtedly, early Republic scholars have noted how Bonaparte's rule generated strong American reactions. But, overall, the existing scholarship focuses rather narrowly on diplomacy, partisanship, and commerce and cannot convey the fullness of Napoleon's impact.[5] A political-cultural examination of

4. Philip G. Dwyer, "Napoleon and the Drive for Glory: Reflections on the Making of French Foreign Policy," in Dwyer, ed., *Napoleon and Europe* (Harlow, U.K., 2001), 118–135; David A. Bell, *The First Total War: Napoleon's Europe and the Birth of Warfare as We Know It* (Boston, 2007), 186–262; Steven Englund, *Napoleon: A Political Life* (Cambridge, Mass., 2004); John A. Lynn, "Toward an Army of Honor: The Moral Evolution of the French Army, 1789–1815," *French Historical Studies*, XVI (1989), 152–173; Owen Connelly, "A Critique of John Lynn's 'Toward an Army of Honor: The Moral Evolution of the French Army, 1789–1815,'" ibid., 174–179; Lynn, "Response to Owen Connelly's Critique," ibid., 179–182; Rafe Blaufarb, *Napoleon, Symbol for an Age: A Brief History with Documents* (Boston, 2008); Christophe Belaubre, Jordana Dym, and John Savage, eds., *Napoleon's Atlantic: The Impact of Napoleonic Empire in the Atlantic World* (Leiden, 2010); Michael J. Hughes, *Forging Napoleon's Grande Armée: Motivation, Military Culture, and Masculinity in the French Army, 1800–1808* (New York, 2012), 51–78; Jarosław Czubaty, "Glory, Honour and Patriotism: Military Careers in the Duchy of Warsaw, 1806–1815," in Alan Forrest, Karen Hagemann, and Jane Rendall, eds., *Soldiers, Citizens, and Civilians: Experiences and Perceptions of the Revolutionary and Napoleonic Wars, 1790–1820* (New York, 2009), 59–76; Karen Hagemann, "Of 'Manly Valor' and 'German Honor': Nation, War, and Masculinity in the Age of the Prussian Uprising against Napoleon," *Central European History*, XXX (1997), 187–220; Hagemann, "German Heroes: The Cult of Death for the Fatherland in Nineteenth-Century Germany," in Stefan Dudink, Karen Hagemann, and John Tosh, eds., *Masculinities in Politics and War: Gendering Modern History* (Manchester, U.K., 2004), 116–134; Robert Morrissey, *The Economy of Glory: From Ancien Régime France to the Fall of Napoleon*, trans. Teresa Lavender Fagan (Chicago, 2014) (originally published as *Napoléon et l'héritage de la gloire* [Paris, 2010]).

5. Edward L. Andrews, *Napoleon and America: An Outline of the Relations of the United States to the Career and Downfall of Napoleon Bonaparte* (New York, 1909); Paul H. Giddens, "Contemporary American Opinion of Napoleon," *Journal of American History*, XXVI (1932), 189–204; Anna C. Clauder, *American Commerce as Affected by the Wars of the French Revolution and Napoleon, 1793–1812* (1932; rpt. Clifton, N.J., 1972); E. Wilson Lyon, *Louisiana in French Diplomacy, 1759–1803*, new ed. (Norman, Okla., 1974); Arthur Preston Whitaker, *The Mississippi Question, 1795–1803: A Study in Trade, Politics, and Diplomacy* (New York, 1934); Joseph I. Shulim, *The Old Dominion and Napoleon Bonaparte: A Study in American Opinion* (New York, 1952); Lawrence S. Kaplan, "Jefferson, the Napoleonic Wars, and the Balance of Power," *William and Mary Quarterly*, 3d Ser., XIV (1957), 196–217; Kaplan, "Jefferson's Foreign Policy and Napoleon's Idéologues," *WMQ*, 3d Ser., XIX (1962), 344–359; Charles Willis Mei-

the concept of glory, however, offers not only a fresh account of American perceptions of Napoleon but also a new perspective on democracy's development in the United States.[6]

More specifically, an investigation of select Bonapartist phenomena—printed accounts of and reader responses to Napoleon; post-Revolutionary soldiers' and sailors' actions, dress, and utterances; a John Wesley Jarvis painting; and gender roles and concepts—illuminates early American democracy's romance with power as expressed in a new culture of war. This new culture held that martial values were superior to civilian ones and depicted warfare as a compelling forum for romantic self-expression and nationalist apotheosis. Those preoccupied with Napoleonic glory were motivated by the idea that extraordinary individuals and nations could make a spectacle of themselves and transcend even as they dramatically altered history. This self-important, exhibitionist streak induced many to indulge preposterous fantasies. Or, as Linda Colley put it in reference to British aristocrats' concurrent cultural makeover, they were "heroes of their own epic."

---

nert, "The American Periodical Press and Napoleonic France, 1800–1815" (Ph.D. diss., Syracuse University, 1960); Alexander DeConde, *This Affair of Louisiana* (Baton Rouge, La., 1976); Alfred W. Crosby, Jr., *America, Russia, Hemp, and Napoleon: American Trade with Russia and the Baltic, 1783–1812* ([Columbus, Ohio], 1965); Robert B. Holtman and Steven G. Reinhardt, eds., *Napoleon and America* (Pensacola, Fla., 1988); Peter P. Hill, *Napoleon's Troublesome Americans: Franco-American Relations, 1804–1815* (Washington, D.C., 2005); Jennifer Newman, "U.S. Public Opinion of Napoleon Bonaparte during the Hundred Days," *The Consortium on the Revolutionary Era, 1750–1850: Selected Papers, 2006* ([Tallahassee, Fla.], 2007), 271–280.

6. For works that start to move beyond Napoleon's impact on American diplomacy, partisanship, and commerce, see Howard Mumford Jones and Daniel Aaron, "Notes on the Napoleonic Legend in America," *Franco-American Review*, II (1937), 10–26; Guillaume de Bertier de Sauvigny, "The American Press and the Fall of Napoleon in 1814," American Philosophical Society, *Proceedings*, XCVIII (1954), 337–376; Mark Patterson, "Emerson, Napoleon, and the Concept of the Representative," *ESQ: A Journal of the American Renaissance*, XXXI (1985), 230–242; Donald D. Horward and William Warren Rogers, "The American Press and the Death of Napoleon," *Journalism Quarterly*, XLIII (1966), 715–721; Matthew Q. Dawson, "The Impact of Napoleon Bonaparte on American Opinion and Policy in 1796 and 1797," *Consortium on Revolutionary Europe, 1750–1850: Selected Papers, 1996* ([Tallahassee, Fla.], 1996), 143–149; Dawson, "Napoleon Bonaparte's Impact on American Opinion and Policy in 1798," *The Consortium on Revolution Europe, 1750–1850: Selected Papers, 1997* ([Tallahassee, Fla.], 1997), 390–397; Dawson, "The Impact of Napoleon Bonaparte on American Opinion and Policy in 1799 and 1800," *The Consortium on Revolutionary Europe, 1750–1850: Selected Papers, 1998* ([Tallahasse, Fla.], 1998), 621–628.

Yet no matter how outlandish, no matter how implausible, and no matter how often military persons and their admirers demonstrated the "faculty," to use Washington Irving's phrasing, "of swelling up nothings into importance," these epics should be taken seriously. In their Napoleonic flights of fancy, a sizable number of Americans powerfully shaped their own lives and the early Republic.⁷

The concept of glory has existed for millennia, but it reemerged with new energy in the early modern era as a description of human monarchs. Louis XIV of France, in particular, invited extensive commentary revolving around the idea of glory, and, through various media, the French royal administration represented the Sun King as the embodiment of magnificence and its offshoots—grandeur, éclat, imperiousness, and brilliance. The French Revolution dealt a blow to the notion of glory in that it toppled the Bourbon dynasty and threatened to upend other monarchies. Yet the concept of glory did not fade away because Napoleon reinvigorated it. The Corsican upstart helped France dominate the Continent, and he did so with a flair that wowed supporters and opponents alike. From his extraordinary rise to power to the speed with which his armies achieved victories, from his innovative use of propaganda to his sometimes subtle, sometimes overbearing statecraft, from his terse, breathless bulletins to his novelistic sensibilities and appreciation of military pomp, and from his ambition and sense of destiny to his conviction that he personified the French Revolution, Napoleon made everyone take notice. Unquestionably, others in the late eighteenth and early nineteenth centuries—including Horatio Nelson, the naval martyr of the British aristocracy—reflected and contributed to the emergent cult of romantic, self-aggrandizing heroism. But no one riveted the imagination like Napoleon.⁸

---

7. Bell, *First Total War;* Nicole Eustace, *1812: War and the Passions of Patriotism* (Philadelphia, 2012); Linda Colley, *Britons: Forging the Nation, 1707–1837* (New Haven, Conn., 1992), 177–193; Washington Irving, "Salmagundi; or, The Whim-Whams and Opinions of Lancelot Langstaff, Esq. and Others," in *History, Tales, and Sketches*, ed. James W. Tuttleton (New York, 1983), 120. See also Irving's comment about "making a mountain out of a mole-hill" (118).

8. Peter Burke, *The Fabrication of Louis XIV* (New Haven, Conn., 1992); Leonora Cohen Rosenfield, "Glory and Anti-Glory in France's Age of Glory," *Kentucky Romance Quarterly*, XXI (1974), supplement 2, *French Renaissance Studies in Honor of Isidore Silver*, 283–307; William Beik, *Louis XIV and Absolutism: A Brief Study with Documents*

The reign of glory supposedly inaugurated by Bonaparte drew strength from the fact that it was, in Steven Englund's words, "monarchical but also democratic." Bolstered by French Revolutionary notions of neo-regal popular sovereignty, which emphasized unity of purpose, transcendent authority, and fearsome force, Napoleon and his supporters crafted a populist regime that enabled the Corsican general to act autocratically. In fact, because Bonaparte enjoyed extensive support, insisted on (partially fraudulent) plebiscites, and purportedly embodied Gallic glory, he was free to assume neo-absolutist powers. Napoleon "reinvented the monarchical principle at its deepest, yet did so within the framework of a [democratic] state of law which seemed to exclude it," Marcel Gauchet wrote. "It was with the title of representative of the nation that Napoleon personified power, and, indeed, declared himself *more* 'representative' than" all other officials.[9]

In an era when the cult of George Washington took on monarchical overtones, and when significant numbers of people began to identify themselves as "democrats," the democratic-monarchical aspects of Napoleon's career necessarily appealed to many Americans, especially Democratic-Republicans.[10] As early as the mid- and late 1790s, there appeared in print not only reprints of Bonaparte's letters and bulletins but also effusive tributes to the French general. In July 1796, the *Windham Herald* reprinted an English editorial exulting that in "18 days" the "admirable efforts" of

---

(Boston, 2000), 199–218; John Lynn, "A Quest for Glory: The Formation of Strategy under Louis XIV, 1661–1715," in Williamson Murray, MacGregory Knox, and Alvin Bernstein, eds., *The Making of Strategy: Rulers, States, and War* (Cambridge, 1994), 178–204; Colley, *Britons*, 177–193.

9. Englund, *Napoleon*, 219–222, 249 (Gauchet quotation), 460; Jeremy Bailey, *Thomas Jefferson and Executive Power* (Cambridge, 2007), 274; Lynn Hunt, *Politics, Culture, and Class in the French Revolution* (Berkeley, Calif., 1984), 94–113; Hunt, "Hercules and the Radical Image in the French Revolution," *Representations*, I, no. 2 (Spring 1983), 95–117; Matthew Rainbow Hale, "American Hercules: Militant Sovereignty and Violence in the Democratic-Republican Imagination, 1793–1795," in Patrick Griffin et al., eds., *Between Sovereignty and Anarchy: The Politics of Violence in the American Revolutionary Era* (Charlottesville, Va., 2015), 243–262.

10. Gordon S. Wood, *Empire of Liberty: A History of the Early Republic, 1789–1815* (New York, 2009), 53–94; Simon P. Newman, *Parades and the Politics of the Street: Festive Culture in the Early American Republic* (Philadelphia, 1997), 44–82; R. R. Palmer, "Notes on the Use of the Word 'Democracy,' 1789–1799," *Political Science Quarterly*, LXVIII (1953), 203–226; Matthew Rainbow Hale, "Regenerating the World: The French Revolution, Civic Festivals, and the Forging of Modern American Democracy, 1793–1795," *JAH*, CIII (2017), 891–920.

Napoleon in the Italian Piedmont "far surpass[ed] even the achievements of [Charles François] Dumourie[z]'s famed six weeks [of] victories [in the fall of 1792], which in their turn surpassed romance itself!" In that same year, self-proclaimed "democratic republican" James Elliott, a twenty-one-year-old Vermonter, lauded Bonaparte as the "HANNIBAL of *France*," who "With his immortal band advance[d]" over "realms of *Alpine* frost and snow." In April 1799, finally, a *Centinel of Freedom* writer argued that the "presence" of French "Generals Berthier, Massena, Cervoni, and others" might "have proved ineffectual" at the Battle of Lodi (1796) "had it not been for the intrepidity of Buonaparte, who, snatching a standard from the hand of a Subaltern, like Caesar on a similar occasion, and placing himself in front, animated his soldiers by his actions and gesticulation" so that "victory once more arranged herself under the Gallic banners."[11]

These early commentaries are striking for how they portrayed Napoleon and his military deeds as glorious, as the embodiment of French Revolutionary notions of neo-monarchical democratic sovereignty. To begin, they reveal a belief that Bonaparte imposed his will on events. Other commanders proved "ineffectual" in the face of obstacles, but the Corsican general refused to succumb and turned the tide of history. These 1790s tributes also focused on the unexpected nature and "rapidity" of Napoleon's actions.[12] Like lightning bolts, Bonaparte's martial exploits seemed to materialize out of nowhere and dazzle everyone who witnessed them. Bonaparte's soldiers, in turn, could not help but be inspired by their leader's singularity and became an "immortal band" made in Napoleon's image and capable of remarkable feats. The triumphs of the French Army of Italy were so astonishing, more-

---

11. "Remarks on Occurences in Italy," *Phenix; Or, Windham Herald* (Conn.), July 9, 1796; James Elliot, *The Poetical and Miscellaneous Works of James Elliot* ... (Greenfield, Mass., 1798), vi, 55–56; "A Syllabus of the Life of General Bonaparte," *Centinel of Freedom* (Newark, N.J.), Apr. 9, 1799. For reprinted Napoleonic letters and bulletins, see "France—Official," *Gazette of the United States, and Philadelphia Daily Advertiser*, Jan. 19, 1799, [2-3]; "France—Official," *Centinel of Freedom*, Jan. 22, 1799, [2-3]; "Intercepted Correspondence, from the Army of General Bonaparte in Egypt," *Spectator* (New York), Mar. 6, 1799, [4]; "Bonaparte's Official Letters," *Independent Chronicle and the Universal Advertiser* (Boston), Jan. 21–24, 1799, [1]; "Bonaparte's Official Letters," *Weekly Companion; and the Commercial Centinel* (Newport, R.I.), Feb. 2, 1799, [1-2]; Dawson, "The Impact of Napoleon Bonaparte on American Opinion and Policy in 1796 and 1797," *Consortium on Revolutionary Europe*, 143–149.

12. Rufus McIntire to John Holmes, Dec. 8, 1813, in John C. Fredriksen, ed., *The War of 1812 in Person: Fifteen Accounts by United States Army Regulars, Volunteers, and Militiamen* (Jefferson, N.C., 2010), 124.

over, that it merited the status of legendary, and American writers scoured the ancient past in an attempt to place its deeds in an appropriate historical context. Noteworthy, in this regard, was the comparison of Bonaparte to Julius Caesar. Untroubled that Caesar wrought the Roman Republic's demise by defying Senate orders, marching on Rome, and accepting the perpetual dictator designation, the *Centinel of Freedom* author eagerly highlighted an instance of Caesarean military heroism that Napoleon purportedly duplicated. Hence only two years after Washington confirmed his iconic status as the prototypical republican leader resistant to dictatorial power by stepping down as president, a newspaper writer blithely praised Bonaparte by linking him to the prototypical antirepublican villain seduced by that type of power.

The dilemma of a republican military hero capitulating to power's charms acquired even greater potency between 1799 and 1804, as Napoleon seized command of the French government, centralized authority, named himself first consul (and, later, emperor), and embarked upon a series of imperialistic wars. Many Federalists responded to these events by denouncing Bonaparte as a usurper akin to the anti-Christ. Democratic-Republican reactions were mixed. Even as some tried to distance their party and the United States from Napoleon, others celebrated the person Baltimorean George Douglas suspected of being "more than mortal" in even more extravagant language, in terms that one historian has characterized as the "*secular marvelous* of the Enlightenment," a phenomenon wherein natural laws were reconciled with exceptional individuals who (supposedly) broke free from those laws. In 1806, Virginian Henry Banks's pseudonymously published *Sketches of the History of France* lengthily eulogized the "splendor" of Bonaparte's "achievements," which elevated "this extraordinary man" to "the highest pitch of military glory." There was, for starters, the "battle of Montinotte; from which time, he led his troops, with the rapidity of lightning, from place to place, and from victory to victory." Within a year of the triumph at Montinotte, Napoleon had further "dazzled the world" by retaking Corsica, adding Sardinia to the French Empire, establishing the Cisalpine republic, and dispersing five armies arrayed against him. "Never did any man before perform so many great actions, or acquire so much glory, in so short a time."[13]

---

13. George Douglas to Henry Wheaton, Oct. 14, [1813], in John Gordon Freymann, "A View of the War and the World from Baltimore, 1813–1815," *Maryland Historical Magazine*, CVII (2012), 493; [Henry Banks], *Sketches of the History of France, from the Earliest Historical Accounts, to the Present Time ... by an American* (Richmond, Va.,

Printed reports of Napoleonic glory found many enthusiastic readers in the United States. As early as 1798, New York City printer Thomas Greenleaf announced that circulating "subscription papers" for a publication called *The Campaign of General Buonaparte in Italy* had resulted in "almost the whole of the edition" being successfully "engaged," which meant that "those" interested in "secur[ing] a copy" should "call soon" at his office. Struggling Vermont farmer Hiram Harwood and ambitious law student John Calhoun both diligently followed the career of Napoleon. George Bourne, the author of an 1806 Bonaparte biography, justified his work's "unadorned" aspect by stating "that [the] patience of investigation which such a work would demand, will not suit the avidity with which the present generation wish to be informed of the wonderful changes which the French emperor is daily producing on the European continent." Henry Wright, finally, wistfully remembered "with what absorbing interest I used to hear and read of [Napoleon's] movements." Despite being "a child," he elaborated,

> my heart always triumphed in his victories, his rapid movements, his sudden encounters with the combined armies of all Europe. It was the fearful daring and energy of the man that kindled up my young heart. Many a stirring speech have I made, in the dreams of my childhood, to an army, to animate them to battle and to victory.[14]

As Wright's reminiscences suggest, reading about Bonaparte often resulted in a desire to enact a Napoleonic version of heroism. Particularly important in this regard was a generation of soldiers and sailors born in the 1770s and 1780s. Burdened by the duty to match American Revolutionaries'

1806), 54–55, 59, 58, 61. For the *"secular marvelous,"* see Morrissey, *Economy of Glory*, trans. Lavender, 68. For Bonaparte as anti-Christ or tyrannical usurper, see Shulim, *Old Dominion*, 182–250; Troy Bickham, *The Weight of Vengeance: The United States, the British Empire, and the War of 1812* (New York, 2012), 73, 190. For more details about Henry Banks's *Sketches*, see Shulim, *Old Dominion*, 203–209.

14. *Daily Advertiser* (New York), June 5, 1798, [3]; *Connecticut Journal* (New Haven), Aug. 8, 1798, [4]; *Carey's United States' Recorder* (Philadelphia), July 7, 1798, [3]; Robert E. Shalhope, *A Tale of New England: The Diaries of Hiram Harwood, Vermont Farmer, 1810–1837* (Baltimore, 2003), 128; John William Ward, *Andrew Jackson: Symbol for an Age* (New York, 1955), 184; [George Bourne], *The History of Napoleon Bonaparte: Emperor of the French, and King of Italy* (Baltimore, 1806), v–vi; Henry Clarke Wright, *Human Life* ... (Boston, 1849), 113–114, excerpted in Louis C. Jones, ed., *Growing Up in the Cooper Country: Boyhood Recollections of the New York Frontier* (Syracuse, N.Y., 1965), 160.

achievements, this post-Revolutionary age cohort latched onto Napoleon in part because he made it possible for younger citizens to establish their anti-British credentials. Bonapartist Anglophobia thus operated as an agent of generational continuity, and copious contemporaneous references to the War of 1812 as a "second war of independence" testified to the difficulty the second generation had emerging from its predecessor's shadow. At the same time, Napoleon mitigated the post-Revolutionary age cohort's psychological burden by engendering a belief that revolutionary nations, when led by a charismatic democratic leader, would perform unprecedentedly glorious deeds. Popular fascination with the Corsican general accordingly served as the cultural mechanism whereby those who hardly remembered (or never knew) George III as their sovereign both made decades-long Anglophobia their own and pioneered a new path. Even as they struggled to emulate their heroic forebears, many born in the 1770s and 1780s approached their martial careers and nation's future with an overweening, melodramatic sanguinity.[15]

This overbearing, theatrical optimism often took shape as military recklessness. According to Gordon S. Wood, Stephen Decatur's (b. 1779) 1804 nocturnal raid of Tripoli harbor—"surrounded [as it was] by a dozen other armed vessels and [sitting] under the castle's heavy batteries"—was a "dangerous, even foolhardy, mission." Oliver Hazard Perry's (b. 1785) choice to leave the flagship *Lawrence* during the 1813 Battle of Lake Erie likewise exposed himself and those who rowed him half a mile to the brig *Niagara* to incredible danger, but, even before that thrilling event, Gerald Altoff writes, Perry's "rashness" and "impetuosity" caused him to make "headstrong decision[s]" and display "a lack of constraint."[16] And then there is Admiral David Porter (b. 1780) and the Battle of Valparaiso. By early 1814, Porter and crew members of the frigates *Essex* and *Essex Jr.* had enjoyed a year of successful

---

15. Steven J. Novak, *The Rights of Youth: American Colleges and Student Revolt, 1798-1815* (Cambridge, Mass., 1977); Glenn Wallach, *Obedient Sons: The Discourse of Youth and Generations in American Culture, 1630-1860* (Amherst, Mass., 1997); Michael Paul Rogin, *Fathers and Children: Andrew Jackson and the Subjugation of the American Indian* (New York, 1975); Lawrence A. Peskin, "Conspiratorial Anglophobia and the War of 1812," *JAH*, XCVIII (2011), 647-669; Sam W. Haynes, *Unfinished Revolution: The Early American Republic in a British World* (Charlottesville, Va., 2010); Hale, "American Hercules," in Griffin et al., eds., *Between Sovereignty and Anarchy*, 243-262.

16. Wood, *Empire of Liberty*, 637; Gerald T. Altoff, "The Battle of Lake Erie: A Narrative," in William Jeffrey Welsh and David Curtis Skaggs, eds., *War on the Great Lakes: Essays Commemorating the 175th Anniversary of the Battle of Lake Erie* (Kent, Ohio, 1991), 9-10; Skaggs, *Perry*, 109-119. The half-mile figure comes from David S. Heidler and Jeanne T. Heidler, eds., *Encyclopedia of the War of 1812* (Annapolis, Md., 2004), 291.

raiding missions against British commercial vessels. Yet, instead of returning home, on March 28, 1814, Porter sought out and attacked the British ships *Cherub* and *Phoebe* off the Chilean coast, resulting in what the admiral characterized as a "dreadfully severe" loss of life. "Porter had no right to fight any battle at all," biographer David Long observed; "he should have continued as a commerce destroyer and naval irritant."[17]

Decatur, Perry, and Porter were motivated in large part by a brazen desire to garner accolades. Before entering Tripoli harbor, Decatur rallied his crew by declaring, à la Shakespeare's Henry V, "The fewer the number the greater the honor." In similar fashion, Perry responded to the possibility that a subordinate might be credited with the victory by blurting out, upon leaving the *Lawrence* for the *Niagara*, "If a victory is to be gained, I'll gain it." Porter, finally, wrote that he was dissatisfied with his successful commercial raids and hoped to conclude his voyage "by something more splendid." Or, as Barber Badger's *Naval Temple* put it in 1816, "Glutted with spoil and havock, and sated with the easy and inglorious captures of merchantmen, captain Porter now felt eager for an opportunity to meet the enemy on equal terms, and to signalize his cruise by some brilliant achievement." Decades later, Charles J. Ingersoll echoed Badger's commentary by stating that Porter went "in quest of a frigate of superior force, for the glory of fighting her."[18]

The prize of glory derived not only from daring military acts but also from the flair with which American sailors and soldiers presented themselves. Just as Napoleonic campaigns prompted, according to Raoul Brunon, "an unparalleled deployment of rich costumes, a veritable explosion of panache" in France, so "the age of Napoleon" in the United States witnessed, in Rene Chartrand's words, "some very elaborate uniforms." Numerous features of

---

17. David Porter, *Journal of a Cruise Made to the Pacific Ocean ...*, 2d ed. (New York, 1822), II, 170; David E. Long, *Nothing Too Daring: A Biography of Commodore David Porter, 1780-1843* (Annapolis, Md. 1970), 143, 162 (quotation); Paul A. Gilje, *Free Trade and Sailors' Rights in the War of 1812* (New York, 2013), 200-201.

18. Adair, "Fame and the Founding Fathers," Colbourn, ed., *Fame and the Founding Fathers*, 33; Charles Morris, *The Autobiography of Commodore Charles Morris, U.S. Navy*, ed. Frederick C. Leiner (1880; rpt. Annapolis, Md., 2002), 27; *Henry V*, ed. Claire McEachern (New York, 199), 4.3.23; Dulany Forrest to M. C. Perry, Jan. 29, 1821, Oliver Hazard Perry Papers, William L. Clements Library, University of Michigan, Ann Arbor (thanks to Jayne Ptolemy for forwarding a scanned copy of this document); David Porter to William Jones, July 3, 1814, in Michael J. Crawford et al., eds., *The Naval War of 1812: A Documentary History*, III (Washington D.C., 2002), 733; [Barber Badger], *The Naval Temple* (Boston, 1816), 121; Charles J. Ingersoll, *History of the Second War between the United States of America and Great Britain ...*, 2 vols. (Philadelphia, 1852), I, 14.

these ornate costumes owed their inspiration to French developments.[19] The dark blue coat, gold epaulets, and gold, oak-leaf embroidery worn by William Henry Harrison (b. 1773) and Henry Dearborn (b. 1751) clearly evoked the sartorial sensibilities of French generals (see Figures 1 and 2). The Governor's Guard Battalion of New York State Artillery completed its costume with Polish caps or *schapska* (tall, four-pointed hats), which were modeled after the headgear of Napoleon's Polish lancers. The uniform of the U.S. Second Regiment of Light Dragoons—with its three rows of buttons, silver shoulder "wings" instead of epaulets, white braided pantaloons, and black leather helmets with white metal and white horsehair mane—was inspired by Gallic cavalry outfits.[20]

Segments of the civilian and military population objected to the lavishness of American soldiers' and sailors' uniforms because they were wasteful, unrepublican, and perhaps even feminine. "A considerable saving would accrue to each corps from" the proscription "of every superfluous ornament of dress," argued a New York writer.

19. Raoul Brunon, "Uniforms of the Napoleonic Era," in Katell le Bourhis, ed., *The Age of Napoleon: Costume from Revolution to Empire 1789-1815*, ed. Katell Le Bourhis (New York, 1989), 179; René Chartrand, *Uniforms and Equipment of the United States Forces in the War of 1812* (Youngstown, N.Y., 1992), 7, 13, 29, 34, 43, 126. Brian Leigh Dunnigan, in "To Make a Military Appearance: Uniforming Michigan's Militia and Fencibles," *Michigan Historical Review*, XV (1989), argued that, in the years before the War of 1812, the Michigan Territory militia was "well, even extravagantly dressed" (33). See Colley, *Britons*, 183-188; John R. Elting, *Napoleonic Uniforms*, 2 vols. (London, 2007), II, 421; Scott Hughes Myerly, *British Military Spectacle: From the Napoleonic Wars through the Crimea* (Cambridge, Mass., 1996). American military personnel also copied the dress of British soldiers and sailors. See John R. Elting, ed., *Military Uniforms in America*, II, *Years of Growth, 1796-1851* (San Rafael, Calif., 1977), 30, 38, 64. Yet, because the British military borrowed so heavily from its Gallic counterpart, it seems reasonable to attribute the primary influence on American martial costumes in the early nineteenth century to Napoleonic France. See Charles Hamilton Smith and Philip J. Haythornthwaite, *Wellington's Army: The Uniforms of the British Soldier, 1812-1815* (London and Philadelphia, 2002), 30-34.

20. Chartrand, *Uniforms*, 15, 29, 41; Elting, *Military Uniforms*, II, 42-43, 58. Hugh Charles McBarron, Jr., states that an 1818 "marble bust of [Henry] Dearborn by [John] Binon, in the Chicago Historical Society, displays on [the oval-gilt, shoulder] plate an eagle of Napoleonic type grasping a thunderbolt in its talons"; see McBarron, "American Military Dress in the War of 1812," *Journal of the American Military Institute*, IV (1940), 55. For additional details regarding the uniforms of the Governor's Guard Battalion of New York State Artillery, see Daniel Tompkins, *Public Papers of Daniel D. Tompkins, Governor of New York, 1807-1817*, I (New York, 1898), 312.

Figure 1. Rembrandt Peale, *William Henry Harrison (1773–1841), 9th President of the USA*. Circa 1815. Oil on canvas, 72.4 × 58.4 cm. National Portrait Gallery, Smithsonian Institution / Art Resource, N.Y.

A round hat should replace the present preposterous 'chapeau bras.' ... The sash reduced to one third its present size would be equally useful; and a plain sabre in strong leather scabbard slung in a black or buff waistbelt, would certainly be a more effective weapon for offence or defence, than the shewey blades which now dangle in gingerbread scabbards and gold stitched morocco at the sides of 'Military men.'"

Figure 2. Gilbert Stuart, *Major-General Henry Dearborn*. 1812. Oil on mahogany panel. 71.5 × 57.1 cm. (28 9/16 × 22 1/2 in.). Friends of American Art Collection, 1913.793. The Art Institute of Chicago

Washington Irving anticipated this negative assessment, using one section of *Salmagundi* to mock "the glare" of military dress, including the *"two tails"* of the lead officer or "bashaw fired with that thirst for glory," the "trappings" of the colonel, the "fine clothes and *feathers*" of infantry units, the nineteen- and twenty-year-olds "most gorgeously equipped in tight green jackets and breeches," and the privates' "pondrous cocked hats, which seemed as unwieldy, and cumbrous, as the shell which the snail lumbers along on his back." Yet another indication of how sartorial magnificence attracted disparagement appeared in the form of a James Akin illustration accompanying the first American edition of the British book *Advice to the Officers of the Army* (see Figure 3). Titled "Dress, the Most Distinguishing Mark of a Military Genius," the print depicts a soldier buried beneath a gigantic, ribboned, feathered bicorn and festooned with epaulets, braided frills, lace cuffs, long coattails, an ungainly sword, a silk fan, and dainty, cockaded shoes. Not only has the officer in this illustration become a caricature of the debonair man in military costume, he has made himself into a dandy. The most severe critics of flamboyant Napoleonic uniforms thus portrayed their targets in Wollstonecraftian terms, as the male counterparts of those "fashionable ladies" so insidiously revered that they functioned as "vain inconsiderate dolls" preoccupied with worthless pursuits like the "frippery of dress."[21]

Partly in response to public censure of excessive ornamentation, the War Department issued in May 1813 regulations that decreed what one historian has described as "an economical and practical style of dress," and the artillery and light infantry uniforms that resulted were some of "the most sober to be found among the armies of the Napoleonic period." Yet, despite official instructions, and despite similarly strict codes of appearance instituted by certain volunteer militias, numerous individuals and groups embellished their outfits with all sorts of nonregulation gewgaws, many that hearkened to French military fashions. The unsanctioned red sword belt with gold-

---

21. *Military Monitor, and American Register* (New York), Jan. 18, 1813, 164–165; Irving, "Salmagundi," in *History, Tales, and Sketches*, ed. Tuttleton, 116–120; [Francis Grose], *Advice to the Officers of the Army* ... (Philadelphia, 1813); Nancy Isenberg, "'The Little Emperor': Aaron Burr, Dandyism, and the Sexual Politics of Treason," in Jeffrey L. Pasley, Andrew W. Robertson, and David Waldstreicher, eds., *Beyond the Founders: New Approaches to the Political History of the Early American Republic* (Chapel Hill, N.C., 2004), 129–158; Kate Haulman, *The Politics of Fashion in Eighteenth-Century America* (Chapel Hill, N.C., 2011); Mary Wollstonecraft, *"A Vindication of the Rights of Men"* with *"A Vindication of the Rights of Woman" and "Hints,"* ed. Sylvana Tomaselli (New York, 1995), 25, 153.

Figure 3. James Akin, "Dress, the Most Distinguishing Mark of a Military Genius." Frontispiece of [Francis Grose], *Advice to the Officers of the Army ...* (Philadelphia, 1813). Courtesy, American Antiquarian Society, Worcester, Mass.

covered plate that the aforementioned Henry Dearborn wore resembled the French Legion of Honor sash (see Figure 2). Army staff officers likewise contravened code by beautifying their uniforms with red morocco leather sword belts. And, in their attempt to imitate French hussars, some members of the U.S. Light Artillery Regiment wore gold-embroidered sabretaches and copious amounts of gold lace, even though the former were unmentioned in official decrees and even though the latter should have been blue cord.[22]

The way in which persons in the War of 1812 era violated policy regarding military dress reveals their affinity for splendor, and soldiers like "Fuss and Feathers" Winfield Scott (b. 1786)—who in 1808 locked himself in a room, placed two mirrors at opposite corners of the room, and "strutted back and forth ... for two hours" admiring himself in his newly tailored uniform—acquired lifelong reputations as gaudy costume aficionados. Yet civilians were also enthralled by stylish accouterment.[23] According to one account, the "splendid uniform[s]" of the "Boston Hussars"—an elite group organized by Josiah Quincy, modeled after the Regiment de Chasseurs a Cheval of Napoleon's Garde Imperiale, and bedecked in gold-embroidered crimson pelisses, gold-embroidered green jackets, "greyish-brown riding breeches, embroidered with sage green and pale brown silk," and tall caps "with black cloth," black cockades, brass-scaled chin straps, brass-bound visors, gold lace, and "a panache or flat plume of green feathers"—"filled the Boston of that day with admiration, and were talked of long after the Hussars were disbanded." Likewise, in his remembrance of the New York militia, Asher Taylor (b. 1800) ranked the units of the War of 1812 era according to their "gallant and brilliant appearance." First, for Taylor, came the aforementioned Governor's Guard Battalion, which "in a few years had acquired

---

22. Chartrand, *Uniforms*, 14, 28–29, 37 (quotation), 41, 42, 48, 117. See also McBarron, "American Military Dress," *Journal of the American Military Institute*, IV (1940), 185–196.

23. E. D. Keyes, *Fifty Years' Observation of Men and Events, Civil and Military* (New York, 1884), 9 (quotation); Timothy D. Johnson, *Winfield Scott: The Quest for Military Glory* (Lawrence, Kans., 1998), 12, 25, 74, 116, 132, 138, 140, 153. See also Alan Taylor, *The Internal Enemy: Slavery and War in Virginia, 1772–1832* (New York, 2013), 146, 276, 313, 345. Note that the Beau Brummell (1778–1840) phenomenon scorned excess but encouraged chic dressing "in the style of a military man," which is unsurprising considering that Brummell's "rise to fame began while he was serving in the Prince Regent's (George IV's) own fashionable regiment ... nicknamed the 'Elegant Extracts.'" See Isenberg, "The 'Little Emperor,'" in Pasley, Robertson, and Waldstreicher, eds., *Beyond the Founders*, 143–144 (quotations); Hubert Cole, *Beau Brummell* (Newton Abbot, U.K., 1978), 44–45, 78–82; Ellen Moers, *The Dandy: Brummell to Beerbohm* (London, 1960), 17–38.

great distinction" for "its Brilliant Uniforms, exceeding in richness and elegance all others in the City—Blue Coats, and White Pantaloons, and tall, white waving feathers—the front of the coats almost covered with gold lace, and the cuffs and collars with gold embroidery." "Next, perhaps, in display and eclat," Taylor wrote, "came the Third Regiment," commanded "by Col. WILLIAM T. HUNTER on his splendid white charger, with full, flowing mane and tail, their uniforms but little behind" the Governor's Guard Battalion "in brilliancy, their feathers white, with red tops." After the Third Regiment, there was the "old ELEVENTH" with its white pantaloons, red-collared blue coats "reaching to the knee," "long 'Suwarrow' boots," and white-topped red feathers, succeeded by "the NINTH" with red feathers, and "following them was the SECOND," adorned "with feathers of dark blue, and red tops." As if this detailed description was insufficient, Taylor appended wistful remarks about how "the bare enumeration" of military display in the War of 1812 era "brings them all up so clearly to the 'mind's eye,' with their gay and gallant appearance, that it makes one almost wish to be a boy again, and, perched up on some stoop railing in Broadway, or jammed in the front rank of the crowd in the Park, enjoying the pleasing sights." For sure, Taylor noted the "solid discipline and real efficiency" of these units. But, ultimately, what mattered most and stimulated his imagination and memory was their reputation in the "walks of fashion."[24]

The attention given to sartorial splendor was particularly meaningful in the United States because it signaled a shift in attitudes about military style. For centuries, elites pronounced the masses incapable of transcending their vulgar origins and disreputable passions, even—or perhaps especially—in battle. Eye-catching self-presentation and wartime laurels accordingly remained the prerogative of nobles and gentlemen. With Napoleon's rise, American officers not only seized the martial finery mantle but also magnified its intensity and scope. By cutting dashing figures, democratic soldiers and sailors supposedly outshone their aristocratic opponents.[25]

Brilliant, too, it seemed, were officers' utterances. Just as Napoleon wrote "laconic, dramatic, hypnotic" bulletins, so American commanders captivated people with succinctly ostentatious jingoistic phrases like "Our Coun-

---

24. Charles Winslow Hall, ed., *Regiments and Armories of Massachusetts* . . . , II (Boston, 1901), 394–395; [Asher Taylor], *Recollections of the Early Days of the National Guard* . . . (New York, 1868), 16–19; Tompkins, *Public Papers*, I, 311.

25. Bell, *First Total War*, 21–51. Likewise, in the social realm, patronage and conspicuous consumption were reserved for elites; see Gordon S. Wood, *The Radicalism of the American Revolution* (New York, 1992), 24–42, 57–77.

try ... right or wrong," "We have met the enemy and they are ours," and "Don't give up the ship!" Decatur spoke that first phrase at a Norfolk, Virginia, dinner honoring naval heroes, and, when he attended a similar affair in nearby Petersburg a few months later, a guest showed how closely heeded officers' utterances were by voicing almost the exact same words. Celebrants of American military victories, meanwhile, demonstrated devotion to those last two phrases by plastering them on huge dining-room-wall placards. Even before those placards were hung, Perry cemented in the popular imagination the "Don't give up the ship!" phrase, which was uttered by his good friend Captain Jacob Lawrence (b. 1781) during the June 1813 ship-to-ship duel between the *Chesapeake* and *Shannon*—another battle instigated by a glory-hungry officer's impetuosity—by emblazoning it on a banner on his Lake Erie flagship, the *Lawrence* (see Figure 4). So it was that various lightning-like, patriotic-military remarks entered the American lexicon and revealed another aspect of the emergent Napoleonic-glory aesthetic.[26]

Perhaps the most revealing manifestation of this aesthetic appeared in the form of a painting, John Wesley Jarvis's *Oliver Hazard Perry* (1816) (see Figure 5). Commissioned by the New York City Common Council as one in a series of War of 1812 portraits, this artwork lavishly portrays the pivotal Battle of Lake Erie moment when Commodore Perry has left the *Lawrence* in order to travel to the *Niagara*. Standing in front of (and partially draped in) the aforementioned "Don't Give Up the Ship!" banner, the Lake Erie hero dominates the scene and captivates his underlings. Perry attracts destiny's lamp, making him brilliant against the smoke-filled clouds. Splashes of red and blue patriotically complement the commodore's luminous white shirt and pants. By striding majestically over two boat seats amid the desperate manual labor, booming cannon fire, and faltering flagship's cracking timber, "Flashing American *Perry*," as one newspaper song called him, represents the United States' glory.[27]

---

26. Englund, *Napoleon*, 308; Robert J. Allison, *Stephen Decatur: American Naval Hero, 1779–1820* (Amherst, Mass., 2005), 183–185; Skaggs, *Perry*, 118; Donald R. Hickey, *Don't Give Up the Ship! Myths of the War of 1812* (Urbana, Ill., 2006), 111–112; Dan Hicks, "Broadsides on Land and Sea: A Cultural Reading of the Naval Engagements in the War of 1812," in Paul Gilje and William Pencak, eds., *Pirates, Jack Tar, and Memory: New Directions in American Maritime History* (Mystic, Conn., 2007), 142. For James Lawrence's rash leadership as a cause of the 1813 *Chesapeake-Shannon* duel, see Heidler and Heidler, eds., *Encyclopedia*, 295–296; Skaggs, *Perry*, 19.

27. "American Perry: A Song," *American Watchman and Delaware Republican* (Wilmington), Sept. 29, 1813, [1].

Figure 4. "Don't Give Up the Ship" Banner. 1813.
Courtesy, United States Naval Academy Museum, Annapolis, Md.

Jarvis's jingoistic rendition of a martial incident departed from even as it hearkened to the history-painting tradition. In Benjamin West's *Death of General Wolfe* (1770), John Singleton Copley's *Death of Major Peirson, 6 January 1781* (1783), John Trumbull's *Death of General Warren at the Battle of Bunker's Hill, 17 June, 1775* (1786), and Arthur William Devis's *Death of Nelson* (circa 1805), the heroes function as martyrs and compositionally recall Christ in Michelangelo's *Pieta* (1498–1499); it is no coincidence that "death" is the common word in these titles (see Figure 6). Furthermore, so cluttered with characters and subplots are those paintings that the significance of each of the central figures is diminished. The larger events themselves, rather than particular individuals, are the true subjects. Even as they garner attention, Wolfe, Peirson, Warren, and Nelson melt into the crowd, emphasizing their redemptive roles. Giving is the overarching theme of these history paintings.[28]

28. Bryan J. Zygmont, *Portraiture and Politics in New York City, 1790–1825: Gilbert Stuart, John Vanderlyn, John Trumbull, and John Wesley Jarvis* (Saarbrücken, Germany,

Figure 5. John Wesley Jarvis, *Oliver Hazard Perry*. 1816.
Oil on canvas, 96 × 60 in. Photograph by Glenn Castellano,
Collection of the Public Design Commission of the City of New York

Figure 6. Benjamin West, *The Death of General Wolfe*. 1770.
Oil on canvas, 152.6 × 214.5 cm. National Gallery of Canada, Ottawa.
Photo © National Gallery of Canada

Conversely, Jarvis's portrait highlights the idea of self-assertion. Perry does not give his life as a sacrifice; he imposes his will. The neo-divine light that illuminates the commodore undoubtedly makes him Christlike. Yet the Christ that Jarvis's painting evokes is the one who commanded winds and waves. Perry does not so much redeem his followers as overawe them with his magnificence. As a result, the painting's supporting actors cannot enliven subplots; they can only absorb, reflect, and be inspired by Perry's glory. In this regard, it is significant that Jarvis purportedly placed himself in the painting as the striped figure on the left unsuccessfully trying to pull his superior toward safety. Perhaps longing to participate vicariously in Perry's victory, the artist does so paradoxically, by showing how a strong-willed indi-

---

2008), 196. For history painting, see, among other works, Dennis Montagna, "Benjamin West's *The Death of General Wolfe:* A Nationalist Narrative," *American Art Journal*, XIII, no. 2 (Spring 1981), 72–88; Ann Uhry Abrams, *The Valiant Hero: Benjamin West and Grand-Style History Painting* (Washington, D.C., 1985).

vidual cannot be suppressed, by suggesting how a Napoleonic hero dictates rather than responds to spectacular, authoritative action.[29]

The greatest American military hero was George Washington, which raises the question of how visual depictions of him compare to Jarvis's *Perry*. Eighteenth-century Washington paintings resemble Jarvis's *Perry* in that they reverentially approach their subject. Yet in the end the differences are conspicuous. Whereas Washington, argued Garry Wills, was depicted in military dress "with great restraint," Jarvis's canvas brims with immoderate self-indulgence. While Wills states that "there was less emphasis on the glory of battle than on dutiful service" in artistic renderings of Washington, the Perry image highlights the former. Bryan Zygmont astutely compares Jarvis's *Perry* to John Trumbull's *George Washington before the Battle of Trenton* (circa 1792–1794) by noting that, whereas Washington looms "above the fray of the battle that roars behind him, Perry is in the middle of a heated skirmish" (see Figure 7).[30]

Eighteenth-century Washington images thus accentuate virtue, which means they operated in a register distinct from Jarvis's *Perry*. The former feature self-sacrifice for the sake of the public good, the latter self-aggrandizement for the sake of individual and national glory. The aesthetic imperative coursing through representations of Washington is meticulous self-control. The one animating *Perry* is grandiose self-expression.

If Jarvis's portrait stands apart from both portrayals of Washington and Anglo-American history paintings, there is nonetheless one image that deserves special scrutiny as precedent and model, Frenchman Antoine Jean Gros's *General Napoleon at the Bridge of Arcole, November 17, 1796* (1796) (see Figure 8). Like Jarvis's *Perry*, Gros's portrait focuses on a dramatic battle moment; depicts a striding, awe-inspiring hero against a dark backdrop that includes a wind-blown banner; emphasizes the patriotic red, white, and blue; shines a heavenly light on the central figure and his military uniform; and evokes physical fitness and achievement rather than sickly martyrdom. These similarities were not fortuitous. At some point during his training at the New York Academy of the Arts (later named the American Academy of the Arts), Jarvis engraved a mezzotint likeness of Gros's *Napoleon*, which he

---

29. Zygmont, *Portraiture*, 195–197; *Blunt's Stranger's Guide to the City of New-York…* (New York, 1817), 57. On strong will, see Ward, *Andrew Jackson*, 151–204.

30. Garry Wills, *Cincinnatus: George Washington and the Enlightenment* (Garden City, N.Y., 1984), 82; Zygmont, *Portraiture*, 196–197.

Figure 7. John Trumbull, *George Washington before the Battle of Trenton*. Circa 1792–1794. The Metropolitan Museum of Art, Bequest of Grace Wilkes, 1922

Figure 8. Antoine Jean Gros, *General Napoleon Bonaparte at the Bridge of Arcole, November 17, 1796*. 1796. Oil on canvas, 73 × 59 cm. Photo: Gérard Blot. Chateaux de Versailles et de Trianon. © RMN-Grand Palais / Art Resource, N.Y.

possibly encountered through Guiseppi Longhi's well-circulated engraving. No matter how Jarvis came across Gros's image, he likely felt grateful toward Napoleon. For, at the instigation of the American minister to France, Robert Livingston, Bonaparte donated to the New York Academy French artwork worth ten thousand dollars. No wonder Jarvis was attuned to the burgeoning Empire style.[31]

Notwithstanding the inspiration Gros's *Napoleon* provided Jarvis, *Perry* was not an unimaginative adaptation. Jarvis's portrait is full-length and approximately double the size (96 × 60 in.) of Gros's three-quarter representation (51 × 37 in.), and the extra 3,873 square inches of canvas give the former a physical presence and grandeur that surpasses that of the latter.[32] The generational and gender characteristics Jarvis imparted to Perry also distinguish his work from Gros's. The androgynous qualities of Gros's Bonaparte—the slender upper body, the long hair, the clean-shaven (or never-shaven) face, and the angular, exquisite facial features—indicate an individual still growing into his body and leadership role. In contrast, Jarvis's *Perry* exudes adult masculinity. The commodore's sideburns, muscularity, broad shoulders, and self-assuredness guarantee that he will not be mistaken for a teenager or young adult. Furthermore, Perry's open-legged stance, tight-fitting uniform pants, moderate pelvic thrust, and tucked-inside-his-belt pistol draw attention to his groin, to the seat of his primal, life-giving, self-aggrandizing masculinity. In this regard, it might not be too much to propose that the Lake Erie hero is so aroused by battle that he metaphorically makes love to the god of war. *Perry* is accordingly an eroticized portrayal of hypermasculinity and its insatiable lust for power, fame, and immortality.[33]

31. Harold E. Dickson, *John Wesley Jarvis, American Painter, 1780–1840, with a Checklist of His Works* (1949; rpt. Breinigsville, Pa., 2011), 71, 78–79.

32. This comparison is based on the Versailles version of Gros's painting. The waist-up Louvre version is even smaller (29 × 23 in.).

33. Todd D. Smith incorrectly claims that the "male body as representational phallus never materialized in the early republic" and that "there was little impetus [among Americans] to glorify" events and people in the War of 1812; see Smith, "The Problematics of Absence: Looking for the Male Body in the War of 1812," in Janet Moore Lindman and Michele Lise Tarter, eds., *A Centre of Wonders: The Body in Early America* (Ithaca, N.Y., 2001), 248–249. On the intertwining of French Revolutionary–Napoleonic love and war, see Eustace, *1812*; Bell, *First Total War*, 186–222; Myerly, *British Military Spectacle*, 58–59; Hughes, *Napoleon's Grande Armée*, 108–135; Philipp Ziesche, *Cosmopolitan Patriots: Americans in Paris in the Age of Revolution* (Charlottesville, Va., 2010), 77–78. See also Adair's comment that "the desire for fame is primarily the desire for immortality" ("Fame and the Founding Fathers," in Colbourn, ed., *Fame and the Founding Fathers*, 12).

In conjunction with the flamboyant deeds, dress, and utterances of post-Revolutionary sailors and soldiers, the hypermasculinty of Jarvis's painting augured a new version of manhood. As Mark Kann has suggested, the founding fathers possessed a vibrant notion of the "Heroic Man" who acted outside the law during emergencies. But this "Heroic Man's" influence was severely curtailed because he "was exquisitely selfless and supremely public-spirited." The Napoleonic hero knew no such limits, giving free reign to his self-involved, exhibitionist ambition. Without doubt, republican virtue still motivated men. But Napoleonic glory's rise in the War of 1812 era sapped the self-regulatory imperative embedded in the masculine ethos of republican virtue. Indeed, considering the prominence of individuals like Decatur, Porter, and Perry, it is worth considering the possibility that the bourgeois self-control iteration of nineteenth-century American manhood that has played such an important historiographical role was less a continuation of republican virtue than a reaction against Napoleonic masculinity's ascendance.[34] Along the same lines, both the 1850s–1860s "martial manhood" phenomenon associated with American filibusters, secessionists, and Civil War soldiers and the oft-cited turn-of-the-century infatuation with Teddy Roosevelt–style muscularity, expansionism, primitivism, and war were, in many ways, reformulations of Napoleonic concepts.[35]

The early-nineteenth-century transformation of masculinity had impor-

---

34. Mark Kann, *A Republic of Men: The American Founders, Gendered Language, and Patriarchal Politics* (New York, 1998), 130–154, esp. 141; E. Anthony Rotundo, *American Manhood: Transformations in Masculinity from the Revolution to the Modern Era* (New York, 1993); Michael S. Kimmel, *Manhood in America: A Cultural History* (New York, 1996).

35. Amy S. Greenberg, *Manifest Manhood and the Antebellum American Empire* (Cambridge, 2005); Stephanie McCurry, *Masters of Small Worlds: Yeoman Households, Gender Relations, and the Political Culture of the Antebellum South Carolina Low Country* (New York, 1995), 259–261; Jim Cullen, "'I's a Man Now': Gender and African American Men," in Catherine Clinton and Nina Silber, eds., *Divided Houses: Gender and the Civil War* (New York, 1992), 76–91; Monica Rico, *Nature's Noblemen: Transatlantic Masculinities and the Nineteenth-Century American West* (New Haven, Conn., 2013); Sarah Watts, *Rough Rider in the White House: Theodore Roosevelt and the Politics of Desire* (Chicago, 2006); Kristin L. Hoganson, *Fighting for American Manhood: How Gender Politics Provoked the Spanish-American and Philippine-American Wars* (New Haven, Conn., 1998); John Higham, "The Reorientation of American Culture in the 1890's," in John Weiss, ed., *The Origins of Modern Consciousness* (Detroit, 1965), 25–48; T. J. Jackson Lears, *No Place of Grace: Antimodernism and the Transformation of American Culture, 1880–1920* (New York, 1981), 97–139.

tant ramifications for male-female relations and concepts of femininity. As Rosemarie Zagarri has argued, the War of 1812 era witnessed a backlash against the idea of political women. Zagarri rightly attributes this counterattack to male politicians' desire to create a nonpolitical group of (female) citizens who could alleviate partisanship's viciousness. But it is necessary to insert the rise of Bonaparte-inspired manhood as another important factor. Napoleonic masculinity's orientation toward militarism and reckless demonstrations of willpower defined women out of politics and encouraged the expansion of various male subcultures revolving around misogyny, sexual license, violence, and devotion to homosocial organizations.[36] The flowering of these subcultures paradoxically facilitated and undermined Victorian femininity's growth. On the one hand, by excluding women from numerous institutions and treating them as delicate objects peculiarly suited to histrionic rescue, sexual surrender, and unstinting support of male pursuits, Napoleonic men contributed to the social and cultural conditions within which the "female world of love and ritual" and the cult of domesticity flourished. On the other, Bonapartist masculinity defied the increasingly accepted idea that women had a special purchase on virtue and thus were essential to men's character development and the well-being of the nation. In the Napoleonic calculus, heroic men and the all-male institutions that they joined were morally self-sufficient and the United States' primary guardians, and women should be valued merely for enhancing men's glory. Hence, even as the Victorian American woman derived a degree of indirect encouragement from the Bonaparte-like man, the egocentric self-assertiveness of the latter stunted the former's potential.[37]

36. Rosemarie Zagarri, *Revolutionary Backlash: Women and Politics in the Early American Republic* (Philadelphia, 2007), 124-136. On nineteenth-century masculine subcultures, see Patricia Cline Cohen, Timothy J. Gilfoyle, and Helen Lefkowitz Horowitz, *The Flash Press: Sporting Male Weeklies in 1840s New York* (Chicago, 2008); Timothy J. Gilfoyle, *City of Eros: New York City, Prostitution, and the Commercialization of Sex, 1790-1920* (New York, 1992), 27-178; Clare A. Lyons, *Sex among the Rabble: An Intimate History of Gender and Power in the Age of Revolution, Philadelphia, 1730-1830* (Chapel Hill, N.C., 2006), 186-236; McCurry, *Masters of Small Worlds*, 239-276; John Mack Faragher, *Women and Men on the Overland Trail*, 2d ed. (New Haven, Conn., 2001), 88-143; James Oliver Horton, "Freedom's Yoke: Gender Conventions among Antebellum Free Blacks," *Feminist Studies*, XII (1986), 51-76; Mary Ann Clawson, *Constructing Brotherhood: Class, Gender, and Fraternalism* (Princeton, N.J., 1989); Marc C. Carnes, *Secret Ritual and Manhood in Victorian America* (New Haven, Conn., 1989).

37. Ruth H. Bloch, "The Gendered Meanings of Virtue in Revolutionary America,"

The manner in which Napoleonic glory imperatives infused gender roles and concepts, Jarvis's *Perry*, and the utterances, military dress, and deeds of young sailors and soldiers suggests that popular infatuation with style was anything but window dressing. In its capacity to stir the mind's subjective elements, Bonapartist activity supposedly pushed people to move beyond the perceived limits of imagination. Or, to put it differently, Napoleon and his disciples not only justified ambition but also enlarged its domain.[38] Bonaparte-inspired occurrences thus complemented—and, in so doing, helped drive—the concurrent cultural transformation of individual economic striving from a dangerous, disgraceful passion to a civic imperative capable of liberating morally upright talent from the provincial demands of rural family life, which is one reason various nineteenth-century businessmen—including Andrew Carnegie, John Rockefeller, J. P. Morgan, James Hill, Edward Harriman, Edward Bok, and P. T. Barnum—idolized Napoleon or were characterized as Napoleons of their respective fields. Similarly, the Corsican general's naked thirst for power—"I too love power," he professed—paralleled and contributed to the rise of unabashed electioneering and questing for office among politicians like Aaron Burr, who, not coincidentally, was a small-in-stature womanizer and former soldier admired by followers for Napoleonic audacity and eroticized self-presentation. In the aura of unprecedented French martial triumphs, self-interested, go-getting soldiering, entrepreneurialism, and politicking seemed to many less a path to military dictatorship, corrosive luxury, and anarchic factionalism than varied means of engendering inspirational heroes and a brilliant inter-

---

Signs: Journal of Women in Culture and Society, XIII (1987), 37–58; Barbara Welter, "The Cult of True Womanhood: 1820–1860," *American Quarterly*, XVIII (1966), 151–174; Nancy F. Cott, *The Bonds of Womanhood: "Woman's Sphere" in New England, 1780–1830* (New Haven, Conn., 1977); Cott, "Passionlessness: An Interpretation of Victorian Sexual Ideology, 1790–1850," *Signs*, IV (1978), 219–236; Lyons, *Sex among the Rabble*, 309–395; Carroll Smith-Rosenberg, "The Female World of Love and Ritual: Relations between Women in Nineteenth-Century America," in *Disorderly Conduct: Visions of Gender in Victorian America* (New York, 1985), 53–76; Clawson, *Constructing Brotherhood*, 185–187; Zagarri, *Revolutionary Backlash*, 159–160; Daniel Walker Howe, *What Hath God Wrought: The Transformation of America, 1815–1848* (New York, 2007), 340–341.

38. David Waldstreicher, "Federalism, the Style of Politics, and the Politics of Style," in Doron Ben-Atar and Barbara B. Oberg, eds., *Federalists Reconsidered* (Charlottesville, Va., 1998), 99–117; Isenberg, "The 'Little Emperor,'" in Pasley, Robertson, and Waldstreicher, eds., *Beyond the Founders*, 129–158; Walter Jackson Bate, *From Classic to Romantic: Premises of Taste in Eighteenth-Century England* (New York, 1961), 153–156.

national reputation. Through the dazzling exploits of Napoleon and likeminded individuals, French-inflected concepts of glory violently instructed American thought.[39]

Without doubt, glory's allure existed before Napoleon's emergence, and a number of Seven Years' War and American Revolutionary War combatants—for instance, James Wolfe, Alexander Hamilton, John Laurens, John Paul Jones, and Benedict Arnold—were just as ambitious and vainglorious as Decatur, Porter, and Perry. Yet what occurred between 1789 and 1815 was different. To begin, Robert Morrissey has demonstrated that Napoleonic glory reconciled democratic equality with a society oriented toward distinction. "Heroes" in the new regime were "as numerous as the nation's soldiers," Morrissey noted, because *"every person"* was "motivated by a 'noble desire.'" An American periodical biographer accordingly interrupted his 1813 account of Stephen Decatur's life to explain not only that the "obscure, unambitious ... poor sailor" who voluntarily took a saber blow intended for Decatur possessed an "innate nobleness of soul" but also that the "poor sailor" was rewarded with a degree of fame and "a pension from government."[40]

In addition, an examination of Readex's digital database America's Historical Newspapers demonstrates that, even after taking into account newspaper culture's growth, the number of references to the words "glory" and "honor," as well as to glory-related terms like "brilliance," "splendor," and "éclat," was higher during the Tripolitan Wars and the War of 1812 than dur-

---

39. J. Christopher Herold, ed., *The Mind of Napoleon: A Selection from His Written and Spoken Words* ... (New York, 1955), 260; J. M. Opal, *Beyond the Farm: National Ambitions in Rural New England* (Philadelphia, 2008); Joseph Frazier Wall, *Andrew Carnegie*, 2d ed. (Pittsburgh, 1989), 790; Grant Segall, *John D. Rockefeller: Anointed with Oil* (New York, 2001), 89; Jean Strouse, *Morgan: American Financier* (New York, 1999), 46–48, 125, 420; Judy Hilkey, *Character Is Capital: Success Manuals and Manhood in Gilded Age America* (Chapel Hill, N.C., 1997), 79–81; Theodore P. Greene, *America's Heroes: The Changing Models of Success in American Magazines* (New York, 1970), 110–165; *Philadelphia Inquirer*, Apr. 10, 1875; A. H. Saxon, *P. T. Barnum: The Legend and the Man* (New York, 1989), 126–128, 159; Phineas T. Barnum, *The Life of P. T. Barnum, Written by Himself* (1855), introduction by Terence Whalen (Urbana, Ill., 2000), 266; Alexis de Tocqueville, *Democracy in America*, ed. Harvey C. Mansfield and Delba Winthrop (Chicago, 2000), 386–387; Isenberg, "The 'Little Emperor,'" in Pasley, Robertson, and Waldstreicher, eds., *Beyond the Founders*, 129–158; Nancy Isenberg, *Fallen Founder: The Life of Aaron Burr* (New York, 2007); Gordon S. Wood, *Revolutionary Characters: What Made the Founders Different* (New York, 2006), 223–242.

40. Morrissey, *Economy of Glory*, 94; "Biography of Commodore Decatur," *Analectic Magazine*, I (1813), 508.

ing the French and Indian War and the colonial rebellion against Britain (see Graphs 1A and 1B). Not every mention of these words between 1801–1805 and 1812–1815 stemmed from American and European warfare coverage. Nevertheless, in combination with Morrissey's analysis and the qualitative evidence previously discussed, the database pattern is sufficiently clear to suggest that the quest for individual and national honor enjoyed enhanced political-cultural cachet in the first two decades of the nineteenth century. Thus, whereas republican virtue's dominance encouraged soldiers, sailors, and their followers in the 1770s and 1780s to check exhibition of personal aspiration, to "think not," as a 1776 song in honor of George Washington put it, that the "thirst [for] Glory, unsheaths our vengeful Swords," the early-nineteenth-century growth in stature of glory produced a more expansive milieu for narcissistic martial pursuits, an environment wherein the *Analectic Magazine* could brazenly trumpet that "glory was the prize for which" Winfield Scott and his soldiers fought, "and their country must bestow it." No wonder James E. Valle found that the "Quasi-War with France and the War of 1812 had yielded a crop of overwhelmingly proud and egotistical young commodores pathologically preoccupied with personal 'honor' and incapable of sacrificing private considerations for the good of the service." And no wonder Samuel J. Watson wrote that "in 1820 the U.S. Army officer corps was ... full of belligerent glory seekers eager to substitute colonial adventures (or individual duels), often on exaggerated pretexts, for the excitement, fame, and potential political advancement of wars now past."[41]

Glory's augmented prestige necessarily prompted a wave of criticism, much of which Montesquieu anticipated with his analysis of how "arbitrary principles of glory" resulted in "tides of blood ... inundat[ing] the earth" during Louis XIV and XV's reigns, most of which came from Federalists and their conservative successors, the Whigs. Six months after the War of 1812 ended, the *New-York Examiner* excoriated "Madison's Glory War" by wondering, "What is Glory, Martial Glory, but expertness in shedding human blood[,] the talent at destroying the human species!" In 1841, artist John Trumbull not only lamented that the American Revolution "was eclipsed in the meteoric glare and horrible blaze of glory of republican France" but

---

41. [Jonathan Sewall], *Gen. Washington, a New Favourite Song* ... (n.p., [1776]); "Biographical Sketch of Major General Winfield Scott," *Analectic Magazine*, IV (1814), 484; James E. Valle, *Rocks and Shoals: Naval Discipline in the Age of Fighting Sail* (Annapolis, Md., 1980), 24; Samuel J. Watson, *Jackson's Sword: The Army Officer Corps on the American Frontier, 1810–1821* (Lawrence, Kans., 2012), 186.

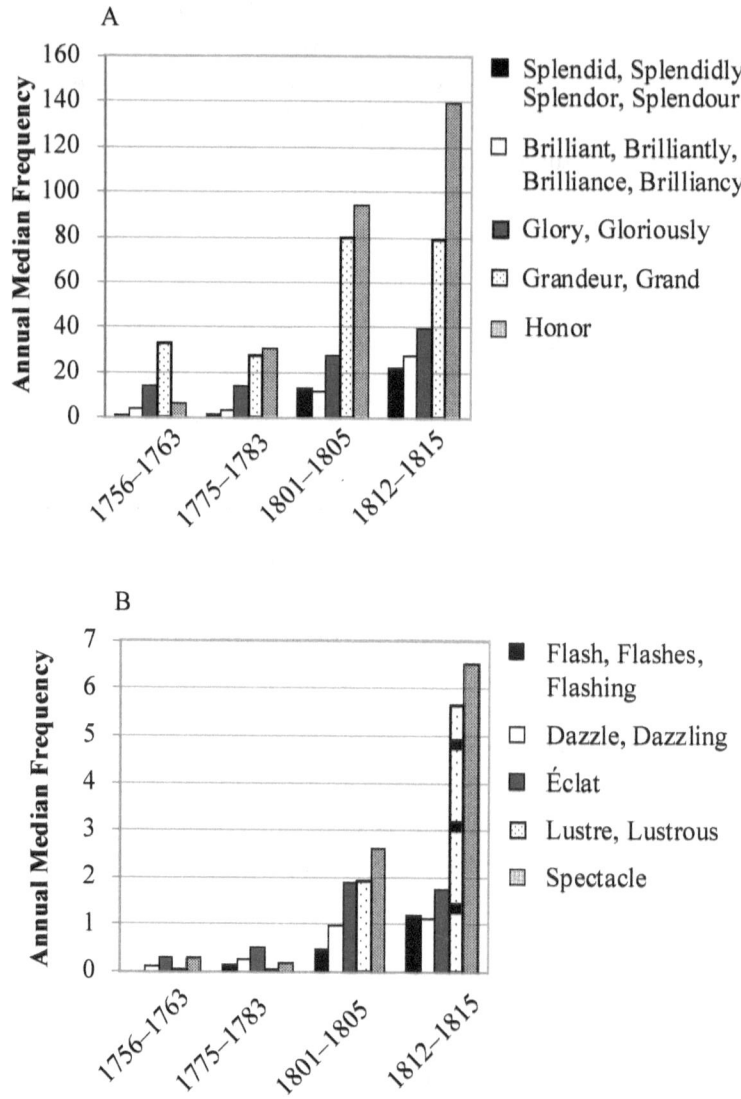

Graphs 1A and 1B. Annual Median Frequency of English-Language Newspaper References to Various Words Associated with the Concept of "Glory" during the Seven Years' War (1756–1763), the American Revolutionary War (1775–1783), the First Barbary War (1801–1805), the War of 1812, and the Second Barbary War (1812–1815). Frequency is equal to the number of references to a particular word or words divided by the number of English-language newspapers in the database published during that particular year. Readex's America's Historical Newspapers database, Series I and II.

also deprecated individuals "who threw up their caps, and cried, 'glorious, glorious, sister republic!'" In *White Jacket* (1850), Herman Melville derided David Porter as the "brainless bravo ... captain" of the Battle of Valparaiso who "continued to fight his crippled ship against a greatly superior force" because he wanted to "crown himself with the glory of the shambles, by permitting his hopeless crew to be butchered before his eyes."[42]

The most sustained critique of glory appeared in Thomas Upham's *Manual of Peace* (1836). According to Upham, glory was defined exclusively as "that species of reputation or honor, which is founded on brave and successful efforts in war." When "an Englishman speaks of the glory of his country," he was "musing, in all probability, on what his country has done nobly and successfully in war; on the splendid names of Blake, Howe, and Nelson, of Marlborough and Wellington." Likewise, "when a Frenchman speaks of the glory of France," he was pondering "the terrible bridge of Lodi, the victory and the sun of Austerlitz." The consequence of this narrow, perverted definition of glory, Upham wrote, was threefold. First, it meant that "a nation's glory is estimated to be nearly in proportion to the national capabilities for destroying the human race in future, and the successful exercise of those capabilities in time past." Second, it transformed military honor into "a sort of personification, a species of animated existence, floating in the air and radiant with celestial hues, and beckoning the beholders onward and upward to the transcendent heights." Third, it implanted in otherwise moderate men an "indescribable fury" and bloodlust. Taken as a whole, Upham asserted, "national glory" was "a source of unspeakable evil" that led "men astray and hurr[ied] them on to deeds of blood."[43]

In light of Rachel Hope Cleves's cogent explanation of how the first nonsectarian peace movement in the United States emerged among northeast-

42. Montesquieu, *The Spirit of the Laws*, ed. and trans. Anne M. Cohler, Basia Carolyn Miller, and Harold Samuel Stone (Cambridge, 1989), 139; "Madison's Glory War," *New-York Examiner*, reprinted in *Alexandria Gazette, Commercial and Political* (Va.), Sept. 14, 1815, [3]; John Trumbull, *Autobiography, Reminiscences and Letters of John Trumbull, from 1756 to 1841* (New York, 1841), 168–169. See also Samuel G. Goodrich, *Recollections of a Lifetime ...*, 2 vols. (1856; rpt. Detroit, 1967), I, 505; Herman Melville, *White-Jacket; or, The World in a Man-of-War*, introduction by Tony Tanner, notes by John Dugdale (Oxford, 1990), 318. For Montesquieu's critique of glory, Louis XIV, and Louis XV, see Paul A. Rahe, *Montesquieu and the Logic of Liberty: War, Religion, Commerce, Climate, Terrain, Technology, Uneasiness of Mind, the Spirit of Political Vigilance, and the Foundations of the Modern Republic* (New Haven, Conn., 2009), 201–207.

43. Thomas C. Upham, *The Manual of Peace ...* (New York, 1836), 186–187.

ern neo-Calvinists dismayed by French Revolutionary violence, it is unsurprising that Upham, a Bowdoin College professor who served for a number of years as vice president of the American Peace Society, was born in New Hampshire and educated as a Calvinist. Nor is it remarkable that his denunciation of national glory appeared in a work insisting that "wars must cease, absolutely and universally." Upham was typical, in other words, of the paradoxically progressive conservative who tried to counter the restless, democratic spirit unleashed in the 1790s. By prompting a negative reaction, American engagement with Napoleonic glory stimulated cultural upheaval.[44]

Unfortunately for reformers like Upham, the upheaval they initiated failed to undermine the cult of Napoleon in the United States. That cult—which included multiple stage plays, a Ralph Waldo Emerson essay, numerous exhibitions and copies of Jacques Louis-David's painting *Napoleon Crossing the Alps* (1800), young women's "story paper" tales celebrating Napoleon and female literary ambition, and an assortment of Gulf Coast inhabitants committed to Napoleon's liberation from Saint Helena, the memorialization of two Bonapartist death masks, and the reestablishment of a neo-Napoleonic American empire—was at bottom a manifestation of early American democracy's fascination with power. Or, better yet, the cult was a reflection of how a compulsion for state and civic capacity was embedded in and gave life to American democracy's development.[45] Forged in the French Revolution, modern democracy at its outset was, as R. R. Palmer demonstrated long ago, an embattled, international crusade preoccupied with national self-

---

44. Ibid., iii; Rachel Hope Cleves, *The Reign of Terror in America: Visions of Violence from Anti-Jacobinism to Antislavery* (Cambridge, 2009), 153–193.

45. Daniel A. Cohen, "Making Hero Strong: Teenage Ambition, Story-Paper Fiction, and the Generational Recasting of American Women's Authorship," *Journal of the Early Republic*, XXX (2010), 114, 118; Lee Kennett, "Le Culte de Napoléon aux États-Unis Jusqu'a la Guerre de Sécession," *Revue de l'Institut Napoléon*, no. 125 (October–December 1972), 147–156, esp. 150; Ralph Waldo Emerson, "Napoleon; or, The Man of the World," in *Essays and Lectures*, ed. Joel Porte (New York, 1983), 727–745; Catherine Wilcox-Titus, "Napoleon and Lafayette in the Print Culture," in Georgia B. Barnhill, ed., *With a French Accent: American Lithography to 1860* (Worcester, Mass., 2012), 49–63; Emilio Ocampo, *The Emperor's Last Campaign: A Napoleonic Empire in America* (Tuscaloosa, Ala., 2009); Rafe Blaufarb, *Bonapartists in the Borderlands: French Exiles and Refugees on the Gulf Coast, 1815–1835* (Tuscaloosa, Ala., 2005); Olivia Blanchard, "The Death Mask of Napoleon at the Cabildo, New Orleans," *Louisiana Historical Quarterly*, VIII (1925), 71–83. On democratic state and civic capacity, see Hale, "American Hercules," in Griffin et al., eds., *Between Sovereignty and Anarchy*, 243–262.

determination and the destruction of corporate privilege. The American iteration of this crusade took shape as a campaign against both British influence and Federalist attempts to construct a British-inspired fiscal-military state.[46] Yet characterizations of Jeffersonian democracy as an altogether decentralizing phenomenon motivated primarily by a loathing of concentrated force miss the mark. If Democratic-Republicans in the late eighteenth and early nineteenth centuries sought to foil British and Federalist power, that does not mean they were averse to power in general. At the heart of the Jeffersonian movement, in fact, was a desire to overturn long-standing assumptions about democracy's weakness by ruthlessly enforcing its standing at home and in the world. Napoleon proved alluring to many Americans because he held out the promise that anti-British, democratic enthusiasts would one day bid defiance to their enemies and rule unopposed. Moreover, dreams of incontrovertible democratic power, especially those entangled with what Lyman Beecher characterized as "intense admiration for Napoleon Bonaparte" and his purported "executive genius," undergirded popular fascination with and an inclination to employ—even at the expense of law, civility, and morality—terrifying, neo-monarchical authority. Even though democracy is often seen as the antithesis of monarchy, it is in many ways its fulfillment and amplification, so that nothing is more democratic than bold, even cruel, assertions of autocratic power.[47]

The most expansive, sublime versions of democratic-autocratic power

---

46. R. R. Palmer, *The Age of the Democratic Revolution: A Political History of Europe and America, 1760-1800*, 2 vols. (Princeton, N.J., 1959 and 1964); Hale, "Regenerating the World," *JAH*, CIII (2017), 891-920; Lance Banning, *The Jeffersonian Persuasion: Evolution of a Party Ideology* (Ithaca, N.Y., 1978); Drew R. McCoy, *The Elusive Republic: Political Economy in Jeffersonian America* (Chapel Hill, N.C., 1980); Lawrence Delbert Cress, *Citizens in Arms: The Army and Militia in American Society to the War of 1812* (Chapel Hill, N.C., 1982); Richard H. Kohn, *Eagle and Sword: The Federalists and the Beginnings of the Military Establishment in America, 1783-1802* (New York, 1975).

47. Lyman Beecher, *Autobiography, Correspondence, etc.*, 2 vols., ed. Charles Beecher (New York, 1865), 531; Hale, "American Hercules," in Griffin et al., eds., *Between Sovereignty and Anarchy*, 243-262. For Napoleon and genius, see Darrin M. McMahon, *Divine Fury: A History of Genius* (New York, 2013), 115-124. Although few scholars have explored the intersection of monarchy and democracy, see Brendan McConville, *The King's Three Faces: The Rise and Fall of Royal America, 1688-1776* (Chapel Hill, N.C., 2006) 139, 314-316; Paul Downes, *Democracy, Revolution, and Monarchism in Early American Literature* (Cambridge, 2002); Bailey, *Thomas Jefferson and Executive Power;* John W. Compton and Karen Orren, "Political Theory in Institutional Context: The Case of Patriot Royalism," *American Political Thought*, III (2014), 1-31.

often materialized in war, and evidence of post-Revolutionary Americans' enthrallment with Napoleonic militarism abounds. For starters, soldiers in various American conflicts fashioned themselves and their conflicts in the image of Napoleon and his conflicts.[48] In addition, martial rituals and principles infused antebellum political and educational culture.[49] Finally, in response to his nine-month journey through the United States in 1831–1832, Frenchman Alexis de Tocqueville astutely contended that there is "a hidden relation between military mores and democratic mores," that there "is no greatness that satisfies the imagination of a democratic people more than military greatness." That idea is anathema to many, and scholarly studies—especially in political science—continue to appear purportedly proving that democracy is more peaceful than other types of government. A historically grounded approach to the problem, on the other hand, suggests that American democracy contains within it a distinct, albeit occasionally obscured, affinity for war.[50]

48. Robert W. Johannsen, *To the Halls of the Montezumas: The Mexican War in the American Imagination* (New York, 1985), 74–77, 249–250; Charles Royster, *The Destructive War: William Tecumseh Sherman, Stonewall Jackson, and the Americans* (New York, 1991), 42, 234–235; Stephen W. Sears, *George B. McClellan: The Young Napoleon* (1988; rpt. New York, 1999); T. Harry Williams, *P. G. T. Beauregard: Napoleon in Gray* (1955; rpt. Baton Rouge, La., 1995); Michael A. Bonura, *Under the Shadow of Napoleon: French Influence on the American Way of Warfare from the War of 1812 to the Outbreak of WWII* (New York, 2012).

49. David Waldstreicher, *In the Midst of Perpetual Fetes: The Making of American Nationalism, 1776–1820* (Chapel Hill, N.C., 1997), 157–166; Marcus Cunliffe, *Soldiers and Civilians: The Martial Spirit in America, 1775–1865* (New York, 1973); Jean H. Baker, *Affairs of Party: The Political Culture of Northern Democrats in the Mid-Nineteenth Century* (1983; rpt. New York, 1998), 287–316; Harry S. Laver, *Citizens More than Soldiers: The Kentucky Militia and Society in the Early Republic* (Lincoln, Nebr., 2007); John F. Kutolowski and Kathleen Smith Kutolowski, "Commissions and Canvasses: The Militia and Politics in Western New York, 1800–1845," *New York History*, LXIII (1982), 4–38; George H. Callcott, "History Enters the Schools," *American Quarterly*, XI (1959), 476; Don Higginbotham, *Revolution in America: Considerations and Comparisons* (Charlottesville, Va., 2005), 163–189.

50. Tocqueville, *Democracy in America*, ed. Mansfield and Winthrop, 629; Steve Chan, "In Search of Democratic Peace: Problems and Promise," *Mershon International Studies Review*, XLI (1997), 59–91; James Lee Ray, "Does Democracy Cause Peace?" *Annual Review of Political Science*, I (1998) 27–46; R. J. Rummel, *The Blue Book of Freedom: Ending Famine, Poverty, Democide, and War* (Nashville, Tenn., 2007). On the integral role of war in American history, see Fred Anderson and Andrew Cayton, *The Dominion of War: Empire and Liberty in North America, 1500–2000* (New York, 2005).

Born in 1767, just two years before Napoleon's natal year, Andrew Jackson embodied the democratic penchant for war, as well as most of the other historical developments discussed in this essay. An early backer of Napoleon—in 1798 he wrote that if "Bonaparte make a landing on the English shore, Tyranny will be Humbled"—Jackson maintained that support throughout his life, accumulating five biographies and a sculpted bust of the Corsican general.[51] During his pre-presidential career, the man known as "Old Hickory" demonstrated: an abiding Anglophobia; a combative personality geared toward reprisal; outsized political and military ambition; an impulsive, self-centered, reckless spirit; a predisposition to violence; a charisma rooted in supreme self-confidence, decisive action, and daring military campaigns; a commitment to territorial expansion, slavery, and homosocial organizations (the military and the Freemasons); a flamboyant disregard of civilian authority; and a concern for stylish military dress and gallantry, which numerous artists, including John Wesley Jarvis, captured in their Napoleonic portraits and busts (see Figures 9–15).[52] Once in the White House, Jackson continued operating in a Bonapartist mode, lambasting British influence, subduing political rivals, inviting his cult-like democratic following to champion him, promoting Indian Removal and slaveholders' interests, and wielding expansive executive prerogative. In response to these authoritarian actions, opponents characterized Jackson as a dangerous man akin to Napoleon and themselves as "Whigs" counteracting "King Andrew." By the same token, democratic enthusiasts beguiled by Jackson's dictatorial ways embraced rather than denied the Bonaparte comparisons.[53]

51. Andrew Jackson to James Robertson, Jan. 11, 1798, in Sam B. Smith and Harriet Chappell Owsley, eds., *The Papers of Andrew Jackson*, I (Knoxville, Tenn., 1980) 165 (quotation); Ward, *Andrew Jackson*, 184; Kennett, "Le Culte," *Revue de l'Institut Napoléon*, no. 125 (October–December 1972), 148.

52. Charles Henry Hart, "Life Portraits of Andrew Jackson," *McClure's Magazine*, IX (1897), 797; James G. Barber, *Andrew Jackson: A Portrait Study* (Washington, D.C., 1991), 37–38, 116; Susan Clover Symonds, "Portraits of Andrew Jackson: 1815–1848" (master's thesis, University of Delaware, 1968), 8–11; Milo M. Naeve, "William Rush's Terracotta and Plaster Busts of General Andrew Jackson," *American Art Journal*, XXI (1989), 19–39; Michael Zakim, *Ready-Made Democracy: A History of Men's Dress in the American Republic, 1760–1860* (Chicago, 2003), 212, 287 n. 2; Robert Remini, *Andrew Jackson and the Course of American Empire, 1767–1821* (Baltimore, 1977); Remini, *Andrew Jackson and the Course of American Freedom, 1822–1832* (New York, 1981).

53. Remini, *Andrew Jackson and the Course of American Freedom*; Robert Remini, *Andrew Jackson and the Course of American Democracy, 1833–1845* (New York, 1984); Andrew Burstein, *The Passions of Andrew Jackson* (New York, 2003); Haynes, *Unfin-*

Figure 9. John Wesley Jarvis, *Andrew Jackson*. 1817. White House Historical Association (White House Collection): 3120

Figure 10. John Wesley Jarvis, *General Andrew Jackson*. 1819.
The Metropolitan Museum of Art, Harris Brisbane Dick Fund, 1964

Figure 11. Jean François de la Vallée, *Andrew Jackson (1767–1845)*. 1815. Watercolor on ivory. Historic Hudson Valley, Potantico Hills, N.Y. Gift of J. Dennis Delafield. MP.91.11 a-b

Figure 12. Charles Willson Peale, *Andrew Jackson*. 1819. Courtesy, The Masonic Library and Museum of Pennsylvania, Philadelphia

Figure 13. Anna Claypoole Peale, *Andrew Jackson*. 1819. Watercolor on ivory. 7.9 x 6.2 cm. Mabel Brady Garvan Collection. Yale University Art Gallery, New Haven, Conn.

Figure 14. William Rush, *General Andrew Jackson*. 1819. Terracotta, 50.5 x 47.9 x 22.2 cm. (19⅞ x 18⅞ x 8¾ in.). Restricted Gift of Jamee J. and Marshall Field, the Brooks and Hope B. McCormick Foundation, and the Bessie Bennett, W. G. Field, Ada Turnbull Hertle, Laura T. Magnuson, and Major Acquisitions Funds. 1985.251. The Art Institute of Chicago

Figure 15. John Vanderlyn, *Andrew Jackson*. 1823.
Oil on canvas, 94 x 64 in. Photograph by Glenn Castellano,
Collection of the Public Design Commission of the City of New York

To study Napoleonic glory imperatives in the early United States is therefore to confront various aspects of American democracy—especially those derived from its initial romance with power—that have received little scholarly attention. Yet only by situating post-Revolutionary occurrences in a Bonapartist framework can we realize the degree to which transatlantic currents impelled American democracy's development. And only by engaging these phenomena can historians conceptualize and depict a more complicated, morally unencumbered version of democracy.

---

ished Revolution, 106–122; Howe, *What God Hath Wrought*, 328–445; Bertram Wyatt-Brown, "Andrew Jackson's Honor," *JER*, XVII (1997), 1–36; David Hackett Fischer, *Albion's Seed: Four British Folkways in America* (New York, 1989), 775. For the response of Jackson's opponents, see Michael Holt, *The Rise and Fall of the American Whig Party: Jacksonian Politics and the Onset of the Civil War* (New York, 1999), 19–32. For that of his proponents, see Ward, *Andrew Jackson*, 123, 161, 183–185; Colin McCoy, "Democracy in Print: The Literature of Persuasion in Jacksonian America, 1815–1840" (Ph.D. diss., University of Illinois at Urbana-Champaign, 2001), 247–251; James Parton, *Life of Andrew Jackson*, 3 vols. (New York, 1860), III, 17, 493.

MILITARY SERVICE AND RACIAL SUBJECTIVITY IN THE WAR NARRATIVES OF JAMES ROBERTS AND ISAAC HUBBELL

James M. Greene

Among the many veterans of the Revolutionary War who published their memoirs, Jonathan Burnham, a colonel in the New Hampshire line, perhaps provided the most glowing account of the war's results in his 1814 text: "Then we had our independence from Great Britain, and peace and plenty and the love of the whole world, and were the happiest nation in the world." If Burnham might have been guilty of a small measure of hyperbole in this account, his rosy recollection of the United States following the Revolution stood in stark contrast to his feelings about the war that he found the nation fighting as he wrote—his narrative closed with the frustrated claim that "America is undone, for if we should take Canada it is not worth the life of one man, to America." Burnham was not alone in describing the War of 1812 as a decline from the glorious era of the Revolution. Other Revolutionary War veterans, such as Samuel Dewees and David Perry, expressed a similar sense of disappointment over a second war with Great Britain and the domestic tension between Federalists and Republicans that accompanied it. Dewees, a fifer, even claimed to have served in both wars, which is a reasonable claim, given that he joined the Continental army as a young orphan and was in early middle age during the War of 1812. The frustration expressed in these narratives indicates how many of the nation's first veterans imagined the Revolutionary War as a moment of collective virtue that had been forgotten as younger Americans pursued their self-interest at the expense of the commonweal. The War of 1812 became a marker for such writers of a moment when the possibilities of the Revolution began to be foreclosed.[1]

1. Jonathan Burnham, *The Life of Col. Jonathan Burnham, Now Living in Salisbury, Mass.; Being a Narrative of His Long and Useful Life* (Portsmouth, N.H., 1814), 7–8; John Smith Hanna, *A History of the Life and Services of Captain Samuel Dewees, a Native of Pennsylvania, and Soldier of the Revolutionary and Last Wars; Also, Reminiscences of the Revolutionary Struggle (Indian War, Western Expedition, Liberty Insurrection in Northampton County, Pa.) and Late War with Great Britain* ... (Baltimore, 1844); David Perry, *Recollections of an Old Soldier; the Life of Captain David Perry, a*

The prevalence of such narratives helps explain the appearance of two other accounts of questionable authenticity that nonetheless tried to spread awareness of the larger truth of post-Revolutionary disillusionment. Isaac Hubbell and James Roberts, two obscure veterans of the Continental army, also claimed to present the experiences of veterans of both the Revolution and the War of 1812 in works published during the antebellum era. These texts shared the concern that the later war represented a compromise in national virtue. To modern readers, however, they lack authenticity as the memories of veterans given the many bold claims and historical inaccuracies they present. Both narratives openly admitted the presence of an amanuensis. Josiah Priest, a prolific author of sensational literature for the popular press, adapted Hubbell's story, and an unnamed collaborator records Roberts's experiences. Further, Priest's tale differs in significant ways from the other written accounts of Isaac Hubbell's war experiences, and no evidence of James Roberts exists apart from the narrative published in his name.[2]

Yet, in their fictional qualities, both texts provide unique insight into the ways that the Revolutionary War and the War of 1812 were represented and understood during the years leading toward an even greater national struggle. They show the ways in which the trope of national decline from the Revolution could be put to competing ideological purposes amid the fight over slavery during the later antebellum period. What these narratives lack in historical reliability is made up in their demonstration of the efforts of antebellum writers to reshape American history in order to narrate the nation's violent past as a warning to an increasingly troubled present.

Although these texts agreed that the War of 1812 marked a symbolic end to the promise of the Revolutionary era, they described this moment through

---

Soldier of the French and Revolutionary Wars; Containing Many Extraordinary Occurrences Relating to His Own Private History, and an Account of Some Interesting Events in the History of the Times in Which He Lived, No-where Else Recorded; Written by Himself (Windsor, Vt., 1822).

2. Josiah Priest, *The Fort Stanwix Captive; or, New England Volunteer, Being the Extraordinary Life and Adventures of Isaac Hubbell among the Indians of Canada and the West, in the War of the Revolution, and the Story of His Marriage with the Indian Princess, Now First Published, from the Lips of the Hero Himself* (Albany, N.Y., 1841); James Roberts, *The Narrative of James Roberts, a Soldier Under Gen. Washington in the Revolutionary War, and Under Gen. Jackson at the Battle of New Orleans, in the War of 1812: "A Battle Which Cost Me a Limb, Some Blood, and Almost My Life"* (Chicago, 1858), *Documenting the American South*, http://docsouth.unc.edu/neh/roberts/menu.html.

contrasting emotions. The narratives of Hubbell and Roberts responded to a nationalist discourse that envisioned liberty as the product of the collective strength of a continental body politic. Both narratives assumed implicitly an ideology of popular sovereignty that remembered the violence of the Revolution as an expression of the will of the American people—with people defined, not as an aggregation of local political communities, but as the association of men from across the colonies joined in communal resistance. The collective will to political violence appeared as the most concrete expression of popular sovereignty, but these texts imagined this collective will as the product of the subordination of the individual to the commonweal. Military service offered a compelling model of this subordination, and both narratives emphasized the individual act of submission to military authority as a means of describing a commitment to the nation. In the racial contrast between the white Hubbell and the black Roberts, however, these accounts also suggested that such a commitment only gains legitimacy through a discourse of white supremacy and racial purity.

Read together, the narratives indicate that racial difference has provided the ideological underpinnings to the history of American Revolutionary violence by imagining the legitimate expression of this violence as the sole domain of the united white men of the United States. Josiah Priest framed Isaac Hubbell's experiences in 1812 as a lament over the loss of the national unity Priest attributed to the Revolutionary conflict. He found this unity embodied in the Continental army, and the account concluded in dismay that the army assembled for the second Anglo-American war lacked the fraternity Priest associated with the army that won the first. Priest told Hubbell's story as that of a white man who abandoned his military service to live as an Indian before ultimately recognizing the error of his ways and returning to the normative racial order—an order figured by Hubbell's membership in the army. Such an ideal anticipated Priest's later writings as a pro-slavery apologist and indicated his desire to locate the ideology of white supremacy within the nation's founding moment. The James Roberts narrative presented its protagonist as a freed slave who served in the armies of George Washington and Andrew Jackson while still in bondage. For Roberts, his service in the War of 1812 established that the liberty he helped win in 1783 extended only to white men. The text read both the Revolutionary War and the War of 1812 as false promises of freedom in order to challenge the founding notion of Revolutionary violence in the United States. As it depicted the broken promises of freedom made to a black man who served in two wars, as well as the mistreatment and disregard for white soldiers in the War of

1812, the narrative implied that Revolutionary violence in the United States has not assured liberty and inclusion in the body politic for those who have fought. Such violence has instead served the imperial interests of America's political and economic elites. It described war and slavery as mutual expressions of domination and found little distinction between the battlefield and the cotton field.[3]

Both texts were published several decades after the War of 1812, with Hubbell's story appearing as Priest's 1841 pamphlet, *The Fort Stanwix Captive* and Roberts's narrative seeing print in 1858. Given this wide gap from even the latest events in the narratives, it should be unsurprising that they both feature their share of inaccuracies, but they also go beyond errors in memory to present plots that border on the fantastic. Priest told Isaac Hubbell's story as a frontier romance in which the brave white soldier is adopted by his Indian captors and marries an Indian "princess." After being taken captive by the British and separated from his wife, Hubbell was reunited by chance with his Indian bride as he attempted to escape to Boston, only to see her tragically drown along with his mixed-blood son as they row out to the boat that will take them to safety. James Roberts was presented as a purportedly 104-year-old former slave who fought along with his master in the southern theater of the Revolutionary War and was promised freedom in exchange for his service in Jackson's army at New Orleans, where he killed six British soldiers in close combat as a 60-year-old man. As a centenarian, Roberts also claimed to have argued for a veteran's pension with both President Franklin Pierce and President James Buchanan.[4]

As authentic records of the voices of veterans of America's first two wars, the narratives of Roberts and Hubbell appear less than reliable. As cultural

---

3. Studies of the social bonds within the Continental army include Caroline Cox, *A Proper Sense of Honor: Service and Sacrifice in George Washington's Army* (Chapel Hill, N.C., 2004); Sarah Knott, *Sensibility and the American Revolution* (Chapel Hill, N.C., 2009); and Gregory T. Knouff, *The Soldiers' Revolution: Pennsylvanians in Arms and the Forging of Early American Identity* (University Park, Pa., 2004).

4. Josiah Priest's writings have received limited scholarly attention. The most thorough study of his work comes from Winthrop Hillyer Duncan's bibliographic essay, "Josiah Priest: Historian of the American Frontier: A Study and Bibliography," American Antiquarian Society, *Proceedings*, XLIV, pt. 1 (1935), 45–102. A more recent study focused on one of Priest's historical romances can be found in De Villo Sloan, "*The Crimsoned Hills of Onondaga:* Josiah Priest's Hallucinatory Epic," *Journal of Popular Culture*, XXXVI (2002), 86–104. The Roberts narrative is discussed briefly in Russ Castronovo, *Fathering the Nation: American Genealogies of Slavery and Freedom* (Berkeley, Calif., 1995), 203–206.

fantasies of the history of U.S. political violence, however, these two texts reveal how a stable form of that history emerged through the interaction of the ideology of white male supremacy and the valorization of the American citizen-soldier. Both stories approach the memory of the nation's first wars as an opportunity to self-consciously arrange that memory into a history that moves forward the political argument their authors present. Josiah Priest rearranged the facts of Isaac Hubbell's life to create a romantic fiction of the progress of white civilization and the tragic disappearance of the Indian; the author of the James Roberts narrative told the fiction of Roberts's life as a lost set of facts that overturns the celebratory history of American nationalism. In both narratives, these fantastic elements bring sharper contrast to the ways each text locates race at the center of the nation's Revolutionary origins.

"A Monument of Heroism and Courage": White Manhood and Service to the Nation

The Fort Stanwix Captive, in setting up its contrast between the Continental army and the army of 1812, drew on two different discourses that promoted national identification in the early United States: the commemoration of the American Revolution and the advancement of theories of white supremacy. Both discourses evolved over the decades between 1800 and the start of the Civil War. The remembrance of the Revolutionary War imparted a sense of national identity almost from the moment the war ended. Public orations and private toasts, especially on the Fourth of July, celebrated the achievement of liberty from Great Britain. Written tributes and ceremonies of mourning marked the sacrifices of American patriots lost to the cause. New American histories, such as those by Mason Locke Weems, Mercy Otis Warren, and David Ramsay, created a class of heroic founding fathers. The wide array of cultural practices for remembering the Revolution as the moment of origin for a new nation allowed Americans to imagine themselves bound by a common identity that was unique from Europe and also transcended local distinctions between the states.[5]

During the same years the nation developed a shared sense of history,

---

5. Mercy Otis Warren, *History of the Rise, Progress, and Termination of the American Revolution* ... (Boston, 1805); David Ramsay, *The History of the American Revolution*, 2 vols. (Philadelphia, 1789). Weems published numerous biographies of participants in the American Revolution, such as George Washington, Benjamin Franklin, and Francis Marion.

many Americans speculated that such unity could only be maintained in a racially homogenous country. In his 1785 *Notes on the State of Virginia*, Thomas Jefferson famously described his belief that those of African descent were by birth inferior to those of European descent and that African Americans should be removed to Africa since they would be less capable of citizenship in the new nation. Many writers during the next decades would further Jefferson's belief that the races could not coexist. The antebellum era would see a proliferation of discourses that sought to demonstrate that white supremacy was the justified result of historical, natural, or divine forces. Liberty was held to be the unique motivation of the Anglo-Saxon race, which had carried this drive from the shores of Britain to the New World. The pseudoscience of phrenology arose from ethnological comparisons between races to claim that the Caucasian race was distinguished by a greater cranial capacity and thus greater intelligence. Supporters of slavery advanced interpretations of the Bible that sought to prove God's intention for the white race to be elevated above others. Such discourses intended to defend in theory a situation that existed in fact: the United States was a nation that extended its benefits nearly exclusively to white men. Identifying as a white man deemphasized class distinctions between the lower classes and the elite by investing all white men with a sense of autonomy that distinguished them from nonwhites and women. Like the commemoration of the American Revolution, white supremacist discourse offered a means of identification that transcended regional and economic divisions between men.[6]

Much of the argument of *The Fort Stanwix Captive* emerged from its effort to draw these discourses together to reimagine national history in a way that would justify white supremacy as a basis for social unity. The narrative's mixture of two popular nineteenth-century literary genres sug-

---

6. Thomas Jefferson, *Notes on the State of Virginia*, ed. Frank Shuffleton (New York, 1999), 144–151. The literature on nineteenth-century white supremacist discourse is vast, but a good overview can be found in George M. Fredrickson, *The Black Image in the White Mind: The Debate on Afro-American Character and Destiny, 1817–1914* (New York, 1971); and Reginald Horsman, *Race and Manifest Destiny: The Origins of American Racial Anglo-Saxonism* (Cambridge, Mass., 1981). On the unifying effect of white supremacy for white men of different economic classes, see Edmund S. Morgan, *American Slavery, American Freedom: The Ordeal of Colonial Virginia* (New York, 1975), 380–381; David R. Roediger, *The Wages of Whiteness: Race and the Making of the American Working Class*, rev. ed. (New York, 1999), 33–36; and Dana D. Nelson, *National Manhood: Capitalist Citizenship and the Imagined Fraternity of White Men* (Durham, N.C., 1998), 29–60.

gests the intersection of these two strands of thought. Priest's deployment of Revolutionary-era commemorative rhetoric appears readily within the text as he portrayed Isaac Hubbell as a forgotten hero of the struggle for nationhood. The text shares the generic features of many veterans' narratives published throughout the nineteenth century by depicting a protagonist who proudly served during the Revolutionary War, only to be mistreated or unacknowledged by his countrymen in later years. Priest's engagement with racist discourses of the time occurs more subtly as *The Fort Stanwix Captive* blended the conventions of the veteran narrative with the traits of a historical frontier romance in the mode of James Fenimore Cooper. As mentioned, Hubbell chose to intermarry and live as an Indian—a decision for which he is symbolically punished over the course of the story, primarily through the death of his Indian wife and child. Hubbell's intermarriage also interrupted his service in the Continental army, yet Hubbell appears to redeem this decision by returning to serve in the War of 1812.

This return served to position Hubbell in contrast to subsequent generations of Americans and implied a decline in national virtue. Despite his dalliance with the Indians, Hubbell symbolized a disinterested commitment to the nation that Priest believed had been lost by 1812. The narrative concludes with a final scene of Hubbell, "full of the old fire of the war of Independence," returning to the army in 1812. This second service ended abruptly, however, when a younger officer who had "[taken] offence at the old man's stories about his deeds in the Revolution" struck Hubbell on the head with a heavy wood cane. In the immediate context of the narrative, this attack suggests a decline in the character of the nation's soldiers, as the man Priest called "a monument of heroism and courage" is assaulted by a "ruthless envious fool." This officer appeared to gratify his emotions of jealousy toward Hubbell, rather than respect the bonds of military camaraderie as well as the figurative debt that he owed to the older man as a veteran of the Revolution. The conclusion of *The Fort Stanwix Captive* thus distinguished between the Revolution and the War of 1812 through a decline of the fellow feeling that bound individuals into an American nation and that Priest sought to locate in the memory of the earlier war. As noted, such arguments were a common feature in the war narratives of Revolutionary veterans. As a commemoration of the Revolution, *The Fort Stanwix Captive* called on its readers to rally around the common sacrifices made by men like Hubbell and to avoid the selfish disregard for such efforts shown by the younger officer.[7]

7. Priest, *The Fort Stanwix Captive*, 64.

This appeal to respect the Revolutionary past stemmed from Priest's presentation of Hubbell at the end of the narrative as an example of disinterested republican virtue. Motivated by the same spirit that led him to war in 1776, Hubbell returned to serve his country once again in 1812. By depicting Hubbell as both a brave young soldier who accomplished many daring tasks in battle during the Revolution and as an older veteran who received the scorn and abuse of a younger generation in 1812, Priest incorporated a cultural image John Resch has described as "the suffering soldier," a dualfaceted figure that simultaneously emphasized the Revolutionary veteran's bravery and endurance during the war and his infirmity and deprivation after its conclusion. Emerging through the many personal narratives and pension testimonies given by Revolutionary veterans during the years after the war, the image of the suffering soldier became a celebration of the heroic sacrifices of those veterans and, as Resch argues, encouraged a shift in national memory regarding the Continental army. Negative portrayals of this force as a collection of social dregs and mercenaries, motivated only by enlistment bounties, gave way to an idealized view of these soldiers as virtuous republican warriors fighting on behalf of the American people. The motif of the suffering soldier allowed soldiers of the Continental army to be perceived as having made a disinterested defense of the will of the people, even if they enlisted out of economic self-interest. Standing armies of professional soldiers that would be beholden to the will of their patron had long been considered a danger to liberty in republican thought, but the reality of fighting a prolonged war often made such soldiers essential. As a result, Americans sought ways to imagine the soldier of the United States that emphasized his autonomy and independence, even as they acknowledged the subordination necessary for military discipline. Unlike the European hireling, the American soldier was imagined to serve, not out of obligation to a powerful commander, but out of what Elizabeth Samet terms "a *liberal obedience*" based in his personal commitment to the cause for which he fought. Even though the soldier of the Continental army received financial compensation for his efforts, he could be imagined to have freely chosen to defend the common good on behalf of his countrymen. This liberal sense of free choice would erase distinctions between a virtuous militia and a potentially corrupt standing army. Part of the utility of the trope of the suffering soldier comes from its deemphasis of the motivations of an individual soldier in favor of attention to his affiliation with the national cause. A soldier might have enlisted for purely self-interested reasons, such as enlistment bounties, a desire to escape an overbearing parent or master, or simple boredom, but his affiliation with the army that fought in the Revolution marked him as a disinterested patriot.[8]

The soldiers of the Revolutionary War thus exemplify an idealized moment of national consensus. In *The Fort Stanwix Captive,* Priest both lamented the loss of that unity and advanced what he saw as the best means to regain it. In place of the struggle for independence from the British, Priest imagined white supremacy as the bulwark to support commitment to the commonweal. The narrative cast the Continental army not just as an example of national solidarity but also as an embodiment of an ideal moment of white male unity. This racial argument developed in large part through the depiction of Isaac Hubbell's earlier lapse from the disinterested sense of service he symbolized at the story's end. Hubbell's intermarriage figured as both a pursuit of his own self-interest and a crossing of racial boundaries. Priest emphasized the tragic death of Hubbell's Indian wife and mixed-blood son so that the protagonist appeared as a white man who chose to live as an Indian and suffered negative consequences as a result of that decision. Unlike the officer of 1812, though, Hubbell corrected his lapse in virtue—in this case by returning to a racially homogenous nation represented by the Continental army.

Over the course of the narrative, Hubbell's career follows a plot of the rise, fall, and ultimate redemption of a forgotten Revolutionary soldier. The early sections of the text present Hubbell not only as a common soldier but also as an exceptional and heroic patriot in order to stress his subsequent decline among the Indians. Like many of the subjects of veteran narratives, Hubbell is introduced to readers as a young man swept up in the patriotic fervor of the opening shots of the war. Hubbell joined a local militia after being inspired by the Boston Tea Party—an event that the narrator states "roused in a moment the slumbering fires of the bosoms of all true patriots, throughout the entire country, and produced the great resolve that America should be free." Hubbell went on to serve in the regular army and participated in the failed invasion of Canada as well as the Battle of Monmouth. Priest depicted Hubbell as a significant participant in the latter battle by claiming that General Washington had handpicked Hubbell for a dangerous individual mission that involved driving a wagon toward a squad of British light horse in

---

8. John Resch, *Suffering Soldiers: Revolutionary War Veterans, Moral Sentiment, and Political Culture in the Early Republic* (Amherst, Mass., 1999), 1–10; Elizabeth D. Samet, *Willing Obedience: Citizens, Soldiers, and the Progress of Consent in America, 1776–1898* (Stanford, Calif., 2004), 6–7.

order to provoke a chase that would lead the enemy cavalry into an American ambush. Priest asserted that this mission was essential in initiating the entire battle and that Washington had personally chosen Hubbell because the general recognized him as "one of those fear-naught kind of men." This claim illustrates both the unreliability of Priest's story as a record of Hubbell's service and the degree to which Priest aimed to present the veteran as an idealized Revolutionary hero. In contrast to Priest's heroic tale, the historical Isaac Hubbell made no mention of the Battle of Monmouth in his application for a federal pension in 1820. Furthermore, he stated that he was a member of Goose van Schaik's Second Regiment of the New York Line. This unit was not included in the force Charles Lee led against the British at the start of the battle. It therefore seems likely that the scene in which Hubbell bravely serves as bait to lead the enemy into a trap was pure invention by Priest. That invention set Hubbell within the discourse of the suffering soldier by firmly establishing his patriotism and his self-sacrificing commitment to the American cause in the early days of the war.[9]

Such a depiction grounded the subsequent theme of Hubbell's personal decline when he chose not to attempt to escape from his Indian captors but rather accepted adoption into the tribe. Priest made it clear that Hubbell made this decision because an Indian way of life granted him far more material and social privileges than he had known before. Hubbell "had now made up his mind to remain for life among the Indians, as he saw from the position he had acquired among them that he could possess himself of wealth and importance; and besides that he loved Estaloee [his Indian wife] as he had never loved before." As the son-in-law of the chief of his adopted tribe, Hubbell chose the comforts of high status among the Indians over the privation he would continue to face as a soldier in the Continental army. Although Priest clearly showed that Hubbell maintained his physical and social superiority over the Indians by besting the tribe's runners in sport and winning the hand of the chief's daughter, his subsequent suffering in British captivity and the death of his Indian family implied this privileged status was unsustainable. The hardships of his life apart from the army suggested that Hubbell had been symbolically punished for choosing to pur-

9. Priest, *The Fort Stanwix Captive*, 5, 16–17; Affidavit of Isaac Hubbell, S. 36601, *Case Files of Pension and Bounty-Land Warrant Applications Based on Revolutionary War Service, Compiled ca. 1800–ca. 1912, Documenting the Period ca. 1775–ca. 1900*, National Archives and Record Administration (NARA), microfilm publication M804, digital images courtesy of "Revolutionary War Pension and Bounty-Land Warrant Application Files," *Fold3*, accessed Oct. 1, 2012, http://fold3.com.

sue his own self-interest, rather than maintaining his commitment to the national struggle. Further, the story coded this choice of self-interest as an act of racial transgression and a violation of the norms of white manhood.[10]

When the plot of Priest's text is compared with other accounts of Isaac Hubbell's war experiences, it becomes much clearer that Priest arranged the plot to define Hubbell's intermarriage as a choice of self-interest over military commitment. In addition to *The Fort Stanwix Captive* and his federal pension application, Hubbell's story can be found in Walter Hubbell's 1881 genealogical history of the Hubbell family. The three accounts of Hubbell's experiences offer slightly different versions of his escape from captivity. The unreliability of an aged man's memory may be the simplest explanation for these differences, but the contrasting details can also be a window onto Priest's intentions as he prepared Hubbell's story for a commercial audience. *The History of the Hubbell Family* and his pension application contend that Hubbell initiated his efforts to escape from the Indians because both assert that he escaped directly from the tribe. Conversely, *The Fort Stanwix Captive* suggests Hubbell was unwillingly removed from the tribe when he was claimed by the British as a prisoner of war. Indeed, the narrator remarks shortly before describing this capture that "Hubbell, as he informed the writer, had now made up his mind to remain for life among the Indians." In contrast, the Hubbell family history claims Isaac Hubbell snuck away from his Indian captors owing to "a constant yearning to see again his friends and relatives" in Connecticut. Priest thus gave greater attention to Hubbell's decision to intermarry and live with the tribe as an indication of the veteran's abandonment of the national struggle as well as his deviation from an ideal of racial purity.[11]

This deviation received further emphasis from another key distinction between the accounts of Hubbell's captivity. Priest dramatized Hubbell's story to repudiate the veteran's conscious decision to live as an Indian. The narrative implied that Hubbell's decision to gratify his interests by going native could only end in tragedy. In Priest's version, Hubbell was miraculously reunited with his Indian wife and child during his escape from British captivity in Montreal. His wife had joined another tribe to be closer to the place where her husband was a captive, and they met by chance when he was de-

---

10. Priest, *The Fort Stanwix Captive*, 43.
11. Affidavit of Isaac Hubbell, S. 36601, *Case Files of Pension and Bounty-Land Warrant Applications*, NARA; Walter Hubbell, *History of the Hubbell Family, Containing a Genealogical Record* ... (New York, 1881), 90–92; Priest, *The Fort Stanwix Captive*, 43.

tained by this band. Hubbell was ransomed to his wife, and they agreed to make their way to Boston. Just when things seemed about to change for the better, Hubbell's wife and child drowned in a canoe accident as the family attempted to row out to a Boston-bound ship. In *The History of the Hubbell Family*, Hubbell left his Indian captors with his family by his side. His family still perished when their canoe overturned, but the account rendered this event as an unfortunate accident, rather than, as portrayed by Priest, the final tragic blow to a pair of star-crossed lovers. This revision places *The Fort Stanwix Captive* squarely within the literary vein of historical romance that became popular in the era between 1820 and 1850.

Writers such as James Fenimore Cooper, William Gilmore Simms, and Lydia Maria Child published novels during this period that worked to forge a national literature from the colonial and Revolutionary past. Such fiction frequently incorporated frontier settings to imagine the nation's history as the progress of civilization moving westward into the wilderness and often included Indian characters condemned to die or otherwise fade into obscurity before the advance of a white society. Lucy Maddox has argued that this literature reflected a popular binary in nineteenth-century American culture that Indians were destined for either extinction or civilization; they could not continue to exist as separate nations apart from the United States. Priest drew on such a line of thought by presenting Hubbell as choosing to willingly live among the Indians and then enduring the tragedy of losing his wife and child before ultimately returning to white society. Child's *Hobomok* offers a comparable literary theme in depicting a Puritan woman who married an Indian man after she believed her white lover has died. When it is revealed that the deceased lover is still alive, the Indian husband nobly sacrificed his own happiness by departing for the West, leaving his wife to a new (white) husband and his mixed-blood son to be raised as a white man. Much like in Child's novel, the interracial marriage in *The Fort Stanwix Captive* cannot be sustained. Further, the choice of self-interest Hubbell appeared to make became associated with a more primitive culture and way of life that the story implied must fade into oblivion.[12]

12. Lucy Maddox, *Removals: Nineteenth-Century American Literature and the Politics of Indian Affairs* (New York, 1991), 8–9. Examples of historical romance include James Fenimore Cooper's *Spy: A Tale of the Neutral Ground*, 2 vols. (New York, 1821), and his series, The Leatherstocking Tales; Lydia Maria Child's *Hobomok, a Tale of Early Times* (Boston, 1824), and *The Rebels; or, Boston before the Revolution* (Boston, 1825); and William Gilmore Simms's *Partisan: A Tale of the Revolution*, 2 vols. (New York, 1835).

By deploying the trope of the vanishing Indian, Priest defined the United States through a contrast between a fading population of Indians and an expanding population of white Americans. Although he did not address this idea directly in *The Fort Stanwix Captive,* this rhetoric underscored that the decline of the Indian nations allowed for the territorial expansion of the United States. As a white American civilization advanced into lands held by Indians, the institution of the nation, especially its power to direct military force, secured these lands for future settlement. Such land represented a potential source of property for the soldiers who served during the Revolution, many of whom were recruited specifically through the promise of land grants upon the completion of their service. This land could provide greater economic opportunity and social autonomy for those who served. Traditionally, the republican citizen-soldier has been distinguished from the mercenary or the soldier in a standing army through reference to property ownership. The citizen-soldier owns property and fights alongside his neighbors to defend it. As J. G. A. Pocock has written in summary of the Renaissance ideal of this individual, in order to value the public good a soldier must have a home of his own and an occupation apart from making war, as only then will he have any motivation to end the fighting quickly. Unlike a professional soldier, an independent, property-holding citizen would be uninterested in maintaining a state of perpetual war that would threaten his home and disrupt his livelihood. Furthermore, the citizen-soldier's independent property allowed him to avoid becoming the pawn of a corrupt tyrant and to go to war with a clear sense of purpose in defending the common good. As mentioned earlier, such an ideal could not be realized in the Revolutionary War, however, and the Continental army included many men who served precisely because they were not property holders. But, as men choosing to serve in the army that makes the acquisition of future lands possible, soldiers without property could see their labor as an essential contribution to the commonweal. Gregory T. Knouff has argued that Revolutionary-era militia requirements that mandated the availability of all white male inhabitants of a community for potential service played a key role in encouraging the perception of white men, regardless of class, as political actors within the public sphere in the years after the war. What a text like *The Fort Stanwix Captive* suggests is that, in place of actual property, the commitment to the nation became a source of autonomy for American soldiers.[13]

---

13. J. G. A. Pocock, *The Machiavellian Moment: Florentine Political Thought and the Atlantic Republican Tradition,* 2d ed. (Princeton, N.J., 2003), 201; Knouff, *The Soldier's*

But this commitment only gained value if the soldier could imagine himself as freely choosing to submit to military discipline—a choice that Priest suggested was coded in racial terms. In place of land or other capital, the American citizen-soldier's control over his own labor became the property that established his independence, and his racial identity as a white man became the guarantee that he enjoyed full title to this property.[14]

The death of Isaac Hubbell's Indian wife and child was presented as the final hardship that brought Hubbell to a state of symbolic repentance that highlighted his restoration to an unintegrated racial order. Hubbell returned to his place in the Continental army just before it disbanded, and he received an honorable discharge along with his comrades. This detail reasserted Hubbell's equality with his fellow soldiers following his intermarriage, especially since Priest wrote that Washington himself was present for Hubbell's return, and the commander-in-chief "[gave] orders that the brave soldier should do no duty, but remain at his leisure, till the army should be disbanded, receiving his rations as the rest received theirs in his regiment." Hubbell's return figured within the text as a moment of redemption, erasing his transgression of racial boundaries and recertifying his status as a white American male—a status the text emphasized through reference to Hubbell's marriage to a white woman after his discharge. This moment also indicated that Hubbell's dalliance from the American fold had ended; he returned to the service that defined him as a virtuous member of a republican body politic. This service now appears less as the kind of participation in the war Hubbell undertook before his captivity and more as a passive form of affiliation and loyalty. Hubbell's redemption developed from his solidarity with his fellow soldiers. More than actual military service, this sense of camaraderie factored as the antithesis to Hubbell's racialized pursuit of self-interest. As Hubbell's example illustrates, the free choice implicit in liberal obedience always threatens political stability since individuals can choose to pursue their own interests over those of the nation. In response to such instability, Priest's story furnished a cohesive sense of affiliation within the nation by

---

Revolution, xv. On the potential western land held for Revolutionary soldiers, see John Shy, *A People Numerous and Armed: Reflections on the Military Struggle for American Independence* (Ann Arbor, Mich., 1990), 252, 258.

14. Cheryl I. Harris has described whiteness as "a shield from slavery"—a form of property that consists of free access to one's legal rights and protection from the legal commodification possible under slavery. See Harris, "Whiteness as Property," *Critical Race Theory: The Key Writings That Formed the Movement*, ed. Kimberlé Crenshaw et al. (New York, 1995), 276–291.

casting race as the source of the unity that bound the Revolutionary generation into a sovereign people.[15]

By reading the ways in which *The Fort Stanwix Captive* integrated white supremacy into the Revolutionary past, we can observe how Priest ultimately framed the story's 1812 conclusion as a cautionary tale for his audience in the 1830s. Isaac Hubbell's character arc of initial virtue declining into self-interest closed with his redemption in the institution Priest treated as the embodiment of white male unity, the Continental army. In contrast to this depiction of a Revolutionary-era soldier who corrected his lapse in virtue, the epilogue of Hubbell's tale portrayed an officer of 1812 who violated the bonds of white male solidarity and provided no moment of redemption or remorse. Priest presented the Revolutionary generation as flawed but ultimately heroic, whereas the generation that fought in 1812 symbolized a national decline. A brief consideration of Priest's later career indicates his concern that this loss of collective virtue had only accelerated from 1812 onward. Although the conflict between Hubbell and the rude officer does not appear to directly relate to racist or white supremacist discourse, from this scene of one white man infringing upon the rights of another we can trace a line to Priest's concern over the growing influence of the abolitionist movement. Priest presented the attack on Hubbell in 1812 as foreshadowing the discord he found in his own time over slavery, which he would describe more fully in the biblical defense of slavery he published two years after *The Fort Stanwix Captive*.

Priest would argue in this text, *Slavery, as It Relates to the Negro, or African Race*, that abolitionists failed to recognize the ancient grounds of African inferiority and that continued division over slavery would eventually lead the sections of the United States into civil war. Maintaining white supremacy became essential to the integrity of the nation. He contended that the English actively encouraged the end of African slavery to cause dissension between the American states in the hope that such division would produce a civil war and allow the English to claim unmatched authority over the continent once again. He therefore accused abolitionists of tacitly col-

---

15. Priest, *The Fort Stanwix Captive*, 64. Laura Doyle describes moments such as Hubbell's loss of his Indian family as the "swoon," a trope used across Anglo-Atlantic writing that presents a protagonist being overwhelmed and losing consciousness (and self-control) before awakening to a new state of (racial) identity. See Doyle, *Freedom's Empire: Race and the Rise of the Novel in Atlantic Modernity, 1640–1940* (Durham, N.C., 2008), 2–3.

laborating with the "bitterest enemy" of America. At one point, Priest drew a line from Abraham, Lot, Job, and Moses to Washington in order to cast American slaveholding as an extension of biblical precedent. Like the biblical patriarchs, Priest noted that Washington observed the divine intention for some to be masters and some to be slaves. The nation Washington established can thus be characterized in part by slaveholding, as could the nation of Israel. This reference set slaveholding as one means of providing the United States, a nation formed in the rupture of Revolutionary violence, with a continuous history emerging from the ancient past. Respecting that past thus required maintaining white supremacy. Like the officer who strikes Hubbell, abolitionists ignored the collective commitment to the commonweal Priest attributed to the Revolutionary era. Read from the perspective of Priest's defense of slavery, *The Fort Stanwix Captive* can be interpreted as an effort to locate white supremacy in the historical origins of the nation. In order to address the divisions within his contemporary society, Priest proffered a fantasy of racial solidarity as the common history of the nation.[16]

"To Stay Here in the Cotton-field, Dying and Never Die": Slavery and the Limits of Revolutionary Violence

This vision of national history not only obscured the contentiousness of an earlier era, of course, but also advanced a false image of racial homogeneity within the American forces during the Revolutionary War. Although a larger number of African Americans joined the British following the offer of emancipation made by the royal governor of Virginia, Lord Dunmore, in 1775, the patriot cause was not without support from black men and women. On the American side, black men were initially barred from combat roles and were limited to serving as laborers, but, as the fighting dragged on and the initial enthusiasm for war cooled among many white men, most states began recruiting blacks as soldiers to meet the pressing need for manpower. This need led the American political and military establishment eventually to accept both free and enslaved black men into the army, with many states offering manumission to those who would enlist, thus creating a dual purpose for many African American soldiers, who fought for both national and

---

16. Josiah Priest, *Slavery, as It Relates to the Negro, or African Race, Examined in the Light of Circumstances, History and the Holy Scriptures; with an Account of the Origin of the Black Man's Color, Causes of His State of Servitude and Traces of His Character as Well as in Ancient as in Modern Times: With Strictures on Abolitionism* (Albany, N.Y., 1843), 288, 295–309.

personal independence. The James Roberts narrative presented its subject as evidence of the failure of many of these soldiers to achieve the latter, even as they valiantly fought to gain the former, and launched a bitter critique of the cultural history of American freedom as the product of the brave sacrifices of white patriots.[17]

Despite its factual inaccuracies, the Roberts narrative framed itself as a historical corrective to the popular myth of Revolutionary violence by asserting that the contributions of black soldiers have been erased from U.S. history because they contradict the ideal of this violence as the achievement of liberty. By using the example of African American soldiers, it challenged the image of the American army as a band of citizen-soldiers who fought to ensure freedom for their countrymen and who neither gained citizenship nor enjoyed liberty as a result of their service. The Roberts story and similar texts also sought to overturn the prevalent argument in the antebellum period that the absence of a large-scale revolt by the enslaved in the United States was evidence that blacks lacked the will to fight against slavery as whites had fought against the British. François Furstenberg has argued that many early national civic texts presented a simple vision of slavery as a choice; one could actively resist being enslaved, even to the point of death, or one could passively accept a life in bondage. The Revolution demonstrated that whites had earned their freedom through violent resistance. Ignoring African American contributions to the war excluded blacks from this reward and suggested that slaves had assented to their condition. The Roberts narrative, in the depiction of its protagonist and in the graphic anecdotes of the acts of resistance it recounted, countered claims that African Americans had passively accepted subjugation. It sought not only to remind its readers of the sacrifices made by African Americans in the cause of liberty, however, but also to demonstrate that such sacrifices ultimately failed to guarantee the achievement of liberty.[18]

In its claim to present the history of a forgotten black veteran, the Roberts

---

17. The standard history of black service in the Revolutionary War remains Benjamin Quarles, *The Negro in the American Revolution* (Chapel Hill, N.C., 1961). Profiles of many individual African Americans who chose to fight for the American cause during the Revolution can be found in Gary B. Nash, *The Forgotten Fifth: African Americans in the Age of Revolution* (Cambridge, Mass., 2006), 1–67. See also Sidney Kaplan and Emma Nogrady Kaplan, *The Black Presence in the Era of the American Revolution* (Amherst, Mass., 1989).

18. François Furstenberg, *In the Name of the Father: Washington's Legacy, Slavery, and the Making of a Nation* (New York, 2006), 192–193.

narrative fits within a larger context of historical recovery among African American writers during the antebellum period. Many of these works sought to locate African American claims to liberty within the rhetoric of the American Revolution. In 1829, David Walker published his *Appeal to the Coloured Citizens of the World* as an indictment of the cruelties endured by both enslaved and free blacks in the United States. He would end his argument by quoting from the Declaration of Independence and its assertion of universal equality in order to ask how far the nation had fallen from this ideal: "Compare your own language ... extracted from your Declaration of Independence, with your cruelties and murders inflicted by your cruel and unmerciful fathers and yourselves on our fathers and on us—men who have never given your fathers or you the least provocation!" Several African American writers took the implications of Walker's reference to the Declaration of Independence even further to argue the similarity between black struggles against slavery and the struggle for American self-government. The 1850s would see the publication of works like Frederick Douglass's novella *The Heroic Slave* and William Wells Brown's novel *Clotel; or, The President's Daughter*, both of which deliberately posed stories of enslaved characters struggling for freedom as historical parallels to the nation's Revolutionary origin. Like Walker's appeal, these works of fiction aimed to display the distance between Revolutionary ideals of liberty and the reality of a slaveholding society.[19]

A more specific line of argument within such antislavery thought worked to reassert African American claims to liberty based on the service of black soldiers during the Revolutionary War. In 1855, African American historian William C. Nell would publish *The Colored Patriots of the American Revolution*, a state-by-state collection of examples of black military service on behalf of the United States from the Revolution to the War of 1812 and beyond that sought to prove the invaluable role of African Americans in the nation's conflicts. William Lloyd Garrison would record multiple examples of this argument in an 1861 publication that included excerpts from abolitionist speeches, comments from members of Congress regarding the bravery of black soldiers during the Revolutionary War, brief anecdotes describing African American men who served, and discussions among the founders on the necessity of enlisting African American soldiers to defeat the British. In 1858, Nell would help to revive a Boston civic tradition of marking March 5

---

19. Peter P. Hinks, ed., *David Walker's Appeal to the Coloured Citizens of the World* (University Park, Pa., 2000), 78–79.

to commemorate the five men killed by British soldiers on that day in 1770, the date remembered as the Boston Massacre and considered the prelude to the Revolution. The renewed commemorations placed special emphasis on the role of Crispus Attucks, a black sailor believed to be the first man shot during the struggle. Nell's emphasis on Crispus Attucks revealed a desire to remember African Americans as essential contributors to the Revolutionary struggle rather than as peripheral actors. This desire could also be found in the popular notion that an African American soldier provided Andrew Jackson with the idea to use cotton bales as the keystones of the makeshift ramparts his army assembled on the field of battle at New Orleans. Such ideas reflected a larger movement to establish a distinctly African American history that would both provide a sense of communal identity and also assert the unrepresented contributions of this community during the nation's founding. Having recognized the rhetoric of Revolutionary violence, African American writers argued that blacks had been co-participants along with whites in the defense of American liberties, and, as a result of this loyal service to the commonweal, they too should enjoy the personal autonomy and political sovereignty that had become the nearly exclusive property of white men.[20]

The Roberts narrative clearly draws on this current of thought in its forceful depiction of a black veteran of two American wars who remains in slavery, his service unacknowledged. It combined elements of the autobiographical slave narrative, as Roberts recalled the horrors of plantation slavery, with the argument of the Revolutionary veteran narrative, as Roberts protested that his time at war had been unappreciated. Unlike *The Fort Stanwix Captive*, however, the Roberts account found no distinction between 1783 and

20. W[illia]m C. Nell, *The Colored Patriots of the American Revolution, with Sketches of Several Distinguished Colored Persons* ... (Boston, 1855); [William Lloyd Garrison], *The Loyalty and Devotion of Colored Americans in the Revolution and War of 1812* (Boston, 1861). For an account of the first of the Boston Massacre commemorations, see "The Boston Massacre, March 5, 1770: Commemorative Festival in Faneuil Hall," *Liberator* (Boston), Mar. 12, 1858. Martin Robinson Delany gives a full account of the story of the cotton-bale ramparts in *The Condition, Elevation, Emigration, and Destiny of the Colored People of the United States; Politically Considered* (Philadelphia, 1852), 80–82. Robin Reilly notes that the widespread notion of ramparts made of cotton bales was likely a distortion of the facts; such ramparts would have easily caught fire from the hot British shot. He asserts that cotton bales covered in heavy mud were used to provide sturdy embrasures for the American artillery but did not form the ramparts of the U.S. fortifications. See Reilly, *The British at the Gates: The New Orleans Campaign in the War of 1812* (New York, 1974), 279–280.

1815 and claimed that Roberts's service in both wars had the same ultimate effect, which was to make the chains of slavery tighter for African Americans. By presenting the Revolution and the War of 1812 as equivalent illustrations of white racism toward blacks, the Roberts's story denied both the ideal of social unity during the Revolution and the idealization of its veterans exemplified in texts like those of Josiah Priest.

Although the Roberts narrative can be easily located within a culture of antebellum African American historiography, solid details regarding its publication history remain elusive. It was published in Chicago in 1858, though Roberts implied that he had prepared an edition as early as 1856 when he described giving his story to James Buchanan to read during a personal meeting with the then president-elect. Roberts also stated that his narrative was written by an unnamed black amanuensis and expressed what he calls the satisfaction "of knowing and seeing one of [his] despised race capable of writing a book, however small." Though written in the first person as the voice of Roberts, the role of this amanuensis is never clarified since the account includes no further details regarding its authorship. These textual references to the narrative's composition obfuscate, rather than clarify, the origins of the work. Did Roberts write a manuscript version (which he could have shared with Buchanan, among others) that his amanuensis later revised? Who was this amanuensis? Was the amanuensis an African American or a white writer adopting a black voice? Did the amanuensis create the written voice of Roberts from a series of oral interviews and transcriptions? Or does the entire work represent the creation of an unnamed writer seeking to offer a counter to the fantasies of white male solidarity found in the likes of *The Fort Stanwix Captive*?[21]

A more direct approach to these questions might be to simply ask: Was James Roberts a real person? Evidence within the text, previously mentioned, indicates that is unlikely, such as Roberts's extraordinarily long life (104 years would be considered impressive today but must be considered doubly so when describing a man born in the mid-eighteenth century under the conditions of chattel slavery), his success in hand-to-hand combat against British soldiers at the age of sixty-one (Roberts claimed to have decapitated six enemies during the fighting), and his multiple encounters with prominent Americans (Roberts argued with Andrew Jackson after the Battle of New Orleans and enjoyed interviews with both Franklin Pierce and James Buchanan). In his foundational study of African American life

21. Roberts, *Narrative*, iii, 30.

writing, William Andrews noted that many of Roberts's claims are of "questionable historical authenticity," especially his contention that enslaved men were armed to fight as soldiers in Jackson's army at New Orleans. As Adam Rothman has argued, widespread anxiety over the possibility of a British-sponsored slave revolt in the Deep South would have likely made most slaveholders highly reluctant to have the enslaved supplied with guns and drilled as a military unit in the way Roberts describes. Although some enslaved men did serve in the American forces during the Revolutionary War, there are no records of a black soldier named James Roberts in the Continental army. Furthermore, no reference to Roberts's original master, Francis De Shields, can be found in the standard reference work on Revolutionary officers, despite Roberts's statement that De Shields held the rank of colonel. As a commissioned officer, De Shields should have left a clear documentary record—especially in light of Roberts's subsequent claim that De Shields was elected as Washington's vice president.[22]

22. William L. Andrews, *To Tell a Free Story: The First Century of Afro-American Autobiography, 1760–1865* (Urbana, Ill., 1986), 184–185 n. 33, 318; Adam Rothman, *Slave Country: American Expansion and the Origins of the Deep South* (Cambridge, Mass., 2005), 144–151. In a review of *Slavery and the Making of America*, Adam Rothman also notes the unreliability of the Roberts narrative as a source; see Rothman, "This Guilty Land," review of *Slavery and the Making of America*, by James Oliver Horton and Lois Horton, *Reviews in American History*, XXXIII (2005), 301–308. The Maryland General Assembly approved the enlistment of slaves as soldiers in October 1780, yet no list has yet been found that includes James Roberts among those who served. See Eric G. Grundset, ed., *Forgotten Patriots: African American and American Indian Patriots in the Revolutionary War: A Guide to Service, Sources, and Studies* (Washington, D.C., 2008), 454. If Francis De Shields was a Continental army officer, he should have been listed in Francis B. Heitman, *Historical Register of Officers of the Continental Army during the War of the Revolution, April 1775, to December, 1783*, rev. ed. (Washington, D.C., 1914). Given the relative obscurity of the Roberts narrative, little scholarship has been devoted to establishing the conditions of authorship. This situation has been compounded, however, by the tendency among some scholars to accept the narrative uncritically as a factual account. For example, Jon Latimer uses the Roberts account as the basis for his claim that enslaved men served in combat in the U.S. army at the Battle of New Orleans. James Oliver Horton and Lois E. Horton also rely on the Roberts narrative to provide nearly their entire description of the African American experience at this battle. Karin L. Stanford uses the work to support the claim that Jackson recruited soldiers from local plantations and that he promised his enslaved African American soldiers equal pay to whites and their freedom after service. William E. Alt and Betty L. Alt also use the Roberts narrative as their primary example of a black soldier's experience of this battle, though they do note that Roberts's account cannot be supported by most historical

The immediate falsity of this latter claim further undermines the credibility of the Roberts narrative, but it also suggests the possibility of reading the text, not as the memoirs of an actual person, but rather as a fantastic imitation of both the slave narrative and the veteran narrative, one that plays with the facts of history in order to draw a continuous thread through the gaps that have erased African Americans from the national story. In its depiction of an enslaved black man whose life spans the existence of the nation, and whose memory recalls its first two wars, the Roberts narrative posited a competing vision of Revolutionary political violence to that found in *The Fort Stanwix Captive;* it suggested that the ideal of the United States as a nation established through the heroic efforts of citizen-soldiers had been a façade to cover the reality of subjugation and exploitation faced by many of those, both black and white, who fought in the Revolution and in 1812.

Roberts argued that his service in both the Revolution and the War of 1812 would be displaced from national history, starting with the treatment he received following the conclusion of the Revolutionary War. He had hoped to be given his freedom for his loyal service but was instead sold to a new owner in Louisiana and separated from his wife and children upon the death of De Shields. Following his arrival in Louisiana, his new master confiscated all of Roberts's clothes, including his regimental uniform. This small indignity reflected the larger denial of Roberts's Revolutionary service, stripping him of the evidence of his participation in the nation's founding. Roberts referred to these events as "the payment of [his] wages, for all of [his] fighting and suffering in the Revolutionary War for the liberty of this ungrateful, illiberal country."[23]

The confiscation of Roberts's regimentals symbolized the effort to erase the military service of African Americans and to deny the claims to freedom such service would inspire. Roberts's experiences during the War of 1812, however, render the most vivid illustration of this effort. Roberts claimed that Andrew Jackson struck a deal with local plantation owners to supply his army with enslaved soldiers and that Jackson came to the fields to person-

---

records and might be questionable. In all of these examples, the Roberts narrative serves as a reliable source that requires little to no corroboration, despite its many dubious elements. See Latimer, *1812: War with America* (Cambridge, Mass., 2007), 387; Horton and Horton, *Slavery and the Making of America* (Oxford, 2005), 82–83; Stanford, ed., *If We Must Die: African American Voices on War and Peace* (Lanham, Md., 2008), 32; Alt and Alt, *Black Soldiers, White Wars: Black Warriors from Antiquity to the Present* (Westport, Conn., 2002), 28–29.

23. Roberts, *Narrative,* 10.

ally recruit men by promising them freedom should there be an American victory. The narrative presented the enslaved soldiers as essential contributors to American success in the battle, but it also stated that, once the fighting was over, Jackson ordered them to return to their masters and protested that he had no authority to free them without the consent of their owners. When many of these men, including Roberts, disputed this treatment, Jackson chose to distract them by taking his enslaved regiment to a local tavern and ordering the landlord to ply the men with unlimited liquor. Near the end of this episode, Roberts reported that Jackson gave a speech warning that black men should never again be armed; according to Roberts, Jackson stated, "We have fooled them now, but never trust them again; they will not be fooled again with this example before them." Roberts's commentary on this speech provided a clear sense of the narrative's efforts to unsettle the history of U.S. political violence as the text challenges the reputation of an American military hero and future president. With regard to Jackson's warning against arming slaves, Roberts asked: "Why was not this speech published in the history of that war? No mention is made of it whatever. Such monstrous deception and villainy could not, of course, be allowed to disgrace the pages of history, and blacken the character of a man who wanted the applause and approbation of his country." Roberts here contrasted the power the victorious Jackson held to shape the history of the battle to the impotence felt by its unacknowledged black participants, whose fighting and suffering had gained them nothing.[24]

Whereas the Roberts narrative proposed a lost example of racist duplicity in its depiction of Jackson at New Orleans, most antislavery discourse of the time looked back to the general's attitude at this moment for a potential recognition of African American equality. Apart from the Roberts account, no evidence has been found to support claims of men held in slavery participating in combat on the American side at New Orleans, but the free black residents of Louisiana did in fact join the fight against the British, many serving with distinction. Two battalions of free men of color served in Jackson's army at New Orleans: a unit of around 280 men under the command of Major Pierre LaCoste, and a unit of approximately 200 men commanded by Major Louis Daquin that was almost entirely composed of refugees from Santo Domingo. Jackson would praise the contributions of his African American soldiers in one of the two proclamations he made addressing the free black men of Louisiana; the first called on African American men to serve on the

---

24. Ibid., 17–18.

American side, and the second celebrated their efforts. In the later proclamation, Jackson stated that he had high expectations for these African American battalions and that his expectations had been exceeded by their conduct: "*You have done more than I expected.* In addition to the previous qualities I before knew you to possess, I found among you a noble enthusiasm, which leads to the performance of great things." These proclamations would become significant texts within African American historical writing. The earlier address inviting free black men to join the fight against the British would gain particular importance because it documented Jackson's describing black men as "sons of freedom" who were part of the national American family and who would receive equal reward to white soldiers for their service on behalf of that family. John Ernest has called these proclamations "a staple of African American historical writing" that were taken as evidence that African Americans should not have to argue for recognition as citizens and should be included in any sense of national identity. Ernest also noted that a large part of the appeal of Jackson's proclamations came from the speaker's reputation as a committed opponent of efforts to end slavery. Indeed, as part of his citation of the proclamations, Martin Delany observed that Jackson respected the manhood of African Americans and simply saw their exploitation as a means to an end; Delany quipped that Jackson "would just as readily have held a white man, had it been the policy of the country, as a black one in slavery." Jackson's proclamations thus positioned the general as a contradictory symbol for African American writers; the same man who could recognize the valor of black soldiers and imagine them as fellow citizens also stood as an advocate of the institution that prevented such equality. The Roberts narrative dissolved this ambiguity around Jackson as a symbol to instead emphasize the impulse toward human commodification implied by Delany's comments.[25]

From the perspective of the Roberts narrative, Jackson's proclamations

---

25. Jackson's proclamations in Nell, *Colored Patriots*, 286–288 (quotations on 286, 288, emphasis in original); John Ernest, *Liberation Historiography: African American Writers and the Challenge of History, 1794–1861* (Chapel Hill, N.C., 2004), 84; Delany, *The Condition, Elevation, Emigration, and Destiny of the Colored People of the United States*, 82. Accounts of African American service during the Louisiana campaign can be found in Gerard T. Altoff, *Amongst My Best Men: African-Americans and the War of 1812* (Put-in-Bay, Ohio, 1996), 149; Roland C. McConnell, *Negro Troops of Antebellum Louisiana: A History of The Battalion of Free Men of Color* (Baton Rouge, La., 1968), 84–85; Rothman, *Slave Country*, 144–146; Kai Wright, *Soldiers of Freedom: An Illustrated History of African Americans in the Armed Forces* (New York, 2002), 45–50.

belied the link between fighting for liberty and being included in the body politic as a full citizen. The appeal to the recognition of a great man such as Jackson suggests that political inclusion emerges, not from collective actions, such as political violence, but rather from the will of those in power. The Roberts account used the Battle of New Orleans less as evidence for black inclusion within the nation than as an illustration of the ways in which an American subjectivity purportedly based in the sovereignty of the people depended far more on the prerogatives of political elites who maintained the authority to encourage deference from their less powerful countrymen. Through the figure of the enslaved soldier, the text challenged an ideology that cast commitment to the commonweal as the basis of inclusion within the body politic. Unlike the white soldier, the black soldier held as a slave had no property to defend, not even his own person, which belonged to another. The enslaved soldier thus disrupted the circle of substitutions that set white supremacy and an idealized Revolutionary history as ideological compensations for an unequal distribution of landed property and other capital within the nation.

Jackson could offer the right to self-mastery through self-defense, but he could also take away that right. The Roberts narrative implied that, in a society that permits slavery, no one can truly have the right to defend his own liberty because that liberty can be commodified and sold to another. The ideal of the republican citizen-soldier served only to obfuscate this reality by giving support to an ideology of whiteness-as-property. The Roberts account invoked that ideology when describing the bargain Jackson struck with the slaveowners of Louisiana to supply his army with slave labor. Roberts claimed to have heard the discussion between his master, Calvin Smith, and Jackson in which Smith reiterated the distinctions of value between white and black bodies. Smith asked Jackson to recruit as many slaves as he could so that Smith's sons would not have to join the fight and closed this plea saying, "If the negroes should get killed, they are paid for; but if [his] children should go and get killed, they cannot be replaced." For a slaveowner like Smith, the enslaved represented the ideal bodies to send to war because their lives had no meaning apart from their economic value, whereas his sons carried an inestimable value to him. The narrative here captures the sense in which whiteness became valuable property through its exclusivity; white lives became priceless through the contrast with black lives, which could be assigned a specific dollar value. Yet Smith's comments also indicate the degree to which war serves to level social differences such as race or class—on the battlefield, his sons were just as likely as his slaves to be killed, thus Smith asserted the uniqueness of his sons against the complete fungibility of his slaves.[26]

The Roberts narrative aimed its challenge to national history at the distance between this fungibility and the ideal of the citizen-soldier. It rooted its criticism of Jackson not only in his broken promise of freedom but also in Jackson's realization that this offer had to be made to inspire black service. By offering freedom to the enslaved individuals who fought, Jackson evinced an understanding of black men as more than just armed brutes to be sent to the battlefield, and such recognition indicated that these soldiers could demonstrate the mental self-possession to serve as defenders of the Republic, even as they lacked the legal self-possession to truly submit out of liberal obedience. Jackson's offer seemed to grant these enslaved soldiers a temporary measure of self-mastery in battle, a freedom to defend themselves from abuse in a way that they lack on the plantation. This invitation to serve stood as a complete ontological transformation—Roberts claimed Jackson asked them, "Had you not as soon go into the battle and fight, as to stay here in the cotton-field, dying and never die?" The phrase Roberts ascribed to Jackson, "dying and never die," defines slavery as an uncanny state between life and death in which the slave lacks the authority to resist his physical exploitation or the abusive whims of his master and thus endures constant suffering.[27]

For the American citizen-soldier, then, self-defense represents the defense of his property, but the right to self-defense is denied to the enslaved since they are the property of another. The narrative illustrates this denial through its depictions of individuals who attempt to fight back against their overseers or owners and receive harsh reprisals. Blacks who asserted their right to self-defense were subject to horrific punishments designed to discourage others from following their examples, as demonstrated through the gruesome story of Ben, an enslaved man who killed an overseer and was subjected to an unspeakably grisly execution. The example of Ben is paired with that of John, a young black man who was whipped to death for having the insolence to tell a white man he would not like to have him for a master. Both scenes reiterate slavery's dependence on denying African Americans the power to defend themselves against the whims of white men, though this

---

26. Roberts, *Narrative*, 13.

27. Ibid., 13. Elizabeth Samet traces the arguments surrounding African American military service during the Civil War, particularly the claim that blacks must have a preexisting conception of freedom in order to fight for it; see Samet, *Willing Obedience*, 140–152.

argument appeared most clearly in Roberts's account of a man called Joe. Joe received repeated whippings one day from an overseer named Coonrood, whom he murdered in retaliation that night. When Roberts, as the field leader of Joe's work party, was about to receive punishment for the overseer's disappearance, Joe promptly took credit for the murder, repeatedly justifying the act as self-defense with the claim, "My life is as sweet to me as his was to him." Roberts stated that, even as Joe was about to be hanged, he refused to apologize for his actions on the scaffold, choosing instead to reassert his basic right to self-defense: "It is no disgrace to me; I die an honorable death. Did not God put these limbs to my body to defend it?" He then advised other African Americans to follow his example: "Let no white man kill you, but you kill him." Joe's fate implied the arbitrary quality of American rhetoric regarding the defense of personal liberties because it indicated that the power of self-defense rests, not in the individual's capability to defend himself, but instead on the legal power of the state.[28]

In its depiction of these African American acts of resistance, the Roberts narrative offered parallels to the political violence on display in its account of the Revolution and the War of 1812, yet it demonstrated that these individual acts stood as illegitimate expressions of rebellion since they could not be considered expressions of the will of a sovereign people. The institution of the nation did not emerge from collective political violence; it instead functioned as a means to define when such action was legitimate by delineating who counts as the body politic.

The Roberts account showed the importance of white supremacy as an ideological cover for the subjugation of ordinary white men. Like men held in slavery, they, too, could become commodities of imperial expansion, but discourses of popular sovereignty and white supremacy intersected in ways that obscured this commodification and celebrated their subordination to an ideal of the nation. Roberts claimed Jackson informed his white volunteers from Kentucky that they were a hindrance more than a help and that the march toward New Orleans would have been less trouble with only black troops: "It would have been far better for us to have had no whites, for there is not a day or night passes that we do not have to dig a hole and bury five or six of you." This statement positioned white men within the same logic of expendability ascribed to black men. By reversing the standard terms of racial comparison and casting whites as inferior to blacks when it came to military endurance in the harsh swamps of Louisiana, the narrative sought to illus-

28. Roberts, *Narrative*, 23–25.

trate the ease with which distinctions between the races could be made and the arbitrary quality of such distinctions. Furthermore, it set depictions of the inhumanity of battle, such as rivers red with the blood of the slain and incapacitated British soldiers buried alive by their American adversaries, alongside the sadistic brutality of the plantation, such as the increasingly grisly execution of rebellious slaves. As Laura Doyle has noted, the subjugation of African slaves and Euro-American soldiers are not comparable, but they do work in tandem as expressions of Anglo-Atlantic imperialism. The position of the enslaved soldier collapses the boundary between these subjectivities by depicting a soldier who fights for a freedom from which he is excluded and a slave who fights to secure the state that holds him in thrall. The Roberts narrative thus sought to establish a continuum between war and slavery as practices that degrade individuals into tools of military or economic expansion in order to suggest the futility of Revolutionary violence. It implies such violence seems to benefit white men only through the deliberate erasure of the ways in which it has not benefited black men.[29]

The real story of Isaac Hubbell would support such a claim. Although Josiah Priest ended his story with the celebration of a patriotic hero, the actual Hubbell experienced little such recognition. His pension application maintained that the infirmities of his wartime service left him unable to work as frequently as necessary to support his family. As a result of fighting for the nation that would recognize his control over his own labor as the source of his independence, Hubbell in fact lost that control and found himself ultimately dependent upon public support. Read together, *The Fort Stanwix Captive* and the Roberts narrative reveal the central role white supremacy has played in maintaining an ideal of Revolutionary struggle as the source of U.S. liberty. For such struggle to be regarded as a transformative moment that secures individual liberty, those who engage in failed acts of political violence must be cast as independent agents acting on their own interests, rather than as representatives of a larger collective. At the same time, those who choose not to actively support the nation must be seen as making a similar act of selfish disregard for the institution that secures their personal autonomy. These two texts suggest that racist discourse supported nationalist history in the effort to establish a cohesive identity for a country riven by the fault-lines of competing interests—fault-lines that run from 1783 to 1812 and, ultimately, to April 12, 1861.

29. Ibid., 14; Doyle, *Freedom's Empire*, 8.

NAVAL BIOGRAPHY, THE WAR OF 1812, AND THE CONTESTATION OF AMERICAN NATIONAL IDENTITY

Tim Lanzendörfer

In September 1813, the Philadelphia magazine the *Port-Folio* published a biography of James Lawrence, an American naval officer who had died on June 1 in the first frigate action that the U.S. Navy had lost during the war. His death and the lost fight had occasioned much mourning, and the *Port-Folio* was not alone in deeming it "a national duty . . . to contribute our efforts to extend and perpetuate" Lawrence's "fame." Yet what the *Port-Folio* produced was more than biography. It kept its reportage of Lawrence's life before the War of 1812 short, extensively reported on the action itself, and commented on proper behavior in wartime. Most strikingly, however, it meditated on American national origins and offered a vision of American national identity. The article denied that any damage to American pride could result from the loss of Lawrence and his ship; far from it, indeed, because the defeat, bought at great cost for the British, could not efface earlier victories: "Even a series of naval losses cannot now control" the determination that, "in all the qualities essential to success on the ocean, the American seamen are not equal, but superior to the British seamen." This belief was grounded in a Buffonesque rendering of Americans: "Nature and circumstances have made them so. . . . The warm and variable climate of the United States has, to a certain degree, melted the original English constitution of our ancestors" and produced a different "race" of men. This new American man still derived, genealogically, from the English, but he had been changed by his new habitat into a superior specimen. Three years later, James Kirke Paulding, in a biography of Commodore Thomas Macdonough written for the *Analectic Magazine*, offered a radically different take; here, the transatlantic journey effaced, if not the fact of English ancestry, then certainly its relevance in a new national mythology. "Few of us can trace our ancestry,"

I would like to acknowledge the splendid staff members at the Historical Society of Pennsylvania, the Library Company of Philadelphia, and the Houghton Library at Harvard University, where much of the research for this essay was conducted.

wrote Paulding, but no matter. "Obliged to build up a name for ourselves," Americans were forced to invent their own origins and their own heroes, particularly the naval officers of the War of 1812.[1]

Dozens of original biographies of American naval officers appeared from early 1813 through 1817. However, studies of biography as well as of the War of 1812 have passed over the biographical work done in periodicals or dismissed it as intellectually minor. The biographies are usually regarded as thoroughly conventional, unequivocal statements in a continuity of American nationalist assertion. But a closer reading of just a small group of these lives reveals something peculiarly different. This essay argues that American periodicals around the War of 1812 used biographies of American naval officers to produce contesting versions of American national identity and competing national genealogies, strongly connected with an awareness of the power of historical memory and the need to produce and affirm the right national memories. These contesting ideas about American national identity played out in a period of recurrent but never stable interest in promoting nationhood. The biographies reveal much about the different underlying conceptions of what could constitute an American nation. Individual biographies served as the canvas on which it was possible to paint a variety of images of the nation, images that manifested themselves both in the depiction of the biographees themselves as well as in the commentaries that went with the texts. The biographies show the versatility of the biographical genre in the construction of contestable versions of American national identity and highlight the contingency of national identity. They also throw a new light on the War of 1812. Rather than ultimately establishing the American nation in a "second war of independence," the War of 1812 was one of those momentary events that catapulted American nationalism to the forefront of public consciousness and produced texts that explicitly avowed a national idea against party politics or regionalisms. In these texts, a variety of conceptions of American "nationness" flourished that could be accommodated, and in fact had to be accommodated, by an unfolding American nationalist discourse.[2]

---

1. "Biography of Captain James Lawrence," *Port-Folio*, II, no. 3 (September 1813), 235, 254; [James Kirke Paulding], "Biographical Sketch of Captain Thomas Macdonough," *Analectic Magazine*, VI (March 1816), 203.

2. Edward H. O'Neill, *A History of American Biography, 1800–1935* (1935; rpt. New York, 1961), 25; Elsie Lee West, "Washington Irving: Biographer," in James W. Tuttleton, ed., *Washington Irving: The Critical Reaction* (New York, 1993), 197–205; Scott Casper, *Constructing American Lives: Biography and Culture in Nineteenth-Century*

Naval issues had played a genuinely critical role in the run-up to the War of 1812, with regard to both foreign policy and domestic politics, and this contributed signally to the possibility of rendering national identity through naval biography. American naval officers were especially suitable as nationalist icons because of the particular nature of the conflict with Great Britain, whose deprivations of American commerce and citizens' rights on the high seas were major reasons for war and whose naval power could stand metonymically for America's perceived inferiority toward the mother country. The War of 1812 is often seen as a "truly" nationalizing event, an interpretation reinforced by Gordon Wood in his *Empire of Liberty:* "The War of 1812 did finally establish for Americans the independence and nationhood of the United States that so many had previously doubted." By contrast, this essay will not contribute to "a consequence-driven historiography of national identity (a historiography concerned primarily with charting long-term effects for the political development of nation-states)," as Timothy Jenks has put it in his discussion of the Royal Navy's role in the creation of a British national identity. Rather, it will explore "the meanings that were articulated by specific political symbols, as well as of the significance of

---

America (Chapel Hill, N.C., 1999), 22. On American nationalism, see Benedict Anderson, *Imagined Communities: Reflections on the Origin and Spread of Nationalism* (London, 2006); Ed White, "Early American Nations as Imagined Communities," *American Quarterly*, LVI (2004), 49–81. That the contestations of American national identity discussed below occur within an entrepreneurial print culture might seem to confirm Anderson's thesis about the "imagined community" created by the experience of reading commonly shared vernacular print products, specifically newspapers (31–36). In fact, however, they call into question several of Anderson's assumptions and conclusions. White rightly calls the structures of the imagined community a "fairly stark relational network," which resists an examination of "the details or content of individual subjectivity and intersubjectivity ... in light of the more general and material experiences of time and space" (53). Anderson's thesis of the nation imagined in the shared belief of simultaneous newspaper consumption (see 62–63) ultimately conflates reception theory—the unprovable claim that readers perceived themselves as part of a simultaneous reading experience—and the postulation of an almost mechanistic determinacy—"the newspaper ... quite naturally, and even apolitically, created an imagined community" (62). Anderson relies exclusively on questions of form and ignores the question of content. Yet content cannot be ignored: American newspapers and magazines before the War of 1812 were anything but apolitical, and their turn to a nationalist rhetoric transcending party lines was the result of the transitory patriotism engendered by the war; in other words, the relationship I see between these two issues relies on reading the interplay between a particular form (the monthly magazine and naval biography) and its particular content.

that articulation itself." The biographies discussed below—published in the Philadelphia-based *Analectic Magazine* between 1813 and 1816—share the belief that the naval victories won by American naval officers during the War of 1812 were national victories capable of uniting a disparate citizenry behind a national idea, but, at the same time, they contest the particulars of a common myth of origin and offer different national genealogies.[3]

As Anthony Smith has noted, "the sense of 'whence we came' is central to the definition of 'who we are'": the mythical histories of descent, the "myths of common ancestry" shape national identity. Rather than creating *a* nation, the War of 1812 permitted the voicing of a variety of approaches to national genealogy, from the admission of lasting genealogical ties with the mother country to a complete denial of such a transatlantic family history and the development of an autochthonous national origin in the War of 1812 itself through the biographies of naval heroes. The periodical biographies thus highlight some of the many possible ways in which Americans strove to fill the idea of the nation with meaning and how disparate their conceptions of national identities were even in the allegedly established postwar American nation. Nationalism, national identity, and the various cognates functioned here as "empty signifiers," the term Ernesto Laclau has suggested for all those objectives that can stand for a perceived societal lack. The "actual content" of those objectives "becomes a secondary consideration." Indeed, the very emptiness of the term *nation* derives from its requisite feature of mirroring Americans' sudden imagination of a larger cohesion in place of the regions, states, parties, and religions that were the foundational collectives of the United States before—and after—the War of 1812. Emptiness does not mean meaninglessness; in fact, to the contrary, it allowed a great variety of meanings to be infused into the national idea. The naval biographies selected here, even as they contested the details, shared the ultimate objective of promoting the nation. The contestation of national identity in the naval biographies published around the War of 1812, then, took the form

---

3. Gordon S. Wood, *Empire of Liberty: A History of the Early Republic, 1789–1815* (Oxford, 2009), 699; Timothy Jenks, *Naval Engagements: Patriotism, Cultural Politics, and the Royal Navy, 1793–1815* (Oxford, 2006), 10. See also George Dangerfield, *The Awakening of American Nationalism, 1815–1828* (New York, 1965); Jon Latimer, *1812: War with America* (Cambridge, 2007); and Lloyd Kramer, *Nationalism in Europe and America: Politics, Cultures, and Identities since 1775* (Chapel Hill, N.C., 2011); David Waldstreicher, *In the Midst of Perpetual Fetes: The Making of American Nationalism, 1776–1820* (Chapel Hill, N.C., 1997).

of a shifting conception of national origins and offered an immediate mythologization of current events.[4]

The biographies emphatically stress the need to nationalize the federal Union far beyond the feelings of the moment, to offer it a common, coherent set of public heroes and mythical origins. They are not interested in civic patriotism, the precarious roof under which the strife-tossed United States had sheltered before the war. They seek to establish a true nation with its foundation in a shared myth of origin and to fill in the necessary *"symbolic content"* for a genuine national identity, as Anthony Giddens phrases it; "Whatever their differences, nationalist ideals tend to tie a conception of the 'homeland'—a concept of territoriality, in other words—to a myth of origin, conferring cultural autonomy upon the community which is held to be the bearer of these ideals." Naval heroes offered American writers the opportunity to create "authentic, native historical memories" capable of figuring as incipient myths from which to date the creation of an American national identity.[5]

The notion of the moment is significant because the biographies, despite sharing the ultimate goal of advancing a national reading of the naval victories and of the future United States, were heavily influenced by the patriotic fervor created by the war. They exploited the contingency of war in a variety of interpretations of iconic lives. The War of 1812 was not the end point of a teleological trajectory toward a genuine American nationality; rather, it was one of the moments in which a nationalist discourse could be foregrounded

---

4. Anthony D. Smith, *National Identity* (Reno, 1991), 22; Ernesto Laclau, *Emancipation(s)* (London, 1996), 44. Smith's emphasis on national symbolisms, "repertoires of shared values, symbols, and traditions" (16), and the mythic, rather than actual, nature of the genealogical ties presumed by nationalist endeavors is what I would like to emphasize here. Smith's primordialist impulse to declare that "the idea that nations exist from time immemorial" (19) is problematic, however, and I am not making any such claim. Smith's argument (and Anthony Giddens's argument, below) is a useful corrective to Ernest Gellner's modernist assertion that "the actual formulation of the idea or ideas" of nationalist endeavors "doesn't matter much"; see Gellner, *Nations and Nationalism* (Ithaca, N.Y., 1983), 121.

5. John M. Murrin, "A Roof without Walls: The Dilemma of American National Identity," in Richard Beeman, Stephen Botein, and Edward C. Carter II, eds., *Beyond Confederation: Origins of the Constitution and American National Identity* (Chapel Hill, N.C., 1987), 333-348 (quotation on 346-347); Anthony Giddens, *The Nation-State and Violence*, vol. II of *A Contemporary Critique of Historical Materialism* (Berkeley, Calif., 1985), 216; Anthony Smith, quoted in Walker Connor, "The Timelessness of Nations," *Nations and Nationalism*, X (2004), 35-47 (quotation on 37).

in preference to competing conceptions of collective identity, especially those of party and region. Some biographies molded the lives they described with the implicit purpose of rendering their subjects as representatives of the causes of the war. Others reinterpreted their biographees as allegorical figures standing for the universal ascendancy of the United States. The periodicals, rather than accepting that they would have to reaffirm, over and over, the nation's newfound ascendancy and identity, took for granted that, once Americans had shown that they could beat the Royal Navy, they no longer needed to feel inferior. The naval biographies thus rhetorically denied the relevance of the war's ultimate outcome for Americans' national identity. This was a particularly fitting solution to the lingering question of American political and emotional independence, and it is by no means coincidental that this rhetorical ploy was effected in naval biography.[6]

American periodicals chose to frame national identities symbolically through individual naval officers, producing what Wilbur Zelinsky has called "eidolons," ideal personifications embodying the "central meanings, values, and aspirations of a large population." Such personifications might be found in the abstracts of Columbia or Lady Liberty, but also in idealizations of living people, George Washington certainly foremost among them in the United States. Such figures, Zelinsky argues, were "the single most powerful device for fabricating a strong sense of nationhood in a hurry." The Royal Navy's potential as a symbol of the nation rested on its institutional history, a history that the U.S. Navy did not have. American periodicals thus recurred to the individual level of the public eidolon to actively construct the iconic personifications of the American nation. The naval heroes of the War of 1812 could stand as national icons in a way that the post-Washington generation of politicians could not. Among the men whom Zelinsky lists as being part of the "Second Generation of Heroes," naval officers Stephen Decatur and Oliver Hazard Perry stand out. Men such as Albert Gallatin, John

---

6. Anthony Smith has emphasized that war could function as a "mobilizer of . . . national consciousness, a centralizing force in the life of the community and a provider of myths and memories for future generations" (*National Identity*, 27). Lloyd Kramer has noted that the "implicit nationalism in the relationships of everyday life becomes more explicit and coercive during wars" (*Nationalism in Europe and America*, 14), and Gopal Balakrishnan makes this point even more strongly: "Most of the time the experience of national membership is faint and superficial. Only in struggle does the nation cease to be an informal, contestable and taken-for-granted frame of reference, and become a community which seizes hold of the imagination" (Balakrishnan, "The National Imagination," in Balakrishnan, ed., *Mapping the Nation* [London, 1996], 210).

Marshall, and John Calhoun, also listed by Zelinsky, could perhaps represent aspects of the "character of the rising nation," but their political roles precluded their use as genuinely national icons. Not surprisingly, victorious Republicans, interested in putting the war in the best possible light, after the war emphasized the struggle's importance for American nationhood. President James Monroe suggested that the "Union has gained strength ... and the nation character, by the contest." The former secretary of the treasury, Albert Gallatin, commented in an 1816 letter to Congressman Matthew Lyon: "The war has renewed and reinstated the national feelings and character which the Revolution had given, and which were daily lessened. The people have now more general objects of attachment with which their pride and political opinions are connected. They are more American; they feel and act more as a nation." If so, however, it was a peculiar nationhood, one based almost solely on party unity, an "Era of Good Feelings" in which the demise of the Federalist Party papered over, for a very short time (until the disputes leading to the Missouri Compromise), the fragility of the national idea in the United States.[7]

By the War of 1812, the struggle between the moribund Federalist Party and the ascendant Democratic-Republicans—territorialized in a Federalist New England, a Republican South, and a small number of battleground states in between—effectively precluded a closer national tie between the opposing factions, and certainly a figure as divisive as Albert Gallatin could hardly have been expected to become a contemporary national icon. Indeed, when the Republican leadership spoke of the nation, party echoed through their conceptions. Thomas Jefferson was perhaps the most prominent Republican when he wrote to Philadelphia editor William Duane in March 1811. Seeking to emphasize the necessity of unity to the "friends of the country," he noted: "If we schismatize on either men or measures, if we do not act in phalanx ... I will not say our *party*, the term is false and degrading, but our *nation* will be undone. For the republicans are the *nation*." By the outbreak of the war, Republicans were convinced that the honor and survival of the nation had become indivisible from the honor and survival of

---

7. Wilbur Zelinsky, *Nation into State: The Shifting Symbolic Foundations of American Nationalism* (Chapel Hill, N.C., 1988), 20, 30, 43; Monroe quoted in Alan Taylor, *The Civil War of 1812: American Citizens, British Subjects, Irish Rebels, and Indian Allies* (New York, 2010), 420; Henry Adams, ed., *The Writings of Albert Gallatin*, 3 vols. (Philadelphia, 1879), I, 700; Daniel Walker Howe, *What Hath God Wrought: The Transformation of America, 1815–1848* (Oxford, 2007), 124, 147–163.

their party, and they conversely assumed that a Federalist revival would ultimately result in a revocation of the Revolution. James Madison and Gallatin were thus celebrating the triumphant vindication of the Republican Party as much as a genuine nationalization of the "loose confederation of regions" that had begun the war in 1812. Indeed, the war had brought the political Union close to the breaking point. "In late 1814," Alan Taylor notes, "national dissolution seemed plausible because Royal Navy commanders were already pressuring vulnerable American coastal communities to drop out of the war." But December's Treaty of Ghent, ratified by Congress in March, ended the struggle before the stability of the Union could truly be put to the test, and news of the successful Battle of New Orleans effectively killed New England's latent anti-Union aspirations.[8]

The political struggle between Republicans and Federalists was reflected in their conceptions of the role of the navy. Stephen Budiansky has aptly summarized the political landscape in which the naval victories became so notably capable of providing unexpected national rallying points: "The Federalists had opposed the war, the Republicans had opposed the navy, and so the one thing they could agree on after it was all over was how gloriously the tiny American navy had triumphed." The U.S. naval victories that so impressed Americans and British in the first year of the conflict did not have to wait until "it was all over" before they became the focal points of a discourse of national identity for many U.S. magazines, perhaps most notably the *Analectic Magazine* of Philadelphia. Indeed, the naval officers who had successfully waged battle against the British provided the *Analectic* with a uniquely national foil against which to read American victories over Great Britain, one that explicitly excluded the party perspective. In an editorial intervention prefacing James Kirke Paulding's biography of Captain Jacob Jones, published by the *Analectic Magazine* in July 1813, Washington Irving wrote, "We consider the victories of our navy as so many subjects for national feeling, in the discussion of which the sordid animosities of party should give way to the nobler sentiment of patriotic exultation." Certainly, the most important reason to see naval officers as uniquely suitable was their success. Unlike the struggling U.S. Army, which had opened the campaign season in 1812 with ignoble defeats on the northwestern frontier, the navy had sur-

8. Taylor, *Civil War of 1812*, 138, 176, 415; Thomas Jefferson to William Duane, Mar. 28, 1811, in H. A. Washington, ed., *The Writings of Thomas Jefferson ...*, V (New York, 1854), 576; Donald R. Hickey, *The War of 1812: A Forgotten Conflict* (Chicago, Ill., 1989), 27; Wood, *Empire of Liberty*, 668–670.

prised most by repeatedly gaining signal victories over the seemingly invincible Royal Navy, a force that was not only vastly larger than the U.S. Navy but also had a string of victorious naval wars going back for centuries.[9]

The navy was in several respects already a national force. In the selection of its officer corps, the U.S. Department of the Navy had a formal requirement for fair geographical distribution of appointments, an endeavor that "implied an active attempt to encourage applications from states and regions that might be underrepresented." When Captain Isaac Hull departed with the *Constitution* on the cruise that ended with the capture of HMS *Guerrière*, his six lieutenants were from Massachusetts, Connecticut, New York, Pennsylvania, Virginia, and South Carolina, with a crew from all seaboard states. If, owing to a shortage of applications from New England and western states, the officer corps tended toward favoring sailors from the middle states, especially Maryland, Pennsylvania, and Virginia, this practice did not diminish the basic understanding of the navy as a national force. Although not every officer would have agreed with Isaac Hull's 1807 comment that "the cloth has no politics," the navy's comparative freedom from sectional divisions enabled it to become the source of a genuinely national imaginary.[10]

For American readers attuned to the naval origins of the War of 1812, the naval conflict could stand for the entirety of the U.S.-British relationship in a way that the army could not: British dominance expressed itself equally in economic power, in cultural metropolitanism, and in naval success and strength. The symbolism of the naval victories much exceeded their material value. The machinery of mythologization worked in a dimension apart from the hard material factors that weighed heavily on strategists: it could transform defeat into victory. Against the long odds the navy faced, its victories had resounded all the more forcefully, and, perhaps more important, they were undeniable and uncontestable. The *Analectic Magazine's* biography of Captain Lewis Warrington, published a year after the conclusion of the war, observed as much in its opening paragraphs. "We have selected," it noted, "the distinguished officers of our navy as subjects for biography, not

---

9. Stephen Budiansky, *Perilous Fight: America's Intrepid War with Britain on the High Seas, 1812–1815* (New York, 2010), xi; [Washington Irving], Editorial Note on "Biography of Captain Jacob Jones," *Analectic Magazine*, II (July 1813), 70.

10. Christopher McKee, *A Gentlemanly and Honorable Profession: The Creation of the U.S. Naval Officer Corps, 1794–1815* (Annapolis, Md., 1991), 44, 65; Linda M. Maloney, *The Captain from Connecticut: The Life and Naval Times of Isaac Hull* (Annapolis, Md., 1986), 14, 169.

only because they naturally came under the notice of this work [the *Analectic Magazine* carried the additional title '*and Naval Chronicle*' during 1816], but because their actions are not liable to doubt or misconstruction, and their victories when gained are unquestionable." Whereas in battles on land doubts might remain about who had carried the victory, at sea "no denial, or opposite claim, on the part of the beaten enemy" could negate that a ship had been captured or sunk, or, alternatively, that both opposing ships remained afloat and under their own banners, thus making the fight a draw. American and British newspapers and magazines, instead of debating the reality of victories, engaged in disputes over their meaning.[11]

In a country in which something like 90 percent of the people were farmers, rural towns and single farms outnumbered the few larger cities on the Eastern Seaboard, and knowledge of the sea must have been severely limited. Even as the sea was the highway on which American goods were shipped, it may be considered strange to suggest any ambitions to read American national identity through naval officers. But, as Timothy Jenks's analysis of the role of the Royal Navy in arguments about British nationhood has suggested, the national identification with a successful fleet could easily transcend the coastal areas, thanks to the communicative powers of print. Printed depictions of naval victories, whether pictorial or textual, could circulate far deeper into the country than could information based on personal acquaintances with the successful officers or news of the public celebrations and gala dinners that took place, for example, in December 1812 in honor of Isaac Hull and Stephen Decatur in Washington and New York.[12]

The British examples collected by Timothy Jenks reveal the unifying potential of printed reportage about a successfully nationalized naval force endowed with almost mythical properties and widely hailed as the chief bulwark of England. Publisher and newspaperman William Cobbett, in his first autobiographical recollections before he moved shortly to the United States, remembered the stories told and retold over and over about the glori-

---

11. "Biographical Sketch of Captain Lewis Warrington," *Analectic Magazine*, VII (January 1816), 1–10.

12. George C. Daughan, *If by Sea: The Forging of an American Navy—From the American Revolution to the War of 1812* (New York, 2008), 427; Brian Jay Jones, *Washington Irving: An American Original* (New York, 2008), 119; Nicole Eustace, *1812: War and the Passions of Patriotism* (Philadelphia, 2012), 27–28. According to Paul E. Johnson, *The Early American Republic, 1789–1829* (Oxford, 2007), 61, in 1790 94 percent of Americans were living in villages and on farms, and 6 percent were living in cities with more than twenty-five hundred inhabitants.

ous deeds of the British fleet: His "heart was inflated with national pride." "Surely," Cobbett remembered thinking, "I had a part in it, and in all its honours." The mythologization of the Royal Navy and the mediated experience through printed stories of the "honours" the navy had won became the basis for an individual's identification with the fleet in a genuinely national experience. "The rustic inhabitants of Cobbett's village of memory identify with an ocean, a navy, a fleet, and sailors that many of them have never seen," Jenks suggests, because they were readers of newspapers and magazines that mediated the experiences of the fleet. The *Analectic Magazine*'s wide-ranging readership—its circulation reached into Georgia, Kentucky, and Maine—could also substitute the stories told about American glory for the direct experience of it, as acknowledged in James Kirke Paulding's "Biographical Notice of Captain Isaac Hull": "Every man appropriates to himself some little portion of the glory acquired by his countrymen." Those audiences whom the *Analectic Magazine* did not reach directly were informed by newspapers and other magazines that reprinted the *Analectic*'s biographies almost immediately after their publication. These reprints added to the wide audience that the biographical texts received and highlighted the public interest evinced by them. Samuel Brown and John Hathaway's 1815 *American Naval Gallantry*, which openly reprinted the *Analectic Magazine*'s biographies, put it succinctly in its short preface: "A cheap volume of this kind is much wanted."[13]

As well as extending the biographies' geographical distribution, the various forms of reprinting increased readership by allowing individual biographies to be published again and again for a considerable amount of time, even granting the small circulation of most of the rural and city newspapers of the day. The biography of Stephen Decatur, for example, was published in June 1813 by the *Analectic Magazine* but remained in circulation for a year and was published as late as September 1815. Reprints like those offered by the *Weekly Aurora*, the digest version of William Duane's immensely successful Philadelphia paper, in July 1813 were invaluable. The *Aurora*, "even according to a hostile observer, was 'universal throughout the United States—and in every hovel of Pennsylvania it is to be found and read.'" Newspaper

---

13. Jenks, *Naval Engagements*, 1–2; [James Kirke Paulding], "Biographical Notice of Captain Isaac Hull," *Analectic Magazine*, I (March 1813), 275; [Samuel] Brown and [John] Hathaway, eds., *American Naval Gallantry; or, Biographical Notices of the Constellation of Heroes, Who Have So Eminently Contributed to the Naval Glory of America* ... (Auburn, N.Y., 1815), [preface].

reprints offered texts the chance to remain in constant circulation, even as magazines, with a readership more attuned to novelty and variety, were forced to offer new texts every month.[14]

The *Analectic Magazine* can be seen as a microcosm of the interactions that determined the shape of naval biography around the War of 1812. Its pages reveal the editorial role in molding essays to fit a common message, the authorial freedoms to envisage slightly different ideas about the nation, and the proprietary interests in publishing material suitable for the passing interests of the audience. In the three years from 1813 to 1816, it produced more interesting biographical material with a wider range of conceptions of national identity than any other single magazine.

Washington Irving's role at the *Analectic Magazine* is key to understanding the popularity of the *Analectic* and the impressive literary quality of its contributions to the discussion of American national identity as well as the ways in which individual authors could operate within the heteronomous field of periodical production. Both Philadelphia, where the *Analectic Magazine* was published, and New York, where Washington Irving lived, were cities that relied heavily on transatlantic commerce; nevertheless, both had voted overwhelmingly in favor of James Madison's Republicans in the 1808 presidential elections, and, by extension, were not entirely unfavorably inclined toward the war. Both cities profited from the war: military and naval supplies secured huge incomes for their banks and merchants. Nothing is known of the politics of Irving's employer, Moses Thomas, but Irving himself was initially an ambivalent observer of the political wrangling leading up to the war. After the declaration of war, though, he became a fervent believer in the U.S. cause. Both publisher and editor clearly operated within their local political constellations; however, the *Analectic Magazine* itself emphatically disavowed party politics. As Irving noted in his headnote to the biography of Jacob Jones, he had excised "several passages of a political nature." The editorial "we" with which he addressed his readers in this note indicated the

---

14. Jeffrey L. Pasley, *"The Tyranny of Printers": Newspaper Politics in the Early American Republic* (Charlottesville, Va., 2001), 440. Because no subscriber lists exist for the *Analectic Magazine*, it is difficult to ascertain the extent to which newspaper reprints widened the geographical distribution of the journal. The Frankfort, Ky., *Argus of Western America* reprinted part of the Perry biography as "Anecdotes of the Battle of Lake Erie" on Apr. 16, 1814. The Charleston, S.C., *Investigator* reprinted Paulding's "Biography of Commodore Decatur" in two parts in its June 21 and 22, 1813, issues. Many New England papers also reprinted the biographies.

magazine's apolitical stance, an editorial policy as much a matter of commercial choice as of personal conviction.[15]

As editor from 1813 to early 1815, Irving had much influence on the printed matter appearing in the magazine, and he wrote several biographies and other short texts himself. Publishing naval biographies was not Irving's idea, however. In December 1812, before he had even taken up the job of editing the *Analectic Magazine,* Irving had written to James Renwick, a longtime friend and fellow member of the New York group of writers known as the Knickerbockers, with loud complaints about Thomas's approach to marketing the magazine and the publisher's plans for the *Analectic*'s content. "My publisher," Irving noted testily, "who seems determined to make a comfortable penny out of me, has been advertizing, every day or two, some new addition and improvement ... of which I have known nothing until I saw the advertisements." The result was, he claimed, a "vile farrago—a congregation of heterogenious [sic] articles, that have no possible affinity to one another." Key to Thomas's plan was the publication of what Irving called "a series of portraits of our Naval Commanders with Biographical Sketches," an ambitious project of American biography that could be contemplated by the *Analectic*'s proprietor because he could count on the patriotic fervor of Americans—or, at the very least, that of enough of his subscribers. The American novelist John Neal, writing about American authors under the pseudonym "X.Y.Z." for *Blackwood's Edinburgh Magazine* in 1825, shrewdly analyzed the situation in his sketch of Washington Irving: "The navy had grown popular, with everybody.... The Analectic Magazine took fire—with an eye to profit; hunted up materials: employed Irving to write a Biography of these naval captains, one after the other; and gave it out, with portrait after portrait, month after month, to the overheated public."[16]

---

15. Taylor, *Civil War of 1812,* 118–123; Hickey, *War of 1812,* 227–228; Andrew Burstein, *The Original Knickerbocker: A Life of Washington Irving* (New York, 2007), 97; Irving, Editorial Note on "Biography of Captain Jacob Jones," *Analectic Magazine,* II (July 1813), 70. Rosalind Remer, *Printers and Men of Capital: Philadelphia Book Publishers in the New Republic* (Philadelphia, 1996), is a useful primer on the business side of magazine publishing in the early Republic. I deal with the whole complex of periodical publication in Tim Lanzendörfer, *The Professionalization of the American Magazine: Periodicals, Biography, and Nationalism in the Early Republic* (Paderborn, Germany, 2013).

16. Washington Irving, *Letters,* ed. Ralph M. Aderman, Herbert L. Kleinfield, and Jenifer S. Banks, The Complete Works of Washington Irving, 4 vols. (New York, 1978–

Neal's analysis highlights the contingent nature of the *Analectic*'s efforts at avowedly national naval biography and stresses the sequence of events that led to the production of biographical short texts. The *Analectic Magazine*'s proprietor was reacting to a larger popular patriotic interest in the naval war. The *Port-Folio* recognized in 1825 that "as the war proceeded, and the navy of America rose high in reputation as in utility, the proprietors of the Analectic Magazine, prevailed on [Irving] to enrich their periodical with the biography of the most illustrious naval officers." "Recent naval victories by U.S. forces," Ralph Aderman and Wayne Kime note, "would make those yet unwritten articles timely": on August 19, Captain Isaac Hull won a spectacular and unexpected victory in a frigate action between his own *Constitution* and the British HMS *Guerrière* off the Canary Islands, news of which had reached the United States in the last days of August. On October 18, Jacob Jones of the USS *Wasp* defeated HMS *Frolic*. And exactly a week later, Commodore Stephen Decatur of the USS *United States* defeated the frigate HMS *Macedonian*. Moses Thomas had only bought the *Analectic Magazine*'s immediate successor, the *Select Reviews*, in November 1812 and had asked Washington Irving to become its editor at about the same time. Within months, then, Thomas had bought a magazine and reshaped its plan to make money from the events of the war, thus "capitaliz[ing] on the public interest." Even in his choice of Irving as editor, Thomas indicated how well he understood the periodical business. As David Dowling has argued, by 1812 Irving and the Knickerbockers had evolved into a "kind of trademark ... a moral passport to its audience's hearts, and thus their wallets." In hiring Irving, Thomas could be sure of both extensive patronage as well as access to the literary talent of Irving's acquaintances. Despite Irving's limited experience in editorship, his name carried weight in literary circles, and Thomas made wide use of Irving's name in advertising his product. Irving's and James Kirke Paulding's fame in New York won them an invitation to a December 1812 banquet honoring Hull, Jones, and Decatur. Not coincidentally, the first biographies published in the *Analectic Magazine* (all written by Paulding) were of these three officers. From the get-go, Irving's editorship of the *Analectic Magazine* as well as the individual contributions to it were involved in a complex field determined by his publisher's expectations of readership interest—including the assumption that, in order to sell, the

---

1982), I, 349; [John Neal], "American Writers, No. IV," *Blackwood's Edinburgh Magazine*, XVII, no. 46 (1825), 62.

magazine would have to advance patriotic ideals—and by the availability of authors and biographical materials.[17]

The texts discussed below—James Kirke Paulding's biography of Isaac Hull, Washington Irving's biographies of James Lawrence and, especially, Oliver Hazard Perry, all published in 1813, as well as Paulding's life of Thomas Macdonough and life of John Shubrick, both published in 1816—thus exist on a trajectory of changing ideas about national genealogy and iconographic possibilities. They also highlight the subordination of the biographical life narrative to their accompanying introductory and concluding material.

17. "Memoir of Washington Irving, Esq.," *Port-Folio*, no. 277 (May 1825), 438; Ralph M. Aderman and Wayne R. Kime, *Advocate for America: The Life of James Kirke Paulding* (Selinsgrove, Pa., 2003), 55; David Dowling, *The Business of Literary Circles in Nineteenth-Century America* (New York, 2011), 29. With a publishing panache similar to Thomas's, Mathew Carey, the Philadelphia publisher, put out Thomas Clark's *Sketches of the Naval History of the United States* ... in mid-1813, in order to "capitalize on [popular interest]" in the navy's victories. As James N. Green notes, Carey used his "editorial skills" to shape the book "into a persuasive argument for a strong navy and for a naval academy"; see Green, *Mathew Carey: Publisher and Patriot* (Philadelphia, 1985), 28. Carey's influence on the exact shape and argument of the book is, however, impossible to determine. Stephen Budiansky has noted that John Adams wrote to Carey suggesting the issue of a second edition with additional material promoting a buildup of the navy, a proposal that Carey accepted; clearly, then, Carey was not unwilling to add to his author's work (Budiansky, *Perilous Fight*, 362–363). With regard to the writing of biographies, Irving lost little time in finding friendly hands to help him. In late November, he wrote to James Renwick, suggesting that, if Renwick could supply a biographical sketch of a recently deceased mutual acquaintance, he would be happy to print it in the first number of his magazine (Irving, *Letters,* ed. Aderman, Kleinfield, and Banks, I, 343). Nothing came of this particular attempt to secure material, but other friends more readily obliged. Irving paid James Kirke Paulding for his contributions to the *Analectic Magazine;* although the details of his arrangement are unknown, in October 1814 he wrote his publisher Moses Thomas that he needed a settlement of accounts, in order that "I may pay Paulding according to my agreement with him" (ibid., 382). He also received help with biographical sketches from Gulian C. Verplanck, another old friend. In January 1815, as he was preparing to leave the magazine, Irving wrote to Verplanck. Thomas had suffered insolvency as a consequence of the failure of the publishing house of Bradford and Inskeep. Irving sought to calm Verplanck, who was facing going unpaid for his contributions: "For the sums which Thomas is indebted to you, You will have your chance with the other creditors" (387).

James Kirke Paulding wrote the first of the *Analectic*'s naval biographies in March 1813, but, like many of the successive efforts in the *Analetic*, his "Biographical Notice of Captain Hull," victor in the fight with *Guerrière*, hardly deserved to be called biography. Only 80 of the 352 lines of the article contained any biographical information on Isaac Hull, and much of that material was more historical in scope than truly biographical. The rest was devoted to a meditation on biography and to offering an interpretation of Hull's victory that firmly established the line the *Analectic* would be taking for the duration of the war, even as it offered a reading of the national identity of the United States that provided a first outline of a national genealogy. Concluding his summary of Hull's life, Paulding began his effort at transmuting the action between Hull's USS *Constitution* and HMS *Guerrière* into something vastly more important than a mere inconsequential naval victory. He noted that it was "one of the most important events that has occurred in the history of this country for many years past." There was, he suggested, "a sort of superstitious reverence" for England in the United States, one owed chiefly to a history rendered in genealogical terms: America was a young country, with the "fond credulity of a child," which received "the most exaggerated impressions of a nation to whom she once looked up as a parent." His parent-child metaphor extended to a life cycle trope of America; as a young nation, its faculties had not yet been tested nor fully developed, and it was as yet influenced by the "opinions implanted early in life," opinions that remained forceful in the minds of Americans even as their basis in fact vanished. Thus, with the United States reaching the end of its metaphorical childhood and standing now "at the very outset of [its] naval career," the habits of "superstitious reverence" had become so ingrained that few could believe they were not outmatched by the British in almost every way. Yet, Paulding continued, in extension of his metaphor, this deference to British naval prowess ignored that Americans had, in point of genealogical fact, "too much ... of Englishmen in our habits to be easily overpowered." It was precisely this English heritage that allowed Americans to succeed so magically (a term Paulding himself suggests) and that enabled them to dissolve "the spectres which had haunted us from the cradle upwards." America had "received into her bosom a spark, which, at some future period, will animate her to deeds that will realize this first promise of [America's] youth."[18]

18. [Paulding], "Isaac Hull," *Analectic Magazine*, I (March 1813), 270–273. Paulding uses the metaphor of the parent-child relationship, but complicates it by making Hull's

Paulding offered his readers a thoroughly conventional view of American identity: Americans were transplanted Englishmen, slowly growing out of their dependence on the parent country but still tied firmly by a transatlantic family history to the British. The victory itself, Paulding noted, was "an object of apparent insignificance," capable neither of denting British naval supremacy nor signally influencing the course of the war. It was by declaring the victory insignificant in point of fact that Paulding was able to make it significant symbolically. Paulding's biography of Isaac Hull rendered the victory over the *Guerrière* as a necessary beginning to the growth of a national character, "the only tie now wanting to secure a union of hearts among every class and denomination," a union that Paulding—and by extension the *Analectic Magazine*—clearly considered lacking.[19]

Paulding concluded in his biography of Hull that "subsequent instances of similar victories will add vigour ... and do much to form a national character," arguing that what Hull's victory had begun—cracking the myth of British superiority at sea—further such successes might continue. Implicit in this contention was the idea that it would be necessary to keep winning victories. In his biography of James Lawrence, published with amazing dispatch in August 1813, Washington Irving suggested that no further victories were in fact needed to reaffirm American national identity. Irving's biography came in the wake of a defeat. On June 1, Captain Lawrence, commanding USS *Chesapeake*, had engaged the British frigate *Shannon* off Boston and soundly lost; mortally wounded, Lawrence died shortly after the battle. The British rejoiced: "the doubts," which had been occasioned by the string of British defeats suffered during the previous year, "could be laughed away," and the right natural order of dominance at sea had been restored. Not so, suggested the *Analectic Magazine:* "The question of naval superiority," which the British now saw reopened, "was in our opinion settled long since, in the course of the five preceding battles ... the nations are equal on the ocean; and the result of any contest, between well-matched ships, would depend entirely on accident." Counterintuitively, Irving suggested sweepingly that there was no further need to affirm anything. The modest war goals of the navy had been achieved by "showing that [Britain's] maritime power was vulnerable," he argued. No matter what happened in the naval war in the future, any successful effort by the British to redeem British hegemony over

---

victory into the "parent of a well-founded confidence in ourselves" (271). As we shall see below, however, the force of the metaphor remains directed at England as the parent.

19. Ibid., 273, 274.

the oceans—to redeem their flag, as Irving had it—required them to "first obliterate from the tablets of our memories, the deep-traced recollection, that we have repeatedly met them with equal force and conquered."[20]

Irving's rhetoric was both a gambit necessitated by events as well as the most important claim the *Analectic* made on American national identity during the war. It persisted in linking the naval war to the greater question of the nation. If, as Irving indicated, American officers had theretofore been "fighting under superior excitement to the British ... eager to establish a name, and ... each has felt as if individually responsible for the reputation of the navy," they echoed a more general American desire to achieve emotional independence from Great Britain. Paulding had asserted in "Hull" that the naval victories had effectively tied the national knot by promoting the national character, by creating a national identity for Americans in a shared identification as benefactors and celebrants of naval heroes. Irving now insisted that this tie was already indissoluble, entirely independent of future events, woven into an indelible national memory that would become the basis of a new national mythology. In fact, Irving recognized that Lawrence was as valuable for the construction of a national identity in death as he would have been in life—perhaps more so: "There is a touching pathos about the death of this estimable officer, that endears him more to us than if he had been successful." Irving was well aware that Lawrence's death meant that he could now be embalmed as a national icon. "The idea of Lawrence, cut down in the prime of his days, stretched upon his deck, wrapped in the flag of his country—that flag which he had contributed to ennoble, and had died to defend—is a picture that will remain treasured up in the dearest recollections of every American." Lawrence, Irving suggested, will become "one of those talismanic names which every nation preserves as watchwords for patriotism and valour" and would lastingly unite the nation behind it.[21]

Irving's biography of Lawrence was a most skillful piece of political propaganda. It was hurried into print "with a precipitation that is understandable," not only because of an entrepreneurial effort to be the first to publish a life of Lawrence. Irving also attempted to deflect the demoralization caused by the defeat of the *Chesapeake* by highlighting the reasons for which Lawrence might yet be deemed a successful role model and by dismissing the

---

20. Ibid.; Ian W. Toll, *Six Frigates: The Epic History of the Founding of the U.S. Navy* (London, 2006), 417; [Washington Irving], "Biography of Captain James Lawrence," *Analectic Magazine*, II (August 1813), 137–139.

21. [Irving], "James Lawrence," *Analectic Magazine*, II (August 1813), 135.

moral importance of the battle. Irving's major recognition in the biography of Lawrence, spelled out in the lengthy final paragraph, is that, thanks to the vast resources of the United States, America would at length become dominant, and the question of the individual superiority of Americans was no longer vital.[22]

Paulding and Irving suggested in their early biographies that the naval victories won during 1812 had established Americans as on the same level vis-à-vis Britain; America was no longer inferior to its erstwhile mother country. In subsequent texts, they moved away from the notion of equality with Britain on the basis of a shared sense of English heritage and began to construct an autonomous American identity grounded in national allegory and incipient national myths. The *Port-Folio*, in its own biography of Lawrence, had noted that there was no shame in the defeat—it was, the magazine averred, an unequal fight anyhow—and that, in fact, the Americans could consider themselves superior to the British individually. Interestingly, the *Port-Folio* also offered a genealogical argument, whose formulation echoed J. Hector St. John de Crèvecoeur: "Nature and circumstances have made them so." The *Port-Folio* adapted James Paulding's genealogical motive and shaped a different interpretation: although the British still functioned as ancestors and, indeed, held that Americans clearly were "generally younger men" (echoing Paulding's family metaphor), significant shifts now made Americans constitutively different from the British:

> The warm and variable climate of the United States has, to a certain degree, melted the original English constitution of our ancestors, till, instead of the broad shouldered and ruddy form of the people of Great Britain, the Americans are a thinner race of men, with less personal strength and stamina, but with more activity, more quickness, more alertness.

Here, again, was the motif of British descent, transmuted into something more, an avowal of a fundamentally different American national identity based in the naturalization of certain imagined physical and psychological

---

22. P. C. Blackburn, "Irving's Biography of James Lawrence—and a New Discovery," *Bulletin of the New York Public Library*, XXXVI (1932), 743; Aderman and Kime, *Advocate for America*, 56. This was also the more practical and level-headed analysis of the secretary of the navy, William Jones. Jones, who had shifted American naval operations toward commerce raiding and away from the glorious but fruitless one-on-one frigate actions, noted in December 1813 to one of his captains that "the Character of the American Navy stands upon a basis not to be shaken" (quoted in Budiansky, *Perilous Fight*, 285).

traits, proven by the victoriousness of the United States Navy in equal combat and not disproven by the unfair fight between Lawrence and the *Shannon*. However, the *Port-Folio* did not offer a way to mythologize the national origins. If Americans were a transmuted race, they were transmuted British. For all its eloquence, this vision was highly conservative. It echoed Paulding's life of Isaac Hull, could trace its intellectual origins back to Jefferson's *Notes on the State of Virginia*, to Crèvecoeur, and to the natural history of the comte de Buffon. Successive efforts in the *Analectic Magazine*, by contrast, would drift toward offering readers visions of an originally American national identity located more explicitly in the War of 1812.[23]

As a first step, in December 1813, Washington Irving himself supplied the most notable biography printed in the *Analectic Magazine* during the War of 1812. Its subject was Commodore Oliver Hazard Perry, who, in September, had won the Battle of Lake Erie, leading a small squadron of U.S. Navy vessels to victory over a slightly stronger British force and securing the western theater of the war for the Americans. For the *Analectic Magazine*, Irving crafted a biography that reimagined American national identity by mythologizing the victory on the lake even as he took care to further emphasize the *Analectic Magazine*'s year-long endeavor to claim America as Great Britain's rightful imperial heir.

The "Biographical Memoir of Commodore Perry" started out, as had be-

---

23. "Lawrence," *Port-Folio*, II, no. 3 (1813), 254. The *Analectic Magazine*'s biography of William Burrows, who had commanded the sloop *Enterprise* in a successful engagement with the British *Boxer* and had died in the fight, is an intriguing example of how the previously established connection between navy and nation worked to render a life allegorical. Burrows was found to "cherish a solitary independence of mind, and to rely as much as possible on his own resources" ([Washington Irving], "Biographical Notice of the Late Lieutenant Burrows," *Analectic Magazine*, II [November 1813], 397). He had long sought to enlist in the navy, but, although he had been commissioned as a midshipman, "it was with difficulty he could be persuaded to wear the naval dress, until he had proved himself worthy of it by his services," and he "felt the novelty of his situation, and shrunk from the exercise of authority over the aged and veteran sailor, whom he considered his superior in seamanship" (397–398). If it is possible to detect echoes here of the larger relationship between Britain, the veteran sailor, and America, the youth who has yet to prove himself on the high seas and in command, this is because of the long standing that the comparison had acquired in the *Analectic Magazine*. Burrows himself, even without the contrast with Britain, becomes a typical figure: "He was proud of spirit, but perfectly unassuming; jealous of his own rights [shades of impressment and free trade!], but scrupulously considerate of those of others. His friendships were strong and sincere" (399).

come customary with the *Analectic Magazine*'s biographies, not with the life of Perry, but rather with a thoroughgoing meditation on the issue of biography as a means of commenting on the ongoing war. It was for this reason that Irving quickly disclaimed "rigid precision and dispassionate coolness" in his narrative and set out to elaborate his conception of how Americans should behave as a consequence of their victories over the British. He recognized the need for, and indeed the propriety of, Americans' exultation over their success "when the triumphs of our navy are the theme," but he cautioned that there was a point "beyond which exultation becomes insulting, and honest pride swells into vanity." Americans should avoid crossing that point, because their gains on the field of battle might suffer if by "fulsome and extravagant paragraphs" in newspapers they were to produce "national faults [and] boastful arrogance" and thus "lessen our triumphs in the eyes of impartial nations." Irving recognized that his position might not be popular, and therefore he clarified his purpose. The point was not to deny "joy ... in seeing the flag of our country encircled with glory"; rather, it was to be careful in what we ended up claiming. "We make no boastful claims to intrinsic superiority, nor seek to throw sneer or stigma on an enemy, whom, in spite of temporary hostility, we honour and admire." As in the life of Lawrence, Irving offered a measured estimate of relative American and British prowess and sought to establish their equality on the seas rather than American superiority. But Irving again took the same line as the previous biographies in subsuming the victory on Lake Erie into a long history of public American grievances. The "unexpected and repeated success" of American naval arms rang more resoundingly because "our memories are still sore with the tales of our flag insulted in every sea, and our countrymen oppressed in every port."[24]

Irving's nationalism was tempered by the recognition that Great Britain's heritage and especially its relationship with America in the present could not easily be disavowed. "For our parts," Irving wrote, "we truly declare that we revere the British nation." "One of the dearest wishes of our hearts," he continued, "is to see a firm and well grounded friendship established between us." Irving steered a careful course in which he tried to negotiate the difficult waters between claiming the naval victories were productive for the "independence of the national character" and that they did not ultimately harm the relationship between the United States and Great Britain

---

24. [Washington Irving], "Biographical Memoir of Commodore Perry," *Analectic Magazine*, II (December 1813), 494, 495, 496.

that he advocated. Thus, he suggested, it was curiously advantageous for a lasting friendship with Britain to stand up to it in combat; indeed, it was the only way of winning the respect on which international friendships could be built. In this middle course between "rancorous hostility on the one side, and blind partiality on the other," he found a position that could hold together Americans and British, even in the middle of a war.[25]

At the same time, Irving also sought to integrate the different parties on the home front by emphatically stressing the national dimension of the struggle and Americans' responsibility to unite in the face of an exterior enemy:

> He who fancies he can stand aloof in interest, and by condemning the present war, can exonerate himself from the shame of its disasters, is wofully [sic] mistaken. Other nations will not trouble themselves about our internal wranglings and party questions; they will not ask who among us fought, or why we fought—but *how* we fought. The disgrace of defeat will not be confined to the contrivers of the war, or the party in power, or the conductors of the battle; but will extend to the whole nation, and come home to every individual.

He considered the continuing struggle affirmatively a "war awfully decisive of the future character and destinies of the nation."[26]

Yet, as the biography of Perry made clear, Irving was not prepared to let the course of the war decide the destinies of the nation without mediation. The biography became an effort to shape the character of the future nation itself by offering it a new conception of its national identity. As Irving summarized in the final paragraph of his lengthy introduction, "In writing these naval biographies, it is our object not merely to render a small tribute of gratitude to these intrepid champions of our honour; but to render our feeble assistance towards promoting that national feeling which their triumphs are calculated to inspire." The biographical sketch of Perry, very much like those already published by the *Analectic Magazine*, spared few words for business unrelated to the Battle of Lake Erie. After a page recounting the first fifteen years of Perry's service, the biography found him in command of a gunboat flotilla at the beginning of the War of 1812. Irving took the opportunity to criticize the Jeffersonian antinavalist policies, noting the

---

25. Ibid., 496, 497.
26. Ibid., 497.

unpleasantness of gunboat duty for "ardent and daring minds ... obliged to skulk about harbours and rivers," and highlighted Perry's desire to be transferred to a more active station. Here, in describing Perry's departure from the "the comforts of home, and the endearments of a young and beautiful wife and blooming child," Irving's greater conception for the biographical essay was introduced. In this description of Perry's leave-taking from his family, Irving began an implicit comparison between Perry and British admiral Lord Horatio Nelson, a connection on which Irving grounded his conception of American succession to British domination. Nelson, Britain's foremost naval hero, became a foil for Perry: similarly successful, a useful point of reference, but less virtuous in private life. Both came to stand as the *pars pro toto* that circumscribed the transfiguration by which America came to succeed Britain as the foremost imperial power in America.[27]

The reference to Nelson in Perry's departure requires some previous knowledge of Nelson's life, but Irving did not gamble on his readers' knowledge. Describing Perry's letter announcing his victory on Lake Erie, Irving claimed that the letter "has been called an imitation of Nelson's letter after the battle of the Nile; but it was choosing a noble precedent, and the important national results of the victory justified the language." The explicit connection here between the British officer and the American commodore highlighted the similar importance accrued both events as well as the prospect of more signal victories still to come. If the Battle of the Nile was Nelson's first true independent victory, his grand triumph at Trafalgar was yet to come; an echo of greater glory for Perry, too, sounded through the phrase. This late explicit paralleling of Perry and Nelson gave force to the previous allusion in the description of Perry's departure for the lakes. And here the editorial opportunities of the periodical were used to the fullest. If the Perry biography requires knowledge of Nelson's life, the *Analectic Magazine*'s December 1813 edition helpfully provided it: it carried a lengthy discussion of Robert Southey's *Life of Nelson*, a review initially published in the *London Critical Review* of July 1813. As was customary for the times, the review includes large sections copied verbatim—as examples of the prose—from the book itself. Nelson's career was summarized, and his status as a great naval officer amply honored, but the sketch concluded with his affair with Lady Hamilton. The reviewer's stance was critical but understanding, acknowledging that "his infirmity has been that of many noble minds" and posing the question of "whether Nelson would have been altogether more estimable if the

27. Ibid., 497, 499.

ingredients of his character had been mingled in different proportions." Nelson was a hero in the fleet but a flawed man in private life, an issue that the reviewer of Southey's life of Nelson did not take to be, in the last resort, critical. It became important only in the connection that Irving established between Nelson and Perry. Not only was the implicit contrast between the ways in which Nelson left his wife for a mistress evident, but Irving emphasized it, without naming names, in the biography of Perry. "It is pleasing," Irving wrote, "thus to find public services accompanied by private virtues; to discover no drawbacks in our esteem; no base alloy in the man we are disposed to admire; but a character full of moral excellence, of high-minded courtesy, and pure unsullied honour." As Nicole Eustace has pointed out, "connubial love, naval service, and national loyalty not only made for an evocative symbolical configuration"; marriage also served as the "best metaphor ... for citizenship." Whereas Nelson combined martial prowess with moral failure, Perry did not; whereas Perry tore himself from the bosom of an intact family, Nelson's final departure was from his mistress and their daughter. Whereas Nelson was a British subject, Perry was an American citizen. The Nelson connection was reinforced wherever possible: Irving explicitly noted that Commodore Barclay, the British commander whom Perry beat, had himself fought at Nelson's great last victory at Trafalgar. And, if it would be too much to claim that the engraved portrait that preceded the biography, showing Perry with his right hand tucked into his coat, was playing on Nelson's empty right sleeve (devoid of the arm that he had lost in the Battle of Santa Cruz in 1797), it would perhaps not be too much to say that the allusion would have been willingly accepted by Irving if it had been pointed out to him (Figure 1).[28]

In juxtaposing biography, portraiture, and review, Irving editorially connected Nelson and Perry. In writing about Perry with implicit reference to the life of Nelson, he placed them in relation authorially. By contrasting Nelson and Perry in the two biographical articles, Irving established a central figure in the myth of British naval dominance in contrast to an American figure whom he wanted to refigure as Nelson's superior successor. The effort to contrast and compare the two men led from the similarity of their victory letters and their contrasting private lives to more obscure but telling refer-

---

28. Ibid., 503, 509; Robert Southey, review of "The Life of Lord Nelson," *Analectic Magazine*, II (December 1813), 472; Eustace, *1812*, 86–87; see also Nicole Eustace, "War Stories and Love Stories: Captain Oliver Perry and the Making of American Patriotism," *Common-Place*, XII, no. 4 (July 2012), www.common-place.org.

Figure 1. Oliver Hazard Perry. From [Washington Irving], "Biographical Memoir of Commodore Perry," *Analectic Magazine*, II (December 1813), preceding 494. Courtesy, American Antiquarian Society

ences and produced a form of hereditary succession: Perry was marked as the successor of Nelson, and, in succeeding Nelson, he became a metonymical stand-in for the United States that succeeds Great Britain.

Irving's editorial and authorial work on a new conception of American national identity did not end with the Nelson parallel. Between the review of the biography of Nelson and the sketch of Oliver Hazard Perry, editor Irving placed an original article called "Hints on the Navy of the United States." Much as discussion in the magazines before the war had emphasized the role that a strong navy could play in cementing American independence and national character, the "Hints" highlighted the ways in which Americans could make use of their natural resources and ingenuity and actively considered the "means by which [the country's] glory may be perpetuated and its successes continued." The article, largely a factual analysis of the various options and opportunities open to a future U.S. Navy, concluded that, if its remarks should "awaken a discussion that will bring to light any of the naval energies of the nation," they would "attain the end proposed," thus echoing the prewar reflections on the synchrony of naval power and national character. And, for readers who went through the magazine front to back, it highlighted once more the importance of Perry's victory, as Perry's victory validated the conclusions of the "Hints."[29]

Irving the editor of the *Analectic* was primarily responsible for this juxtaposition of texts with a similar outlook. Irving the author was responsible for the conclusion of Perry's biography. For nine months, the *Analectic Magazine* had been dealing with a simple problem: whenever it had claimed that American naval victories had shown American equality, if not superiority, at sea in a one-on-one fight, the British had responded derisively that American frigates—heavier, stronger, and armed with more guns—had always outclassed the British ships, rendering American victories essentially meaningless as far as a comparison of naval prowess was concerned. Now, Irving gleefully noted that "in this battle, we trust, incontrovertible proof is given ... that the success of our navy does not arise from chance, or superiority of force"; rather, it comes from the sheer ability of American seamen. The Battle of Lake Erie had shown Americans able "to face the foe in squadron, and vanquish him even though superior in force." The December issue of the *Analectic Magazine* thus neatly concluded the narrative that had begun with the sketch of the biography of Captain Hull by removing from the British "every excuse in which [they] sought to shelter" themselves.[30]

Irving did not just present a summary of the value of Perry's victory for the immediate circumstances of the War of 1812 or as a fitting conclusion to the series of biographies published during 1813; he also offered his readers a proleptic view of American grandeur. In America's future, the present victory on Lake Erie would be transformed into a mythical past in which Perry played the role of the "warrior" in a "heroic story," "streaming like a meteor through the fight, and working wonders with his single arm." The historical legacy of the Battle of Lake Erie would thus become much more than a momentary shift in control of a body of water. "Naval warfare," Irving wrote, "has been carried into the interior of a continent," and American victory on

---

29. "Hints on the Navy of the United States," *Analectic Magazine*, II (December 1813), 484, 494.

30. Irving, "Perry," *Analectic Magazine*, II (December 1813), 506.

Lake Erie had sounded "the expiring note of British domination." The lakes, Irving's vision suggested, would soon "be embosomed within a mighty empire," no longer "the separating space between contending nations" thanks to the "ocean warriors that came from the shores of the Atlantic." Irving's striking and romantic prose read Perry's victory, apart from the real-world consequences for the War of 1812 that he had already enumerated, as the prefiguration of a new American empire, one in which Canada would belong to the United States. The movement into the wilderness of Lake Erie from the Atlantic reimagined the westward movement of empire, and the peal that rang out signaling the end of English domination could be heard not only over Lake Erie but also through the metaphorical connection between Perry and Nelson, in individual naval victories and America's consequent assumption of the role of Britain's successor, and in the new myth of origin for the American empire. Paulding's life of Hull had emphasized the parent-child relationship between Great Britain and the United States, a relationship that had stressed the literal "Englishness" of Americans. By contrast, Irving constructed a metaphorical form of genealogy, one that sought to reaffirm good relations with Great Britain at the same time as it conceived of American victory, and especially American victors, as symbolic of America's supersession of Great Britain. It also built an origin myth for the United States in the present of the War of 1812: "In future times," Irving noted,

> when the shores of Erie shall hum with busy population; when towns and cities shall brighten where now extend the dark and tangled forest; when ports shall spread their arms, and lofty barks shall ride where now the canoe is fastened to the stake; when the present age shall have grown into venerable antiquity, and the mists of fable begin to gather round its history; then will the inhabitants of Canada look back to this battle we record, as one of the romantic achievements of the days of yore. It will stand first on the page of their local legends, and in the marvellous [sic] tales of the borders.

In the Battle of Lake Erie and the figure of Oliver Hazard Perry, Irving found suitable material for a mythical construction of national identity. His proleptical musings on the effects of the Battle of Lake Erie transposed the events of war into the diction and realms of the mythical. The inhabitants of Canada, who as we have seen, would already have been integrated into a vast American empire, would make this battle their *fons et origo*, and they, too, would stand for a future United States whose shape and identity as heir to Britain's empire stemmed directly from the Battle of Lake Erie and the personified heir to Britain's naval glory, Oliver Hazard Perry. Yet, just as future Americans would be able to draw on this mythical past through the medium of the magazine and the unifying power of the national navy, so could contemporaries benefit.[31]

Contemporary Americans could see themselves as the forefathers of those future Americans who would draw on them for their mythical genealogy. Irving's readers were enjoined to constitute their own national identity through their descendants: they, after all, were the ancestors of those Americans whose national identity would be traceable from the shared inaugural, quasi-mythical victory on Lake Erie and who would be looking back for their national origins to the time of the War of 1812. It is toward this goal that the mildness of the biography's rhetoric was chiefly directed. Irving's methodical essay neatly recognized that its efforts to establish a new American genealogy would suffer if Americans persisted in viewing themselves as naturally superior while ridiculing their enemies. American naval triumphs could be valuable only against an enemy who was not intrinsically inferior— to claim a naturalized superiority would have devalued the victory. When Irving wrote of the "national feeling" that the naval victories were "calculated to inspire"—even as he attempted to rein in precisely those national feelings that the victories *had* inspired, the "vulgar joy and coarse tauntings of the rabble"—he indicated the complicated nature of the particular construction of American national identity that he sought to install. With a bit of cheek, Irving fully acknowledged the ulterior motives that prompted the writing of the biography:

---

31. Ibid., 505, 510. The reference to a single arm is a bit mystifying. Irving had previously spoken of Captain Barclay, who had indeed lost an arm in battle, but the paragraph is clearly speaking of Perry, who remained uninjured throughout the action. Irving is probably suggesting here that the hero in the story is usually working with a single arm (a sword or a spear), and so he is not directly referencing Perry. But, of course, the echo of Nelson is unavoidable, and the confusion may be intentional. Irving's metaphor of the movement into the wilderness may also echo looming debates about the construction of a canal from the Hudson River to Lake Erie, a project that the New Yorker Irving was certainly aware of and that had been framed initially as a "national" project worthy of the support of the entire Union (see John Lauritz Larson, *Internal Improvement: National Public Works and the Promise of Popular Government in the Early United States* [Chapel Hill, N.C., 2001], 73–74).

> We have seized this opportunity to express the foregoing sentiments, because we thought that if of any value, they might stand some chance of making an impression, when accompanied by the following memoir. And, indeed, in writing these naval biographies, it is our object not merely to render a small tribute of gratitude to these intrepid champions of our honour; but to render our feeble assistance towards promoting that national feeling which their triumphs are calculated to inspire.

Here, biography became a vehicle for editorial policy; the biography, ostensibly the article proper, came to merely "accompany" the political statements, and its value for the production of national identity was explicitly affirmed. Americans could at once consider themselves the legitimate heirs to Great Britain, which was fairly beaten in its own element, and locate their own mythical origin precisely from the time of this victory over the erstwhile motherland, an origin that implied a lack of direct antecedents. This was the approach that James Kirke Paulding would pursue in 1816.[32]

Washington Irving left the editorship at the *Analectic Magazine* in February 1815. The magazine then passed into the hands of Thomas Isaac Wharton, a longtime contributor to the *Port-Folio*, whose editorial policies did not correspond with Irving's, although they were genial to James Kirke Paulding. After Irving had exercised his editorial prerogative to rein in Paulding's political stance in the biography of Jacob Jones, Paulding had not written anything resembling the political essay that was the biography of Hull. Irving had used his editorial role at the *Analectic* to mediate between the ultranationalist position that assumed the victories of 1812 to be evidence of inherent American supremacy and the British opinion that they signified nothing at all. Unlike, for example, the *Port-Folio*'s biographer of Lawrence, Irving cautioned his readers not to assume anything more than parity with

---

32. Irving, "Perry," *Analectic Magazine*, II (December 1813), 495, 497. Irving's rhetoric suggests a thinly veiled classism on his part and the more immediate purpose to chastise or at least educate his fellow Americans. Likewise, Irving's latent Anglophilia (he had to forego a planned trip to England because of the war) here may be argued to sit uneasily with his momentary promulgation of a decisively American future. As the argument of the essay develops, however, it becomes clear that Irving is not merely criticizing the nature of his contemporaries' vulgarities but in particular their shortsightedness: the immediate exultation over their victories obscures their longer-term meaning. In this longer-term meaning, too, the immediate insult that might be perceived to Irving's Anglophile sensibilities (his fellow writers' "tauntings" of the British) is rendered moot, as these meanings are largely without reference to Britain.

Britain, despite the victories attained in 1812. Although James Paulding was on a "literary campaign against the British," Irving moderated Paulding's vicious attacks in his direct editorial influence on the biography of Jacob Jones and in his own writings. Irving realized Paulding's stance toward the British full well, writing to Henry Brevoort with friendly irony in August 1815 that Napoleon's defeat at Waterloo and the French Restoration "will be sore blows to Jims [sic] plans—they will materially delay the great object of his life—the overthrow of the British Empire." There can be little doubt that Irving was chiefly responsible for holding back Paulding: soon after Irving's departure, Paulding's biographies of Commodore Thomas Macdonough and Lieutenant John Templar Shubrick showed what Paulding thought of America's British relations.[33]

Paulding's biography of Thomas Macdonough began by setting out a theory of biography that contrasted the practice in "legitimate monarchies" and in "a simple republic." A monarchical biographer, Paulding averred, had an advantage over a republican one because, if he found his subject unsuitable for lack of "any thing worth recording," he could resort to describing the lives of his subject's ancestors, "to whose exploits [the biographee] is fully entitled by the theory as well as the practice of hereditary succession." This made it "worth a man's while to perform great actions, since he thereby not only ennobles himself and his wife, but all the rogues and blockheads of his posterity forever and ever." Paulding's acerbic commentary then turned to the question of a biography's worth in republics. Honors were "exclusively paid to his [the subject's] own merit," so biography did not need to consider family history, an argument that Paulding had previously made in a biography of another naval officer, John Shubrick. In that piece, the lowly lieutenant's biography was justified by the simple formula that "honour should be paid where honour is due," since words of praise would render it possible for subjects to "gain ... individual distinction." The notion that honoring a deserving individual through the publication of a biography was the only adequate republican form of paying homage to him was common in the early Republic, but, in the essay on Macdonough, Paulding expanded it into a theory of genealogical descent. Even if American biographers were inclined to reduce their subjects to the achievements of their forebears, such an effort was de facto impossible. Aside from the mytho-religious origins of the Bible, in which "few of us can trace our ancestry higher than Adam," Americans did

33. Aderman and Kime, *Advocate for America*, 57; Irving, *Letters*, ed. Aderman, Kleinfield, and Banks, I, 418.

not have a heritage. "Family trees," Paulding noted, "are exceedingly scarce ... containing at most not more than three or four generations. Our ancestors unluckily forgot their pedigrees."[34]

Emigration to America for Paulding became the crossing of a Lethean stream, a journey at whose end lay a new identity:

> Not one of our ancestors, that we know of, came over with William the bastard to conquer England.... We are consequently obliged to build up a name for ourselves, as the first settlers of this country were obliged to build houses.... It is believed ... that this undignified republic cannot boast of a single man the merits of whose ancestors can make amends for his own want of merit.

The motif of memory was present, too, in Paulding's qualification "that we know of," but, more important, he denied a shared mythical origin with the British by rejecting any connection with the events of 1066. This denial is best understood, not as a refusal of Norman heritage, which would still allow Americans to trace their origins back to Anglo-Saxon roots, but as a refusal of heritage as such. Paulding also noted that "we cannot trace back to those glorious times when a man was ... immortalized, like young Lochinvar," an allusion to Walter Scott's popular poem *Marmion*, set in a mytho-historic Scottish past. Paulding thereby distanced himself from imported mythologies generally, whether based on historical data or contemporary efforts to create them anew. Instead, for Paulding, as previously for Irving, the here and now became important, when Americans were "undignified" by the titles of which the British boasted, and each and every deserving individual could come to serve as an example for building "a name for ourselves." For Paulding, the first American settlers, instead of figuring as colonial Englishmen, were first and foremost the ancestors of current Americans. Their pioneering work of constructing physical shelters for themselves was a type for American's contemporary endeavor to establish their national identity, their "name." America had granted both the "first settlers" and their descendants, from whom Paulding claimed descent, a chance for a new myth of origin, an original national identity.[35]

---

34. [Paulding], "Macdonough," *Analectic Magazine*, VII (March 1816), 201, 202, 203; [James Kirke Paulding], "Biographical Sketch of Lieutenant John Templar Shubrick," ibid., VIII (September 1816), 247, 248.

35. [Paulding], "Macdonough," *Analectic Magazine*, VII (March 1816), 203–204.

[This vignette, cut in wood by Anderson, from a design by Sully, represents Columbia seizing the trident of Neptune.]

Figure 2. Columbia Seizing the Trident of Neptune. From *Analectic Magazine*, VI (September 1815), 231. Courtesy, American Antiquarian Society

The *Analectic Magazine* neatly illustrated the periodicals' insistence that Americans had taken from the British what would not, could not be returned in a woodcut that accompanied its biography of Macdonough, an image that also prefaced the *Analectic*'s September 1815 "Introductory Essay" for its brand-new feature "The American Naval Chronicle" (Figure 2). Here, helpfully for those not gifted with great interpretative powers, an editorial comment stressed how to read the picture: "This vignette, cut in wood by Anderson, from a design by Sully, represents Columbia seizing the trident of Neptune." The woodcut shows the figure of Columbia looking toward a lunging Neptune. Columbia's outstretched arm holds Neptune's trident, symbol of maritime power, away from Neptune, who apparently seeks to reacquire

---

Paulding might have made a more radical claim than the one I suggest here: that the American Republic's insistence on individual merit meant that ancestry had become entirely meaningless, whether transatlantic or not. This is certainly a valid reading of Paulding's point, yet, by invoking the first settlers, he himself placed Americans in a lineage of lineage-less men, a paradox that he does not ultimately resolve.

it. Behind her, the waves crest in the form of horses; beneath her, fishes carry the seashell in which she floats. Neptune's shell, by contrast, is drawn by two white horses, who are orienting themselves toward the left side of the frame. There, the sky is turning ominously dark. To Columbia's right, the clouds are lighter—sunshine can almost be imagined breaking through at any moment. Columbia has taken Neptune's station and tends toward a glorious future. Neptune, by contrast, is reduced to desperate leaps in order to have any hope of escaping the darkness of maritime obscurity. The intended symbolism was left to the discerning reader, but forewent subtlety: Britain's loss of maritime dominance to the United States is heralded, bringing with it a golden dawn for the latter and the looming threat of obscurity for the former.[36]

The *Analectic Magazine*'s engraver allegorized the magazine's insistence on the unalterable ascendancy of the United States. Beating the British in their own domain, Americans could read a general American ascendancy into naval victory, figuring that, precisely because the British tied their sense of national worth so tightly to their fleet, success at sea was a mere precursor to success elsewhere. Having appropriated the British trident in graphic and in rhetoric, Americans likewise appropriated the rhetoric of national identity from British examples. Ironically, in attempting to reinvent a national identity from the deeds of the U.S. Navy's officers, American authors were adopting and adapting the British strategies that Timothy Jenks has outlined. They were, so to speak, at their most British in asserting their American national identity. While Elsie West commends Washington Irving for "allowing the facts to speak for themselves and ... eliminating secondary purposes and digressive material," it is in fact precisely those digressions—by no means eliminated at all!—that allow Irving to make his biographies a means to the greater end of shaping American national identity. In this reading, the specific subjects of the biographies—their biographees—become subordinate to the ways in which their lives can be used as a metaphor for the development of the U.S.-British relationship, specifically the genealogi-

---

36. "The American Naval Chronicle: Introductory Essay," *Analectic Magazine*, VI (September 1815), 231. I am indebted to Nicole Eustace for pointing out another level of symbolism. Representing Britain through Neptune (rather than female Britannia) heightens the engraving's tension by adding a dimension of sexual danger, the lecherous assault by an old man on a young woman. This idea may be compared, again, to the issue of sexual vice versus sexual virtue inherent in the comparison between Horatio Nelson and Oliver Hazard Perry, above.

cal relationship between the two nations as a consequence of the events of the War of 1812.³⁷

Many histories of the War of 1812 have emphasized the incomplete nationhood of the United States in the aftermath of the American Revolution and sought to identify in the subsequent decades the progress of American nationalism. Yet, as Jack P. Greene suggests, "the powerful state identities inherited from the colonial era and the deep-seated provincial loyalties, habits, and prejudices they expressed represented a formidable challenge for those who hoped to create a durable national union" in the direct aftermath of the Revolution and beyond. This essay has framed national identity as a rhetorical trope, a contingent figure within a discourse that waxed and waned in importance compared to those other identities that existed in the early Republic. By early 1817, the public interest in naval officers' biographies had clearly waned enough to make it increasingly unprofitable to keep publishing and writing them. Indeed, as early as January 1816, the *Analectic*'s author of the biography of Lewis Warrington noted: "As it is probable that for some time to come there will occur but few opportunities of gaining distinction in the service ... our biographical labours may possibly be brought nearly to a close."³⁸

The purpose of biography was to herald "distinction in the service of [the] country," advancing the heroic individuals who could figure as public eidolons and whose ability to do so depended in no small part on the external enemy capable of genuinely uniting the disparate communities of the United States. War had catapulted American nationalism and American naval officers into public interest. Peace relegated those officers to their "ordinary duties" and Americans' national identity to one affiliation among many, and by no means a *primus inter pares*. As Alan Taylor has recently summarized, the war had not been fought because of American nationalism. Rather, it had at best engendered a fleeting nationalism that postwar histories extended backward and transmuted from a result into a cause—and that modern histories too often essentialize as a more-than-momentary, lasting impact of the War of 1812.³⁹

Even at a period of heightened nationalism, Americans were hardly in

37. West, "Washington Irving," in Tuttleton, ed., *Washington Irving*, 200.
38. Jack P. Greene, "State and National Identities in the Era of the American Revolution," in Don H. Doyle and Marco Antonio Pamplona, eds., *Nationalism in the New World* (Athens, 2006), 77; "Warrington," *Analectic Magazine*, VII (January 1816), 7.
39. "Warrington," *Analectic Magazine*, VII (January 1816), 7; Taylor, *Civil War of 1812*, 458.

agreement about what precisely constituted their national identity. Periodicals—indeed, even just one magazine and one genre of text, written by just two authors—offered their readers various conceptions of American national identity. Some texts reflected the British heritage of Americans and avowed the lasting and profound ties as parent and child, coequal friends, or, at the very least, equals in ability and spirit, while others firmly disavowed any remaining connection with Britain. Even as these texts shared a general sense of American nationhood, they contested the particular form that nationhood should take. Indeed, as we have seen, Democratic-Republicans thought that the best form of the nation coincided with an identification with their own party.

Americans could use the naval biographies to identify themselves with the victorious heroes, explicitly presented to them as examples of American virtue. They could view the individual struggles and victories of the naval officers as synecdoches for the nation, and, in turn, see themselves as part of the nation. These representations of the nation through naval officers, however, were the result of a temporary upsurge of national feelings brought about by war, reflecting merely one moment in the burgeoning history of the United States. Beneath this upsurge lay conflicting and incompatible conceptions of how Americans should see themselves, as evidenced by the contrasting genealogies the *Analectic Magazine* and the *Port-Folio* offered their readers during the War of 1812 and in the two years afterward. Not that it mattered: as the glory of the naval war vanished into the haze of the past, politics, sectionalism, and racial and social strife reared their heads again. As Maurizio Viroli has suggested, "the only kind of commitment that is compatible with the pluralism of American society is a commitment to the republic; it is a political allegiance," rather than the kind of ethno-mythical national identity envisaged in the biographies in the *Analectic Magazine*. With the diminishing of the patriotic fervor that had fueled nationalist politics for two or three years after the War of 1812, Americans found themselves back in a union of separate states, the individual goals of which trumped the national spirit and all conceptions of national identity.[40]

---

40. Maurizio Viroli, *For Love of Country: An Essay on Patriotism and Nationalism* (Oxford, 1995), 179.

THE SELF-ABSTRACTING LETTERS OF WAR
MADISON, HENRY, AND THE EXECUTIVE AUTHOR

Eric Wertheimer

Calculating the probability that New England would secede from the union if the U.S. Congress were to declare war on Britain, John Henry, the British spy, seemed to understand what it took to move the powerful to action. In an encrypted letter dated March 7, 1809, he took a jab at James Madison's constitutional authority: "The truth is, the common people have so long regarded the Constitution of the United States with complacency, that they are now only disposed in this quarter to treat it like a truant mistress, whom they would, for a time, put away on a separate maintenance, but, without further and greater provocation, would not absolutely repudiate." Henry rhetorically figured the public hopelessly trapped by an erotic embarrassment—the great defining text now a rogue inconvenience, threatening authority at all levels. But, even as he documented the people's waning devotion to the Constitution, he took care not to overstate the possibility of either a declaration of war or a subsequent rupture of the union. Despite his evident pleasure in reporting the "hopes and expectations that animate the friends of an alliance between the Northern States and Great Britain," Henry asserted, "I have abstracted myself from all the sympathies these are calculated to inspire; because, notwithstanding that I feel the utmost confidence in the integrity of intention of the leading characters in this political drama, I cannot forget that they derive their power from a giddy, inconstant multitude; who ... will act inconsistently and absurdly."[1]

I thank Nicole Eustace, Virginia Chew, Fredrika Teute, and Sohinee Roy for their help in refining this essay.

1. There are many repositories for the complete set of letters from John Henry to Sir James Craig, along with James Madison's Message to the Senate and House of Representatives of the United States, Mar. 9, 1812, summaries of congressional commentary about the letters, and correspondence between Henry, Henry Ryland, and various British agents in London. Primary sources on Henry are held at the Library of Congress and the Public Archives of Canada and are published in *Vermont State Papers; Being a Collection of Records and Documents, Connected with the Assumption and Establishment of Gov-*

What does Henry mean by "abstracted myself"? He likely intends something more than a calm dispassion, a rationalist disembodied perspective of the sort advanced by any number of eighteenth-century political theorists. It also has to do with a mindset adopted in specific ways by political executives, a prototype of the ways modern nations organize themselves politically for war through the office of the presidency. Henry "abstracted" himself in order to rethink the connections between public opinion and foreign policy. This is a critical instance of political theory finding its way, through the helpful suggestion of figurative language, into policy—a textually disseminated concept and argument moving to the material enactment of war.

The following discussion relies on that metanarrative of abstraction to produce a conversation between actors. Though Henry wrote his letters on Federalist activities to Sir James Craig, governor-general of the Canadas, he saved copies for his own use. Ultimately, he found the means to sell them to James Madison in February 1812, a moment when the president was equally keen to know of the activities of his political opponents. Madison published the letters almost as soon as he received them. In some sense, then, the Henry letters, though addressed to Craig, were written for Madison. And Madison's own subsequent rhetorical and legal moves toward war came in conversation with Henry.

Rather than have a nation anxiously captive to mixed obligations and allegiances, Henry wants Madison to remember the Constitution and then use it as a device to recapture affect. In that recollection he will be able to direct the nation's citizens, to move people to action via textual protocol; implicitly, then, the Constitution should be a technique to return Americans to unitary authority, at last in control of the affective connections that too often can divide and defeat directed action. If Henry can abstract himself, he can understand the manifold drama that constitutes the irrational nation and thereby offer an executive model for Madison, a way to manage the connections between power and feeling. Henry instructs Madison in authorizing the text Madison himself had drafted. Henry does not persuade Madison; rather, he offers a culturally effective moment for Madison to use, one that

---

ernment by the People of Vermont..., ed. William Slade (Middlebury, Vt., 1823). I have relied throughout on the Library of Congress's digital edition of *Debates and Proceedings in the Congress of the United States*..., *Annals of Congress*, 12th Congress, Session 1 (Washington, D.C., 1853), http://memory.loc.gov/cgi-bin/ampage?collId=llac&fileName=023/llaco23.db&recNum=577. For Henry's Mar. 9, 1809, letter to Craig, see *Annals of Congress*, 1172.

Madison had no trouble imagining given the political and rhetorical cultures he inhabited.

Henry was a remarkably interesting instructor. In the late winter of 1809, not long after the repeal of the Embargo Acts, Henry (former captain in the U.S. Army and one-time editor of *Brown's Philadelphia Gazette*) found himself in Burlington, Vermont, documenting the possibilities for a national Federalist resurgence, or, at the very least, a consolidation of Federalism in New England. A naturalized American, born in Ireland (he is described by Francis Gore, lieutenant governor of Upper Canada, as an "Irish Adventurer"), Henry had exiled himself to Montreal in 1806 in reaction to Jeffersonian rule; the extremity of such dissent was of a piece with the Essex Junto, the Hartford Convention, and assorted other radical Federalist renegades throughout the antebellum and war years. Henry Adams points out that New England Federalists, by 1808, were in open league with the leader of the House of Commons, George Canning, and it is likely, from John Henry's claims, that Henry's letters and their intelligence reached as far as the foreign secretary, Lord Castlereagh, and leader of the House of Lords, the earl of Liverpool, Robert Jenkinson.[2]

Henry's mysteriously networked subversion took place against the backdrop of a Constitution in manifest need of reauthorization. His desired Constitution implies that the public is a genre to be mastered—the giddy, inconstant multitude reframed axiomatically—with a fictional shape and substance, a drama with characters and motive; it is itself a categorical abstraction necessary to thinking about legitimate war. It both denies and embraces the sentimental nation. Henry sees the need to erase the gendered individual (anxiously subject as *he* is to truant mistresses) from the national construct; instead, he summons the reasonable nation as a self that is at once collective, depluralized, transcending gender, and emotionally definitive.[3]

---

2. Henry Adams, *History of the United States of America during the Administrations of Madison* (New York, 1986); E. A. Cruikshank, *The Political Adventures of John Henry: The Record of an International Imbroglio* (Toronto, 1936), 15 (quotation). For the Essex Junto, the Hartford Convention, and the Federalists, see Richard Buel, Jr., *America on the Brink: How the Political Struggle over the War of 1812 Almost Destroyed the Young Republic* (New York, 2005).

3. This line of thinking is deeply influenced by Elaine Scarry's work on the relationship between language, war, and the body. See Scarry, *The Body in Pain: The Making and the Unmaking of the World* (New York, 1985). For an important discussion of emotion and national politics, see Sarah Ahmed, *The Cultural Politics of Emotion* (New York,

Henry abstracts authority and the public to avoid risking the ruin of the fictive and novelistic aspects of the public; instead, he hopes to harness them and their mediational effects. That harnessing redefines the relationship between the people and the Constitution, from the irrationally voiced nation, which diffuses authority, to a proper realignment with presidential power. The move contains the role of individual selfhood in naming national interests and declaring war. The republican devotion to bottom-up persuasive transparency, idealized in the contemporaneous media of letters, print, and opinion, is critically diminished. He invites us to consider how late-eighteenth-century networks of information—letters, secret communiqués, war messages to Congress—abstract the self (its "absurd" opinions, its "inconsistent" rationales) to the benefit of a new (masculinized) executive. The executive model of authority will replace the irregular multitude of republican political culture.

Such recurring and complex embarrassment connecting self and nation is especially important to assess for those interested in matters of identity, representation, and interpretation in early U.S. history. That the Constitution might have been viewed as an inconvenience or as a source of jealous contention raises a question about national policy: What are the conditions under which textual matters (scripted forms of emotion, strategy, and economy—war undertaken after the Constitution) are translated into action, a kind of consummation that aligns national interest with "abstracted" textual and technical imperatives? That it took roughly twenty-five years for the Constitution to have its injunctions respected is part of the answer to the question of how a war policy actually happens. Republics require an emergency, a representational charge carried through the media apparatus of the new polity. And crises are painstaking affairs, at many levels.

Madison's personal rejection of the Monroe-Pinkney Treaty of 1806 was arguably the true writing on the wall when it came to pursuing war as president. Nonetheless, wresting a declaration of war from Congress, in accordance with the Constitution's protocols, was something of an ominous puzzle for the administration. The solution meant spending much of that first term searching for pretexts that would turn "public opinion"—the self-

---

2004). It is also, of course, part of a wider discourse of emotion and political thought in the eighteenth century, which can be broadly viewed as an attempt to derive a political algorithm for containing political multiplicity/pluralism.

abstracted master and now unaccountably misplaced force of nature in the republican print sphere. In authoring the Constitution, Madison had moved declarations of war from executive purview to the legislative realm, in effect deauthorizing his future self. Madison the president thus made an uneasy heir to Madison the architect of the Constitution. In 1812, Madison had to turn to the public to reauthorize powers he himself had once enjoyed the authority to allocate.[4]

With the public at last reconciled and voicing consensus—released from the bonds of regional and party matrimonies—congressional action would come, all under the aegis of constitutional meaning and method. A majority in Congress, with the help of Henry Clay, John Calhoun, and the reintroduction of the Embargo Acts, had to be made to see the justice and inevitability of military action. War as a strict legal reality would otherwise be impossible—and this truth should not be underestimated. As Madison puts it in his June 1 war message, he viewed himself as addressing "a solemn question, which the Constitution wisely confides to the Legislative Department of the Government." James Trenchard's 1788 engraving for the second volume of the *Columbian Magazine or Monthly Miscellany* offers an emblem of that solemnity; in the updated classical tableau, the Constitution, borne by Cupid, was to be a pacifying, visibly ordering text in the republican world (Figure 1).[5]

Although Eric Slauter has deftly read this image as a document of ambiguity, of conflict overwritten, it is taken here at its word, viewed as symbolizing the absolute power of mediation to pacify. Rather than the fragility of fabric, and indeed fabrication, the scene highlights connectivity. From written constitutionality emerges one voice, serving peaceful arts, irresistible even to its enemies, who are persuaded (like Concordia herself, standing) by the new regime of connections. The temple of liberty is made meaningful by a network of interdependent understandings, which exclude an executive/president empowered to stand above all others; fabric and paper mediate the tableau, account for flaws (the cracked pillar), and deepen its dimensions. The evidence at hand is decentralized but unified, and all arms and hands (Cupid's, Concordia's, and Clio's) are indexing, relaying, extending, recording, and acknowledging this truth as a function of nexus. Instead

---

4. See Donald R. Hickey, "The Monroe-Pinkney Treaty of 1806: A Reappraisal," *William and Mary Quarterly*, 3d Ser., XLIV (1987), 65–88.

5. James Madison, Message to the Senate and House of Representatives of the United States, June 1, 1812, *Annals of Congress*, 1629.

Figure 1. James Trenchard, *Temple of Liberty*. Frontispiece of *Columbian Magazine or Monthly Miscellany*..., II (Philadelphia, 1988). Courtesy, Library of Congress, Rare Book and Special Collections Division, Washington, D.C.

of divulging the instability of the fabric of peace, the poem underwrites the scene like a descriptive contract, like the Constitution itself. It makes for an ideal that is undeniable and everywhere to be learned—war and the Republic are opposed because the Constitution arranged a harmonized, fixed network for collocation.[6]

Despite the stabilizing effects of the Jay Treaty of 1793, and the pacifist orthodoxy of republican symbology, Indian and postcolonial European conflicts flared along contested borders, coastlines, and on the high seas throughout the early national period. During the last two years of the eighteenth century, the nation waged the Quasi-War with France, never formally declared and carried on almost entirely at sea. The conflict may be viewed as presenting a Federalist version of the situation before 1812—neutrality as sacrosanct, the insult of an indignity (the "XYZ Affair"), the threat of ciphers, communiqués, and cryptography ("xyz")—with France substituting for Great Britain as the designated enemy. This set of pretexts did not result, however, in a formal declaration, a testament to the power of the Federalists to maintain Washington's proclamation of neutrality as a beacon for official policy and constitutional practice. But the shift to the Jefferson administration did not mean a rush to war with the British either, as many Federalists had feared. There was something about a formal declaration or decree—a matter of policy beyond the informal practice of violence conducted remotely from civilian life—that continued to defy the expected practices and partisan energies of the new republic of letters.[7]

Madison's understanding of the Constitution's war protocols, embodied most powerfully in his Federalist essays and approximating a liberal constitutionalism, made his pursuit of war a little more difficult, since for him the theory of constitutional textuality ordained a natural reluctance to bel-

---

6. Eric Slauter, *The State as a Work of Art: The Cultural Origins of the Constitution* (Chicago, 2009), 83–84. There is a variation on this tableau in the frontispiece to John Brown, *The Self-Interpreting Bible* ... (New York, 1792), in which the characters are similarly positioned, but with Brown's own annotated Bible as the offering to America. It can be read as a religious gloss on the easy national receptivity to republican textuality. A liberty pole is grounded (held by Concordia?), rather than positioned at the apex of the portico as it was in Trenchard's version; behind the seated figure of America is a tree with the names of George Washington, Thomas Jefferson, Henry Clinton, Richard Montgomery et al. carved on it.

7. It is arguable that even the Patriot War of early 1812 was but a pretext to the War of 1812 later that year, but Madison's impatience with its instigators marks it as a conflict carried on within the confines of professed neutrality.

licosity. Indeed, Madison's Constitution would act as a kind of break on all future need for reasons to go to war. Or, as he puts it quite curiously, it is the "pretext" that displaces the need for any other (more dangerous) pretexts. He had written in "*The Federalist* Number 41" that America's prudence and circumspection precludes the dangers of unnecessary pretexts to war—and that would amount to the impossibility of unnecessary war *tout court*. From there, Madison puts the word "pretext" through various rationales meant to buttress the image of America as an antimilitarist nation that would forever be without need of pretexts:

> The clearest marks of this prudence are stamped on the proposed Constitution. The Union itself, which it cements and secures, destroys every pretext for a military establishment which could be dangerous. America united, with a handful of troops, or without a single soldier, exhibits a more forbidding posture to foreign ambition than America disunited, with a hundred thousand veterans ready for combat.

Following the logic of pretexts in his argument, Madison proceeds to map the Constitution as protective document onto the geographical contingencies of both Britain and America, contingencies that perform similar strategic functions. The Constitution here is the ultimate pretext, first and last, establishing the geographical imaginary that precludes international conflict and an established peacetime military. It is, as well, a "cement[ing]" of republican textuality that secures the nation against the instability of representational posturing and divisiveness. An antimilitarist constitutional union precedes the geographical fortress with its standing armies and tendency to belligerence; without that union the sovereign nation would be subject to all manner of dangerous pretexts to offense or defense.[8]

Madison acknowledges a parallel argument about national insularity obtained in Britain, but to the opposite effect—putting Britain onto a permanent war footing with a standing army. Madison's rejoinder is to point to the transoceanic divide that makes U.S. insularity singularly different from

---

8. *The Federalist Papers: Alexander Hamilton, James Madison, John Jay*, ed. Ian Shapiro (New Haven, Conn., 2009), 208. Interestingly, Madison uses the word "cement" again in reference to the Constitution in his Mar. 4, 1809, inaugural address (*Annals of Congress*, 11th Congress, 4th Session, 464, http://www.memory.loc.gov:8081/cgi-bin/ampage?collId=llac&fileName=019/llac019.db&recNum=229). One could be forgiven for thinking that Madison overreached for a metaphor that would ease the instabilities surrounding the powers implied by the text.

Great Britain's (along with the federalizing nature of the constitutional union). His theory seems to underwrite Washington's subsequent neutrality stratagem in ways that make constitutional textuality the primary facet of neutrality's policy virtues.

> It was remarked, on a former occasion, that the want of this pretext had saved the liberties of one nation in Europe. Being rendered by her insular situation and her maritime resources impregnable to the armies of her neighbors, the rulers of Great Britain have never been able, by real or artificial dangers, to cheat the public into an extensive peace establishment. The distance of the United States from the powerful nations of the world gives them the same happy security. A dangerous establishment can never be necessary or plausible, so long as they continue a united people. But let it never, for a moment, be forgotten that they are indebted for this advantage to the Union alone. The moment of its dissolution will be the date of a new order of things.

Admittedly, Madison is pushing the virtues of Federalism to the point of hyperbole, but the antimilitarist register of his republican faith is compelling. Here is American exceptionalism joined to a republican appeal to unity, all in the service of some kind of nationalist quietism; its synthetic neutrality is perhaps the best expression of the paradoxical hand that, to paraphrase Henry Adams, wrote both *The Federalist* and the Virginia Resolution.[9]

But that neutralizing perspective clearly changed by 1809. So what happened for Madison that necessitated a "new order of things" on his own watch? How did the strained pacifism of the new constitutional order give way to the necessary executive authorizing of war? How did the ideology of republican America fail to secure this "new order of things"?

As secretary of state, Madison's paper trail tends to bear out his desire to maintain the given order of rhetorically pervasive, antimilitarist neutrality. It registers a statesmanlike reserve, regarding skeptically any pretext to war as unlikely to be successful given the geopolitical factions of the nation. And, in the service of a nation, republican ideology demanded a compelling legal brief that would countermand the natural mythos of isolation and consensus. Carefully calibrating, via texts and media, emotion with the abstracted self would be essential.

More specifically, the fundamental theory of the relation between the

9. *Federalist Papers*, ed. Shapiro, 87.

people and their representatives would be tested in the turning of inchoate public sentiment to a corresponding political voice that triggered state violence. But, as the ambivalent ungainliness of the undeclared Quasi-War would indicate, there existed a deep skepticism about attaining that concurrence in which the executive and legislative branches joined in formalizing war as a declaration; perhaps that level of self-abstraction was beyond the capabilities of rationalized republics. Madison reiterates variations on the natural mythos of isolationism and consensus that he valued everywhere in "*The Federalist* Number 41." Given the nation's, and Madison's, somewhat skittish evolution toward a declaration of war as a rhetorical and legal event, the case of the War of 1812 put the nature of republican, indeed national, war making to the test of theory; as historians, it puts us to the task of finding that point of inflection between neutrality and hostility.

It was in a pair of letters, written in late January and early February 1809, that Henry was commissioned by Henry Ryland, his "handler," secretary to the governor-general of British America, Sir James Craig. Henry received a letter of instruction, a letter of "credence" (credentials to be presented to appropriate informants), and a cipher for encoding particularly sensitive intelligence. One might suppose that gathering intelligence about public opinion in New England would not be too difficult were one to read the popular press and follow electoral patterns. Craig's true intention, according to his commissioning letter, was for Henry to assess, and perhaps lay the groundwork for, the secession of the northeastern states should the nation choose war with Great Britain; the idea of secession had been around at least since the Essex Junto, but, for Craig, Henry's voluntarist intelligence might have been a chance to gauge just how much Canada would be needed as protection for an independent New England in case of war. Once in Vermont, Henry began meeting with Federalist officials, taking subversive notes that were then transmitted via designated couriers, either in epistolary prose or enciphered. He betrayed the British when he was unable, after much back and forth by letter and finally a trip to London, to obtain his reward; the exchange of letters documenting the negotiations about remuneration, sent between Henry, Ryland, and various British agents in London, are part of the full suite of documents presented to Congress.

After delivering the letters with the help of a mysterious French intermediary (the self-titled Comte de Edouard de Crillon, whose real name was

Paul Emile Soubiran) to the Madison administration, in the person of James Monroe, Henry makes an eloquent, and at times disingenuous, declaration of his political interests. In the introduction letter he emphasizes for Monroe/Madison the difficulty of attaining political consent for war, positing the peculiar power of letters—his letters—to motivate public opinion. Henry explains:

> Much observation and experience have convinced me, that the injuries and insults with which the United States have been so long and so frequently visited ... have been owing to an opinion entertained by foreign States, *"that in any measure tending to wound their pride, or provoke their hostility, the Government of this Country could never induce a great majority of its citizens to concur."*—And as many of the evils which flow from the influence of this opinion on the policy of foreign nations, may be removed by any act that can produce unanimity among all parties in America, I voluntarily tender to you, sir, such means, as I possess, towards promoting so desirable and important an object; which, if accomplished, cannot fail to extinguish, perhaps forever, those expectations abroad, which may protract indefinitely an accommodation of existing differences, and check the progress of industry and prosperity in this rising Empire.

This passage is remarkable because Henry is working with a rhetoric of victimhood ("injuries," "insults," "wound," "pride," "provoke"). This rhetoric is interwoven with abstracted vocabulary suggesting rationalist diplomacy ("foreign states," "progress," "prosperity," "measure," "majority," "concur"). "Hostility" bridges both discourses—emotional and rational, self and schematic. The American public needs a mode that will allow it to envision and speak about a body politic with specific wounds. Although the first decade of the new century was replete with hostilities, Henry instructs the Madison administration to put the rhetoric to incendiary tactics, lest we delay "indefinitely."[10]

---

10. John Henry to James Monroe, Feb. 12, 1812, *Annals of Congress*, 1163 (emphasis added). I share observations about source material with a previously published essay, but I have attempted here to reframe them appropriately. See Eric Wertheimer, "Pretexts: Some Thoughts on the Militarization of Print Rationality in the Early Republic," *Canadian Review of American Studies*, XLII (2012), 21–35.

Madison saw the opportunity and quickly began to understand a rhetorical advantage. He writes somewhat cryptically to Jefferson on March 9, 1812, after laying the letters before Congress:

> I send you a copy of ... the Documents among which are the original credential and instructions from the Governor of Canada, and an original despatch from the Earl of Liverpool to him approving the conduct of the secret agent. This discovery, or rather formal proof, of the co-operation between the Eastern Junto and the British Cabinet, will, it is to be hoped, not only prevent future evils from that source, but extract good out of the past.

Madison's formal proof of a secessionist conspiracy afoot among the Essex Junto and Great Britain promises to turn that betrayal into a weapon. The debate that followed in Congress turned on the ability of the members to think, not about self, but abstractly about the data, which proved particularly important for the war votes of the Quids, or Old Republicans. As one of those Quids, Nathaniel Macon put it, "They expose an attempt, not to stab an individual, but to stab a nation." John Randolph was especially eloquent as he argued on behalf of publication to the Committee for Foreign Relations: "The character ... of the whole nation ... was implicated in this affair."[11]

Within the letters generally there is a fundamental challenge to the transparent functioning of the republican political system, whereby the general will of the public and its sphere of opinion and surveillance are accurately reflected, or at least deliberately wrestled with, in the press and then acted upon legislatively. As Henry writes to Sir James Craig, on March 5, 1809, by way of proposing the surreptitious promotion of a policy favorable to British interests in both the states and London:

> If it could not be done formally and officially, nor in a correspondence between Ministers, still, perhaps, the administration in the Parliament of Great Britain might take that ground, and the suggestion would find its way into the papers both in England and America.

---

11. See James Madison to Thomas Jefferson, Mar. 9, 1812, in *Letters and Other Writings of James Madison, Fourth President of the United States*, II, *1794–1815* (Philadelphia, 1865), 530; *Annals of Congress*, 1186, 1190. The manuscript version of Madison's letter to Jefferson is not in the Library of Congress's collection, though Madison's list of letters sent to Jefferson includes the entry: "1812: March 9 — Henry disclosures."

It cannot be too frequently repeated, that this country can only be governed and directed by the influence of opinion, as there is nothing permanent in its political institutions; nor are the populace, under any circumstances, to be relied on, when measures become inconvenient and burdensome.

The revelation that public opinion was the tail that wagged the government dog, in lieu of a strong legal and political apparatus, would seem to be painfully accurate for Madison. The unreliability, not to say infidelity, of American public opinion—its proneness to division and divided affections, its surprising distortions in its informational networks—is everywhere referenced in Henry's letters. At some level, Henry understood the value of the letters as material symbols that Madison needed to transform the public's understanding of itself, and its obligations, given that its affections had grown inattentive and its boundaries porous. Madison and his administration found in the revelation of Henry's offering the vocabulary for summoning a congressional will ready to vote for war. He turned sentiment into national interest, strategy into consent, and then consent into a declaration of war, and his communiqués were worth fifty thousand dollars to the State Department to acquire. Perhaps most important, Henry offered Madison a deflection from his own authorship of a war message by providing, in the most incendiary form of evidence—betrayal itself—the rhetorical and affective means to political consent.[12]

Again, Henry's attention in the introductory letter to Monroe is fully on the problem facing Madison—using textual persuasion, founded on anger and resentment, to promote the accommodation of differences and save the nation from the jealous meddling of European powers. Evident in Henry's statement is a persistent appeal to ideas of insult, injury, pain, and degradation, and even, in some sense, the truant mistress, all of which will prove instrumental to dissolving partisan interests.

> I have the honor to transmit herewith the documents and correspondence relating to an important mission in which I was employed by Sir James Craig, the late Governor General of the British provinces in North America, in the Winter of the year 1809....

---

12. Henry to Sir James Craig, Mar. 5, 1809, *Annals of Congress*, 1172. The vote on the June 18 war resolution was the closest in American history, with no Federalists tallying in favor. The vote in the House was 79 to 49 and in the Senate, 19 to 13.

> In contributing to the good of the United States by an exposition which cannot (I think) fail to solve and melt all division and disunion among its citizens, I flatter myself with the fond expectation that when it is made public in England it will add one great motive to the many that already exist, to induce that nation to withdraw its confidence from men whose political career is a fruitful source of injury and embarrassment in America; of injustice and misery in Ireland; of distress and apprehension in England; and contempt everywhere. In making this communication to you, sir, I deem it incumbent on me distinctly and unequivocally to state that I adopt no party views; that I have not changed' any of my political opinions; that I neither seek nor desire the patronage nor countenance of any Government nor of any party; and that, in addition to the motives already expressed, I am influenced by a just resentment of the perfidy and dishonor of those who first violated the conditions upon which I received their confidence; who have injured me and disappointed the expectations of my friends, and left me no choice but between a degrading acquiescence in injustice, and a retaliation which is necessary to secure to me my own respect.
>
> This wound will be felt where it is merited; and if Sir James Craig still live, his share of the pain will excite no sympathy among those who are at all in the secret of our connexion.[13]

Secret connections incite pain in the appropriate enemy, and the realization of a new enemy in Craig will engender no sympathy because the connection explains the value of its emotional instruction. Henry's rhetoric migrates from the diplomatic and political sins of the British ministries to the personal honor due not only the U.S. national self-imagination but also himself. The private world of republican honor is embodied in the double-crosser double-crossed, a kind of parody of republican transcendence of personal interest used to preserve, and indeed augment (ironically), personal interest. Henry's letters conspire to not only reveal an even more actively hostile and crafty British proxy in Canada than most had imagined; they pay witness to an insecurity within public and official political opinion about the nature of public opinion itself.

A consequence of Madison's laying the letters before Congress in March 1812—the bombshell before his war message—was a series of interposed debates, not about the message, but about the medium. Much of the argument

---

13. Henry to Monroe, Feb. 20, 1812, *Annals of Congress*, 1163.

centered on whether to publish the letters widely and officially, as part of a test of the public's ability to function as republican theory dictated. Some worried that the letters incriminated particular Federalists and, more generally, that they were untruthful about the speculated secessionist mission. The absence of named accomplices and informants only fueled doubt about the authenticity of the letters' purported mission, if not their originality as documents. Democratic-Republican William Widgery made the point that

> it by no means followed, because [Henry] had been a spy, that he could not tell the truth.... Let the papers be printed ... and every one will be able to judge for themselves. Are we to shut our proceedings from the public view in this way, by refusing to publish these things? It is one of the most important communications made to Congress at the present session, and why should not the people see it?[14]

Despite Widgery's confidence in the essential truthfulness of Henry's letters and their appropriateness for fair public assessment, we get the sense that the debate opened a deeper matter that media and representative apparatuses of publication and congressional review could not adequately decide. That is, how to assess the proper response to the "things" themselves? Henry Adams's theory about the letters is still persuasive—that they were likely the product of a French ruse, using Napoleon's agents (the cryptonymous Crillon) to concoct a set of letters that could only be recreations of the originals—had there indeed been originals. Nonetheless, their true origin (or their original truths) was never an issue when it came to their final usefulness, and that is the point.[15]

---

14. Response to the Report of the Secretary of State, Mar. 12, 1812, *Annals of Congress*, 1182–1183. As an indication of the geographical dissemination of the letters, they were, in whole or in part, published widely in the weeks following the congressional discussion—from New York City's *Commercial Advertiser* and *New-York Herald*, to the *Salem Gazette*, to Virginia's *Enquirer* (Richmond).

15. See Adams, *History of the United States during the Administrations of James Madison*, 416–420. Federalists poured great energy into investigating the conspiratorial nature of the affair, first with the Hartford Convention and then in the subsequent publication, Theodore Dwight, *History of the Hartford Convention: With a Review of the Policy of the United States Government, Which Led to the War of 1812* (New York, 1833). There is also a text of mysterious provenance called *Facts Relative to John Henry and His Negotiation* (Washington, D.C.[?], 1812[?]), held by the Library of Congress. This short book is a fascinating example of early political investigative journalism, replete with all manner of paper trails and chronologies—from depositions with the likes of Crillon, to

During these debates, the letters are often referred to as "things," "transactions," and "communications," words chosen (consciously?) to deflect from the matters contained within their intelligence. They also suggest their degraded charge as truths that emerged from something other than the idealized republican proving ground of opinion. In some sense, the letters became conveyances, not of truth about intelligence or strategy, but of the idea of the nation's capacity to feel as one, despite carrying the obvious burdens of a conflicted individual, like Henry or Madison. Madison used the letters to construct and then seize a moment of emergency, to bring self and nation into expressive proximity. What became visible in that challenge to the emotional nation — authentic letters or not, published or not — was that constitutional and political narratives were, in their truancy, at this moment of crisis, politically fragile, and thus necessary to defend.[16]

That disorientation, not to say fictionalizing, of the peaceful neutral order (to which Jefferson refers contemptuously as a "sublimated impartiality" in a May 30 letter to Madison) had Madison as its final orchestrator. It exposed the absurdity of waiting for the voice of the public to enable executive action. And executive action, in the wake of the letters, flowed downward to shape public/congressional opinion, not the other way around. Madison was able to claim a kind of veiled executive authorship over the letters and the law itself; such authority both underwrote constitutional injunctions and overwrote them as they disclosed the degree to which modern war, as a drama of emotional legitimacy, needed the executive to search out new techniques of power.[17]

There is an important moment in Clement Fatovic's study of executive

---

receipts signed by Albert Gallatin, to incriminating timelines meant to prove the administration's complicity with the French.

16. The term "transaction" appears in the report issued by the Committee on Foreign Relations and published, among other places, in Dwight, *History of the Hartford Convention*, 205.

17. See Jefferson to Madison, May 30, 1812, in *The Writings of Thomas Jefferson ...*, ed. Andrew A. Lipscomb et al., XIII (Washington, D.C., 1904), 154. For an excellent discussion of the history of the executive power in American politics, see Clement Fatovic, *Outside the Law: Emergency and the Executive Power* (Baltimore, 2009). Fatovic's discussion of Madison's shift from drafter of executive powers in the Constitution to practitioner of presidential prerogative is helpful here. He argues that Madison (along with Alexander Hamilton, interestingly) looked to Niccolò Machiavelli, John Locke, and David Hume for explanations of the role of character in good executive action, irrespective of the procedures of republican government (see 87, 189).

power and emergency in which he makes a startling point about Madison, linguistic ambiguity, and constitutional directives:

> [Madison] never developed a theory that might have explained the complex and mutually constitutive relationship between objects and words. Madison never developed the point that certain objects are constituted in and through language, that they have no independent existence outside the realm of human thought. His persistent (and persistently ignored) exhortation to define executive power was put to fellow delegates in a manner suggesting that the Convention had to *discover* rather than define or revise the meaning of executive power.

The letters help us understand the moving target that was republican governance, especially when language, identity, and communication were realized to be so deeply unfixed, theoretically and practically, by emotion and intrigue. Madison had to learn for himself that the executive found his authority in the events of political life, which provided, not rational and univocal lines of action, but ciphers, usable pasts, and drama.[18]

The letters might have been ineffectual in that they were deemed to be of dubious provenance and contained intelligence that could have been had just as easily by reading the regional press. But they put the mystique of covert representation, language separated from and disguised from its objects, in the service of a new kind of executive thinking that answered to a new conception of the Constitution. Madison managed to surpass the plurality of region, opinion, and representation, using the letters to salvage a narrower vision of Trenchard's constitutional rendering of oneness, wresting the quill of Clio into the scripting of a cause for war. The Constitution's inauguration of war had reauthorized it as an executive's document, shattering the conception of an autonomously definable network of arguments and replacing it with a set of jagged filaments that illuminated the dangerous immateriality of the declaring nation.

Ultimately, Henry's letters provoked anger in Democratic-Republicans and embarrassment in Federalists—irreconcilable emotions that nonetheless were politically effective in ways determined by a uniquely disassociated authorial calculation. And, although Federalists like Josiah Quincy urged the use of "reason" in the "temple of our liberties . . . according to the evi-

---

18. Fatovic, *Outside the Law*, 170.

dence before us," the debate threw into doubt the pacifying paper edifice of the great neutrality moment of 1793. The letters themselves—material evidence that a British agent was fomenting secession—secured war's necessity and the president's discovery of a new self-abstraction: author.[19]

19. Response to the Report of the Secretary of State, Mar. 12, 1812, *Annals of Congress*, 1184. Congress had arrived at a state of public influence described by H. M. Brackenridge in *History of the Western Insurrection in Western Pennsylvania, Commonly Called the Whiskey Insurrection, 1794* (Pittsburgh, 1859): "The fear of public opinion among themselves was even greater than that of the threatened march of an army" (249).

"CAN YOU BE SURPRISED AT MY DISCOURAGEMENT?"
GLOBAL EMULATION AND THE LOGIC OF COLONIZATION AT THE NEW YORK AFRICAN FREE SCHOOL

Anna Mae Duane

An 1819 valedictory address at the New York African Free School (NYAFS), spoken by a fourteen-year-old student named James Fields, but written by white trustee Ruben Leggett, told a tale of a thwarted journey:

> I crave your sympathy for my Self and for my School mates, for I feel that we need it. Had I the mind of a *Lock[e]* and the eloquence of a Chatham Still would there not be in the minds of some an immense distance that would divide me from one of a White Skin—What, signifies it. Why should I strive hard, and acquire all the constituents of a Man, If the prevailing genious of the land admits one as such, but in an inferior degree,—Pardon me if I feel insignificant and weak—Pardon me if I feel discouragement to oppress me to the very earth, Am I arrived at the end of my education?...What are my prospects? and to what turn my hand? Will I be a mechanic? No one will employ me, White Boys won't work with me—will I be a merchant? no one will have me in his office—White clerks won't associate with me,—Drugery and servitude then are my prospects—can you be surprised at my discouragement?

Put simply, James was a good student in a good school telling that school's benefactors that education will make absolutely no difference. As perplexing as it might seem, Fields's valedictory address reflected the conflicted environment of the NYAFS in the 1810s and early 1820s and of the reformist

---

The author wishes to thank the editors of this volume for their support of this piece, the anonymous readers of this essay for their generous feedback, and Mary Kelley, Karen Sánchez-Eppler, Jeff Allred, Sophie Bell, Sarah Chinn, Joseph Entin, Hildegard Hoeller, and Jennifer Travis for their kind readings and canny suggestions.

philosophies that influenced the school, and the nation, in the early years of the nineteenth century. This baffling performance offers a glimpse of some of the wider contradictions emerging in the era, among them the rise of the American Colonization Society (ACS) and its insistence that African Americans were inherently resistant to improvement in the United States but were yet somehow qualified to improve all of Africa. This essay seeks to illuminate why Fields's scripted lament would have seemed a logical pitch to make to the funders of the very school Fields described as a futile exercise. Doing so involves understanding two transnational endeavors that interlocked at the school Fields attended. First, the school's administrators promoted the school as a showcase for the ideas of Joseph Lancaster, the English schoolmaster whose early desire to "teach the poor blacks to read" had developed into a global system of education. Second, the school's board members, many of whom would become members of the ACS, increasingly saw the school as a point of intellectual embarkation for black migrants leaving the United States. Both Joseph Lancaster's global vision of education and the ACS's transatlantic emigration scheme were part of an interpretive framework in which a tale featuring a hero doomed to walk in circles could be read as a success story.[1]

If early Americanists have been tempted to read the first fifty years of U.S. history much like a novel in which one can chart the development of a national character and the exclusion of its doppelgängers, the story behind James Fields's valedictory speech offers a different way of reading the era. In this version, early American elites were enamored with a picaresque narrative in which character evolution is unlikely and perpetual remove displaces linear progress. Many scholars have read the War of 1812 and its aftermath as the catalyst for a nationalist policing of borders, but the school James Fields attended represents a diffusionist, globalist impulse warring for American attention. Rather than the narrative of investment in national borders and evolution that has become so familiar, this story tells of vacillating movements from origin to destination and back again. Much like the Lancasterian system that educated them, the students at the NYAFS were told that they would be able to change locations like pieces of moving machinery. In the vision of the ACS, African American students would move from their ancestors' African past to absorb the lessons of American "civilization" in the

---

1. "New-York African Free School Records, 1817–1832," III, "Addresses and Pieces Spoken at Examinations," [27–29], New-York Historical Society; "Joseph Lancaster," *Littell's Living Age* (Boston), XIX, no. 233 (Nov. 4, 1848), 216.

present United States, and then they would somehow "return" to an Africa they had never visited to remake the continent in the image of the place they had never truly belonged. Colonizing arguments often referred to the settlement of America as a precedent. Indeed, the first ACS ship headed toward Liberia was deemed the *Mayflower of Liberia*. Once there, the plan was for African American labor to enhance Liberia's ability to engage in legal Atlantic trade, allowing African resources to once again flow across the ocean, only this time in a virtuous fashion.[2]

For both black and white people struggling to determine the role of free blacks in the new nation, the gravitational pull of slavery was so strong that it threatened to make progress impossible. As Fields's speech indicated, when it came to the problem of prejudice, Americans were in a rut. Matthew Carey's fatalism about the need for African colonization in an 1832 pamphlet claiming that "no merit, no services, no talents can ever elevate them [freed blacks] to a level with the whites" drew from a tradition articulated two generations earlier by Thomas Jefferson, who had lamented the "deep rooted prejudices entertained by the whites" and "ten thousand recollections, by the blacks, of the injuries they have sustained." For Jefferson, who was an advocate for colonization, and for the members of the NYAFS school board, human progress stopped short when faced with the specter of white prejudice.[3]

If education was the Lockean answer to the problem of seeming inequality, prejudice was its antithesis: a force immovable by either time or instruction. Even as post-Revolutionaries recoiled from the dangers of what they deemed partiality and prejudice, and thereby sought solutions (which included, as we shall see, embracing Lancasterian pedagogy), they saw racial prejudice as impervious to change. "It is sufficient for our misfortune and embarrassment," one editorial read in an 1805 issue of the *Democrat*, "that they [feelings of prejudice] exist, and are perhaps so deeply rooted, and so interwoven with the feelings and opinions of the whites, that the exterminating hand of time may never be able to eradicate them." In such a climate,

---

2. See, for example, Howard Dodson, with Christopher Moore and Roberta Yancy, *Becoming American: The African-American Journey* (New York, 2009), 19, 29; David Kazanjian, "The Speculative Freedom of Colonial Liberia," *American Quarterly*, LXIII (2011), 866–867.

3. M[atthew] Carey, *Reflections on the Causes That Led to the Formation of the Colonization Society: With a View of Its Probable Results* ... (Philadelphia, 1832), 16; Thomas Jefferson, *Notes on the State of Virginia*, in Merrill D. Peterson, ed., *Writings* (New York, 1984), 264.

it is little wonder that Fields faced such difficult prospects. Indeed, his story would have struck the audience as all too common. As an 1819 editorial in the *Westchester Herald* argues, because "prejudice" "cuts them off from the prospect of any considerable height in the scale of society," black children have little reason to receive an education. A black father would come to realize that "his children can never hope to obtain distinction or preferment in political life, and that a superior degree of refinement will render them disqualified for the only society they can partake of, that of their own colour." Thus, the funders of the NYAFS, the New York Manumission Society, faced a paradox—why fund a black school even when members of your own circle insist that black education does not matter? Such questions made manifest the incongruity that plagued many white reformers who sought to reconcile the Enlightenment ideals of progress with ingrained racial inequity that seemed destined to only grow more pronounced as the nation moved into the future.[4]

The impasse between promise and prejudice, so movingly set forth in Fields's valedictory speech, had been enabled by the structure of eighteenth-century education itself. The NYAFS, in accordance with the ideas of Joseph Lancaster, placed particular pedagogical emphasis on emulation, a process through which a student's affective world is remade in the image of teachers and mentors. Yet reliance on emulation as the foundation of education often placed nonwhite students at a nearly insurmountable disadvantage. As critic William Huntting Howell explains, "To emulate—'to imitate with hope of equality, or superiour excellence,' . . . is to become oneself by becoming more like a commonly held model—perhaps even more like the model than the model itself." Whether it was Benjamin Franklin patiently transcribing and "improving" on passages from the *Spectator* or George Washington copying more than 110 maxims for gentlemanly conduct from a sixteenth-century etiquette book, the educational aesthetic of the late eighteenth and early nineteenth century illustrated that, in Karen Sánchez-Eppler's phrase, "copying is not a neutral act." Rather, copying, reciting, and repeating were the royal road to a deep personal transformation. A book in use at the NYAFS, Lindley Murray's popular *English Reader,* emphasized the importance of students entering into an emotional conversation with the text and, by extension, its author. "It is essential to a complete reader, that he

---

4. "Extract from Joseph's Memorandums, Under the Head of Slavery," *Democrat* (Boston), Oct. 23, 1805, [1]; "For the Westchester Herald, On Slaves and Free Blacks," *Westchester Herald* (Mount Pleasant, N.Y.), May 11, 1819, [3].

minutely perceive the ideas, and enter into the feelings of the author, whose sentiments he professes to repeat: for how is it possible to represent clearly to others, what we have but faint or inaccurate conceptions of ourselves?" Jean Jacques Rousseau, who famously asserted that he would become the character about whom he was reading, is an oft-cited exemplar of this sort of transformation. To effectively read an author's words, one must be capable of "enter[ing] into the feelings" of the author himself, effacing one's own particular emotions in the emulation of the model.[5]

For Adam Smith and those influenced by his work, proper emulation would inevitably evoke feelings of sympathy that could overcome prejudice. As David Hogan writes, for Smith, "sympathy and emulation were complementary rather than contradictory 'passions.'" After all, the "anxious desire that we ourselves should excel" stems from "our admiration of the excellence of others." Students wanted to do well because they desired the approval of those they admire. When it came to educating children like James Fields, however, the aesthetics of emulation became a deeply complex exercise. If black students could perfectly emulate their white teachers' intellectual, emotional, and religious sentiments, then, arguably, they would evoke the very sympathy that had engendered their own remarkable transformation, thus verifying their claim to future citizenship. But, when faced with the academic performances of black students, white observers often chose to respond by placing still more emphasis on their own sympathies—or lack of them. Again and again, white evaluators would find some subjective element missing. Yes, a black student might have been able to recite just as well as a white student, but, observers often noted, there was some ineffable quality lacking. In short, critics would argue that nonwhite students simply never made the jump from imitating Western subjectivity to inhabiting it. Missionaries stretching back to the celebrated Puritan John Eliot were hard-pressed to demonstrate that their converts were not merely going through

---

5. William Huntting Howell, "Spirits of Emulation: Readers, Samplers, and the Republican Girl, 1787–1810," *American Literature*, LXXXI (2009), 499; Karen Sánchez-Eppler, "Scraps, Schoolbooks, and Homemade Books: Childhood Studies in the Archives, *Society for the History of Children and Youth Newsletter*, XIII (Winter 2009) 22, http://www.history.vt.edu/Jones/SHCY/Newsletter13/Issue13.pdf; Lindley Murray, *The English Reader; or, Pieces in Prose and Poetry* ... (New York, 1810), [v]. I am indebted to Jordan Stein's work on Benjamin Franklin for the insight on Franklin's transcribing passages from the *Spectator*. For more on Rousseau and the aesthetics of reading he enacted, see Nicholas Paige, "Rousseau's Readers Revisited: The Aesthetics of *La Nouvelle Héloïse*," *Eighteenth-Century Studies*, XLII (2008), 131–154.

the motions but were deeply transformed by emulating their leader's interior states, in particular his spiritual piety. "Praying Indians" were often seen as clever performers rather than true converts.[6]

In 1706, Elias Neau learned that teaching African Americans in New York City required securing evidence that his students were capable of moving beyond mere repetition to show that they were fully, affectively, inhabiting the materials of the catechism. His makeshift school for teaching enslaved New Yorkers was criticized for having students merely pay lip service to the texts when they should have been experiencing a true change of heart. Faced with a class of exhausted students, Neau struck upon music as an effective method of instruction. "I observe with pleasure," Neau wrote, "that they strive who shall sing best." Contemporary accounts told of singing so beautiful that crowds would gather outside the classroom to listen. But the Society for the Propagation of the Gospel in Foreign Parts, for whom Neau worked, worried that such musical instruction was evidence of superficial imitation rather than testimony of a truly educated, and thus converted, interior. The prospect of supposedly ignorant heathens who could movingly sing psalms raised the specter of what Homi Bhabha would call hybrids, being "the same, but not quite" as pious white churchgoers. Their supposedly superficial performance thus threatened to undermine the spiritual power of the words by repeating them without feeling. Ultimately, the Society insisted that the Lord's Prayer and other psalms "'ought not to be Invoked by a people who know it not.'"[7]

It was with an eye to the importance of emulation that Benjamin Franklin noted the feelings of the black students he visited in 1763 as minutely as he recorded their "considerable Progress in Reading." Franklin notes that they "behav'd very orderly, showd a proper Respect and ready Obedience to the

---

6. David Hogan, "The Market Revolution and Disciplinary Power: Joseph Lancaster and the Psychology of the Early Classroom System," *History of Education Quarterly*, XXIX (1989), 401; Adam Smith, *The Theory of Moral Sentiments*, ed. D. D. Raphael and A. L. Macfie (Indianapolis, Ind., 1982), 50, 52, 114.

7. Elias Neau to John Chamberlain, July 24, 1707, in Letterbooks of the Society for the Propogation of the Gospel in Foreign Parts, microfilm, Widener Library, Harvard University; Homi K. Bhabha, *The Location of Culture* (London, 1994), 85; Thelma Foote, *Black and White Manhattan: The History of Racial Formation in Colonial New York City* (New York, 2004), 129–130. Later New Yorkers would worry that Neau's students had indeed imbibed too much of white sensibility. Neau's school was blamed in the aftermath of the 1712 riots for giving black students access to reading and writing, and hence the ability to access works about freedom.

Mistress, and seem'd very attentive to, and a good deal affected by, a serious Exhortation with which Mr. Sturgeon concluded our Visit." In his attentions to what his Massachusetts forebears called the "religious affections," Franklin reflected the still-prevalent belief that a true education required both emotional and cognitive development. Seemingly satisfied in this regard, Franklin wrote that the school visit had changed his opinion about the "the natural Capacities of the black Race." Here and elsewhere, the success of a nonwhite student depended largely on how whites felt about that student. A major evaluation tool for early republican schools, black and white, was the appreciation of an audience who would attend public student demonstrations (like the one at which Fields delivered his speech or the one Benjamin Franklin attended in Philadelphia). A school's reputation was partially measured by the public's response to student performances. If a true education involved inhabiting the affective and even spiritual state of one's mentor, then successful students and teachers would, of necessity, be tied with bonds of deep sympathy. Both teachers and observers would register such strong feelings—as Franklin did when he noted that black Philadelphia students were "a good deal affected by" their teacher's exhortations. Arguably, if a student were fully affected by his education, and could properly emulate his mentor, both his mentor and outside observers would be able to find their own sensibilities mirrored in the student.[8]

Thus, emulation, like sympathy, can be considered a reciprocal relationship. If the student never gains the approbation of the admired model, the circle is incomplete. The mentor—the distributor and the stand-in for Western wisdom and culture—and his peers must bestow or withhold such approval based on their assessment of a student's largely unquantifiable ability to inhabit the subjectivity they've been copying. The failure of whites to feel this tug of recognition can be considered evidence that the education just didn't take. In the tautological assertions of the ACS, the prejudice that whites still had, which is portrayed over and over as unshakeable and immutable, was proof positive that black education is effectively impossible. If whites were unmoved, as they are in Fields's speech and as they were in countless testimonials lamenting the immutability of white prejudice, blacks

---

8. Benjamin Franklin to John Waring, Dec. 17, 1763, in Leonard W. Labaree et al., eds., *Papers of Benjamin Franklin*, X (New Haven, Conn., 1966), 395–396; Carolyn Eastman, *A Nation of Speechifiers: Making an American Public after the Revolution* (Chicago, 2009). I use gender-exclusive language here purposely, as the dynamic I describe was deeply invested in a masculine model of citizenship.

have fallen short, unable to escape the realm of mimicry. For Fields, the speech taught him that the work of emulation cannot be his. He himself might indeed replicate the models of Western civilization—he might have "the mind of a *Lock[e]* and the eloquence of a Chatham," but he will never be able to occupy their place in society. Even as he spoke the words his scriptwriter had prepared for him, he enacted the difference between individual and model. In sum, Fields's speech, given at a school that urged its students to embrace the spirit of emulation, provided instruction in how race creates an unbridgeable gap between the individual and the exemplar.

Joseph Lancaster and the Work of Global Emulation

When NYAFS board members decided to embrace the Lancasterian model of education in the first decade of the nineteenth century, they were signing on to a worldwide trend that promised to deploy emulation to eradicate the problem of prejudice. This result would come about, Joseph Lancaster promised, through radically redirecting the energies of emulation and, by extension, altering the structure by which both knowledge and feelings were transmitted from adult to child. The implications of the system were nothing short of world-shaking. In the same decade that featured anti-British rhetoric inflammatory enough to fuel a devastating war, hundreds of schools would be erected in the United States that proudly touted their connection to an English system. Certainly, the United States was not alone in its enthusiasm. Thousands of schools would be built on this system throughout the world, including Europe, the Americas, Asia, and Africa. Joseph Lancaster became world famous, enjoying praise and support by European royalty and American politicians such as the mayor of New York and the president himself. Lancaster began his career by teaching orphans in London, and he created a system in which the parental relationship extolled by earlier models was replaced by an educational arrangement capacious enough to accommodate the world's fatherless masses.[9]

Rather than depending on the intense relationship between master and

---

9. Joseph Lancaster, *Improvements in Education, as It Respects the Industrious Classes of the Community* ... (London, 1803); [Lancaster], *The British System of Education: Being a Complete Epitome of the Improvements and Inventions Practised by Joseph Lancaster* ... (Washington, D.C., 1812); Patricia Crain, "Children of Media, Children as Media: Optical Telegraphs, Indian Pupils, and Joseph Lancaster's System for Cultural Replication," in Lisa Gitelman and Geoffrey B. Pingree, eds., *New Media, 1740–1915* (Cambridge, Mass., 2003), 70.

student that had characterized schooling for much of the late eighteenth century, Lancaster delegated much of the teaching authority to students themselves. Older children, often called monitors, would continually quiz the others in small groups. Children who performed well during such tests could then earn the chance of eventually becoming instructors, or monitors, themselves. If they wanted to keep their coveted status as monitors, they would have to consistently outperform other students. Lancaster's revision of the work of the schoolhouse was certainly cost-effective. It also changed the dynamics of education in which the schoolmaster was the sole guardian of true education. Lancaster did not, however, disregard emulation. He, like educators before him, felt that the emotional relationship between master and student was a powerful force:

> The influence a master has over his scholars is very great; the veneration wherewith they regard him is almost equal to idolatry, and that simply by his conduct in his station; so much so, that they are all his willing servants, and doubly proud to be his ambassadors on trivial occasions; his smiles are precious, and even bitter things are sweet, when bestowed by his hand.

The difference now was that such emulation could be moved from an intense, personal relationship between adult teacher and young student and channeled along a series of smaller conduits, diffusing it throughout hundreds of students, allowing it to circulate even when cut off from the initial source. Indeed, once the system was in place, Lancaster promised, the headmaster needn't be present at all. "On my plan," Lancaster insisted, "when the master leaves school, the business will go on as well in his absence as in his presence because the authority is not *personal*." In 1811, a report indicated that, when Lancaster had fallen ill at the famous Borough Road School in London, "an interesting boy of fourteen" named Maurice Cross "took charge of and governed the school in a most pleasing and gratifying manner." Even in New York City, where black children were doubly disempowered by race and youth, the Lancasterian shift in sympathy allowed a space for agency and authority. In 1822, a visitor to the NYAFS reported that the school was being run, not by the absent schoolmaster, but instead by student "Robert Gray, Monitor of order, a boy of 13 years of age."[10]

10. Lancaster, *Improvements*, 49; [Lancaster], *British System*, 93; *Report of J. Lancaster's Progress from the Year 1798, with the Report of the Finance Committee for the Year*

Supporters all over the world hailed the decentralized authority offered by Lancaster's model as the answer to partisan divides. "When *the pupils*, as well as the schoolmaster, understand how to act and learn on this system," Lancaster promised, "*the system*, not the master's vague, discretionary, uncertain judgment, will be in practice." Divested of the intense emotional connections that might be generated in a smaller classroom, a truly Lancasterian curriculum would be devoid of the ideological or political prejudices of individual schoolmasters. An account of an 1811 meeting of the Lancasterian Society, the minutes of which were republished in at least five different American newspapers, featured members of the British aristocracy who wholeheartedly applauded the monitorial system's ability to bridge ideological (and arguably, cultural) divides. The support of Lancaster, the duke of Bedford asserted, "was no party question; all ranks were interested in it, from the Monarch on the throne to the meanest individual of the community." Similar support would come from the leaders of Russia, France, and Spain, who sponsored the spread of Lancaster's model throughout South America. Here then, was one possible answer for partiality of all kinds, and perhaps even an answer for the prejudice that seemed so intractable. The appeal of a standardized system, creating uniform, nonpartisan students, caught the imagination of the NYAFS board and of many other American leaders that embraced the system.[11]

This vaunted impartiality promised to reshape national as well as religious and ethnic divides. In an era when the nation would embark on what might be called a second American Revolution, many U.S. leaders found solace in a version of education devised to combat the danger of the very rebellious autodidacts peopling the young Republic's evolving origin myth. Indeed, the 1803 version of Lancaster's treatise *Improvements in Education* refers explicitly to Benjamin Franklin, that Revolutionary problem child, to make the case for the need for proper education:

1810; to Which Is Prefixed an Address of the Committee for Promoting the Royal Lancasterian System for the Education of the Poor (London, 1811), 11; "New-York African Free School Records," I, "Regulations, By-laws, and Reports, 1817–1832," Jan. 11, 1822, NYHS.

11. [Lancaster], *British System*, 93; "From a Late London Paper: Lancaster Meeting," *Commercial Advertiser* (New York), July 25, 1811, [2]. The Society for Promoting the Lancasterian System for the Education of the Poor was formed in 1808 to promote Lancaster's system in the hope of expanding free education. In 1814, the Society was renamed the British and Foreign School Society for the Education of the Labouring and Manufacturing Classes of Society of Every Religious Persuasion.

The effects of approbation, or the contrary, expressed by the senior boys to lesser, seem to carry a degree of weight, almost similar to that of their master. Whenever a neat, ingenious trick, of a mischievous nature, has been played, we may be sure some arch wag, who officiates as captain of the gang, perhaps a Franklin, was the original and life of the conspiracy.

In case the reader skimmed over the reference, Lancaster provided a footnote in which he reproduced the entire excerpt from the *Life and Works* detailing young Franklin's naughty decision to build a wharf in spite of adult prohibitions. The argument is clear—Franklin's natural, and unchecked, leadership is productive of mischief. By citing Franklin, Lancaster cannily evoked both the lingering fear and grudging admiration such a Revolutionary master of "ingenious trick[s]" would likely call up in the minds of British readers in 1803. Indeed, Lancaster immediately followed the anecdote with the warning that the "predominant feature in the youthful disposition is an almost irresistible propensity to action; this, if properly controlled by suitable employment, will become a valuable auxiliary to the master, but, if neglected, will be apt to degenerate into rebellion." Certainly, we can imagine the appeal of preventing the rise of any future Franklins for a British audience, who were living with the threat of the French Revolution on its borders and with the specter of a rising generation of unaffiliated orphans within the nation.[12]

Perhaps more surprising is the great enthusiasm with which American leaders, including New York mayor DeWitt Clinton, Secretary of War John C. Calhoun, and Presidents John Adams and James Monroe, would embrace the system, illustrating their own desire to head off any unaffiliated Franklinesque wags at the pass in favor of a standardized global populace. By the

---

12. Lancaster, *Improvements*, 50–52. The selection can be found in *The Private Life of the Late Benjamin Franklin* ... (London, 1793), 11. Lancaster's quotation deviates slightly from this 1793 edition of *The Private Life*, which refers to a causeway rather than a wharf. For arguments that cast the War of 1812 as the catalyst for American nationalism and the emphasis on Manifest Destiny that would grow from it, see Donald R. Hickey, *The War of 1812: A Forgotten Conflict* (Urbana, Ill., 1990). As Hickey writes in the 2012 edition, "As America's second and last war against Great Britain it echoed the ideology and issues of the American Revolution" (2–3). For contemporary arguments that the War of 1812 was a second American Revolution, see the *National Intelligencer* (Washington, D.C.), July 8, 1812; and the New York *National Advocate*, particularly the issues of Dec. 15, 1812, and May 22, 1813.

time the Englishman Lancaster arrived in New York in 1818 to a hero's welcome, there were at least 150 U.S. schools established on his world-spanning system. The most patriotic of publications made the case that American children needed to be educated in a system that had nothing particularly American about it. In March 1812, three months before the United States declared war on England to maintain American independence, the Yankee publication the *Green-Mountain Farmer* featured an editorial written by the self-styled "Spirit of '76" who extolled Lancaster's system, not because it lent itself to American sensibilities, but rather because it crossed boundaries of both time and space, dissolving national and historical borders. The writer took pains to praise Englishman Lancaster's choice to turn away from the Enlightenment's fascination with written text and instead tap into ancient Indian pedagogy. Noting that Lancaster largely avoids books and paper, the writer pointed out:

> This is by no means a modern improvement, for it may be traced up to remote antiquity, as a proof which we read in the voyages of Francisco Bartolemeo to the East-Indies. In his first chapter, treating of the birth and education of children, he says 'the education of youth in India, is much simpler and not near so expensive as in Europe; the children assemble half naked, under the shade of a cocoa nut tree, place themselves in rows on the ground, and trace out [letters] in the sand....['] This method of teaching writing, was introduced into India 200 years before the birth of Christ: therefore, the public are indebted to Mr. Lancaster, for the adoption of this very simple, tho' comprehensive course.

Rather than a narrative of progress in which Anglo-Americans led the way, "The Spirit of '76" provided a circular, picaresque tale in which nineteenth-century Yankees emulated ancient Indian youth. According to this self-styled representative of the Revolution that made the United States independent, the salvation of American youth could be found in copying the "half naked" students of nonwhite people halfway across the world. To move forward, it seems, American youth needed to circle back through space and time.[13]

13. "The Spirit of '76," "Letter I. To the Friends of the Lancasterian System of Education," *Green-Mountain Farmer* (Bennington, Vt.), Mar. 10, 1812, [4]. DeWitt Clinton's advocacy of the system is well known and is largely acknowledged as the foundation of the New York public school system. Monroe and Calhoun were deeply invested in the establishment of the Lancasterian Cherokee School. For more on Lancaster's reception

In this respect, the craze for Lancasterian teaching offers intriguing evidence of modern globalization's long and varied history. As Frederick Cooper reminds us, "The highpoint of intercontinental labour migration was the century after 1815," not the century after 1915. C. L. R. James has demonstrated that the structures of time management and mass labor that enabled the growth of global capitalism were developed on Caribbean plantations as well as in English factories. Lancaster's educational system was one vital mechanism through which these structures were transported across national and continental borders, through the philanthropic language of charity replete with the emotional hook of aiding the world's orphans. The fantasy of impersonal replication that would transcend class, creed, and even nation—what Jacqueline Rose has called the "postmodern predicament—belonging everywhere and nowhere at the same time"—was one of the system's greatest promises.[14]

It is hardly a coincidence that the appeal of a uniform populace who could move smoothly through both time and space appears alongside the growth of the Industrial Revolution and the factory workers it would require. As theorists from Michel Foucault to John Lea to David Hogan have illustrated, the exercise of diffused competitive discipline was a prerequisite, if not a cause, of capitalism's market revolution. Certainly, contemporaries were pleased with how neatly the Lancasterian method lent itself to metaphors of factories humming with self-sustaining industry.[15]

The *Edinburgh Review* marveled at the way, within the monitorial sys-

---

in the United States, see Henry Barnard, *American Journal of Education*, X, no. 25 (June 1861), 362.

14. Frederick Cooper, "What is the Concept of Globalization Good For? An African Historian's Perspective," *African Affairs*, C, no. 399 (2001), 194; C. L. R. James, *The Black Jacobins: Toussaint L'Ouverture and the San Domingo Revolution*, 2d ed. (New York, 1989); Jacqueline Rose, *States of Fantasy* (1996; rpt. New York, 1998), 2.

15. Although Michel Foucault generally demurs on thinking through the extensive reciprocity of capitalism and disciplinary power, his interest in wide-scale mechanisms of discipline that organize bio-politics of the population is central to understanding the mechanisms of industrial capitalism itself. For Foucault, the monitorial system of education that Lancaster pioneered emerged as a vital piece of evidence in his argument about disciplinary regimes. See Foucault, *Discipline and Punish: The Birth of the Prison*, trans. Alan Sheridan (New York, 1995), 136–138, 222; Hogan, "Market Revolution," *History of Education Quarterly*, XXIX (1989), 393 n. 29; John Lea, "Discipline and Capitalist Development," in Barry Fine et al., eds., *Capitalism and the Rule of Law: From Deviancy Theory to Marxism* (London, 1979), 79–81.

tem, "every boy seems to be the cog of a wheel—the whole school is a perfect machine." As Paul Gilmore has argued, machines certainly worked as instruments of social and economic production. But, when it came to the Lancasterian system, the vaunted machine occupies a global, as well as a national, role. The worldwide embrace of this model reflects a remarkable aesthetic of interchangeability, a picaresque logic in which markets and capital spread across borders, circling back and forth with no discernible denouement. Rather than being shaped by national or personal destiny or development, the subject created by Lancasterian schooling was designed for a story devoid of clear teleology, one in which, as John Lea writes, market forces work "against, and without reference to, the conscious decisions of the individuals who are its bearers." In Lancaster's model, students can substitute for teachers; African American New Yorkers can substitute for orphans in London. That the co-discoverer (and eventual competitor) of Lancaster's system, Andrew Bell, first encountered the monitorial system in India (and arguably based his model on Hindu educational strategies) testifies to the colonial fantasy of endlessly reproducible polities where knowledge and resources can move effortlessly across distances, with origins constantly being replaced and renamed. For, if the schoolmaster is interchangeable, then so is the schoolhouse; the system itself transcends physical and national boundaries, with energy moving from one node in the network to another. As educational historian Carl F. Kaestle writes, the Lancasterian system "was not simply 'efficient,' as a single machine is, but, like the machine, it was infinitely replicable."[16] If one place offers a richer, or more appropriate, set of resources, then students, like flowing water, or, to use the metaphor Benjamin Franklin provided forty years earlier, like electricity, would simply move through available channels until equilibrium might be found. Certainly, the

---

16. Review of [Sarah] Trimmer, *A Comparative View of the New Plan of Education Promulgated by Mr. Joseph Lacaster ...*, Edinburgh Review, or Critical Journal, IX, no. 17 (October 1806), 182; Paul Gilmore, "Republican Machines and Brackenridge's Caves: Aesthetics and Models of Machinery in the Early Republic," *Early American Literature*, XXXIX (2004), 299–322; Lea, "Discipline and Capitalist Development," in Fine et al., eds., *Capitalism and the Rule of Law*, 81; Carl F. Kaestle, ed., *Joseph Lancaster and the Monitorial School Movement: A Documentary History* (New York, 1973), 7, 14; Andrew Bell, *Elements of Tuition, Part II, The English School; or, The History, Analysis, and Application of the Madras System of Education to English Schools*, new ed. (Edinburgh, 1814), 13; Jana Tschurenev, "Diffusing Useful Knowledge: The Monitorial System of Education in Madras, London, and Bengal, 1789–1840," *Paedagogica Historica*, XLIV (2008), 245–264.

advocates of the Lancasterian system saw it as part of the scientific revolution in which Franklin played such an exemplary role. John Griscom, a chemist from New York and a fan of Lancaster, praised the system as an example of "the *science* of education," a science that worked toward "*simplifying* and *accelerating* the acquisition of knowledge."[17]

Lancaster's popularity offers a different reading for Benjamin Rush's oft-cited wish for education to "convert men into republican machines," one in which the machine has a global, rather than a national, function. Sari Altschuler has convincingly demonstrated that Rush's vision was designed, not to cast republicans as self-contained automatons, but instead to render them as part of "dynamic living systems." It is important to remember that, as Colleen Terrell has argued, "for Rush, as for so many of his contemporaries, men were already understood to *be* machines, in a scientific tradition tracing back through the Scottish Enlightenment to the seventeenth-century universities of Holland, to Newtonian mechanics, Cartesian philosophy, and, ultimately, to William Harvey's landmark 1628 analysis of the circulation of the blood." Harvey's analysis is a particularly relevant analogy here—in both Harvey's and Lancaster's models, the beauty of the system comes not only from the soundness of its parts but also from the alacrity with which those parts can function as they circulate throughout space and time. As Patricia Crain has demonstrated in her analysis of the elaborate set of physical cues used to move students through various tasks in the Lancasterian classroom, "only when the student performs the cued action can the network proceed." "The Lancasterian child is thus positioned not only inside of but as *a moving part* within a kind of knowledge machine."[18]

In Rush's model for education, what constitutes a well-running machine

---

17. John Griscom, *Monitorial Instruction: An Address* ... (New York, 1825), 10. Many of the experiments in Benjamin Franklin's *Observations* focus on electricity's movement through various mediums. Experiment III discusses how a silk thread dangled over an electrified bottle "fetches and carries fire from the top to the bottom of the bottle, 'till the equilibrium is restored"; see Franklin, *Experiments and Observations in Electricity, Made at Philadelphia in America* ... (London, 1751), 5.

18. Benjamin Rush, *Essays, Literary, Moral, and Philosophical* (Philadelphia, 1798), 14; Sari Altschuler, "From Blood Vessels to Global Networks of Exchange: The Physiology of Benjamin Rush's Early Republic," *Journal of the Early Republic*, XXXII (2012), 210, 212; Colleen E. Terrell, "'Republican Machines': Franklin, Rush, and the Manufacture of Civic Virtue in the Early Republic," *Early American Studies*, I, no. 2 (Fall 2003), 103; Crain, "Children of Media," in Gitelman and Pingree, eds., *New Media*, 70 (emphasis added).

is precisely the parts' interchangeability. There could be no loyalty to particular aspects of the machine, Rush argued, but rather a subsuming of the part to the better functioning of the whole. A well-instructed child should "be taught that he does not belong to himself, but that he is public property." "Let him be taught to love his family," he continued, "but let him be taught, at the same time, that he must forsake, and even forget them, when the welfare of his country requires it." Rush's vision, amplified in Lancasterian education, allows for a dislocation of local and filial connections in favor of membership in a larger organization that might well require an act of self-orphaning as the child, now public property, would simply shift his energies to where he was most needed. For Lancaster, it was not only the "welfare of his country" that should generate a child's break from local ties but also the welfare of the entire world.[19]

As Lancaster's monitorial system built upon existing models of circulation, even as it provided new ways to conceptualize interchangeability, its dominance, like the workings of slavery, was (to borrow Paul Gilroy's phrase) predicated on routes rather than roots. In this fantasy, relations are not wrought through ancestral ties to one place, to one family, or to one teacher. Instead, both knowledge and populations can be shifted from place to place without substantial loss. As Walter Benjamin would contend more than a hundred years after the Lancasterian method spread like wildfire across the globe, "by making many reproductions," one "substitutes a plurality of copies for a unique existence." For Benjamin, at least, the result is a "tremendous shattering of tradition." With the importance of the original dismantled, Lancaster's school could be imported to a dizzying array of locales and populations and still remain intact. In the United States, the Lancasterian model was put to use all over the country, deployed to educate poor white immigrant children in Philadelphia, black children in New York, and Cherokee children in Tennessee. Lancaster himself had an ambitious global itinerary for promoting his system, as he traveled extensively throughout Europe, South and Central America, the Caribbean, and the United States. In a Lancasterian context, history—of origins, of succession, of the "aura" attached to a particular spot of land—became reimagined through continual repetition and substitution.[20]

19. Rush, *Essays*, 11–12.
20. Paul Gilroy, *The Black Atlantic: Modernity and Double Consciousness* (London, 1993); Walter Benjamin, *The Work of Art in the Age of Mechanical Reproduction* (Scottsdale, Ariz., 2010), 14.

Colonization and Education: Circulating Bodies, Circulating Histories

Lancaster's remarkable success at selling a vision of continual circulation, detached from the personal histories of those circulating, fostered a cognitive framework that rendered the official rise of the ACS in 1816 another variation on a popular theme. Of course, the idea of African colonization predated Lancaster's reign: Lancaster did not cause the rise of the ACS. Rather, Lancaster's popularity and the rise of the ACS as an institution were both part of an emergent way of understanding how to shape the future by both dislocating and duplicating the past. Certainly, the ACS model appealed to the same people who were animated by Lancasterian education. At the NYAFS, schoolmaster Charles C. Andrews and many members of the board were enthusiastic subscribers to both schemes, as was President Monroe, Henry Clay, and a host of other prominent reformers.

Although the work of the ACS shared many of the exclusionary motives behind Indian removal, if we place the ACS in conversation with the Lancasterian ethos at the NYAFS we can also trace the echoes of Lancaster's circulatory, self-replicating logic. In short, we are mistaken if we read Lancaster and African colonization as wholly divergent means of exerting power. To use the Foucauldian terminology Lancaster so often inspires, at first glance it is easy to see the NYAFS as a "plague city," in which individuals learn to internalize disciplinary regimes through ever-increasing surveillance. On the other hand, African colonization—particularly as it emerges in African Americans' virulent resistance to it—might appear as Foucault's leper colony, in which the unwanted are cast out and disciplined solely through exile and neglect. But the work at the NYAFS prompts us to see these two trends as deeply intertwined philosophies appealing to the imaginations of those who saw themselves as crusaders against prejudice. Although the desire to remove blacks from the nation undoubtedly was one impetus behind the movement, many supporters imagined African colonization, not as exile, but as an act of national replication that could atone for history's wrongs.[21]

Certainly, many NYAFS administrators and trustees saw Lancasterian education and African colonization as mutually enabling endeavors. The

---

21. Michel Foucault, *Abnormal: Lectures at the Collège de France, 1974-1975* (New York, 2004), esp. 44-48. I am grateful to the anonymous reader of this essay for urging me to engage the relationship between Lancsterian education and the ACS in these terms.

ACS was quite proud of erecting a Lancasterian school in Monrovia, the capital of Liberia in 1827. By 1828, The NYAFS had struck a deal with the ACS in which they would train two black students, Cecil Ashman and Washington Davis, in Lancasterian pedagogy to teach in the colony. In 1829, when John B. Russwurm, co-editor of *Freedom's Journal,* a black newspaper that frequently sang the praises of the NYAFS, decided to go to Liberia, Charles Andrews, the NYAFS schoolmaster, offered to instruct him in school administration. When Russwurm arrived in Liberia, he rendered the diffusion of American black people as a means to replicate acts of American history, only this time with African Americans doing the pilgrim's work. "When I look around [Liberia]," he wrote to Edward Jones in 1830, "an aspiration rises to the Heaven that my friend may become a second Brainerd or Elliot." The language of replication through removal would persist well into the nineteenth century. In his efforts to persuade Frederick Douglass to convert to the colonization cause, Benjamin Coates would cast the coast of Liberia as a second Plymouth Rock. "Do you blame the pilgrims who settled New England," he challenged, "or the followers of Fox and Penn, who, to escape persecution in England colonized Pennsylvania? Would they have accomplished more by remaining in England?" As late as 1886, Thomas McCants Stewart, an African American lawyer and associate of Booker T. Washington, would refer to Africa's Cape Mesurado as the "Plymouth Rock of Liberia." The colonizationist model, at its heart, was a fantasy in which the middle passage could be reversed. This circling back in space and time would efface the coercion and trauma that accompanied the initial disruption from home and bloodline.[22]

A shifting American origin story animates both Lancasterian and colonizationist schemes, and in 1820 no less than Thomas Jefferson himself—largely considered the father of the colonizationist movement—would distill this fantasy into a justification that equated the spread of slavery with liberation from it. In a letter to the marquis de Lafayette, a staunch opponent of slavery, Jefferson worked mightily to cast the Missouri Compromise, and the spread of slavery it allowed, as a movement toward freedom. "All

22. See Benjamin Quarles, *The Black Abolitionists* (1969; rpt. New York, 1991), 12; John B. Russwurm to Edward Jones, Mar. 20, 1830, in *Black Abolitionist Papers,* III, *The United States, 1830–1846,* ed. Peter Ripley et al. (Chapel Hill, N.C. 1991), 72; Benjamin Coates, letter to the editor, June 17, 1850, *North Star* (Rochester, N.Y.), June 27, 1850, [3]; T[homas] McCants Stewart, *Liberia: The Americo-African Republic: Being Some Impressions of the Climate, Resources, and People, Resulting from Personal Observations and Experiences in West Africa* (New York, 1886), 12.

know," Jefferson penned, "that permitting the slaves of the South to spread into the West will not add one being to that unfortunate condition, that it will increase the happiness of those existing, and by spreading them over a larger surface, will dilute the evil everywhere, and facilitate the means of finally getting rid of it." The idea that allowing the slaves to "spread" to the West will "increase the happiness" of those existing in a state of slavery is almost as counterintuitive as the notion that the growth of slavery will hasten the spread of freedom. It only makes sense in a model in which attachment to a particular plot of land is the enemy of liberation. The capacity to disperse over a "larger surface," for Jefferson, enhances both personal and racial emancipation. Of course, the particularity of Jefferson's vision exposes the racial and class hierarchies underlying the supposedly neutralizing discourse of space. In other contexts, Jefferson was a staunch advocate of an agrarian ideal in which farmers gain independence through attachment to, rather than distance from, the land. Thus, the expansive vision of mobile freedom he advocates—and that manifested in both Lancasterian and colonizationist schemes—applies best to those who have something they need to escape.[23]

We can see a similarly amnesiac logic at work in the writings of Robert Finley, one of the founders of the ACS. The best remedy for the traumatic loss of connections wrought by the slave trade, Finley believes, is another upheaval, one that will disrupt the memories ingrained in the hearts of both white and black Americans. If blacks do not leave the country, Finley warns in 1817, "the recollection of their former servitude will keep alive the feeling that they were formed for labor" and that whites should be exempt from it. In an era where the dangerous pull of old obligations was still fresh in the memory of white Americans—and, indeed, renewed by the War of 1812—memories are a danger to the future. The longer African Americans remained in one place, the deeper the mnemonic rut will become, with the stubborn traumas of the past shaping a dangerous future. "The evil therefore increases every year," Finley worries, "and the gloomy picture grows darker continually, so that the question is often and anxiously asked—*What will be the end of all this?*" In opposition to this "gloomy picture" forged by the local attachments that lend memory the force of habit, a vision of diffuse

---

23. Thomas Jefferson to the marquis de Lafayette, Dec. 26, 1820, in Albert Ellery Bergh, *The Writings of Thomas Jefferson* (Washington, D.C., 1907), XV, 301. For more on how Jefferson, in alliance with French physiocrats, aligned freedom with circulation, see Nicole Eustace, *1812: War and the Passions of Patriotism* (Philadelphia, 2012).

interchangeability, enacted by Lancaster and advocated by the ACS, creates a capacious narrative in which the traumas of the past can be diffused through movement and in which peer emulation would naturally draw the cogs of the global wheel to the sections of the machine where they would be most useful. For Finley, as for Jefferson, however, that magnetism operates along strict racial lines.[24]

Yet, even with their embedded hierarchies, both Lancasterian and colonizationist visions promoted a freewheeling picaresque identity resistant, rather than conducive, to a form of nationalism dependent on particularities of land and blood. For at least one commentator in the 1817 *National Review*, the most disturbing problem with the project of African American colonization was how it threatened to dislocate American loyalties through the colony's ability to "amalgamate" British imperialism with American enterprise. For this writer, the vision of an unaffiliated global populace — a vision shared by both colonizationists and Lancasterians — effaces the possibility of an independent and innovative American identity: "We object to the American association leaning on the support or aids of British means, British information, or even British humanity itself; thus transferring to that nation all the glory and greatness of an enterprize which had its origins in the bosoms of independent Americans." If colonization was to take place, it needed to do so "unaided by Britain and heedless of the frowns or the smiles of all the potentates of Europe, from the autocrats of Russia to the mock majesty of a Ferdinand itself." Although American missionaries might travel to Great Britain, the writer "religiously hopes" that they may not in any manner "amalgamate themselves" with the British who were unworthy of "American imitation." These worries about American emulation of, and amalgamation with, European models would have been equally apt in a discussion of Lancasterian educational schemes as they were in a renunciation of the colonization project. For, in fact, "the autocrats of Russia," the king of Britain, and the "potentates" of Spain and France, among others, were smiling, along with the American president, on the Lancasterian system, which boasted of equal applicability to "independent" Americans, dependent British orphans, and abject Russian serfs.[25]

James Fields, who went to a school situated at a vortex of international

---

24. [Robert] Finley, "Thoughts on the Colonization of Free Blacks" (1816), in *African Repository and Colonial Journal*, IX (1834), 334.

25. "The Colonization of the Free Blacks," *National Register* (Washington, D.C.), IV, no. 19 (Nov. 8, 1817), 289–290.

models celebrating displacement and exchange, was taught to value a model in which remove was the solution to disappointment. Indeed, Fields's schoolmaster, Charles C. Andrews, a man noted for colonizationist sympathies and the school historian, writes with passion of Isaac, another star student, who like James could not find work in either New York or Philadelphia. In true picaresque fashion, young Isaac simply leaves his native country and finds another. "Far from uttering a word of angry disappointment," Andrews tells his readers, Isaac resolves "to leave the country and go to the Colony of Liberia." Arguably, Issac's Lancasterian education prepared him well for the trip.[26]

Amid the nest of oppressions that animated the lives of Fields and his fellow students at the NYAFS, their experiences reveal some aspects of Lancasterianism that were, in fact, liberatory. In contrast to the earlier model of emulation, in which students must transform their interiors to inhabit the subject position of an (almost always white) teacher, the Lancasterian system dismantled the concentration of both power and judgment. Within the NYAFS, students were not expected to inhabit the affective and cognitive register represented by a white schoolmaster. Rather, the system of student teachers created a situation in which they were emulating fellow African American students. At their school, as well as at other Lancasterian schools, children of color were taught daily by authorities that looked like them. Lancaster's famed system did indeed dismantle the authority of the schoolmaster. So, arguably, in the United States it worked to dismantle the aura of originality—the power that whiteness lends—that the schoolmaster might possess. For the NYAFS students, it was the responsive praise of a fellow black student, rather than the sympathetic assent of a white teacher, that provided evidence of success. If we are to judge by the careers of the school's alumni, who would go on to become the first generation of leaders in a host of fields including acting, medicine, missionary work, and abolitionist activism, the leadership skills they learned as children competing for the right to teach one another shaped their lives in ways unforeseen by the white trustees.[27]

26. Charles C. Andrews, *The History of the New York African Free-Schools, from Their Establishment in 1787, to the Present Time; Embracing a Period of More than Forty Years ...* (New York, 1830), 119.

27. NYAFS alumni include James McCune Smith, the first African American to earn an M.D., Henry Highland Garnet, the first African American to address Congress, and Ira Aldridge, the first African American to perform Shakespeare on a London stage. Other notables include Alexander Crummell, Issiah De Grasse, and Patrick and Charles

Not surprisingly, critics of Lancaster's system found this movement of authority from master to student a dangerous precedent, and this worry contributed to the system's fall in favor in the 1830s and 1840s, a fall as spectacular as its rise in popularity a generation earlier. In 1805, Sarah Trimmer, a British opponent of the Lancasterian system, found the work of copying potentially radical, taking place in "training schools for the army of the approaching revolution." Trimmer is especially concerned by Lancaster's "Order of merit," in which each member is distinguished by a silver medal worn on a chain around his neck—the sort of distinction that for Trimmer lays a bad foundation:

> When one considers the *humble rank* of the boys of which common *Day Schools* and *Charity Schools* are composed, one is naturally led to reflect whether there is any occasion to put notions concerning the *'origin of nobility'* into their heads; ... Boys, accustomed to consider themselves as the *nobles of a school,* may in their future lives, from a conceit of their own *trivial merits,* unless they have very sound principles, aspire to be *nobles of the land,* and to take place of the *hereditary nobility.*"

For Trimmer, at least, the plurality of copies does indeed shatter tradition. In contrast to the vision in which replacement and relocation works to disrupt painful memories, Trimmer worries that globalized students will learn to see themselves as originals in their own right. As students are able to emulate what she calls "the *'origin of nobility,'*" those very origins become demystified and ultimately dislodged from their privileged site. Trimmer's particularly British fears of students' taking on the claims of landed gentry runs counter to Lancaster's colonizing vision of loosening the ties of property and heredity in favor of global replication and circulation. But her prediction of an underclass that lays claim to their land prophesied one unintended reaction to the expansive visions of both Joseph Lancaster and the ACS.[28]

In 1818, American reformers who saw themselves as cultivating a model in

---

Reason. For more on the lives of NYAFS alumni, see Carla L. Peterson, *Black Gotham: A Family History of African Americans in Nineteenth-Century New York City* (New Haven, Conn., 2011).

28. Elie Halévy, *England in 1815,* vol. I of *A History of the English People in the Nineteenth Century* (New York, 1913), 531, quoted in Harold Silver, *The Concept of Popular Education: A Study of Ideas and Social Movements in the Early Nineteenth Century* (New York, 1965), 47; [Sarah] Trimmer, *A Comparative View of the New Plan of Education Promulgated by Mr. Joseph Lancaster ...* (London, 1805), 39.

which loyalties could be dispersed among cutting-edge systems rather than rooted in the particularities of land and history found that vision rejected by those considered least able to resist it. In an early and well-publicized African American response to the newly formed ACS, Philadelphia's black community, led by business leader James Forten, came together to evoke the very hereditary claims to the land that both Lancasterian and colonizationist rhetoric sought to loosen.

> But if the emancipation of our kindred shall, when the plan of colonization shall go into effect, be attended with transportation to a distant land, and shall be granted on no other condition; the consolation for our past sufferings and of those of our color who are in slavery, which have hitherto been, and under the present situation of things would continue to be, afforded to us and to them, will cease for ever. The cords, which now connect them with us, will be stretched by the distance to which their ends will be carried, until they break; and all the sources of happiness, which affection and connexion and blood bestow, will be ours and theirs no more.

In this response, distance does not expand possibility and liberation. The network James Forten and others envision does not allow for a resettlement that will somehow both undo American crimes against Africa and reenact American settler colonialism. Rather, they see their future embedded in locally connected "cords" that depend on proximity. Peace and happiness are not portable—they are grounded in the palpable presence of "affection and connexion and blood."[29]

Ultimately, the vast majority of African Americans, including the families and students of the New York African Free Schools, would reject the ACS and the white school leadership that embraced both the ACS and the Lancasterian model. The students who were educated in a school whose board members sought to instill social control and an embrace of Lancasterian mobility instead rose up to make claims for the validity of familial community and national ties. The African American community's largely negative response to the enthusiasm of European and American elites for a world-spanning system sheds light on how this vision of interchangeable world

29. James Forten, "To the Humane and Benevolent Inhabitants of the City and County of Philadelphia" (1818), in Dorothy Porter, ed., *Early Negro Writing, 1760–1837* (1971; rpt. Baltimore, 1995), 266.

citizenship effectively ignored and effaced—even as it was arguably modeled on—Atlantic slavery's stark rebuttal of the utopia of a mobile, interchangeable labor force. Lancasterian models, largely embraced by schools for racial minorities and the poor, promised a uniform populace whose ability to work would be unhindered by attachments to particular religious or political parties. Ostensibly, they would also be untroubled by the notion of rights that often accompanied membership in such parties. The political activism of NYAFS alumni would indicate otherwise.[30]

James Fields, that fourteen-year-old who lamented his lack of options in the United States, would grow up to organize against the ACS, picking up where Forten and others began. He, too, would argue for the pull of "connexion and blood" against the vision of interchangeability that animated both the Lancasterian and colonizationist agendas that profoundly shaped his education. In 1834, he presided as secretary in the meeting of the Fourth Annual Convention for the Improvement of Free People of Color, held in Chatham Street Chapel, not far from African Free School Number 2, where he gave his valedictory speech fifteen years earlier. Here, rather than performing the script of white reformer Ruben Leggett, he recorded the speech of black activist William Hamilton. Fields noted the Convention's derision of the ACS's ability to adapt across geographical and regional borders.

> But as long at least as the Colonization Society exists, will a convention of colored people be highly necessary.... That society has spread itself over this whole land, it is artful, it suits itself to all places. It is one thing at the south, and another at the north; it blows hot and cold; it sends forth bitter and sweet.

Suspicious of any logic that promises it could "[suit] itself to all places," the Convention would instead favor the individual ties and talents of the black community.[31]

The resistance of African Americans to the colonizationist scheme was, without doubt, a major element in its downfall. Black critiques of the ACS,

---

30. In 1832, a boycott led by African American parents incensed by Andrews's "colonizationist views" led to his resignation. For more on this incident, see Anna Mae Duane, "'Like a Motherless Child': Racial Education at the New York African Free School and in *My Bondage and My Freedom*," *American Literature*, LXXXII (2010), 461–488.

31. William Hamilton, *Address to the Fourth Annual Convention of the Free People of Color of the United States; Delivered at the Opening of Their Session in the City of New-York, June 2, 1834* (New York, 1834), 5.

and indeed black refusals to cooperate with the organization, changed the minds of other white reformers and ultimately required another model for what freedom would look like. William Lloyd Garrison's scathing and ultimately influential attack on the ACS pointed out that African American resistance to the scheme predated his own by several years. Garrison, never one to downplay his own powers of persuasion, vigorously denied having any influence on this count. In response to critics who accused him of turning blacks against the ACS, Garrison asserted: "No conversions were necessary. Their sentiments were familiar to me long before they knew my own." No, the work of thwarting the "concentrated energies of the mightiest men in the land" and the "perpetual labor of fifteen years" was accomplished within the African American community itself long before Garrison and other whites got on board.[32]

The eloquence and cohesion with which the African American community resisted the powerful and influential ACS is, of course, remarkable in itself. If we consider how pervasive the vision of global mobility and individual dispersal was in the first few decades of the nineteenth century, African American responses to the ACS's pitch for "freedom" represent a paradigm shift of great historical significance. Scholars of later periods have taught us that African American activists, including alumni of the NYAFS, would be instrumental in the discrediting of both the ACS and of the slavery system. A closer look at the understudied era in which they grew up and were educated—the heyday of enthusiasm for Lancaster and the ACS—reveals the extent to which their resistance was a striking reversal of powerful intellectual trends about the United States' place in the global order.[33]

As free blacks critiqued and resisted the logic of dispersal and exchange that energized the Lancasterian system, the ACS, and the global capitalism that undergirded both enterprises, they contributed to an antislavery emphasis on the trauma of forced upheaval and dispersal, a discourse that would ultimately shape the path of the nation. That story would be told by alumni of the New York African Free Schools, including James McCune Smith, Henry Highland Garnet, Alexander Crummell, Ira Aldridge, and others. Their lives and works would alternate between arguing (as James

---

32. William Lloyd Garrison, *Thoughts on African Colonization* ... (Boston, 1832), part II, 8.

33. John Stauffer, for example, explores the antislavery activism of alumnus James McCune Smith; see Stauffer, *The Black Hearts of Men: Radical Abolitionists and the Transformation of Race* (Cambridge, Mass., 2002). See also Manisha Sinha, ed., *The Slave's Cause: A History of Abolition* (New Haven, Conn., [2016]).

McCune Smith did) for enfranchisement within the United States and, alternately (as Henry Highland Garnet and Alexander Crummell did), for a capacious vision of international black affiliation. Young men and women facing the frustrations James Fields expressed in 1819 extended and reworked the warring Americas of their youth. The arguments of these students and their contemporaries, ranging from David Walker to Frederick Douglass, would help shape not just the question of where black identity could reside but also the question of where the United States belonged in the world.

PART III

EXPANSION AND THE INTIMACY OF BORDERS

WIDENING THE SCOPE ON THE INDIANS' OLD NORTHWEST

Jonathan Todd Hancock

In early 1814, a delegation of Sioux leaders, including a man named Red Wing, met with British captain Thomas G. Anderson near the confluence of the Mississippi and Wisconsin Rivers. Having long traded with the Sioux and accompanied them on summer raids against their indigenous enemies in the region, Anderson sought their support for Great Britain's ongoing war with the United States. Although rumors of U.S. military power had led many in the delegation to return medals signifying their alliance with the British, he convinced all but Red Wing to restore their support for the crown. Anderson pressed Red Wing to explain his neutral stance. Red Wing, the "head of a large band, and a numerous family connection" who "was famed, too, as a great prognosticator," related an allegorical vision of the future. He explained that, although "all the blood in my heart is English," he saw the war as a struggle between a British lion and an American eagle. The lion and the eagle "will scold at each other for a while; but they will finally make up and be friends, and smoke the pipe of peace. The lion will then go home, and leave us Indians with our foes."[1]

A major Sioux military force never mustered alongside the British. But,

---

For comments and suggestions, I am grateful to the anonymous readers, Fredrika J. Teute, Nicole Eustace, Kathleen DuVal, and participants in the Triangle Early American History Seminar in North Carolina, the Carolina Seminar on American Indian Studies, and a session at the 2014 meeting of the Organization of American Historians. I also appreciate the support of the UNC Royster Society of Fellows, the Huntington Library, and the Newberry Library.

1. Thomas G. Anderson, "Personal Narrative of Capt. Thomas G. Anderson," *Report and Collections of the State Historical Society of Wisconsin*, IX (1882), 197–198. "Sioux" is an umbrella term that refers to the large, complex confederation of decentralized bands that gradually came to control the northern and central Great Plains in the eighteenth and nineteenth centuries. On Sioux terminology and history in this period, see Richard White, "The Winning of the West: The Expansion of the Western Sioux in the Eighteenth and Nineteenth Centuries," *Journal of American History*, LXV (1978), 319–343; Jeffrey Ostler, *The Plains Sioux and U.S. Colonialism from Lewis and Clark to Wounded Knee* (Cambridge, 2004), 21–25.

like other Indian groups closer to the Anglo-American fighting, the Sioux continued to influence the conflict. Later that summer, a young warrior, Little Crow, the grandfather of the 1862 Dakota War leader of the same name, arrived at a British fort with one hundred soldiers ready to attack their Potawatomi and Ojibwa enemies as well as any American soldiers that they encountered along the way. The British, fearing the raids would destabilize the crown's alliances with the Potawatomis, Ojibwas, and other Indians hostile to the Sioux, prevented Little Crow's proposed sweep through the south. By the fall, however, Americans remained concerned about the threat of another powerful intertribal force that was neither the Sioux nor the famous Ohio Valley movement led by Shawnee brothers Tecumseh and Tenskwatawa. From Saint Louis, U.S. Indian agent Thomas Forsyth estimated that the British "can at any time raise from three to four thousand Indians without including the Sioux, or the Mississippi, or any of the Missouri Indians," resulting in "an indiscriminate massacre" of the city's inhabitants. The British corroborated the basis for American fears. On the same fall day in 1814, Anderson noted in his journal that the Sioux also were circulating a pipe and wampum across the upper Midwest in a bid "to request all Indians, of what nation soever, to join hands, and not allow an American to come this far."[2]

The War of 1812 brought the complex nature of tribal politics and diplomacy into full relief. Red Wing's vision coupled with Forsyth's concerns about a major intertribal force gathering west of the Mississippi River nearly a year after Tecumseh's death show that there were important and more distant indigenous forces shaping the early-nineteenth-century contest for the Old Northwest. By casting the conflict as a final showdown between intertribal militants and the U.S. Army, William Henry Harrison and the Shawnee brothers tried to simplify this complexity for political purposes. For Harrison, the myth of a unified Indian menace justified Native land cessions and the territorial extension of the United States. Like other U.S. officers, namely Andrew Jackson and Richard Mentor Johnson, this characterization also benefited Harrison's national political career. Through and beyond the Mississippi Valley, Tecumseh and Tenskwatawa circulated an all-or-nothing proposition: purge white people and their goods and join in an intertribal

---

2. T. G. Anderson, "Capt. T. G. Anderson's Journal, 1814," *Report and Collections of the State Historical Society of Wisconsin*, IX (1882), 233–238; Thomas Forsyth to Rufus Eaton, Sept. 18, 1814, "Letter-Book of Thomas Forsyth—1814-1818," ed. Reuben G. Thwaites, *Collections of the State Historical Society of Wisconsin*, XI (1888), 334–335.

defense of Native land. Anything less than total Indian unity was accommodation. For building a coalition of disparate people, some of whom had been ancient enemies, constructing these strict, oppositional categories was diplomatically necessary but difficult to actualize.[3]

That Red Wing cited a vision in his argument against war shows that some Indian authorities' special spiritual access led them to caution against the Shawnee brothers' militancy. The larger conflict between Native Americans and the United States was not a simple matter of Native American spirit versus American greed, nor was it a "holy war" between religiously inspired visions of the Ohio Valley. Communities across early-nineteenth-century North America intertwined concerns about territory, culture, politics, and spirit. The Shawnee brothers' spiritual imperative for conflict needs

---

3. American fascination with Tecumseh and Tenskwatawa's movement continued into the mid-nineteenth century with Benjamin Drake's 1841 biography of the Shawnee brothers. See Drake, *Life of Tecumseh, and of His Brother the Prophet; with a Historical Sketch of the Shawanoe Indians* (Cincinnati, 1841). Gregory Evans Dowd's path-breaking work has established prophetic, intertribal militancy as a major Indian strategy for reckoning with colonial British and later U.S. expansion. See Dowd, *A Spirited Resistance: The North American Indian Struggle for Unity, 1745-1815* (Baltimore, 1992); Dowd, "Thinking and Believing: Nativism and Unity in the Ages of Pontiac and Tecumseh," *American Indian Quarterly*, XVI (1992), 309-335. Pitting American Indian "nativists" against "accommodationists," Dowd's interpretive model importantly recognized the prophetic roots of intertribal resistance from the mid-eighteenth through the early nineteenth century. While not diminishing the importance of this brand of intertribal militancy, I argue that the persistent historiographical focus on the Shawnee brothers and previous nativist militants has overshadowed a wider spectrum of Indian strategies and tribal particularities in the War of 1812 era. For studies of American Indians in the War of 1812 with a similar focus on the Shawnee brothers, see R. David Edmunds, *The Shawnee Prophet* (Lincoln, Nebr., 1983); Edmunds, *Tecumseh and the Quest for Indian Leadership* (New York, 1984); John Sugden, *Tecumseh's Last Stand* (Norman, Okla., 1985); Sugden, *Tecumseh: A life* (New York, 1998); Alfred A. Cave, "The Shawnee Prophet, Tecumseh, and Tippecanoe: A Case Study of Historical Myth-Making," *Journal of the Early Republic*, XXII (2002), 637-673; Adam Jortner, *The Gods of Prophetstown: The Battle of Tippecanoe and the Holy War for the American Frontier* (New York, 2012). Edmunds's more recent work on the topic has highlighted the Shawnees' divided courses in the War of 1812. See Edmunds, "'A Watchful Safeguard to Our Habitations': Black Hoof and the Loyal Shawnees," in Frederick E. Hoxie, Ronald Hoffman, and Peter J. Albert, eds., *Native Americans and the Early Republic* (Charlottesville, Va., 1999), 162-199; and Edmunds, "Forgotten Allies: The Loyal Shawnees and the War of 1812," in David Curtis Skaggs and Larry L. Nelson, eds., *The Sixty Years' War for the Great Lakes, 1754-1814* (East Lansing, Mich., 2001), 337-351.

to be more fully situated within a larger matrix of wartime considerations and strategies in Indian country. For instance, varying Indian understandings of major earthquakes on the Mississippi River in late 1811 and early 1812 point to how connected and unbalanced the human, natural, and spiritual orders seemed during these tumultuous months. Their readings of the related natural and human upheaval underscored tremendous interpretive and strategic diversity among Trans-Appalachian Indians as they confronted the new century's challenges.[4]

Extending the temporal and geographical boundaries of American Indian participation in the War of 1812 reveals the multivalent nature of Indian authority and a wide spectrum of strategies at play. Wartime upheaval necessitated Indian decisions on tribal, village, or even individual levels that often defied the strict battle lines that military leaders sought to demarcate. Some Shawnees found alliance with the United States preferable; other communities sought to remain neutral. When joint Indian and British forces made gains in late 1812, many more Indians in the Ohio Valley and beyond became receptive to fighting alongside the British, but their enthusiasm waned with losses in 1813. On the Illinois plains, northwest of the war's hotspots, Native groups such as the Potawatomis and Sauks constituted sprawling and complex forces that threatened and confounded the Americans, British, and Shawnee brothers alike. The Potawatomis had a prophet of their own who opposed the United States but ultimately refused to comply with the Shawnee brothers' strict social codes and centralized political organization. At the same time, another major Potawatomi leader spied for the Americans. Well after dashed dreams of a unified, intertribal front, American Indians

---

4. For an interpretation of the conflict that focuses on religion, see Jortner, *Gods of Prophetstown*. In a synthesis of American Indian prophetic movements, Alfred A. Cave also has emphasized the divisiveness of the Shawnee brothers' movement and the limits of their authority. See Cave, *Prophets of the Great Spirit: Native American Revitalization Movements in Eastern North America* (Lincoln, Nebr., 2006), 86–105. Other studies have looked beyond the Shawnee brothers' movement to consider how tribally based resistance and Indian strategies during the War of 1812 did not fit neatly into the nativist-accommodationist framework. See Stephen Warren, *The Shawnees and Their Neighbors, 1795–1870* (Urbana, Ill., 2005), 6–42; John P. Bowes, "Transformation and Transition: American Indians and the War of 1812 in the Lower Great Lakes," *Journal of Military History*, LXXVI (2012), 1129–1146; Patrick Bottiger, "Prophetstown for Their Own Purposes: The French, Miamis, and Cultural Identities in the Wabash-Maumee Valley," *JER*, XXXIII (2013), 29–60; Karim M. Tiro, "The View from Piqua Agency: The War of 1812, the White River Delawares, and the Origins of Indian Removal," *JER*, XXXV (2015), 25–54.

continued to influence the conflict on their own, often on more tribally specific terms.

Widening the scope on the Indians' Old Northwest to capture a greater range of strategies, alliances, and rivalries need not diminish the Shawnee brothers' historical stature. They found sympathetic audiences across the continent's interior and advanced a vision of intertribal unity that has remained an important historical force. As far away as the northern plains, Native people fondly remembered their influence one century later. "The excitement spread from tribe to tribe until all the Indians from Hudson's Bay and even to the Rocky mountains were affected by it," related a Sioux man in 1910. But that the Shawnee brothers' famous message of militant unity ranged so widely was more of a testament to the cosmopolitanism of Native North America than the willingness of Indians to join them.[5]

The Material and Strategic Bases for War

Specific material factors and American military policies drove Indians unconvinced by the Shawnee brothers to fight alongside the British in 1812. Chief among these were American trade policy, Indian opportunism after British military gains, and William Henry Harrison's raids against neutral Indian villages. These examples are useful reminders that the spiritual impulse for intertribal resistance should be situated among a constellation of factors that Indians weighed as they considered the most effective strategy for maintaining their lands, cultures, and communities.

Wartime interruptions in trade galvanized some Indians who were unconvinced about the spiritual imperative for conflict. Americans were unable to replace the British as a reliable source of goods for Indians. In June 1812, an American man in Cahokia wrote to Illinois governor Ninian Edwards about an impending trade crisis there. He explained that, if the United States re-

---

5. Doane Robinson, "A Sioux Indian View of the Last War with England," *South Dakota Historical Collections*, V (1910), 398. In his article "The Winning of the West: The Expansion of the Western Sioux in the Eighteenth and Nineteenth Centuries," *JAH*, LXV (1978), Richard White noted, "The failure of Indians to unite has been much easier to deplore than to examine" (320). For examples of scholarship that track shifting inter-Indian rivalries and alliances and highlight their geopolitical significance in trans-Appalachian North America, see Kathleen DuVal, *The Native Ground: Indians and Colonists in the Heart of the Continent* (Philadelphia, 2006); Brett Rushforth, *Bonds of Alliance: Indigenous and Atlantic Slaveries in New France* (Chapel Hill, N.C., 2012); Michael Witgen, *An Infinity of Nations: How the Native New World Shaped Early North America* (Philadelphia, 2012).

fused to allow the British to supply Indians, "then all those tribes, amounting to some thousands, will consider themselves as abandoned and as it were, dead, and through despair immediately they will assemble all the nations around them, determined to conquer or die, and destroy us, our wives and children, before necessary assistance can be obtained." He urged the United States to "send factors or traders among those Indians to supply them with merchandise and powder, etc., to support them and their families ... then and not till then will they be peaceful." This was not a plea for charity; Indians would have gladly exchanged furs for the goods. When Americans prevented them from supporting their own communities through trade, however, they went to war alongside the British.[6]

Long after the War of 1812, the famed Sauk leader Black Hawk remembered a similar desperation for trade goods. Americans originally told his village leaders that, like the British, they would supply goods on credit. Assured that trade would not be interrupted by conflict, Black Hawk recounted: "Every thing went on cheerfully in our village. We resumed our pastimes of playing ball, horse racing, and dancing, which had been laid aside when this great war was first talked about." The Americans later recanted on their promise, and British boats "loaded with goods" soon arrived at Black Hawk's village. "Here ended all hopes of our remaining at peace—having been *forced into* WAR *by being* DECEIVED!" he wrote. In their bluster about the British inciting the Indians to war, Americans misinterpreted an Indian act of survival as a British act of incitement. The British certainly traded with Indians for strategic reasons, but their military alliance was not foreordained. According to Edwards's American correspondent and Black Hawk, who were on opposite sides of the war, Americans could have secured at least Indian neutrality through trade. From Black Hawk's perspective, his people's participation in the conflict was an economic calculation, not a divinely ordained directive nor a manipulative British conspiracy. The ability to provide for his community through trade dwarfed arguments about the spiritual necessity for war.[7]

Many Indians did not ally with the British until the fall of 1812, when the British and their earliest Native allies made major incursions into the United

---

6. Jarrott to Ninian Edwards, June 29, 1812, in Ninian W. Edwards, ed., *History of Illinois, from 1778 to 1833; and Life and Times of Ninian Edwards* (Springfield, Ill., 1870), 330.

7. Black Hawk, *Life of Black Hawk, or Mà-ka-tai-me-she-kià-kiàk* ... (1833), ed. J. Gerald Kennedy (New York, 2008), 24–25.

States. These easy and early gains surprised the British. "That a consequence so deeply injurious to the United States, as their expulsion from such an immense tract of the Indian Country, should have resulted almost instantaneously as it were ... must not only have exceeded the expectation, it can hardly have been within the contemplation of our most sanguine friends," reported a British traveler in November. By December, Secretary of War William Eustis resigned in embarrassment after the seizures of Forts Detroit and Wayne.[8]

The year 1813 brought more American losses: a joint force destroyed an army attachment of nearly two thousand soldiers, taking six hundred prisoners in an engagement remembered by Americans as the "River Raisin Massacre." American agent John Johnston feared that the sweeping British-Indian victory would inspire more Indians to fight. He explained to Harrison: "Above all things I dread the effects it will produce on the Indians[.] Such a victory will transport them beyond measure. the news will fly thro' their Country like lightening and will gather them in Swarms to Detroit in the Spring, expecting to reap a Similar harvest of plunder and glory." Rather than a final act of desperation, as intertribal militancy in the War of 1812 is commonly portrayed, mass Indian participation in the conflict's northwest theater was a measured, strategic decision made only after early gains by the British and their Indian allies.[9]

It was Harrison, by raiding previously neutral villages, who incited some Indians to war. The case of the Miamis illustrates how Harrison's decisions, coupled with internal tensions over leadership following the death of Little Turtle, the famed 1790s militant turned peacemaker, transformed neutrals into combatants. At a gathering in September 1811, a speaker for one branch of the Miamis contrasted his people's caution with the impulsiveness of the Shawnee brothers' followers. "We the Miamies, are not a people that are passionate.... Our hearts are as heavy as the earth! Our minds are not easily irritated," he explained, adding that they would defend their land under invasion and "be angry but once." Little Turtle asked Harrison "not to bloody our ground, if you can avoid it." He granted that, although Tenskwatawa

---

8. T. Tackle to Lord Henry Bathurst, Nov. 24, 1812, "The Fur-Trade in Wisconsin, 1812–1825," ed. Reuben Gold Thwaites, *Collections of the State Historical Society of Wisconsin*, XX (1911), 3.

9. Jno. Johnston to William Henry Harrison, Feb. 4, 1813, *Papers of William Henry Harrison, 1800–1815*, ed. Douglas Clanin and Ruth Dorrel (Indianapolis, Ind., 1999) (hereafter cited as *WHH*), microfilm, reel 7, 417.

might have lived and traveled in Miami lands, he did so without their permission. By January 1812, Little Turtle anticipated military conflict, but he pledged solidarity with the United States. He explained: "The clouds appear to be rising in a different quarter, which threatens to turn our light into darkness. To prevent this, it may require the united efforts of us all.—We hope; that none of us, will be found to shrink from the storm."[10]

Relations between the Miamis and the United States remained steady into the spring of 1812, although a report of Miami thefts against settlers and a coalescing alliance between the British and some Indian bands made the diplomatic situation volatile. At an intertribal council in May, Miamis warned potentially hostile Potawatomis, Shawnees, Kickapoos, and Winnebagos to "keep their warriors in good order." Once the British formally declared war against the United States in June, the battle lines hardened rapidly. With Indian violence intensifying and the British appealing for military assistance, Miami chief Picon aptly characterized his people's dilemma as one of being caught "between two fires." The fires pointed toward war, but Picon simply wished to protect his community. He turned to his "red brethren, but could see no safety there." Sensing danger in joining with other Indian groups and decrying deception from both the Americans and the British, Picon and the Miamis felt the mounting pressure of neutrality.[11]

The space between competing British and American fires narrowed after Little Turtle's death on July 14, 1812. The loss of this elder statesman and staunch advocate of neutrality almost certainly tilted the delicate Miami balance toward war against the United States. Nevertheless, after the joint British-Indian siege of Fort Wayne, Harrison made the Miamis' decision for them by ordering attacks on Miami towns on the Wabash River. He wrote to

---

10. "Speeches of Miami, et al. Chiefs," Sept. 4, 1811, *WHH*, reel 4, 758, 761; Little Turtle to Harrison, Jan. 25, 1812, J[osiah] Snelling to Harrison, Apr. 14, 1812, "Meeting with Miami, et al. Chiefs," [April 17, 1812], all in *WHH*, reel 5, 299, 491–493, 519–523. On early-nineteenth-century Miami diplomatic maneuvers and their rivalry with the intertribal coalition before the Battle of Tippecanoe, see Bottiger, "Prophetstown for Their Own Purposes," *JER*, XXXIII (2013), 33–41, 47–56.

11. William Wells to Harrison, May 24, 1812, in Logan Esarey, ed., *Governors Messages and Letters: Messages and Letters of William Henry Harrison [Concluded]*, II, *1812–1816* (Indianapolis, Ind., 1922), 53; "Journal of the Proceedings of the Commissioners Plenipotentiary, Appointed on Behalf of the United States of America, to Treat with the Northwestern Tribes of Indians," July 12, 1814, *American State Papers: Documents Legislative and Executive, of the Congress of the United States*, IV (Washington, D.C., 1832), 831.

Eustis that he had "no evidence" of Miami participation at Fort Wayne and granted that many Miami leaders were "no doubt desirous of preserving their friendly relations with us, but as they are unable to control the licentious part of their tribe it is impossible to discriminate and we have no alternative but operating upon their fears by severe chastisement." Furthermore, Harrison reasoned that, since the Miami villages were near Fort Wayne, the corn crops that were cut down and left to rot would prevent Indians from gathering near the fort again. One of the villages destroyed had been Little Turtle's. In knowingly sacrificing Miami neutrality, Harrison both avenged the loss of Fort Wayne and expanded the amount of Indian land eligible for seizure and redistribution to soldiers after the war. For Indians grappling with early-nineteenth-century U.S. expansion, this incident was a small episode in a slowly unfolding revelation about the central contradiction in Jeffersonian agrarianism: Indian farming no longer justified indigenous claims to landownership.[12]

On Miami hostility one month later, Harrison wrote that "the revolution in thier [sic] affairs and in thier disposition towards us was very Sudden." But he was too savvy to be genuinely surprised. On the battlefield and in Harrison's letters, the Miamis became increasing menaces. Americans and Miamis traded attacks, and, beginning in early 1813, Americans plotted assaults against Miami winter camps. By September 1813, the Miami transformation from neutral to enemy was complete. Feigning betrayal, even though he had ordered attacks without evidence that they had participated in the siege of Fort Wayne, Harrison singled out the Miamis and Potawatomis for particular punishment. He wrote: "The Miamis and Potawatimies deserve no mercy—they were the tribes most favored by us. they have been, (the latter particularly) our most cruel and inveterate enemies." Although American propaganda blamed the British for inciting Indians, in the Miamis' experience, that distinction belonged to Harrison. Once his army destroyed the very crops that Jeffersonian agrarians should have praised, the Miamis

---

12. B[enjamin] F. Stickney to Harrison, July 21, 1812, *WHH*, reel 5, 687–689; Harrison to [Isaac] Shelby, Sept. 18, 1812, and Harrison to William Eustis, Sept. 21, 1812, *WHH*, reel 6, 184–187, 203–204. On contradictions in Jeffersonian agrarianism, see Daniel H. Usner, Jr., "Iroquois Livelihood and Jeffersonian Agrarianism: Reaching Beyond the Models and Metaphors," in Hoxie, Hoffman, and Albert, eds., *Native Americans and the Early Republic*, 200–225. The classic work on Jeffersonian Indian policy is Bernard W. Sheehan, *Seeds of Extinction: Jeffersonian Philanthropy and the American Indian* (Chapel Hill, N.C., 1973).

defended themselves from the "two fires" engulfing the region by taking up arms against the United States.[13]

Other Prophets and Tribal Agendas

Harrison's grouping of the Potowatomis with the Miamis is curious, because, along with the Kickapoos, the Potawatomis from the Illinois plains were avowedly hostile to both the United States and their long-standing Native enemies nearby. Indeed, the main locus of Indian militancy in the Old Northwest during the War of 1812 might have been in Illinois country, west of the Shawnee brothers and their followers. Thanks to sparse American settlement and less American monitoring of Indian affairs there, the region's indigenous inhabitants could more freely gather forces to attack east of the Illinois River and retreat back across the river.

Illinois territorial governor Ninian Edwards continually sought to remind Harrison and other American officials farther east that Indians in his area, most of whom "were not in the battle of Tippecanoe," constituted a major threat to Americans occupying lands in the Ohio Valley and beyond. In May 1812, he warned Secretary of War Eustis that their "force is superior to the Prophet's." Following scattered murders early that year, which Edwards believed were part of a strategy to avoid engaging the American army in a pitched battle, his reports became increasingly alarmist. "If the Illinois Indians become hostile, they will over-run this Territory," he wrote to Eustis in June 1812.[14]

By July, Edwards's concerns boiled into panic. He cautioned U.S. military officials in the Ohio Valley that the focus on the Indian threat there ignored other regions of gathering resistance and "hitherto the seat of the most imminent danger has not been well understood." He believed that the British were seeking to make peace between the warring Sioux and Ojibwas in order to amass a northern force that could travel to the eastern side of the Illinois River in ten days. Indeed, Tenskwatawa previously had visited the Ojibwas and promised them that, if they followed his rules of obedience to the Great Spirit, they would be protected from the Sioux. The Sioux attacked the Ojibwas in the summer of 1812, however, ensuring that neither would

---

13. Harrison to Eustis, Oct. 13, 1812, *WHH*, reel 6, 374–386; John B. Campbell to Harrison, Dec. 25, 1812, *WHH*, reel 7, 25–39; Harrison to John Armstrong, Oct. 10, 1813, *WHH*, reel 9, 342–346.

14. Edwards to Eustis, May 12, June 2, 1812, in Edwards, ed., *History of Illinois*, 319, 325; Harrison to Eustis, June 3, 1812, *WHH*, reel 5, 621–623.

engage in the Anglo-American dimension of the conflict, though British and American authorities remained wary of both the Sioux and the Ojibwas into 1815. The nearby Potawatomis were Edwards's most immediate concern. Although he was more prone to distress in his letters than his contemporaries, other reports corroborated his accounts of more distant Indian threats, less well known than the Shawnee brothers and not altogether loyal to them.[15]

Despite the Americans' perception that all Indians allied against them, Potawatomi bands enacted their own agendas during the war. The origins of Potawatomi divides with the intertribal coalition, as well other indigenous groups in the region, long pre-dated the establishment of the United States. There also was a rivalry between Tenskwatawa and Main Poc, a Potawatomi shaman and war chief who spread the Shawnee's message through Illinois country in 1808. Though he remained hostile to the United States, Main Poc ultimately broke his alliance with Tenskwatawa.[16]

There were two likely factors behind this rift: one was long-standing and diplomatic, the other a more immediate problem with the way of life and political centralization that Tenskwatawa demanded from his followers. In March 1812, the *Louisiana Gazette* reported that Main Poc was preparing for war against the Osages. In his grand tour of Indian country in the fall of 1811, Tecumseh had visited the Osages and sought their support. Seventeenth-century Osage expansion had created many Indian enemies in this period, and news that Tecumseh sought an alliance with the Osages likely hurt the Shawnee brothers' standing among other potential western allies like Main Poc's band. Futhermore, an American official suggested that the Potawatomis "in the course of one season got tired of this strict way of living, and declared off and joined the Main Poque." The Prophet's ban on traditional cultural forms like medicine bags and songs, as well as Euro-American ob-

---

15. Edwards to [Charles] Scott, July 23, 1812, *WHH*, reel 5, 696; John Tanner, *A Narrative of the Captivity and Adventures of John Tanner* (1830), reprinted as *The Falcon: A Narrative of the Captivity and Adventures of John Tanner*, with an introduction by Louise Erdrich (New York, 1994), 145–147; Anderson, "Personal Narrative of Capt. Thomas G. Anderson," *Report and Collections of the State Historical Society of Wisconsin*, IX (1882), 83–90.

16. On Main Poc and his historiographical overshadowing, see R. David Edmunds, "Main Poc: Potawatomi Wabeno," *American Indian Quarterly*, IX (1985), 259–272. On Anglo-American fears of broad alliances among American Indians and enslaved people and the effects of those fears on policy making, see Robert M. Owens, *Red Dreams, White Nightmares: Pan-Indian Alliances in the Anglo-American Mind, 1763–1815* (Norman, Okla., 2015).

jects and conventions, fueled Indian dissent because the ban violated specific tribal conventions. By leaving the Shawnee brothers for a prophet from among their own people, Potawatomis remained concerned about American expansion without making the major sacrifices that the intertribal militants demanded.[17]

Main Poc's break from the Shawnee brothers shows that the competition for authority among Indian leaders in the Old Northwest did not hinge solely on how they approached the United States. Despite their shared, prophetic opposition to the United States, Main Poc refused to cede spiritual and political authority to the Shawnee brothers. In the years before the war, the Shawnee brothers had violently consolidated their power by demanding absolute loyalty from a diverse group of followers. As a U.S. official described, Tenskwatawa was "always reserving the Supreme authority to himself, viz, that he (the Prophet) might be considered the head of the whole of the different Nations of Indians, as he only, could see and converse with the Great Spirit." He claimed to manipulate and predict natural phenomena, and he used this divine mandate to eliminate rivals, often by identifying and ordering the executions of witches. This violent insistence on absolute authority compromised the movement's military might. In the case of Main Poc's band, among a host of other groups, the Shawnee brothers' methods alienated Indian people who were sympathetic to the cause of repelling the United States but refused to dismantle the political and religious establishment within their tribes.[18]

The outbreak of war in the region and their departure from the intertribal coalition allowed the Potawatomis to settle old scores with Indian enemies. At the end of 1812, an American agent reported that Potawatomis, Ottawas, and Ojibwas were fighting Miamis, Weas, Piankashaws, and Peorias. This intertribal conflict, precisely what Tecumseh sought to avoid by uniting tribes and consolidating power, was nonetheless a persistent fea-

---

17. R. David Edmunds, *The Potawatomis: Keepers of the Fire* (Norman, Okla., 1978), 166–169; *Louisiana Gazette* (Saint Louis), Mar. 21, 1812; Forsyth to William Clark, May 27, Dec. 23, 1812 (typescript), Tesson Family Papers, Missouri History Museum, Saint Louis. On Tecumseh's alleged visit to the Osages, see John Sugden, "Early Pan-Indianism: Tecumseh's Tour of the Indian Country, 1811–1812," *American Indian Quarterly*, X (1986), 292; Sugden, "Tecumseh's Travels Revisited," *Indiana Magazine of History*, XCVI (2000), 164–165. On Osage conflicts with other regional Indians in the period, see DuVal, *Native Ground*, 196–215.

18. "Thomas Forsyth to William Clark, St. Louis, December 23, 1812," ed. Dorothy Libby, *Ethnohistory*, VIII (1961), 194.

ture of the War of 1812. But Americans remained fixated on the perception that a unified Indian menace—manipulated by the British—threatened the nation's existence. "I am informed that every Nation has Declared war against the United States even the Chickesaws + Chocktaws that has so long been friendly. The British had made Tecumshe the Prophets brother a Brigidier General," wrote a man in northern Kentucky. Governor Edwards worried about a wider conspiracy. "The union of Indians, negroes, disaffected French people, other choice spirits and a British force from the West-Indians will give our government employment enough on our southern frontier," he wrote to another Illinois official. At the western edges of American settlement, rumors led American people to imagine all manner of threatening alliances, which proponents of the War of 1812 exploited to mobilize popular American support for the war.[19]

Potawatomis, Kickapoos, and others undoubtedly communicated with the Shawnee brothers and shared some of their objectives, but, like other Ohio Indians with their own tribal agendas, they were late to join the War of 1812. Many abandoned the intertribal cause well before Tecumseh's death, but they remained concerned about the American and British militaries alike into 1814 and 1815. When Americans accused them of treachery, they frequently demurred, blaming their young men's involvement on youthful impetuousness and the seductive lies of Tenskwatawa. Before the Battle of Tippecanoe, a Potawatomi chief acknowledged that some young men were "foolish enough to believe what he said." He argued, however, "that their faults shall not be charged to our nation." After reports that Potawatomis had killed American settlers in the spring of 1812, their anti-Tenskwatawa rhetoric intensified. In a council they explained that the "pretended prophet" had encouraged the attacks and sought to "detach" the youth from their traditional leaders. "We have no control over these few vagabonds, and consider them not belonging to our nation; and will be thankful to any people that will put them to death, wherever they are found," they added.[20]

By denying official involvement in the conflict, groups like the Potawato-

19. Ibid., 188; Joseph Bunker to his uncle, Sept. 18, 1812, Hite-Bowman Papers, box 29, folder 5, Indiana Historical Society, Indianapolis; Edwards to Nathaniel Pope, August 1813, "Letter of Ninian Edwards to Nathaniel Pope," *Journal of the Illinois State Historical Society*, X (1917), 277. On mobilizing popular American support for the War of 1812, see Nicole Eustace, *1812: War and the Passions of Patriotism* (Philadelphia, 2012).

20. "Speeches of Miami, et al. Chiefs," Sept. 4, 1811, *WHH*, reel 4, 760, 762; "Speeches of Indians at Massassinway," May 15, 1812, in Esarey, ed., *Governors Messages and Letters*, II, 51.

mis and Kickapoos sought to hedge their bets on the outcome of the War of 1812. They were hardly the absolute enemies of the United States that the Shawnee brothers claimed to be. But, as in the case of Harrison's attack on the Miamis near Fort Wayne, Americans became increasingly unwilling to distinguish between outwardly neutral or friendly villages and the young combatants who lived there.

The Indians' refrain that their young men were uncontrollable was common, suggesting that the War of 1812 spurred generational conflict within tribes and scrambled Indian battle lines even further. For example, the threats and opportunities that the war posed to Wyandot sovereignty starkly divided them. Americans noted their presence at Tippecanoe, but the Wyandots quickly disavowed their allegiance to the Shawnee brothers. The Wyandots appealed to the Americans' Christian and material sensibilities, arguing that, because they allowed missionaries, built "valuable houses," and improved their land, they should remain on it. As other Ohio Indians agitated for war in the spring of 1812, Wyandots used their status as an "elder" tribe to urge restraint, instructing their *"younger brothers"* to "put an entire stop to the effusion of blood." Nevertheless, certain Wyandots broke from the tribe's professions of peace. In August 1813, Wyandot chief Round Head led one of three major detachments to assault Fort Meigs, and Americans exchanged Wyandot captives for Kentucky militiamen taken in the stalemate. Other Wyandots, however, assumed a much more active role in supporting the Americans than tribes that claimed to be friendly or at least neutral. During the same year, a Wyandot chief seized Ottawa spies for the British and alerted Harrison to a hostile force gathering to attack a post at Sandusky. Like others in the region, Wyandots collectively resisted expectations about their absolute commitment to one side or another during the War of 1812.[21]

U.S. Alliance or Neutrality: The Ottawa, Shawnee, Delaware, and Otoe Cases

Alliance with the United States or neutrality constituted other strategies for preserving sovereignty in this geopolitically tumultuous time and place. Despite the aforementioned spy for the British, the Ottawas were the most

---

21. "The Wyandots, Communicated to the House of Representatives, February 28, 1812," *American State Papers*, IV, 795; Wells to Harrison, May 24, 1812, in Esarey, ed., *Governors Messages and Letters*, II, 50; Harrison to Armstrong, Aug. 4, 1813, *WHH*, reel 8, 849–851; Stickney to Harrison, Apr. 7, 1813, *WHH*, reel 7, 849–851.

committed Native opponents of the Shawnee brothers. An American official described them as "inveterate enemies to the Shawanoe Prophet" and claimed that, "had the United States a few years ago, shewn the least inclination, the Ottawas alone would have routed the Prophet and his party from the Wabash" long before the intertribal coalition revealed its hostile intentions to the Americans. To the British, the Ottawa chiefs who joined Harrison at Detroit were "avowed Yankees."[22]

Of the Shawnees that actively participated in the War of 1812, most fought or spied for the Americans. Shawnee chief Logan died on the Americans' side during the December 1812 attacks on Miami villages ordered by Harrison, who called him "a Victim to his Zeal for our cause." In the winter of 1813, Shawnee chiefs offered intelligence about Tecumseh gathering a force for a spring offensive. While the chiefs were reluctant to dispatch their soldiers, an American official "informed them the service already rendered had been acceptable." One month later, Harrison ordered an agent to hire twenty-four Shawnee spies. On their spying, Harrison reported that the Shawnees had "given a Strikeing proof of their fidelity." Along with the Kentucky militiamen captured in the attack on Fort Meigs, four Shawnees were returned to the United States. These captives recounted being saved by Tecumseh when Wyandots wanted to execute them.[23]

Shawnees who fought for the United States continually apologized for the actions of their hostile tribesmen. When chiefs discovered a young man had killed an American soldier in July 1813, they explained to Harrison that they were "all very much hurt at our hearts" and promised to deliver him in accordance with the Treaty of Greenville. Although they acknowledged that his fate was the Americans' prerogative, they also sought American mercy

---

22. "Thomas Forsyth to William Clark, St. Louis, December 23, 1812," ed. Libby, *Ethnohistory*, VIII (1961), 189-190; Jno. Askin, Jr., to Louis Grignon, Jan. 28, 1812, "Lawe and Grignon Papers, 1794-1821," ed. Lyman C. Draper, *Report and Collections of the State Historical Society of Wisconsin*, X (1888), 101.

23. Harrison to Eustis, Dec. 14, 1812, *WHH*, reel 6, 809; John Payne to Harrison, Feb. 7, 1813, and "Order to John Johnston," Mar. 4, 1813, *WHH*, reel 7, 438, 659; John Wingate to Harrison, June 15, 1813, Harrison to Armstrong, July 23, 1813, *WHH*, reel 8, 399-408, 593-596; Harrison to Armstrong, July 23, 1813, reel 8. On Shawnee allies to the United States during the War of 1812, see Edmunds, "Black Hoof and the Loyal Shawnees," in Hoxie, Hoffman, and Albert, eds., *Native Americans and the Early Republic*, 162-199; Edmunds, "Forgotten Allies," in Skaggs and Nelson, eds., *The Sixty Years' War*, 337-351.

for a number of reasons. They explained that the young man had killed the soldier to avenge his friend's death, "the devil had taken possession of his mind at that moment," he was "in deep sorrow for what he has done," and, if pardoned, he promised to fight for the Americans. This Shawnee plea and Tecumseh's protection of the Shawnee captives at Fort Meigs were significant because they revealed that tribal bonds could withstand the internal divisions created by the conflict. It would have been much more diplomatically expedient for the chiefs to distance themselves from an individual who threatened relations with a large nation already mobilized for war.[24]

Although the War of 1812 splintered allegiances in most tribes across the Ohio Valley, the Delawares remained the most avowedly neutral. At a council in May 1812, they described the Shawnee Prophet's teachings as destructive for Indians and Americans alike. Increasing murders in the Ohio Valley were evidence that "both the red and white people had felt the bad effect of his counsels." They wished instead to "proclaim peace through the land of the red people." When war was officially declared and the British advanced into U.S. territory, the Delawares remained unwilling to join the burgeoning cause. Because of "the bravery of their Warriors" and "intimate acquaintance" with American settlements, Harrison recognized the importance of preserving Delaware neutrality. Although rumors implicated them in killings, he praised their "Uncommon faithfulness." And, unlike his approach to the Miamis, Harrison urged "every proper forbearance" in American dealings with them. Through the end of the war, Americans remained concerned about wavering Delaware neutrality, but their fears never materialized.[25]

Delaware oral traditions and their leaders' existing rivalries with Tenskwatawa offer insight into their reasons for neutrality. They could have, after all, drawn from their long tradition of participation in militant, intertribal resistance to Euro-American settlement in the Ohio Valley. The Delaware prophet Neolin had been one of the first leaders to advocate for intertribal unity, and his teachings inspired Pontiac's War, following the Seven Years' War. But the Shawnee brothers' brand of militant unity did not accommodate the Delawares' religious leadership and their tribally specific ceremo-

24. Harrison to Armstrong, May 26, 1813, Shawnee Chiefs to Harrison, July 17, 1813, and Harrison to Armstrong, July 23, 1813, *WHH*, reel 8, 316–320, 547–548, 593–596.

25. Harrison to Eustis, Apr. 15, 1812, "Message to the Delawares," [circa Apr. 17, 1812], and Harrison to Eustis, Apr. 29, 1812, *WHH*, reel 5, 495–497, 513–514, 542; Wells to Harrison, May 24, 1812, in Esarey, ed., *Governors Messages and Letters*, II, 52; Stickney to Harrison, Oct. 11, 1812, *WHH*, reel 6, 361–362; Stickney to Harrison, Mar. 16, 1813, and Johnston to Harrison, Mar. 31, 1813, *WHH*, reel 7, 698–702, 814–818.

nialism. Only a few years before hostilities escalated into war, Tenskwatawa had ordered witch hunts against Delaware leaders.[26]

The combination of warfare and earthquakes in the Ohio Valley also held special significance for the Delawares, who turned to a unique ritual known as the Big House Ceremony to handle these cosmological disruptions internally. According to their oral tradition, the first Delaware Big House Ceremony began after a major earthquake in Delaware country. Whether the ceremony was an ancient tradition or a more recent innovation, the original earthquake predated those in 1811 and 1812. Deciding that the earthquake was a sign that "the Great Spirit was very seriously angry with them," many people reported a common dream in which they were told to construct a building and conduct an annual ritual of purification and thanksgiving. The result became known as the Big House Ceremony, an elaborate, twelve-day process that was the highlight of their ritual calendar. Despite their continual dislocations west from their homelands in the mid-Atlantic, the ceremony gave the Delawares a steady sense of place inside the Big House. When three major earthquakes and countless aftershocks rocked the region between December 1811 and March 1812, American newspapers printed stories of an Indian explaining that "this calamity was foretold by the Shawanoe Prophet for the destruction of the whites!" Tenskwatawa previously had claimed the ability to predict and manipulate forces, and the earthquakes became a way for him to reassert spiritual authority undermined by his miscalculations at the Battle of Tippecanoe in November. He used the shaking as a dramatic recruitment tool, and the Shawnee brothers reinvigorated their movement before declaring war on the United States in July. Unswayed by the Shawnee brothers' spring resurgence and wary of relinquishing tribal customs, especially after the witch hunts a few years prior, Delawares instead looked inward. Rather than participating in a conflict with an uncertain and likely short-term outcome, they addressed these troubling and related signs of human and natural disorder inside the Big House.[27]

26. On Tenskwatawa's witch hunts and claims to predict and control natural phenomena, see Edmunds, *The Shawnee Prophet*, 2–49; Jay Miller, "The 1806 Purge among the Indiana Delaware: Sorcery, Gender, Boundaries, and Legitimacy," *Ethnohistory*, XLI (1994), 245–266; Alfred A. Cave, "The Failure of the Shawnee Prophet's Witch-Hunt," ibid., XLII (1995), 445–475.

27. Frank G. Speck, *A Study of the Delaware Indian Big House Ceremony*, in native text dictated by Witapanóxwe (Harrisburg, Pa., 1931), 81. On recorded versions of the Big House Ceremony and its origins, see ibid.; and Robert S. Grumet, ed., *Voices from the Delaware Big House Ceremony* (Norman, Okla., 2001). For American newspapers attrib-

Much farther west on the Great Plains, the Otoes attributed the earthquakes to American violence and expansion, but they remained unwilling to commit to the intertribal coalition. Their interpretation of the tremors was significant enough that an American expedition traveling up the Missouri River recorded it nearly a decade after the war. In 1811, a "son of the Master of Life" rode a white horse through a nearby forest. Some Americans "of a sanguinary disposition" shot and killed the mystical figure on horseback. Otoes explained that earthquakes were "the effect of supernatural agency, connected, like the thunder, with the immediate operations of the Master of Life." For killing a divine messenger, the American assailants enraged the Master of Life, and "it was certainly owing to this act that the earth was now trembling before the anger of the great Wahconda [Master of Life]." Whether the "son of the Master of Life" was an emissary from the Ohio Valley or a local spiritual leader, the Otoes clearly blamed American violence for the earthquakes. But, when Tenskwatawa sent wampum to invite them to join the intertribal alliance, the Otoes refused. They explained that "they could make more by trapping beaver than making war against the Americans."[28]

The Otoes' case epitomized the array of considerations that all American Indians had to take into account when deliberating about whether to join the Shawnee brothers. On the one hand, even Native groups as far west as the Otoes already had witnessed the violent consequences of American expansion. From the Great Plains to the Ohio River and from the Great Lakes to the Gulf of Mexico, the Shawnee brothers' bid for alliance found sympathetic audiences across the continent's interior. But, on the other, although Indians agreed that the new nation threatened their lands and people, the United States was not their sole concern in the daily rhythms of early-nineteenth-century Native trade and diplomacy. For those Ohio Valley Indians who were

---

uting the earthquakes to Tenskwatawa, see *Virginia Argus* (Richmond), Feb. 2, 1812, [2]; *Columbian* (New York), Feb. 14, 1812, [2]. On Delaware mobility and the Delawares' adaptable sense of homeland in the Ohio Valley, see Dawn Marsh, "Creating Delaware Homelands in the Ohio Country," *Ohio History*, CXVI (2009), 26–40.

28. Edwin James, *Account of an Expedition from Pittsburgh to the Rocky Mountains* ..., 3 vols. (London, 1823), reprinted as *James's Account of S. H. Long's Expedition, 1819-1820*, in Reuben Gold Thwaites, ed., *Early Western Travels, 1748-1846* ..., XV (Cleveland, Ohio, 1905), 57; "The Following Interesting Narrative of the Expedition of Mr. Hunt, Mentioned in This Work, Is Extracted from the Missouri Gazette," appendix in John Bradbury, *Travels in the Interior of America in the Years 1809, 1810, and 1811*, 2d ed. (1819; rpt. Lincoln, Nebr., 1986), 227.

the foundation of the Shawnee brothers' intertribal militancy, the situation indeed seemed more desperate. Coupled with rumors of war between the Americans and the British, the earthquakes deepened many people's sense of alarm and urgency. Even among those living closest to American settlements in Ohio and Indiana territory, however, the decision to relocate and cede all spiritual and political authority to the Shawnee brothers was not an easy one. Like most Native Americans in the War of 1812 era, the Otoes worried about signs of imbalance in the natural, human, and spiritual orders without committing to intertribal militancy.

Although the rhetoric of the intertribal militants conveyed a sense of absolute Indian commitment to their cause, most Indian participation in the War of 1812 proved to be much more situational. After early British victories, they sensed an opportunity to check the growth of the expansionist early Republic, but they were careful not to stake their futures in the region on British success. Indeed, Harrison noted that Indians had committed "less mischief" against settlers during the war than before it.[29]

Direct Indian involvement in the conflict seems to have peaked in late 1812 and early 1813, when joint British and Indian forces attacked a series of American forts and committed what Americans regarded as "massacres" against American armies. As an American official later noted, "The fall of Detroit and defeat of Gen. Winchester's army at River Raisin, raised the spirits of the Indians to such a pitch that they really thought that nothing could conquer them." By October 1812, however, Winnebagos had reportedly deserted the Shawnee Prophet's forces and "returned home disgusted" after a failed attempt to seize Fort Harrison. The pro-British Indian front splintered further during the next spring, when another failed siege prompted the Shawnee brothers to lead their group north into Canada. Between sixteen hundred and two thousand Indians immediately withdrew from the British and the Shawnee brothers. The Weas stole horses from the Prophet, and bands of Miamis, Kickapoos, and others appealed to the United States for peace and goods.[30]

---

29. Harrison to Eustis, Oct. 22, 1812, *WHH*, reel 6, 430–435.

30. Forsyth to Eaton, Sept. 18, 1814, "Letter-Book of Thomas Forsyth," ed. Thwaites, *Collections of the State Historical Society of Wisconsin*, XI (1888), 331; Harrison to Eustis, Oct. 13, 1812, and Johnston to Harrison, Oct. 23, 1812, *WHH*, reel 6, 374–386, 441–445; Johnston to Harrison, Mar. 31, 1813, *WHH*, reel 7, 814–818; Harrison to Armstrong, May 13, 1813, and June 8, 1813, *WHH*, reel 8, 247–254, 350–354; R[ichard] M[entor] Johnson to Harrison, Sept. 20, 1813, Harrison to Armstrong, Sept. 30, 1813, Oct. 10, 1813, *WHH*, reel 9, 249–253, 342–336.

Coping with dwindling Indian support, Tecumseh felt similarly aggrieved by the British in September 1813. He likened their conduct to a "fat Animal" that ran away with its tail between its legs when threatened. His death at the Battle of the Thames on October 5, 1813, launched American celebrations and political careers. In recounting the battle, a British official described Tecumseh's multiethnic force: "Tecumseh, with his party—some Ottawas, Chippewas, Delawares, Sauks, Folle Avoines [Menominees], and some Hurons followed." Though British and American authorities struggled to identify Indian people in a region this diverse, Potawatomis were noticeably absent from the list. Among a host of other Native actors, however, the Potawatomis continued to influence this theater of war. Most histories of Indian participation in the War of 1812 end at the Battle of the Thames or pivot south to discuss the Red Stick uprising among the Creeks. Widening the scope beyond this time and place, however, reveals an international dimension of the conflict that extended into the Great Plains: a western web of Native alliances and hostilities as dynamic and contested as those in Napoleonic Europe.[31]

Threats and Conflicts among the Potawatomis, Sioux, and Sauks
Divergent Indian strategies and certain inter-Indian conflicts, particularly between the Potawatomis and Sioux, ensured that Indians did not form the powerful, post-Tecumseh confederacy that Americans feared. Indians nonetheless remained essential actors in the war well after Tecumseh's death. The continued militancy of the Sauks as well as recurrent American and British concerns about Potawatomi and Sioux participation in the conflict show that an emphasis on Ohio Valley intertribal militancy does not fully capture the range of tribally based strategies that continued through the duration of the war.

Much to the frustration of American and British officials, who complained that Indian statements and actions were duplicitous, Indians continued to use wartime instability to negotiate optimal trade and diplomatic relationships among American, British, and Native powers. What Euro-Americans on both sides of the conflict regarded as treachery was in fact flexible policy making based on the changing nature of the war and relations among a com-

---

31. "Speech of Tecumseh to Henry Proctor," Sept. 18, 1813, *WHH*, reel 9, 358–364; Askin to Grignon, Dec. 1813, "Lawe and Grignon Papers, 1794–1821," ed. Draper, *Report and Collections of the State Historical Society of Wisconsin*, X (1909), 99.

plicated network of Native groups. This network extended much farther north and west than the war's hotspots in the Ohio Valley.

Though they did not launch any large-scale attacks after 1813, the Potawatomis remained a constant concern for the British and the Americans. Their threats and diplomatic machinations prevented both the British and the Americans from diverting all of their attention and resources to fronts farther south and east, where the conflict had shifted. At the beginning of the war, U.S. Indian agent Thomas Forsyth foreshadowed later authorities' frustrations with the Potawatomis when he described them as numerous, geographically diffuse, and "a deceitfall, treacherous people." They had been the primary assailants at the American Fort Dearborn in 1812, a siege seared into nineteenth-century American memory as an icon of supposedly inherent Indian savagery. After seizing the fort, the Potawatomis disagreed about the fate of their American captives. Later-nineteenth-century Potawatomi activist and writer Simon Pokagon reminded American readers of this fact when he questioned why Indian attacks were always considered "massacres" when, for example, Andrew Jackson's assault on Horseshoe Bend had been a "battle." Pokagon's recounting of Potawatomi differences at Fort Dearborn revealed the decentralized nature of Potawatomi authority. With bands spread across the Midwest, Potawatomis looked to a range of leaders with markedly different diplomatic strategies for relating with the United States, from the militant spiritual leader Main Poc to Gomo, a chief who supplied the United States with wartime intelligence.[32]

Despite their diffuse leadership, wartime strategies, and geographical dispersal, the Potawatomis continued to exert a major geopolitical influence on the Illinois plains. In 1814, British and American authorities worried that, although some bands had made peace with the Americans, they were playing both sides, and their twelve hundred warriors could not be easily ignored. Explaining that they "have always been villains to both parties and will continue so untill the end of the Chapter," British trader and Indian agent Robert Dickson expected them to attack in the winter of 1814. When a few Potawatomi emissaries arrived at his camp in February to ask for goods, Dickson "asked them what they were; and told them in a stern matter if they were

---

32. "Thomas Forsyth to William Clark, St. Louis, December 23, 1812," ed. Libby, *Ethnohistory*, VIII (1961), 188; Simon Pokagon, "The Massacre of Fort Dearborn at Chicago, Gathered from the Traditions of the Indian Tribes Engaged in the Massacre and from the Published Accounts," *Harper's New Monthly Magazine*, XCVII (1899), 649–656.

Pottawatomies, they should walk off immediately." That Dickson had to inquire "what they were" demonstrates Euro-Americans' difficulty in identifying specific Indian groups in a diverse region. In this case, their reputation preceded them, and Dickson rejected their request for goods. He went on to draft a detailed list of thirty-four reasons the British could not trust the Potawatomis. Among the reasons, they had promised to fight for the British in the fall of 1813, "and[,] putting it off under different pretexts from time to time," they negotiated peace with the Americans. Furthermore, despite Main Poc's avowed opposition to the United States, Dickson found him unreliable and untrustworthy. Although the Potawatomis never attacked the British in the conflict's later stages, they nonetheless kept the British guessing about their intentions, a useful strategy while the war's outcome was still in doubt.[33]

Although they had negotiated an armistice, Americans were no less suspicious of the Potawatomis. Ninian Edwards, who had so vociferously warned Americans about them at the onset of war, instructed Forsyth to order a Potawatomi attack on the British to prove their loyalty. In May 1814, he wrote that "experience has fully convinced us that there can be no neutrality with savages," and "we have found them faithless in all their promises." As with a previous agreement with the Americans to attack the Winnebagos, the Potawatomis did not comply with U.S. wishes. By the fall of 1814, Forsyth wondered if they were turning to the British for gunpowder and ammunition. Needing to hunt before winter, the Potawatomis were surrounded by Indian allies of the British who had helped the British seize an American fort in July 1814. If they did receive hunting supplies from the British, the Potawatomis nonetheless refrained from attacking the Americans. In exchange for honoring the armistice, they then appealed for the United States to lower the prices of goods at trading posts. Instead they received U.S. surveyors, who arrived in Potawatomi territory in 1815 to survey bounty land for War of 1812 veterans. As for Main Poc, Forsyth reported a year later that the leader was sickly and had lost his hearing. As his health waivered, so, too, had his influence.[34]

33. R. Dickson to John Lawe, Feb. 4, 1814, "Dickson and Grignon Papers—1812–1815," ed. Thwaites, *Collections of the State Historical Society of Wisconsin*, XI (1888), 290–291; Dickson to Lawe, Feb. 4, 1814, and Dickson, "Remarks on the Bad Intentions of the Pottawatomies, March 2, 1814," both in "Lawe and Grignon Papers, 1794–1821," ed. Draper, *Report and Collections of the State Historical Society of Wisconsin*, X (1909), 103, 109. On Europeans struggling to identify Indians and misunderstanding the nature of their social and political organization in this region, see Witgen, *An Infinity of Nations*.

34. Edwards to Forsyth, May 16, 1814, Forsyth to Edwards, Sept. 3, 1814, Forsyth to

The British and the Americans were not the only major foreign powers with which the Potawatomis had to contend. The threat of Sioux involvement, coupled with their hostility toward the Potawatomis and Ojibwas, made the northwestern periphery of this theater even more volatile. The British and the intertribal militants both recruited the Sioux, who were sympathetic to the anti-American cause. Although they remained a military presence with which the Americans, British, and other Indians had to reckon during the war, a number of factors influenced their decision not to fight. First, disease and famine racked the northern plains in the early 1810s. Winter counts listed a smallpox outbreak in the winter of 1810–1811, followed by famine in 1812 and whooping cough in 1813. As access to British trade goods motivated Black Hawk to fight, the Sioux's material deficits surely tempered their enthusiasm for the alliance. Early-nineteenth-century U.S. expansion had not affected Sioux trade and territory as much as it had for Indian communities farther south and east, and the Sioux had less to gain from repelling this distant eastern power. Rumor also had it that the United States dispatched a Spanish trader from Saint Louis to outfit the Teton Sioux at the Big Bend of the Missouri River. Furthermore, as enemies of the Potawatomis and Ojibwas, the Sioux needed to protect their communities from indigenous foes whose threats were much more long-standing and proximate than the United States. Early-twentieth-century Sioux people remembered the potential conflict with the Potawatomis as the major reason the Sioux avoided the War of 1812. Finally, Red Wing's vision of the British lion abandoning Indians after making peace with the American eagle gave Sioux neutrality a spiritual impulse. Red Wing joined the Delawares and the Shawnee brothers in claiming special spiritual access to orient wartime strategies. And those strategies, which took spiritual, material, and social circumstances into account, often did not lead Indians to war.[35]

The Sioux constituted an important peripheral influence on this theater in the same way that antiwar Federalists in New England were an impor-

---

Eaton, Sept. 18, 1814, Forsyth to James Monroe, Apr. 13, 1815, Forsyth to Edwards, Mar. 31, 1816, all in "Letter-Book of Thomas Forsyth," ed. Thwaites, *Collections of the State Historical Society of Wisconsin*, XI (1888), 316–347; James D. Walker, introduction to *War of 1812 Bounty Lands in Illinois* (Thomson, Ill., 1977), xi.

35. Linea Sundstrom, "Smallpox Used Them Up: References to Epidemic Disease in Northern Plains Winter Counts, 1714–1920," *Ethnohistory*, XLIV (1997), 315–317; Robinson, "A Sioux Indian View of the Last War with England," *South Dakota Historical Collections*, V (1910), 398–400; Anderson, "Personal Narrative of Capt. Thomas G. Anderson," *Report and Collections of the State Historical Society of Wisconsin*, IX (1882), 197–198.

tant northeastern faction on the American side, even if both groups did not actively participate in the fighting. In the summer of 1812, the Sioux attacked the Ojibwas, which undoubtedly contributed to the Ojibwa decision also to refrain from the military engagements farther south. Two years later, younger Sioux leaders became more active in the conflict. Motivated by their desire for British gunpowder and the need to prove themselves as young men, some of them traded intelligence for British supplies and offered to hunt Americans and American-allied Indians. It was for this reason that Little Crow arrived at a British fort with 100 "young men" and their families in September 1814. "He regarded every Indian and white soldier, no matter of what color, as long as they were British subjects as his brother—the rest his inveterate enemies, and would act with greatest vigor towards both accordingly," a British officer noted. Because raids would threaten their alliances with Indians who were hostile to the Sioux, the British talked Little Crow out of his proposal. He and his band were content to remain well supplied by their foreign allies. With the British and Tecumseh's forces courting the Sioux, who in turn influenced the wartime strategies of their Ojibwa and Potawatomi enemies, a conflict associated with American vulnerabilities on the East Coast also had major international dimensions in the West.[36]

Late in the War of 1812, the Battle of New Orleans and the burning of Washington demonstrated both U.S. weakness at the seat of government and the new nation's commitment to retaining the portal to the Mississippi basin located at its territorial periphery. While these dramatic coastline events became icons of the war, a core struggle among Indian powers, Great Britain, and the United States for control of that basin was still ongoing. As Indian polities considered how best to maintain their territories and sovereignties, they continued to influence this struggle in ways beyond the battlefronts.

In spite of triumphal press reports, the United States remained vulnerable during the final year of the war. From his vantage point in Michigan in early 1814, the British agent Dickson remarked that the world seemed "convulsed." Dickson believed that Spanish and British military maneuvers in the Deep South, combined with the Red Stick uprising, would bring the Americans "on their knees to Britain." The Red Sticks also could force American

---

36. Anderson, "Personal Narrative of Capt. Thomas G. Anderson," *Report and Collections of the State Historical Society of Wisconsin*, IX (1882), 183–190; Dickson to Lawe, Feb. 4, 1814, "Dickson and Grignon Papers—1812–1815," ed. Thwaites, *Collections of the State Historical Society of Wisconsin*, XI (1888), 290; Anderson, "Anderson's Journal," *Report and Collections of the State Historical Society of Wisconsin*, IX (1882), 219–249.

troops away from Saint Louis, rendering the city vulnerable to takeover. This scenario was what had led Forsyth to estimate that three to four thousand Indians could attack Saint Louis in 1814. Forsyth noted that his calculation did not include nearly five thousand more Indians to his south and west, a force he believed that the Spanish could mobilize. Well into 1814, American and British officials took Indians seriously as tribal and intertribal threats to their western outposts.[37]

Of the Indian groups that remained prominent geopolitical players through the conclusion of the war, the Sauks were the most avowedly hostile to the United States. Although some bands had the British guessing about them "playing a double game," the Sauks continued to attack Americans into 1815. In accordance with Black Hawk's initial motivation for war, they leveraged their opposition to the Americans for a favorable trade and military relationship with the British. With twelve hundred warriors in 1814, more than double Tenskwatawa's army at the Battle of Tippecanoe in 1811, the Sauks matched the Potawatomis' forces in size. Perhaps because the Potawatomis agreed to stop fighting after an armistice with the Americans, the Sauks stole their horses. As the largest anti-American force of Indians in the region, they sought to translate their loyalty into more British trade goods and weapons. When they appealed for more trading partners in late 1814, a British commander regretted that he could not coordinate independent traders, but he assured them he "would even go so far as to take powder from the big guns, to assist them." He continued to reward their loyalty with ammunition until he learned that the Treaty of Ghent had ceased hostilities between the Americans and the British. "I gave them some ammunition, provisions, with a hearty shake of the hand, and we parted sorrowfully," he remembered about his farewell with Black Hawk and his band. This exchange stood in stark contrast to Tecumseh's claim that the British ran away like a "fat Animal" less than two years earlier.[38]

---

37. Dickson to Lawe, Feb. 4, 1814, "Dickson and Grignon Papers—1812-1815," ed. Thwaites, *Collections of the State Historical Society of Wisconsin*, XI (1888), 291–292; Forsyth to Eaton, Sept. 18, 1814, "Letter-Book of Thomas Forsyth," ed. Thwaites, ibid., 335.

38. Dickson to Lawe, Jan. 23, Mar. 31, 1814, "Dickson and Grignon Papers—1812-1815," ed. Thwaites, *Collections of the State Historical Society of Wisconsin*, XI (1888), 287, 302; Forsyth to Edwards, July 6, 1814, "Letter-Book of Thomas Forsyth," ed. Thwaites, ibid., 320; Anderson, "Personal Narrative of Capt. Thomas G. Anderson," *Report and Collections of the State Historical Society of Wisconsin*, IX (1882), 201; Anderson, "Anderson's Journal," ibid., 250. Sugden has estimated Tenskwatawa's force at the Battle of Tippecanoe at five hundred men; see Sugden, *Tecumseh*, 231–232.

Sauk appeals to the British and attacks on the Americans nonetheless continued after the Treaty of Ghent. In an April 1815 speech, Black Hawk requested a British cannon for protection. He received guns and ammunition instead, a gift that infuriated the Americans in light of the treaty. Though the region's "color" was about to change from red (war) to white (peace), Black Hawk also vowed to continue fighting, as the United States had not concluded peace with the Sauks: "I now see the time is drawing near when we shall all change color; but, my Father, our lands have not yet changed color—they are red—the water is red with our blood, and the sky is cloudy. I have fought the Big Knives, and will continue to fight them until they retire from our lands." One month later, his assault on American troops just northwest of Saint Louis, known as the Battle of the Sink Hole, signaled his unwillingness to relent.[39]

On his plans to attack Fort Wayne in the fall of 1812, Tecumseh told Miamis "to step on one side, for his feet were verry large, and required much room." "If they did not he might step upon them." For the study of Native Americans in the War of 1812 era, the Shawnee brothers' footprints are equally large. Widening the scope on the Indians' Old Northwest and beyond reveals the need to resituate the Shawnee brothers among a range of Indian tactics and motivations in this era. The War of 1812 heightened the sense of urgency among those Indians living closest to the steadily encroaching early Republic. But most Native people did not accept the assessment of Tecumseh, and indeed of Harrison, that this was a final, epic battle for control of the Old Northwest. Many Indians chose neutrality or alliance with the United States as the most viable strategy for navigating the War of 1812. Most of those who did fight against the United States did so because they sensed an immediate opportunity to check U.S. expansion, not because they were absolutely loyal to the Shawnee brothers or incited by the British. When the British-Indian alliance faltered, many Indians quickly abandoned that strategy and sought to maintain their territories and sovereignties in other ways. For an era so

---

39. "Speech of L'Epervier, or Sparrow Hawk, Better Knowd as Black Hawk, Principal War Chief of the Sauks, Delivered before Peace Was Known, at Prairie du Chien, April 18th, 1815, and Taken Down by Capt. T. G. Anderson," "Prairie du Chien Documents, 1814-'15," *Report and Collections of the State Historical Society of Wisconsin*, IX (1882), 278; Forsyth to Monroe, Apr. 13, 1815, "Letter-Book of Thomas Forsyth," ed. Thwaites, *Collections of the State Historical Society of Wisconsin*, XI (1888), 337.

closely associated with Indian prophecy and millenarianism, pragmatism most often reigned.[40]

Furthermore, when the American nation and its expansion are the primary referents around which histories of the struggle for the early-nineteenth-century Mississippi basin are written, American Indians risk being portrayed as mere obstacles or enablers of the early Republic. A closer examination of intertribal rivalries and coalitions as well as political tensions within Indian polities reveal a broader spectrum of Indian agendas in action than the false choice between joining the Shawnee brothers or accommodating to the United States during the War of 1812. In fact, it was the Shawnee brothers who demanded many cultural and political accommodations from their followers as they sought to consolidate authority in the region. That so many Indian people were sympathetic to their concerns but ultimately unwilling to join their intertribal coalition suggests that veterans of prior conflicts with the United States already had recalibrated their strategies.

And, for a conflict whose international dimensions have been so closely associated with the Atlantic coast, Red Wing's vision, Black Hawk's intransigence, and Forsyth's fears point to important international forces and agendas among Indians west of the Mississippi River. Concerns about trade, international diplomacy, and the link between natural and geopolitical instability as well as contentious experiments in new forms of governance extended well beyond the early Republic in early-nineteenth-century North America. From Prophetstown all the way out to the Great Plains, American Indians negotiated the threats and opportunities posed by another round of imperial war.

---

40. Stickney to Harrison, Sept. 29, 1812, *WHH*, reel 6, 293.

DOMESTIC FRONTS IN THE ERA OF 1812
SLAVERY, EXPANSION, AND FAMILIAL STRUGGLES FOR SOVEREIGNTY IN THE EARLY-NINETEENTH-CENTURY CHOCTAW SOUTH

Dawn Peterson

While working on Choctaw homelands in the lower Mississippi Valley, U.S. Indian agent Silas Dinsmoor began to imagine himself as a father to Choctaw people. In the spring of 1807, as he put the African men and women he enslaved to work on the plantation farm he ran as part of his newly relocated Choctaw agency, Dinsmoor saw himself as mirroring, like a good father, the patriarchal agrarian life to which he believed Choctaw women and men should aspire. For, when his cattle wandered into his agency grounds once again shot full of arrows, Dinsmoor complained to his wife Mary of his "de[vil]ish children." Choctaw resistance to his instructions in the central tenets of U.S. "civilization" did not thwart his paternalism. It enhanced it. By January 1808, Dinsmoor began to playfully refer to Silas, Jr., his infant son in New Hampshire, as Choctaw. "Kiss our young Chaktaw for me," he relayed in letters home, before sending love to the rest of the family. Around 1811, Dinsmoor even took over the guardianship of a Choctaw boy named James McDonald. He incorporated the ten- or eleven-year-old youth into his new family home, a slaveholding household located roughly one hundred miles southwest of Dinsmoor's Pearl River Choctaw agency, in the burgeoning U.S. planter town of Washington, Mississippi. McDonald would live there for the next two and a half years before Dinsmoor took him to Washington, D.C., to pursue an education with Baltimore Quakers.[1]

For their insightful comments on this essay, I would like to thank the editors and anonymous reviewers of this volume; the Five Colleges Writing Group, including Barbara Krauthamer, Edward Melillo, Khary Polk, Elizabeth Pryor, and Tanisha Ford; members of the Rocky Mountain Seminar in Early American History, especially Jenny Pulsipher, Eric Hinderaker, and Matthew Mason as well as Paul T. Conrad, J. Kēhaulani Kauanui, Alyssa Mt. Pleasant, and Elena Schneider.

1. Silas Dinsmoor to Mary Gordon, Mar. 29, 1807, Silas Dinsmoor to Mary Gordon Dinsmoor, Jan. 6, May 18, 1808, James McDonald to Silas Dinsmoor, Nov. 6, 1820, all in

Dinsmoor's paternalistic rhetoric and unexpected domestic arrangements unfolded on the eve of the War of 1812, a moment when federal elites redoubled efforts to crush American Indian resistance to U.S. expansion. The image of Dinsmoor's cows shot full of arrows provides a glimpse into tensions in the first decades of the nineteenth century between U.S. officials and settlers such as Dinsmoor and the Native people whose lands they occupied. By the time Dinsmoor brought James McDonald into his plantation household, the Shawnee-Creek leader Tecumseh had traveled to the Southeast in an effort to firmly ally Southeast Indian nations with a broader pan-Indian movement armed against U.S. settler expansion, leading U.S. federal elites to prepare for possible war. One of Dinsmoor's roles as Indian agent was to try to prevent such an alliance from taking place. Why in this lead-up to war would the federal agent embrace a fatherly role with respect to Choctaw people, so much so that he would desire the presence of a Choctaw youth within the space of his own home? More than this, Dinsmoor found local support for some of his actions. To be more precise, he received the cooperation—or even the encouragement—of James McDonald's mother, a Choctaw woman named Molly McDonald. Why would Molly McDonald place her son under the care of the unpopular federal agent who occupied her homelands?[2]

The federal career of Silas Dinsmoor and its eventual convergence with the lives of James McDonald and his Choctaw mother, Molly, opens a window onto domestic battles for Native lands. It reveals that, as the United States worked to claim western Indian territories, the gendered and racialized kinship arrangements and physical locations supporting white households oriented federal Indian policy writ large and, in turn, shaped its messy and contested implementation on the ground. More specifically, Dinsmoor's attempts to claim Choctaw lands for U.S. plantation slavery illuminates how the particular familial structures supporting racial slavery became signally important to both U.S. whites and a select group of Southeast Indians in their struggles to impose and resist U.S. imperial rule. Colonial records re-

---

the Silas Dinsmoor Papers, 1794–1853, reel 1, Kansas Historical Society, Topeka; James McDonald to Thomas McKenney, Aug. 9, 1819, *Secretary of War: Letters Received*, microfilm 221, roll 86, frames 3921–3922, National Archives, Washington, D.C. (hereafter cited as NA).

2. On Tecumseh's travels south and how his organizing efforts connected to broader pan-Indian movements during the era of the War of 1812, see Gregory Evans Dowd, *A Spirited Resistance: The North American Indian Struggle for Unity, 1745–1815* (Baltimore, 1993), 144–148, 167–173, 181–190.

vealing these struggles for land and power are heavily imbalanced, largely relating the vantage point of colonial elites. Yet, when read for what they say about family and slavery—intertwined technologies in the politics and practices of settler colonialism—these sources bring into focus important sites of war. Thus emerges not only a more complicated picture of the ways that leading whites fought to extend slaveholding colonial settlements into new southern regions but also a very brief glimpse of how at least some Native people, including one Choctaw woman, navigated dispossession.[3]

Building on scholarship examining formations of race, gender, kinship, and sexuality within and across colonial contexts, this essay places ideas and practices concerning kinship at the heart of post-Revolutionary North American history. Revisiting early U.S. federal Indian policy, it highlights the gendered, spatial, and racial familial regimes that informed Dinsmoor's early career in Choctaw territories. It then considers how Dinsmoor specifically drew upon the kinship arrangements that supported both Native dispossession and black servitude to claim Choctaw space as his own. Living in the Southeast during critical years in the late eighteenth and nineteenth century, Dinsmoor transformed himself from a New England federal official to a local Mississippi settler. Initially invested in federal Indian policies and programs, he became disillusioned with his work in light of Choctaw responses—and, in some cases, hostilities—to his controversial presence in their homelands. Presented with an opportunity to establish a plantation household of his own, he recalibrated his ambitions. Rather than working to extend mastery over all Choctaw people, he began to focus his energy on containing individuals, including one Choctaw youth, within a private space of his own. As Dinsmoor turned to plantation settlement, he exemplified the processes undergone by many other U.S. settlers during this era. Although only a small proportion of U.S. whites came to incorporate Native youth into their homes, Dinsmoor's behaviors reflect a broader set of practices in which family and slavery became central to claims to territory.

Dinsmoor's actions were informed by U.S. imperial arrogances deeming Euro-Americans, particularly those hailing from the United States, as inherently superior to people of African and American Indian descent and characterizing Native people as essentially desirous of inclusion into the United States. As a result, he appears to have believed that his promotion of U.S.

---

3. My thinking about domesticity and warfare is heavily informed by work in slavery studies, particularly that of Thavolia Glymph, *Out of the House of Bondage: The Transformation of the Plantation Household* (Cambridge, 2008).

domestic regimes among Choctaw people both within and beyond the space of his home would transform Choctaws into tractable and pliable Native subjects happy to subsume themselves within an expanding United States. Not only would he encounter diverse forms of resistance to his assumptions concerning assimilation, but also his endeavors would eventually pave the way for new contests over land and slave-driven commercial interests in the first decades of the nineteenth century.

James McDonald's mother, Molly, had her own ideas about what it meant to situate her son in Dinsmoor's plantation home. A brief coda addressing her choices with respect to her son indicates how the colonial anxieties and paternal arrogances inspiring and supporting civilization initiatives opened doors to a select few who hoped to beat colonists at their own game. As Dinsmoor struggled to assert his patriarchal authority over Choctaw lands, he inadvertently supported one Native woman's efforts to harness black servitude in her household to bolster her economic influence and retain territorial and political sovereignty in a changing colonial world. Molly McDonald's decisions subsequently demonstrate the yawning gap between imperial agendas and colonial realities as Native people found new ways to maintain control over their homelands. When glimpsed alongside the actions of Silas Dinsmoor, her actions make clear that U.S. settler expansion, Native dispossession, and black servitude did not simply evolve out of the public successes or failures of a few great politicians or military heroes—or villains. Rather, the war to control land and labor was also a familial contest unfolding in the shared and local spaces in which people labored and lived.[4]

Indian Agent to the Choctaw Nation

When Silas Dinsmoor was appointed Indian agent to the Choctaw Nation in May 1802, he received a set of instructions from the U.S. secretary of war. "The motives of the Government for sending Agents to reside with the Indian Nations," wrote Henry Dearborn, "are the cultivation of peace and harmony between the U. States, and the Indian Nations generally; the detection of any improper conduct in the Indians, or the Citizens of the U. States, or others relating to the Indians, or their lands, and the introduction of the

---

4. Writing about the Cherokee Nation, scholar Tiya Miles makes the argument that, by adopting the property regimes supporting racial slavery, Cherokee slaveholders similarly hoped to stem the tide of colonial dispossession by using colonial technologies against U.S. colonizers. See Miles, *Ties That Bind: The Story of an Afro-Cherokee Family in Slavery and Freedom* (Berkeley, Calif., 2005), esp. 83–84.

Arts of husbandry, and domestic manufactures." In other words, as a federal Indian agent, it would be Dinsmoor's job to serve as a diplomat, policeman, and educator among Choctaw people. He was to monitor relations between members of the Choctaw Nation and their white and Indian neighbors while encouraging Choctaw women and men to take up the various domestic "Arts" his federal supervisors associated with the "plan of civilization." This was five years before letters appear in which Dinsmoor cultivated scenarios of himself parenting Choctaw people—and longer still before he established a relationship with Molly McDonald's son James. The logics and expectations contained within Dearborn's instructions, however, would directly impact Dinsmoor's later visions for his domestic space.[5]

Dearborn's requests reflected broader U.S. designs with respect to Native territories in general and Choctaw lands in particular. Before the Revolution, British settlers had set their sights on acquiring new Native lands east of the Mississippi, from the Great Lakes region in the north, through the Ohio and Mississippi River valleys in the continental interior, to the southern shores of the Gulf Coast. From the days of the Continental Congress, a wide range of actors committed their emergent nation to expansion. Revolutionary soldiers and civilians saw in war with Great Britain an opportunity to invade and claim neighboring Indian lands for settlement. Meanwhile, a strong contingent of well-heeled political elites believed their push for political independence was the beginning of an inevitable history in which North America—including Canada—would come under the new nation's imperial reach. Abolitionist pressures quickly shaped the ways in which this expansionist vision unfolded, with Native lands above the Ohio River reserved for "free" settlement, while southern elites and their northern allies ensured that the rich agricultural lands of the Southeast would become part of an extended slaveholding South. By the late 1780s, aspiring and established slaveholders were flooding into Shawnee, Cherokee, Creek, Chickasaw, and Choctaw homelands, largely expecting that the federal government would eventually validate their land claims. Dinsmoor was to live on some of the most coveted territories of these migrants and speculators. Not only did Choctaw land prove highly compatible for the production of short-staple cotton, a burgeoning cash crop in transatlantic markets, but,

5. The Secretary of War [Henry Dearborn] to Silas Dinsmoor, May 8, 1802, in Clarence Edwin Carter, ed., *The Territorial Papers of the United States*, V, *The Territory of Mississippi, 1798–1817* (Washington, D.C., 1937), 146, 148. A copy is also transcribed in the Silas Dinsmoor Papers, 1794–1853.

stretching from the banks of the Mississippi River to the Tombigbee—in much of what is now the state of Mississippi—their slow-moving southerly rivers provided efficient transportation networks from inland farms to the Gulf of Mexico, where they could be shipped across the Atlantic world. By the time of Dinsmoor's appointment, the federal government had taken its first steps toward claiming Choctaws' landed and riverine resources through the 1795 Treaty of San Lorenzo. In 1798, Congress formally recognized this region as its nation's "Mississippi Territory."[6]

By cultivating "peace and harmony" and promoting the "plan of civilization" among Choctaw people, Dinsmoor was to work in concert with other federal Indian agents to carefully recalibrate the political terrain of western Indian country, a necessary step toward the realization of settler and federal ambitions. Native people from the Great Lakes to the Gulf Coast were deeply embedded in political networks and trade economies that crisscrossed North America and stretched across the Atlantic world. By the late eighteenth and early nineteenth century, Choctaw, Cherokee, and Creek people participated in commercial markets deeply interwoven with those of Britain, Spain, and France. These Native communities had played these empires off of one another, leveraging European commercial interests in white-tailed deer and competing territorial claims in the region to obtain favorable trade relations and military alliances and to thwart settler expansion. Although the British, Spanish, and French empires variously withdrew from parts of the Southeast over the course of the second half of the eighteenth century, federal elites hesitated about creating costly territorial wars with Native nations and their remaining commercial and military allies. Military invasion also threatened to consolidate pan-Indian unity movements stretching across the continental interior, including those that would eventually inspire the actions of Tecumseh and his brother Tenskwatawa. In the words of Henry

---

6. Colin G. Calloway, *The American Revolution in Indian Country: Crisis and Diversity in Native American Communities* (Cambridge, 1995), 20–25, 55, 280; Woody Holton, *Forced Founders: Indians, Debtors, Slaves, and the Making of the American Revolution in Virginia* (Chapel Hill, N.C., 1999), 3–36; Anthony F. C. Wallace, *Jefferson and the Indians: The Tragic Fate of the First Americans* (Cambridge, Mass., 1999), 21–74, 161–165; Reginald Horsman, "The Dimensions of an 'Empire for Liberty': Expansion and Republicanism, 1775–1825," *Journal of the Early Republic*, IX (1989), 1–20; Adam Rothman, *Slave Country: American Expansion and the Origins of the Deep South* (Cambridge, Mass., 2005), 9, 18–35, 45–54; Daniel H. Usner, Jr., "American Indians on the Cotton Frontier: Changing Economic Relations with Citizens and Slaves in the Mississippi Territory," *Journal of American History*, LXXII (1985), 298.

Knox, George Washington's secretary of war, engendering such a European-backed Indian alliance would create an "impassable barrier" to expansion.[7]

To avoid this scenario, it was Dinsmoor's job to acquire Choctaw territory for his nation by imposing upon Choctaw people the commercial systems, familial structures, and spatial economies popularly associated with Anglo-American households. He was to encourage Choctaw men to give up the hunting economies that fueled transatlantic exchange and Choctaw women to forgo the agricultural practices and matrilineal family structures that underpinned Native women's autonomy and communal landownership. In their stead, he was to inspire the adoption of the male-headed farming traditions, patriarchal nuclear family relations, and private property values idealized within Revolutionary governance philosophies—even if they were not perfectly or uniformly performed by U.S. families. As Secretary of War Dearborn put it, Dinsmoor was to use "Suitable measures ... for introducing the use of the plough, and the growth of Cotton as well as Grain" among Choctaw men and to hire "A woman" to teach Choctaw women "spinning and weaving, and other household Arts." Through compelling these labor transitions, the new agent was to recognize Choctaws' ownership of their own homelands while simultaneously persuading Choctaw communities to consolidate themselves upon small, privately owned, and male-run farmsteads and, in turn, to consensually yield territories to the United States.[8]

---

7. Dowd, *A Spirited Resistance*, esp. 90–115; Kathleen DuVal, *The Native Ground: Indians and Colonists in the Heart of the Continent* (Philadelphia, 2006), 1–28; Daniel K. Richter, *Facing East from Indian Country: A Native History of Early America* (Cambridge, Mass., 2003), 6–7, 41–68; Daniel K. Richter and Troy L. Thompson, "Severed Connections: American Indigenous Peoples and the Atlantic World in an Era of Imperial Transformation," in *The Oxford Handbook of the Atlantic World: c. 1450–c. 1850*, ed. Nicholas Canny and Philip Morgan (New York, 2011), 499–515; Michael Witgen, *An Infinity of Nations: How the Native New World Shaped Early North America* (Philadelphia, 2012), esp. 325–332; James Taylor Carson, *Searching for the Bright Path: The Mississippi Choctaws from Prehistory to Removal*, Indians of the Southeast (Lincoln, Nebr., 1999), 26–50; Richard White, *The Roots of Dependency: Subsistence, Environment, and Social Change among the Choctaws, Pawnees, and Navajos* (Lincoln, Nebr., 1988), 1–146, esp. 69–96; H[enry] Knox to George Washington, July 7, 1789, in *American State Papers: Documents, Legislative and Executive, of the Congress of the United States*, IV (Washington, D.C., 1832), 52.

8. Secretary of War Henry Dearborn to Silas Dinsmoor (copy), May 8, 1802, Silas Dinsmoor Papers, 1794–1853. Dinsmoor was preceded as Indian agent by Samuel Mitchell, who served as agent to the Choctaw and Chickasaw Nations between 1797 and 1799, and by John McKee, who ran the Choctaw agency from 1799 until Dinsmoor's

There were reasons specific family formations informed attempts to consolidate and claim native territories. Many Revolutionary elites considered male-headed family structures and private property systems the very building blocks of human civilization. They positioned private property ownership and masculine authority as foundational to successful human propagation, Christian respectability, and material and temporal progress. These beliefs had deep colonial implications, for progress required more than the subordination of white women and children to a household patriarch. It moved from the assumption that those individuals characterized as unwilling or unfit to govern their own male-headed homes—namely people of American Indian and African descent—were like children who would benefit from white male instruction. This racial paternalism justified the enslavement of Africans and African Americans in white homes. It also helped to undermine Native sovereignty. Dubious descriptions outlining the supposed inefficiencies and hardships endured by Native women and men within their own familial economies inspired and legitimated U.S. oversight of and interventions into Native people's social, political, and commercial lives.[9]

1802 arrival. See John D. W. Guice, "Face to Face in Mississippi Territory, 1798–1817," in Carolyn Keller Reeves, ed., *The Choctaw before Removal* (Jackson, Miss., 1985), 161–162. Historian Theda Perdue aptly sums up the so-called civilization program: "Guided by an idealized view of men and women in their own society," those promoting Indian "civilization" "sought to turn men into industrious, republican farmers and women into chaste, orderly housewives." See Perdue, *Cherokee Women: Gender and Culture Change, 1700–1835*, Indians of the Southeast (Lincoln, Nebr., 1998), 109. On the tensions between the realities of U.S. domestic life and the tenets of civilization, see also Daniel K. Richter, "'Believing That Many of the Red People Suffer Much for the Want of Food': Hunting, Agriculture, and a Quaker Construction of Indianness in the Early Republic," *JER*, XIX (1999), esp. 616–618. For one account of disparities between nuclear ideals and bonds of affection and lived practices within U.S. households, see Joan E. Cashin, *A Family Venture: Men and Women on the Southern Frontier* (New York, 1991), 11. For overviews of the roles of Indian agents, see William G. McLoughlin, *Cherokee Renascence in the New Republic* (Princeton, N.J., 1992), 35; Wallace, *Jefferson and the Indians*, 189–191; Carson, *Searching for the Bright Path*, 66–67.

9. As Dearborn put it to Silas Dinsmoor in 1802, the agent's educational initiatives were the very "means of producing, and diffusing" among Choctaw people "the blessings attached to a well regulated civil Society." See [Dearborn] to Silas Dinsmoor, May 8, 1802, in Carter, ed., *Territorial Papers of the United States*, V, 146. On representations of indigenous people and federal Indian policy, see Roy Harvey Pearce, *Savagism and Civilization: A Study of the Indian and the American Mind* (Berkeley, Calif., 1988), 82–96; Bernard W. Sheehan, *Seeds of Extinction: Jeffersonian Philanthropy and the American Indian* (Chapel Hill, N.C., 1973), 19–20; Dawn Peterson, "Unusual Sympathies: Settler

The terms *patriarchal agrarianism* and *reproductive philanthropy* effectively encapsulate the ideological and physical terrain upon which such interventions unfolded. By teaching U.S. kinship formations and agrarian ideals, Indian agents were to save Native people from a supposedly inevitable population demise. Male-headed farming putatively supported more people on smaller swaths of land than did hunting. Federal officials believed it had proven highly successful in existing colonies, so much so that it created the populations that pressed into Indian lands. In 1789, Secretary of War Henry Knox revealed his opinion of how settler expansion would eventually impact Native people. "As population shall increase, and approach the Indian boundaries," Knox wrote in reference to U.S. whites, "game will be diminished." Erasing Native women's own farming practices—which provided the nutritional foundation of many Native diets east of the Mississippi—he insisted that the end result would be Indians' starvation and, in turn, their eventual extinction. The adoption of patriarchal agrarianism would prevent this tragic fate. "How different would be the sensation of a philosophic mind to reflect, that, instead of exterminating a part of the human race by our modes of population," Knox declared, "we had preserved, through all difficulties, and at last had imparted our knowledge of cultivation and the arts to the aboriginals of the country."[10]

Imperialism, Slavery, and the Politics of Adoption in the Early U.S. Republic" (Ph.D. diss., New York University, 2011), esp. 30–59. My thinking on patriarchy, household, and reproduction in the context of Anglo-American colonialism is indebted to the work of Jennifer L. Morgan, Kathleen M. Brown, Kirsten Fischer, Carole Shammas, and Michael Paul Rogin. See Morgan, *Laboring Women: Reproduction and Gender in New World Slavery* (Philadelphia, 2004); Brown, *Good Wives, Nasty Wenches, and Anxious Patriarchs: Gender, Race, and Power in Colonial Virginia* (Chapel Hill, N.C., 1996); Fischer, *Suspect Relations: Sex, Race, and Resistance in Colonial North Carolina* (Ithaca, N.Y., 2002); Shammas, *A History of Household Government in America* (Charlottesville, Va., 2002); Rogin, *Fathers and Children: Andrew Jackson and the Subjugation of the American Indian* (New York, 1975). For scholarship emphasizing the ways in which people of African and American Indian descent were characterized as children in the post-Revolutionary era, see Eugene Genovese, "'Our Family, White and Black': Family and Household in the Southern Slaveholders' World View," in Carol Bleser, ed., *In Joy and in Sorrow: Women, Family, and Marriage in the Victorian South, 1830–1900* (Oxford, 1991), 69–87; Rogin, *Fathers and Children*, esp. 6, 47, 113–125.

10. Knox to Washington, *American State Papers*, IV, 53. On women's-centered agriculture and nutrition, see Michelene E. Pesantubbee, *Choctaw Women in a Chaotic World: The Clash of Cultures in the Colonial Southeast* (Albuquerque, N.M., 2005), 124–125; Richter, "'Believing That Many of the Red People Suffer Much for the Want of

By framing expansion as the natural result of male-headed household formations, Knox obscured a deeper truth: for pro-expansionists, U.S. population growth was intentional strategy. Settlers committed themselves to reproducing their numbers precisely as a means to strengthen illegitimate claims to Native space. Meanwhile, reproductive philanthropy itself was a direct strategy to gain Indian land. Male-centered farming and women's housewifery among Cherokee, Creek, Chickasaw, and Choctaw people was supposed to redirect Native interests from the transatlantic fur trade to less threatening small-scale farming enterprises. As Thomas Jefferson would make explicit in 1803, through the cultivation of political isolation and attachments to U.S. markets, the United States could use economic dependency to coerce land cessions.[11]

When Dinsmoor took up his position as agent to the Choctaw Nation, he well understood that it was his role to promote U.S. domestic ideals on Choctaw lands. He had already spent three years as an assistant U.S. agent to the Cherokee Nation. Appointed to this post in 1796 at roughly thirty years of age, he sought to quell violent confrontations erupting between Cherokee people and the white settlers who crowded into their homelands. Meanwhile, he promoted the "arts" of U.S. patriarchal agrarianism and white domesticity by distributing plows to Cherokee men and spinning wheels, cotton cards, and looms to Cherokee women. Dinsmoor received recognition for changes in the political economy of the Cherokee Nation during this time. During his tenure, the Cherokee national council, an emerging Cherokee governing body, created a centralized police force to establish and punish new crimes within their territories, including the theft of settlers' horses and retributive attacks against those who had murdered Cherokee relations.

Food,'" *JER*, XIX (1999), esp. 612–616. For one of the most thorough overviews of how post-Revolutionary philanthropy justified interventions into Native societies, see Sheehan, *Seeds of Extinction*. For an emphasis on how ideas about reproduction and propagation influenced ideas about philanthropy, see Peterson, "Unusual Sympathies," 48–59.

11. Thomas Jefferson to William Henry Harrison, Feb. 27, 1803, in Barbara B. Oberg et al., eds., *The Papers of Thomas Jefferson*, XXXIX (Princeton, N.J., 2012), 589–593. On population and settler colonialism, see Nicole Eustace, *1812: War and the Passions of Patriotism* (Philadelphia, 2012), esp. 31–35, 118–121. On efforts to pull Indian people out of a global economy into smaller-scale semicommercial endeavors, see Richter, "'Believing That Many of the Red People Suffer Much for the Want of Food,'" *JER*, XIX (1999), 601–628. See also Richter and Thompson, "Severed Connections: American Indigenous Peoples and the Atlantic World in an Era of Imperial Transformation," in *Oxford Handbook of the Atlantic World*, ed. Canny and Morgan, 507–508.

According to historian Theda Perdue, a number of Cherokee women also "seized the opportunity to manufacture their own clothes." If Dinsmoor took credit for these changes, his understanding of Cherokee agency was limited. Cherokee cultural adaptations had more to do with the Cherokees' own interests in innovating their economies in response to settler encroachment and land loss than they did to any particular persuasiveness on Dinsmoor's part. Moreover, Cherokee women and men incorporated the trappings of civilization on their own terms. The Cherokee national council was all too aware that violence against white people and their property brought devastating reprisals. Counter to Dinsmoor's initial intentions to inspire male-headed agriculture, Cherokee women grew cotton in their own agricultural fields, cultivating the fibers that might lessen their "dependence on the declining deerskin trade."[12]

Nonetheless, Dinsmoor's perceived accomplishments made him an attractive candidate for the position of Choctaw agent when it opened in 1802. Thomas Jefferson's presidential administration was certainly pleased with his work. When it redoubled federal commitments to acquiring Southeast Indian lands in the first years of the nineteenth century, it not only reappointed Dinsmoor to live among the Choctaws but also asked him to intervene in conflicts arising in Chickasaw territories as he made his journey into Choctaw lands. Dinsmoor could not have known it as he accepted these requests and began his travels west, but his years working as agent to the Choctaw Nation would not go smoothly. He not only struggled to promote the Anglo-American kinship roles and gender-based labors idealized within the "plan of civilization," but he also had a hard time maintaining these idealized roles for himself. It was these challenges that set the stage

---

12. In historian William McLoughlin's assessment, "Dinsmoor was an able and conscientious agent who did his best to help the Cherokees adjust to a new way of life." See McLoughlin, *Cherokee Renascence in the New Republic*, 42–45 (quotation on 43). For Dinsmoor's age, see *New Hampshire, Births and Christenings Index, 1714-1904*, Ancestry.com, 2011, http://search.ancestry.com/search/db.aspx?dbid=2559. For more on horse raids and Cherokee justice systems, see McLoughlin, *Cherokee Renascence in the New Republic*, esp. 12–13, 44. Historian Theda Perdue astutely documents and sums up Cherokee men's and women's engagement with civilization programs. As she puts it, "The response of Native people to 'civilization' varied by tribes and individuals, but the pattern is remarkably similar. People adopted aspects of 'civilization' that seemed useful to them and avoided practices that challenged deeply held values and beliefs." See Perdue, *"Mixed Blood" Indians: Racial Construction in the Early South* (Athens, Ga., 2005), 78. See also Perdue, *Cherokee Women*, 117.

for his paternalistic desires, as well as his eventual encounters with James McDonald around 1811.[13]

Choctaw Agency

In August 1802, Silas Dinsmoor made his way to Choctaw territories. Traveling south from Chickasaw to Choctaw lands in the late summer heat, the thirty-six-year-old agent passed into an undulating terrain of slow-moving rivers and swamps, lowland oak forests, and pine-ringed highland prairies. He took a road called the Natchez Trace, which the United States government had expropriated from the Chickasaw and Choctaw Nations just a year before his arrival. Chickasaw and Choctaw leaders granted this right of way through the heart of their territories in exchange for the promise of "two thousand dollars in goods and merchandise," in the Choctaws' case, and, for the Chickasaws, "goods to the value of seven hundred dollars." Weakened by declining deer populations and circumscribed access to transatlantic trade routes, these leaders hoped to generate new commercial opportunities through interactions with migrating settlers.[14]

U.S. whites popularly referred to the Natchez Trace as the "Wilderness Road," actively erasing the presence of the Native people whose lands it traversed. Yet, as Dinsmoor journeyed along the Trace, he encountered some of the roughly 11,500 Choctaw people whose territories spanned to its east and west and whose hundreds of towns and countless agricultural fields of corns, beans, and pumpkins dotted the highland terrain. There are no detailed records of Dinsmoor's 1802 journey; other accounts from this time,

---

13. R. S. Cotterill, *The Southern Indians: The Story of the Civilized Tribes before Removal* (Norman, Okla., 1954), 142 n. 7.

14. United States, *Indian Affairs: Laws and Treaties*, II, Treaties, ed. Charles J. Kappler (Washington, D.C., 1904), 55–58 (quotations on 55, 57). For descriptions of Choctaw topography, see Daniel H. Usner, Jr., *Indians, Settlers, and Slaves in a Frontier Exchange Economy: The Lower Mississippi Valley before 1783* (Chapel Hill, N.C., 1992), 170; H. S. Halbert, "Bernard Romans' Map of 1772," Mississippi Historical Society, *Publications*, VI (1902), 415–439; Edward Mease, "Narrative of a Journey through Several Parts of the Province of West Florida in the Years 1770 and 1771," ibid., Centenary Ser., no. 5 (1925), 82. The history and purpose of the Natchez Trace are detailed in John R. Finger, *Tennessee Frontiers: Three Regions in Transition* (Bloomington, Ind., 2001), 4; Carson, *Searching for the Bright Path*, 48–49; Greg O'Brien, *Choctaws in a Revolutionary Age, 1750–1830* (Lincoln, Nebr., 2005), 100–101. See also William C. C. Claiborne to James Madison, Dec. 20, 1801, in Dunbar Rowland, ed., *The Mississippi Territorial Archives, 1798–1803* (Nashville, Tenn., 1905), 363.

however, report of Choctaw women selling produce along the roadway and indicate the presence of roadside taverns run by white resident traders and their Choctaw wives, places where a traveler such as Dinsmoor could find a hot meal and perhaps even a comfortable bed after a long day's journey. It is possible that Silas Dinsmoor encountered James McDonald's extended kin as the Trace wound its way south through Choctaw territories (James McDonald would have been around one or two years old at the time). If their paths did cross, however, their meeting would have been brief. For Dinsmoor ended his journey into Choctaw country roughly one hundred miles due east of the Pearl River valley, the region in which the McDonalds reportedly lived.[15]

In this fertile valley stretching east from the banks of the Chickasawhay River—near present-day Quitman, Mississippi—Dinsmoor established his first agency. Sources fail to mention why this became the specific site for his settlement. The location was most certainly one in which Choctaw leaders agreed to let him reside. A Chickasawhay settlement also suited U.S. imperial ambitions, particularly when it came to monitoring Choctaws' participation in transatlantic trade. From there, Dinsmoor had opportunities to keep tabs on the large Choctaw towns in the area, which stood just north of the Spanish at Mobile Bay. Dinsmoor had expressed concerns about transatlantic affiliations between Choctaws and the Spanish. Just before he established the agency, he and the Mississippi territorial governor exchanged fears over "the traffic trade" that the Spanish "carried on with the Choctaws from Mobile, and the lake contiguous to Orleans."[16]

15. On the Natchez Trace becoming synonymous with "the Wilderness Road," see George Strother Gaines, *The Reminiscences of George Strother Gaines: Pioneer and Stateman of Early Alabama and Mississippi, 1805-1843*, ed. James P. Pate (Tuscaloosa, Ala., 1998), 159; William Lattimore to the Secretary of War, Mar. 9, 1814, in Carter, ed., *Territorial Papers of the United States*, VI, *The Territory of Mississippi, 1809-1817* (Washington, D.C., 1938), 425; Gideon Fitz to the President, Feb. 17, 1804, in Carter, ed., *Territorial Papers of the United States*, V, 308. On Choctaw spatial orientations and town structures, see Usner, *Indians, Settlers, and Slaves*, 170. The estimated size of the Choctaw Nation in the late eighteenth and early nineteenth century is from Usner, "American Indians on the Cotton Frontier," *JAH*, LXXII (1985), 298 n. 2. For Dinsmoor's possible encounters, see Carson, *Searching for the Bright Path*, 72-73; O'Brien, *Choctaws in a Revolutionary Age*, 89-90. On the McDonald family's location, see Herman J. Viola, *Thomas L. McKenney: Architect of America's Early Indian Policy, 1816-1830* (Chicago, 1974), 44; W. H., *History of Copiah: Recollections of an Old Citizen by W.H. (Attributed to William Haley) c. 1876, from the "Mississippi Democrat" Newspaper*, ed. Paul Cartwright (n.p., 2000).

16. On the location of Dinsmoor's first agency, see Gaines, *Reminiscences*, ed. Pate, 47. For U.S. concerns regarding Choctaw-Spanish interactions, see William C. C. Claiborne

Although evidence is also lean concerning Dinsmoor's day-to-day actions at the site, it appears that he resumed similar strategies to those pursued in Cherokee country. He passed out spinning wheels and cotton cards to women and ploughs and hoes to men, and he hired white men and women to help him establish a "model farm" to demonstrate the domestic roles associated with patriarchal farm life. George Gaines, the federally appointed trader to the Choctaw Nation, provides one account of Dinsmoor's labors. According to Gaines's remembrances, Dinsmoor hired a retinue of employees, including blacksmiths and wheelwrights, inspiring these workers "with an ardent desire for the improvement of the Indians." Gaines failed to report that along with Dinsmoor's civilization efforts came demands for territory. In addition to distributing agricultural tools and manufactures for homespun, Dinsmoor helped his government flex growing economic and territorial power over Choctaw communities. In October 1802, he negotiated a treaty in which the United States pressured Choctaw division leaders to cede rights to fifty thousand acres of land. Three years later, in 1805, he pushed for the cession of the southeast portion of Choctaw territories to cover trade debt. Another three years after that, he continued demands for land, once again using debt as leverage to glean the Choctaws' easternmost territories for the United States.[17]

Dinsmoor's combined efforts to promote the work of civilization and obtain land led to his mixed reception among Choctaw people. When Dinsmoor distributed cotton cards, seed, and looms or encouraged families to keep livestock, he was—at least in part—bolstering an indigenous semi-subsistence economy adapting to the specific pressures that came with U.S. settler colonialism. As with the Cherokees, Choctaw women and men selec-

---

to Silas Dinsmoor, Jan. 28, 1803, Series 0483, Journal of the Superintendent, 1803–1808, frames 2–5, Mississippi Department of Archives and History, Jackson.

17. Gaines, *Reminiscences*, ed. Pate, 47. The Mississippi territorial governor ordered "thirty pair of Cards" for Dinsmoor to distribute to Choctaw women in February 1803. See Claiborne to Silas Dinsmoor, Feb. 28, 1803, Series 0483, Journal of the Superintendent, 1803–1808, frames 8–9, Mississippi Department of Archives and History. Land cessions are documented in Robert B. Ferguson, "Treaties between the United States and the Choctaw Nation," in Reeves, ed., *The Choctaw before Removal*, 215–218; Usner, "American Indians on the Cotton Frontier," *JAH*, LXXII (1985), 302–304; United States, *Indian Affairs: Laws and Treaties*, II, 63–64; *Message from the President of the United States, Transmitting a Treaty of Limits between the United States of America and the Choctaw Nation of Indians; January 30, 1808; Referred to the Committee of Ways and Means* (Washington, [D.C.], 1808).

tively engaged the U.S. agent in order to accommodate changing economic circumstances and circumscribed territorial resources. For at least a decade before his arrival, Choctaw women were already enlarging their fields to grow cotton alongside corn, beans, potatoes, and pumpkins and began to keep chickens to sell to migrants passing through their territories or to settlers in Mobile and New Orleans. Both women and men raised livestock such as hogs, horses, and cattle as deer became scarce for their own subsistence and for trade with whites. They assimilated this small-scale production of cotton and stock raising into enduring matrilineal hunting and agricultural economies.[18]

A few saw in Dinsmoor additional opportunities to support their own ambitions for private wealth. Over the latter half of the eighteenth century, British, Scottish, and French traders had married the matrilineal relatives of prominent chiefs, an arrangement that secured transatlantic commercial alliances through the bonds of kinship. Although these men frequently adopted Choctaw customs of dress and diplomacy, many continued to value the gendered and racialized property regimes of their imperial nations, claiming private ownership of Choctaw lands and holding African-descended people as chattel slaves. Matrilineal customs designated the children of these unions as fully Choctaw, giving Choctaw mothers and their clan relatives a great deal of control over the upbringing of the children. Nonetheless, some of the men and women who grew up under white traders' paternal orbit replicated their fathers' economic practices, particularly after inheriting Choctaw territory and black people as alienable property. By the first years of the nineteenth century, white traders and their bicultural sons and daughters were tending "huge herds of black-faced cattle," "shipping bales of cotton downriver to Spanish Mobile," and "establishing themselves as innkeepers and ferrymen along the early frontier roads and horsepaths." These men and women were not alone among Choctaws in their interests in holding black slaves and Choctaw lands as private property. Their commercial and kinship ties to influential Choctaw chiefs, however, converged with their paternal influences to place them at the forefront of the Choctaw Nation's small but growing plantation economy. From Silas Dinsmoor, these individuals acquired resources to expand their economic ventures. Not only did the agent recognize their private holdings in land and labor, but he also proved a potential resource for the mass production of cotton. In the early-nineteenth-century cessions that both Dinsmoor and his predecessor helped

18. Carson, *Searching for the Bright Path*, 51–56, 73–74.

to negotiate, Choctaw chiefs requested ploughs, hoes, cottonseed, and even a cotton gin explicitly for the bicultural descendants of prominent traders. Many of these Choctaw slaveholding families clustered in the rich Pearl River delta, where fertile agricultural lands and proximity to the Natchez Trace facilitated trade in slaves and cotton. The young James McDonald and his mother Molly were part of this cohort of emerging Choctaw elites in the Pearl River region, a reality that would shape both the young man's and his mother's respective interactions with Dinsmoor by the close of the decade.[19]

Despite cultivating careful alliances with this small group of Choctaw families, Dinsmoor still struggled to obtain the broader accommodations to his teachings that he sought. Enough Choctaw people recognized Dinsmoor's ambitions and rejected the ideas that his teachings in civilization would lead to their personal and collective improvement to inspire Dinsmoor's chagrin. His neighbors shunned him and continued to practice both the distributive economies and the gendered divisions of labor that shaped their own matrilineal kinship relations and household arrangements. That is, even as they adapted to social, environmental, and economic changes in the lower Mississippi Valley, women owned, farmed, and shared the harvests of the land as their kin had done for generations. Young men made their feelings for Dinsmoor violently explicit, targeting his agency in the horse and cattle raids they reserved for white settlers and potentially one resident white trader and his bicultural wife. From Dinsmoor's continuing

---

19. O'Brien, *Choctaws in a Revolutionary Age*, 80-82, 88-90; W. David Baird, *Peter Pitchlynn: Chief of the Choctaws* (Norman, Okla., 1972), 6-8; Samuel J. Wells, "The Role of Mixed-Bloods in Mississippi Choctaw History," in Wells and Roseanna Tubby, eds., *After Removal: The Choctaw in Mississippi* (Jackson, Miss., 1986), 47 (quotations); Carson, *Searching for the Bright Path*, 79-80; Perdue, *"Mixed Blood" Indians*, 58-59; Christina Snyder, *Slavery in Indian Country: The Changing Face of Captivity in Early America* (Cambridge, Mass., 2010), esp. 182-212; [Sarah Tuttle], *Conversations on the Choctaw Mission* (Boston, 1830), I, 84-85; White, *The Roots of Dependency Subsistence*, 103-104. Historian Theda Perdue reveals circumstances when women and their clan relatives foiled traders' ambitions to privatize Choctaw resources. See Perdue, *"Mixed Blood" Indians*, 2. On matrilineal childrearing, see ibid., 25. Discussions involving the paternal influences of Euro-American fathers in the Native Southeast and debates about race thinking can be found in Tiya Miles, *The House on Diamond Hill: A Cherokee Plantation Story* (Chapel Hill, N.C., 2010), 59; Barbara Krauthamer, *Black Slaves, Indian Masters: Slavery, Emancipation, and Citizenship in the Native American South* (Chapel Hill, N.C., 2013), 30-31; Theda Perdue, "Race and Culture: Writing the Ethnohistory of the Early South," *Ethnohistory*, LI (2004), 701-723; Saunt et al., "Rethinking Race and Culture in the Early South," ibid., LIII (2006), 399-405.

complaints of attacks on his cattle, it is even possible that the agent's farm was one of the more popular targets in the lower Mississippi Valley. As he modeled U.S. civilization for Choctaw people and demanded land cessions, Dinsmoor and his Chickasawhay agency might have become the very symbols of U.S. imperial aggression.[20]

Silas Dinsmoor took note of these combined "failures." Disinclined to consider either the arrogance of his imperial ventures or the cultural and economic violence underpinning them, he blamed his lack of success on the supposed frailties of Choctaw "character." As he framed it, Choctaws were an "ignorant people." The men were "too proud to labour for the subsistence of themselves or families," leaving agricultural labors up to women, whom he declared did not execute them properly. They are "poor devoted people," he concluded in 1807, "devoted to self destruction and total extinction." If Knox and Jefferson framed their civilization program in terms of saving Indian people from population decline, for Dinsmoor this initiative was doomed to failure. Reproductive philanthropy—at least on a large scale—was hopeless.[21]

Dinsmoor declared that Choctaw disinclinations to heed his lessons in civilization informed his exasperation with his job. Yet the previous year had also been something of a turning point for him. In 1806, he married a white woman from New England, purchased black slaves, and established a plan-

20. Either willfully or ignorantly disregarding Choctaw women's efficient crop management systems, Dinsmoor complained after riding through a Choctaw town in 1807 that "the women perform all the labour, are principally employed in cultivating wild roots, and preparing them for food, which is at best but [edible], and the corn fields too generally lie neglected." See Silas Dinsmoor to Mary Dinsmoor, May 24, 1807, Silas Dinsmoor Papers, 1794–1853. After his participation in treaty negotiations in 1805, John Pitchlynn—an influential resident trader, slaveholder, and Dinsmoor's interpreter—and his British-Choctaw wife, Sophia, suffered damage worth twenty-five hundred dollars, which appears to have been the result of an attack on their farm. In the words of one imperial observer, as Dinsmoor pushed for new land cessions in treaty negotiations in 1805, "some turbulent young Choctaws" destroyed his "stock and other property" at the Chickasawhay agency. See James Parton, *Life of Andrew Jackson*, 3 vols. (New York, 1861), II, 579. See also Cato West to Silas Dinsmoor, Feb. 15, 1805, Series 0483, Journal of the Superintendent, 1803–1808, frames 79–80, Mississippi Department of Archives and History; *American State Papers*, IV, 749. For analyses of Choctaw plantation raids, see James Taylor Carson, "Horses and the Economy and Culture of the Choctaw Indians, 1690–1840," *Ethnohistory*, XLII (1995), 495–513; Carson, "Native Americans, the Market Revolution, and Culture Change: The Choctaw Cattle Economy, 1690–1830," *Agricultural History*, LXXI (1997), 7; O'Brien, *Choctaws in a Revolutionary Age*, 84.

21. Silas Dinsmoor to Mary Gordon Dinsmoor, May 24, 1807, Silas Dinsmoor Papers, 1794–1853.

tation household of his own. In doing so, he began to think of himself not only as a federal Indian agent but also as a local Mississippi settler. This transformation inspired a new kind of racial paternalism, one that deviated from his earlier efforts. He abandoned widespread programs aimed at teaching Choctaw people Anglo-American kinship values and instead used the politics of race and kinship to transform Choctaw lands into his own private space. Possibly lured by trade connections from the Natchez Trace and—just as centrally—the presence of prominent Choctaw chiefs and other influential slaveholding Choctaw families, Dinsmoor moved his agency to the Pearl River valley, where he would encounter Molly McDonald and her young son. There he worked to transform the Choctaw landscape into a plantation home. It was precisely as he struggled to maintain both his position as an Indian agent and as a plantation master that he began to imagine that he could safely contain Choctaw bodies within his household.

Settler Paternalism

Dinsmoor's transformations around 1806 and his eventual decisions with respect to James McDonald were less a reflection of unique experiences or psychological traits than they were the outcome of overlapping yet competing ambitions on the part of federal elites and slaveholding settlers. Those who deployed him to Choctaw territories coveted these lands for the United States. However, they were crucially aware of the geopolitical dance necessary to avoid military conflict. Settler desires for territories could be less cautious. Already laying claim to Native homelands, many U.S. migrants felt an imperative to quickly erase an indigenous presence in order to naturalize their own occupation. Ideas around patriarchy and paternalism, race, and kinship informed both government and settler aims. Yet, when Dinsmoor began to think of himself as a federal agent and a local planter, he straddled competing interests. He was supposed to carefully persuade Choctaw people to transform into small-scale landholders at the very same moment he was also trying to assert his own belonging in Choctaw space. Dinsmoor worked out these conflicts through the paternalistic discourse that shaped both federal Indian policy and plantation governance, eventually incorporating James McDonald into his home in an attempt to resolve the tensions of his competing responsibilities and ambitions.[22]

Initially, like other federal observers and policy makers, Dinsmoor had

---

22. For useful overviews of the logics underpinning settler colonialism, see the citations in Note 24, below.

a tendency to position Indian territories and U.S. settlements in diametric opposition to one another. One had all the creature comforts of family, society, and technology; the other supposedly suffered from the chaos of kinlessness and ancient environmental conditions. In 1794, while working within the Cherokee Nation, Dinsmoor wrote a fantastical letter to his future wife Mary Gordon comparing life in Cherokee society to the life he imagined he was missing in New Hampshire, where he was raised. "Now behold me," he asked of Gordon, "cross legged sitting on a Panther's hide or Bear's skin, or in a mat of Boughs ... surrounded by a group of tawny savages, jealous and revengeful.... Not a friend to whom I may with confidence unbosom, and lay my thoughts in open view before him." This was a far cry from his life in the Northeast, where he enjoyed the company of "worthy gentleman whose minds intent upon their several objects" were "like bees which on a sunny day seek precious honey dew from opening flowers," striving "contentedly to gain the boon of rational delights." For Dinsmoor, hunting economies went hand in hand with petty and foolish behavior, whereas the agricultural practices popularly associated with a national U.S. yeomanry allowed men to enjoy more "rational" inquiries in bucolic homosocial settings. That he was in Charleston when he wrote this letter mattered little to his description of his surroundings. His language had more to do with proving a disjuncture between U.S. and Indian territories—not to mention his masculine bravery and intellectual acuity to the object of his affection—than with accurately describing his material surroundings and personal company.[23]

After he began to build his own household around 1806, he moved away from comparing Southeast Indian society to white gentility in New Hampshire. Instead, he took on a different colonial narrative, emphasizing the processes through which Choctaw territories could be made to resemble a suitable home for his family. Rather than highlighting the potential civilization and assimilation of Choctaw people into U.S. society, he emphasized their replaceability by U.S. whites. The comforts he associated with U.S. society would come, not from remaking Choctaw men and women in the white family's image, but by establishing on Choctaw territories a white family of his own. Dinsmoor's transformation parallels that of other North American

23. Silas Dinsmoor to Mary Gordon, Aug. 16, 1794, Silas Dinsmoor Papers, 1794–1853. U.S. settlements were, of course, still Indian territories. For a critique of the erasure of an indigenous presence from New England in particular, see Jean M. O'Brien, *Firsting and Lasting: Writing Indians out of Existence in New England* (Minneapolis, Minn., 2010).

settlers. Through these politics of kinship, he in fact exemplified the processes of settler colonialism. As scholars have made clear, settlers have historically claimed new territories by making indigenous people foreigners in their own homelands. By characterizing Choctaw people as inherently lacking in the patriarchal kinship structures that were supposed to foster large-scale agriculture and human population, Dinsmoor positioned them as an anarchic and anachronistic presence on their ancestral lands. In Dinsmoor's mind, Choctaw people failed to appreciate the kinship structures and reproductive systems supporting United States civilization. As a result, they were to be supplanted by those who did.[24]

Dinsmoor's efforts to assert his personal reproductive claims to Choctaw territories were not without problems. He needed family to claim Choctaw space, yet, ironically, the agent's very presence upon Southeast Indian territories worked against his ability to realize the male-headed nuclear family structures he so actively promoted. As he aggressively pursued Gordon's hand in marriage, she expressed fears of having to live on Native lands, which were exacerbated by the unfavorable counsel of friends. Although Gordon's letters are not preserved, according to Dinsmoor's correspondence Gordon's social circle "drew ... a horrid picture" of the agent's "situation" within the Choctaw Nation, complete with "savage beasts," "more savage men," and "the deprivation of all ... friendly connexion." In fact, echoing Dinsmoor's own reliance upon popular depictions of Indian people, Gordon's community raised such doubts about Dinsmoor's "ability to afford the necessary comforts in life" that Gordon initially rejected the agent's proposals. Dinsmoor did manage to persuade Gordon to overcome her fears of social dishonor enough to marry him, which she did at the end of the summer of 1806. Yet, even after their marriage, she still hesitated to join him at the agency, wishing she might instead "dream" her husband "out of the wilderness."[25]

---

24. My reading of these sources is deeply indebted to theorizations of settler colonialism, particularly those of Jean O'Brien, J. Kēhaulani Kauanui, and Patrick Wolfe. These scholars have emphasized the ways that settler colonists claim territories by imposing the social and spatial structures of the colonial "home" on Native space through civilization programs and displacement. Of course, New England was also a Native space, one that Dinsmoor disavowed. See O'Brien, *Firsting and Lasting;* Kauanui and Wolfe, "Settler Colonialism Then and Now: A Conversation between J. Kēhaulani Kauanui and Patrick Wolfe," *Politica e Società,* II, no. 2 (June 2012), 235–258; Wolfe, "Settler Colonialism and the Elimination of the Native," *Journal of Genocide Research,* VIII (2006), 387–409.

25. Silas Dinsmoor to Mary Gordon, June 10, 19, 1806, Silas Dinsmoor to [unad-

If marriage and cohabitation were essential to Dinsmoor in making Choctaw lands into his own home, so was black servitude. Indeed, both were intertwined, as people of African descent not only created the agricultural vision Dinsmoor imagined but also the creature comforts he believed his family required. In October 1806, a few months after traveling back to New Hampshire to marry Gordon, and upon the eve of the closing of the transatlantic slave trade, Dinsmoor rushed to Charleston to purchase African women and men who had just survived the Middle Passage. "My object is to purchase some Africans," he then wrote his new wife, "and [I] shall not forget to procure a nice made *[sic]* for you." Through buying an enslaved woman, Dinsmoor might create the domestic conditions that could ease his wife's preconceived notions about life in Native territories.[26]

Purchasing slaves presented a challenge to his understanding of himself as a philanthropic gentleman, however, albeit one from which he quickly recovered. Two weeks after announcing his decision to acquire slaves for his and Mary's home, he engaged in what he called "a horrid traffic of purchasing negroes." Dinsmoor's horror was not over the conditions endured by newly enslaved Africans; instead it was because he was "obliged to have intercourse with the most unprincipled people" who sold them, a common sentiment expressed by gentlemen slave buyers as they were forced to confront the realities of the slave market. In the end, Dinsmoor purchased sixteen people, whom he sent ahead of him with a slave driver. After his foray into Charleston slave markets, it did not take him long to console himself with the paternalistic discourses justifying enslavement. "I shipped my flock of black sheep," he told Mary from Charleston, drawing on Christian imagery to position himself as a benevolent overseer. By January 1807, two of these people had died. Revealing slaveholder beliefs that the principles of Christianity and the racialized property values supporting chattel slavery could quite easily coexist, Dinsmoor relayed the news to his wife in "a painful talk." "My property has sustained a revers *[sic]*, since I wrote you last, by the death

---

dressed], July 10, 1806, Silas Dinsmoor to Mary Gordon Dinsmoor, Jan. 18, 26, 1807, all in Silas Dinsmoor Papers, 1794–1853. Silas begins to refer to Gordon as Mary Gordon Dinsmoor in a letter to her dated Aug. 14, 1806 (ibid). The marriage was announced in the major Mississippi newspaper on Sept. 30, 1806; see *Misissippi* [sic] *Herald & Natchez Gazette*.

26. Silas Dinsmoor to Mary Gordon Dinsmoor, Oct. 12, 1806, Dinsmoor Papers, 1794–1853. On black servitude and the making of white domesticity, see Walter Johnson, *Soul by Soul: Life Inside the Antebellum Slave Market* (Cambridge, Mass., 1999), esp. 78–116.

of two of my Africans." "No foresight could have prevented the loss," he continued, absolving himself of wrongdoing. "I [submit] without a murmur to this frown of Providence."²⁷

It might seem odd that Silas Dinsmoor, a New Englander, saw slavery as crucial to setting up his household for his new family. But the business of slavery was nothing new to the Indian agent. Before he even arrived in Choctaw territories and witnessed their burgeoning U.S. plantation settlements, his time in Cherokee country had exposed him to both white and Cherokee families who owned African and African American slaves. Slavery had come to shape visions of wealth and prosperity for aspiring white men, and, indeed, served to shore up and even create elite white status itself. Moreover, census records from 1790 indicate that his own father, a settler from Ulster Ireland, still held three slaves in New Hampshire at the close of the eighteenth century, signaling a likeliness that Dinsmoor grew up in a household run by African American labor. In fact, as gradual abolition circumscribed slaveownership over the first decade of the nineteenth century for younger men such as Dinsmoor, life with slaves in an the expanding plantation South might have felt more in line with visions of their futures than did life in New England without them.²⁸

The names and histories of the two enslaved people who lost their lives in January 1806 are not preserved in the archives, nor are the direct causes of their deaths. The psychic and physical exhaustion brought on by the horrors of the Middle Passage, however, combined with the intense labors required to build Dinsmoor's plantation were almost certainly contributing factors. In the winter of 1806–1807, a matter of months after purchasing the sixteen African women and men from Charleston and "driving" them to Choctaw territory, Dinsmoor relied upon their labors to move his agency

---

27. Silas Dinsmoor to Mary Gordon Dinsmoor, Oct. 26, 1806, Jan. 18, 1807, Silas Dinsmoor Papers, 1794–1853. With regard to Dinsmoor's views of slave traders, as historian Walter Johnson argues, slave buyers worked to "maintain an artificial and ideological separation of 'slavery' from 'the market.'" See Johnson, *Soul by Soul*, 24.

28. *Population Schedules of the First Census of the United States, 1790,* microfilm roll 5, *New Hampshire, Volumes 1 and 2* (Washington, D.C., 1965), 121. On late-eighteenth-century slaveownership among Cherokee people, see Miles, *Ties That Bind*, esp. 25–41; Theda Perdue, *Slavery and the Evolution Cherokee Society, 1540–1866* (Knoxville, Tenn., 1987), 36–39. On slavery and the production of whiteness, see Johnson, *Soul by Soul*, 81–94. On gradual emancipation in New Hampshire, see Joanne Pope Melish, *Disowning Slavery: Gradual Emancipation and "Race" in New England, 1780–1860* (Ithaca, N.Y., 1998), 64, 66, 76–77.

one hundred miles west of Chickasawhay to the Pearl River valley. At this location, Dinsmoor again depended on his slaves to prepare sixty acres "for culture" and to build, in the words of one early-twentieth-century historian, an agency house of "a very fine structure." As Gaines, the U.S. government trader, would remember it, this structure and its surroundings quite explicitly resembled "a large plantation."[29]

As the cold winter days slowly warmed and lengthened in the spring of 1807, the presence of the fourteen remaining African women and men at Dinsmoor's new agency plantation home changed the Indian agent's relationship to the Choctaw landscape. For the first time in his correspondence, he began to write with a sense of pleasure in his surroundings. Scanning a horizon in which the boughs of "upwards of a hundred fine young peach trees" spread their blooms, 112 cattle and 64 hogs roamed in search of food, and where even "two domesticated deer cut fantastic symbols," Dinsmoor celebrated his "little rustic domain." He even wrote of the pleasure he felt from work in his garden, performed alongside his slaves or, more than likely, simply involving overseeing their labors. The agent celebrated the planting of peas, "irish" potatoes, leeks, asparagus, and oats—vegetables popular among white settlers—as well as Native corn. Even Choctaw people seemed less hostile to him, "more respectful than usual," leaving his cattle alone and sending along good wishes to his wife. For Dinsmoor, only Mary could complete the transformation of his Indian agency into a fully "domesticated" familial home. ("Without my Mary," he asserted, "society is a *wilderness*, or a *desert!!!*") He explicitly saw himself as creating an orderly plantation household, one that literally beckoned his wife "home." For, even as they were barred the legal status of kinship, slaves were the very beings whose labors enabled domestic space. Indeed, they were synonymous with the household itself. "My household are in perfect health, docile and tractable," Silas told Mary, in reference to his own perception of the well-being and actions of those he enslaved, one that must have required a great deal of willful blindness. "When shall my Mary join me," he queried in closing, "to view this wilderness blossom as a rose"? Slaves made the household. Dinsmoor just needed a companion with whom to share it.[30]

---

29. Silas Dinsmoor to Mary Gordon Dinsmoor, Mar. 29, 1807, Silas Dinsmoor Papers, 1794–1853; Charles S. Sydnor, *A Gentleman of the Old Natchez Region, Benjamin L. C. Wailes* (Durham, N.C., 1938), 55; Gaines, *Reminiscences*, ed. Pate, 65.

30. Silas Dinsmoor to Mary Gordon Dinsmoor, Feb. 14, Mar. 21, 29, 1807, Silas Dinsmoor Papers, 1794–1853.

Dinsmoor's paternal confidence greatly expanded through the establishment of this plantation space. As he drew on slaveownership to "domesticate" the Choctaw agency, he began to imagine his household as a kind of container through which he could more effectively assert his authority over Choctaw people. He had never used paternalistic language in his letters before, but, after establishing his plantation agency, the Choctaw men who continued to "depredate" his cattle over the spring of 1807 were suddenly his children. And when Mary Dinsmoor gave birth to Silas, Jr., in the summer of 1807 and began to make preparations to join her husband at the new plantation agency over the following year, the child became a "young Chaktaw." Scholars have cogently argued that, when colonial elites imagined white children as Native offspring, they revealed anxieties about descendants exhibiting the so-called savage traits of the Native peoples whose lands they occupied. Yet Dinsmoor's playful rhetoric can simultaneously be read in terms of governance and desire in a Native world he could not control. If Dinsmoor felt ineffective as an Indian agent, reimagining Choctaw people as helpless infants living within the space of his own home was one way to reconstitute authority.[31]

Dinsmoor's tone in his letters was playful, but his paternalism was inherently violent. Just as he disguised the violence of slavery through providential accounting and fatherly sentiment, his discourse with regard to Choctaw people reflected his inclinations to assert power by infantalizing those he sought to dispossess. The full extent of Dinsmoor's disregard for Choctaw lives became clear in March 1807. After paying "130 dollars" to "mend" a Choctaw woman whose mouth was "disfigured and mangled" in a "riot" on Choctaw lands the winter before, Dinsmoor wrote to his wife, rather pleased with the exchange. "I thought it a good bargain," he told Mary, "for I have a piece of her jaw with two teeth in it in my desk." Dinsmoor's actions reflected a growing interest on the part of U.S. whites to collect signifiers of Indian

---

31. Silas Dinsmoor to Mary Gordon Dinsmoor, Mar. 21, 1807, ibid. See also Silas Dinsmoor to Mary Gordon Dinsmoor, Mar. 29, 1807, ibid. On Mary's migration with Silas Junior and Nancy, Silas's ward, to live with Dinsmoor at the agency, see Silas Dinsmoor to Mary Gordon Dinsmoor, May 16, 1808, ibid. On referring to European-descended children as "savage," see, for example, Amy Kaplan, *The Anarchy of Empire in the Making of U.S. Culture* (Cambridge, Mass., 2005), 32; Ann Laura Stoler, *Race and the Education of Desire: Foucault's History of Sexuality and the Colonial Order of Things* (Durham, N.C., 1995), 141. Scholar Michael Rogin notes that Andrew Jackson's own paternalistic rhetoric vis-à-vis Indian people emerged after his victories over the Seminoles and their transatlantic allies in 1818. See Rogin, *Fathers and Children*, 198–199.

identity and culture as they believed in and promoted Indian disappearance. For Dinsmoor, the "bargain" was not the price of caring for this woman's body; it was obtaining the object that emerged from it, a reminder of his own physical distinctness from Choctaw people, whose bodies he believed did not merit the same sanctity and memorialization as white ones did.[32]

Imagining Choctaw bodies within his home and then physically relocating them there shored up Dinsmoor's efforts in still other ways. It allowed the agent to cease the large-scale pedagogical efforts that had been so widely disregarded and, instead, to continue his work at home. There he could spend his energies on smaller-scale projects over which he believed he had greater control. He could address pressures from his federal superiors while focusing on the domestic life he longed for.

The larger Dinsmoor's plantation agency grew, the more he withdrew from Choctaw politics. Gaines—the federal trader who remarked on Dinsmoor's early labors in Choctaw country—remembered seeing "but little of Col. Dinsmore after he removed his agency" from Chickasawhay to Pearl River. By January 1809, Dinsmoor again moved with his wife, children, and at least some of those he enslaved to live one hundred miles farther southwest, in the U.S. planter town of Washington, Mississippi. In February 1809, Dinsmoor further expanded his landholdings, purchasing a three-hundred-acre plantation along the Mississippi River in Concordia Parish for thirty-four hundred dollars. Dinsmoor's absences from Choctaw lands became so prolonged that they attracted the attention of Secretary of War William Eustis. When Tecumseh traveled the Southeast in 1811 to court Choctaw, Creek, Cherokee, and Chickasaw alliances, Eustis dashed off a note to his missing agent. "Inconveniences to the public service having arisen from the absence of the Choctaw Agent from his Agency; and late circumstances having rendered his personal residence in the nation indispensible to the due exertions of his duties," Eustis chastised, "you will be pleased after the

---

32. Silas Dinsmoor to Mary Gordon Dinsmoor, Mar. 21, 1807, Silas Dinsmoor Papers, 1794–1853. On late-eighteenth- and early-nineteenth-century interests in collecting human remains and other sacred objects associated with Indian people, see Wallace, *Jefferson and the Indians*, 75–107. My thinking on Dinsmoor here is directly informed by continuing struggles over remains and sacred objects, on which there is a broad activist and scholarly literature. See, for example, Kathleen S. Fine-Dare, *Grave Injustice: The American Indian Repatriation Movement and NAGPRA* (Lincoln, Nebr., 2002), 13–46; Ruth B. Phillips, *Museum Pieces: Toward the Indigenization of Canadian Museums* (Montreal, 2011); Susan Sleeper-Smith, ed., *Contesting Knowledge: Museums and Indigenous Perspectives* (Lincoln, Nebr., 2009).

receipt of this letter, to repair thither without delay; and in future consider yourself as permanently resident among them." Dinsmoor begrudgingly accepted, relocating himself, at least part-time, to the agency, focusing his attentions on ensuring U.S. slaveholders' legal ownership of the people of African descent they brought through Choctaw lands.[33]

It was in 1811 that the agent interacted with Molly McDonald long enough to obtain her child and then send the ten- or eleven-year-old boy to his home in Washington, Mississippi. In so doing, Dinsmoor demonstrated commitments to his work as a civilizer, surrounding James McDonald with the patriarchal familial structures he as an agent was meant to impose. Dinsmoor's later actions indicate his desires to showcase his work with McDonald. In 1813, he traveled with McDonald to Washington, D.C., presenting the twelve- or thirteen-year-old youth to the secretary of war, John Armstrong, Jr., with the hope of securing further schooling for him in the region. At precisely this moment, political winds were working against Silas Dinsmoor, with Andrew Jackson waging a campaign for his removal. (Jackson was incensed at the agent's demands for written proof of slaveownership when enslavers passed by the agency with people of African descent.) Within this context, McDonald's presence in the federal capital would have been a way for the beleaguered agent to garner favor, demonstrating commitments to civilization even as he concentrated on securing his position in Mississippi land, slave, and cotton markets.[34]

Dinsmoor's gamble ultimately failed. In 1813, as the war of 1812 raged in the Southeast, a new agent was appointed to reside in the Choctaw Nation during Dinsmoor's travels to and from the federal capital. Nonetheless, the struggling agent's actions highlight the relationship between domesticity, slavery, settlement, and war. The kin-based logics legitimating both American Indian and African American dispossession shaped a multifaceted war for Indian territories while simultaneously providing Dinsmoor with the

33. Gaines, *Reminiscences*, ed. Pate, 65; Dowd, *A Spirited Resistance*, 145–147; the Secretary of War to Silas Dinsmoor, Feb. 22, 1811, Carter, ed., *Territorial Papers of the United States*, VI, 178; Parton, *Life of Andrew Jackson*, II, 351–352. The "Indenture" was signed on Feb. 9, 1809; see Dinsmoor Papers, 1794–1853. Silas Dinsmoor began to address letters to Mary Gordon Dinsmoor in Washington, Mississippi, on Jan. 24, 1809 (ibid). On Dinsmoor's investments in slaveholders' proof of ownership of people of African descent, see Parton, *Life of Andrew Jackson*, I, 350–351.

34. On pressures for Dinsmoor's dismissal, see William Lattimore to the Secretary of War, Mar. 9, 1814, in Carter, ed., *Territorial Papers of the United States*, VI, 424–425; Remini, *Andrew Jackson and the Course of American Empire*, 162–164, 170.

structures that supported his ambitions as a planter in the lower Mississippi Valley. It is no wonder, then, that he went to the space of his own household to work through clashes between his personal goals and his public mandate. Family became the site through which mastery was both created and destroyed. Those whose families were recognized became the symbols of patriarchal agrarianism and reproductive success. Moreover, their households were the very locations through which violence was remade in the image of philanthropy.[35]

Silas Dinsmoor positioned himself as a benefactor to enslaved people of African descent and Choctaw people. And he might very well have believed that he was. As the federal government moved toward more explicit removal policies in the aftermath of Andrew Jackson's virtual elimination of British, Spanish, and pan-Indian collaborations in the era of 1812, Silas Dinsmoor apparently described "the policy of our government towards the Indian tribes" as "a harsh one." Nonetheless, he remained unable to resist the lures and logics of settlement and slavery in an expanding U.S. South. As Jackson negotiated the very first treaty exchanging Choctaw lands in the east for lands west of the Mississippi, Dinsmoor stood to receive a tract of his own to compensate him for the loss of livestock while living in Choctaw territories. If Choctaw lands were to become U.S. slave country, he was going to make sure he held a stake in it.[36]

Molly McDonald

Whereas U.S. colonial archives preserve Silas Dinsmoor's letters, there are only a few existing sources pertaining to Molly McDonald—and she produced none of these by her own hand. In fact, almost all of the information about her comes through writings between her son James and U.S. federal elites years after his transfer to Dinsmoor's care. As a result, those concerned with her story are met with a series of resounding silences, leaving more questions than answers. When and where was Molly McDonald born? Who did she call family? How did she spend the early years of her life? In what

---

35. Remini, *Andrew Jackson and the Course of American Empire*, 163; Rogin, *Fathers and Children*, 41–42; Parton, *Life of Andrew Jackson*, I, 358–359.

36. For Dinsmoor's statements on Jackson, see Parton, *Life of Andrew Jackson*, II, 577–578. For his land grants, see "Extract of the Journal of the Conference between Colo. John McKee United States Agent to the Chaktaws, and the Mingoes, Leaders and Warriors of the Chaktaws, Chaktaw Agency, December 15, 1815," folder 7, 4026.176, Peter Pitchlynn Papers, Gilrease Museum, University of Tulsa; Remini, *Andrew Jackson and the Course of American Empire*, 392.

ways did her experiences in the late eighteenth and early nineteenth century shape the ways she saw the world? How did her vantage point as a Choctaw woman inform the decisions she made with respect to herself, her family, and her broader communities? Sources do not even provide information regarding how she met the Indian agent appointed to live in her nation or what she thought of the man whose plantation agency sprawled across sixty acres of her tribal lands.[37]

While archival material pertaining to Molly McDonald is thin, it is not entirely absent. When she placed her son in the care of Silas Dinsmoor, she established a documented relationship with the U.S. colonial state, allowing for possible narratives about the ways she navigated the expansion of U.S. plantation settlements in the early nineteenth century. Surviving documentary fragments indicating that McDonald supported her son's education in the United States and her connections to the U.S. plantation economy illuminate possible scenarios in which she took advantage of Dinsmoor's anxious efforts to reproduce Anglo-American colonial values on Choctaw lands to enter into, or further entrench herself within, the specific racial and spatial economies that increasingly yielded political and economic influence in the South. They allow us to speculate on how her son's presence in Dinsmoor's home helped her as a Choctaw woman to stand at the forefront of changing race, gender, and property relations in Choctaw homelands that were quickly becoming absorbed into the U.S. cotton kingdom.

From extant evidence, it is clear that in the early nineteenth century Molly McDonald lived in or around the Pearl River valley, where Silas Dinsmoor would eventually establish his plantation agency. By 1800 or 1801, she was the mother to at least two children, both sons. The younger one was James, born right at the dawn of the century—within a year or two before Silas Dinsmoor made his way into Choctaw territories. The elder, born in the late eighteenth century, was known by the name of Alexander Hamilton. Molly McDonald married three white men—most likely European traders—over the course of her life, the second of which went by the surname McDonald. However, James McDonald never mentioned his father, suggesting that, whoever this man was, he played a small role in both his and his mother's daily lives by the 1810s, if he played a part in them at all. In 1819, six years after he had left Choctaw lands for Washington, D.C., James McDonald wrote that he traveled from Washington, Mississippi, to the U.S.

37. McDonald was likely born between the mid-1860s and early 1880s because she was of childbearing age in the first years of the nineteenth century.

capital with Silas Dinsmoor "in obedience to the wishes" of his mother, signaling that Molly not only approved of but also encouraged her son's migration to the United States. By 1824, her younger son's correspondence reveals that she owned a one-mile private reserve on Choctaw lands, which Alexander Hamilton and James McDonald, respectively, secured for her in treaties with the United States. She also owned at least one black slave, a man she had purchased by credit for more than $650 from white slave traders. In 1826, four years before the United States implemented Choctaw removal to lands that would become known as the state of Oklahoma, she ran a farm on her reserve, where people of African descent cultivated cotton and raised cattle for southern markets.[38]

From these sources, it is possible to argue that Molly McDonald saw both her son and plantation slavery as powerful familial resources in a world in flux. In one scenario, we can imagine her using Dinsmoor to allow herself—and her son—to enter into the practices of racial slavery and plantation management. Through ethnohistorical accounts, we can draw a possible picture of the Choctaw economy of her earlier years, when Choctaw people occupied much of their original ancestral homelands in the lower Mississippi Valley. The most influential men in her life, including her father and her matrilineal uncles, hunted these territories for white-tailed deer and other wild game, whose skins they exchanged with British, Spanish, and French traders for the manufactured goods upon which their communities had come to rely. Meanwhile, her mother owned the house and lands upon which she lived, providing food for her family by farming corn, beans, squash and other indigenous and European vegetables alongside other women from her matrilineal clan and selling surplus to traders and settlers in the region.

38. Viola, *Thomas L. McKenney*, 41, 44; Thomas Loraine McKenney to John C. Calhoun, Apr. 15, 1818, in *Secretary of War: Letters Received*, M221, roll 78, 1817–1818, frames 9072–9077, NA; McKenney to Richard Mentor Johnson, n.d., *Records of the Office of Indian Affairs: Letters Sent*, II, *May 4, 1825–May 31, 1826*, M21, roll 2, frame 469, NA; Eron O. Rowland, *History of Hinds County Mississippi, 1821-1922* (Jackson, Miss., 1922); James McDonald to McKenney enclosed in McKenney to Calhoun, Aug. 10, 1819, in *Secretary of War: Letters Received*, M221, roll 86, 3918–3920; McKenney to William Ward, Choctaw Agent, Feb. 23, 1825, McKenney to Calhoun, Feb. 23, 1825, *Letters Sent by the Office of Indian Affairs, 1824-1881*, I, *March 18, 1824–May 3, 1825*, M21, roll 1, 371–372, NA; United States, *Indian Affairs: Laws and Treaties*, II, 191–195; James McDonald to Calhoun, Nov. 9, July 10, 1824, *Letters Received by the Office of Indian Affairs, 1824-81*, M234, roll 169, frames 89–91, 93–97, NA; Robert Jones to J. L. McDonald, Sept. 15, 1826, *Letters Received by the Office of Indian Affairs, 1824-81*, M234, roll 773, frames 356–357, NA.

This world of McDonald's youth was already deeply affected by centuries of colonialism. As she grew older, however, the increasing regional power of the United States led to new concerns and colonial tensions. Plantation slavery began to engulf her homelands, driving away game and threatening Choctaw territorial sovereignty. By the turn to the nineteenth century, she was acutely aware of the growing threats—and opportunities—presented by U.S. planters. Prescient of the United States' growing regional power, she named her first child Alexander Hamilton, after the famous U.S. figure. Beginning in 1801, after she married a Scotch-Irish trader and gave birth to her second son, who they named James, she had no choice but to interact with the thousands of settlers who poured through the newly established Natchez Trace because it ran through the river valley in which she lived. When U.S. treaty commissioners began to chip away at the boundaries of the Choctaw Nation by leveraging trade debt between Choctaws and the United States in 1801, 1802, and 1805, she became acutely aware of the economic opportunities and political resources racial slavery generated. With her husband dead or departed from Choctaw lands, she connected herself to her slaveholding Indian agent by placing her son in Dinsmoor's care. For, through him she might gain the farming and spinning implements, and perhaps even the enslaved human beings, that helped yield economic power in a changing southern landscape.[39]

Yet it is also possible that Molly McDonald's exposure to slavery came earlier and, as she grew older, she expanded on her commitments to the practice as the United States expanded its own southern slave economy. Choctaw communities had been embedded in North American and transatlantic slave trades long before the arrival of U.S. settlers. Over the course of McDonald's late-eighteenth-century youth, Choctaw men continued the long-standing Native practice of capturing outsiders, mostly women and children, during war raids. Although Choctaw women adopted a great many of these captives into matrilineal kinship networks in order to foster international alliances and to replace family members lost through disease or war, some were denied the bonds of kinship and, instead, were valued as a source of labor or as

---

39. As one historian argues, "Choctaw belief in the power of Euro-Americans ... surfaced in the names of some of their leaders and villages.... borrowing of foreign appellations probably served metaphorically to unite dissimilar peoples as well as honor the recipients with foreign epithets that connoted power." See O'Brien, *Choctaws in a Revolutionary Age*, 77. For one estimate on the numbers migrating through the Trace, see Secretary of the Treasury to Williams, Nov. 5, 1805, in Carter, ed., *Territorial Papers of the United States*, V, 425.

tradable prestige commodities. In the decades before the Revolution—right around the time when Molly McDonald was born—these practices were increasingly inflected by race. As British, French, and Spanish settlers gained ground in the lower Mississippi Valley, Choctaw people, along with other Southeast Indians, became aware of the high price people of African descent brought in Euro-American markets. Black captives, considered valuable trade commodities throughout the Southeast, especially as the deerskin trade declined, were less likely to be incorporated into Choctaw families as kin, and black slaves became important status symbols. The settlement of British traders on Choctaw lands further expanded the presence of racial slavery. These men frequently held and traded African and African American slaves, normalizing black servitude in the eyes of their neighbors as well as in those of their Choctaw wives and children. Molly McDonald's presence in the Pearl River valley strongly connects her to these families. If McDonald spent her childhood in such a bicultural setting or, later, created one through marriage, her father or her husband exposed her to this "new and particular form of exploitation." Perhaps, then, as U.S. plantation slavery began to envelope Choctaw lands, McDonald further committed herself to racial servitude by purchasing additional black slaves and establishing a plantation of her own.[40]

As historians of slavery in Indian country have emphasized, when Southeast Indians began to own black people as chattel slaves they were both resisting and contributing to the physical, economic, and racial violence of colonialism. By becoming slaveholders and planters, these individuals worked to defend themselves and their Native communities against wholesale dispossession by white slaveholders. Through the slave-driven production of export agriculture and the construction of respectable plantation spaces, they exhibited their "civilized" status, a powerful resource for women and men trying to undo the narratives of savagery that delegitimated their rights to hold land. By the same token, holding slaves became a way to accrue economic and political power for tribal nations within an expanding cotton kingdom that not only eagerly claimed Indian territories but also that increasingly circumscribed trade and economic opportunity. As Native slaveholders pushed back against the United States, however, they did so by drawing on the violent practices that exploited people of African descent, that undermined other Native-centered kinship and labor systems, and that supported the polarization of wealth in their communities. Most narratives,

---

40. Snyder, *Slavery in Indian Country*, 13–45, 182–212; Miles, *The House on Diamond Hill*, 59 (quotation).

however, have largely focused on the pro-slavery interests of Native men. Molly McDonald provides a rare glimpse into the ways in which one Choctaw woman stood at the forefront of emerging race and gender practices in the Native South. In fact, Choctaw society largely recognized McDonald's matrilineal rights to oversee the upbringing of her son, and it was precisely these rights that allowed her to take advantage of Dinsmoor's own efforts to use race and family to claim Choctaw space.[41]

To have a son living in Washington, Mississippi—the planter town in which the Dinsmoor family resided—created for Molly McDonald extended personal and kinship ties that lubricated economic transactions, credit networks, and business alliances. Meanwhile, James McDonald's schooling there exposed him to the language and literacy regimes that undergirded the ownership of human and landed property in the United States. By providing her son with these individual connections and colonial schooling opportunities, Molly not only worked to advance James's position within a southern slave economy but also created a masculine intermediary for herself in an increasingly patriarchal landscape.[42]

Indeed, drawing on both Choctaw and Euro-American ideas about kinship and servitude, Molly McDonald worked to resist individual dispossession. As a Choctaw woman, she had fewer opportunities to directly participate in the treaty negotiations that granted U.S. whites and some Native men ownership of private property and political power on Mississippian territories traditionally belonging to Choctaw women. A son raised to manhood in the United States could serve as her representative and liaison in those political and economic spaces in which her right to belong would not automatically be recognized. That Molly McDonald eventually relied on both her

---

41. For scholarship examining the complexities of slavery in Indian country and its entangled relationship with U.S. colonialism, see Krauthamer, *Black Slaves, Indian Masters*; Miles, *Ties That Bind*; Miles, *The House on Diamond Hill*; Celia E. Naylor, *African Cherokees in Indian Territory: From Chattel to Citizens* (Chapel Hill, N.C., 2008); Claudio Saunt, *A New Order of Things: Property, Power, and the Transformation of the Creek Indians, 1733–1816* (Cambridge, 1999); Saunt, *Black, White, and Indian: Race and the Unmaking of an American Family* (Oxford, 2005); David A. Chang, *The Color of the Land: Race, Nation, and the Politics of Landownership in Oklahoma, 1832–1929* (Chapel Hill, N.C., 2010).

42. On the importance of kinship networks in the U.S. South, see, for example, Remini, *Andrew Jackson and the Course of American Empire*, esp. 68; Cashin, *A Family Venture*, 9–10, 17–20. As Cashin writes with respect to the South, "The family was of paramount importance, even for those who wished to escape it" (10).

sons to help her secure Choctaw lands and African American labor is clear. Not only did Alexander Hamilton and James McDonald ensure her rights to her plantation farmlands during U.S.-Choctaw treaty negotiations; James McDonald also successfully demanded compensation for his mother when the white traders from whom she had purchased an enslaved man of African descent repossessed him at gunpoint.[43]

Decisions on the part of Molly McDonald would come to exemplify the ultimately reciprocal vectors that shaped battles over territory in the era of 1812. For, when Dinsmoor participated in his own familial contests for Native space, he inadvertently supported her efforts to use matrilineal kinship relationships with her son for her own ends. As it would turn out, the messy constellation of intimate exchanges unfolding between individuals like Silas Dinsmoor and Molly McDonald would reshape the Southeast, not only over the course of the War of 1812 but also in the lead-up to Indian Removal. As the War of 1812 effectively severed Southeast Indians' connections to the transatlantic markets that had empowered them against United States territorial expansion, the numbers of Southeast Indian women and men entering into the plantation economy swelled. Some worked closely alongside the African American women and men around whose enslavement southern domesticity unfolded. According to one missionary report, by the 1820s roughly a thousand migrant and semi-migrant Choctaw people picked cotton for wages across the Deep South. A small—but growing—group of elites, however, expanded their interests in slave-driven export commodities. Although men such as Dinsmoor might have appreciated diplomatic relationships with these established and aspiring planters in the short term, in later years their strategies began to agitate U.S. governing elites. With Southeast Indian planter nationalists consolidating their political and economic power over the course of the 1820s, they presented new barriers to expansion, ones that would reshape federal Indian policy over the latter half of the century.[44]

---

43. James McDonald to Calhoun, July 10, 1824, *Letters Received by the Office of Indian Affairs*, M234, roll 169, frames 94–97, NA; McKenney to Calhoun, McKenney to Ward, Feb. 23, 1825, *Letters Sent by the Office of Indian Affairs*, M21, roll 1, frames 371–372, NA.

44. See Tuttle, *Conversations on the Choctaw Mission*, 47–48; Usner, "American Indians on the Cotton Frontier," *JAH*, LXXII (1985), 305.

"BORDERS THICK AND FOGGY"
MOBILITY, COMMUNITY, AND NATION IN A NORTHERN INDIGENOUS REGION

Karen L. Marrero

In 1838, a senator from the newly established state of Michigan received a letter from an anxious citizen. The nation's borders, the writer advised, were "rather hairy or squally, thick and foggy, and perhaps some may say cloudy, stormy, and even tempestuous." To the south, the country was troubled by the "Mexican affair" that gave rise to a "sleepless jealousy"; to the east, by the "boundary question"; to the west, by "Indian maneuvers"; and, to the north, at the Canadian border, by the so-called Patriots, "who create some uneasiness." Having raised the specter of a nation in imminent danger from menacing forces pressing in on all sides, the writer shifted his stance. He made a bold prediction that, despite these perceived threats, the country would not only prevail but also grow stronger. "But fear not," he concluded, "when foreign enemies come, as the heart of one man we will raise the stripes, crown our warrior with the stars, and put such a cruel mark upon their mortified back as will long take from them the blessed privilege of being forgotten." The writer's allusion to stars and stripes reflected the ambiguous nature of collective belonging and the basis on which it could be established. There remained the veiled threat of monarchical governments, suggested by the writer's reference to a "crown," while the metaphoric use of "stripes" as the "cruel mark" of the lash on the "mortified back" of the nation's enemies infused his commentary with the violent imagery of slave mastery. But his invocation of the stars and stripes also suggested his belief that a core American nationalism would triumph.[1]

The writer stoked fears that a still-nascent and vulnerable nation would lose itself, only two decades after the inconclusive and divisive War of 1812

I would like to thank Benjamin Johnson and Alan Taylor (who with the author participated in the National Endowment for the Humanities Summer Seminar "Bridging National Borders in North America," Newberry Library, June 2014) as well as the anonymous reviewers of this essay and Niki Eustace for suggestions and guidance.

1. Andrew M. Bradley to Hon. Lucius Lyon, Sept. 13, 1838, Lucius Lyon Papers, William L. Clements Library, University of Michigan, Ann Arbor.

with Great Britain. But he also hoped that a cohesive sense of national purpose gained through vigilant protection of these vaguely defined borders would triumph over local threats. Just a year earlier, in relation to the "Mexican affair," the member of Congress to whom this letter had been addressed received a memorial signed by more than four hundred Michigan men opposed to the annexation of Texas by the United States. The eastern boundary question, which referred to the lack of a firm border between British Canadian New Brunswick and Maine, threatened to lead to war between the United States and Britain and would remain unresolved for another decade. Like the Texas colonists at the southern border a few years earlier, the Patriots in the north were citizens defying federal authority by organizing themselves into military units. The Texans had provoked the Mexican government into waging war, and the Patriots all across the northern border from Vermont to Michigan, despite a neutrality agreement between the United States and Britain, were similarly attempting to instigate hostilities. In both cases, citizens came together to liberate a population they viewed as enslaved by despotic foreign governments. For the Patriots, this entailed assisting their northern neighbors in Upper and Lower Canada (the present-day provinces of Ontario and Quebec, respectively) in a revolt against a British oligarchy. Finally, the Indians of whom the letter writer expressed some uneasiness lived not only at what he perceived as an indeterminate and peripheral western edge but, in the case of the Potawatomi and other Anishinaabe, throughout Michigan. In 1838, many of the Potawatomi would also defy the federal government, in their case by resisting forced removal west and relocating to Canada, thereby keeping their options for residence open.[2]

The intersection of these large-scale movements and the challenge posed to national boundaries, still fluid and undefined a quarter century after the War of 1812, made the northern border a particularly contested region. U.S. and British Canadian imperial officials attempted to discern and enforce the limits of nation by controlling the movement of local populations whose sympathies and loyalties to national projects remained uncertain.

This essay will consider Patriots and Potawatomi as they used the fluidity of the northern border to challenge these efforts by national governments. Their mobility helped to maintain a porous buffer zone where loyalty to nation was in flux and where alternative forms of community developed. Patriots and Potawatomi hailed from various points across this territory,

---

2. Memorial signed by Michigan men, enclosed in Doct. N. M. Thomas to Hon. Lucius Lyon, Sept. 8, 1837, Lucius Lyon Papers.

and the reactions of residents located at the points where they crossed the border were varied. The Patriots would force open still unresolved political issues between the United States and Britain that hovered decades after the War of 1812 and formed a backdrop to the movement of indigenous peoples across the border. During this period, the year 1838 saw increased incursions by Patriots at the border and the largest number of Potawatomi of Michigan, Illinois, Indiana, and Wisconsin who would cross the same border to seek alternative living arrangements.

To better understand how these movements affected local residents, this essay will also examine the effects of the Potawatomi relocation on the indigenized French, who had long-standing ties to Native communities through marriage and trade. The communities of which they were part had been established over the course of the eighteenth century. Indeed, these people of mixed French-indigenous blood and culture were so thoroughly integrated into both white settler and Native communities they could not be easily expelled from either world. The indigenized French had traditionally maintained an allegiance to family over ties to nation. They, too, would defy imperial efforts by following the trajectory of their kin networks across borders, even when expulsion from Anishinaabe territory by Euro-American officials displaced them. Patriots, Potawatomi, and indigenized French would act out their own versions of collective belonging to counter imperial efforts at control.[3]

3. For the inability of the state to expel mixed-race people because of their ties to both indigenous and settler communities, see Michael Witgen, *An Infinity of Nations: How the Native New World Shaped Early North America* (Philadelphia, 2013), 365. Witgen and others use the term "Métis" to refer to mixed French, Scottish, Cree, Ojibwa, and Saulteaux communities that formed in the nineteenth century in the northwestern provinces and states of Canada and the United States and that maintain a distinct culture today. Although Jacqueline Peterson used "Métis" more broadly to describe people of mixed race and culture in the Great Lakes ("Prelude to Red River: A Social Portrait of the Great Lakes Métis," *Ethnohistory*, XXV [1978], 41–67), influencing subsequent scholars, she has since narrowed her definition to refer to the northwestern Métis ("Red River Redux: Métis Ethnogenesis and the Great Lakes Region," in Nicole St-Onge, Carolyn Podruchny, and Brenda Macdougall, eds., *Contours of a People: Metis Family, Mobility, and History* [Norman, Okla., 2012], 22–58). Other scholars of Great Lakes indigenous people (including Lucy Murphy, Susan Sleeper-Smith, and Rebecca Kugel) have discussed terminology in making reference to individuals of mixed race or Native-French cultures of the southern Great Lakes and Ohio Valley who were shaped politically, economically, and culturally by their integration into indigenous societies. I use the term "indigenized French" to distinguish these peoples from the Métis (for a seminal work on the Métis,

By examining the activities of these three groups, it is possible to see how still-elastic categories of community, nation, and race were being negotiated and solidified in a decade bookended on one side by the Indian Removal Act of 1830 in the United States and on the other by the Act for the Protection of the Lands of the Crown in This Province from Trespass and Injury of 1839 in Upper Canada. Disguised as efforts to protect indigenous nations from the ravages of white civilization, these pieces of legislation were part of mandates aimed at acquiring Native land through a proprietary relationship. In attempting to lay claim to the same indigenous bodies and indigenous land, both governments inadvertently reaffirmed a disputed buffer zone as an indigenous space. Because indigeneity and territoriality became intertwined concepts for American and British governments eager to expand and protect their nations, the performance of indigeneity became a method for manipulating and defying these Euro-American polities. Euro-American nationhood could be the cruel mark that compelled collective fidelity as it obliterated locally based loyalties. It might also be a code inscribed on the psyche at birth that allowed a distant monarch to claim ownership of a body wherever it might wander. Or it could cling to the land as a feature of place, in each possible scenario becoming a decisive and divisive issue in this era. Ultimately, Euro-American nationhood would be challenged by well-established indigenous concepts of nation and by indigenous agents who understood the points at which these competing notions intersected.

Indigenous Bodies and the Limits of Nation in the Buffer Zone
In the waning years of the War of 1812, as British and American plenipotentiaries met in Ghent to negotiate an end to hostilities, the interdependent nature of indigenous peoples and borders assumed a position of central importance. The Treaty of Paris of 1783, which had ended war between the United States and Britain, acknowledged the middle of waterways between the United States and Canada as a boundary line. In spite of this demarcation, Britain had maintained control of a handful of strategic forts, including those at Detroit and Niagara, which were deemed by Americans to be on U.S. ground. Ten years later, the Jay Treaty of 1794 had forced the British to finally abandon those posts. In the interim, however, the two Euro-American national claims, along with those long-standing claims of local indigenous groups, had existed simultaneously, one nullifying the other, cre-

---

see Chris Andersen, *"Métis": Race, Recognition, and the Struggle for Indigenous Peoplehood* [Vancouver, 2014]).

ating a transitional space where allegiance to community or nation was in flux and where the loyalty of any person could be called into question.

The Jay Treaty had recognized indigenous peoples dwelling on both sides of the border as a distinct population and preserved their right to freely travel between the United States and Canada, reaffirming an indigenous buffer zone that had challenged American and British territorial ambitions. Owing to confusion over what constituted the halfway point, and to which country the islands existing in this nebulous zone belonged, British negotiators at the Treaty of Ghent planned to call for the further delineation of the border through Lake Saint Clair and the Detroit and Saint Clair Rivers, the bodies of water that separated Michigan Territory and Upper Canada, by two appointed commissioners. It would take several years for the boundary commission to make its final recommendations. Ultimately, the British negotiators dropped the requirement for a formal buffer zone, settling for upholding indigenous possession of territory as it had existed in 1811.[4]

The British were intent on maintaining this unique space by making the maintenance of boundaries synonymous with the status of indigenous peoples. In initial correspondence and talks with their American counterparts, the British negotiators at Ghent argued that a strong and lasting peace could not be achieved without the involvement of indigenous groups as allies and co-signatories to a peace treaty. After all, the British purported, Indians had entered the war against the United States independently of British involvement and as a result of the "spirit of encroachment on their boundaries," which the American government had not only "practiced everywhere" but also continued to "assert as their right and defend as essentially necessary."[5]

British foreign secretary Robert Stewart advised his designates that the best prospect for future peace required that the two governments mutually agree to respect the integrity of indigenous territory. This territory would act as a "useful barrier between both states" and would prevent their collision. As such, the countries would have a "common interest" in rendering Native peoples "peaceful neighbours to both states." The British wanted to

---

4. Phil Bellfy, "Cross-Border Treaty Signers: The Anishnaabeg of the Lake Huron Borderlands," in Karl S. Hele, ed., *Lines Drawn upon the Water: First Nations and the Great Lakes Borders and Borderlands* (Waterloo, Ontario, Canada, 2008), 24; Francis M. Carroll, *A Good and Wise Measure: The Search for the Canadian-American Boundary, 1783-1842* (Toronto, 2001), 28; Dean Jacobs, "Land Claims Research Paper: Walpole Island Indian Reserve" (n.p., Association of Iroquois and Allied Indians, [1973?]), 166.

5. Henry Bathurst, 3d Earl Bathurst, to Henry Goulburn, Sept. 27, 1814, Henry Goulburn Papers, Clements Library.

distinguish a barrier region between their North American territory and the United States and sought to legally recognize the permanent existence of independent indigenous nations for this purpose. These independent nations would ostensibly remain neutral. But the British were most interested in maintaining trade routes and an economic foothold through their indigenous allies in Canada, alliances that they had been building since the middle of the eighteenth century. They were alarmed at the growth of the United States and the speed with which American merchants were taking over or rerouting trade routes. For its part, the United States balked at efforts by a European power to check its growth and limit its future economic possibilities. American plenipotentiaries refused to use the word *nation* in referring to indigenous groups, declaring instead that their country was interested in recognizing Indian *tribes* as independent as long as their interests did not conflict with those of the United States and for the purpose of engaging in binding legal transactions for the sale of land. U.S. representatives reinforced this stance by excluding indigenous agents as signatories of the Treaty of Ghent.[6]

Although these two perspectives on nomenclature and indigenous peoples were in conflict, for both sides indigenous bodies became the penultimate markers of the limits of nation in an era of hardening Euro-American boundaries. The British regarded national identity as residing in and inseparable from the person who possessed it by birth and therefore as "antecedent and paramount" to any other state of being, ontological or political, that the individual might encounter or adopt. An 1814 proclamation had declared that "the natural-born subjects of His Majesty cannot, either by swearing allegiance to other Princes or States, or by any other their own acts, or by the acts of foreign Princes or States ... discharge themselves, or be discharged, from the natural allegiance which, from their birth, they owe to His Majesty." British national identity could not be separated from the body, even if that break was sought willingly by its possessor. This body could wander, but it maintained its inherent connection to the king nonetheless.[7]

---

6. American Commissioners (Adams, Bayard, Clay, Russell, and Gallatin) to British Commissioners for restoring peace (Gambier, Goulburn, and Adams), Oct. 13, 1814, Henry Goulburn Papers. For discussion of the basis for this decision and its antecedents, see Phil Bellfy, *Three Fires Unity: The Anishnaabeg of the Lake Huron Borderlands* (Lincoln, Nebr., 2011); and Dwight L. Smith, "A North American Neutral Indian Zone: Persistence of a British Idea," *Northwest Ohio Quarterly*, LXI (1989), 46–63.

7. "A Proclamation, for Recalling, and Prohibiting His Majesty's Natural-Born Sub-

The British had followed this logic in their practice of impressing American seamen deemed to be "perpetual subject[s]" in neutral waters before and during the War of 1812. They also established a system for classifying and enumerating indigenous peoples that reflected this philosophy, distinguishing "Resident Indians" from "Visiting Indians." A third category of "Wandering Indians" was established after 1836 to address the movement of large numbers of Native people of the Old Northwest in the era of treaty making, when land cessions divided them from their domiciles. Indeed, this category was specifically created to include those who were relocating from the United States to Canada but who had not yet settled on a particular reserve. The acknowledgement of this third category allowed the British to claim ties to indigenous bodies as they traveled and wherever they might relocate.[8]

In contrast, American northern border territories of the Old Northwest that were transitioning to statehood in the first decades of the nineteenth century sought to combine citizenship and residence. While Michigan underwent this process between 1835 and 1837, its representatives carefully debated the matter at their conventions. The right to participate as an elector was attached to place at the federal, state, and local levels. An article proposed that every white male inhabitant over the age of twenty-one who had resided in the United States for a year and in Michigan for six months could vote in elections. More specifically, the inhabitant could only vote in the county, township, or district in which he lived. Ultimately, an externalized concept of national identity dependent on place triumphed over embodied versions of nationhood. "Aliens," in the language of the article, could vote as noncitizens, as long as they took an oath to repudiate all other foreign heads of state and agreed that they would seek citizenship in the future. Some of the Michigan representatives objected to the use of the term *alien*, declaring that it classified "respectable men" with "Negroes and Indians." They further

---

jects from Serving in the Sea or Land Forces of the United States of America," *London Gazette*, Aug. 2, 1814, 1553.

8. For "perpetual subject," see Alan Taylor, *The Civil War of 1812: American Citizens, British Subjects, Irish Rebels, and Indian Allies* (New York, 2012), 102. For British impressment of American seamen in the War of 1812, see ibid., 102–106; and Denver Brunsman, *The Evil Necessity: British Naval Impressment in the Eighteenth-Century Atlantic World* (Charlottesville, Va., 2013). For British categorization of indigenous people, see James A. Clifton, *The Prairie People: Continuity and Change in Potawatomi Indian Culture, 1665–1965* (Lawrence, Kans., 1977), 306. On the "Wandering Indians" category, see Bellfy, *Three Fires Unity*, 112.

discussed the possibility that indigenous peoples could attain citizenship as long as they were either attached to the land as agriculturalists or possessed some drop of white blood in their ancestry. In either case, land and the status of yeoman farmer coalesced to mark race and nationhood. The state used and manipulated the apparent acknowledgement of indigenous political identity as a vehicle for consolidating its own authority.[9]

But, for some time to come, delineation of the status of indigeneity in order to settle the northern border would continue unresolved, and the boundary would remain stubbornly fuzzy and indeterminate. This state of uncertain national identity turned rivers and lakes that had existed previously as conduits into national borders and rendered the land on either side a topographical symbol of sovereignty. Despite the U.S. government's efforts to police and patrol these areas by employing customs officials, local residents circumvented these new impediments and continued to trade and travel, keeping the transitional zone open. The act of moving back and forth across the border carved a plethora of alternative paths that maintained the region as intrinsically multinational.[10]

Rebels on Both Sides: Patriots and the Upper Canada Rebellion
Visitors to the border region remarked on the extensive integration of the disparate communities located across its vast territory. Traveling through the Talbot settlement located on the Canadian side of Lake Saint Clair, one European visitor expressed his surprise at encountering a "mixed assemblage of persons" in the same house. He described "sullen" Scotch Highlanders speaking only Gaelic; New Englanders who "talked volubly about politics, [and] recounted many incredible stories of their own prowess";

---

9. For a discussion of indigenous peoples and citizenship, see Harold M. Dorr, ed., *The Michigan Constitutional Conventions of 1835-36, Debates and Proceedings* (Ann Arbor, Mich., 1940), 244–247. For conflation of race and nationhood, see Deborah A. Rosen, *American Indians and State Law: Sovereignty, Race, and Citizenship, 1790-1880* (Lincoln, Nebr., 2007), 131–133; and Witgen, *An Infinity of Nations*, 355. Witgen points out that denial of citizenship to Indians and Africans was based on conditions imposed on them by the state. Africans were deemed unfit because of their "acceptance" of slavery, and Indians were perceived to have rejected "civilization" because they fought to preserve their way of life (363). For manipulation of Native political identity by the state, see Mark Rifkin, *Manifesting America: The Imperial Construction of U.S. National Space* (New York, 2009), 3.

10. Catherine Cangany, *Frontier Seaport: Detroit's Transformation into an Atlantic Entrepôt* (Chicago, 2014), 197.

and Indians "in full hunting costume." The setting for this multinational gathering was the extensive territory owned by Thomas Talbot, an officer from Ireland's elite who had emigrated to the Canadian side of Lake Erie. Talbot acquired large swaths of land, originally gained by the British government from Algonquian and Iroquoian nations. He then doled out plots to emigrating Scots, Irish, and Americans. Talbot grew rich and powerful and bankrolled the creation of a road that linked Lake Ontario to the Detroit River in order to encourage further Euro-American settlement.[11]

It was the concentration of land, resources, and power in the hands of Talbot—described by contemporaries as an "absolute despot"—and other Anglo political elites, collectively known as the Family Compact, that would drive some residents of Upper Canada to revolt against the British in 1837 and 1838. Among the disaffected were immigrants from the United States whose political and economic ideals lingered from the first break with the British in 1776. Similar rebellions had been taking place in Lower Canada (Quebec), where the discontented were predominantly composed of French Canadians who sought to maintain their economic and cultural systems against a small number of privileged English politicians and businessmen. Their successes encouraged residents of Upper Canada sympathetic to the idea of republican government to launch public demonstrations, most notably in Toronto, and conduct raids in regions along the border.[12]

On the American side of the border, men organized into militias, adopted a distinct uniform, and labeled themselves Patriots. They established their own version of a republican government for Upper Canada, appointing members to cabinet positions that included president, vice president, secretary of the treasury, and secretary of war. Others were given military titles, including commander-in-chief of the Patriot army in the west, commodore of the Patriot navy on Lake Erie, and commodore of the Patriot navy on Lake Ontario and Saint Lawrence. British subjects, including those of French descent, and Americans met on both sides of the border, in one another's homes and at local taverns, in order to plan invasions and raise funds, creating a "regional republican community." This binational collective, its provisional shadow government, and the armed forces that protected it existed as semi-

---

11. John Howison, *Sketches of Upper Canada, Domestic, Local, and Characteristic: To Which Are Added, Practical Details for the Information of Emigrants of Every Class; and Some Recollections of the United States of America* (Edinburgh, 1821), 180–181.

12. For Talbot as despot, see John Clarke, *Land, Power, and Economics on the Frontier of Upper Canada* (Montreal, 2001), 377.

illusory structures maintained by men whose authority resided solely in the transitional space between the United States and Upper Canada.[13]

William Putnam, nephew of Revolutionary general Israel Putnam, traveled to Detroit, where he organized a local group of Patriots composed of men who came from as far away as Kentucky to invade Canada over the Detroit River. Putnam would be killed in that campaign by the British. Another raid, launched from Vermont into Quebec, was led by Charles Grandison Bryant, who brought his Missisquoi Division over Lake Champlain. Fellow Patriots must have placed faith in Bryant's abilities because he had founded a military school in Maine that was used to recruit and train volunteers for the northern rebellion. Bryant was ultimately unsuccessful in his efforts to invade Lower Canada and was arrested on charges of breaking the neutrality agreement. He jumped bail and made his way to the Republic of Texas. When Bryant engaged in a campaign to repulse Mexican attacks and later joined the Texas Rangers, he reinvented and glorified his record of service on the northern border, claiming to have been captured and sentenced to death before managing to escape. A number of men from northern states would parlay their experiences with the Patriots into military campaigns during the Mexican-American War ten years later.[14]

The Patriot movement was not confined solely to military initiatives. The shared political ideologies of the men led to the formation of fraternal organizations that together became known as Hunter Lodges. These groups existed in Upper Canada, Lower Canada (where they were known as "Fréres Chasseurs"), and the United States. Members hailed predominantly from professional and elite social stations and included physicians, lawyers, accountants, judges, political figures, and members of state militias. They demanded complete discretion and used a complex system of signs and symbols and a coded written language to distinguish members from those who might be spies. The ranks or degrees, known as "Snowshoe," "Beaver," and

---

13. Oscar A. Kinchen, *The Rise and Fall of the Patriot Hunters* (New York, 1956), 39. For "regional republican community," see Tom Dunning, "The Canadian Rebellions of 1837 and 1838 as a Borderland War: A Retrospective," *Ontario History*, CI (2009), 140.

14. Kinchen, *Rise and Fall of the Patriot Hunters*, 65, 80–82; *Handbook of Texas Online*, s.v. "Bryant, Charles Grandison," by Christopher Long, accessed June 30, 2014, http://www.tshaonline.org/handbook/online/articles/fbrcb. Bryant became acting commissary at the U.S. post at Corpus Christi in 1849; see H. P. N. Gammel, ed., *The Laws of Texas, 1822–1897*, III (Austin, Tex., 1898), 457. I am grateful to Jay Gitlin for bringing Bryant's participation in the northern rebellion to my attention.

"Grand Hunter," were a nod to indigenous peoples and the fur trade culture, with its image of the rugged woodsman. Many of the same men who were playing the role of the fur trapper, with its roots in European and indigenous encounters, were simultaneously facilitating the cession of land in their own states and territories and the relocation of indigenous nations westward.[15]

In 1838, the activities of the Patriots and their desire to incite war between the United States and Britain threatened well-established cross-border trade relations between Michigan and Upper Canada. Patriots had begun gathering at Detroit and arming themselves in 1837. Because Detroit was the capital of the fledgling state of Michigan, and it was located directly across from the Canadian town of Sandwich, many of its residents felt at risk. In January 1838, the mayor of Detroit, Colonel Henry Mack, described the situation as an "attempted revolution in Canada" that had "entirely absorbed public and private attention" in the city. One visitor proclaimed that the Patriots "endangered the peace and safety" not only of Detroit but of the United States as well and that "none can tell how it may end and whether this city may not be in ruins ere long." Public meetings for and against the cause of the Patriots were held, causing disturbances in the streets. Guns were fired day and night, and local taverns did a brisk business. The Patriots were denigrated as wandering vagrants with no desire other than that of plundering the countryside; their dangerous efforts, many believed, had been stopped by yeomen superior in number and character who were defending their land.[16]

Not all Americans were anxious to engage in hostilities with their northern neighbors. The Patriots were outnumbered by local residents in both Canada and the United States and by agents of the British Canadian and American governments who were determined to uphold the neutrality that existed between Great Britain and the United States. A local Detroit doctor heralded the "two thousand effective men" he met while visiting the British camps at Fort Malden and Sandwich on the Canadian side of the Detroit River. Among this number were reformers and volunteers who spurned the idea of revolt and sought instead to "redress their grievances in a constitutional way." The doctor had greater sympathy for British Canadian men

---

15. Kinchen, *Rise and Fall of the Patriot Hunters*, 27, 56–57, 63.

16. Col. Henry Mack to Hon. Lucius Lyon, Jan. 15, 1838, Lucius Lyon Papers; Joshua Toulmin Smith, Detroit, Jan. 8, 1838, *Journal in America, 1837-1838*, ed. Floyd Benjamin Streeter (Metuchen, N.J., 1925), 25; John C. Schneider, "Urbanization and the Maintenance of Order: Detroit, 1824–1847," *Michigan History*, LX (1976), 268.

dedicated to preserving peace than he had for fellow Americans dedicated to destroying it.[17]

The local group of Patriots at Detroit made several attempts to invade Canada in order to assist a similarly armed contingent of Canadians who were launching their own assault. During one of these raids in February 1838, Patriots advanced as far as Pelee Island, part of British Canada, in a partially frozen Lake Erie, and seized the island. Their victory was short-lived when British militia met them on the ice and inflicted heavy casualties. Many were killed outright, and those who managed to make it to Ohio on the opposite shore of Lake Erie were met by American troops who had been ordered to stop their movements. Similar inter-border engagements took place on islands in the Detroit River, with British attacks forcing Patriot retreat to Michigan, where the men were captured by U.S. forces. The Patriots were literally caught in a transitional zone between two governments opposed to their activities.

American president Martin Van Buren was determined to honor the neutrality agreement and the "peace and order of a neighboring country" by criminalizing the activities of the Patriots. He faced harsh criticism from federal officials who opposed U.S. efforts to uphold the neutrality agreement for the same reasons declared by the Patriots. Senator Caleb Cushing pronounced that, in prohibiting trade in arms and munitions across the northern border, the government of the United States proclaimed to the world that it "prevent[ed] forever the further spread of republican institutions in North America." Cushing pointed out that such controls on trade had not been exercised when Texas declared independence from Mexico, so why, he asked, did the government submit on bended knee to Britain? According to Cushing, Britain had not prevented the arms trade from its side of the border, choosing instead to supply guns to Indians who were "pensioners of Great Britain, under old war treaties," thereby keeping them in a state of readiness for invasion of the United States.[18]

British imperial agents were equally alarmed by the possibility of invasion,

17. Dr. Z. Pitcher to Hon. L. Lyon, Jan. 18, 1838, Lucius Lyon Papers.

18. Martin Van Buren, "Second Annual Message, December 3, 1838," in James D. Richardson, [comp.], *A Compilation of the Messages and Papers of the Presidents, 1789-1897*, III (New York, 1896), 486; Kenneth R. Stevens, *Border Diplomacy: The Caroline and McLeod Affairs in Anglo-American-Canadian Relations, 1837-1842* (Tuscaloosa, Ala., 1989), 44-45; Caleb Cushing, *Remarks of Mr. Cushing of Massachusetts on the Neutrality Bill Delivered in the House of Representatives, March 6 and 9, 1838* (Washington, D.C., 1838), 3-4.

not by Indians, but by Americans. However poorly organized and militarily ineffective the Patriots were in their attempts to invade Canada, the British Canadian government feared that Canada could fall to the United States. Upper Canadian lieutenant governor Sir George Arthur conjectured that, if this happened, Americans would "pour in" as they had in Texas. Arthur therefore took seriously the activities of the Patriots, imprisoning and, in some cases, executing individuals who sought to overthrow the governments of Upper and Lower Canada. As a result, Patriots and their Canadian sympathizers found themselves prisoners on both sides of the border, regardless of the country to which they claimed citizenship.[19]

Upper Canadian newspaperman and former elected official William Lyon MacKenzie, who was the highest-profile activist against the Canadian government, was jailed in the United States after fleeing to New York to avoid capture by the British. As his health declined in prison, he wrote to Van Buren, asking to be released and offering to live in any U.S. state or the Republic of Texas. Edward Theller, an Irishman who had emigrated first to Upper Canada and then to Detroit, had taken part in an attack on Sandwich and was captured by British militia and sentenced to hang. During his trial in Toronto, his consistent protestations that his status as a naturalized American citizen rendered his trial for treason illegal in Canada were ignored. His prosecutor replied that any rights possessed in his adopted country "ceased the moment he was found in arms against the government of his birth" and that, "having been born in her majesty's dominions, no subsequent act of his could release him" from perpetual allegiance; indeed, such an act amounted to "moral treason." Hundreds of American Patriots, including Theller, were sentenced alongside Canadian agitators to serve time at Van Diemen's Land (Tasmania), a British penal colony. Efforts of the American government—including Van Buren's son, working behind the scenes—to obtain the freedom of the Americans were rebuffed until the border turmoil had settled several years afterward.[20]

British officials and pro-British Canadian newspapers condemned the Patriots, referring to them as "godless American rabble" and labeling them

---

19. Stevens, *Border Diplomacy*, 7. Five years later, British minster to the United States Henry Fox would go so far as to conjecture that northern states would annex Canada as a free state to balance Texas's incorporation into the union as a slave state.

20. Charles Lindsey, *The Life and Times of Wm. Lyon Mackenzie* ..., 2 vols. (Toronto, 1862), II, 258; E[dward] A[lexander] Theller, *Canada in 1837-38*, 2 vols. (Philadelphia, 1841), I, 202-204; Tony Moore, *Death or Liberty: Rebels and Radicals Transported to Australia, 1788-1868* (Millers Point, New South Wales, Australia, 2010), 267-271.

"uncivilized" and therefore not fit to meet British soldiers. Instead, officials urged that Indians be organized to repel the invaders. Indeed, both British Canadian and Patriot leaders would ultimately seek the assistance of indigenous men all along the border during the rebellions. Hundreds of Mohawk, Wendat, and Anishinaabe (Odawa, Ojibwa, and Potawatomi) warriors joined with Upper Canadian militias in readiness to defend against Patriot incursions north of Toronto. The Patriots, for their part, actively sought an alliance with indigenous nations. In early 1839, there were reportedly 1,500 indigenous men and 1,750 Americans, Canadians, Irish, and Dutch ready for military action with the Patriots in an area that stretched from Missouri to the Illinois and Fox Rivers. Patriot general Henry Handy boasted that he had "a general knowledge" and a "social and friendly alliance" with indigenous nations in the Territories of Mississippi, Illinois, Missouri, and Wisconsin as well as with some west of the Mississippi River whom he could ostensibly persuade to fight under the Patriot banner. He had held a meeting with indigenous leaders at Detroit who, according to Handy, assured the Patriots of their military support if they would be financially compensated. There were British reports, ultimately unsubstantiated, that Michigan-based indigenous men had destroyed homes and stolen guns west of Toronto near London while shouting slogans in support of William Lyon MacKenzie and Louis-Joseph Papineau, the leaders of the rebellions in Upper and Lower Canada, respectively. The Patriots also used rumors of the destruction of local property by British-allied indigenous peoples to instill fear in and garner support from Upper Canadian residents.[21]

Patriots would go further than using the image of the indigenous warrior as a tool to gain adherents to their cause. They would also assume the identity of the mythic warrior to give symbolic meaning to their activities. In December 1837, a group of twenty Patriots, made up of both Canadians and

21. Albert B. Corey, *The Crisis of 1830-1842 in Canadian-American Relations* (New York, 1941), 92; Rev. Saltern Givins to Samuel Peters Jarvis, Dec. 13, 1837, and Colin C. Ferrie to W. H. Draper, Dec. 22, 1837, both in Colin Read and Ronald J. Stagg, eds., *The Rebellion of 1837 in Upper Canada: A Collection of Documents* (Toronto, 1985), 287–288, 333–334; Jacobs, "Land Claims Research Paper," 16; Henry Handy, quoted in Lindsey, *Life and Times of Wm. Lyon Mackenzie*, II, 236–237; Bellfy, *Three Fires Unity*, 95–96. At Coldwater, Missouri, 1,500 Indians and 500 volunteers gathered under General J. B. Stewart. At Chicago, 560 Catholic Irish came together under A. Smith. At Kankakee, 140 French Canadians were brought together under Francis Brodieau. On the Illinois and Fox Rivers, Major Luddington gathered 300 Canadians, Dutch, and Irish (Lindsey, *Life and Times of Wm. Lyon Mackenzie*, II, 237–238).

Americans and led by New York resident and former federal customs agent Bill Johnston, donned make-shift Indian costumes and attacked a British steamboat in American waters that was bound for Oswego, New York. Shouting, "Remember the Caroline," the men forcibly removed passengers and unloaded cargo before setting fire to the vessel. With their cries, the men referenced a previous incident in which the Patriot-commandeered U.S. steamboat *Caroline* had been destroyed by the British in American waters. The episode had caused large-scale condemnation in the United States and a surge of support for the Patriots by the local populace in New York. For several months afterward, Johnston and his followers continued their protests, looting and burning houses and barns. At a Patriot Congress held the next year in Cleveland, Ohio, where members from across the United States and Upper Canada met in large numbers, Bill Johnston arrived dressed again in Indian clothing and accepted the position of commodore of the Patriot navy on Lake Ontario and the Saint Lawrence River.[22]

In all likelihood, Johnston intended to replicate the symbolic acts of rebellion of the fraternal organization Sons of Liberty, whose members had donned Indian dress in 1773 and stormed a British ship in Boston's harbor, destroying the ship's cargo in protest over the levying of excessive taxes. By "playing Indian," as Philip Deloria has pointed out, Johnston transformed himself and the nature of his activities in order to solidify an abstract concept of American national identity. Johnston and the Patriots pressed carefully selected images of indigeneity into service to maintain cross-border fraternal ties and to give symbolic meaning to their rebellion against what they perceived a corrupt government. At this same point in time, Anishinaabe would follow traditional paths across the same borders, reaffirming the indigeneity of their traditional homeland and pressing into service British categorization of indigenous peoples to reconfigure communities and resist imperial control.[23]

Moving Marks of Loyalty: Potawatomi Escape to Upper Canada
Michigan's indigenous nations had reason to challenge the federal government while it attempted to maintain peace and neutrality in the face of the Patriot activities. Funds promised from treaties already settled that would have allowed them to improve their land had not been forthcoming. They were well aware that, in failing to make improvements, they risked losing

22. Corey, *Crisis of 1830–1842*, 70–71.
23. Philip J. Deloria, *Playing Indian* (New Haven, Conn., 1998), 6–7.

their acreage to speculators. In January 1837, a series of scuffles took place between Michigan Potawatomi and white settlers near Coldwater in southwestern Michigan. The Michigan Potawatomi had ceded some of their lands, but individuals of that nation still maintained holdings and a presence in the area. So, while Patriots on both sides of the border rallied to challenge the British government and evade capture by American and British forces, the Potawatomi and other Anishinaabe nations sought their own solution to white encroachment, managing as well to avoid capture by American troops and efforts of the American government to control their movements. That year, some of the Potawatomi of southwestern Michigan decided to accept the invitation of Ojibwa and Odawa groups residing at Bkejwanong (Walpole Island reserve) in Upper Canada to move to Walpole as an alternative to and escape from the policy of Indian Removal in the United States.[24]

British acceptance of the American Potawatomi in Upper Canada partly resulted from changes in the nature of the relationship between the government and indigenous nations. In 1830, lieutenant governor and colonial secretary Sir George Murray officially transferred jurisdiction of Indian Affairs in Canada from military to civilian authority. This move reflected a shift in policy from viewing indigenous peoples as allies in times of war to peoples who had to be "reclaim[ed]," as Murray described, "from a state of barbarism" and introduced to "the industrious and peaceful habits of civilized life." Murray held two distinct but equally popular ideas about the place of indigenous peoples in early-nineteenth-century society, both in the United States and Canada. One saw removal of indigenous peoples from areas of white settlement as the best hope for their survival. The other proposed their "assimilation" into settler culture. Murray would eventually decide that assimilating Indians into British culture was best. He did so at the same time the United States was proclaiming its official policy toward indigenous groups with the Indian Removal Act of 1830.[25]

Murray's successor, Sir Francis Bond Head, reversed this position during his tenure from 1836 to 1838, implementing a policy of Indian removal that had not been sanctioned by the home government in London. Head was

---

24. E. Lyon Esq. to Hon. Lucius Lyon, Jan. 25, 1838, Lucius Lyon Papers; R. David Edmunds, *The Potawatomis, Keepers of the Fire* (Norman, Okla., 1978), 261.

25. Theodore Binnema and Kevin Hutchings, "The Emigrant and the Noble Savage: Sir Francis Bond Head's Romantic Approach to Aboriginal Policy in Upper Canada, 1836–1838," *Journal of Canadian Studies/Revue d'études canadiennes*, XXXIX, no. 1 (Winter 2005), 117–118.

enamored with the idea of primitivism and the notion of the noble savage, concepts that were popular in Britain. He believed that British colonial culture was adversely affecting indigenous peoples and for their benefit they should be removed from this influence. The British and Foreign Aborigines Protection Society agreed with Head's general views and, in a voluminous report published in 1837, accused settlers of having unjustly expropriated indigenous land and of abusing indigenous peoples. The Committee, however, did not believe removal was the answer. It instead took a paternalistic tone in suggesting that indigenous groups could remain in place but needed to be protected from the greed of British settlers. The British considered Walpole crown land and wished to maintain control over the area's development by upholding the crown's proprietary relationship with Anishinaabe residents.[26]

British imperial authorities recognized the Potawatomi as Anishinaabe and therefore former British allies. Potawatomi had begun migrating to Upper Canada in 1835, when Milwaukee-based groups traveled north through Lake Michigan and into Lake Huron, arriving eventually in Penetanguishene in northern Upper Canada. More than two hundred arrived at Amherstburg, across the river from Detroit, and another small group made its way to Toronto. All of these Potawatomi pressed claims based on having assisted the British during the War of 1812. Indeed, a year earlier, the Potawatomi had foreseen the need to keep their relationship with the British in play. When they were threatened by American government agents with confiscation of the medals that had been bestowed upon them by the British, they had left these objects temporarily with a British Indian agent at Penetanguishene. Proof of their alliance with the British was sometimes literally imprinted on their bodies. Potawatomi leader Standing Spirit bared his chest to British Indian agents, exhibiting seventeen wounds that had been inflicted on his person in his defense of British interests in the war. What the citizen anxious to defend thick and foggy borders would have categorized as "cruel marks" meted out by the U.S. government in the defense of a burgeoning American nationalism would have signified something entirely different to Standing Spirit. These same marks acted as visual text that inscribed the man's bravery, served as his war history, and communicated his defiance of that same American nationalism.[27]

26. Ibid., 121, 130; *Report of the Parliamentary Select Committee on Aboriginal Tribes* ... (London, 1837), 5–8.
27. Clifton, *Prairie People*, 305; Mairin Odle, "The Human Stain: A Deep History

The Potawatomi who migrated to Walpole came as entire village communities organized around long-standing lineages. They arrived with a determination to maintain traditions and to resist attempts to missionize and educate them according to Euro-American standards. Unlike some of the Ojibwa and Odawa among whom they settled, they had not converted to Christianity and instead practiced the Midewiwin (spiritual customs of the Grand Medicine Society), alarming Baptist and Methodist missionaries at Walpole. They had not Europeanized their names, and British agents noted that there were very few "half-breeds" among them. For years to come, they would continue to live in bark and mat homes, rather than the log and frame cabins of other Anishinaabe around them. Moreover, because the Potawatomi had emigrated from the United States, they did not bear the British designation of "Treaty Indians" and were therefore not allowed to draw annuities. But they were entitled to settle at Bkejwanong nonetheless as a result of a unique stipulation made decades beforehand.[28]

Named by visiting early Europeans for the "warpoles," or carved wooden staves they observed there, Walpole, known as Bkejwanong ("where the waters divide" in Anishinaabemowin) to Anishinaabe, comprised seventeen thousand acres of diverse wetlands and fifty-eight thousand acres of land that stretched across six islands. Its location on Lake Saint Clair, bordering Michigan and Upper Canada and part of the Great Lakes water system, also allowed for easy access to Lakes Huron and Erie. During the War of 1812, several key skirmishes took place in its vicinity, making it a thoroughfare for indigenous and Euro-American groups. After that war, there was a persistent migration of groups of Potawatomi, Odawa, Sauk, Mesquakie (Fox), Kickapoo, and Ho-Chunk (Winnebago) through the area. Walpole was one of two reserves that had been set aside for the future occupation of Anishinaabe during the indeterminate period when the British and Americans held overlapping claims to land that straddled the border between Michigan and Upper Canada. When the Jay Treaty had drawn a more definite border, the status of the reserves and their purpose remained intact. This land helped to maintain the multinational character of the buffer zone and kept it propped open for the arrival of the Potawatomi.[29]

---

of Tattoo Removal," *Atlantic*, Nov. 19, 2013, http://www.theatlantic.com/technology/archive/2013/11/the-human-stain-a-deep-history-of-tattoo-removal/281630.

28. Clifton, *Prairie People*, 307–308.

29. Dean M. Jacobs, "'We Have but Our Hearts and the Traditions of Our Old Men': Understanding the Traditions and History of Bkejwanong," in Dale Standen and David

The Ojibwa, Odawa, and Potowatomi reaffirmed their status as the people of the three fires, resulting in a strengthened Anishinaabe presence in that area. When the Potawatomi of Michigan and eventually Indiana and Illinois accepted the invitation of the Odawa and Ojibwa to come to Bkejwanong, they traveled not only a well-worn and familiar route but also one that offered an alternative to forcible removal. The Indian agent at Walpole reported that three hundred Indians had come over from the American shore and that they had never wavered in their allegiance to the British, wishing to "remain under the protection of their great Father the King." The agent also made certain to mention that the Potawatomi had promised to "leave off their roving habits and become permanent residents" and that they had met with Walpole Indians to determine what tracts of land would be available. Michigan superintendent of Indian affairs Henry Rowe Schoolcraft closely observed the movement of the Potawatomi, reporting to the American government his belief that regular visits of Indians to Canada were "calculated to foster sentiments of hostility to the United States in the Indian mind." The Potawatomi had moved north and east through the buffer zone rather than west. Indeed, at the same moment they were making their journey, many Indiana Potawatomi who stayed back would be coerced in 1838 by American forces to leave their homes and travel more than six hundred miles to Kansas. Eighty people, most of them children, died of typhoid fever on this forced march. The two migrations represented two vastly different reactions to government policies calculated to control the movement and settlement of indigenous nations.[30]

The Limits of Family: The Indigenized French

The decision by the Potawatomi to relocate to Canada and reaffirm migration routes they had followed for centuries would affect other populations at Walpole and its vicinity. In 1839, several indigenized French families abandoned Walpole Island. Their departure resulted from the passage by the Upper Canada provincial legislature in 1839 of the Act for the Protection of the Lands of the Crown in This Province from Trespass and Injury. The

---

McNab, eds., *Gin Das Winan: Documenting Aboriginal History in Ontario* . . . , Occasional Papers of the Champlain Society, no. 2 (Toronto, 1996), 1; Clifton, *Prairie People*, 307–309.

30. William Jones to Colonel James Givens, July 7, 1837, William Jones Letterbook, microfilm reel MS 296, Archives of Ontario; Henry Schoolcraft, quoted in Cushing, *Remarks*, 4–5; Edmunds, *The Potawatomis*, 266–267.

Act called for the appointment of a commissioner to investigate and remove trespassers from lands set aside for the residence of designated indigenous groups and upheld the rights of the Anishinaabe to exclusive use of Bkejwanong. The land made available by the removal of those deemed trespassers would be designated for the Potawatomi, who were arriving in large numbers. The Act and resulting expulsions proved ultimately ineffective in halting squatting and improper use of indigenous land, but it did catch in its net many indigenized French who were integrated into Anishinaabe society and who were resident at Walpole.[31]

Families of the indigenized French of southern Michigan and Upper Canada had been established in the eighteenth century in the Great Lakes. Some had mobilized in the interests of their trade and families against the British during the American Revolution, although others had chosen to align themselves with British imperial interests. This brand of provisional loyalty had frustrated American and British governments in the last decade of the eighteenth century, when Euro-American and indigenous nations vied for control of the southern Great Lakes and the Ohio Valley. The indigenized French had also supported both sides in the War of 1812, maintaining a devotion to members of their extended kin networks and a hybrid identity over loyalty to a particular Euro-American nation. One such community referenced their sense of a distinct culture, proclaiming that "the English say that the French Canadians are their people and the land is theirs, but it's no such thing, we have nothing to do with the English, we are a separate people—this land is ours." The allegiance of indigenized French to family and community overrode loyalty demanded by Euro-American concepts of nation and citizenship.[32]

---

31. Richard H. Bartlett, "Mineral Rights on Indian Reserves in Ontario," *Canadian Journal of Native Studies*, III (1983), 257. David T. McNab notes that illegal use of land by non-Native outsiders continued unabated throughout the nineteenth century (McNab, *Circles of Time: Aboriginal Land Rights and Resistance in Ontario* [Waterloo, Ontario, Canada, 1999], 160–161).

32. Laplante's Speech to the Indians, Oct. 31, 1794, Miscellaneous Intercepted Correspondence, 1789–1814, *"War of 1812 Papers" of the Department of State, 1789–1815*, M588, roll 7, National Archives, Washington, D.C. I am grateful to Dennis Au for bringing this correspondence to my attention. For the unique culture of the French of the greater Detroit area, see Dennis M. Au, "The Mushrat French: The Survival of French Canadian Folklife on the American Side of *Le Détroit*," in Marcel Bénéteau, *Le Passage du Détroit: 300 ans de présence francophone / Passages: Three Centuries of Francophone Presence at Le Détroit*, ed. Marcel Bénéteau, Working Papers in the Humanities, XI (Windsor, 2003), 167–180.

The Drouillard family represented one of many extended indigenized French kinship networks with a foot in both European and indigenous worlds. François Xavier Drouillard had been born in 1806 on the southwest shore of the Detroit River, where the Jesuits had established a mission among the Huron-Petun peoples in the second decade of the eighteenth century. François's birth occurred six weeks after his cousin George Drouillard, born at Detroit of a French father and Shawnee mother, had completed his paid tenure as a guide, hunter, and interpreter on the Lewis and Clark Expedition. George's father Pierre had acted as a Huron language interpreter at Detroit and had been instrumental—much to the chagrin of British officials in the latter part of the eighteenth century—in participating in and helping to organize indigenous resistance to white settlement in the Ohio Valley. After their arrival in the Detroit area in the mid-eighteenth century, some members of the Drouillard family had made their way north and east to the area on Lake Saint Clair in the vicinity of Bkejwanong. François and his nine siblings were all raised there, along with his Uncle Thomas and Thomas's children.[33]

All members of the extended Drouillard family appear to have abandoned Walpole Island at the same time in 1839. François, his brother Joseph, and their uncle Thomas were reported by the Indian agent at Walpole as having been expelled by 1840. The family had fallen through the cracks that existed in complicated and ineffective attempts at policy making with regard to indigenous groups in Canada. Ironically, by acting or being designated "British" in matters regarding landownership, the Drouillard family might have contributed to its own expulsion from Walpole.

François's uncle Thomas had been a captain in the British army during the War of 1812. Like many military men in Canada, he had been rewarded with a gift of land after the war for his service to the crown, and the land he obtained was located at his place of residence on Walpole Island. In the larger efforts of Anishinaabe at Walpole to maintain rights to what had always been their land, and of the crown to "protect" the Anishinaabe and its own interests from unscrupulous settlers and land speculators, Thomas Drouillard, his children, nephews (including François), and niece along with other indigenized French families were likely designated as both non-Indians and

33. Christian Denissen, *Genealogy of the French Families of the Detroit River Region, Revision, 1701–1936,* 2 vols., ed. Robert L. Pilon (Detroit, 1987), I, 380; Elizabeth L. (Warner) Droulard, comp., *Genealogy of the Drouillard Families of St. Clair Co., Mich.* (Algonac, Mich., 1979), 23.

British, despite ties to Walpole. In exchange for territory lost at Walpole, the Drouillard family was given land at what would be known as Drouillard Point, located on the southeastern shore of the Detroit River where it met the Saint Clair River. Drouillard Point would eventually be populated by members of the extended Drouillard family, including François and successive generations, some of whom are still resident there today.[34]

Despite their expulsion, members of the family maintained their connection to Walpole and to the Anishinaabe even while living away from the reserve. A son of Thomas (also named Thomas) lived for periods in both Michigan and Ontario at locations close to Walpole Island. He was described as having knowledge of the languages of several tribes as well as English and French. Anishinaabe residents of Walpole made the trek across Lake Saint Clair to his home in Algonac, Michigan, walking over the ice in winter to obtain supplies and occasionally staying at his residence. Thomas's nephew François was described in his old age as "a commanding figure" with "piercing dark eyes" in "high boots, riding breeches and familiar red woolen shirt, which all guides wore to distinguish them in the woods." He was said to have had successful dealings with Indians, "with whom he was most familiar." François's son (also named François) had been born at Walpole and was nearly ten years old when the family was expelled. In his older age, the younger François would be known as a raconteur of "Indian stories" who was capable of speaking several Native languages. Indeed, when the family left Walpole, ten-year-old François was unable to speak French and only capable of speaking Anishinaabowin.[35]

Family stories relate that Anishinaabe visitors came frequently to shore at Drouillard Point and traded with the elder François. As a boy, the younger François spent several weeks at a time with the Anishinaabe, who gathered him up at Drouillard Point and took him in their canoes. As time passed, the elder François made a pivotal shift in the expression of his dual-cultured identity. He began to play the part of an Indian in a highly ritualized ceremony designed to entrench his Frenchness and Catholicism. His actions can be read as the first cracks in a gap between the French and indigenous cultural signifiers that he had combined while at Walpole and for a time after his relocation to Drouillard Point. François became a devout Roman Catholic and joined the Saint Jean Baptiste Society, an organization born during the turbulent years of the Upper and Lower Canada rebellions. During

---

34. Droulard, comp., *Genealogy of the Drouillard Families*, 26.
35. *Border Cities Star* (Windsor, Ontario), July 22, 1933.

the ceremonies of the Saint Jean Baptiste Festival, held every year on June 24, he would dress in "full Indian costume" and speak "in their language." The younger François eventually shared the role of Indian, the costume, and membership in the Society with his father. This shift reflected the mutable nature of indigeneity at play in the northern border region and the myriad ways its enactment enabled resistance to imperial governments.[36]

The Société Saint-Jean-Baptiste had been founded by the French journalist Ludger Duvernay during the ceremonies of the Saint Jean Baptiste Festival in Montreal in June 1834 as a fraternal and charitable organization composed of leading French politicians and businessmen. Its primary purpose was to encourage French Canadian men to unite to preserve their language, culture, and Roman Catholic religion against the onslaught of the English language, British customs, and Protestantism. French Canadians had imported the celebrations of Saint Jean Baptiste from France when they arrived in North America in the seventeenth century. The Saint Jean Baptiste Society elevated these celebrations to a symbolic representation of French Canadian identity in the nineteenth century, adding parade floats, plays, and picnics to the traditional lighting of bonfires and attendance of morning mass. It is difficult to know what part François and his son would have played as an Indian in the Saint Jean Baptiste Festival at Drouillard Point. If the celebrations resembled those enacted in early-twentieth-century festivals in Quebec, it might have called for the men to perform as a seventeenth-century Indian greeting French explorers and Catholic missionaries as they arrived in North America.[37]

The Society had political roots through its founder in the Patriot movement and the rebellions in Upper and Lower Canada in 1837 and 1838. Although the rebellions were ultimately quashed by the British, the Patriots succeeded in shaping a "Canadien" identity. The symbols of this identity included the maple leaf, originally adopted as the logo of the Saint Jean Baptiste Society, the song "O Canada," composed in French by a member of the

36. Interview with Diana LaBute Marrero, great-granddaughter of Francois Drouillard, Jr., May 2002 (family story); *Border Cities Star*, July 22, 1933.

37. *The Canadian Encyclopedia*, s.v. "Société Saint-Jean-Baptiste," by Richard Jones, http://www.thecanadianencyclopedia.com. H. V. Nelles describes dramatic events enacted in the summer of 1908 in Quebec to commemorate the anniversary of the arrival of Samuel Champlain. Members of local indigenous communities camped on the grounds of the festival and played the role of "grateful" and "supplicant" Indians welcoming Champlain in 1608. See Nelles, *The Art of Nation-Building: Pageantry and Spectacle at Quebec's Tercentenary* (Toronto, 1999), 164–168.

Society for the Saint Jean Baptiste Festival, and the image of the fleur-de-lis, which would eventually form part of the flag of the Province of Quebec. Like other fraternal organizations founded in the nineteenth century, including the Hunter Lodges of the British and American Patriots, the Saint Jean Baptiste Society was a civic fraternity that offered a "symbolic domain of filiation," where membership derived from a shared vision of race and nation and was "protected from the undeserving." Indigenous peoples were the farthest thing from the minds of fraternity members, but many of these organizations integrated the character of the Indian and related symbols into their rituals to signify the group's ancient and codified knowledge.[38]

François Xavier Drouillard and his son, as well as members of the Hunter Lodges and the Patriots, performed the role of Indian to challenge and at times openly rebel against British and American governments. At the same time that these groups used a symbolic concept of indigeneity in defiance of Euro-American imperial policy, the Potawatomi were reactivating the bonds of historic alliance with the British and reentering an Anishinaabe space. When Standing Spirit bared his chest to British authorities, he offered the marks on his body as a visual record of past military campaigns and resisted efforts to hold the Potawatomi within the borders of either American or British Canadian nations. By traveling the routes their families had traversed for centuries and thereby maintaining the indigeneity of the northern region, the Potawatomi kept their options open. It was, in fact, the very nature of their mobility that allowed their cultural identity to remain in play. They maintained multiple nationalities by storing their medals—the literal and material symbols of Americanness and Britishness—in the northern region. They capitalized on the British concept of portable citizenship (the idea that national identity was imprinted on the body) and carried the marks of their multiple loyalties on their person wherever they traveled.

The indigenized French of Walpole had traditionally straddled Native and Euro-American worlds, but a British Canadian government forced apart their hybridity when it legislated against their opportunity to remain part of the Native community at Walpole. Although they were designated as non-Native and relegated to a new place of residence, they would defy imperial efforts to control them by reconstituting their ties to Bkejwanong. When they joined a fraternal society that had its roots in French defiance of Anglo-Canadian politics, however, the nature of that defiance would change. As

---

38. Dana D. Nelson, *National Manhood: Capitalist Citizenship and the Imagined Fraternity of White Men* (Durham, N.C., 1998), 93; Deloria, *Playing Indian*, 60.

members of the Saint Jean Baptiste Society acting in the role of a symbolic Indian, they pledged themselves to the cause of French Canadian opposition against an Anglo-British government, rather than preserved their ties to Walpole.

Patriots, Potawatomi, and the indigenized French were thus openly expressing their desire to remain "in play" at a time when North American borders were taking shape. At this crucial moment in political relations between the United States and Britain, they traversed national boundaries, creating new communities or resituating old communities in new places. By acting out, they challenged imperial efforts to harden national borders and kept the northern region open and permeable. For Patriots and indigenized French, however, this accessibility would be only temporary.

Postscript—Tecumseh's Bones and the Reinscription of Indigeneity in the Northern Region

Lake Saint Clair, known in Anishinaabemowin as Wabasajonkasskapawa, is a heart-shaped, almost circular, body of water at the center of the Upper Canada–Michigan border region. It adjoins both the state of Michigan and the Province of Ontario and empties into the Detroit River, which in turn flows into Lake Erie. It figures as a prime location in multiple and often conflicting indigenous and Euro-American stories of the death in battle and burial of the Shawnee leader Tecumseh during the War of 1812. In 1840, American Thomas Moore crossed the border at Detroit and made his way along Lake Saint Clair, close to Walpole Island. Moore was a colleague of William Henry Harrison, and he was determined to retrieve specific material evidence that would bolster Harrison's political reputation. Harrison had been "credited" with killing Tecumseh, and Moore had come to Upper Canada to seize Tecumseh's bones as concrete proof of Harrison's fitness for the American presidency. By the time he completed his mission, Moore had not managed to locate Tecumseh's remains, but he had disinterred and transported the portions of several indigenous bodies to Detroit.[39]

According to historian Guy St-Denis, various Americans seeking public office in the years following the death of Tecumseh boasted of having killed him. Although Tecumseh's death had gone virtually unnoted by non-Native Canadians—and some of them had aided Moore in his grisly exploits—

---

39. McNab, *Circles of Time*, 154–155; Guy St-Denis, *Tecumseh's Bones* (Montreal, 2005), 10–12; Michelle A. Hamilton, *Collections and Objections: Aboriginal Material Culture in Southern Ontario, 1791–1914* (Montreal, 2010), 95–97.

Moore's escapades, when reported in Canadian newspapers, caused a collective sense of national indignation. Canadians consoled themselves that, because the location of the slain warrior's grave could not be definitively ascertained, Moore could not have succeeded in his purpose. Moore's activities set off a flush of patriotism among Canadians, who launched their own searches for Tecumseh in order to build monuments in his honor. Locating his bones and commemorating Tecumseh would become something of a cottage industry in Upper Canada in the nineteenth century. There remained multiple and conflicting stories surrounding the death and burial of Tecumseh. Local persons profited by acting as guides to the bones for the benefit of curious outsiders, but Anishinaabe continue to claim that Tecumseh's indigenous comrades buried his body soon after his death at Bkejwanong.[40]

Harrison would attain the presidency, with the support of members of Hunter Lodges across the northern border who roundly denounced Martin Van Buren, Harrison's rival, as a traitor to the Patriot cause. Ultimately, however, the Patriots were condemned as unruly, dangerous, and a threat to peace and the thriving business climate between the two countries. The Hunter Lodges ceased to exist within a few years of the end of the rebellions, and the eastern border between the United States and Canada would be finally settled with the Treaty of Webster-Ashburton in 1841. Movement across the northern boundary would continue, but the nature of that mobility, as a mindful strategy to defy or problematize citizenship, had changed. Traversing the border had kept it thick and foggy and open to a multitude of national possibilities. More than thirty years after the discussions of negotiators in Ghent, British Canadian and American imperial officials continued their efforts to mark the boundaries of nation and national identity through the manipulation of Native bodies, and indigenous peoples continued to thwart these efforts. The Haudenosaunee in New York, Ontario, and Quebec and the Anishinaabe on either side of Lake Saint Clair and the Great Lakes would press for and reinstate their own version of sovereignty, thereby appropriating a northern border created by Euro-American nations to contain them.

---

40. R. David Edmunds, *Tecumseh and the Quest for Indian Leadership* (Boston, 1984), 214–215. See also Rick Garrick, "Tecumseh Statue Unveiled on Walpole Island," *Anishinabek News*, Oct. 30, 2015, http://anishinabeknews.ca/2015/10/30/tecumseh-sculpture-unveiled-on-walpole-island (my thanks to Christy Peters for bringing this article to my attention).

"HINDOO MARRIAGE" AND NATIONAL SOVEREIGNTY IN THE EARLY-NINETEENTH-CENTURY UNITED STATES

Brian Connolly

In 1810, readers of the inaugural issue of the *Philadelphia Repertory*, a short-lived literary review, would have found—nestled among Treasury reports on American manufacturing, an open letter from Robert Fulton to the U.S. Congress concerning the navy's use of torpedoes, diplomatic reports from the House of Representatives, various accounts of "foreign intelligence," marriage and death lists, and a biography of Vladimir the Great—an account titled "Naptial Ceremonies among the Hindoos." Quasi-ethnographic, the account initially focused on the seemingly exotic rituals of the ceremony. The bride was "given" to the bridegroom by her father as a "donation"; the bridegroom clothed the bride, at which point they were tied together; "oblations to fire" were made, after which the bride tread on a "stone and mullar," then circled the fire in seven steps with the bridegroom. After all the spectators were dismissed and the marriage was "complete and irrevocable," the bridegroom identified the "polar star" for the bride, which served as "an emblem of stability." The couple remained at the bride's father's home for three more days, after which they made their way, in "solemn procession," to the home of the bridegroom, where they were "welcomed by his kindred."[1]

Accounts like this one of Hindoo marriage and Hindoo kinship were common in the first decades of the nineteenth century. Yet what are we to make of them? And what are we to make of the context of such an article like that in the *Philadelphia Repertory*, surrounded as it was by the goings on of the state and the economy? The editor explained that "religion and morality are the great pillars of national prosperity." What might stories of Hindoo marriage have to do with the politics of sovereignty that were being played out in the other articles? Moreover, what was the relationship between the duty

---

I would like thank Joan Scott, Anver Emon, Nicole Eustace, and the two anonymous readers for critical commentary.

1. The Editor, "Preliminary Observations," *Philadelphia Repertory*, May 5, 1810, 1; Asiatic Researcher, "Naptial Ceremonies among the Hindoos," ibid., 8.

and obligations of Hindoo kinship and the duty and obligations to be found in the legal discourse of early-nineteenth-century domestic relations?[2]

At first glance, the article appears to be an exotic account of a foreign marriage, one more instance in the annals of Orientalism. And it may well be that, but in the early nineteenth century it was something more, too. These descriptions of Hindoo marriage were regulatory—they articulated the limits of legitimate marriage and kinship by describing what fell on the other side of that limit. Such representations offered a kind of negative pedagogy; duty and obligation were also paramount but in ways incompatible with liberal democracy, particularly in terms of consent. If that was one manner in which Hindoo marriage worked, it was also relevant in relation to international law and national sovereignty. Across the first decades of the nineteenth century, the law of nations and private international law were undergoing profound transformations. These changes were particularly apparent with regard to marriage.

In the initial description of the ceremony, the entire marriage was ensconced in a broad, collective network of kinship—the bride was given to the bridegroom by her father as a donation, suggesting the lineaments of a gift economy; the couple stayed at the bride's father's home and then moved to the bridegroom's home, where they were met by all his kin. The author then offered some contextual analysis of Hindoo marriage. "Among the Hindoos," the author wrote, "a girl is married before the age of puberty." More than custom, "the law … censures the delay of her marriage beyond the tenth year." Because the bride was so young, as, frequently, was the bridegroom, it was "rare that a marriage should be consummated until long after its solemnization." Moreover, the author suggested that such young marriages were related to something analogous to original sin, which marked the marriage as explicitly and primarily religious. "The recital of prayers on this occasion constitutes it a religious ceremony; and it is the first of those that are performed for the purpose of expiating the sinful taint which a child is supposed to contract in the womb of its mother."[3]

Even as this arranged child marriage worked to create distance between American marriage and Hindoo marriage, the author noted the "laudable motive" of the father. It arose "from a sense of duty incumbent upon a father"—the obligation to find a husband was a "debt" he owed his daughter, a "notion … strongly inculcated by Hindoo legislators." This complex of duty,

---

2. The Editor, "Preliminary Observations," ibid., May 5, 1810, 1.
3. Asiatic Researcher, "Naptial Ceremonies," ibid., 8.

obligation, and debt had its problems, however; parents "do not, perhaps, sufficiently consult [the daughter's] domestic felicity." If her husband died young, for instance, she would be, by law, "condemned to virgin widowhood for the period of her life." And yet, if both survived into adulthood, they might never outrun "the habitual bickerings of their infancy." Arranged child marriage, then, was both a laudable action by a duty-bound father and one that, in ignoring the daughter's situation and dispensing with any notion of consent, took duty and obligation too far, in part as an effort to negotiate a situation brought on by laws and legislators.[4]

The first three decades of the nineteenth century were particularly vexatious in terms of national community, nationalism, and national sovereignty. The War of 1812, sitting at the midpoint of this period, signified the problems for both national community and national sovereignty. The United States waged a popular but controversial war, one that Alan Taylor has referred to as a civil war. The print culture that has been influentially linked to the rise of nationalism by Benedict Anderson was in formation, but, although it perhaps was beginning to envision a nation, it was not yet close to constituting that imagined national community. Indeed, as Trish Loughran has argued, the emergent print culture was regionally rather than nationally oriented. And national sovereignty, on the global stage, was being asserted and potentially secured in conflicts like the War of 1812 and imperial projects like the Louisiana Purchase. The Barbary conflicts tested U.S. sovereignty in the Mediterranean, and, in 1823, the Monroe Doctrine, for all of its subsequent influence, stood as something of a compensatory performative utterance. Which is to say, even if the nation is never a fully secured and stable entity, this early period in the nineteenth century was particularly troublesome. How an emergent liberal democracy was to establish and consolidate the nation and maintain its attendant sovereignty, especially at a moment in which sovereignty had shifted, at least in part, to the individual and the people as opposed to the state or the monarch, remained an open question.[5]

---

4. Ibid.

5. Alan Taylor, *The Civil War of 1812: American Citizens, British Subjects, Irish Rebels, and Indian Allies* (New York, 2011). See also Nicole Eustace, *1812: War and the Passions of Patriotism* (Philadelphia, 2012). On regional print culture, see Trish Loughran, *The Republic in Print: Print Culture in the Age of U.S. Nation Building, 1770–1870* (New York, 2007). Carroll Smith-Rosenberg has argued that early national political periodicals and newspapers were sites of contestation on national identity; see Smith-Rosenberg, *This Violent Empire: The Birth of an American National Identity* (Chapel Hill, N.C., 2010). The Barbary conflicts also foregrounded American engagement with

This essay addresses cultural preoccupations with Hindoo marriage as a response to a crisis of sovereignty in a liberal democracy that, far from being resolved in formal law, was there exacerbated. Marriage was frequently invoked as a stabilizing institution—it regulated romantic love and desire, modeled consensual relations, organized the transmission of property, and, in ratifying the conjugal couple, created a nuclear family organized around duty, obligation, and affection that would, ideally, produce proper liberal democratic citizens. Yet, that complex of duty and obligation was never particularly clear. In what manner would the duties and obligations produce consenting liberal subjects, proper citizens of the democratic Republic, and when would those duties and obligations slip into an antiliberal, antidemocratic authoritarianism, reproducing a kind of sovereignty in the father that had supposedly been dispensed with by the Revolution and the rise of popular sovereignty?

In both interstate law and international law, jurists and treatise writers codified a legal doctrine in which a marriage legally contracted or celebrated in one U.S. state or in one nation was to be recognized as valid, with few exceptions, everywhere. Although this doctrine has been addressed with regard to interstate issues—the federal disorder of domestic relations law was one of its signal features—less attention has been paid to its international context. This doctrine potentially opened American borders to a plethora of marital forms that would have violated U.S. marriage and domestic relations laws. Representations of Hindoo marriage, in this context, worked as supplements to the law, resolving this constitutive contradiction in national

---

Islam in the early Republic. Although outside the scope of this essay, it is worth noting that the "Mahometan" was frequently conflated with the Hindoo. On the Barbary conflicts, see Lawrence A. Peskin, *Captives and Countrymen: Barbary Slavery and the American Public, 1785–1816* (Baltimore, 2009). On American representations of Islam, see Timothy Marr, *The Cultural Roots of American Islamicism* (Cambridge, 2006). For a cultural reading of the Monroe Doctrine, one that has influenced my approach here, see Gretchen Murphy, *Hemispheric Imaginings: The Monroe Doctrine and Narratives of U.S. Empire* (Durham, N.C., 2005). Liberal democracy is a common enough term, one that suggests the confluence of property rights, market relations, and equal representation before the law. Yet here the term registers the conflict between the liberal individual and the democratic people. The aims and desires of the liberal subject and the collective subject of democracy were not always analogous and were frequently in conflict with one another. The discourse of marriage, broadly construed, aimed to resolve this tension so that individual desire was channeled into monogamous, consensual marriage, which would, again ideally, lead to the production of the nuclear family and the virtue therein necessary to the order of the collective, democratic subject.

sovereignty. If marriage ideally stabilized individuals, then this legal doctrine potentially opened U.S. borders to marital forms that would undermine the conservative and regulative force of marriage in making liberal democratic citizens.[6]

The era of the War of 1812 was a particularly fertile juncture for thinking through issues of marriage, sovereignty, law, and U.S. relations with India. The early nineteenth century was a period of change for domestic relations law. On the one hand, as the United States pursued imperial expansion westward, a number of new states entered the Union with their own particular domestic relations laws, ones that would, at times, be in conflict with the laws of other states. Moreover, the understanding of domestic relations law was itself transforming. As Holly Brewer notes, the late eighteenth and early nineteenth century witnessed "the development of democratic-republican ideas about consent" that would greatly affect legal norms of marriage and domestic relations. On the other hand, this change was mirrored by the broad discourse on the relationship between marriage and the nation. As Nicole Eustace puts it, "Lacking true natal ties, nationalists in the era of the early republic had to develop deliberately the feelings they could not inherit naturally.... Promoting patriotism in a new democracy, they decided to foreground the future over the past, the chosen love of heterosexual romance over the obligatory obeisance of filial duty." The negative examples of Hindoo marriage worked to normalize love and heterosexual romance while also policing the boundaries of international marriage law.[7]

At the same time, consent and democracy suggested dramatic changes in sovereignty, from a more classical, pre-Revolutionary notion associated with a sovereign to the increasingly democratic popular sovereignty that teetered on the brink of licentiousness. Proper marriage and kinship would, according to many, curtail that license. Moreover, the War of 1812, with its attempted imperial land grab and insistence on neutrality rights, suggested the precariousness of U.S. sovereignty, one most tenuous and negotiable with regard to European nations (as Native Americans were excluded from these contests over sovereignty while being wholly implicated in them). The debates over international marriage laws coupled with representations of

---

6. Michael Grossberg, *Governing the Hearth: Law and the Family in Nineteenth-Century America* (Chapel Hill, N.C., 1985); Hendrik Hartog, *Man and Wife in America: A History* (Cambridge, Mass., 2000).

7. Holly Brewer, "The Transformation of Domestic Law," in Michael Grossberg and Christopher Tomlins, eds., *The Cambridge History of Law in America*, 3 vols. (New York, 2011), I, 322; Eustace, *1812*, 28–29.

Hindoo marriage provided another space for working out national sovereignty while reinforcing that such sovereignty was implicitly white and secular. Finally, it was in the early nineteenth century that U.S. writings about India shifted from those primarily penned by ministers attempting to establish commercial relations to those crafted by missionaries who evinced a greater interest in the ethnography of kinship as an index of civilization.[8]

Sovereignty and the Law

Before exploring the American construction and uses of Hindoo marriage, it will be useful to review the place of marriage within international law. In a critique of the concept of sovereignty, the anthropologist Brian Goldstone has written of "the innumerable doors upon which the word sovereignty is inscribed." By the late eighteenth century, sovereignty was inscribed on at least four doors in the United States: the people (popular sovereignty / democracy), the individual, the states, and the nation. These were overlapping spheres of sovereignty—particularly after the Constitution replaced the Articles of Confederation, there was a productive tension between the states and the nation, which made for a federal union. The seemingly commonplace notion of power being derived from the people was, as numerous scholars have noted, not simple. One can see this complexity, to give one instance, in the odd temporality of the Constitution—in precisely that moment at which the Constitution claimed to derive its power from "the People," it also constituted the people as an (in)coherent body. Few people ever believed that there was an easily discerned voice of the people, of course, but this notion was even further complicated as more and more emphasis, in the political, social, and cultural domains, was placed on the autonomous individual, or liberal subject. The coherence of the people was increasingly fractured by individual desire.[9]

---

8. On Native Americans and the law of nations, see Eliga H. Gould, *Among the Powers of the Earth: The American Revolution and the Making of a New World Empire* (Cambridge, Mass., 2012), 182. On this shift from merchant to missionary accounts of the Indian subcontinent, see Michael A. Verney, "An Eye for Prices, An Eye for Souls: Americans in the Indian Subcontinent, 1784–1838," *Journal of the Early Republic*, XXXIII (2013), 397–431.

9. Brian Goldstone, "Life after Sovereignty," *History of the Present: A Journal of Critical History*, IV (2014), 97, 100. Goldstone enters a long-standing debate on sovereignty in political theory by engaging with Michel Foucault's well-known claim in a 1977 interview that "what we need ... is a political philosophy that isn't erected around the problem of sovereignty, nor therefore around the problems of law and prohibition" (Fou-

This disjuncture in sovereignty, where each location of sovereign power slipped to another one, not through a hierarchical series, but rather through a network, was not necessarily figured as a problem. Indeed, it was the condition of political sovereignty in the United States. As Michael Hardt and Antonio Negri write, modern U.S. sovereignty offers a break with the religious, transcendent notions of the past: "The new sovereignty can arise ... only from the constitutional formation of limits and equilibria, checks and balances, which both constitutes a central power and maintains power in the hands of the multitude." This is well-tread ground, but it is worth noting that such a conception of sovereignty both allows for the consolidation of power in national and state representative bodies while also holding out the possibility of more democratic, dispersed sovereignty. One might think, for example, of Shays's Rebellion in the late eighteenth century as an instance of power residing in the multitude and precipitating a crisis in sovereignty.[10]

These issues of sovereignty overlap with one another, and they do so of necessity—it is precisely that tension, not only between state and nation but also between individual and people, that constituted sovereignty in the

---

cault, "Truth and Power," in *Power/Knowledge: Selected Interviews and Other Writings, 1972–1977,* ed. Colin Gordon, trans. Gordon et al. [New York, 1980], 120–121). Goldstone, following from Foucault, is critical of the reinvigoration of work on sovereignty, especially the work of German political philosopher Carl Schmitt. See, for example, Schmitt, *Political Theology: Four Chapters on the Concept of Sovereignty,* trans. George Schwab (Chicago, 2005); Giorgio Agamben, *Homo Sacer: Sovereign Power and Bare Life,* trans. Daniel Heller-Roazen (Stanford, Calif., 1998). For a statement on modern sovereignty that invokes the U.S. Constitution as a model, see Michael Hardt and Antonio Negri, *Empire* (Cambridge, Mass., 2000), 160–172. For a classic statement on medieval sovereignty, in which sovereign power rested squarely in the figure of the sovereign/monarch, see Ernst H. Kantorowicz, *The King's Two Bodies: A Study in Mediaeval Political Theology* (Princeton, N.J., 1997). On this temporality, or paradox, in popular sovereignty, Michael Warner writes, "By constituting the government, the people's text literally constitutes the people.... writing gives original existence to its author." See Warner, *The Letters of the Republic: Publication and the Public Sphere in Eighteenth-Century America* (Cambridge, Mass., 1990), 102. This type of paradox, contradiction, or instability in sovereignty lies at the heart of this essay, which tracks the international problems of assuming marriage will resolve the paradox. For more on this feature of sovereignty, see Jason Frank, *Constituent Moments: Enacting the People in Postrevolutionary America* (Durham, N.C., 2010).

10. Hardt and Negri, *Empire,* 161. For a less theoretical and more empirical documenting of this articulation of sovereignty, and one that is quite important to my own discussion of the law of nations below, see Peter Onuf and Nicholas Onuf, *Federal Union, Modern World: The Law of Nations in an Age of Revolutions, 1776–1814* (Madison, Wis., 1993). For a more expansive study, see Gould, *Among the Powers of the Earth.*

early Republic. As multiple scholars have pointed out, the U.S. Constitution and the principles of federal union that follow from it were a radical break with past conceptions of sovereignty, but they were not a rejection of sovereignty as such. Of particular concern here is the place of marriage and family, which do not figure into discussions of sovereignty and international law frequently. Yet marriage and family were of great significance at both the people / individual level and the state / nation level of sovereignty.

Consensual, monogamous marriage and the affectionate nuclear family it was presumed to produce were pedagogic institutions for the production of liberal democratic citizens and subjects. The private, intimate space of the nuclear family was a product of proper marriage, and as such it cultivated consenting, affectionate individuals with proper attachments to the nation and the virtuous sensibilities necessary to the ordered workings of popular sovereignty. As the literary critic Elizabeth Maddock Dillon has written, "The public sphere produces privacy insofar as it looks to the intimate sphere as both origin and end of freedom: exercising freedom of choice in love and marriage, for instance, serves to illustrate the freedom and basic humanity of the bourgeois subject." Here, then, marriage regulated both the democratic mass and the liberal individual.[11]

Moreover, crises of national sovereignty were frequently represented in terms of marriage. As Nicole Eustace has argued in relation to the War of 1812, the impropriety of British aggression, particularly concerning impressment, was frequently represented as a violation of marriage, with sailors and soldiers separated from their wives and families. If marriage worked to produce proper liberal democratic (and republican) citizens, citizens whose consent was not only recognized in marriage but who were trained in its proper exercise by being reared in the affectionate family that supposedly followed from such marriages, then the potential for breaking up families through impressment and other acts of sovereign aggression threatened the family and consent itself. Marriage thus sat athwart questions of sovereignty in this period: although it was on the margins of formal discussions of state sovereignty, it nonetheless was the primary mechanism for establishing an

---

11. Elizabeth Maddock Dillon, *The Gender of Freedom: Fiction of Liberalism and the Literary Public Sphere* (Stanford, Calif., 2004), 35. The literature on marriage in the early Republic is vast; most relevant here is Nancy F. Cott, *Public Vows: A History of Marriage and the Nation* (Cambridge, Mass., 2000), chap. 1. For a classic statement, see Jan Lewis, "The Republican Wife: Virtue and Seduction in the Early Republic," *William and Mary Quarterly*, 3d Ser., XLIV (1987), 689–721.

elusive notion of order among the people and individuals and thus, in holding out the possibility of order and a pedagogy of consent, was central to the articulation of sovereignty.[12]

Questions of state and national sovereignty, however, were of a seemingly different order. Since the Declaration of Independence, the United States had sought not only the conditions of individual liberty but also the conditions of national sovereignty within an international community of nations. Indeed, in the words of the Declaration, the United States sought to be counted "among the powers of the earth." This desire necessitated engagement with the law of nations, or what came to be called "international law" after Jeremy Bentham's invention of the term in 1780. From the late eighteenth century through the first decades of the nineteenth century, the law of nations was radically revised, owing in no small part to the emergence of the United States on the international scene, the French Revolution, and the Napoleonic Wars in Europe. The law of nations, as presented in Emmerich de Vattel's influential *Law of Nations; or, The Principles of Natural Law Applied to the Conduct and to the Affairs of Nations and of Sovereigns* (1758), was derived from and often synonymous with the law of nature. It was a series of principles that ideally guided interactions between nations but, derived as it was from the law of nature, transcended and preceded the existence of nations themselves. Thus, the law of nations was more principle than law. For Vattel and others, its enforceability derived from the perpetuation of a balance of power in Europe. The law of nations would help to perpetuate peace, but its existence rested on a balance of power, making it a rather tautological proposition. The law of nations, for the most part, dealt with the business of international politics—treaties, commerce, maritime rights, and war.[13]

With the Napoleonic Wars, the balance of power in Europe, already quite fragile, disappeared. Many commentators saw the law of nations as doomed, an increasingly irrelevant relic from a prior era of naturalism. Bentham, however, just as the United States was emerging as an independent nation, renamed the law of nations "*international* law," envisioning its basis as posi-

---

12. Eustace, *1812*, 76–92.

13. Jeremy Bentham, *An Introduction to the Principles of Morals and Legislation, Printed in the Year 1780, and Now First Published* (London, 1789), 6; David Armitage, "The Declaration of Independence and International Law," *WMQ*, 3d Ser., LIX (2002), 39–64. As Eliga Gould puts it, "The law of nations ... was neither coherent nor binding"; see Gould, *Among the Powers of the Earth*, 5.

tive law. Both Bentham and Immanuel Kant described international bodies of positive law that would regulate international relations, presumably to compensate for the haziness and imprecision, the incoherence, even, of the naturalistic version of the law of nations.[14]

In the early nineteenth century, the United States, particularly in the person of James Madison, contributed to these articulations of a positivist international law (although in the United States the use of the term "law of nations" persisted). These changes in international law recapitulated two long-standing issues. First, if the basis of international law was changing, its preoccupations remained relatively the same—treaties, commerce, maritime rights, and war. Second, international law remained a mechanism by which national sovereignty was established, ostensibly creating a community of nations that could recognize and acknowledge national sovereignty on an international stage.

The American intervention here was important for both the future of international law and the relationship between marriage law and national sovereignty. For Madison, the solution to the crisis in the law of nations was not simply a reliance on positive law, although that was quite important. Positive international law, for Madison, included "learned treatises, treaties, customary ministerial practices, and even judicial decisions." For positivism to work in the law of nations—and, to be clear, positivism rested on positively enunciated and codified laws created by nations rather than the ambiguities of a natural law that would be realized by the use of reason—Madison argued for a principle of "federal union," of which the United States was the model. As Peter Onuf and Nicholas Onuf write, "A regime of law depended on the persistence of *artificial* conditions—a balance of power, a community of interests among sovereigns, a common set of values." The new artificial condition that Madison proposed was, essentially, that the form of the United States, the relationship between states and nation realized and constituted in the Constitution, be universalized, particularly in Europe. The

---

14. This paragraph and the next one draw on Armitage, "Declaration of Independence," *WMQ*, 3d Ser., LIX (2002), 54–62; and Onuf and Onuf, *Federal Union, Modern World*. For a good overview of the long history of the United States and international law, see Eileen P. Scully, "The United States and International Affairs, 1789–1919," in Grossberg and Tomlins, eds., *Cambridge History of Law in America*, II, 604–642. It is worth noting that the law of nations, despite the historical shift of the period under consideration here, still has great bearing on law today. For a deft handling of the subject, see Jeremy Waldron, *"Partly Laws Common to All Mankind": Foreign Laws in American Courts* (New Haven, Conn., 2012).

principle of union, the networked notion of sovereignty, would, according to Madison, make an international body of law more likely to work than something like a balance of power. That this federal union, or republic of Europe, never materialized as the basis of international law is largely irrelevant. That Madison proposed the federal structure of U.S sovereignty as the basis of international law matters a great deal.[15]

Marriage was not part of the general discourse of the law of nations for the simple reason that it was considered part of the law of persons, not the law of nations. Nations could enter into treaties with one another, they could maintain commercial relations with one another, but they could not marry one another. Yet its absence from the law of nations does not mean that there were no international legal issues concerning marriage; moreover, some of the same issues that haunted the law of nations, particularly the paradox in national sovereignty, animated international marriage law, or what would later in the nineteenth century come to be called private international law. Thus, the absence of marriage from the law of nations has sequestered marriage in discussions of national sovereignty, but not because it lacks importance. On the contrary, it was the figuration of marriage as a special kind of contract that separated it from the law of nations. As the legal scholars Janet Halley and Kerry Rittich write,

> Family and family law are often treated as occupying a unique and autonomous domain—as exceptional—and for a wide variety of reasons: they are unique because (unlike the market) they house intimate, private, emotional, and vulnerable relationships; they are unique because they preserve (against modernity and/or the global and foreign) the traditional, the national, the indigenous; they are unique because (as against the secular) they derive from sacred command.

This is a useful summary of the ideological pretensions of marriage and marriage law in the early Republic, yet the legal record also exceeds it. The exceptional and supposedly private status of marriage and family did not insulate it from international law and the concerns of national sovereignty. Indeed, the discussions of interstate and international marriage law sounded quite

---

15. Onuf and Onuf, *Federal Union*, 193, 202. Madison's ideas were quite influential to the American lawyer Henry Wheaton, who wrote one of the most important works on international law of the nineteenth century. See Wheaton, *Elements of International Law: With a Sketch of the History of the Science*, 2 vols. (London, 1836).

similar to those of the law of nations. It was precisely the special status of marriage that opened the borders of the United States to foreign marriages in a bid for international recognition of American sovereignty. Moreover, this relative openness of the border was derived, in part, from the conflation of the interstate and the international in terms of marriage law.[16]

A paradox should be apparent here, one that mattered as much in the law of nations as it did in international marriage law. To claim national sovereignty does not mean absolute authority, even though most commentators insisted on the inviolability of national sovereignty. Rather, to claim national sovereignty meant consent to subordinate a nation to an international body of law, even if international law had no formal power to enforce its laws within the borders of any individual nation. In other words, to be a sovereign nation was to consent to limits on one's own sovereignty. And, with this gap in sovereignty, constituted precisely in the legal ordering of marriage, more fluid forms of cultural policing would work to shore up the boundaries of sovereign power.

Marriage and the Conflict of Laws

To get at the legal discourse on marriage and sovereignty in the early Republic, and why something like representations of Hindoo marriage were needed as a supplement to the law, the following discussion will focus on two trials from the second decade of the nineteenth century in Massachusetts

---

16. Janet Halley and Kerry Rittich, "Critical Directions in Comparative Family Law: Genealogies and Contemporary Studies of Family Law Exceptionalism," *American Journal of Comparative Law*, LVIII (2010), 754. It is worth noting that Halley and Rittich offer this summary of domestic ideology and separate spheres in order to unpack its binary assumptions. The shift from the law of nations to international law complicated this ideology with the emergence of private international law. So, for example, whereas Vattel only incidentally mentioned marriage, Henry Wheaton addressed international marriage law in the context of the broader field, as did Joseph Story in *Commentaries on the Conflict of Laws* ... (Boston, 1834), discussed below. And, as Nancy Cott has persuasively demonstrated, marriage was and is not a private relation; it is a public one constituted by the state. Cott writes: "In the form of the law and state enforcement, the public sets the terms of marriage, says who can and cannot marry, who can officiate, what obligations and rights the agreement involves, whether it can be ended and if so, why and how.... From the founding of the United States to the present day, assumptions about the importance of marriage and its appropriate form have been deeply implanted in public policy, sprouting repeatedly as the nation took over the continent and established terms for the inclusions and exclusion of new citizens." See Cott, *Public Vows*, 2.

and New York, respectively, and on an influential treatise from the 1830s that systematized the legal principles outlined in these two cases. Taken together, the legal cases—one involving poor laws, paupers, race, and marriage, and the other concerning the marriage of "lunatics"—at the local and state level enunciated the means by which foreign marriages could demand recognition and legitimacy in the United States. The treatise, Joseph Story's influential *Commentaries on the Conflict of Laws*, organized these decisions into a principle of adjudicating conflicting marriage laws at both the interstate and international levels.

The trials and Story's treatise all relied on the exaggerated force of marriage to establish order in the early Republic. As Theophilus Parsons, chief justice of the Massachusetts Supreme Judicial Court, wrote in an opinion from 1810, "Marriage is unquestionably a civil contract, founded in the social nature of man, and intended to regulate, chasten and refine the intercourse between the sexes; and to multiply, preserve and improve the species." Emphasizing its importance to civil society, Parsons was insistent on its relation to "the civil magistrate . . . to guard against fraud, surprise and seduction." Parsons's opinion was emblematic precisely because it was so derivative—legists, jurists, treatise writers, and lawyers during this period all argued that a legally recognized marriage was valid everywhere, regardless of its offense to local morals or social practices.[17]

This legal conundrum was apparent in an 1818 case that ultimately found its way to the Massachusetts Supreme Judicial Court and became something of a touchstone for subsequent discussions of marriage and conflict of laws. Sometime before 1770, Ishmael Coffee, a mixed-race man living in Massachusetts, and a white woman (unnamed in the case report) desired to marry each other. Massachusetts, however, prohibited interracial marriages. In order to get around this legal prohibition, Coffee and the woman went to Rhode Island, where such marriages were not legally prohibited, married each other, and then returned to Massachusetts. Later, they were legally deemed paupers, and the town of Medway sued the town of Needham, their place of legal residence, for support. In order to avoid the expense, Needham claimed their marriage was void because it violated the law of Massachusetts both at the time they were married and at the time of trial. The judge in the initial trial, held in 1818, declared that a marriage legally contracted in Rhode Island was, of necessity, to be recognized in Massachu-

---

17. Milford v. Worcester, 7 Mass. 48, 52–53 (1810).

setts, regardless of whether it was legal in Massachusetts or of the manner in which the conjugal couple had gone about the marriage. In this case, the judge suggested that whether or not Ishmael Coffee and his wife had simply gone to Rhode Island to avoid Massachusetts's law was, from a legal standpoint, irrelevant.

The Supreme Judicial Court upheld the verdict and did so in rather expansive language. The chief justice of the Court, Isaac Parker, wrote, "It is a principle adopted for general convenience and security, that a marriage, which is good according to the laws of the country where it is entered into, shall be valid in any other country." This was no casual interpretation. Rather, "this principle is considered so essential, that even when it appears that the parties went in to another state to evade the laws of their own country, the marriage in the foreign state shall nevertheless be valid in the country where the parties live." Parker, dealing with a case of interstate marriage, slipped easily from the language of states to the language of nations, suggesting that the legal doctrine that adjudicated the conflict of marriage laws between states was equally applicable to similar cases between nations. Here, Madison's principle for the law of nations, whereby federal union became the basis for international law, was played out in marriage law, or private international law. Moreover, Coffee's marriage threatened the racial order of the state and the nation. The law nonetheless found the marriage legitimate because it was legally contracted in another state.[18]

This case suggested a specific approach to conflicting marriage laws: if they were legally recognized, in the proper manner, where celebrated, they were to be recognized nearly everywhere. Parker's slip from state to nation suggested that this was both an interstate and international issue. The history of marriage law and the disorder from state to state is well known. Yet, if this was disorder, it was, as both Parsons and Parker suggested, in the service of greater stability. It was better to let a marriage legally contracted elsewhere stand, even if it violated state law, than to risk introducing the specter of arbitrary separations by the state. The international issue offered a potentially greater threat: if a marriage was legally recognized in another nation, yet violated a U.S. statute, should it be recognized in the United States? If so, were there any limits to this recognition? Parker suggested a limit in his 1819 opinion. This principle, "if without any restriction, then it might be that incestuous marriages might be contracted, between citizens of a state where

---

18. Medway v. Needham, 16 Mass. 157, 159 (1819).

they were held unlawful and void, in countries where they were not prohibited." This, Parker suggested, could not be tolerated, but he did little in 1819 to set the legal groundwork for such an exception.[19]

That groundwork was left to Chancellor James Kent, who, in 1820, in a case of lunatic marriage before the New York State Court of Chancery, elaborated on the exceptions to the principle underlying the conflict of laws. Put simply, only incest and polygamy were universal exceptions, meaning that, if an incestuous or polygamous marriage was legally recognized somewhere in the United States or the world, it did not require legal recognition in any state in America. Although the trial itself concerned the annulment of the marriage of a "lunatic," Kent's opinion was much more concerned with the jurisdictional expansion of the court of chancery. It ranged over a broad expanse of marriage and domestic relations law and became a touchstone of domestic relations law in the nineteenth century. According to Kent, what constituted legitimate marriages could vary from nation to nation (or state to state), but both incest (a very narrow definition of incest, which included only consanguine relatives in the lineal line and siblings) and polygamy were universally prohibited.[20]

Unlike most marriage laws, the prohibition of incest (and polygamy, which occasioned much less commentary from Kent) was "of absolute, uniform, and universal obligation." It was put in place to ensure the purity, obligations, and hierarchies of the family.

---

19. Medway v. Needham, 16 Mass. 161 (1819). Hendrik Hartog writes: "Disorder may have been the rule in law and in many personal lives. Nonetheless, this was the country in which Americans lived their marital lives—one with many jurisdictions with imperfect forms of policing and regulation, with a national post office and a developing communication structure, yet with inadequate and locally based forms of property and marriage recordation." See Hartog, *Man and Wife in America: A History* (Cambridge, Mass., 2000), 19. See also Michael Grossberg, *Governing the Hearth: Law and the Family in Nineteenth-Century America* (Chapel Hill, N.C., 1985).

20. Wightman v. Wightman, 4 Johns. Ch. 343, 348 (1820). "Lunatic" was a legal category here. Lack of the use of reason was one of the common law incapacities that made marriages void *ab initio*. Kent's opinion in a case that would otherwise have been lost to obscurity was cited in many influential legal treatises in the nineteenth century. A partial list includes Story, *Commentaries;* Joel Prentiss Bishop, *Commentaries on the Law of Marriage and Divorce, and Evidence in Matrimonial Suits* (Boston, 1852); James Schouler, *A Treatise on the Law of Husband and Wife* (Boston, 1882). I discuss Kent's opinion at greater length in *Domestic Intimacies: Incest and the Liberal Subject in Nineteenth-Century America* (Philadelphia, 2014), 99–107.

> It grows out of the institution of families, and the rights and duties, habits and affections, flowing from that relation, and which may justly be considered as part of the law of our nature, as *rational* and *social* beings. Marriages among such near relations, would not only lead to domestic licentiousness, but by blending in one object, duties and feelings incompatible with each other, would perplex and confound the duties, habits, and affections proceeding from the family state, impair the perception and corrupt the purity of moral taste, and do violence to the moral sentiments of mankind.

Kent claimed the universality of the incest prohibition as a means to ensure the proper duties and obligations of the family. He assumed these were self-evident, as did many writers on the topic in this era. Yet, in an era that increasingly lauded consent, autonomy, and the desire of the liberal subject, what exactly did Kent mean when he wrote of duties and obligations in the family? Which kinds of obligations and duties were incompatible with the production and effective regulation of the liberal democratic subject?[21]

The Legality of Marriage and the Sovereignty of Nations

Kent's opinion was shot through with questions of jurisdiction, territoriality, and sovereignty. In particular, similar to the problem of the law of nations, especially insofar as it was derived from the natural law, it was unclear where the jurisdictional authority came from to enforce such a universal prohibition against incest and polygamy. Moreover, how did this question of jurisdictional authority affect the sovereignty of nations and the territorial mobility of legally contracted marriages? These questions were most clearly answered in Joseph Story's 1834 *Commentaries on the Conflict of Laws*, which systematized decades of American, English, and Continental legal thought. If Vattel, Madison, and others who attempted to articulate a transcendent body of international law were concerned with nations, Story, in summarizing the conflict of laws was, in large part, concerned with national law and the mobility of persons. Put differently, what kinds of laws governed the actions of migrants? Were the laws that had governed them in the nation in which they were subjects or citizens still in force when they entered a new nation? Moreover, if they were still in force, what might this mean for the new nation in which the migratory person had taken up residence? Although, according to Story, the "Earth has long since been divided

---

21. Wightman v. Wightman, 4 Johns. Ch. 350 (1820).

into distinct nations," the necessity of a doctrine to adjudicate the conflict of laws was of relatively modern provenance. "In the present times, without some general rules of right and obligation, recognised by civilized nations to govern their intercourse with each other," Story wrote, "the most serious mischiefs and most injurious conflicts would arise." "The conflict of laws," then, would be a heuristic device for adjudicating those moments when the laws of two nations, or two states or provinces within a nation, were in conflict with each other.[22]

Although the conflict of laws concerned nations, it was primarily addressed to the law of persons. Indeed, Story even called it "private international law, since it is chiefly seen and felt in its application to the common business of private persons, and rarely rises to the dignity of national negotiations, or national controversies." In short, the conflict of laws, like the law of nations, worked from the presumption that membership in the community of civilized nations necessitated recognition of the validity of foreign law within the boundaries of the nation, especially with regard to foreign residents. As Story noted, summarizing the views of Continental jurists (of which he was sympathetic), "Personal statutes are held ... to be of general obligation and force every where." This conviction was important because of the mobility of persons, populations, and property, often along the circuits of the movement of international capital. As Story put it,

> Commerce is now so absolutely universal among all countries; the inhabitants of all have such a free intercourse with each other; contracts, marriage, nuptial settlements, wills, and successions, are so common among persons, whose domicils are in different countries, having different and even opposite laws on the same subjects; that without some common principles adopted by all nations in this regard there would be an utter confusion of all rights and remedies; and intolerable grievances would grow up to weaken all the domestic relations, as well as to destroy the sanctity of contracts and the security of property.

In the name of comity, the legal borders of the nation, with regard to contracts, marriages, wills, and property, needed to be porous in order to ensure the international reciprocity constitutive of national sovereignty.[23]

At the same time that Story was arguing that nations needed to recognize

22. Story, *Commentaries*, 1, 4–5.
23. Ibid., 5, 9, 12.

the domestic laws of other nations, he offered compensatory language on the inviolability of national sovereignty. "It is plain, that the laws of one country can have no intrinsic force, *proprio vigore*, except within the territorial limits and jurisdiction of that country." Story followed this compensatory gesture with the necessity of submitting to the international community: "Whatever extra-territorial force they are to have is the result, not of any original power to extend them abroad, but of that respect, which from motives of public policy other nations are disposed to yield to them, giving them effect ... with a wise and liberal regard to common convenience and mutual necessities." That is, the possibility of the force of domestic laws in foreign nations derived, not from any absolute national sovereignty that could extend across the globe, but from the existence of the community of nations.[24]

As previously noted, marriage was often invoked to stabilize the nation, as a special, consensual relation. Story wrote: "Marriage is treated by all civilized nations as a peculiar and favored contract. It is in its origin a contract of natural law." Or, more evocatively, Story called marriage "the parent, and not the child of society." As the parent of society, marriage was, according to Story and countless others, a foundational relationship. Yet marriage law varied from nation to nation and, within the United States, from state to state. Thus, legal conflict around the legitimacy of certain marriages was bound to ensue. There was one overriding principle in adjudicating the conflict of laws. "The general principle certainly is ... that between persons, *sui juris*, marriage is to be decided by the law of the place, where it is celebrated. If valid there, it is valid every where. It has a legal ubiquity of obligation. If invalid there, it is equally invalid every where." Citing Kent's opinion, Story reaffirmed that only incest and polygamy were universally prohibited. Although local and moral objections may arise to certain marriages, there was greater harm to be done in violating the sanctity of already-contracted marriages.

> All civilized nations allow marriage contracts.... and the subjects of all nations are equally concerned in them. Infinite mischief and confusion must necessarily arise to the subjects of all nations ... if the respective laws of different countries were only to be observed, as to marriage contracted by the subjects of those countries abroad; and therefore all nations have consented, or are presumed to consent, for the common belief

24. Ibid., 7–8.

and advantage, that such marriages shall be good or not, according to the laws of the country where they are celebrated. By observing this rule, few, if any, inconveniences can arise. By disregarding it, infinite mischiefs must ensue.

Moreover, Story expanded the definition of legitimate marriage found in the 1810 Massachusetts case discussed above, arguing that "it is a contract so completely of natural and moral law, that when celebrated by savages, in places where there are no established laws, it will be recognised as good in other countries." This was an important point, as it shifted the terms of recognition of marriage. Story, like his predecessors, usually wrote in terms of civilized nations, a flexible term generally associated with Europe. Yet here, precisely because marriage followed from natural and moral law, it appeared that marriages celebrated anywhere in the world could be recognized, opening the borders of the United States to marriage contracted in so-called savage societies.[25]

Following from this series of decisions and Story's treatise, the borders of the United States were potentially open to other forms of marriage. As Story noted, commerce and the global movement of capital and persons created the conditions by which nearly anyone could end up in the United States. This was further substantiated by Story's willingness to grant legitimacy to savage marriages. Moreover, in the law, as these two cases and Story's treatise made clear, religion was of little importance. Parker, as we have seen in his opinion from 1819, insisted on marriage as a civil contract. Kent, in defending his narrow interpretation of the incest prohibition, dismissed the Levitical prohibition, which had been the basis of most incest law in the United States, as "not binding, as a rule of municipal obedience." Kent went further, classifying "injunctions of religion" with "manners and opinion." Story followed on this logic as well. "The common law of England (and the like law exists in America) considers marriage in no other light than as a civil contract. The holiness of the matrimonial state is left entirely to ecclesiastical and religious scrutiny." As Kent privatized religion in the delimitation of marriage, Story noted its common presence in various marital practices around the globe but called it "superadded," noting its legal irrelevance to marriage in the United States. All of which is to say that marriage and the

25. Ibid., 100, 103–104, 112, 115. Story drew on Phillipe-Antoine Merlin's *Repertoire universel et raisonné de jurisprudence*, 4th ed., 17 vols. (Paris, 1812–1825).

family were not removed from the domain of religion but that, in issues of law and national sovereignty, religious concerns were of a different order.[26]

The conflict of laws and articulation of national sovereignty left the borders of the United States open to marital and family forms that might not have been compatible with the production of liberal democratic citizens. This was a constitutive contradiction in sovereignty—to have the sovereign power of the United States recognized by an international community of nations required that the nation give up some of its sovereignty. That this contradiction applied to the domain of marriage potentially threatened the very institution that was supposed to channel the passions of individuals and the people, to order popular and individual sovereignty by producing virtuous citizens. How, then, would the institution of marriage be protected, if the law was unable to do so? It is here that we turn to Hindoo marriage as a supplement to marriage law in securing national sovereignty.

Hindoo Marriage

Representations of Hindoo marriage and kinship formations, from arranged child marriages to suttee (or sati, widow immolation), circulated extensively in the first two decades of the nineteenth century, frequently as part of missionary accounts. Given the absence of South Asian populations in the United States, these accounts clearly signified concerns with the global distribution of marriage and kinship. Although they generally described practices considered beyond the bounds of monogamous, consensual marriage and the affectionate, nuclear family, they nonetheless used language similar to that found in descriptions of marriage in the United States. Given that these accounts were not attempts to define kinship and marriage in ways relevant to subordinating marginal populations within the territorial United States or on its immediate horizon, such as Native Americans or enslaved African Americans, what was the significance of this preoccupation with Hindoo marriage in this period? If marriage was central to producing proper liberal democratic citizens and subjects, but the contours of national sovereignty and the conflict of laws opened the borders of the nation to marriages contrary to that goal, then these representations supplemented the law at precisely the point where the law threatened its own regulative power.[27]

26. Story, *Commentaries*, 100–101; Wightman v. Wightman, 4 Johns. Ch. 350–351 (1820).

27. There has been relatively little work on the Hindoo in the early Republic, but see, for instance, Rosemarie Zagarri, "The Significance of the 'Global Turn' for the Early

"The Hindoo" functioned as a synecdoche in these texts. It did a great deal of political and cultural work, performing two important tasks, in particular. First, the Hindoo reduced South Asia to the religious. Although there were occasionally other terms used—references to India and Bengal and component parts like the Brahman and the maharaja—the Hindoo did the work of making the Indian subcontinent wholly inscribed in religion. As one missionary argued in 1818, it was difficult to convert the Hindoo because "with them theology is so blended with the whole moral and civil obligations of life, that enters into every habit, and sanctions almost every action." In doing so, Hindoo marriage became an entirely religious affair, in contradistinction to marriage as a civil contract on which American legists insisted. Second, figuring the Indian subcontinent as abstractly Hindoo mostly erased the British colonial presence, thus reducing the marital and familial practices of the Hindoo to something outside the limits of modernity. Moreover, it tended to present these familial and kinship forms as static, when they were, in fact, anything but that. As India and the populations there were inscribed in religion through the figure of synecdoche, the legal, kinship, and marital practices of the Hindoo were relegated to a premodern condition incompatible with the liberal democratic order.[28]

American Republic: Globalization in the Age of Nation-Building," *JER*, XXXI (2011), 1–37; Verney, "An Eye for Prices," *JER*, XXXIII (2013), 397–431. For a slightly later period, and the connection between American slavery and British imperialism in India, see Elizabeth Kelly Gray, "'Whisper to Him the Word "India"': Trans-Atlantic Critics and American Slavery, 1830–1860," *JER*, XXVIII (2008), 379–406. Representations of Hindoo marriage were also quite common in the late nineteenth century, but such martial practices did not become manifestly legal and political issues until the first migration from Punjab to the western United States in the early twentieth century. See Nayan Shah, "Adjudicating Intimacies on U.S. Frontiers," in Ann Laura Stoler, ed., *Haunted by Empire: Geographies of Intimacy in North American History* (Durham, N.C., 2006), 116–139; Shah, *Stranger Intimacy: Contesting Race, Sexuality, and the Law in the North American West* (Berkeley, Calif., 2011). In thinking through the relationship between intimacy and governance, I draw on Lisa Lowe's argument that, "insofar as *bourgeois intimacy* was precisely a biopolitics through which the colonial powers administered the enslaved and colonized and sought to indoctrinate the newly freed into forms of Christian marriage and family," we must think of it as "part of the microphysics of colonial rule." If the United States was not directly involved in the colonial project, American evangelicals were nonetheless establishing missions in India and producing a geopolitical distribution of kinship and marriage that facilitated both colonial rule and national sovereignty. See Lowe, "The Intimacies of Four Continents," in Stoler, ed., *Haunted by Empire*, 195.

28. "Religion of the Hindoos, from Forbes' Oriental Memoirs," *Weekly Visitor, and*

If we think of the conflict of laws as a legal hermeneutic that created an opening in the borders of the nation for marital forms contracted elsewhere, forms that might be acceptable because of a sovereign desire to be part of a legally constituted community of nations, then the cultural focus on Hindoo marriage functioned as a supplement to the law, working to resolve (or at least mask) the constitutive contradiction in sovereignty. The Hindoo as synecdoche linked illiberal obligations and duties, kinship (as opposed to family), marriage, and religion. As Wai Chee Dimock has argued with regard to the nineteenth-century novel and its relation to the law, the novel had "signifying latitude both as a residual supplement to the contracting boundaries of the criminal law and as an index to the more general problems of polity and morality." This was a consequence, Dimock argues, of the separation of religion and law. A similar secularity can be discerned in the marriage law considered here.[29]

To read these cultural representations together with the law allows us to think through the relation between the production of norms and law. To trace the production of marriage norms, one needs to move across multiple fields, including the law and cultural representations. Thus, case reports and legal treatises produced a notion of marriage as a special contract, one in which the possibility of an ordered, virtuous society was codified. But, by speaking in rather vague and grandiloquent language of duties and obligations and rights, the legal archive leaves us, in some sense, with the form of marriage but little of its content. The law, then, was one vector along which marriage was normalized, but it was neither the only nor the most important one. With sovereignty dispersed not only across states and the nation

---

Ladies' Museum (New York), Aug. 22, 1818, 262. On the presence of the British in the articulation of late-eighteenth- and nineteenth-century practices of intimacy in India, see Durba Ghosh, *Sex and the Family in Colonial India: The Making of Empire* (New York, 2008); Rochona Majumdar, *Marriage and Modernity: Family Values in Colonial Bengal* (Durham, N.C., 2009). On pre-colonial marriage and family relations in India, see Indrani Chatterjee, "Introduction," in Chatterjee, ed., *Unfamiliar Relations: Family and History in South Asia* (New Brunswick, N.J., 2004), 3–45.

29. Wai Chee Dimock, "Criminal Law, Female Virtue, and the Rise of Liberalism," *Yale Journal of Law and the Humanities*, IV (1992), 210. To clarify, I do not want to suggest that marriage was undergoing something like secularization, which implies a linear process from sacred to secular. Rather, as John Lardas Modern writes, "Rather than signal a decreasing influence of the religious, secularism names a conceptual environment—emergent since at least the Protestant Reformation and the early Enlightenment—that has made 'religion' a recognizable and vital thing in the world." See Modern, *Secularism in Antebellum America*... (Chicago, 2011), 7.

but also through the people and individuals, the production of the marital norm occurred across multiple domains as well. In this sense, then, despite both the persistence and emergence of kinship forms in the nineteenth century, both the law and the discourse of Hindoo marriage worked to produce a normative concept of marriage and family, one that was consensual, secular, and marked by affectionate obligations and duties in line with the regulative demands of a democratic society.[30]

The norm and the law, then, were not opposed to each other but congruent; the law and the norm constituted multiple avenues for the workings of power in a liberal democracy. We must think beyond what Michel Foucault called juridical power—that form of power that works primarily through the law, which is conceived of as the effect of the sovereign in the form of the monarch—but we must not necessarily oppose the law and the norm. Although Foucault argues that in the modern deployment of power the norm replaces the juridical, the law does not necessarily become less important for the functioning of nonjuridical sovereignty. Indeed, the consolidation of norms is effected through the multiplication of laws. The law is not simply the expression of the sovereign's power but rather a wide field across which sovereignty is dispersed. The proliferation of laws and legal treatises alongside the cultural representations of Hindoo marriage can be seen as one conjunction where the marital norm was produced as a way of articulating sovereignty.[31]

This emphasis on sovereignty might seem at once derived from Foucault's conceptualization and at odds with it, given that his engagement with sovereignty was drawn from Continental statutory legal traditions, which were and are frequently opposed to the English common law tradition so influential in the early national United States. Indeed, when Foucault writes of the common law and "Saxon right" interchangeably as attempts to disavow the historical event of the Norman conquest, he argues that the seventeenth-century invention of common law was an effort to derive Norman sover-

---

30. On kinship in the nineteenth century, see, on demography and the extended family, Steven Ruggles, *Prolonged Connections: The Rise of the Extended Family in Nineteenth-Century England and America* (Madison, Wis., 1987); on Mormonism and polygamy, Sarah Barringer Gordon, *The Mormon Question: Polygamy and Constitutional Conflict in Nineteenth-Century America* (Chapel Hill, N.C., 2002).

31. François Ewald, "Norms, Discipline, and the Law," *Representations*, no. 30 (Spring 1990), 138. For Foucault's articulation and critique of juridical power, see Foucault, *The History of Sexuality*, 3 vols., trans. Robert Hurley (New York, 1978), I, 87–91, 133–159.

eignty from Saxon sources. The tension between Norman and Saxon history in the invention of the common law would seem to mark a sharp division between the two forms of legality, and there certainly are distinctions. However, Foucault writes, "The fact remains that you see here the first formulation of the idea that any law ... every form of sovereignty ... and any type of power ... has to be analyzed not in terms of natural right and the establishment of sovereignty, but in terms of the unending movement—which has no historical end—of the shifting relations that make some dominant over others." The conjunction of marriage law and representations of Hindoo marriage and kinship worked to constitute a marriage norm that was one vector through which democratic sovereignty and dominance were established. Given the dispersal and persistence of sovereignty in a democratic republic, these "shifting relations" were intimately tied to sovereignty. Moreover, although the common law was perhaps dominant in American legality, it worked with and against statutory law, which is evident not only in the codification movement of the 1820s through 1840s but also in the increasing combination of common law and statutes in the legal elaboration of marriage in the early nineteenth century. Writing on the conflict of laws—in which Kent and Story were stalwart defenders of the common law—drew liberally from Continental legal codes and legal theorists in order to establish legal doctrine. In the conjunction of law and representation, then, is the configuration of a norm appropriate to the workings of democratic sovereignty.[32]

If the Hindoo served to locate all South Asian marital practices and legal regimes within the religious, then the location of marriage within dense structures of kinship, frequently religiously justified, served to make marriage, even if monogamous, something incompatible with the liberal democratic form of the American nation. As the anthropologist Elizabeth Povinelli has written, "If the magical features of the intimate event [love, marriage, the conjugal couple, in all their liberal configurations] are to be animated socially and psychically, then others must be trapped in liberal intimacy's

32. Michel Foucault, *"Society Must Be Defended": Lectures at the Collége de France, 1975–76*, eds. Mauro Bertani and Alessandro Fontana, trans. David Macey (New York, 2003), 106, 109. Foucault's most extensive comments on the common law stretch across the lecture of Feb. 4, 1976 (87–114). On the codification movement and the transformation of common law in the nineteenth-century United States, see Kunal M. Parker, *Common Law, History, and Democracy in America, 1790–1900: Legal Thought before Modernism* (New York, 2011), esp. chaps. 3, 4. On marriage, common law, and statutes, see Cott, *Public Vows*, 7.

nightmare—the genealogically determined collective." Hindoo marriage represented that nightmare, in which all intimacies—marital and conjugal—were inscribed in kin networks and thus genealogically determined. As such, these intimacies were not conducive to the proliferation of marital forms necessary in a democracy.[33]

Representations of Hindoo marriage frequently turned on the absence of women's consent in marriage. In an 1812 account of Hindoo religion, for instance, the author, writing under the pseudonym "A Christian," wrote that Hindoo women "are truly an unfortunate part of the community, and greatly to be pitied." "Receiving no education; disposed of in marriage without their own consent, or knowing any thing of the person to whom they are to be given, they are immured for life, and made mere servants in the family of their despotic lord." This was an effect of the oppressive structure of kinship, something that women could not escape. "If barren, or bearing only daughters, they are neglected; and not always released from oppression even when death removes the husband; for they are then frequently reduced to the alternative of sinking into a state of infamy, or of burning themselves with his dead body." Such representations worked to make certain forms of conjugality incompatible with American sociality and polity; moreover, they made the place of American women in marriage and the family, which was one of constraint, seem, by contrast, consonant with consent.[34]

The despotism of kinship and religion and the absence of consent were compounded by the caste system. Indeed, it was the inscription of marriage and kinship within a caste system that made Hindoo marriage incompatible with liberal forms of intimacy in the United States. If the consent of the conjugal couple, conceived of as a ratification of romantic desire, legitimated the obligations, duties, and rights of marital and familial life, the rigidity of caste foreclosed the individual desire and voluntarism of liberal intimacy. In some instances, it was the possibility of losing caste that disrupted the supposedly stabilizing function of marriage and family. As *Robinson's Magazine*, a literary magazine published in Baltimore, reported in 1818, a man who lost caste (which was, according to the author, an often capricious affair) was "dead to the world." "By losing his cast [sic], the Hindu is bereft of friends and relations, and often of wife and children, who will rather forsake

---

33. Elizabeth A. Povinelli, *The Empire of Love: Toward a Theory of Intimacy, Genealogy, and Carnality* (Durham, N.C., 2006), 182–183.

34. A Christian, "Religious Communications," *Christian Observer*, XI, (May 1812), 261, 266, 272.

him than share in his miserable lot." His wife and children might forsake him, but that did not absolve them of his ignominy. "If he has marriageable daughters they are shunned. No other girls can be approached by his sons." The effects of the caste system were inescapable—even if his wife and children chose to sever ties, they were nonetheless genealogically bound to his transgression.[35]

The caste-based determination of kinship and the way in which kinship was laced through caste were usually understood to be religiously organized, and thus inescapable for the Hindoo. So overdetermined by genealogy and kinship, the figures in these stories could not be educated in the necessity of volition and consent in the articulation of marital and familial obligations and duties. Caste simply reinforced this absence of consent. As the *Religious Intelligencer* reported in 1817, for instance, a court in Bombay expelled "a man and his wife" from their caste because her "*father* ... ate, on a certain occasion, contrary to the rules of the cast." Not only was the father's action potentially punished (although that is not clear), the daughter and her husband were also punished, exemplifying the genealogical determination of kinship elsewhere. Moreover, the caste-determined marriages can be read in relation to emergent concerns over aristocratic forms of marriage in the United States driven by the desire for the consolidation of property in specific lineages, both among the merchant elite of the North and the planter class of the South.[36]

The sociality implied in James Kent's formulation of the natural law, in which individuals left their natal origins to enter society, were here foreclosed by the inscription of marriage in a kinship network. The despotic nature of obligation and duty in Hindoo kinship and marriage were, in this discourse, aggravated by the caste system. A gruesome tale of cross-caste marriage laid bare the extent to which a genealogically determined society exerted excessive control over marriage. In a tale from 1825, a lower-caste Hindoo boy persuaded a girl "of superior beauty" and a higher caste to elope with him and marry in his village. After her family discovered the transgression, the girl's mother invited her back to their home, promising forgiveness. At first, her brother and father received her warmly. However, she grew sus-

---

35. "Description of the Character, Manners, and Customs of the People of India, and of Their Institutions, Religious and Civil," *Robinson's Magazine; a Repository of Original Papers, and Selections from English Magazines*, Aug. 15, 1818, 74.

36. "Domestic Intelligence: American Missionaries; from the Panoplist," *Religious Intelligencer*, Jan. 11, 1817, 520.

picious and attempted to escape. She was overtaken by her brother, who feigned sympathy, but, when in a secluded area, he "drew his sword, (the meanest peasant in these provinces wears a sword,) and severed her head from the body." The father and brother were apprehended, confessed, and "exulted in the accomplishment of it." Yet they went unpunished because parents were invested with "unlimited authority over their children, even to the depriving them of life." Here, liberal intimacy in the form of romantic love was punished by death for violating the obligations and duties of kinship.[37]

On rare occasions, cross-caste marriage was possible, but it was marked by a series of rituals to obviate the transgression, which in turn aligned the state with kinship. An 1820 article in *Philanthropist*, for example, recounted the marriage of "his Highness Mulha Row Holkar and Clauder Bye." The bride was of a higher caste than the bridegroom, and thus a particular ceremony was used to legitimate the marriage. Rather than a direct marriage between the bride and bridegroom, performed by a Brahman, the cross-caste nature of the marriage necessitated a substitution. In the place of the maharaja (Mulha Row Holkar), "a sword was substituted ... and the bride was formally married to the sword." The sword, so the author claimed, was a symbol of the state; "the signification of this strange ceremony is said to be, that the sword of state prevails over the consideration of cast" (contrary to the previous story, in which the swords of caste prevailed over conjugal desire). Unlike in the United States, where, at least in the legal domain, marriage was a civil contract, here the state was an actual marital partner. In effect, the desire of the state, in the figure of the maharaja, was not to be denied by considerations of caste. Further, when the maharaja returned to the assembly, reassuming his position within the state, his bride, who was "between nine and ten years of age, and very good looking," was brought before the assembly wearing a veil. She then removed the veil, allowing "the assembly to judge" for themselves her beauty and reputation and, by extension, the legitimacy of the marriage. For American readers, increasingly reared, at least among the white middle class, on notions of consent and affection in marriage, this story outlined the place of hierarchy and obligation in an arranged child marriage over which the state had absolute authority.[38]

Both of these stories suggested that desire might escape the determinations of caste and kinship; one was met with death, and the other required

---

37. "Hindoo Caste," *Western Recorder* (Utica, N.Y.), Mar. 8, 1825, 37.
38. "Hindoo Marriage," *Philanthropist*, Feb. 12, 1820, 253–254.

the intervention of the state. Even a tale of seduction, that allegory of democracy and signifier of the moment at which liberty slid into licentiousness, was nearly impossible to imagine in the kinship-dominated Hindoo society. Seduction, one author noted in 1811 in the *Observer*, "not uncommon in the brilliant and more enlightened society of Europe," was comparatively rare in Hindoo society. Unlike in Europe and America, "the fair sex is regarded with inferior consideration, and secluded from the intercourse of general society." When Sunkeree, the wife of Ishan Dauss, disappeared one morning, she was immediately assumed dead, drowned in a river or perhaps "devoured by an alligator." The presumption of death intimated the metaphorical condition of the woman; in reality, she had eloped with another man. However, it was a case of seduction, and the man soon abandoned her. She had been secreted through several families and, even after being abandoned, her husband could not find her, most likely because she was with another family. Although this was a scandal, it was unusually public, since "seeking redress in courts of law for such domestic calamities, is utterly repugnant to the practice of the Hindoos." Indeed, the entire affair was confined to the privacy of multiple families—Sunkeree, the seduced woman, was never in public. Even a tale of seduction occurred wholly in the realm of kinship.[39]

Marriage and the grid of kinship were also structured by violence. Although the violent retribution for cross-caste marriage was brutal, it was also incidental. Other forms of violence, in particular suttee and infanticide, were structural conditions of kinship in the genealogically, religiously determined society. In this familial violence, there might have been more in common with the private, intimate family of the United States than many authors and readers would have imagined. As Ruth Bloch has persuasively argued apropos the law, "The growing idealization of the family as a distinctively private domain ... opened the way to stronger rationalizations of wife beating." The private family frequently associated with sentiment and affection also created the conditions for the legitimation of domestic violence. The sensationalism of reports of suttee and infanticide, however, distinguished the violence of Hindoo kinship from that of the American family. If suttee and infanticide were types of familial violence incompatible with the liberal democratic order, then wife beating, as it was increasingly protected by the American legal system, was presumably compatible with the duties and obligations of family. Here, if the specter of structural violence

39. "Hindoo Conjugal Disloyalty and Elopement," *Observer* (New York), Mar. 3, 1811, 99.

in the form of suttee and infanticide delegitimized Hindoo marriages in the American imaginary, it also created a limit point of violence within the family, making practices like wife beating acceptable precisely because they were neither genealogically nor religiously determined.[40]

Suttee was frequently represented in the periodical press. This practice, perhaps more than any other, constituted the outer limits of kinship debt and obligation. Suttee was controversial in both pre-colonial and colonial India; the obligation for a widow to burn herself to death after the death of her husband was a point of contention in Hindu law. Although suttee was one of the loci of colonial discourse and contestation (it was outlawed by the British in 1829), in the United States, which had less of a direct stake in that colonial project, the discourse looked quite different. Suttee was a familial and religious obligation, born of marriage, which took obligation too far. And, again, through the figure of the Hindoo, suttee became a religious marker of India, a hidebound tradition that marked Hindoo intimacy. It was not a site of contestation; rather, it was a site of disapprobation that supplemented the regulation of legitimate marriage in the United States. If there was contestation, and several accounts included dissenters, it was more a product of Christian missionary wish fulfillment: the dissenters represented the possibility that the Hindoo could be converted.[41]

Accounts of suttee frequently attempted to distance Hindoos from the practice while also making it an inevitable part of Hindoo kinship, one that structured kin relations in both this world and the next. So, for instance, in one account of a voluntary widow burning published in 1816, just before immolation the widow "prays ... that the heavenly dancers may wait on her and her husband ... and that, by this act of merit, all her father's and husband's ancestors may ascend to heaven." Another potential suttee found that the perpetuation of kin ties beyond death was precisely a reason not to engage in the practice. In an 1803 account of suttee in Smyrna, which at the time was under the government of the "Mahomedans," the widow of a recently deceased Brahman petitioned the government to be allowed to immolate herself. According to the author, in areas under Muslim rule widow burn-

---

40. Ruth H. Bloch, "The American Revolution, Wife Beating, and the Emergent Value of Privacy," *Early American Studies*, V (2007), 229.

41. On suttee and the politics of British colonialism and Indian contestation, see Lata Mani, *Contentious Traditions: The Debate on* Sati *in Colonial India* (Berkeley, Calif., 1998); Gayatri Chakravorty Spivak, *A Critique of Postcolonial Reason: Toward a History of the Vanishing Present* (Cambridge, Mass., 1999), 285–302.

ing had been mostly eliminated; however, Hindoos in the area could petition for an exception. This widow repeatedly petitioned with the support of Brahmans in the area. In the final instance, a Brahman petitioning on her behalf claimed that "great, great will be her reward, great her recompence for it in the other world! there she will be re-joined to her husband, by a sacred marriage, and live with him to all eternity." It was at this point that the widow backed away. "'What,' exclaimed she, 'shall I indeed find my husband in heaven?'" This claim was too much, as her husband had treated her poorly in life. "Since the god Brama will reunite me to my husband," she told the governor, "I renounce him and his religion forever, and embrace yours." These accounts tell conflicting stories. On the one hand, kin ties were absolute, and the link between this world and the next worked across the immolation of widows and led the widow to consent to the practice. Consent was thus something that needed to be learned through proper marital practices. Yet, on the other, that women showed agency through consent held out the hope of conversion in missionary accounts. Hinduism was a corruption that produced despotic kin forms, but one that could be shed.[42]

An account from 1810, reported in the *Weekly Visitor*, encapsulated the ambivalence that lay, perhaps surprisingly, at the heart of accounts of suttee in the early Republic. The report initially discounted the possibility that a widow would willingly submit to immolation. "It is generally a received belief, that in the sacrifice of Hindoo widows," the author wrote, "the victim is previously rendered almost insensible by stupifying and intoxicating drugs." This claim of drug-induced stupefaction was an anomaly in the early Republic, but it suggests the seeming inconceivability of suttee to the American imagination. Despite the assumption of drug use, the author reported that he was drawn to attend a suttee near his home in the vicinity of Calcutta "by a strong and natural curiosity, to observe narrowly the deportment of a human being about to take a voluntary and public leave of existence." The ambiguity—did the widow voluntarily consent to her immolation, or was she drugged into subordination?—captured something of the problem of consensual marriage followed by duties and obligations. Moreover, although this author would go on to recount a particularly brutal instance of widow burning, he did so, he claimed, "to record at least one instance on the other side of the question." The telling of this story was of great necessity because the author did not "recollect to have seen any account of a suttee that did not,

---

42. "On the Burning of Women in India," *Lay-Man's Magazine*, Aug. 1, 1816, 299; "A Hindoo Anecdote," *Boston Weekly Magazine*, July 9, 1803, 151.

upon the whole, tell rather favourably for the humanity of those" subject to "an imperious ordinance of religion."[43]

In this account of a suttee, there was ambivalence around the consent of the widow, thus registering the anxiety that consent in the context of familial obligation did not necessarily lead to virtue. Although most in attendance did not believe she would go through with the immolation, in part because of her three-year-old child, "the widow preserved the utmost, the most entire fortitude and composure, or rather apathy, and was unmoved, even at parting with her child." There was something particularly appealing to this writer about the widow's consent to the dictates of religious and familial obligation, which was then countered with the reference to "apathy" rather than "fortitude and composure." Finally, as a mechanism by which to rectify this rather ambivalent account, the author relayed the affectless reaction of the spectators to this religiously and kin-based act of violence. "I ought to observe, that the utmost indifference, without any symptom of the remotest compassion, prevailed among the whole of the spectators, not excepting the mother and sister of the widow." Seemingly aware that he was dangerously close to sanctioning this kind of subordination to the dictates of religion and kinship, the author left his readers with the apathy of the widow and the spectators, suggesting that such a reaction was ultimately misplaced consent to the obligations of family.[44]

For all of the ambivalence around consent, suttee was also represented as the end result of a violent and oppressive kin network, one in which the consent of the wife was irrelevant. In 1810, the *Adviser; or, Vermont Evangelical Magazine* included a brief report of a widow immolation. The "young widow," whose older husband had recently died, was the daughter of a "very holy man." When the time for suttee arrived, the widow "revolted, and struggled to get out of the flames." Her father refused to let her escape from the funeral pyre, enlisting "the people who stood by with bamboos in their hands to *beat her back*." There was no resistance from the spectators, who "instantly obeyed, and literally beat out her brains while she was endeavouring to escape!" Here, the spectators conspired with the father to ensure that his authority, and the obligations of kinship, were not thwarted.[45]

If suttee should be read, in the U.S. context, in relation to the constella-

---

43. "Burning of a Hindoo Widow," *Weekly Visitor*, July 21, 1810, 166.
44. Ibid., 167–168.
45. "Further Effects of Superstition in India," *Adviser; or, Vermont Evangelical Magazine*, II (August 1810), 250.

tion of familial consent and obligation, it also certainly would have conjured manifest anxieties over suicide in the early Republic. As Richard Bell has noted, "More and more Americans of status and standing now perceived a strong and binding link between the alarming frequency of suicides described in the early national press and the individualistic and disintegrative impulses of this budding capitalist society." If suicide registered liberal capitalist anxieties, suttee registered suicide as an effect of women's encryption in kinship. Indeed, a wife's suicide (attempted or otherwise) signified a sense of agency in the face of a difficult familial situation, whereas suttee, as figured in the missionary-ethnographic accounts, was the culmination of a proper marriage and an untimely spousal death. Here the conjunction of suicide and family in the figure of Hindoo marriage/suttee shored up the American family as the affection base of liberal democratic life.[46]

If suttee constituted one form of obligation and duty that resulted in death, infanticide was the other form of structural violence. In both cases, kinship was aligned with death. Infanticide followed from the debt that fathers owed their daughters, a debt that could only be paid in finding a husband. This debt was represented as difficult to fulfill, and thus infanticide of female children was figured as endemic to Hindoo society. "Without alleging any other reason than the difficulty of providing for daughters in marriage," one author wrote in 1809, "the mothers starve their female infants to death." The author claimed that in some parts of India "not one half of the females are permitted to live." Like with suttee, the duties and obligations of monogamous marriage and kinship were linked, not to morality or the production of virtue, nor were they the effect of consenting to marriage, but rather to the structural conditions of despotic genealogy.[47]

Even when a glimmer of affection and sympathy in the family forestalled infanticide, death was not put off entirely. An 1813 account of infanticide captured both the force of death in the debt-laden kin network and the way in which the Hindoo foreclosed difference in representations of India. This account of infanticide was drawn from the Sikh community, who were represented as an alternative form of Hinduism. "The Hindoos, who form the bulk of the population in this district, seem to be infinitely less attached to their religion than the Hindoos of the other parts of the country." That they were Sikhs seemed to be incidental to this account. According to the author

46. Richard Bell, *We Shall Be No More: Suicide and Self-Government in the Newly United States* (Cambridge, Mass., 2012), 12; on spousal suicide, see 7, 13.
47. "Hindoo Superstitions," *Philadelphia Repertory*, Jan. 18, 1812, 279.

of this report, suttee was not practiced, but infanticide was common. The account of infanticide here initially demonstrated the power of sympathy. "One of these fellows had been induced, by the tears and entreaties of his wife, to spare the life of a daughter born to him." Sentimentality in the form of tears saved the infant daughter, but the debt still remained. "The girl grew up, and had arrived at the age of thirteen, but, unfortunately for her, had not been demanded in marriage by any one." Her father was concerned about bringing "disgrace upon the family" as a result of his unmarried daughter and resolved to kill her. The final reckoning of his debt was gruesome and potentially a result of social ridicule of him for his failed obligation. "Shortly after forming this atrocious design, he either overheard, or pretended to have overheard some of his neighbours talking of his daughter in a way that tended to increase his fears, when, becoming outrageous, he rushed upon the poor girl and cut her head off." The "native magistrate" imprisoned him for one year and seized all of his property. The father's only crime, according to the article, was that his daughter was marriageable. If he had killed her as an infant, it would have been acceptable. The debts and obligations of kinship were, then, linked to death for the helpless daughter.[48]

These were among the most common representations of Hindoo marriage and the debts, duties, and obligations that followed from such marriages. Tales of child marriage, caste, suttee, infanticide, and gruesome murder provided content for the language of duties and obligations and rights and affection that suffused marriage discourse in the United States. These Hindoo practices were monogamous but not consensual—or at least not consensual in the normative terms of American marriage—and as such could not be tolerated in the United States. If they constituted the limits of obligation and violence in the consenting affectionate family, they also supplemented a legal system that potentially opened the national borders to Hindoo marriage, thereby threatening the sovereignty of the nation. Although the legal system might not have been able to prohibit a child marriage legally contracted in India, these cultural representations constituted a national marital imaginary that had no room for Hindoo marriage, thus regulating the flow of persons and marital forms on the circuits of commerce and international capital.

---

48. "Manners of the Shikhs, Communicated in a Letter to Brother Chamberlain, from a Friend at Ludhana, in the Shikh Country," *Christian Monitor, and Religious Intelligencer,* June 19, 1813, 807–808.

Conclusion

As the literary scholar Mark Rifkin has argued, "More than bearing an analogical relationship to each other, kinship and sovereignty are intertwined, the former providing a way of variously managing, containing, and/or disassembling social formations that do not readily fit the dominant ideological and institutional matrix of Anglo-American governance." Rifkin usefully gets us beyond the nation as family in order to think about the ways in which national sovereignty was articulated and managed by its relationship with kinship. Hindoo marriage was fully implicated in and contained by kinship, which provided a counterpoint to the more liberal forms of marriage and family deployed in domestic relations law in the early nineteenth century. Yet it did more in the context of international marriage law. If the sovereignty of the people, the individual, and the nation was dependent on a specific configuration of marriage as bourgeois intimacy, yet was simultaneously dependent on the place of the United States in an increasingly global community of nations (which implied the global circulation not only of individual persons but of married couples), the production of Hindoo marriage and kinship shored up national sovereignty and regulated potential immigrants.[49]

Hindoo marriage, even as it presented itself in a quasi-ethnographic form, had little to do with an engagement with either Hinduism or the Indian subcontinent. Rather, it had everything to do with forms of filiation and affiliation in the early Republic. What the discourse of Hindoo marriage supplemented was not a flaw in the legal regime of marriage; it was a constitutive feature of national sovereignty, an opening that both the law and the nation needed. That is not to say that there was a desire for those marital and kinship forms associated with the Hindoo; rather, the Hindoo policed the spaces of international marriage law that the law itself could not regulate.

---

49. Mark Rifkin, *When Did Indians Become Straight? Kinship, the History of Sexuality, and Native Sovereignty* (New York, 2011), 17.

CONFERENCE PROGRAM

Warring for America, 1803–1818, March 31 and April 1, 2011, Mumford Room, The James Madison Memorial Building of the Library of Congress, Sponsored by the Omohundro Institute of Early American History and Culture, the History Department of New York University, and the Henry E. Huntington Library

SESSION 1. *The International in Nationalism.* Chair: Andrew Cayton, Miami University. Carroll Smith-Rosenberg, University of Michigan, emerita, "White Slaves / Black Revolutionaries: Haiti, Barbary Captives, and the Construction of U.S. Citizenship." Joseph Rezek, McNeil Center for Early American Studies, University of Pennsylvania, and Boston University, "Hail to the Chief: Walter Scott and the Americanization of Scottish Nationalism during the War of 1812." Caitlin Fitz, McNeil Center for Early American Studies, University of Pennsylvania, "The Hemispheric Dimensions of Early U.S. Nationalism: The War of 1812 and Spanish American Independence." Comment: Adam Rothman, Georgetown University.

SESSION 2. *Repositioning Race and Nation.* Chair: Jan Lewis, Rutgers University—Newark. James M. Greene, West Virginia University, "Military Service and Racial Subjectivity in the War Narratives of James Roberts and Isaac Hubbell." David Waldstreicher, Temple University, "Minstrelization and Nationhood: Revisiting 'Backside Albany.'" Anna Mae Duane, University of Connecticut, "'Can You Be Surprised by My Discouragement?' Education and Colonization at the New York African Free School." Comment: François Furstenberg, Université de Montréal.

SESSION 3. *Imperial Margins.* Chair: Claudio Saunt, University of Georgia. Guillaume Teasdale, University of Ottawa, "Old Friends and New Foes: French and Indians in the Detroit River Region, 1796–1815." Sean P. Harvey, American Antiquarian Society and Seton Hall University, "Linguistic Difference, Jeffersonian Taxonomy, and Indian Unity." Nathaniel Millett, Saint Louis University, "Reconsidering the Origins, Course, and Consequences of the First Seminole War." Comment: Kathleen DuVal, University of North Carolina, Chapel Hill.

SESSION 4. *Colonial Legacies Revised*. Chair: Elizabeth Maddock Dillon, Northeastern University. Joseph Eaton, National Cheng Chi University, "'Every Free-Woman in This Country Is a Voter': New Jersey Female Suffrage in the Anglo-American Paper War." Duncan Faherty, Queens College, City University of New York, "'Warmed with a Noble Enthusiasm for the Rights and Liberties of the Citizens of Columbia': American Literature in the Canonical Interregnum, 1800–1820." Joshua Ratner, University of Pennsylvania, "Transatlantic Tennis: Volleys over Inchiquin: The Jesuit's Letters." Comment: Catherine O'Donnell, Arizona State University.

SESSION 5. *Marshalling Patriotism*. Chair: Jason Opal, McGill University. Tim Lanzendörfer, University of Mainz, "Magazine Biographies of Naval Officers and the Contestation of National Identity during the War of 1812." Eric Wertheimer, Arizona State University, "The Self-Abstracting Letters of War: Madison and Henry." Matthew Rainbow Hale, Goucher College, "American Glory: Napoleonic Imperatives in the Early Republic." Comment: Nicole Eustace, New York University.

SESSION 6. *The Calculus of Commerce and Power*. Chair: Toby Ditz, Johns Hopkins University. William Bergmann, Northern Michigan University, "'This Institution Could Be Made Serviceable to the Government': The U.S. Treasury and Banks in the Early West, 1804–1816." Christen Mucher, University of Pennsylvania, "Reconsidering 1812: The Case of the Bordeaux Slave Trade." Brian Murphy, Baruch College, City College of New York, "War Machines: Henry Miller Shreve and the Western Challenge to the Fulton-Livingston Steamboat Monopoly." Comment: Jane Kamensky, Brandeis University.

CONTRIBUTORS

BRIAN CONNOLLY is associate professor of history at the University of South Florida. He is the author of *Domestic Intimacies: Incest and the Liberal Subject in Nineteenth-Century America* (Philadelphia, 2014) and editor of *History of the Present: A Journal of Critical History.*

ANNA MAE DUANE is associate professor of English at the University of Connecticut. She is the author, editor, or co-editor of four books focusing on childhood in early American literature and culture. She is the co-editor of *Common-place: The Journal of Early American Life.*

NICOLE EUSTACE is professor of history at New York University. She is the author of *Passion Is the Gale: Emotion, Power, and the Coming of the American Revolution* (Chapel Hill, N.C., 2008), and *1812: War and the Passions of Patriotism* (Philadelphia, 2012).

DUNCAN FAHERTY is associate professor of English and American studies at Queens College and The Graduate Center of the City University of New York. He is the author of *Remodeling the Nation: The Architecture of American Identity, 1776–1858* (Durham, N.H., 2007), and he is at work on a book about the Haitian Revolution and early U.S. print culture.

JAMES M. GREENE is assistant professor of English at Pittsburg State University. His work has appeared in *Early American Literature,* and his book project focuses on the relationship between writing, violence, and sovereignty in the personal narratives of Revolutionary War veterans.

MATTHEW RAINBOW HALE is associate professor of history at Goucher College. His book, *The French Revolution and the Forging of Modern American Democracy,* will be published by the University of Virginia Press.

JONATHAN TODD HANCOCK is assistant professor of history at Hendrix College. He has published work in the *Journal of the Early Republic* and *The Princeton Companion to Atlantic History,* ed. Joseph C. Miller (Princeton, N.J., 2015), and he is working on a book about responses to the New Madrid earthquakes of 1811–1812.

TIM LANZENDÖRFER is assistant professor of American studies at the University of Mainz. He is the author of *The Professionalization of the American Magazine: Periodicals, Biography, and Nationalism in the Early Republic* (Paderborn, 2013) and co-editor of *American Lives: An Anthology of Transatlantic Life Writing from the Colonies to 1850* (2015).

KAREN L. MARRERO is assistant professor of history at Wayne State University and a comparative and transnational historian of the United States and Canada. Her work explores cross-cultural and cross-gendered interactions between indigenous peoples and Euro-Americans of the Great Lakes in the eighteenth and nineteenth centuries.

NATHANIEL MILLETT is associate professor of history at Saint Louis University. He is the author of *The Maroons of Prospect Bluff and Their Quest for Freedom in the Atlantic World* (Gainesville, Fla., 2013).

CHRISTEN MUCHER is assistant professor of American studies at Smith College. Her co-translation of *Stella* (1859), the first Haitian novel, appeared with New York University Press in 2015.

DAWN PETERSON is assistant professor of history at Emory University. Her research focuses on the intersections of African American and American Indian history in the post-Revolutionary era and is the author of *Indians in the Family: Adoption and the Politics of Antebellum Expansion* (Cambridge, Mass., 2017).

CARROLL SMITH-ROSENBERG is the Mary Frances Berry Collegiate Professor Emerita, University of Michigan. She is the author of "The Female World of Love and Ritual: Relations between Women in Nineteenth-Century America," *Signs*, I (1975), 1–29, *Disorderly Conduct: Visions of Gender in Victorian America* (New York, 1985), and *This Violent Empire: The Birth of an American National Identity* (Chapel Hill, N.C., 2010). Her recent work examines the origins of modern citizenship, focusing on tensions between universal promises and exclusionary practices.

FREDRIKA J. TEUTE is editor of publications, emerita, at the Omohundro Institute of Early American History and Culture, having held that position from 1989 to 2015.

DAVID WALDSTREICHER is Distinguished Professor of History at The Graduate Center of the City University of New York. He is the author of

In the Midst of Perpetual Fetes: The Making of American Nationalism, 1776-1820 (Chapel Hill, N.C., 1997), *Runaway America: Benjamin Franklin, Slavery, and the American Revolution* (New York, 2004), and *Slavery's Constitution: From Revolution to Ratification* (New York, 2009).

ERIC WERTHEIMER is professor of English and American studies at Arizona State University. He is the author of *Imagined Empires: Incas, Aztecs, and the New World of American Literature, 1771-1876* (Cambridge, 1999) and *Underwriting: The Poetics of Insurance in America, 1722-1872* (Stanford, Calif., 2006).

INDEX

Page numbers in italics refer to illustrations.

Abolitionists, 77–78
Act for the Protection of the Lands of the Crown in This Province from Trespass and Injury, 422, 437
Act to Prohibit the Importation of Slaves, 129, 133
Act to Protect the Commerce of the United States and Punish the Crime of Piracy, 129
Adams, Henry, 4–6, 321–322
Adams, John, 101, 341
Adams, John Quincy, 194, 196–197, 315
Adams-Onís Treaty, 198
Aderman, Ralph, 291
Advice to the Officers of the Army (Grose), 219, *220*
Affecting History of the Captivity ... Seven Years a Slave in Tripoli (Velnet), 71
African Colonization Society, 19
African Institution, 138
African Theatre, 52, 54
Age of Revolution, 57–58, 93–94, 167
Agnew, Jean-Christophe, 9
Agrarianism, Jeffersonian, 349, 367
Agriculture: culture and, 7
Akin, James, 219, *220*
Aldridge, Ira, 355
Algerine Captive, The (Tyler), 79–86
Algonquins, 427
Allen, Andrew Jackson, 49–50, *51*, 52
Altoff, Gerald, 214
Altschuler, Sari, 345
Ambrister, Robert, 189–190, 194–195, 197
Amedie decision, 138–139, 142, 148–151
American Colonization Society (ACS), 332–333, 337, 347–349, 352–355

American Naval Gallantry (Brown and Hathaway), 288
American Revolution: comparison of, to War of 1812, 55, 250–252, 256; Burnham on, 250; and postwar disillusionment, 250–251; and commemorative rhetoric, 254, 256
Analectic Magazine: Irving at, 285, 289–292, 306–307; and mythologizing the Royal Navy, 288; Wharton at, 306; "The American Naval Chronicle" introduction, 309; "Columbia Seizing the Trident of Neptune," *309*, 309–310
Analectic Magazine, naval biography of: and the shaping of national identity, 278, 297; Thomas Macdonough, 278–279, 292, 307, 309; Jacob Jones, 285, 289, 306–307; Lewis Warrington, 285–286; Stephen Decatur, 288; Isaac Hull, 288, 292–295, 297, 303–304; plan for, 289–291; James Lawrence, 292, 294–297, 298; Oliver Hazard Perry, 292, 297–305; John Shubrick, 292, 307
Anderson, Benedict, 447
Anderson, Thomas G., 359
Andrew (ship), 146
Andrew Jackson (Jarvis), 241, *242*
Andrew Jackson (Peale), *245*, *246*
Andrew Jackson (Vallée), *244*
Andrew Jackson (Vanderlyn), *248*
Andrews, Charles C., *347*, 351
Andrews, William, 270
Andros Island, 200
Angola settlement, 185–187, 189, 196, 199
Anishinaabes, 432–440, 442, 444

485

INDEX

Antislavery, 16, 94, 109–110, 114–115, 138, 174–187, 189, 195, 264–266, 333, 343, 348–349, 352, 387, 390, 393, 415
Appeal to the Coloured Citizens of the World (Walker), 267
Appleby, Joyce, 3
Arbuckle, Mathew, 192
Arbuthnot, Alexander, 190, 193–195, 197
Army, U.S., 285
Arnold, Benedict, 234
Arthur, George, 431
Arthur Mervyn (Brown), 122
Ashley, Mary, 182, 200
Ashman, Cecil, 348
Assimilation, Indian, 386–390, 397–398, 401, 403, 411–414, 418, 434
Attucks, Crispus, 268
Aurora, 288
Authentic Narrative of the Shipwreck and Sufferings of Mrs. Eliza Bradley, Wife of Capt. James Bradley (Bradley), 71–72

Bache, Benjamin Franklin, 79
"Backside Albany" (Hawkins), 29, *30*, 31–34, *35*, *36*, 37–42, 44–49, 55
Badger, Barber, 215
Banks, Henry, 212
Barbary captivity narratives: federal weaknesses exposed by, 60–61; nation building and the, 60–62; and system of Othering, 61, 73–75; emergence of, 62; and treatment of captives, 63–69, 74, 82–83; and liberty-acceptance of slavery binary, 64–66, 69–71, 75, 86–92; and nationalism and national identity, 65, 69–70, 72; by women, 65–66, 68–71, 76; and collapse of racial distinctions, 66; women in, 67, 86–92; fictional, 71–72, 79–93; white vs. black binary in, 75–84; universalist vision in, 83–85; miscegenation in, 86, 90–91; and inversion of gendered roles, 86–92; and challenge to hierarchical systems of difference, 86–92. *See also* Captivity narratives

Barbary corsairs: attack strategies of, 63
Barclay, Robert Heriot, 301
Barnum, P. T., 233
Bathurst, Henry, 172
Battle of Bladensburg, 41, 42
Battle of Horseshoe Bend, 379
Battle of Lake Champlain, The, 43–44
Battle of Lake Erie, 214–215, 223, 297–299, 303–305
Battle of Lodi, 210
Battle of Monmouth, 258–259
Battle of New Orleans: in "Original Jim Crow" (Rice), 32–33, 50, 52; in "Hunters of Kentucky" (song), 33, 47–49; Jackson and the, 47–49, 193, 205, 268–270, 272, 274, 276; black soldiers in, 170, 268–274, 276; and *Narrative of James Roberts*, 268–270, 272, 274; New England secession and, 285; federal weaknesses exposed by, 382
Battle of Plattsburgh, 29, 33, 41
Battle of Santa Cruz, 301
Battle of Suwannee, 195–196
Battle of the Nile, 300
Battle of the Sink Hole, 384
Battle of the Thames, 378
Battle of Tippecanoe, 371–372, 375, 383
Battle of Trafalgar, 300
Battle of Valparaiso, 214–215
Battle of Waterloo, 307
Beecher, Lyman, 239
Beizat and Jean (Bordeaux firm), 159
Bell, Andrew, 344
Bell, Richard, 476
Benezet, Anthony, 75
Benjamin, Walter, 346
Bentham, Jeremy, 453–454
Bhabha, Homi, 336
Big House Ceremony, 375
Bkejwanong (Walpole Island Reserve), 434, 436–437, 439–440, 442–444

INDEX 487

Blackface minstrelsy: theatrical dimensions of, and the War of 1812, 29, *30*, 31–34, *35*, *36*, 37–42, 44–49, 55; wartime origins of, 32–33; and Battle of New Orleans, 32–33, 50, 52; nationhood and, 33–34; nationalist idioms of, 46–47; damage done by, 55
Black Hawk, 364, 381, 383–385
Black history: movement to establish a, 267–269
Black patriotism, 42
Black sailors, 43–44, 48–49, 52, 54. *See also* Sailors
Black soldiers: and claims to liberty, 18, 266–267; Madison administration and, 48; in New Orleans army, 48–49; in First Seminole War, 165, 179, 188–189, 197; in Nicolls's army, 170, 180, 189–190, 197; in Battle of New Orleans, 170, 268–274, 276; and veteran narratives, 251–252, 262–263, 265–277; accounts of bravery of, 267–268. *See also* Soldiers
Blake, William, 75, 237
Bloch, Ruth, 472
Bok, Edward, 233
Borders: indigenous movement across, 20, 420–426, 433–438, 442–443; of sovereignty, 21; of national authority, 21–22; of exclusion, 22–23; Patriot movement and the northern, 419–421, 426–434, 442–444; Texas, 420; and the limits of nation in the buffer zone, 422–426
Bosquet, Jean, 145–146, 161
Bosquet, Peter, 160
Boston Hussars, 221
Boston Massacre, 268
Boston Tea Party, 38–40, 45, 258
Bourne, George, 213
Bowlegs, 185–187, 191, 194
Bowlegs Town, 193
Bradley, Eliza, 71–72
Brevoort, Henry, 307
Brewer, Holly, 449

British and Foreign Aborigines Protection Society, 435
Brown, Charles Brockden, 100, 122
Brown, Samuel, 288
Brown, William Alexander, 52
Brown, William Hill, 118
Brown, William Wells, 267
Bruce, Dickson D., Jr., 45
Brunon, Raoul, 215
Bryant, Charles Grandison, 428
Buchanan, James, 253, 269
Budiansky, Stephen, 285
Buffon, Georges-Louis Leclerc, comte de, 297
Burgett, Bruce, 124
Burleigh (pseud.), 95–99, 102–105
Burnham, Jonathan, 250
Burr, Aaron, 97, 123, 233

Cadwalader, Lambert, 111
Caesar, Julius, 211–212
Calhoun, John C., 193, 196, 199, 213, 284, 317, 341
Canning, George, 315
Cappachimico, 172
Captivity narratives, 109–110, 125. *See also* Barbary captivity narratives
Carey, Mathew, 67–68, 70, 78–79, 85, 333
Caribbean-U.S. interconnectedness, 105–111, 114, 118–119, 121–124
Carnegie, Andrew, 233
Caroline (ship), 433
Carrying trade, 135
Caste system, 469–472
Cayton, Andrew, 106
Champagny, François-Joseph de, fourth duke of Cadore, 147
Charlotte Temple (Rowson), 118
Chartrand, Rene, 215
Cherokee, 390–391, 395–396, 399, 404, 407, 410
Cherub (ship), 215
Chickasaws, 371, 390, 395–397, 410
Child, Lydia Maria, 261

Child marriage, 445–447
Chippewas, 378
Choctaw Nation, Indian agents to the, 386–392, 396–405, 411–412
Choctaws, 371, 395, 397
Circum-Atlantic networks of association, 105–111, 114, 118–119, 121–124
Citizenship: and strategies for inclusion, 11; military service as a path to, 18; for blacks, 18, 44–45; racial exclusion and, 18, 44–45, 56–57, 273–274, 426; formation of democratic, 57; in Federalist literature, 116–117, 121; British, conferred on blacks by Nicolls, 181–187; British, for Prospect Bluff and descendants, 181–187, 189–190, 200; residence and, 425–426; for Indians, 426; portable, 442
Citizen-soldier, ideal of the, 254, 257, 262–263, 266, 271, 274–275
Clarissa; or, The History of a Young Lady (Richardson), 101
Clay, Henry, 205, 317, 347
Cleve, Rachel Hope, 237–238
Clinton, DeWitt, 341
Clotel; or, The President's Daughter (Brown), 267
Coates, Benjamin, 348
Cobbett, William, 92, 287–288
Cochrane, Alexander, 171, 180
Coffee, Ishmael, 457–458
Colley, Linda, 208
Colonization movement, 19–20, 45, 332–333, 337, 347–355
Colored Patriots of the American Revolution, The (Nell), 267–268
Columbia, 24, 283
Columbia Seizing the Trident of Neptune *(Analectic Magazine)*, *309*, 309–310
Commentaries on the Conflict of Laws (Story), 457, 460–463
Commodification of people, 113, 120, 150–151, 263, 273–274, 276, 416

Commodities, slave produced, 136, 144, 418
Common law, 11, 467–468
Constitution (ship), 286
Constitution of the United States, 13, 57, 313–317, *318*, 319–320, 450–452
Cook, James, 6
Cooper, Frederick, 343
Cooper, James Fenimore, 119, 256, 261
Copley, John Singleton, 224
Coquette, The (Foster), 118
Coudère, François, 155
Courrier d'Elbing, Le (ship), 154
Craig, James, 314, 322, 324–326
Crain, Patricia, 345
Creeks, 20, 170, 172–173, 199–200, 378, 390–391, 395, 410
Creek War, 49, 164, 171
Creole (ship), 169–170
Creolization of the United States: fears of, 96–100, 105–107
Crèvecoeur, M. G. St. J. de (J. Hector St. John), 296–297
Crillon, Edouard de, 322, 327
Cross, Maurice, 339
Crummell, Alexander, 355–356
Cuba, 182
Cullen, Thomas, 145–146, 157, 160
Cultivate: defined, 7
Curtin, Philip, 142
Cushing, Caleb, 430

Dakota, 360
Daquin, Louis, 272
Dauss, Ishan, 472
Dauss, Sunkeree, 472
Daut, Marlene L., 105
Davis, Washington, 348
Dearborn, Henry, 216, *218*, 221, 389, 392
Death of General Warren at the Battle of Bunker Hill, 17 June 1775 (Trumbull), 224
Death of General Wolfe (West), 224, *226*

Death of Major Peirson, 6 January 1781 (Copley), 224
Death of Nelson (Devis), 224
Decatur, Stephen, 214–215, 223, 231, 234, 283, 287, 288, 291
"Defence of Fort McHenry, The" (Key), 41
Delany, Martin, 273
Delaware, 374–375, 378, 381
Deloria, Philip, 433
Democracy: racial exclusion and, 56–58; dangers of, in Federalist literature, 100–102; development of modern, 238–239, 249; power and, 238–240, 249; Jeffersonian, 239
Democratic-Republicans, 98–99, 102, 119, 122, 209–210, 239, 284
De Shields, Francis, 270–271
Devis, Arthur William, 224
Dewees, Samuel, 250
Dickson, Robert, 379–380, 382
Difference: and defining the Other, 61; and system of Othering, 73–84; disruption of racialized categories of, 73–84; challenge to hierarchical systems of, 86–92
Dillon, Elizabeth Maddock, 105, 118, 452
Dimock, Wai Chee, 466
Dinsmoor, Mary (née Gordon), 386, 404, 406, 408–409
Dinsmoor, Silas: as agent to the Choctaw Nation, 386–392, 396–405, 411–412; plantation settlement of, 388, 402–403, 406–413; as agent to the Cherokee Nation, 395–396, 404, 407
Dinsmoor, Silas, Jr., 386, 409
Dispossession: justification of, 10; Native strategies to fight, 21, 417–418. *See also* Territorial expansion
Domestic relations law, 448–449
Domination and the Arts of Resistance (Scott), 9
"Don't Give Up the Ship!" (Lawrence), 223, *224*

Dorset (ship), 139
Douglas, George, 212
Douglas, Mary (later Dinsmoor), 92
Douglass, Frederick, 127–130, 132, 162, 267, 348, 356
Dowling, William C., 119
Doyle, Laura, 104, 277
Doyle, William, 192
"Dress, the Most Distinguishing Mark of a Military Genius" (Akin), 219, *220*
Drexler, Michael, 105
Driver (ship), 158
Drouillard, François Xavier, 439–442
Drouillard, George, 439
Drouillard, Joseph, 439
Drouillard, Pierre, 439
Drouillard, Thomas (father), 439
Drouillard, Thomas (son), 440
Drouillard family, 439–443
Duane, William, 284, 288
Du Barry, John, 160
Dubois, Laurent, 58
Du Bois, W. E. B., 138–139, 143, 157
Ducornau, Jean, 154
Dumoriez, Charles François, 210
Duvernay, Ludger, 441

Eagle (ship), 146
Earthquakes, 362, 375–377
Education for blacks, 19, 332, 334, 338–355
Edwards, Lewis, 199
Edwards, Ninian, 363–364, 368–369, 371, 380
Eighth of January (Smith), 50
Eliot, John, 335–336
Elliott, James, 210
Eltis, David, 131–132, 139, 156–158
Embargo Act (1807), 72, 98, 133, 135, 315, 317
Emerson, Ralph Waldo, 238
Empire of Liberty (Wood), 280
Emulation, 334–343, 350–351
English language, 1–2, 23–24

English Reader (Murray), 334
Englund, Steven, 210
Enlightenment liberalism, 57–58, 83–85
Equality, 17, 25, 56, 58–59, 72, 121, 166, 180, 184, 234, 263, 267, 272–273, 296, 298, 303, 334
Equal rights, 333–334
Equiano, Olaudah, 94
Era of Good Feelings, 284
Ernest, John, 273
Essex (ship), 214–215
Essex Jr. (ship), 214–215
Essex Junto, 315, 322–324
Estaloee, 256, 258–261, 263
Eustace, Nicole, 301, 449, 452
Eustis, William, 365, 367, 368, 410
Exceptionalism, 23, 321
Exclusion: racialized and gendered, 11, 13, 56–58; borders of, 22–23

Family: in Federalist fiction, 100, 119–122, 124; normative concept of, 467–469. *See also* Kinship structures
Family Compact, 427
Fatovic, Clement, 328–329
Federalism, 321; in Federalist fiction, 15, 104, 119–122, 125–126
Federalist, The (Madison), 320, 322
Federalist fiction: Federalism endorsed in, 15, 104, 119–122, 125–126; tropes of, 100; goal of, 100, 103; and fashioning a new social order, 100, 111, 114, 119–122, 124; seduction and virtue in, 100–101, 104–107, 110, 112–119; dangers of democracy in, 100–102; temporal modality in, 103, 108–109, 114–115, 120–121; and companionate marriage as lynchpin of social cohesion, 105–106; and circum-Atlantic networks of association, 105–111, 114, 118–119, 121–124; color line in, 106; and threats to the privileges of whiteness, 107, 118; national identity and, 107–108, 121–122, 124–125; slavery in, 109–110, 114–115; plantation system in, 109–110, 114–116; and captivity narratives, 109–110, 125; colonial imaginary in, 114–115; and right to self-determination, 115–116; citizenship in, 116–117, 121; isolationist imaginary in, 118, 122

Federalist Party: on military confrontation, 5; and opposition to war, 11, 285, 319, 381; and opposition to the Democratic Party, 14; and power during the War of 1812 era, 14, 111, 239, 284–285; on slave representation, 44; opposition to, 57, 250; and opposition to Jefferson, 72, 95–99; and position on immigration, 73; on Bonaparte, 212; and secession of the New England states, 313–315, 322–329

Female Association of Philadelphia, for the Relief of Women and Children, in Reduced Circumstances, 125
Female Quixotism (Tenney), 100
Fernando Pó, 169
Fichtelberg, Joseph, 111
Fields, James, 331–334, 337–338, 350–351, 354, 356
Finley, Robert, 349–350
First Seminole War: black and Indian resistance in, 16–17, 183, 185, 188–189, 192–194, 200–201; Allen and, 49; territorial expansion and, 164; racialization of, 164–165; events underlying the outbreak of, 165, 174, 185, 192, 197; and individuals shaping the conflict, 165–166, 183, 185, 196–201; U.S. goal in, 194; War of 1812 and, 195–196; end of, 196
First Treatise of Government (Locke), 76, 89
Floridas: annexation of, 165, 171–172, 191, 193, 195–201
Folle Avoines, 378
Forbes, Robert P., 44

Forbes and Company, 183
Forrest, Edwin, 50, 54
Forsyth, Thomas, 360, 379–380, 383, 385
Fort Dearborn, 379
Fort Detroit, 365
Forten, James, 353, 354
Fort Harrison, 377
Fort Malden, 428–429
Fort Meigs, 372–374
Fort Scott, 191, 193
Fort Stanwix Captive, The (Priest), 253–265, 268–269, 271, 277
Fort Wayne, 365–367, 372, 384
Foss, John, 63, 65, 69, 76
Foster, Hannah Webster, 118
Foucault, Michel, 343, 467
Fourth of July, 127–130, 254
Fox (ship): captains and registrations of, 140–141, 145–146, 158–161; Piesch ownership of, 146–147, 160–161
Fox, le (ship), 159
Fox tribe, 436
France: independence movement's alliance with, 10–11; U.S. trade relations with, 135–137, 145–147, 151–158; and slave trade, 143–144; glory and, 209; and kinship structures, 439–443
Francophilia: Jeffersonian, 96–97
Franklin, Benjamin, 78–79, 124, 334, 336–337, 340–341
Fraud of the flags, 147–150
Freedom: whiteness and, 14; inclusive cause of, 24–25; of the sailor, 43; racial exclusion and, 76–77; promise of, for black soldiers, 252, 265–277; spread of slavery as a movement toward, 348–349
Free trade, 16, 43. *See also* Slave trade; Trade
French and Indian War, 235
French Revolution, 11, 109, 167, 209
Frontier romance, 253–254, 256
Fulton, Robert, 445
Furstenberg, François, 266

Gabriel's Rebellion, 97
Gadsden, James, 196
Gaines, Edmund, 173, 191–192, 194, 408, 410
Gaines, George, 399
Gallatin, Albert, 283–285
Garnet, Henry Highland, 355–356
Garrison, William Lloyd, 267, 355
Gauchet, Marcel, 210
Gender: and systems of exclusion, 31, 56, 61, 70, 387–388, 400, 413–417; and American allegories, 69, 315; roles, 86, 208, 230–233; and danger, 117; and models of citizenship, 337n; and labor, 396, 401
General Andrew Jackson (Jarvis), *243*
General Andrew Jackson (Rush), *247*
General Napoleon at the Bridge of Arcole, November 17, 1796 (Gros), 227, 229, 230
George Washington before the Battle of Trenton (Trumbull), 227, *228*
Giddens, Anthony, 282
Gilje, Paul, 43
Gilmore, Paul, 344
Gilroy, Paul, 346
Glory: growth in stature of, 17, *236;* and War of 1812 era, 205–208; and Louis XIV era, 209; French Revolution and, 209–210; use of term, in the press, 234–235, *236;* denunciations of, 236–238; in naval biography, 288. *See also* Napoleonic glory
Goldstone, Brian, 450
Gomo (Native chief), 379
González Manrique, Mateo, 174
Gordon, Mary, 404, 406
Gore, Francis, 315
Goudie, Sean, 104
Government: and presidential authority, 18–19, 313–317, 319–322, 328–330; Barbary pirates and weakness of, 60–61; public opinion and the, 324–325; Battle of New Orleans and weakness of, 382

Governor's Guard Battalion of New York State Artillery: uniforms of, 216, 221–222
Gray, Robert, 339
Great Britain: U.S. trade relations with, 135; Age of Revolution changes in, 167–168; and alliance with Indians, 171–173; blacks as citizens of, 181–187; Prospect Bluff citizens of, 181–187, 189–190, 200
Green, Jack P., 311
Greenleaf, Thomas, 213
Griscom, John, 345
Gros, Antoine Jean, 227, *229*, 230
Grose, Francis, 219, *220*
Groves, Samuel, 142, 148–150

Hadjo, Hillis, 193
Haiti, trade with, 105
Haitian Constitution, 185
Haitian Revolution, 11, 57–58, 60, 78, 86, 94, 96–98, 105, 167
Hall, Prince, 77
Halley, Janet, 455
Hambly, Edmund, 192
Hambly, William, 183
Hamilton, Alexander, 234
Hamilton, William, 354
Handy, Henry, 432
Hardt, Michael, 451
Harriman, Edward, 233
Harrison, William Henry, 216, *217*, 360, 363, 366–368, 372–374, 377, 384, 443–444
Hartford Convention, 315
Harvey, William, 345
Harwood, Hiram, 213
Hathaway, John, 288
Haudenosaunees, 444
Hawk (ship), 146
Hawkins, Micah, 29, *30*, 31–34, *35*, *36*, 37–42, 44–49, 55
Head, Francis Bond, 434–435
"Heart of Oak" (song), 43
Henry, John, 313–316, 322–330

Henry, Robert, 175–176
Hepoeth Micco, 172
Heroic Slave, The (Douglass), 267
Hewlett, James, 52
Hill, James, 233
Hindoo marriage, 445–447, 464–477
Historical novels, 102
History of the Hubbell Family, The (Hubbell), 260–261
HMS *Frolic*, 291
HMS *Guerriere*, 286, 291, 293–294
HMS *Macedonian*, 291
Hobomok (Child), 261
Ho-Chunks (Winnebagos), 436
Hogan, David, 335, 343
Hopoy Micco, 172
Howell, William Huntting, 334
Hubbell, Isaac, 251–265, 268–269, 277
Hubbell, Walter, 260–261
Hull, Isaac, 206, 286–288, 291–295, 303–304
Humanity in Algiers; or, The Story of Azem: By an American, Late a Slave in Algiers, 84–86
Humphrey, David, 69
Hunter, William T., 221–222
Hunter Lodges, 428–429, 442, 444
"Hunters of Kentucky" (song), 33, 47–49, 52
Huron-Petun peoples, 439
Hurons, 378

Iannini, Christopher P., 104
Identity: American, 3–6; Indian, 21; black, 37; white American, 46; Federalist fiction and formation of, 107–108, 121–122, 124. *See also* National identity
Immigration, 73
Impressment, 41–42, 425
Improvements in Education (Lancaster), 340
Incest law, 458–460, 463
Indian agents: to the Choctaws, 386–392, 396–405, 411–412; function of,

389–390; to the Cherokees, 395–396, 404, 407; territorial expansion by, 402–403, 406–413
Indian bodies, 409–411
Indian Removal Act, 418, 422, 434
Indian removal policy, British, 434–435
Indian-white intermarriage, 256, 258–261, 263
Inequality, 73–75, 333
Infanticide, 472–473, 476
Ingersoll, Charles J., 215
Interchangeability, 344–346, 350, 353–355
Interesting Narrative, The (Equiano), 94
International law, 22, 446, 453–455, 458
Iroquois, 427
Irving, Washington, 209, 219, 285, 289–292, 294–308, *302*, 310

Jackson, Andrew: and Battle of New Orleans, 47–49, 193, 205, 268–270, 272, 274, 276; emergence of, as national figure, 48, 360; Allen and, 49–50; impersonations of, 49–50; military attire of, 50; and blackface minstrelsy, 50, 52; and Pensacola assault, 170; and treaty with the Creeks, 173; and Creek War, 190; and First Seminole War, 193, 195–199; and celebrity, 193, 205–206; as Florida's territorial governor, 199; and Angola settlement raid, 199–200; and Napoleonic characteristics, 241; paintings of, 241, *242–246, 248;* bust of, *247;* in *Narrative of James Roberts*, 252, 269, 274–276; and black soldiers, 268–274, 276; and Horseshoe Bend assault, 379; and removal of Dinsmoor, 411; mention of, 412
Jackson, James, 78
Jacksonianism, 48
Jack Tars, 42–44
James, C. L. R., 343

James Madison (ship), 154
J. A. Morton (Bordeaux firm), 153
Jane Talbot (Brown), 100
Jarvis, John Wesley, 208, 223–227, 230–231, 233, 241, *242, 243*
Jay, John, 3
Jay Treaty, 134, 319, 422–423, 436
Jefferson, Thomas: election of, 95–99, 102–104; and circum-Atlantic concerns, 122; *Notes on the State of Virginia*, 122, 255, 297; and belief in African American inferiority, 255; on national unity, 284; and Madison's letters on secessionist conspiracy, 324, 328; colonization position of, 333, 348; on spread of slavery as movement toward freedom, 348–350
Jefferson (Thomas) administration: and Embargo Act, 72, 98, 135; mention of, 111; and Act to Prohibit the Importation of Slaves, 129; antinavalist policies of, 299–300; exiles from, 315; war policy of, 319; Indian policy of, 395–396, 402
Jeffersonian Republicans, 73
Jenkinson, Robert, 315
Jenks, Timothy, 280, 287, 310
Jesus, son of Mary, 224–225
Johnson, Richard Mentor, 360
Johnson, Samuel, 23–24, 93
Johnston, Bill, 433
Johnston, John, 365
Jolly Jack Tar stereotype, 43
Jones, Edward, 348
Jones, Jacob, 285, 289, 291
Jones, John Paul, 234

Kaestle, Carl F., 344
Kann, Mark, 231
Kant, Immanuel, 454
Kent, James, 459–460, 463, 468, 470
Kentucky Rifle, The, 52
Kerber, Linda K., 89
Key, Francis Scott, 33, 48
Kickapoos, 366, 368, 371–372, 377, 436

Kime, Wayne, 291
Kinache (Seminole chief), 191, 193
Kinship: Hindoo, 445–447, 464–477; beyond death, 472–477; sovereignty and, 478. *See also* Family
Kinship structures: Indian, 20–21, 392–395, 400–401, 404–405, 414–415, 417; indigenized French, 436–443; French, 439–443; caste-based, 469–472; violence in, 472–473; debt and obligation in, 476–477
Knickerbockers, 290, 291
Knouff, Gregory T., 262
Knox, Henry, 391–392, 394–395, 402

Laclau, Ernesto, 281
LaCoste, Pierre, 272
Lady Liberty, 283
Lafitte, Jean, 142
Lainé, Honorat, 153
Lancaster, Joseph, 332, 334, 338–355
Lancasterian Society, 340
Language: Webster on, 1–2, 23–24
La Rochefoucauld-Liancourt, François-Alexandre-Frédéric, duc de, 3
Laurens, John, 234
Laussat, Anthony, 160
Law: international, 446, 448–449; the norm and, 467
Law of nations, 446, 453–455
Law of Nations (Vattel), 453
Law of persons, 455, 461
Lawrence (ship), 214–215, 223, *224*
Lawrence, Jacob, 223
Lawrence, James, 278, 292, 294–296
Lea, John, 343–344
Lee, Charles, 259
Lee, William, 154
Leggett, Ruben, 331, 354
Lestapies, Adrian, 160–161
Lestapies and Cie (Bordeaux firm), 160
Liberal rights: universality of, 58
Liberty: ideal of, v, 10–11, 95, 100, 121, 252–254, 257, 277, 317, 453; as justifying acts of aggression, 10; as justifying dispossession, 10; compromises of, 14, 17, 472; and slavery binary, 15–16, 25, 56–58, 64–66, 69–71, 75, 86–92, 97, 128, 178, 255; British claims to advance, 167, 178; sacrifice as a guarantee of, 266; black soldiers's claims to, 266–267; Revolutionary ideals of, vs. reality of slavery, 169, 266–267
Life of Nelson (Southey), 300–301
Light Artillery Regiment: uniforms of, 221
Light Dragoons: uniforms of, 216, 222
Little Crow (chief), 360, 381
Little Crow (grandfather), 360
Little Turtle, 365–367
Livingston, Robert, 230
Locke, John, 76, 89
Logan (Shawnee chief), 373
Long, David, 215
Longhi, Guiseppi, 230
Lossing, Benson J., 29
Lott, Eric, 33
Loughran, Trish, 447
Louis XIV, 209, 235
Louis-David, Jacques, 238
Louisiana Purchase, 97, 447
Lower Canada rebellion, 427, 441
Lyon, Matthew, 284

McDonald, Alexander Hamilton, 413–415, 418
McDonald, James, 386–387, 389–390, 397–398, 401, 403, 411–414, 418
McDonald, Molly, 387–390, 401, 403, 411–418
Macdonough, Thomas, 44, 278–279, 292, 307, 309
MacGregor, Gregor, 189
Mack, Henry, 428–429
MacKenzie, William Lyon, 431, 432
Macomb, Alexander, 29, 44
Macon, Nathaniel, 324
McPherson, William, 176, 178
Maddox, Lucy, 261

INDEX 495

Madison, James, 18–19, 48, 139, 235, 285, 289, 313–329, 454, 460
Main Poc (Potawatomi shaman and war chief), 369–370, 379–380
Major-General Henry Dearborn (Stuart), *218*, 221
Manual of Peace (Upham), 237
Margaretta; or, The Intricacies of the Heart (Read), 104, 106–126
"Margaretta; or, The Village Maid" (Read), 111
Marmion (Scott), 308
Marriage: in Federalist fiction, 100, 105–106, 126; whiteness and, 106; white-Indian, 256, 258–261, 263, 400; Hindoo, 445–450, 464–477; white-black, 457–458; legitimate, 458–459, 463; incestuous, 458–460, 463; lunatic, 459; polygamous, 459; caste-determined, 469–472
Marriage law, 22, 448–450, 452–464, 467–468
Marshall, John, 283–284
Masculinity, Napoleonic, 230–232
Mayflower of Liberia (ship), 333
Mazot, José, 195
"Meaning of July Fourth for the Negro, The" (Douglass), 127–130, 132, 162
Mélanie, La (ship), 155
Melville, Herman, 237
Menominees, 378
Meranze, Michael, 9
Meredith, Samuel, 111
Mesquakies, 436
Mexican-American War, 428
Miamis, 365–367, 370, 372, 373, 377, 384
Military attire: and Andrew Jackson, 50; Napoleonic glory and, 215–216, *217–218*, *219*, *220*, *221–222*
Military discipline, 256–257, 263
Military recklessness, 214–215
Military utterances, 222–223, *224*
Minstrelization, 33–34, 46, 52. *See also* Blackface minstrelsy

Miscegenation, 86, 90–91
Mississippi Territory, 391
Missouri Compromise, 284, 348
Mitchell, David, 197
Mohawks, 432
Monima (Read), 109, 111
Monroe, James, 196, 284, 323, 341, 347
Monroe Doctrine, 447
Monroe-Pinkney Treaty, 315
Montesquieu, Charles-Louis de Secondat, baron de La Brède et de, 235
Moore, Thomas, 443–444
Moreland Vale; or, The Fair Fugitive, 100
Morgan, J. P., 233
Morris, Gouverneur, 3
Morrissey, Robert, 234–235
Morton, John Archer, 153
Morton and Russell (Bordeaux firm), 153
Murray, George, 434
Murray, John (Lord Dunmore), 265
Murray, Lindley, 334
Muscogee nation, 172

Napoleon, 143, 146–147, 207–212, 239–241, 327
Napoleon Crossing the Alps (Louis-David), 238
Napoleonic glory: preoccupation with, 208–209; in the press, 210–211, 213; writers on, 212; emulation of, among post-Revolutionary age cohort, 213–214; military recklessness and, 214–215; military attire and, 215–216, *217–218*, 219, *220*, 221–222; military utterances and, 222–223, *224;* in paintings, 223, 224, *225–226*, 226–227, *229;* hypermasculinity and, 230–232; democratic equality and, 233–234; economic striving and, 233–234. *See also* Glory
Napoleonic Wars, 133–140, 168, 453
Narrative, of a Five Years' Expedition, against the Revolted Negroes of Surinam (Stedman), 75

Natchez Trace, 397–398, 415
National identity: War of 1812 and, 4–6, 33, 282–285, 293–312; as imprinted on the body, 21, 442; minstrelized, 33–34, 37, 46–47, 52; sailors as symbols of, 43–44; Barbary captivity narratives and, 61–62, 65, 69–70, 72; in Federalist fiction, 107–108, 121–122, 124–125; remembrances of the Revolution in, 254; shaping of, by naval biography, 278–283, 287, 289, 293–312; British, 424–425; as dependent on place, 425–426; "Canadien," 441–442. *See also* Identity
Nationalism: racialized, 34n, 37, 45–46, 55n, 350; Barbary captivity narratives and, 65, 69–70, 72; print culture and, 279–284, 298, 447; and war, 311, 341n; Native American relations and, 419, 435
Natural law, 453, 460–464, 470
Natural rights, 11
Naval biography: and James Lawrence, 278; and the shaping of national identity, 278–283, 287, 289, 293–312; influence of war patriotism on, 282–285, 291; officers selected for, 286–287; glory in, 288; audience for, 288–289; purpose of, 311–312. *See also Analectic Magazine*
Naval Temple (Badger), 215
Navy, U.S., 72–75, 285–286, 294–296, 303. *See also* War of 1812; *specific battles*
Neal, John, 290–291
Neamathla (leader of Fowltown), 191–192
Neau, Elias, 336
Negri, Antonio, 451
Negro Fort, 41, 174, 188
Nell, William C., 267–268
Nelson, Horatio, 209, 224, 237, 300–304
Neolin (Delaware prophet), 374

Nero, 187, 192, 193, 195
Neutrality, Indian: in the War of 1812, 359, 362–367, 370, 372–378, 384
Neutrality treaties, 134–135, 158–161, 319, 321, 430
New England states: secession of, 313–315, 322–327
New York African Free Schools (NYAFS), 19, 331–332, 334, 338, 347–348, 351, 353
New York Manumission Society, 334
Niagra (ship), 214–215, 223
Nicholson, Thomas, 64–65, 68, 81
Nicolls, Edward: and antislavery plan, 16, 174–187, 189, 195; and Red Sticks and Seminole alliance to restore their lands, 16, 172–173, 197–198; role of, in First Seminole War, 165–166, 170, 173, 197–201; and antislavery beliefs, 166–167, 169–170, 180; background of, 166–169; Fernando Pó incident and, 169–170; at Prospect Bluff, 170–171; ties of, to Angola settlement, 196
Noah, Mordecai M., 54
Non-Intercourse Act, 135
North Africa: in Barbary captivity narratives, 69–70
North African corsairs: number of sailors seized by, 62
Notes on the State of Virginia (Jefferson), 122, 255, 297

O'Brien, Richard, 62
"O Canada" (song), 441–442
Odawas, 432, 434, 436–437
Ohio Valley movement, 360
Ojibwas, 360, 368–370, 381–382, 432, 434, 436–437
Old Hickory; or, A Day at New Orleans, 50
Oliver Hazard Perry (Jarvis), 223–224, 225, 226–227, 230–231, 233
Olson, Joel, 56
Onuf, Nicholas, 454
Onuf, Peter, 454

Orders in Council (U.K.), 133, 135–136, 147–148, 151, 158
"Original Jim Crow" (Rice), 32–33, 50, 52
Osages, 369
Otoes, 376–377
Ottawas, 370, 372–373, 378
Overton, John, 197

Paine, Thomas, 72, 74, 117
Pakenham, Edward, 48
Palmer, R. R., 238
Papineau, Louis-Joseph, 432
Parker, Isaac, 458–459, 463
Parsons, Theophilus, 457–458
Paternalism, racial, 386–387, 392–394, 403–412
Patriarchal agrarianism, 386, 394–395, 399
Patriarchy, 6, 21, 86, 109, 417; white, 11, 92; legal, 13; Christian, 22, 84, 265; and households, 392–393
"Patriotic Diggers" (song), 41
Patriotism, 42, 132, 162–163, 256, 442, 444
Patriots, 419–421, 426–434, 441–444
Patriot War, 164, 198
Patty (ship), 156
Paulding, James Kirke, 278–279, 285, 288–289, 291–295, 297, 303–304, 306–309
Paz (ship), 139
Peace movement, 237–238
Peale, Anna Claypoole, *246*
Peale, Charles Willson, *245*
Peale, Rembrandt, *217*
Pelee Island, 430
Pennsylvania Society for Promoting the Abolition of Slavery, 78
Penrose, William, 67
Pensacola, 170, 195
Peoria, 370
Perdue, Theda, 396
Perry, David, 250
Perry, Oliver Hazard, 206, 214–215, 223–227, 230–231, 233–234, 283, 292, 297–305, *302*
Peskin, Lawrence A., 132
Phoebe (ship), 215
Phrenology, 255
Piankashaws, 370
Picon (Miami chief), 366
Pierce, Franklin, 253, 269
Piesch, Abraham, 160
Pintado, Vicente, 176–180
Pioneers; or, the Sources of the Susquehanna, The (Cooper), 119
Plantation system: Caribbean, 96; and kinship structures, 99; in Federalist fiction, 109–110, 114–116; expansion of, 165, 183, 198, 415; and threat of racialized violence, 191, 198, 200; violence in, 274–277; of Indian agents, 388, 402–403, 406–413; Indian, 416–418
Pocock, J. G. A., 262
Pokagon, Simon, 379
Political violence, 252, 254, 271–272, 274, 276–277
Polly (ship), 63
Pontiac's War, 374
Porpoise (ship), 142
Porter, David, 214–215, 231, 234, 237
Port-Folio, 278, 291, 296–297
Portraiture of Domestic Slavery, in the United States, A (Torrey), 23–24
Positivism, 454
Potawatomis, 20–21, 360, 366–371, 378–381, 383, 420–421, 432–438, 442–443
Povinelli, Elizabeth, 468
Power of Sympathy (Brown), 118
Prejudice, racial: antiblack, 46, 47; education as response to, 333–334; emulation as a response to, 334–340
Presidential authority, 18–19, 313–317, 319–322, 328–330
Prevost, George, 38–39
Priest, Josiah, 251–265, 268–269, 271, 277

Prince's Island, 169
Print culture, 12-13, 447
Private international law, 446, 455, 458, 461. *See also* Marriage law
Property, 23; whiteness as, 18, 57, 76, 94, 274; enslaved people and, 25, 57-58, 150-151, 200, 275, 389n, 400, 406; children as, 346, 477
Property rights: and Native American title, 7, 188, 396, 400, 417; of white men, 10-11, 14, 98, 268, 393, 470; and women, 22, 448; vs. rights of man, 60; Revolutionary guarantees of, 95, 262-263, 352, 392, 417, 432, 461
Prospect Bluff Fort, 170, 185, 188-189
Prospect Bluff settlement: black and Indian soldiers recruited from, 165, 170-171; Spanish expeditions to retrieve slaves from, 175-180; and British status, 181-187, 189-190, 200; refugees from, 182, 185-187, 191, 199-200; departure of the British from, 183-184
Putnam, Israel, 428
Putnam, William, 428

Quasi-War, 235, 319, 322
Quincy, Josiah, 221, 329-330

Ramsay, David, 254
Randolph, John, 324
Ray, William, 66-67, 70, 72-76, 80
Raynal, Guillaume-Thomas Raynal, abbé de, 75
Read, George, 111
Read, John, 111
Read, Martha Meredith, 104, 106-126
Rebecca (ship), 139
Red Sticks, 165, 171-173, 185-186, 190, 382-383
Red Stick War, 41, 378, 382
Red Wing, 359-361, 381, 385
Regiment de Chasseurs a Cheval: uniforms of, 221

Religion: marriage and, 463-466
Renwick, James, 290
Reproductive philanthropy, 394, 402
Republican Party, 73, 250, 285
Resch, John, 257
Resident Indians, 425
Revolutionary violence, 238, 252-253, 265-266, 268, 277
Revolution of 1800, 95-104, 118-119, 124-125
Ribaut, John, 160
Rice, T. D., 32-33, 50, 52
Richardson, David, 156-158
Richardson, Samuel, 101
Rifkin, Mark, 478
Rights of Man (Paine), 117
Riley, Padraig, 56-57
Rittich, Kerry, 455
River Raisin Massacre, 365, 377
Roberts, James, 251-252, 266-277
Rockefeller, John, 233
Rosa (ship), 139
Rose, Jacqueline, 343
Rothman, Adam, 270
Round Head (Wyandot chief), 372
Rousseau, Jean Jacques, 335
Rowson, Susanna, 86-93, 104, 118
Royal Navy, 146, 280, 283, 285-288
"Rule, Britannia" (song), 43
Rush, Benjamin, 345-346
Rush, William, *247*
Russell, Gillian, 43
Russwurm, John B., 348
Ryland, Henry, 322

Sailors: in blackface minstrelsy, 37-43; national identities of, 41-42; and War of 1812 impressment practices, 41-42, 425; in contemporary British theater, 43; enthusiasm for dramatic performances of, 43; freedom of, 43; and poverty as reason for enlistment, 72-73; and self-Other binary, 73-74; treatment of, 73-75. *See also* Barbary captivity narratives; Black sailors

St-Denis, Guy, 443
Saint Domingue: and slave uprising, 78, 86, 94, 96–98
Saint Jean Baptiste Festival, 440, 442
Saint Jean Baptiste Society, 440–443
St. Marks, 192–193
Saint Thomas, 169
Sally (ship), 143
Salmagundi (Irving), 219
Samet, Elizabeth, 257
Sánchez-Eppler, Karen, 334
Sandwich, Canada, 429, 431
Sansay, Leonora, 122–123
Saucy Jack (ship), 139, 143, 157
Sauks, 360, 364, 378, 383–384, 436
Saxton, Alexander, 52
Schoolcraft, Henry Rowe, 437
Scott, James, 9
Scott, Robert, 192–193
Scott, Walter, 308
Scott, William, 142, 149–150
Scott, Winifield, 221
Secession: and New England states, 313–315, 322–327
"Second Vindication, A" (Read), 111
Secret History; or, The Horrors of St. Dominogo (Sansay), 122–123
Seduction: kinship and, 472
Seduction and virtue in Federalist fiction, 100–101, 104–107, 110, 112–119
Self-defense: right to, 196, 274–276
Self-determination: right to, 115–116
Seminoles, 190. *See also* First Seminole War
Semiramis (ship), 148
Seven Years' War, 234, 374
Shankman, Andrew, 57
Shannon (ship), 223, 294, 297
Shapiro, Stephen, 104–105
Sharp, Granville, 75
Shawnees, 366, 373–374, 390
Shawnee brothers, 360–363, 365, 368–378, 381–385, 387, 391, 410, 443–444
Shays's Rebellion, 451
She Would Be a Soldier (Noah), 54

Shklar, Judith N., 56
Short Account of Algiers, and of Its Several Wars (Carey), 67–68, 70, 78
Shubrick, John, 292, 307
Siege of Plattsburg, The, 48
Sierra, Eugenio, 176, 178
Sierra Leone colony, 138
Simms, William Gilmore, 261
Sioux, 359–360, 368–369, 378, 381–382
Sketches of the History of France (Banks), 212
Slauter, Eric, 317
Slave narratives, 268, 271
Slavery, as It Relates to the Negro, or African Race (Priest), 264–265
Slaves in Algiers; or, A Struggle for Freedom (Rowson), 86–93
Slave soldiers, 41–42, 268–277
Slave trade: clandestine period of, 16; Douglass on, 127–130, 132; criminalization of, 129–130, 133, 136, 138, 142–143; War of 1812 and, 131–132, 161–162; effect of neutrality treaties on, 136–138; and fraud of the flags, 138–139; and *Amedie* decision, 138–139, 142, 148–151; and post-abolition acts, 139, 142–143, 158–161; re-legalization of foreign, 140; data available on, 140, 156–158, 162–163; and Charleston, 140–142; French, 143–144; effect on, of right of mutual search, 161. *See also* Trade
Slave Trade Act (1807), 129, 133, 136
Smith, Adam, 335
Smith, Anthony, 281
Smith, Calvin, 274–275
Smith, Edward, 141
Smith, James McCune, 355–356
Smith, Richard Penn, 50
Sobel, Mechal, 46
Société Saint-Jean-Baptiste, 440–443
Society for the Propagation of the Gospel in Foreign Parts, 336
Soldiers: slaves as, 41–42, 268–277; in contemporary British theater, 43; en-

thusiasm for dramatic performances of, 43; decline in the character of, 256; citizen- vs. mercenary, 257, 262; property ownership for, 262–263. *See also* Black soldiers; Veteran narratives
Sons of Liberty, 433
Soubiran, Paul Emile, 323
Southey, Robert, 300–301
Sovereignty: borders of, 21; marriage law and national, 22, 452–464; and Indians, 386–387, 392–394, 403–412; crisis of, 447–449, 451; spheres of, 450; and marital norm, 467; non-juridical, 467; democratic, 468; kinship and, 478
Sovereignty of nations, 460–464
Spencer, Robert, 176–177, 180
Spiegel, Gabrrielle M., 7
Spirit of '76 (pseud.), 342
Stamp Act Crisis, 93
Standing Spirit (Potawatomi leader), 435, 442
"Star-Spangled Banner" (Key), 33, 41, 48
Statutory law, 468
Stedman, John, 75
Steinberg, Saul, 38
Stephen, Isaac, 62
Stephen, James, 136–137, 148, 151, 153
Stevens, James, 69–70
Stewart, Robert, 423
Stewart, Thomas McCants, 348
Story, Isaac, 65, 70
Story, Joseph, 457, 460–463, 468
Stuart, Gilbert, *218*, 221
Suffering soldier, 257, 259
Suicide, 476
Suppression of the African Slave Trade, The (Du Bois), 138–139, 143
Suttee, 472–477

Talbot, Thomas, 427
Tasmania, 431
Taylor, Alan, 41, 285, 311, 447
Taylor, Asher, 221–222
Tea party trope, 38, 40
Tecumseh, 360, 363, 370–371, 373–374, 378, 382, 384, 387, 391, 410, 443–444
Temple of Liberty (Trenchard), 317, *318*
Tenney, Tabitha, 100
Tenskwatawa, 360, 363, 365, 369–371, 375, 383, 391
Terrell, Colleen, 345
Territorial expansion: slavery and, 390, 415; Indian agent's role in, 391–394, 399; patriarchy and paternalism in, 394–395, 399, 403–412; and economics, 395, 399, 415; reproductive philanthropy as strategy for, 395, 402, 412; by Indian agents, 402–403, 406–413; legislation in support of, 422. *See also* Dispossession
Territorial expansion, Indian response to: First Seminole War, 16–17, 183, 185, 188–189, 192–194, 200–201; and War of 1812, 359–385, 423, 435; and cultural / economic adaptations, 396–398, 400–401
Teton Sioux, 381
Texas, 420, 430–431
Theller, Edward, 431
Thomas, Moses, 289–291
Thompson, E. P., 6, 9
Tocqueville, Alexis de, 240
Tompkins, Daniel, 42
Torrey, Jesse, 23–24
Trade: free, and sailor's rights, 16, 43; enslavement of Americans and, 60–62; effect on, of neutrality treaties, 134–138, 153–155, 158–161; and fraud of the flags, 137–138, 145–151; in disguise, 151–158; disruptions in, during 1807–1814, 151; and Indians, 363–364, 381; cross-border, 429. *See also* Slave trade
Trade neutralization, 134–138, 153–155, 158–161
Treaty Indians, 436

INDEX 501

Treaty of Amity, Commerce, and Navigation, 134–135
Treaty of Fort Jackson, 171–173, 189, 191, 197
Treaty of Ghent, 171–173, 285, 383–384, 422–424, 444
Treaty of Greenville, 373
Treaty of Paris, 422
Treaty of San Lorenzo, 391
Treaty of Webster-Ashburton, 444
Treaty with the Creeks, 173
Trenchard, James, 317, *318*, 329
Trimmer, Sarah, 352
Tripolitan Wars, 234
Troup, George, 205
Trumbull, John, 224, 227, *228*, 235
Twiggs, David, 191
Tyler, Royall, 79–86, 93

Upham, Thomas, 237, 238
Upper Canada rebellion, 426–433, 441
Urcullo, José, 175–176
USS *Chesapeake*, 41, 44, 223, 294–295
USS *Constitution*, 291, 293
USS *Philadelphia*, 62, 66, 72–73
USS *United States*, 291
USS *Wasp*, 291

Valle, James E., 235
Vallée, Jean François de la, *244*
Van Buren, Martin, 430–431, 444
Vanderlyn, John, *248*
Van Diemen's Land (Tasmania), 431
Van Schaik, Goose, 259
Vattel, Emmerich de, 453, 460
Velnet, Mary, 65–66, 68–71, 74, 76, 81
Veteran narratives: of black soldiers, 251–252, 262–263, 265–277; *Narrative of James Roberts*, 251–252, 266–277; *The Fort Stanwix Captive* (Priest), 251–265, 268–269, 271, 277; and lamenting of loss of national unity, 252; popular sovereignty ideology in, 252; and war and slavery as mutual expressions of domination,

252; on the false promise of freedom, 252, 265–277; as a frontier romance, 253–254, 256; and valorization of the citizen-soldier, 254; white male supremacy ideology in, 254–265; suffering soldier in, 256–257, 259
Victimhood rhetoric, 323–324
View of the World from Ninth Avenue (Steinberg), 38
Villanueva, J. G., 160
Violence: plantation, 274–277; familial, 472–473
Virginia (ship), 153
Viroli, Maurizio, 312
Virtue: shift from self-sacrificing, 17; and images of Washington, 227; republican, 231–232, 235, 257; in men's character development, 232; glory vs., 235; national, 250–251, 256; intermarriage as a lapse in, 258, 260, 263; redemption of, 263–264; loss of collective, 264
Visiting Indians, 425
Voltaire, 72
Voters: black, 44–45; residence and, 425–426
Voyages: The Trans-Atlantic Slave Trade Database (Eltis and Richardson), 156–158

Waldstreicher, David, 56
Walker, David, 267, 356
Walpole Island Reserve (Bkejwanong), 434, 436–437, 439–440, 442–444
Wandering Indians, 425
War: presidential authority and, 18–19, 313–317, 319–322, 328–330; public opinion and, 19, 324–325; theatrical dimensions of, 32–33, 50, 52; culture of, 208; democratic penchant for, 240–241; Henry letters and, 313–316, 322–330; legal reality of, 317, 322; Constitution as pretext to, 320–321
War in Disguise; or, The Frauds of the Neutral Flags (Stephen), 136–137

War of 1812: and national identity, 4–6, 33, 282–285, 293–312; theatrical dimensions of, 29, *30*, 31–34, *35, 36*, 37–42, 44–49, 55; black soldiers in, 34, 37, 41–42, 48–49, 54–55, 268, 271–274; black identity and, 37; comparison of, to American Revolution, 55, 250, 256–257; slogan of, 129–130; and slave trade/Atlantic slavery, 130–133, 161–162; free trade and, 133–140, 144; factors underlying outbreak of, 144, 146–147, 160, 280; First Seminole War and, 165, 195–196; Burnham on, 250; consequence to, of Battle of Lake Erie, 304; and national borders, 332; Indian militancy in, 359–385, 423, 435; impressment practices of, 425, 452; indigenized French in, 438; and crisis of sovereignty, 449. *See also specific battles*

Warren, Mercy Otis, 254
Warrington, Lewis, 285–286, 311
Washington, Booker T., 348
Washington, George, 210, 212, 227, *228*, 235, 252, 258–259, 263, 265, 270, 283, 319, 334, 392
Washington, D.C.: burning of, 24–25, 41, 42, 382
Watson, Samuel J., 235
Weas, 370, 377
Webster, Noah, 1–5, 7, 23–24
Weems, Mason Locke, 254
Wendats, 432
West, Benjamin, 224, *226*
West, Elsie, 310
Wharton, Thomas Isaac, 306
White, Ashli, 105
White, Ed, 124
White, Robert, 192
Whiteface minstrelsy, 54
White Jacket (Melville), 237
Whiteness, 14, 18, 45–46, 56–57, 106, 107, 118, 255, 263, 274, 351, 407

White slavery, 63–69, 74, 82–83, 114–115
White supremacy, 254–264, 273–274, 276–277, 388–389
Widgery, William, 327
Wilberforce, William, 136
William Henry Harrison (Peale), *217*
Wills, Garry, 227
Winnebagos, 366, 377, 380, 436
Wives, 97; enslaved women as, 81; Native American women as, 364, 393n, 398, 416; as participants in consensual contracts, 452
Wolfe, James, 234
Wollstonecraft, Mary, 111
Women: and strategies for inclusion, 11; Indian, 21, 392, 413–418; as cultural symbols, 24; enslaved African American, 49, 68, 77, 356, 386, 406–408; as revolutionaries, 57–60, 92, 117, 265; as authors, 65, 111, 238; in Barbary captivity narratives, 67, 86–92; and patriarchy, 86, 115–116; roles and images of, 87, 90–93, 255; commodification of, 120; as objects of charity, 125; in warfare, 192, 195, 415–417; and War of 1812 era, 230–232; and politics, 232–233; Choctaw, 386–390; and economy and family structure, 392–402; in plantation economy, 418; in marriage, 469, 474; and suttee, 472–477
Wood, Gordon S., 4–5, 214, 280
Woodbine, George, 170–171, 189–191, 198
Words: as weapon, 1–2
Wright, Henry, 213
Wyandots, 372–373

XYZ Affair, 319

Zagarri, Rosemarie, 92, 232
Zelinsky, Wilbur, 283–284
Zygmont, Bryan, 227

www.ingramcontent.com/pod-product-compliance
Lightning Source LLC
Chambersburg PA
CBHW021414300426
44114CB00010B/489